The Sundance Reader

Second Edition

The Sundance Reader

Second Edition

MARK CONNELLY

MILWAUKEE AREA TECHNICAL COLLEGE

HARCOURT BRACE COLLEGE PUBLISHERS

Fort Worth Philadelphia San Diego New York Orlando Austin San Antonio
Toronto Montreal London Sydney Tokyo

PUBLISHER	Earl McPeek
ACQUISITIONS EDITOR	Julie McBurney
MARKET STRATEGIST	John Meyers
PROJECT EDITOR	Kathryn M. Stewart
ART DIRECTOR	Sue Hart
PRODUCTION MANAGER	Angela Williams Urquhart

ISBN: 0-15-508052-0

Library of Congress Catalog Card Number: 99-65350

Copyright © 2000, 1997 by Harcourt, Inc.

Address for Domestic Orders
Harcourt, Inc., 6277 Sea Harbor Drive, Orlando, FL 32887-6777
800-782-4479

Address for International Orders
International Customer Service
Harcourt, Inc., 6277 Sea Harbor Drive, Orlando, FL 32887-6777
407-345-3800
(fax) 407-345-4060
(e-mail) hbintl@harcourtbrace.com

Address for Editorial Correspondence
Harcourt College Publishers, 301 Commerce Street, Suite 3700, Fort Worth, TX 76102

Web Site Address
http://www.harcourtcollege.com

Harcourt College Publishers will provide complimentary supplements or
supplement packages to those adopters qualified under our adoption policy. Please
contact your sales representative to learn how you qualify. If as an adopter or
potential user you receive supplements you do not need, please return them
to your sales representative or send them to:
Attn: Returns Department, Troy Warehouse,
465 South Lincoln Drive, Troy, MO 63379.

Printed in the United States of America

9 0 1 2 3 4 5 6 7 8 016 9 8 7 6 5 4 3 2 1

Harcourt College Publishers

To Stanley Felber

The Sundance Reader contains over eighty readings drawn from a range of academic disciplines and professions. The collection of essays and articles organized by rhetorical modes includes both classic and contemporary authors such as George Orwell, E.B. White, Joan Didion, Rene Denfeld, Kesaya Noda, and Juliet B. Shor. In addition to writing from the disciplines of law, medicine, and science by writers such as Alan Dershowitz, Oliver Sacks, and Carl Sagan, *The Sundance Reader* offers students practical advice on résumé writing and job interviews. Applied readings at the end of each chapter demonstrate how writers use the rhetorical modes beyond the classroom. Entries such as "The Reconstructed Logbook of the Titanic," "Interrogation of Lee Harvey Oswald," and "Cleaning Battery Terminals" illustrate various writing tasks students will face in future courses and in their careers.

The Sundance Reader's wide variety of topics on the environment, culture, social issues, and business make the textbook suitable for thematic courses. Individual chapters include self-contained units on current issues, and the thematic table of contents lists a number of topics that can be explored in depth.

With its wealth of readings and four-part questioning strategy following each entry, *The Sundance Reader* provides students a unique perspective on how writing is shaped in different contexts.

The Sundance Reader has several features that make it a useful teaching tool for college instructors:

- *A range of readings*   Each chapter opens with brief, readable entries which clearly demonstrate the rhetorical mode, followed by longer, more challenging essays. Each chapter highlights a model "blending" the modes showing how writers often use several methods of development to tell a story or explain a process. Samples of applied writing appear at the end, illustrating how writers use the mode in different professions. Instructors have flexibility in assigning readings best suited to their student populations.
- *Brief entries suitable for in-class reading*   Many of the essays are short enough to be read in class and used as writing prompts, reducing the need for handouts.
- *An emphasis on writing*   *The Sundance Reader* moves students from *reading* to *writing*. Chapters open with reading questions and conclude with writing strategies and

lists of suggested topics. Each chapter ends with a checklist of common writing problems.

- **Writers on writing**   The readings include William Zinsser's "The Transaction" and Peter Elbow's "Desperation Writing," which examine writing as both a process and a product. Fran Martin's "Documentation Tips" explains how nurses should word reports to prevent malpractice suits. In "Resumes That Rate a Second Look," Anne Weisbord demonstrates the importance of writing skills to job seekers.

- **An emphasis on critical thinking**   *The Sundance Reader* stresses critical thinking by including James Austin's article about the role of chance in scientific research. Samuel Scudder's essay "Take This Fish and Look at It" dramatizes the importance of detailed observation. Darrell Huff's "How to Lie with Statistics" heightens student awareness of how statistics are misused and manipulated.

- **Pro and con entries**   Instructors have found that presenting essays with contrasting viewpoints can stimulate class discussions and prompt writing activities. *The Sundance Reader* presents pairs of pro and con articles on three critical issues: the "abuse excuse," global warming, and cultural identity.

- **Focus on diversity**   Over a third of the selections are written by women. African-American, Hispanic, Native American, and Asian writers are represented. In addition to social commentaries by Gloria Steinem and Martin Luther King Jr., women and minorities are featured in nontraditional areas such as business and technology.

- **Writing across the curriculum**   *The Sundance Reader* demonstrates how each mode is developed by writers working in several disciplines, including law, medicine, psychology, history, law enforcement, and business.

- **Writing beyond the classroom**   Each chapter includes a section illustrating how writers use the modes in "the real world." Advertisements, brochures, government documents, and a résumé introduce elements of business and technical writing to composition students. In addition, several of the entries taken from academic and professional journals are reproduced with full documentation.

- **Collaborative writing**   Writing suggestions following the readings include directions for collaborative writing activities. The introduction provides useful guidelines for successful group writing.

- **Advice on the job search**   *The Sundance Reader* contains articles offering students practical advice on writing résumés, succeeding in job interviews, and evaluating job offers. Other articles provide recommendations for entrepreneurs and business managers.

Above all, *The Sundance Reader* has been designed to encourage students to read and develop confidence as writers.

NEW IN THIS EDITION

Student Papers. Each chapter concludes with a student paper, providing students with realistic examples of the type of writing expected in composition courses.

 WebTutor

www.harcourtcollege.com/english/sundance

The Sundance Web site provides online support. The site provides links to other sources, interactive grammar exercises, additional writing topics, and assistance for writing research papers.

ACKNOWLEDGMENTS

I would like to thank the following reviewers for their critiques and recommendations:

Michel A. de Benedictus, Miami Dade Community College—Kendall Campus; David Elias, Eastern Kentucky University; Frederick Gracobazzi, Kirkland Community College; Joyce Marie Miller, Collin County Community College; Peggy J. Pavlisin, Lincoln Land Community College; Harry R. Phillips, Central Piedmont Community College.

All books are a collaborative effort. My special thanks goes to Earl McPeek and Julie McBurney at Harcourt for their perception, editorial judgment, and enthusiasm for *The Sundance Reader*. Mark Gallaher was especially helpful in suggesting additional readings and developing the table of contents. His guidance was critical for giving *The Sundance Reader* its final shape. In addition, I would like to thank the talented Harcourt production team: project editor, Kathryn Stewart; production manager, Angela Urquhart; Sue Hart, art director, and market strategist John Meyers. I am very grateful for the efforts of Tom Hartman in creating the Sundance Web site.

Contents

PREFACE   vii

1 INTRODUCTION   1

How We Write   1

The Writer   3

   The Writer's Purpose   4

   The Writer's Role   7

The Reader   8

   Individual Readers   9

   Extended Readerships   10

   The Perceptual World   10

The Discipline   12

   Writing Contexts   14

The Writing Process   15

   Prewriting   15

   Moving from Topic to Thesis   19

How to Write an Essay   20

   Strategies for Creating a Composing Style   22

Writing the Whole Composition   22

   Prewriting   22

   Planning   23

   First Draft   24

   Revision   24

   Revision Notes   25

   Second Draft   25

Writing on a Computer   27

   Strategies for Writing on a Computer   27

Collaborative Writing   28

   Strategies for Collaborative Writing   29

Writer's Block   30

   Strategies for Overcoming Writer's Block   30

Reading Critically   32

   Strategies for Critical Reading   33

Cornel West *Black Political Leadership*   35

Using *The Sundance Reader*   37

Web Tutor: See for further information on writing   38

2   **NARRATION: RELATING EVENTS**   39

What Is Narration?   39

   The Writer's Purpose   39

   Focus   42

   Chronology   42

Strategies for Reading Narration   43

   Meaning   43

   Strategy   44

   Language   44

Samuel Scudder *Take This Fish and Look at It*   45

Instead of lecturing, a famous scientist repeats a simple command to his
new student—"look, look, look."

Nathan McCall *The Lesson*   51

Entering an integrated school, the author of *Makes Me Wanna Holler*
receives his first lesson in racism.

Molly Ivins *A Short Story about the Vietnam War Memorial*   57

Remembering her dead lover, a young woman knelt before the black
marble wall. "His name leaped out of her. It was like being hit."

Ramon "Tianguis" Perez *The Fender-Bender*   62

A minor traffic incident reveals the tenuous existence of undocumented
aliens in America.

Richard Preston *Ebola River*   67

In 1976 a new deadly virus claimed its first victim. Ebola was not AIDS,
but it foreshadowed the deadly epidemic to come.

George Orwell *Shooting an Elephant*   72

Although an armed officer, Orwell recounts how a crowd pressured him
to act against his will.

Blending the Modes

Oliver Sacks *The Man Who Mistook His Wife for a Hat*   81

A neurologist explains the baffling case of a music professor disabled by
a rare psychological disorder.

Writing beyond the Classroom

Federal Bureau of Investigation *Interrogation of Lee Harvey Oswald*   93

A suspected assassin's account of his movements is recorded with tearse
accuracy.

Walter Lord *The Reconstructed Logbook of the Titanic*   98

Lord provides a minute by minute account of the famed luxury liner's doomed maiden voyage.

Strategies for Writing Narration   101

Suggested Topics for Writing Narration   101

Student Paper *Spare Change*   103

A trip across the Mexican border leads a student to alter his views of poverty.

Narration Checklist   105

Web Tutor: See for further information on writing narration   105

3   DESCRIPTION: PRESENTING IMPRESSIONS   106

What Is Description?   106

Objective and Subjective Description   107

The Language of Description   109

Strategies for Reading Description   113

Meaning   113

Strategy   113

Language   113

Truman Capote *Out There*   115

The opening pages of *In Cold Blood* describe a remote Kansas town that became the scene of an infamous mass murder.

Luis Alberto Urrea *Border Story*   118

For Central Americans seeking a better life, the border between Mexico and the United States is a war zone of poverty and violence.

Joan Didion *Marrying Absurd*   122

Open twenty-four hours a day, the wedding chapels of Las Vegas offer instant marriage with the efficiency of fast food restaurants.

José Antonio Burciaga *My Ecumenical Father*   127

Burciaga recounts how his Mexican father, who worked as a custodian in an El Paso synagogue, risked his life for the Jewish faith.

Carl T. Rowan *Unforgettable Miss Bessie*   131

A noted columnist recalls the teacher who reminded him and other disadvantaged students that "what you put in your head . . . can never be pulled out by the Ku Klux Klan or Congress . . ."

N. Scott Momaday *The Way to Rainy Mountain*   137

Returning to his homeland to attend his grandmother's funeral, a poet and artist encounters his past and a lost language.

Edward Abbey   *The First Morning*   143

Viewing the empty desert, Abbey announces, "This is the most beautiful place on earth."

Blending the Modes

E. B. White   *Once More to the Lake*   151

Describing a vacation trip, White compares past and present and realizes his sense of mortality.

Writing beyond the Classroom

Frank Pilipp and Charles Shull   *TV Movies of the First Decade of AIDS (Abstract)*   159

A brief summary of an article serves as a valuable research tool

3M *Pharmaceutical Sales Representative Want Ad*   161

A want ad describes the ideal job candidate

Monica Ramos   *The Résumé of Monica Ramos*   163

A job applicant details her skills and experience in response to a want ad.

Strategies for Writing Description   166

Suggested Topics for Descriptive Writing   167

Student Paper   *Cities of the Dead*   168

The tombs of New Orleans' above-ground cemeteries form a city of miniature mansions and slums.

Description Checklist   170

Web Tutor: See for further information on writing description   170

4   DEFINITION: ESTABLISHING MEANING   171

What Is Definition?   171

Methods of Definition   173

The Purposes of Definition   174

Definition in Context   174

Strategies for Reading Definition   175

Meaning   175

Strategy   175

Language   176

Eileen Simpson   *Dyslexia*   177

A psychotherapist defines a reading disability by detailing her own experiences as a dyslexic.

Janice Castro, Dan Cook, and Cristina Garcia   *Spanglish*   183

Castro offers a colorful definition of a new language emerging from the blending of two cultures.

Jonathan Ritter *The World View of a Computer Hacker* 187

Viewing data as weapons and programs as delivery systems, hackers see themselves as modern privateers.

John Ciardi *What Is Happiness?* 192

Poet and translator John Ciardi defines the elusive concept of happiness and asserts that it is never more than partial.

Gretel Ehrlich *A Storm, the Cornfield, and Elk* 197

"All through autumn we hear a double voice: one says everything is ripe; the other says everything is dying."

Terry Tempest Williams *Yucca* 203

Williams defines the yucca plant as being essential in Navajo culture, for the "yucca and Navajo are relatives."

Blending the Modes

Edward Dolnick *Deafness as Culture* 212

Instead of viewing themselves as victims of a handicap, a growing number of deaf people define themselves as a minority group with a unique language and culture.

Writing beyond the Classroom

Two Definitions of Depression 230

The Encyclopedia of Psychology *Depression* 230

An academic reference book defines the concept of depression for physicians and psychologists.

Don D. Rosenberg *What Is Depression?* 231

A mental health clinic brochure defines depression for its clients and the general public.

Strategies for Writing Definitions 233

Suggested Topics for Writing Definitions 233

Student Paper *Disneyland Dads* 235

The Disneyland Dad is the divorced father who offers his estranged children material goods they want but not the parenting they need.

Definition Checklist 237

Web Tutor: See for further information on writing definition 237

**5 COMPARISON AND CONTRAST: INDICATING
SIMILARITIES AND DIFFERENCES** 238

What Is Comparison and Contrast? 238

The Purposes of Comparison and Contrast 239

Organizing Comparison and Contrast Papers 239

Strategies for Reading Comparison and Contrast 243

Meaning 243

Strategy 243

Language 243

Yi-Fu Tuan *Chinese Space, American Space* 245

Unlike the Chinese, "Americans have a sense of space, not place."

William Zinsser *The Transaction* 248

Zinsser compares the working styles of two writers. For one, writing is "fun"; for the other, it is "hard and lonely work."

Bruce Catton *Grant and Lee* 254

Meeting at Appomattox, the two famous generals of the Civil War were studies in contrast who were "under everything else very much alike."

Steven D. Stark *A Tale of Two Sitcoms* 259

Though different, *Seinfeld* and *Home Improvement* revealed much about the America of the 1990s.

William Ouchi *Japanese and American Workers: Two States of Mind* 267

Ouchi, an expert on business management, compares the Japanese collective spirit with the American drive for individuality.

Amy Tan *The Language of Discretion* 275

A Chinese writer compares her native language to English, noting that "word-for-word translation is not enough to translate meaning or intent."

Blending the Modes

Rene Denfeld *The New Victorians* 284

Like the Victorians, today's feminists, according to Denfeld, depict women as both sexually pure and helpless.

Writing beyond the Classroom

Peggy Kenna and Sondra Lacy *Communication Styles: United States and Taiwan* 290

Two consultants offer business travelers a chart contrasting American and Taiwanese communications styles.

Strategies for Writing Comparison and Contrast 294

Suggested Topics for Comparison and Contrast Writing 294

Student Paper *Parallel States: Israel and Ireland* 295

Despite obvious differences, Israel and Ireland are both homelands to a great Diaspora and share similar histories, social conflicts, and battles with terrorism.

Comparison and Contrast Checklist 298

Web Tutor: See for further information on writing comparison 298

6   ANALYSIS: MAKING EVALUATIONS   299

What Is Analysis?   299
     Subjective and Objective Analysis
     Detailed Observation
Critical Thinking for Writing Analysis   303
Strategies for Reading Analysis   304
     Meaning   304
     Strategy   305
     Language   305
Juliet B. Schor   *Addicted to Plastic: The Overspent American*   306
     The ease of credit cards has led millions of Americans to live beyond
     their means—at a terrible price.
William Raspberry   *The Handicap of Definition*   310
     A popular commentator asserts that widely held definitions of "blackness"
     have crippling effects on young African-Americans.
Michael Zielenziger   *Black is Beautiful: Tokyo Style*   314
     In Zielenziger's analysis, the current Japanese fascination with
     African-American culture is based on image rather than substance
Joel Connelly   *A Growing Awareness: Environmental Groups and the Media*   319
     Connelly examines how environmentalists have transformed
     dramatic images into "visual lobbying."
Darrell Huff   *How to Live with Statistics*   326
     This 1950 article remains an accurate study of the ways statistics are used
     to "sensationalize, inflate, confuse, and oversimplify."
Louis R. Mizell Jr.   *Who's Listening to Your Cell Phone Calls?*   337
     Easily monitored, even the most innocent cellular phone messages can
     aid criminals and stalkers.
Frank Pilipp and Charles Shull   *TV Movies of the First Decade of AIDS*   343
     TV movies about AIDS rely on stereotypes to depict "the worlds of the
     immune and the implicated."
Blending the Modes   358
Richard Rodriquez and Lauren Greenfield   *Growing Up Old in LA*   358
     "The great postwar, postmodern, suburban city in Dolby sound was built
     by restless people who intended to give their kids an unending spring."
Writing beyond the Classroom   366
Kimberly Crawford, J.D.   *Surreptitious Recording of Suspects' Conversations*   366
     An attorney analyzes the legality of secretly recorded conversations
     for an article in the *FBI Law Enforcement Bulletin*.

Strategies for Writing Analysis   378
Suggested Topics for Writing Analysis   378
Student Paper   *Nostalgia: Why We Need and Love the Past*   379
We love the past because it reminds us of our youth and because it is
safe—whatever problems the Thirties, Fifties, or Seventies posed, we
survived them.

Analysis Checklist   382
Web Tutor: See for further information on writing analysis   382

7   **DIVISION AND CLASSIFICATION: SEPARATING INTO PARTS
    AND RATING CATEGORIES**   383
What Are Division and Classification?   383
    Division   383
    Critical Thinking for Writing Division   384
    Classification   385
    Critical Thinking for Writing Classification   386
Strategies for Reading Division and Classification   387
    Meaning   387
    Strategy   387
    Language   387
Russell Baker   *The Plot Against People*   388
Inanimate objects frustrate people by not working, breaking down, and
getting lost.

Mary Mebane   *Black Wasn't Beautiful*   392
Growing up in the segregated South, dark complexioned
African-American women faced limited choices.

Kesaya E. Noda   *Growing Up Asian in America*   397
Noda reveals the range of identities she faced growing up in America.

Martin Luther King Jr.   *The Ways of Meeting Oppression*   401
Oppressed people can confront their situation in three ways: through
acquiescence, with violence, or by non-violent resistance.

Meg Greenfield   *Why Nothing Is "Wrong" Anymore*   406
Greenfield provides five reasons why people no longer can simply label
behavior as being "wrong."

James Austin   *Four Kinds of Chance*   411
A scientist classifies the kinds of chance that occur in scientific research.

John Holt   *Three Kinds of Discipline*   417
Children encounter discipline from three sources: nature, society, and
superior force.

Blending the Modes

Northrop Frye *Our Three Languages*   422

Humans use language for self-expression, social participation, and
imagination.

Writing beyond the Classroom

Black's Law Dictionary *Homicide*   427

Rinehart Guide to Grammar and Usage *Kinds of Sentences*   431

Sentences are classified by the number and type of clauses.

Strategies for Division and Classification Writing   434

Suggested Topics for Division and Classification Writing   434

Student Paper *Hispanics on Campus*   435

Hispanic students do not form a homogenous group, but range from
Spanish-speaking immigrants to highly assimilated "invisible"
Hispanics.

Division and Classification Checklist   438

Web Tutor: See for further information on writing division and
classification   438

8 PROCESS: EXPLAINING HOW THINGS WORK AND GIVING DIRECTIONS   439

What Is Process?   439

Explaining How Things Work   439

Critical Thinking for Writing Explanations   440

Giving Directions   441

Critical Thinking for Writing Directions   442

Strategies for Reading Process   443

Meaning   443

Strategy   443

Language   444

Elizabeth Kolbert *Birth of a TV Show: A Drama All Its Own*   445

Television shows go through a complex and baffling process that takes
them from pitched idea to pilot to program.

Armond D. Budish *Fender Bender Do's and Don't's*   451

A consumer reporter offers step-by-step advice to motorists involved in
minor accidents.

Marvin Harris *How Our Skins Got Their Color*   456

Sunlight, Vitamin D, and skin cancer caused people to develop lighter
and darker complexions.

Peter Elbow *Desperation Writing*   461

A writing expert offers advice on how to write under stress.

Fran Martin *Documentation Tips* 466

To avoid charges of malpractice, healthcare professionals must document their actions with detailed accuracy.

Anne Weisbord *Résumés That Rate a Second Look* 471

A career counselor offers eight tips for creating effective résumés.

Eugene Raudsepp *Seeing Your Way Past Interview Jitters* 474

Job applicants can improve their interview performances by using a psychological technique called visualization.

Liz Grinslade *Evaluating a Job Opportunity* 479

Accepting the wrong job can be worse than not being hired.

Blending the Modes

Charles N. Jamison Jr. *Why My Business Failed* 484

In this *Black Enterprise* article, an advertising executive offers advice to fellow entrepreneurs.

Writing beyond the Classroom

Lucille Treganowan *Cleaning Battery Terminals* 493

The author of *Lucille's Car Care* provides instructions on car repair.

Strategies for Process Writing 496

Suggested Topics for Process Writing 496

Student Paper *Securing Your Home* 498

Homeowners can deter robbers by following a few simple tips.

Process Checklist 500

Web Tutor: See for further information on writing process 500

**9   CAUSE AND EFFECT: DETERMINING REASONS
        AND PREDICTING RESULTS** 501

What Is Cause and Effect? 501

Deduction and Induction 502

Establishing Causes 504

Predicting Results 505

Critical Thinking for Cause-and-Effect Writing 507

Strategies for Reading Cause and Effect 508

Meaning 508

Strategy 508

Language 508

Michael Marriott *CyberSoul Not Found* 509

Although African-Americans have embraced new technologies such as cellular phones, few have taken advantage of the Internet, which is still perceived as "white."

Gloria Steinem   *Words and Change*   514

"Now, we have terms like *sexual harassment* and *battered women*. A few years ago, they were just called *life*."

Blending the Modes

Jeff Gammage   *Why More Women Are Going to Prison*   522

Gammage offers reasons why the arrest rate for women is increasing at three times the rate of men.

Pro and Con Views: "Abuse Excuse"

Alan Dershowitz   *The "Abuse Excuse" Is Detrimental to the Justice System*   528

A noted defense attorney argues that the "abuse excuse" encourages vigilantism.

Leslie Abramson   *The Abuse Defense Balances the Justice System*   533

The defense attorney who achieved fame during the Menendez trial asserts that abuse defense results in greater justice for victims.

Pro and Con Views: Global Warming

Jodi Jacobson   *Swept Away*   538

Global warming will melt polar icecaps, flood coastal cities, and sink islands unless greenhouse gases are stemmed.

Jocelyn Tomkin   *Hot Air*   549

Far from being a threat, the greenhouse effect, Tomkin claims, makes life on earth possible.

Writing beyond the Classroom

Thomas Jefferson, et. al.   *The Declaration of Independence*   556

Jefferson details the reasons why the American colonies must sever ties with Great Britain.

Hewlett-Packard   *Solving Printer Operation Problems*   561

An owner's manual provides a simple cause-and-effect chart to remedy common problems.

Strategies for Cause-and-Effect Writing   567

Suggested Topics for Cause-and-Effect Writing   567

Student Paper   *Can the Devon Be Saved?*   568

Outlining the effects proposed development will have on a local river, a student questions if the waterway can be preserved.

Cause-and-Effect Checklist   571

WebTutor: See for further information on writing cause and effect   571

10   ARGUMENT AND PERSUASION: INFLUENCING READERS   572

What Is Argument and Persuasion?   572

Persuasive Appeals   574

Appealing to Hostile Readers   576

Critical Thinking for Writing Argument and Persuasion   577

Strategies for Reading Argument and Persuasion   578

    Meaning   578

    Strategy   578

    Language   578

Wilbert Rideau *Why Prisons Don't Work*   579

  The editor of a prison newsmagazine argues that, at best, prisons can play only a limited role in fighting crime.

Leonce Gaiter *The Revolt of the Black Bourgeoisie*   583

  In this *New York Times* article, Gaiter decries negative images that suggest that in order to be genuine, black males must be poor and ignorant.

Carl Sagan *Why We Need to Understand Science*   589

  "I'm haunted by the vision of a generation of Americans unable to distinguish reality from fantasy . . . unequipped to even frame the right questions or to recognize the answers."

David Blankenhorn *Fatherless America*   598

  Blackenhorn argues that in the future Americans will be divided not by race, class, or gender but by paternity. Those who grow up with fathers will have privileges and benefits denied to the fatherless.

Blending the Modes

Nat Hentoff *Should This Student Have Been Expelled?*   604

  Hentoff asks when does "speech" become an "action" that can be punished as a crime?

Pro and Con Views: Cultural Identity

Rendón *Kiss of Death*   611

  Resisting assimilation, a Chicano writer embraces his heritage to escape what he falls the "vacuum of the dominant society."

Barbara Ehrenreich *Cultural Baggage*   617

  Ehrenreich rejects her ethnic background and is proud that her children see themselves as belonging to the "race of none."

Writing beyond the Classroom

Albert Einstein *Letter to President Roosevelt, August 2, 1939*   622

  At the outbreak of World War II, America's most famous scientist alerted President Roosevelt about the potential of nuclear weapons.

The Irish American Partnership *Irish Need Apply*   626

  Using a headline recalling racist "No Irish Need Apply" notices, a fund raising ad urges affluent Irish Americans to donate to their homeland.

Student Paper   *Why a Black Student Union?*   631
   Responding to critics, a student defends the existence of a black student
   union on his campus.
Argument and Persuasion Checklist   634
WebTutor: See for further information on writing argument and
   persuasion   634

Credits   C-1
Index   I-1

THEMATIC CONTENTS

ART AND ENTERTAINMENT

A Tale of Two Sitcoms, Steven D. Stark (comparison)   259

Black Is Beautiful: Tokyo Style, Michael Zielenziger (analysis)   314

TV Movies of the First Decade of AIDS, Frank Pilipp and Charles Shull (analysis)   343

Birth of a TV Show, Elizabeth Kolbert (process)   445

AUTOBIOGRAPHY

Take This Fish and Look at It, Samuel Scudder (narration)   45

The Lesson, Nathan McCall (narration)   51

Shooting an Elephant, George Orwell (narration)   72

The Fender-Bender, Ramon "Tianguis" Perez (narration)   62

The Way to Rainy Mountain, N. Scott Momaday (description)   137

The First Morning, Edward Abbey (description)   143

Once More to the Lake, E. B. White (description)   151

The Transaction, William Zinsser (comparison)   248

Black Wasn't Beautiful, Mary Mebane (division/classification)   392

Growing Up Asian in America, Kesaya E. Noda (division/classification)   397

Kiss of Death, Armando Rendón (argument/persuasion)   611

Cultural Baggage, Barbara Ehrenreich (argument/persuasion)   617

BIOGRAPHY

A Short Story about the Vietnam War Memorial, Molly Ivins (narration)   57

The Man Who Mistook His Wife for a Hat, Oliver Sacks (narration)   81

My Ecumenical Father, José Antonio Burciaga (description)   127

Unforgettable Miss Bessie, Carl Rowan (description)   131

Grant and Lee, Bruce Catton (comparison)   253

BUSINESS AND ECONOMICS

Japanese and American Workers: Two States of Mind, William Ouchi (comparison)   267

Communications Styles: United States and Taiwan, Peggy Kenna and
    Sondra Lacy (comparison)   290
Addicted to Plastic: The Overspent American Juliet B. Schor (analysis)   306
Birth of a TV Show, Elizabeth Kolbert (process)   445
Why My Business Failed, Charles Jamison Jr. (process)   484

CHILDHOOD
The Lesson, Nathan McCall (narration)   51
My Ecumenical Father, José Antonio Burciaga (description)   127
Once More to the Lake, E. B. White (description)   151
Growing Up Old in LA, Richard Rodriquez and Lauren Greenfield
    (analysis)   358
Black Wasn't Beautiful, Mary Mebane (division/classification)   392
Growing Up Asian in America, Kesaya E. Noda (division/classification)   397
Three Kinds of Discipline, John Holt (division/classification)   417
Fatherless America, David Blankenhorn (argument/persuasion)   598

CIVIL RIGHTS
Black Political Leadership, Cornel West (comparison)   35
The Lesson, Nathan McCall (narration)   51
The Fender-Bender, Ramon "Tianguis" Perez (narration)   62
Unforgettable Miss Bessie, Carl Rowan (description)   131
Deafness as Culture, Edward Dolnick (definition)   212
The Handicap of Definition, William Raspberry (analysis)   310
Black Wasn't Beautiful, Mary Mebane (division/classification)   392
The Ways of Meeting Oppression, Martin Luther King Jr.
    (division/classification)   401
How Our Skins Got Their Color, Marvin Harris (process)   456
The Revolt of the Black Bourgeoisie, Leonce Gaiter
    (argument/persuasion)   583

COMMUNITY AND CULTURE
The Lesson, Nathan McCall (narration)   51
The Fender-Bender, Ramon "Tianguis" Perez (narration)   62
Shooting an Elephant, George Orwell (narration)   72
Marrying Absurd, Joan Didion (description)   122
My Ecumenical Father, José Antonio Burciaga (description)   127
The Way to Rainy Mountain, N. Scott Momaday (description)   137

Spanglish, Janice Castro, Dan Cook, Christina Garcia (definition)   183
Yucca, Terry Tempest Williams (definition)   203
Deafness as Culture, Edward Dolnick (definition)   212
The Handicap of Definition, William Raspberry (analysis)   310
Black Is Beautiful: Tokyo Style, Michael Zielenziger (analysis)   314
Growing Up Old in LA, Richard Rodriquez and Lauren Greenfield
    (analysis)   358
Black Wasn't Beautiful, Mary Mebane (division/classification)   392
Growing Up Asian in America, Kesaya E. Noda (division/classification)   397
CyberSoul Not Found, Michel Marriott (cause/effect)   509
The Revolt of the Black Bourgeoisie, Leonce Gaiter
(argument/persuasion)   583
Kiss of Death, Armando Rendón (argument/persuasion)   611
Cultural Baggage, Barbara Ehrenreich (argument/persuasion)   617
Irish Need Apply, Irish American Partnership (argument/persuasion)   626

CRITICAL THINKING

Take This Fish and Look at It, Samuel Scudder (narration)   45
How to Lie with Statistics, Richard Huff (analysis)   326
Four Kinds of Chance, James Austin (division/classification)   411
Why We Need to Understand Science, Carl Sagan
    (argument/persuasion)   589

DIVERSITY

Black Political Leadership, Cornel West (comparison)   35
Border Story, Luis Alberto Urrea (description)   118
My Ecumenical Father, José Antonio Burciaga (description)   127
The Way to Rainy Mountain, N. Scott Momaday (description)   137
Spanglish, Janice Castro, Dan Cook, Christina Garcia (definition)   183
Deafness as Culture, Edward Dolnick (definition)   212
Chinese Space, American Space, Yi-Fu Tuan (comparison)   245
Japanese and American Workers: Two States of Mind, William Ouchi
    (comparison)   267
The Language of Discretion, Amy Tan (comparison)   280
Communications Styles: United States and Taiwan, Peggy Kenna and
    Sondra Lacy (comparison)   290
Growing Up Asian in America, Kesaya E. Noda (division/classification)   397
CyberSoul Not Found, Michel Marriot (cause/effect)   509

EDUCATION
Take This Fish and Look at It, Samuel Scudder (narration)   45
The Lesson, Nathan McCall (narration)   51
Unforgettable Miss Bessie, Carl Rowan (description)   131
Dyslexia, Eileen Simpson (definition)   177
Three Kinds of Discipline, John Holt (division/classification)   417
Should This Student Have Been Expelled?, Nat Hentoff   604

ENVIRONMENT
Ebola River, Richard Preston (narration)   67
First Morning, Edward Abbey (description)   143
A Growing Awareness: Environmental Groups and The Media,
     Joel Connelly (analysis)   319
Swept Away, Jodi Jacobson (cause/effect)   538
Hot Air, Jocelyn Tomkin (cause/effect)   548

HEALTH AND MEDICINE
Ebola River, Richard Preston (narration)   67
The Man Who Mistook His Wife for a Hat, Oliver Sacks (narration)   81
Dyslexia, Eileen Simpson (definition)   177
Deafness as Culture, Edward Dolnick (definition)   212
Two Definitions of Depression (definition)   230
TV Movies of the First Decade of AIDS, Frank Pilipp and Charles Shull
     (analysis)   343

HISTORY
Black Political Leadership, Cornel West (comparison)   35
Interrogation of Lee Harvey Oswald, Federal Bureau of Investigation
     (narration)   93
The Reconstructed Logbook of the *Titanic*, Walter Lord (narration)   98
Grant and Lee, Bruce Catton (comparison)   247
The Declaration of Independence, Thomas Jefferson et al. (cause/effect)   556
Letter to President Roosevelt, August 2, 1939, Albert Einstein
     (argument/persuasion)   622

JOB INTERVIEWS
3M Pharmaceutical Sales Representative Want Ad, *The Times-Picayune*,
     July 31, 1994 (description)   161

Résumé of Monica Ramos, Monica Ramos (description)   163
Resumes That Rate a Second Look, Anne Weisbord (process)   471
Seeing Your Way Past Interview Jitters, Eugene Raudsepp (process)   474
Evaluating a Job Opportunity, Liz Grinslade (process)   479

LANGUAGE
Dyslexia, Eileen Simpson (definition)   177
Spanglish, Janice Castro, Dan Cook, Christina Garcia (definition)   183
The Language of Discretion, Amy Tan (comparison)   274
Our Three Languages, Northrop Frye (division/classification)   422
Kinds of Sentences, *Rinehart Guide to Grammar and Usage*
    (division/classification)   431
Words and Change, Gloria Steinem (cause/effect)   514
Kiss of Death, Armando Rendón (argument/persuasion)   611

LAW AND CRIME
Interrogation of Lee Harvey Oswald, Federal Bureau of Investigation
    (narration)   93
Who's Listening to Your Cell Phone Calls?, Louis Mizell Jr. (analysis)   337
Surreptitious Recording of Suspects' Conversations,
    Kimberly Crawford (analysis)   366
Homicide, *Black's Law Dictionary* (division/classification)   427
Fender Bender Do's and Don't's, Armond Budish (process)   451
Why More Women Are Going to Prison, Jeff Gammage (cause/effect)   522
The "Abuse Excuse" Is Detrimental to the Justice System,
    Alan Dershowitz (cause/effect)   528
The Abuse Defense Balances the Justice System, Leslie Abramson
    (cause/effect)   533
Why Prisons Don't Work, Wilbert Rideau (argument/persuasion)   579

MATHEMATICS
How to Lie with Statistics, Richard Huff (analysis)   326

MEDIA AND IMAGE
A Tale of Two Sitcoms, Steven D. Stark (comparison)   253
Black Is Beautiful: Tokyo Style, Michael Zielenziger (analysis)   314
A Growing Awareness: Environmental Groups and the Media,
    Joel Connelly (analysis)   319

TV Movies of the First Decade of AIDS, Frank Pilipp and Charles Shull
(analysis)   343
Birth of a TV Show, Elizabeth Kolbert (process)   451

MINORITY EXPERIENCE

Black Political Leadership, Cornel West (comparison)   35
The Lesson, Nathan McCall (narration)   51
The Fender-Bender, Ramon "Tianguis" Perez (narration)   62
Border Story, Luis Alberto Urrea (description)   118
The Way to Rainy Mountain, N. Scott Momaday (description)   137
Yucca, Terry Tempest Williams (definition)   203
The Handicap of Definition, William Raspberry (analysis)   310
Black Is Beautiful: Tokyo Style, Michael Zielenziger (analysis)   314
Black Wasn't Beautiful, Mary Mebane (division/classification)   392
Growing Up Asian in America, Kesaya E. Noda (division/classification)   397
CyberSoul Not Found, Michel Marriott (cause/effect)   509
The Revolt of the Black Bourgeoisie, Leonce Gaiter
(argument/persuasion)   583
Kiss of Death, Armando Rendón (argument/persuasion)   611
Cultural Baggage, Barbara Ehrenreich (argument/persuasion)   617
Irish Need Apply, Irish American Partnership (argument/persuasion)   626

NATURE

Ebola River, Richard Preston (narration)   67
First Morning, Edward Abbey (description)   143
A Storm, the Cornfield, and Elk, Gretel Ehrlich (definition)   197
Yucca, Terry Tempest Williams (definition)   203

POLITICS

Black Political Leadership, Cornel West (comparison)   35
A Short Story about the Vietnam War Memorial, Molly Ivins
(narration)   57
Shooting an Elephant, George Orwell (narration)   72
The New Victorians, Rene Denfeld (comparison)   284
A Growing Awareness: Environmental Groups and the Media,
Joel Connelly (analysis)   319
The Ways of Meeting Oppression, Martin Luther King Jr.
(division/classification)   401

Why More Women Are Going to Prison, Jeff Gammage (cause/effect)   522
The Declaration of Independence, Thomas Jefferson et al. (cause/effect)   556
Why Prisons Don't Work, Wilbert Rideau (argument/persuasion)   579
Should This Student Have Been Expelled?, Nat Hentoff
    (argument/persuasion)   604

PSYCHOLOGY AND HUMAN BEHAVIOR
The Man Who Mistook His Wife for a Hat, Oliver Sacks (narration)   81
Shooting an Elephant, George Orwell (narration)   72
Dyslexia, Eileen Simpson (definition)   177
What Is Happiness?, John Ciardi (definition)   192
Deafness as Culture, Edward Dolnick (definition)   212
Depression, Donald Rosenberg (definition)   231
Chinese Space, American Space, Yi-Fu Tuan (comparison)   245
Japanese and American Workers: Two States of Mind, William Ouchi
    (comparison)   267
Addicted to Plastic: The Overspent American, Juliet B. Schor (analysis)   306
Black Is Beautiful: Tokyo Style, Michel Zielenziger (analysis)   314
The Plot Against People, Russell Baker (division/classification)   388
Three Kinds of Discipline, John Holt (division/classification)   417
Seeing Your Way Past Interview Jitters, Eugene Raudsepp (process)   474

SCIENCE AND TECHNOLOGY
Take This Fish and Look at It, Samuel Scudder (narration)   45
Ebola River, Richard Preston (narration)   67
The World View of a Computer Hacker, Jonathan Ritter (definition)   187
Who's Listening to Your Cell Phone Calls?, Louis Mizell Jr. (analysis)   337
Four Kinds of Chance, James Austin (division/classification)   411
CyberSoul Not Found, Michel Marriott (cause/effect)   509
Swept Away, Jodi Jacobson (cause/effect)   538
Hot Air, Joceyln Tomkin (cause/effect)   549
Why We Need to Understand Science, Carl Sagan
    (argument/persuasion)   589

SOCIOLOGY
Black Political Leadership, Cornel West (comparison)   35
Deafness as Culture, Edward Dolnick (definition)   212
Chinese Space, American Space, Yi-Fu Tuan (comparison)   245

Japanese and American Workers; Two States of Mind, William Ouchi
    (comparison)   267

TV Movies of the First Decade of AIDS, Frank Pilipp and Charles Shull
    (analysis)   343

Growing Up Old in LA, Richard Rodriquez and Lauren Greenfield
    (analysis)   358

Words and Change, Gloria Steinem (cause/effect)   514

Fatherless America, David Blankenhorn (argument/persuasion)   597

VALUES

My Ecumenical Father, José Antonio Burgiaga (description)   127

What Is Happiness?, John Ciardi (definition)   192

Addicted to Plastic: The Overspent American, Juliet B. Schor (analysis)   306

Why Nothing Is Wrong Anymore, Meg Greenfield
    (division/classification)   406

Three Kinds of Discipline, John Holt (division/classification)   417

Fatherless America, David Blankenhorn (argument/persuasion)   598

Should This Student Have Been Expelled?, Nat Hentoff
    (argument/persuasion)   604

Kiss of Death, Armando Rendón (argument/persuasion)   611

Cultural Baggage, Barbara Ehrenreich (argument/persuasion)   617

WOMEN AND MEN

A Short Story about the Vietnam War Memorial, Molly Ivins
    (narration)   57

Marrying Absurd, Joan Didion (description)   122

The New Victorians, Rene Denfeld (comparison)   284

Black Wasn't Beautiful, Mary Mebane (division/classification)   392

Words and Change, Gloria Steinem (cause/effect)   514

Why More Women Are Going to Prison, Jeff Gammage (cause/effect)   522

Fatherless America, David Blankenhorn (argument/persuasion)   597

WORK AND CAREER

Japanese and American Workers: Two States of Mind, William Ouchi
    (comparison)   266

Birth of a TV Show, Elizabeth Kolbert (process)   445

Documentation Tips, Fran Martin (process)   466

Why My Business Failed, Charles Jamison Jr. (process)   484

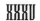
WRITING

The Transaction, William Zinsser (comparison)   248

Our Three Languages, Northrop Frye (division/classification)   422

Kinds of Sentences, *Rinehart Guide to Grammar and Usage*
    (division/classification)   431

Desperation Writing, Peter Elbow (process)   461

Documentation Tips, Fran Martin (process)   466

Resumes That Rate a Second Look, Anne Weisbord (process)   471

Words and Change, Gloria Steinem (cause/effect)   514

The Sundance Reader

Second Edition

1

INTRODUCTION

HOW WE WRITE

In the summer of 1939 scientist Leo Szilard was worried. As Americans enjoyed the New York World's Fair, the exiled physicist followed events in Europe with growing anxiety. His experiments proved that a nuclear chain reaction could create an atomic bomb. German scientists had split the atom, and the Nazis had seized rich deposits of uranium in Czechoslovakia. As a Jew who had escaped on the last train out of Nazi Germany, Szilard was horrified at the prospect of Hitler obtaining nuclear weapons. Now living in New York, he tried to warn the American government, but officials in Washington were unwilling to fund atomic research. A refugee without resources or political contacts, Szilard sought help from his old friend Albert Einstein, a Nobel Prize winner with an international reputation. Szilard hoped the government would listen to Einstein. Although the idea of a nuclear chain reaction had never occurred to him, Einstein quickly grasped its implications and suggested writing to President Roosevelt. Einstein dictated a letter and asked Szilard to revise it. Szilard wrote a new version then telephoned Einstein, who requested another meeting. Accompanied by fellow physicist Edward Teller, Szilard met Einstein at a summer cottage to discuss the letter. The scientists soon became frustrated. Einstein realized their abstract theories would be difficult to explain to a nonscientist. Equally frustrating was the fact that English was a second language to all three scientists. Einstein dictated a new draft to Edward Teller in German. Leo Szilard wrote two more letters in English and mailed them to Einstein. After reviewing them carefully, Einstein selected the longer version and signed it. Just eight paragraphs long, the letter began with a simply worded declaration of Einstein's concerns:

Sir:

Some recent work by E. Fermi and L. Szilard, which has been communicated to me in manuscript, leads me to expect that the element uranium may be turned into a new and important source of energy in the immediate future. Certain aspects of the situation which has arisen seem to call for watchfulness and, if necessary, quick action on the part of the Administration. I believe therefore that it is my duty to bring to your attention the following facts and recommendations:

This letter (see page 622 for the full version) was presented to President Roosevelt and helped launch the Manhattan Project and the nuclear age.

The story behind Einstein's letter demonstrates important elements about writing. Writing is a complex process and does not occur in a vacuum. It takes place in a *context* formed by three factors:

1. The writer's purpose and role
2. The knowledge base, attitudes, needs, expectations, and biases of the reader
3. The conventions, history, and culture of a particular discipline, profession, organization, publication, situation, or community

Writing, as the creation of Einstein's letter shows, is often *collaborative*, a product of a group activity. Writing may reflect the ideas of more than one person. Einstein's letter also illustrates a common dilemma writers face in a technological society. Experts frequently have to communicate with readers outside their discipline, people with little understanding or appreciation of the writers' subjects.

Context explains why a newspaper article about an airplane crash differs from a Federal Aviation Administration (FAA) report or the airline's condolence letter to the victims' families. Stated simply and printed in narrow columns for easy skimming, a newspaper account briefly describes current events for general readers. An FAA report detailing the causes of a plane crash runs hundreds of pages and includes extensive data and testimony of witnesses and survivors. Directed to aviation safety experts, the report is stated in technical language largely incomprehensible to the average reader. The airline's letter to victims' families addresses people enduring confusion, grief, and anger. Carefully worded, it attempts to inform readers without appearing callous or falsely sympathetic.

You may have noticed how context affects your own writing. The notes you take in class for personal use look very different from the in-class essay you submit for a grade. The words you choose when adding a line to a birthday card for your seven-year-old cousin differ from those used on a job application or in a note to your roommate. Almost unconsciously, you alter the way you write depending on your purpose, reader, and circumstances. To be an effective writer in college and in your future career, it is important to increase your understanding of the three elements that form a writing context.

1. Can you recall writing situations where you had difficulty expressing your ideas because you were unsure how your reader would react? Did you have problems finding the right words or just "getting your thoughts on paper"?
2. Have you found that teachers and professors have different attitudes about what constitutes "good writing"? How is writing a paper in English literature different from writing a paper in psychology or economics?
3. Have you observed that magazines often have strikingly different writing styles? What do articles in *Cosmopolitan, Car and Driver*, or *The Wall Street Journal* reveal about their intended readers?

THE WRITER

All writing has a goal. A shopping list serves to refresh your memory. A memo informs employees of a policy change. Research papers demonstrate students' knowledge and skills. Résumés encourage employers to call applicants for job interviews. Even essays written for self-expression must contain more than random observations. To be effective an essay must arouse interest, provide readers with information they can understand, and offer proof to support the writer's thesis.

The Writer's Purpose

Students and professionals in all fields face similar writing tasks. The way they present their ideas, the language they use, and even the physical appearance of the finished document are determined in part by their purpose. Although every writing assignment forms a unique context, most writing tasks can be divided into basic modes or types:

narration *To relate a series of events, usually in chronological order.* Biographies, histories, and novels use narration. Business and government reports often include sections called *narratives* that provide a historical overview of a problem, organization, or situation. Letters to friends usually consist of narratives detailing recent events or experiences.

description *To create a picture or impression of a person, place, object, or condition.* Description is a basic element in all writing and usually serves to provide support for the writer's main goal. Descriptions may be wholly factual and objective, as in an accident report or parts catalog. Others may contain personal impressions emphasizing what the writer saw, thought, or felt. A novelist describing a city is more likely to focus on his or her "feel" of the streets and people rather than on statistics and census figures.

definition *To explain a term, condition, topic, or issue.* In many instances definitions are precise and standard, such as a state's definition of second-degree murder or a biology book's definition of a virus. Other definitions, such as that of a good parent or an ideal teacher, may be based on a writer's personal observation, experience, and opinion.

comparison/contrast *To examine the similarities and differences between two or more subjects.* Textbooks often employ comparison/ contrast to discuss different scientific methods, theories, or subjects. Comparisons can be made to distinguish topics or to recommend one subject as superior to others. Consumer magazines frequently use comparison to highlight differences among competing products.

analysis *To evaluate a subject and identify its essential elements, impact, effectiveness, or qualities.* Writers of a formal analysis can follow a standard method. Stockbrokers, medical examiners, building inspectors, archaeologists, botanists, criminologists, and other professionals generally use uniform methods of studying subjects and presenting their conclusions. Essayists and newspaper columnists, on the other hand, analyze issues from an entirely personal perspective, relying on anecdotal evidence and individual observation. A reviewer's column about a new movie, a sports writer's column about a coach's performance, and a pollster's view on the president's popularity are examples of personal analysis.

division   *To name subgroups or divisions in a broad class.* Writers seek to make a large or complex topic understandable or workable by dividing it into smaller units. Insurance can be divided into life, health, homeowner's, and auto policies. A zoology text divides animals into fish, birds, mammals, and reptiles.

classification   *To place objects into different classes or levels according to a single measurement.* Writers classify with a scale to grade subjects. Homicides are classified as first-, second-, or third-degree according to circumstances and premeditation. Burns are classified as first-, second-, or third-degree based on the severity of tissue damage.

Like analysis, division and classification can be based on professional standards or personal evaluation. A financial adviser might rate mutual funds by risk and performance using commonly accepted criteria. A movie critic, however, could grade films on a one-to-five-star scale based solely on his or her tastes.

process   *To explain how something occurs or to demonstrate how to accomplish a specific task.* A nuclear power plant, the human heart, and inflation can be described as processes. By examining each stage, a writer can make a complex mechanism or event easier to understand. A recipe, the owner's manual of a computer, and a first-aid book offer step-by-step instructions to complete specific tasks.

cause and effect   *To trace the reasons for or results of an occurrence.* A writer can list causes for an increase in crime, for the return of an endangered species, or for the success or failure of an advertising campaign. Similarly, he or she could list the effects crime has on a community, the response to rescued wildlife, or the impact of television commercials. Physicians refer to medical books that explain the causes of disease and the effects of drugs.

persuasion and argumentation   *To influence reader opinion, attitudes, and actions.* Writers persuade with logical appeals based on factual evidence, with ethical appeals based on values or beliefs, or with emotional appeals that arouse feelings to support their views. A fund-raising letter persuades readers to donate money to a charity. An engineer's report presents an argument why a building should be condemned or an engine redesigned. Essayists and columnists try to influence readers to accept their opinions on topics ranging from abortion to welfare reform.

QUESTIONS

1. Consider how you have organized papers in the past. Did any assignments lend themselves to one of the modes? Could following one of these methods make it easier to present and organize your ideas?
2. Do you use modes such as *comparison, classification,* or *cause and effect* in organizing your thoughts and solving problems? Do you *compare* apartments before deciding which one to rent or *classify* courses you want to take next semester by difficulty or desirability?

The way writers achieve their goals depends greatly on the other two elements of context: their readers and the discipline. Each chapter of *The Sundance Reader* focuses on one of these modes, illustrating how writers use it in different contexts.

A Note about Modes

Modes refer to the writer's basic goal. Often writing cannot be neatly labeled. Few writing tasks call for the use of a single mode. A dictionary entry is pure definition, and a parts catalog offers simple product descriptions. But a movie review *analyzing* a new release will first *describe* the film and possibly *compare* it to the director's previous work. It might use *narration* to explain elements of the plot and *classification* to rank it with other films in its genre. Some writing can easily fit two or more categories. The Declaration of Independence, for instance (page 556), is an example of both *cause and effect* and *persuasive writing.*

The Writer's Role

An important aspect of context is the writer's role. As a student your role is much like that of a freelance writer. Your essays, reports, and research papers are expected to reflect only your own efforts. In general, your work is judged independently. A low grade on a first paper should not affect your chances of earning a higher grade later in the semester. What you write in psychology has no influence on your grades in English. Your comments on controversial issues are not likely to be raised at future job interviews.

Outside of academics, however, your role is more complicated. Often you act as an agent of a larger organization, corporation, or profession. Business letters, memos, and reports are assumed to express the views of the employer, not a single employee. Expressing personal views that conflict with corporate practices or administrative policy can jeopardize your position. Frequently, you will have an ongoing relationship with your readers. Comments made in one letter or report affect how readers will respond to your ideas in the future.

Probably the most obvious aspect of a writer's role concerns *perspective,* or the writer's position in the paper. Writing in a newspaper's sports section, a columnist may be free to offer personal opinion: "Given poor ticket sales and the age of the stadium, I predict this town will lose its ball club within two years." A front-page article, however, would be weakened by the use of first person. A reporter would express the same view in more objective terms: "The decline in ticket sales and the age of the stadium indicate the city is in danger of losing its baseball team."

When writing as a member of a group or as an agent of an organization, remember that the ideas you express will be considered the ideas of the group. Refrain from stating anything that would alienate other members or expose your organization to liability. If you state personal views, make sure you clearly identify them as being your opinions.

In many instances your profession will dictate a role that will greatly shape what is expected in your writing. Police officers and nurses, for example, are required to provide objective and impersonal records of their observations. Fashion consultants, decorators, and advertising executives, who are esteemed for their creativity, are more likely to offer personal insights and make first-person statements.

QUESTIONS

1. Consider the jobs you have had and the businesses you have worked for. What writing style would be appropriate for professionals in these fields? Is objective reporting required, or are employees free to offer personal impressions and suggest innovations?

2. What type of writing do you expect to confront in your career? How does writing in engineering and accounting differ from writing in public relations, sales, or nonprofit charities? Does your future profession demand adherence to governmental regulations and industry standards, or does it allow for individual expression?

THE READER

Writing is more than self-expression; it is an act of communication. To be effective your message must be understood. The content, form, and tone of your writing are largely shaped by the needs and expectations of your readers. A medical researcher announcing a new treatment for AIDS would word an article for *Immunology* very differently from one for *Newsweek* or *Redbook*. Each magazine represents a different audience, a different knowledge base, and a different set of concerns. Fellow immunologists would be interested in the author's research methods and would demand detailed proof of his or her claims. Readers of *Immunology* would expect to see extensive data and precise descriptions of experiments and testing methods. Most readers of nonmedical publications would require definitions of scientific terms and would expect brief summaries of data they would be unable to evaluate. Readers of *Newsweek* could be concerned with issues such as cost, government policy, and insurance coverage. Subscribers to a women's magazine like *Redbook* might wonder if the treatment works equally well for both sexes or if the treatment would be suitable for pregnant women with HIV.

Audiences often differ within a discipline. The medical researcher writing for the *New England Journal of Medicine* would be addressing practicing physicians, not laboratory researchers. Doctors would be interested in the practical aspects of the treatment. What drugs does it interact with? What are the side effects? Which patients should receive the drug and in what doses? An article in *Nursing* would focus on the concerns of nurses who closely monitor patients for reactions. What effect does the treatment have on a patient's physical and psychological well-being? Are there special considerations for patients with unrelated disorders, such as hypertension and diabetes?

As a writer you will have to determine how much knowledge your readers have about your subject. Do technical terms have to be defined? Does your writing include historical or biographical references requiring explanation? Do you use concepts that general readers might misunderstand or find confusing? In addition to your readers' level of understanding, you must consider your readers' needs and expectations in relation to your own goal. What information do your readers want from you? Is your audience reading for general interest, curiosity, or entertainment, or do they demand specific information in order to make decisions or plan future actions?

It is also important to take into account how your readers will respond to your ideas. Is your audience likely to be favorable or hostile to you, your ideas, or the organization you might represent? Defense attorneys and prosecutors have different attitudes toward illegally obtained evidence. Environmentalists and real estate developers have conflicting philosophies of land use. Liberals and conservatives have opposing concepts of the proper role of government regulation. When presenting ideas to audiences with undefined or differing attitudes, you will have to work hard to overcome their natural resistance, biases, and suspicions.

Individual Readers

The papers you write in high school and college are usually read by a single teacher or professor who is evaluating your work in the context of a particular course. Instructors form a special audience because they are counted on to read your work and remain objective. Beyond the classroom, however, you may have to persuade someone to read your résumé or proposal. Few of these readers will even attempt objectivity. Unlike the papers you write for instructors, your reports and letters seek more than a grade. In many instances, you will ask an employer for a job or attempt to persuade a client to buy a product. In accepting your ideas, your reader may be investing substantial resources on your behalf, conceivably placing his or her career in your hands. In writing to these individuals, you will have to analyze their needs and concerns very carefully.

Extended Readerships

Many contexts involve two audiences: the immediate person or persons who receive your document and a second, extended readership. When you write as a student, most of your work is returned to you. In most jobs your correspondence, reports, and publications are retained for future reference. The safety inspection report you write in April may be routinely skimmed by your supervisor, filed, and forgotten. But if a serious accident occurs in May, this report will be retrieved and closely examined by state inspectors, insurance investigators, and attorneys. If you engage in a dispute with a customer or another employee, your writing may be reviewed by a supervisor or, in the case of litigation, introduced into court as evidence. Many professionals practice "defensive writing," precisely wording their thoughts and observations, understanding that whatever they write may be examined by adversaries. In court, police officers and physicians are often asked to explain and defend comments they wrote months or years before.

When you write outside of academics, bear in mind who else may see your writing. This is a critical consideration whenever you are writing as an employee or agent of others. Think carefully before making remarks that might be misunderstood out of context.

The Perceptual World

To learn how readers respond to ideas, it is helpful to understand what communications researchers call the *perceptual world,* the context in which people perceive new information and experiences. As individuals or groups, readers base their reactions on a number of factors that have varying significance and often operate simultaneously:

- **Past experiences** influence how people respond to new information and situations. Readers who have lost money in the stock market will be more skeptical of an investment offer than those who have enjoyed substantial returns. A labor union with a harmonious relationship with management will view contract offers differently from a union with a history of stalled talks, bitter negotiations, and strikes.
- **Education,** both formal and informal, affects people's reading ability, background knowledge, and understanding of terminology. Training in specific

disciplines will also influence how readers evaluate the evidence writers present as support. Scientists and mathematicians may be more skeptical of advertising claims using statistics than the general public.

- **Professional experience,** along with training and job responsibilities, shapes people's attitudes. An economics professor with tenure may exhibit a greater ability to be objective about a new tax policy than a small-business owner struggling to meet a weekly payroll. Police officers and emergency-room doctors may be less sympathetic to drunken drivers than people who rarely see the harm they cause.
- **Status** or amount of investment influences people's response to potential change. An entry-level employee is less likely to be concerned about a change in pension plans than is one nearing retirement. Homeowners have more invested in their neighborhoods than renters and may show greater interest in crime or pollution.
- **Values,** whether religious, political, or cultural, help shape readers' responses. Often these values are unspoken but deeply held. People's attitudes about money, sexual conduct, drug use, child rearing, the role of government, and many other issues affect how they react to new ideas.
- **Reference groups** include people or institutions readers respect and to whom they defer. A physician who is unsure about prescribing a new drug may base his or her decision on the opinion of the American Medical Association. A student thinking of changing his or her major might seek advice from parents and friends.
- **Social roles,** such as being a parent, civic leader, or property owner, influence how a person evaluates ideas. A thirty year old with two small children will have different concerns from someone of the same age without children. A shop steward plays a special role and may be expected to react differently than other employees.
- **Age** affects reader attitudes in two ways. People are products of the times they have lived through. Men and women who came of age during World War II have different views than those who grew up during the Vietnam War. In general, older readers have more invested in existing institutions than younger readers and may be more cautious about change.

Other aspects of the perceptual world include gender, ethnic background, and income. In determining your readers' perceptual world, it is important to avoid basing assumptions on common stereotypes. Not all older people are conservative, and not all African Americans endorse Affirmative Action. Many elements of the perceptual world are unconscious and cannot be easily ascertained. No doubt you have been surprised by the reactions of friends you believed you knew very well.

QUESTIONS

1. How would you describe the perceptual world of your parents, coworkers, or friends? How do their common experiences, values, roles, and education affect their attitudes? How would they respond to a letter urging them to donate money to the homeless, to support a handgun ban, or to picket an abortion clinic? Which issues would be difficult to present to them? Why?

2. Have you ever tried to understand someone you hoped to influence in some way? In practicing a presentation, preparing for a job interview, or seeking the right words to discuss a difficult issue with a friend or family member, did you consider how that person might react? Is understanding people's perceptual worlds something we engage in every day?

THE DISCIPLINE

The communication between writer and reader occurs within a particular discipline, setting, culture, publication, or situation. Each academic discipline has a unique history. Some disciplines, such as literature and mathematics, have slowly evolved over thousands of years. Students still read *Oedipus* and study Euclid's principles of geometry. In contrast, the fields of computer science and bioengineering are so new that many of their founders are still actively developing the nature of the discipline.

Every discipline has its own communications style and methods of measuring data, weighing results, and presenting conclusions. In the humanities, research is generally oriented to examining specific works. Whether the researcher is studying Bach, Shakespeare, or Georgia O'Keeffe, the artist's work is the central focus. Disciplines often contain several schools of thought or types of criticism. In literature, for example, some scholars interpret a novel in light of the author's life and thoughts. Other critics would analyze the book in terms of its historical position or political message. Some critics specialize in feminist or Marxist interpretations of literature. But no matter what their approach, literary critics essentially present an educated opinion based on interpretations of the text.

In the sciences, such as biology, chemistry, and physics, scholars base their evaluations on the principles of laboratory research and experiments. Scholars making new assertions in these fields must demonstrate where they obtained their data and prove that other scientists can repeat their experiments and obtain the same results. Although the sciences can seem exact, personal opinion can play a significant role in setting up experiments and interpreting data.

The social sciences of psychology, sociology, criminology, political science, and economics blend some of the features of the humanities and sciences. Although psychologists and criminologists can conduct experiments and often use scientific evidence, many of their conclusions are based on data that can be collected and interpreted in a number of ways.

As a college student you can appreciate the nature of each discipline by examining your textbooks, particularly introductory chapters that often provide a history of the field.

Each profession forms its own context of historical experience, technical training, areas of concern, responsibilities, and political and social outlooks. Corporate executives charged with obtaining investor capital for expansion and research develop different attitudes toward capital-gains taxes than social workers assisting low-income families. The medical profession has a strict tradition of relying on standardized treatment and research methods. Physicians tend to be skeptical of anyone claiming to have a cure for a disease unless the claims can be clearly supported by research and not simply by anecdotal endorsements. Professions measure success differently, praising creativity, sales, or communications skills. Law enforcement officers approach a case of suspected child abuse with the goal of determining if evidence indicates a crime has been committed. A mental health professional is more interested in the child's well-being, whether the situation meets the definitions of legal abuse or not. To a therapist even an imagined incident would be treated seriously if it caused the child distress.

The discipline, profession, or situation creates different methods of using and looking at writing. David Ogilvy, a noted advertising executive, devoted his career to writing ad copy, coming up with snappy, creative, innovative ways of grabbing consumers' attention and boosting sales of his clients' products. For him, writing is a tool to project an image, gain attention, and, above all, sell:

> Always try to inject *news* into your headlines, because the consumer is always on the lookout for new products, or new ways to use an old product, or new improvements in an old product.

> The two most powerful words you can use in a headline are FREE and NEW. You can seldom use FREE, but you can almost always use NEW—if you try hard enough.

Fran Martin, a nurse who serves as an expert witness in medical malpractice trials, offers a very different kind of writing advice to nurses. Unlike ad writers whose success depends on creativity or originality, nurses are counted on to maintain precise records:

> You communicate with other health care providers through the chart and, obviously, incorrect data doesn't give an accurate picture of your patient's condition. That could lead to life-threatening errors. It also raises the specter of fraud, which could make your actions appear not just negligent, but also criminal.

Writing Contexts

The contexts in which writers operate are limitless, but a few general patterns follow:

1. **Expert to general reader:** Most books and articles are written by experts to people reading for information or enjoyment. An attorney preparing a university brochure on date rape would have to anticipate that most student attitudes have been largely formed by the media. He or she might have to dispel common misconceptions and explain terms and legal procedures.
2. **Expert to expert within a discipline:** Law reviews, medical journals, and trade magazines are largely read by professionals within a specific field. Writers for these periodicals can assume readers will understand basic concepts and terminology. Advanced textbooks in biology or criminal law rarely provide the introductory material found in first-year books. The letters, reports, and documents generated within a corporation or government agency may adopt a unique style and format that almost become a code few outsiders can understand. But writers in these situations should always keep an extended readership in mind. An audit, budget review, or investigation could circulate as a memo or letter to a wider audience.
3. **Expert to expert in different disciplines:** This is perhaps one of the most challenging contexts writers face. Einstein's letter to Roosevelt is a classic example of this context—a world-famous scientist attempting to explain a discovery to a powerful leader with minimal knowledge of

physics. How does an engineer explain the practical difficulties to a designer interested in style and creativity? How does an economist persuade a politician facing reelection to raise taxes or cut benefits? In communicating with professionals in different disciplines, it is important for writers to establish trust, to address their readers' concerns, and to explain unfamiliar concepts clearly.

THE WRITING PROCESS

Writing is a process as well as a product. Good writing respects each of the three elements of context. When you plan a writing project, determine your purpose, evaluate your readers, and follow the conventions of your discipline. Many college instructors provide requirements for writing assignments. In a professional situation you can benefit from examining samples of the writing tasks you are undertaking.

Prewriting

Writing is not only a means of preparing a finished document but is also a way of thinking and exploring. You can use a number of planning techniques to discover topics, define your thesis, and list needed items.

Freewriting records thoughts and impressions without interruption and without any concern for spelling, grammar, or punctuation. Freewriting should not be confused with writing a rough draft. Freewriting is like talking to yourself. It may have no direction, it may skip from topic to topic, and it may contradict itself. Freewriting is a bit like making a series of fast sketches before determining the subject matter of a large painting. The goal of freewriting is not writing a "paper" but simply discovering possible topics.

Overhearing a claim that the government was behind the influx of drugs in the inner city, a student sat at her computer and rapidly recorded a stream of thoughts on the topic of conspiracy theories:

The CIA is behind the drug epidemic. The US government pays South Koreans to set up grocery stores in the inner city. Every president since Nixon has lied about MIA's held captive in Southeast Asia. The airforce lies about UFO sitings. The number of conspiracy theories is limitless. The lumber industry is against legalizing marijuana because hemp makes better paper than woodpulp. Roosevelt knew the Japanese were going to bomb Pearl Harbor but let it happen. Conspiracies are endless. They are populair. They sell a lot of newspapers and create a lot of TV shows & employ an army of theoriests who move from talk show to talk show touting their books and their latest proof that the CIA or blacks or the Fortune 500 is responsible for some horrible deed or social threat. No doubt some mad scienist in a govt lab created AIDS and loosed it on the world. No doubt someone has cured cancer and has been kidnapped or killed so millions of doctors and thousands of drug companies won't go out of business. Why? Why do people love these theories?

Some people to need to believe that no lone assassin could have killed JFK. They cling to this belief, no matter what the evidence. Why? Maybe we need to believe in conspiracy theories. It makes the evil in the world less frightening. We are not victims of random chaos, but evil people who can theoretically be located and exposed. To abandon conspiracy theories means accepting chaos. Also it allows us to escape blame. If we blame all our problems on mysterious forces beyond our control, then we can dodge personnal responsibility.

Although this freewriting is loose, repetitive, and misspelled, it moves from listing conspiracy theories to speculating about why people need to believe in them. The student now has something to focus on and a possible title: "Why We Need Conspiracy Theories."

Brainstorming is another prewriting process that can help you generate ideas and identify possible topics for further writing. As in freewriting, list your ideas as quickly as possible. Do not bother to worry if your ideas are repetitive or irrelevant. Again, your purpose is not to outline a paper but simply to develop ideas.

Brainstorming can be used to discover a topic for an essay or to help a professional identify details that need to be included in a business letter or report. A composition student assigned a comparison/contrast essay might list as many ideas as possible in hopes of discovering a topic:

high school teachers/college professors
male/female attitudes about first dates
American/Japanese ideas about privacy
Puerto-Ricans vs. Mexican-Americans
Mexican-born vs. 1st generation Mex-Americans
English only vs. Bilingual
Mexican-born English/1st gen. Mex-Am attitudes

Through brainstorming or listing, the student has run through a number of ideas before focusing on a topic suited for a short paper comparing the attitudes of Mexican-born Americans and their children toward English.

Even when the topic is defined, brainstorming can help writers identify what they should include. The third-shift supervisor of a warehouse who is planning a report following a forklift accident could use brainstorming to make sure he or she produces a complete report that managers can use to examine the firm's legal liability, safety policies, employee training, and equipment use:

time/date/location of accident.
Injured personnel--Alex Bolton, Sara Lopez
    (Medical Status)
911 call--get time from dispatcher
Bolton's forklift--last inspection (service log)
forklift load--stability (check manual)
Use of helmets, earplugs
surveillance cameras (tapes)
accident witnesses

From this list, the supervisor identifies the information needed to meet the needs of the readers.

WRITING ACTIVITIES

1. *Freewriting:* Select one of the following topics, and write for at least ten minutes. Do not worry about making sense or maintaining logical connections between ideas. Remember, this is not the rough draft of a paper but an attempt to develop ideas and discover topics.

your worst job	blind dates	television talk shows
job interviews	marriage	capital punishment
recycling	censorship	student loans
campus housing	car repair	media images of women

2. *Brainstorming:* Select one of the columns of ideas and build on it, adding your own ideas. Jot down your thoughts as quickly as possible. Do not worry if some of your ideas are off the topic.

men/women	success/money	vacation plans
dating	careers	plane/car
expectations	salary/income	hotel/meals
conflicts	risk/reward	budget/costs

Clustering represents a more visual method of developing ideas. Instead of complete sentences or listed ideas, topics are grouped in circles and boxes. Visual markers such as arrows, question marks, and ink color can be used to organize and link ideas. A student writing about the information superhighway clustered the following topics:

Information Superhighway

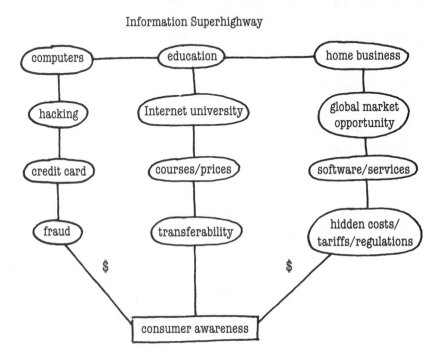

Drawing clusters helps the student focus on a topic: consumer awareness and the Internet.

Asking questions is a method used by reporters and investigators to help identify critical information. For generations newspaper reporters have been trained to ask the "Five Ws": Who? What? When? Where? Why? Asking questions can help you identify topics and narrow your focus. A student considering writing a paper about Arthur Miller's *Death of a Salesman* might list the following questions to help identify a topic for a short analytical paper:

Death of a Salesman

What are Willy's values?
Is Willy a victim of society or of his own delusions?
What role does Uncle Ben play?
Is Willy's suicide caused by despair or a last attempt at success?

What impact does Willy's infidelity have?
Biff steals a suit and a fountain pen. What do these objects represent?
Linda knows Willy has lost his salary but does not confront him about it. Why?
Why does Miller pose Willy and Biff next to Uncle Charlie and Bernard?
Is the play an attack on the American dream?
Why does Willy refuse to take a job from Charlie?
This play is world famous but the hero is abusive, selfish, and short-tempered. Why is the play so popular?
What is the purpose of the requiem at the end?
How would the play be different without it?

By posing lists of questions, you can often identify key issues and provoke critical thinking that will lead to developing a thesis.

1. *Clustering:* Select one of the following topics. Use a large piece of paper to record and arrange your ideas. Group related ideas with circles or squares. Use arrows to connect ideas. You may use different colors, switch from pen to pencil, or mark major ideas with a highlighter. Whatever method you use, do not allow your artwork to overshadow your goal of developing ideas for a paper.

year-round school	computer hacking	nutrition
gay rights	the American dream	women in combat
airports	working out	childless couples
aging	being laid off	divorce

2. *Asking questions:* Select one of the following topics, and write a list of questions. Write as quickly as possible, and do not worry about being repetitive. Try to ask as many questions as you can to explore as many avenues as possible.

recent hit movie	gangs	television violence
day care	welfare reform	suburbs
role models	teen pregnancy	corporate downsizing
labor unions	singles' bars	drunk driving

Moving from Topic to Thesis

A paper is never "about" something; it must make a clear statement. The student who begins writing "about *Death of a Salesman*" may either find himself or herself facing an endless number of issues or end up creating nothing more than a plot summary. Writing should have a focus, a direction. The word *thesis* refers to the writer's main idea. A good thesis makes a clear point that is supported by the body of the writing. In some writing the thesis is the central idea or controlling statement. In argumentative writing the thesis is clearly articulated. In descriptive or narrative writing the thesis can be implied. A writer who offers a powerful description of the homeless may assume readers will be moved to take action.

A thesis makes a strong statement about a topic:

TOPIC: Consumers and the Internet
THESIS: Users of the Internet unknowingly expose themselves to consumer fraud.

TOPIC: Conspiracy theories
THESIS: Like ancient mythology, today's conspiracy theories serve to explain the unexplainable and reduce fear of chaos.

TOPIC: *Death of a Salesman*
THESIS: Willy Loman commits what psychologists call altruistic suicide.

Once you have determined your thesis, you can begin writing. Writers work in many different ways. Some make elaborate outlines and carefully write a draft, perfecting each paragraph or section until they complete a text ready for proofreading. Others make few plans but write several complete drafts, writing and revising key areas over and over again.

Many writers go through a five-stage process that helps improve their writing and save time. As a beginning writer you can benefit from following these guidelines. With experience, you can personalize your method of writing.

HOW TO WRITE AN ESSAY

1. **Plan—establish context.** Once you have established your goal and thesis, determine how you will develop your paper in light of your readers' needs and the conventions of the discipline. Develop an outline listing the items needed to achieve your goal. Your opening should attract attention, announce the topic, and prepare readers for main ideas presented in the body of the work. The conclusion should bring the paper to a logical end, using a final observation, quote, or question to make a strong impression.

2. **Write—get your ideas on paper.** After reviewing your plans, write as much as possible without stopping. Writing the first draft can be considered controlled freewriting. As you write, new ideas may occur to you. Record *all* your thoughts. Do not pause to check spelling or look up a fact because it may break your train of thought. Underline words you think are misspelled or sentences that contain grammatical errors. Leave gaps for missing details. Place question marks next to items you want to double-check.

3. **Cool—put your writing aside.** It is difficult to evaluate your work immediately after writing because much of what you wish to say is still fresh in your mind. Set your work aside. Work on other assignments, read, watch television, or take a walk to clear your mind. Afterward, you can return to your writing with greater objectivity.

4. **Revise—review your writing in context.** Before searching your paper for misspelled words or grammatical errors, examine it holistically. Review your goal and plan. Examine any instructions you have received. Then read your paper. Does it clearly express your goal and support your thesis? Is it properly directed to your audience? Does it violate any principles in the discipline? Revision can mean rewriting the entire paper or merely reworking certain details.

5. **Edit—correct mechanical errors and polish style.** When you have a completed paper, examine your writing for missing words, grammatical errors, and misspelled words. In addition, review your diction. Eliminate wordy phrases and reduce repetition. Make sure ideas flow evenly and smoothly. *Reading a paper aloud can help identify errors and awkward sentences.*

These five stages are not neatly isolated. Writing, according to current research, is *recursive*—the steps overlap and occur simultaneously. As you write you will find yourself brainstorming, editing, correcting, spelling, and freewriting.

Each writing assignment is unique. For example, a narrative requires attention to chronology, while a division paper demands clear organization, and persuasion depends on the skillful use of logic. Each discipline represents a distinct discourse community. In literature courses students are expected to provide original interpretations of literary works such as plays and novels. Students in the sciences are required to follow strict standards for gathering data, analyzing results, and presenting conclusions. Undoubtedly, you may find some papers more challenging than others. Because it is often difficult to determine how hard a particular assignment may be, it is advisable to start writing as soon as possible. Just ten minutes of prewriting will quickly reveal how much time and effort you need to devote to any paper.

Strategies for Creating a Composing Style

1. **Review your past writing.** Consider how you have written in the past. Which papers received the highest and lowest grades in high school? Why? What can you recall about writing them? What mistakes have you made? What comments have teachers made about your work?
2. **Experiment with composing.** Write at different times and places, using pen and paper or a computer. See what conditions enhance your writing.
3. **Study returned papers for clues.** Read your instructors' comments carefully. If your papers lack a clear thesis, you should devote more attention to prewriting and planning. If instructors fill your papers with red ink—circling misspelled words and underlining fragments—devote more time to editing.

WRITING THE WHOLE COMPOSITION

The stages of the writing process are illustrated here by a student developing a paper for a freshman composition class. Having read and discussed several essays concerning criminal justice, the class was instructed to turn in a short commentary debating the merits of a current legal issue.

Prewriting

The student began by exploring topics through prewriting. Note that her work blends several techniques, including brainstorming, free-writing, and clustering:

Topics: Criminal justice (issues)
capital punishment pro/con
gun control
Courtroom TV
What is the impact of televised trials?
Do TV trials educate the public?
How does media attention affect juries?
Victims and crime—are they forgotten?
Who speaks for victims?
Do prosecutors properly speak for victims?

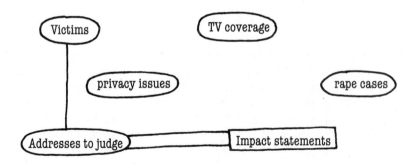

Victim impact statements are increasingly a feature of modern trials as people are allowed to state their feelings about the crime and the criminal after he/she is convicted. Judges can consider the impact of the crime on the victim in sentencing. Sometimes victims ask for harsh punishment and sometimes they even ask for leniency and give the criminal, especially a young person a 2nd chance........

Who is most impressive?
What about victims who can't speak well or don't know English?
What about families of homicide victims?
Victims without mourners? Less important?

Topic: Victim impact statements
Thesis: Although victim impact statements are supposed to empower the victims of crime, they may serve only to further marginalize the most helpless among us.

Planning

Victim Impact Statements
INTRO: Background of impact statements
          Definition

PRO: -- empowers victims who feel forgotten
          -- helps heal victims by addressing criminal
          -- helps people regain control over their lives & move on
          -- makes the human cost of a crime part of the sentencing decision.

CON: Question?
          Whose impact is more effective?
          Middle class professional vs. Welfare mom

END: Question, helpful or hurtful to victims?

First Draft

Across America today more and more victims of crime are being allowed to address the court in terms of making what is called a victim impact statment. This written or oral presentation to the court allows victims to express their feelings to the judge after someone has been convicted of a crime.

Advocates of victim impact statements point to key advantages. First, these statements give victims' a voice. For years, victims have felt helpless. Prosecutors represent the state, not the crime victim. Victims have been dismayed when prosecutors have aranged plea bargains without their knowledge. Some victims are still recovering from their injuries when they learn the person who hurt them has plead to a lesser charge and received probation.

Therapists who work with victims also say that being able to adress the court helps with the healing process. Victims of violent crime can feel powerless and vulnerable. Instead of suffering in silence, they are given the chance to address the criminal, to clear their chests, and get on with the rest of their lives.

Impact statements allows judges to consider what sentences are appropriate. In one case a judge who planned to fine a teenager for shoplifting accepted the store owner's suggestion of waving the fine if the defendant completed his GED.

But giving victims a chance to speak raises some issues. What about the victim who is not articulate, who doesn't even speak English? In murder cases the victim's relatives are given a chance to speak? Does this mean that a middle class professional victim with a circle grieving friends and family members will be granted more significance than the homeless murder victim who leaves no one behind?

Victim impact statements may help empower victims who are educated, personally impressive, and socially promient. But they may also allow forgotten victims to remain voiceless.

After completing the first draft, the student set the paper aside for several hours before returning to examine it. As a rough draft it clearly captured the writer's main ideas, but it could be improved to make a greater impression on readers. Note the student's marginal comments; "SP" refers to a misspelling. The editing process is still incomplete in this stage.

Revision

wordy
SP

Across America today more and more victims of crime are being allowed to address the court in terms of making what is called a victim impact statment. This written or oral presentation to the court allows victims to express their feelings to the judge after someone has been convicted of a crime.

Advocates of victim impact statements point to key advantages. First, these statements give victims\a voice. For years, victims have felt helpless. Prosecutors represent the state, not the crime victim. Victims have been dismayed when prosecutors have (aranged) plea bargains without their knowledge. Some victims are still ~~SP~~ recovering from their injuries when they learn the person who hurt them has (plead) ~~SP~~ to a lesser charge and received probation.

Therapists who work with victims also say that being able to (adress) the court ~~SP~~ helps with the healing process. Victims of violent crime can feel powerless and vulnerable. Instead of suffering in silence, they are given the chance to address the criminal, to clear their chests, and get on with the rest of their lives. ~~cliché~~

Impact statements allows judges to consider what sentences are appropriate. In one case a judge who planned to fine a teenager for shoplifting accepted the store owner's suggestion of (waving) the fine if the defendant completed his GED. ~~SP~~

But giving victims a chance to speak raises some issues. What about the victim ~~weak~~ who is not articulate, who doesn't even speak English? In murder cases the victim's relatives are given a chance to speak? Does this mean that a middle class professional victim with a circle of grieving friends and family members will be granted more significance than the homeless murder victim who leaves no one behind?

Victim impact statements may help empower victims who are educated, personally impressive, and socially (promient) But they may also allow forgotten victims ~~SP~~ to remain voiceless.

Revision Notes

Needs better opening -- needs attention-getter
Sharper definition
Clearer examples
Tighter conclusion

Second Draft

The courtroom scene was riveting. One by one, the survivors of a deadly commuter-train shooting took the stand and addressed the man who had maimed them. Their voices quivering with emotion, they told the court how the gunman's actions changed their lives forever. Spouses and parents of the dead spoke of loss. There were tears, moments of intense anger, and quiet despair. Victim impact statements have become a common feature of criminal proceedings. Spoken in court or submitted in writing, these statements provide an opportunity for victims to be heard before sentencing.

Advocates of victim impact statements believe these declarations give victims a voice, an opportunity to be heard. Traditionally, victims have appeared in court only as witnesses subject to cross-examination. Prosecutors, victims soon learn, represent the state and not individuals. Still hospitalized after a brutal beating, a New Jersey restaurant owner learned from reading a newspaper that his assailants had plea-bargained to a lesser charge and received probation. Joining with other victims, he became an advocate for victims' rights, including impact statements.

Therapists who counsel victims of crime believe that addressing the court and taking an active role in the legal process instead of remaining a passive witness helps people recover from a sense of helplessness and regain a measure of self-respect.

Impact statements allow judges to consider appropriate sentences. In a Florida case, a judge who intended to fine a teenager for shoplifting agreed with the store owner's suggestion that the fine be waived if the defendant completed his GED.

But giving victims a chance to speak has led to ugly courtroom scenes which seem inappropriate in a democracy. In Milwaukee a sister of a young man murdered by Jeffrey Dahmer wailed and shrieked in contortions of pure rage. The relative of another murder victim shouted that he would execute the killer himself. Bailiffs had to restrain him as he begged the judge, "Just gimme five minutes with him!" Defense attorneys argue these harangues are unnecessary. What need is there to heap abuse upon a person about to lose his or her life or liberty? Can anger and harassment be considered healing?

But even restrained, well-reasoned impact statements raise troubling questions. What about the victim who is too impaired, too frightened, or too wounded to speak? Is his or her absence judged as indifference? What about those whose English is limited? What of those without friends or family? Should the drunk driver who kills a young professional missed by friends, family, and colleagues receive a tougher sentence than the drunk driver who kills a homeless man who dies unmourned, unmissed, and uncounted? Do we really want our courts and society to suggest that some lives are more significant than others?

Victim impact statements may help empower victims, especially the educated, the personally impressive, and the socially prominent. But these statements, unintentionally, may also further marginalize the most helpless among us, allowing forgotten victims to remain voiceless.

QUESTIONS

1. What have you found most challenging or difficult about writing? Discovering ideas? Getting started? Revising?
2. What comments have instructors made about your writing? Does a pattern exist? Have they suggested areas for improvement?
3. What writing habits do you have? What could aid you in improving your work and meeting deadlines? What ideas in this chapter might you adopt to write more effectively?

WRITING ON A COMPUTER

If you have never written on a computer take advantage of whatever opportunities your campus offers to learn word processing. Modern computer programs are user-friendly, and learning to utilize them will make your college career easier as well as prepare you for your future profession. Almost every career today requires computer literacy. If you find yourself overwhelmed by technology, as many professional writers do, consider taking a computer course. Many colleges offer one credit courses or free seminars. If no course is available, ask a friend or classmate to show you how he or she uses a computer to write.

Strategies for Writing on a Computer

1. **Appreciate the advantages and limitations of using a computer.** Computers can speed up the writing process, allow you to add ideas, correct spelling, and delete sentences without having to retype an entire page. Computers will not automatically make you a better writer, however. They cannot refine a thesis, improve your logic, or enhance critical thinking. *Don't confuse the neatness of the finished product with good writing.* An attractively designed document must still achieve all the goals of good writing.
2. **Learn the features of your program.** If you are unfamiliar with writing on a computer, make sure you learn how to move blocks of text, change formats, check spelling, and, most importantly, master the *print* and *save* functions. *Find out if your program has an* Undo *key. This can save the day if you accidentally delete or "lose" some of your text.* This key simply undoes your last action, restoring deleted text or eliminating what you just added.
3. **Write in single space.** Most instructors require that papers be double-spaced, but you may find it easier to compose your various drafts in single space so you can see more of your essay on the screen. You can easily change to double space when you are ready to print the final version.
4. **Save your work.** If your program has an automatic save function, use it. Save your work to a floppy disk or hard drive. If you are working on a college or library computer and do not have a disk, print your work after a writing session. Don't let a power shortage or a keystroke error cause you to lose your work!
5. **Label your files clearly.** Because many programs limit the number of characters you can use in a file title, choose your names carefully. Develop a clear notation system such as ENG1 or PSYCH2. If you wish to save a new version of your first English essay you can name it ENG1A.

6. **Print drafts of your work as you write.** Computer screens usually allow you to view less than a page of text at a time. Although it is easy to scroll up and down through the text, it can be difficult to revise on the screen. You may find it easier to work with a hard copy of your paper. Consider double or even triple spacing before you print, so you will have plenty of room for handwritten notations.

7. **Keep backup disks of your work.** Floppy disks are fragile. Store them in a case and keep them clear of dust and debris. Do not leave them near a television or stereo as electrical fields can disturb the data you have stored. *Store important data on more than one disk or save printed copies.*

8. **Make use of special features.** Most word processing applications allow you to count the number of words, check spelling, and use a built-in thesaurus. Some programs will aid you with grammar and usage rules.

9. **Use spell and grammar checks but recognize their limitations.** Spell checking will go through your document and flag words it does not recognize, quickly locating many mistakes you might overlook on your own. *Spell checks do not locate missing words or recognize errors in usage, such as confusing* there *and* their *or* adopt *and* adapt. *Grammar checks sometimes offer awkward suggestions and flag correct expressions as errors.* Reading your text aloud is still the best method of editing.

COLLABORATIVE WRITING

Writing often occurs in groups. Even when produced by a single person, writing may have to reflect the views of many people. Thomas Jefferson wrote the Declaration of Independence, but a committee including Jefferson, John Adams, Benjamin Franklin, and two others made forty-seven changes. Franklin replaced Jefferson's original phrase (in italics) "we hold these rights to be *sound and undeniable*" with "*self-evident.*" More changes occurred when the declaration was presented to the entire Continental Congress. Jefferson's impassioned attack on slavery was eliminated to appease southern representatives. In all, eighty-seven alterations were made to Jefferson's declaration before it was unanimously accepted. By the time John Hancock stepped forward to sign the Declaration of Independence, a quarter of Jefferson's original draft had been changed or deleted.

As a college student, you may be called on to work in a writing group. More and more professors are teaching collaborative writing because writing in groups is common in business and industry. Most professionals work in groups or committees. The partners of a small software company seeking a new personnel director have to agree on the wording of a want ad. The sales team introducing a new product must determine what language to use in its brochures. Volunteers seeking government funding for a day care center must work together on a proposal.

Working in groups poses additional challenges in the writing process. The writing must reflect the ideas of different people. Viewpoints and personalities may clash. Even scheduling time for the group to meet may be difficult. Because people regard their writing as personal expression and are accustomed to working alone, it can be difficult for them to accept criticism.

But whether you are writing alone or in a group, the basic process remains the same. The writing must address the issue, meet the needs of the readers, and respect the conventions of the discipline or discourse community. To be effective, writing groups must achieve the "Three Cs" of group dynamics: *cohesion, cooperation,* and *compromise.* Members must have a clearly defined goal or task. They must be willing to meet and to work outside the group. Finally, and often most difficult, individuals must be willing to accept that their opinions may not prevail and be willing to drop or alter ideas they greatly value.

Strategies for Collaborative Writing

1. **Work to establish cohesion by stressing the goals, intended readers, and requirements of the writing project.** It is important for members of a writing group to feel trust so they can share ideas. In addition, they must be willing to offer and accept criticism.
2. **Keep the group focused on the task by creating a timeline.** People enjoy talking. Discussions can easily become generalized forums for spirited debate or the latest gossip. A target timeline can help keep the group on track by outlining expected outcomes and reminding members of the deadline. The timeline should reflect stages in the writing process.
3. **Make meetings productive by setting goals and assigning tasks.** Meetings can easily degenerate into a series of discussion sessions, which, though interesting, may not help produce the needed writing. Members should be assigned specific responsibilities: gathering research, conducting interviews, writing sample drafts. Each meeting should open with a goal statement of what is to be achieved. Meetings should end with a summary of what has been completed and an announcement of what must be accomplished at the next meeting.

4. **Designate one member to serve as a moderator or recorder.** One member of the group should serve as chair or recorder to document the progress of the group and serve as secretary to exchange messages between meetings.
5. **Avoid personalizing disagreements.** It is important to discuss opposing viewpoints in neutral terms. Avoid attaching ideas to individuals, which can lead to "*us* against *them*" conflicts.
6. **Take advantage of technology.** Students often have trouble finding common times to meet for social activities, let alone assignments. Consider how the group can maintain links through telephone conferences, fax machines, and the Internet.

WRITER'S BLOCK

At some time almost everyone experiences writer's block, the inability to write. With a paper due in a few days, you may find yourself incapable of coming up with a single line or even unable to sit at your desk. You can feel frustrated, nervous, bored, tired, anxious. The more time passes, the more you think about the upcoming assignment, the more frustrated you can become.

Even professional authors sometimes find themselves unable to write. There is no magic cure for writer's block. But although there is nothing that will make your writer's block disappear, there are some tactics you can try.

Strategies for Overcoming Writer's Block

1. **Recognize that writer's block exists.** When you have the time to write, write. Don't assume if you have two weeks to complete an assignment that you will be able to write well for fourteen days. Get as much writing as possible done when you can. If you delay work, you may find yourself unable to write as the deadline nears.
2. **Review your assignment.** Sometimes the reason you feel that you have nothing to say is that you have not fully understood the assignment. Read it carefully and turn the instructions into a series of questions to spark your thinking.
3. **If you are having trouble selecting a topic, review the assignment for key words and search the Internet.** See what Web pages these key words produce. If you don't have access to the Internet, look for these

words in a dictionary or encyclopedia. Even wholly unrelated references can sometimes spark your imagination and help you develop ideas.

4. **Write anything.** The longer you delay writing, the harder it will be to start. If you have trouble focusing on your assignment, get into the mood for writing by sending an e-mail or a letter to a friend. Use an online chat room to get into the rhythm of expressing yourself in writing.

5. **Talk to a friend and discuss your assignment or goal.** Talking with a friend can often boost your confidence and reduce your anxiety about an assignment. A spirited discussion can spark free associations about your topic, helping you to view your subject from new angles.

6. **Force yourself to write for five minutes.** Sit down and write about your topic for five minutes nonstop. Let one idea run into another. If you have trouble writing about your topic, write about anything that comes to mind. Even writing nonsense will help you break the physical resistance you may have to sitting down and working with a pen or keyboard. Try to steer your experimental writing to the assigned task. If your draft is going nowhere, save your work and stop after five minutes. Take a walk or run some errands, then return to your writing. Sometimes seeing a word or phrase out of context will lead to significant associations.

7. **Lower your standards.** Don't be afraid to write poorly. Write as well as you can, making notes in the margin as you go along to remind yourself of areas that need revision. Remember that writing is recursive and even badly written statements can form the foundation of a good paper.

8. **Don't feel obligated to start at the beginning.** If you find yourself unable to develop a convincing opening line or a satisfactory introduction, begin writing the body or conclusion of the paper. Get your ideas flowing.

9. **Switch subjects.** If you are bogged down on your English paper, start work on the history paper due next month. Writing well on a different subject may help you gain the confidence you need to return to a difficult assignment.

10. **Record your thoughts on tape or note cards.** If you find writing frustrating, consider talking into a tape recorder or listing ideas on index cards. You may find working with nonwriting materials an effective method of getting started.

11. **Try writing in a different location.** If you can't work at home because of distractions, go to the library or a quiet room. If the library feels stifling and intimidating, move to a less formal environment. You may discover yourself doing your best work while drinking coffee in a noisy student union.

12. **If you still have problems with your assignment, talk to your instructor.** Try to identify what is giving you the most trouble. Is it the act of writing itself, finding a topic, organizing your thoughts, or developing a thesis?

1. Choose one of the following topics and use the five-step method described in this chapter to draft a short essay. *As you write, note which stages of the process pose the greatest challenges. Alter your composing style in any way that improves your writing.*

roommates	mandatory courses	televised trials
step-parents	campus security	buying a car
current fashion	"outing" gays	personal privacy
the insanity defense	college sports	favorite television show/band/film

2. Select an upcoming assignment and write a rough draft. Use this experience to identify topic areas that require the most attention. *Save your notes and draft for future use.*

3. Write a letter or e-mail to a friend about a recent experience. Before sending it, set the letter aside, letting it "cool." After two or three days, examine your draft for missing details, awkward or confusing phrases, misspelled words, or repetitious statements. *Notice how revision and editing can improve your writing.*

READING CRITICALLY

As a student you are accustomed to reading to gain information. Cramming for a history exam, you read a textbook, hoping to extract the dates, facts, and concepts that will appear on the test. Reading a novel, you may allow yourself to be swept away by an exciting plot or an intriguing character. But as a writer, you need to read critically; you need to read with a "writer's eye."

While most diners simply savor a new gourmet item, a cook wants to know the recipe. Visitors to a new office tower may marvel at the atrium, but an architect analyzes the support structure. Moviegoers gasp at an exciting car chase as film students review the director's editing technique. As a writer, you need to look at writing in much the same way. In addition to determining *what* an essay says, it is important to note *how* it is organized, how the writer overcame problems, and how language and detail contribute to its effect.

Strategies for Critical Reading

When you pick up a magazine, you rarely read every article. You flip through the pages, letting your eyes guide you. A headline, a photograph, a chart, or a familiar name makes you pause and begin reading. If bored, you skip to the next article. While reading your textbooks, you often skim, moving over familiar material so you can devote more time to items that are new to you. If you read *The Great Gatsby* in high school, for a college literature course you will probably find yourself reviewing it rather than reading it.

In this course, however, you should read *all* the assigned selections carefully. Reading with a writer's eye, you will examine familiar works differently than readers seeking information. Critical reading, like writing, occurs best in stages.

1. **Look ahead and skim entries.** Do not wait until the night before to examine assigned readings. Check your syllabus and skim through future readings to get a general impression. Often, if you think about the authors and their issues, you can approach an essay more critically. The more you bring to the reading, the more effective your analysis will be.
2. **Study the headnote and introduction.** Consider the author, the issue, and the context of the reading.
3. **For the first reading, read the entire work.** Just as in writing the first draft, it is important to complete the entire essay. Do not bother to look up unfamiliar words. Instead, try to get the "big picture" and understand the writer's main goal.
4. **Read with a pencil or pen in your hand.** Make notes and underline sentences that strike you as interesting, odd, offensive, or troubling. Reading while holding a writing tool will prompt you to write, to be an active reader rather than a passive consumer of words.
5. **For the first reading, focus on understanding the author's meaning.** Summarize, in your own words, what the essay is about. Identify the thesis and the main types of support.
6. **For the second reading, begin with the questions following the essay.** Considering the questions can help you focus on a closer, analytical reading of the work. The questions are arranged in three groups:

    Understanding Meaning   What is the author's purpose? What is the thesis? What is the author trying to share with his or her readers?
    Evaluating Strategy   How does the author make his or her point? What support is used? How does the writer organize ideas?

Appreciating Language   How does the writer use words? What does the language reveal about the intended reader? Does the language reflect the writer's attitudes?

7. **Summarize your responses in a point or two for class discussion.** Consider how you will express your opinions of the essay to fellow students. Be prepared to back up your remarks by citing passages in the text.
8. **Most important, focus on what this essay can teach you about writing.** How can this writer's style, way of organizing ideas, or word choice enrich your own writing? Though you may not want to imitate everything you see, you can pick up techniques to broaden your personal array of skills.
9. **Think of how writers wrestle with the same problems you face.** If you have trouble making an outline and organizing ideas, study how the essays in this book are arranged. If your instructor returns papers with comments about vague theses and a lack of focus, examine how the writers in this book state their theses.
10. **Above all, read to learn.**

Read the following essay by Cornel West, and study how it has been marked during a critical reading. West is a highly organized writer who blends the use of several modes in this comparison essay on the current state of African-American political leadership.

CORNEL WEST

Cornel West was a religion professor and Director of Afro-American Studies at Princeton University before he was appointed to the faculty at Harvard University. The author of Keeping Faith, Prophetic Fragments, *and other books, West has specialized in writing on race in America.*

Black Political Leadership

"Black Political Leadership" appeared in West's best-selling 1994 book Race Matters. *In this section, West compares the current generation of black political leaders with leaders of the Civil Rights era. Although West's purpose is to compare, he uses a number of modes to develop his ideas.*

1   Black political leadership reveals the tame and genteel face of the black middle class. The black dress suits with white shirts worn by Malcolm X and Martin Luther King Jr., signified the seriousness of their deep commitment to black freedom, whereas today the expensive tailored suits of black politicians symbolize their personal success and individual achievement. Malcolm and Martin called for the realization that black people are somebodies with which America has to reckon, whereas black politicians tend to turn our attention to *their* somebodiness owing to *their* "making it" in America.

2   This crude and slightly unfair comparison highlights two distinctive features of black political leaders in the post–Civil Rights era: the relative lack of authentic anger and the relative absence of genuine humility. What stood out most strikingly about Malcolm X, Martin Luther King Jr., Ella Baker, and Fannie Lou Hamer was that they were almost always visibly upset about the condition of black America. When one saw them speak or heard their voices, they projected on a gut level that the black situation was urgent, in need of immediate attention. One even gets the impression that their own stability and sanity rested on how soon the black predicament could be improved. Malcolm, Martin, Ella, and Fannie were angry about the state of black America, and this anger fueled their boldness and defiance.

[margin notes]
thesis/ opening

clothes as symbolic

compare

note use of italics

division

provides examples

shift/   3
transition

use of
repetitive
wording for
emphasis

contrast

      4

supplies
personal
definition

cause and
effect

      5

division

definition

      6

analysis

In stark contrast, most present-day black political leaders appear too hungry for status to be angry, too eager for acceptance to be bold, too self-invested in advancement to be defiant. And when they do drop their masks and try to get mad (usually in the presence of black audiences), their bold rhetoric is more performance than personal, more play-acting than heartfelt. Malcolm, Martin, Ella, and Fannie made sense of the black plight in a poignant and powerful manner, whereas most contemporary black political leaders' oratory appeals to black people's sense of the sentimental and sensational.

Similarly, Malcolm, Martin, Ella, and Fannie were examples of humility. Yes, even Malcolm's aggressiveness was accompanied by a common touch and humble disposition toward ordinary black people. Humility is the fruit of inner security and wise maturity. To be humble is to be so sure of one's self and one's mission that one can forego calling excessive attention to one's self and status. And, even more pointedly, to be humble is to revel in the accomplishments or potential of others—especially those with whom one identifies and to whom one is linked organically. The relative absence of humility in most black political leaders today is a symptom of the status-anxiety and personal insecurity pervasive in black middle-class America. In this context, even a humble vesture is viewed as a cover for some sinister motive or surreptitious ambition.

Present-day black political leaders can be grouped under three types: race-effacing managerial leaders, race-identifying protest leaders, and race-transcending prophetic leaders. The first type is growing rapidly. The Thomas Bradleys and Wilson Goodes of black America have become a model for many black leaders trying to reach a large white constituency and keep a loyal black one. This type survives on sheer political savvy and thrives on personal diplomacy. This kind of candidate is the lesser of two evils in a political situation where the only other electoral choice is a conservative (usually white) politician. Yet this type of leader tends to stunt progressive development and silence the prophetic voices in the black community by casting the practical mainstream as the only game in town.

The second type of black political leader—race-identifying protest leaders—often view themselves in the tradition of Malcolm X, Martin Luther King Jr., Ella Baker, and Fannie Lou Hamer. Yet they are usually self-deluded. They actually operate more in the tradition of Booker T. Washington, by confining themselves to the black turf, vowing to protect their leadership status over it, and serving as power brokers with powerful nonblack elites (usually white economic or political elites, though in Louis Farrakhan's case it may be Libyan) to "enhance" this black turf. It is crucial to remember that even in the fifties, Malcolm X's vision and practice were international in scope, and that after 1964 his project was transracial—though grounded in the black turf. King never confined himself to being solely the leader of black America—even though the white press attempted to do so. And Fannie Lou Hamer led the National Welfare Rights Organization, not the Black Welfare Rights Organization. In short, race-identifying protest leaders in the post–Civil Rights era function as figures who white Americans must appease so that the plight of the black poor is overlooked and forgotten. When such leaders move successfully into elected office—as with Marion Barry—they usually become managerial types with large black constituencies, flashy styles, flowery rhetoric, and Booker T. Washington–like patronage operations within the public sphere.

7   Race-transcending prophetic leaders are rare in contemporary black America. Harold Washington was one. The Jesse Jackson of **examples** 1988 was attempting to be another—yet the opportunism of his past weighed heavily on him. To be an elected official and prophetic leader requires personal integrity and political savvy, moral vision and prudential judgment, courageous defiance and organizational patience. The present generation has yet to produce such a figure. We have neither an Adam Clayton Powell Jr., nor a Ronald Dellums. This void sits like a festering sore at the center of the crisis of black leadership—and the predicament of the disadvantaged in the United States and abroad **final effects** worsens.

USING *THE SUNDANCE READER*

The Sundance Reader is organized into nine chapters focusing on writers' goals. The readings in each section illustrate how writers achieve their purpose in different contexts. Each chapter opens with an explanation of the goal or mode. The first few readings in each chapter are brief, clear-cut examples of the mode and can serve as models for many of your composition assignments. The middle readings are longer and more complex and demonstrate writing tasks in a range of disciplines and writing situations. Each chapter ends with samples of applied writings taken from business, industry, and government to illustrate how writing is used beyond the classroom.

When reading entries, keep these general questions in mind:

1. **What is the writer's purpose?** Even writers pursuing the same goal—to tell a story or explain a process—have slightly different intentions. What is the purpose of the story—to raise questions, to motivate the reader to take action, or to change his or her point of view?
2. **What is the writer's thesis?** Does a clear thesis statement exist that you can highlight, or is it implied? Can you restate the thesis in your own words?
3. **Who are the intended readers?** Note the source of the article. What does it tell you about the readers? Does the writer direct it to a specific group or a general audience? What assumptions does the writer seem to make about the reader? What terms or references are defined? What knowledge does the writer expect his or her audience to possess?
4. **What evidence does the writer use to support the thesis?** Does the writer provide personal observation, statistics, studies, or the testimony of others to support his or her views?
5. **What is the nature of the discipline, profession, or writing situation?** What discipline is the writer addressing? Is he or she working within a discipline or addressing readers in another discipline? Is the writer addressing general readers? Do special circumstances guide the way the writer develops the thesis, presents ideas, and designs the physical appearance of the writing?
6. **How successful is this writing—in context?** Does the writer achieve his or her goals while respecting the needs of the reader and the conventions of the discipline or situation? Do special circumstances explain why some aspects of the writing appear to "break" the rules of what most English courses consider "good writing"?

 WebTutor

Throughout *The Sundance Reader* WebTutor provides links to online support, offering additional information, answers to common questions, and help for writing each mode.

2

Narration

WHAT IS NARRATION?

Narration seeks to answer the basic question "What happened?" The goal of narration is to tell a story. The Bible, Greek myths, Native American fables, novels, short stories, diaries, autobiographies, and history books are examples of narration. Narrative writing forms the heart of most newspaper articles. Narration is also one of the most common types of professional writing. Physicians write narration to record a patient's history or outline a course of treatment. Attorneys use narrative writing to relate the details of a crime or explain the rationale for a lawsuit. Government reports, grant proposals, sales brochures, and business plans generally include a section labeled "narrative" that provides the history of an organization or a summary of a current project.

The Writer's Purpose

Narration can be subjective or objective, depending on the writer's goal and context. Subjective narration focuses on personal impressions, thoughts, insights, and feelings. Often the writer is at the center of the narrative, either as a principal character or key witness. In "The Lesson" (page 51) Nathan McCall relates his first encounter with racism while attending a previously segregated school:

It was the beginning of my sixth-grade school year, and I was walking down the hall, searching for my new class, when a white boy timed my steps, extended his foot, and tripped me. The boy and his friends nudged each other and laughed as I stumbled into a locker, spilling books and papers everywhere. "Hey, nigger," the boy said. "You dropped something."

McCall's purpose is to share a deeply personal experience of pain and humiliation, impressing readers with what he thought and felt. His emotional reactions form the core of the narrative:

I was sitting on the gym floor with the rest of the student body, watching a school assembly program, when a group of rowdy white upperclassmen began plucking my head and ridiculing me. I got confused. *What should I do?* To turn around and say something to them would start another fight. To get up and leave would require me to wade through a sea of hostile white students to reach the nearest exit. With nowhere to go, I sat there and took the humiliation until I broke. Tears welled in my eyes and started running, uncontrollably, down my face. I sat silently through the remainder of the assembly program with my vision blurred and my spirit broken. That was the only time, then or since, that I've been crushed so completely.

Objective narration, on the other hand, is usually stated in the third person to give the writer's views a sense of neutrality. In objective narration, the author is not a participant but a collector and presenter of facts. In "Ebola River" (page 67) Richard Preston chronicles the outbreak of a deadly virus in Sudan:

It hit the hospital like a bomb. It savaged patients and snaked like chain lightning out from the hospital through patients' families. Apparently the medical staff had been giving patients injections with dirty needles. The virus jumped quickly through the hospital via the needles, and then it hit the medical staff. A characteristic of a lethal, contagious, and incurable virus is that it quickly gets into the medical people. In some cases, the medical system may intensify the outbreak, like a lens that focuses sunlight on a heap of tinder.

Authors do use first person in objective narration, particularly when they have directly participated in or witnessed events. However, unlike Nathan McCall, who focused on his *internal reactions* to situations, a scientist like Oliver Sacks stresses *external events*, making professional rather than personal judgments. In "The Man Who Mistook His Wife for a Hat," Sacks relates his experience with Dr. P., a highly talented professor of music who had begun exhibiting bizarre symptoms. Recounting his initial examination, Sacks objectively records his findings:

> I stilled my disquiet, his perhaps, too, in the soothing routine of a neurological exam—muscle strength, coordination, reflexes, tone. . . . It was while examining his reflexes—a trifle abnormal on the left side— that the first bizarre experience occurred. I had taken off his left shoe and scratched the sole of his foot with a key—a frivolous-seeming but essential test of a reflex—and then, excusing myself to screw my ophthalmoscope together, left him to put on the shoe himself. To my surprise, a minute later, he had not done this.
>
> "Can I help?" I asked.
>
> "Help what? Help whom?"
>
> "Help you put on your shoe."
>
> "Ach," he said, "I had forgotten the shoe," adding, *sotto voce*, "The shoe? The shoe?" He seemed baffled.
>
> "Your shoe," I repeated. "Perhaps you'd put it on."
>
> He continued to look downwards, though not at the shoe, with an intense but misplaced concentration. Finally his gaze settled on his foot: "That is my shoe, yes?"
>
> Did I mis-hear? Did he mis-see?
>
> "My eyes," he explained, and put a hand to his foot. "*This* is my shoe, no?"
>
> "No, it is not. That is your foot. *There* is your shoe."
>
> "Ah! I thought that was my foot."
>
> Was he joking? Was he mad? Was he blind? If this was one of his "strange mistakes," it was the strangest mistake I had ever come across.
>
> I helped him on with his shoe (his foot), to avoid further complication. Dr. P. himself seemed untroubled, indifferent, maybe amused. I resumed my examination. His visual acuity was good: he had no difficulty seeing a pin on the floor, though sometimes he missed it if it was placed to his left.

Though mystified by the patient's odd behavior, Sacks focuses less on his personal responses than on his professional evaluations as a doctor and scientist. When he mentions himself in the narrative, the commentary is limited to explaining his role in conducting a medical examination.

In an effort to create a greater sense of objectivity, many writers avoid using the first person by documenting personal actions in passive voice. Instead of stating, "I took photographs of the crash site," they report, "Photographs of the crash site were taken." Rhetoricians, English instructors, and editors often object to passive voice because it is wordy and less precise. Passive voice deletes the actor from the action, in this case failing to state who took the photographs. Still, many writers insist on using passive voice to deliberately avoid personalizing their narratives.

Focus

Related to the writer's purpose is the narrative's focus. A biography of Abraham Lincoln can be a general account of his entire life or a psychological study of his problem with depression during the Civil War. A book about World War II could concentrate on military activities or on the role of women in the defense industry. An article on recycling may provide a survey of national trends or an in-depth study of a single city's program.

Focus determines the kinds of details the writer includes in the narrative and the types of evidence on which he or she relies. In writing a popular history about the sinking of the *Titanic*, Walter Lord based much of his narrative on memories of the survivors. This gave his book human interest and created a tense series of dramas as he recounted the ship's last hours. A nautical engineer writing a technical article explaining the sinking of the "unsinkable" luxury liner would pay attention to mechanical details, specific measurements, and statistics.

Chronology

Chronology, or time, is a central organizing element in narrative writing. Writers do not always relate events in a straight timeline. A biography, for instance, does not have to begin with birth and childhood. Writers often alter the time sequences of their stories to dramatize events or limit their topic. A biographer of Franklin D. Roosevelt might choose to highlight a key event or turning point in his life. The narrative might open with his polio attack, flash back to his childhood and early political career, then flash forward to his recovery and election to the presidency. Other writers find it more dramatic to begin a narrative at the end and then explain what led to this final event. The first chapter of a book about Czar Nicholas II could describe his execution and then flash back to the events leading to his downfall and death.

Each method of organizing a narrative has distinct advantages and disadvantages:

- **Beginning at the beginning** creates an open-ended narrative, providing readers with little direction to later events. Writers who relate complex stories with many possible causes can use a straight chronology to avoid highlighting a single event. Using a direct beginning-to-end approach is the most traditional method of telling a story. One of the difficulties with this method can be determining exactly when the narrative should start. Often the beginning of a story consists of incidental background information that readers may find uninteresting.
- **Beginning at the middle or at a turning point** can arouse reader interest by opening with a dramatic scene. This method of organization can focus the chain of events, persuading readers to concentrate on a particular issue. This is a common pattern in nonfiction articles, biographies, and histories written for a general readership. Critics, however, can view this alteration of chronology as distorting. Not all historians, for instance, may agree that Roosevelt's illness was the "turning point" of his life. Some biographers might feel that focusing on his physical disability ignores his intellectual development or downplays his political role.
- **Beginning at the end** serves to dramatize the final event. When everything is presented in flashback, readers see events, actions, and thoughts in hindsight. The elements of suspense and randomness are removed, providing a stronger sense of cause and effect. Some readers will object to this method because it implies the final outcome was inevitable, when, in fact, events just as easily could have led to alternative endings.

STRATEGIES FOR READING NARRATION

When reading the narrations in this chapter, keep these questions in mind.

Meaning

1. What is the author's narrative purpose—to inform, enlighten, share a personal experience, or provide information required by the reader?

2. What is the writer's role? Is the author a participant or direct witness? Is he or she writing in a personal context, focusing on internal responses, or in a professional context, concentrating on external events?
3. What readership is the narration directed toward—general or specific? How much knowledge does the author assume readers have?
4. What is the nature of the discipline, discourse community, or writing situation? Is the narration objective or subjective? Does the original source of the narrative (newsmagazine, scientific journal, or government document) reveal anything about the context?

Strategy

1. What details does the writer select to highlight? Are some items summarized or ignored?
2. What kind of support does the writer use—personal observation or factual documentation?
3. What is the sequence of events? How is the narration organized? Does the writer begin at the beginning, the end, or a midpoint?
4. Does the writer use flashbacks and flash-forwards?
5. What transitional devices does the writer use to advance the narrative? Does the author use time references such as "later that day" or "two months later"?

Language

1. What does the level of language suggest about the writer's role, intended readers, and the nature of the discipline or writing situation?
2. How does the writer use words to create tone and style? What do word choices suggest about the writer's attitude toward the subject?

Samuel Scudder (1837–1911) was born in Boston and attended Williams College. In 1857 he entered Harvard, where he studied under the noted professor Louis Agassiz. Scudder held various positions and helped found the Cambridge Entomological Club. He published hundreds of papers and developed a comprehensive catalog of three centuries of scientific publications in mathematics and the natural and physical sciences. While working for the United States Geological Survey, he named more than a thousand species of fossil insects. Although later scientists would question some of his conclusions, much of Scudder's work is still admired for its attention to detail.

Take This Fish and Look at It

Today educators stress critical thinking, which begins with close observation. In this famous essay, Scudder relates the lesson in observation he learned under Professor Agassiz, whose teaching method was simple. Instead of lecturing, he directed his young student to "look again, look again."

1   It was more than fifteen years ago that I entered the laboratory of Professor Agassiz, and told him I had enrolled my name in the Scientific School as a student of natural history. He asked me a few questions about my object in coming, my antecedents generally, the mode in which I afterwards proposed to use the knowledge I might acquire, and, finally, whether I wished to study any special branch. To the latter I replied that, while I wished to be well grounded in all departments of zoology, I purposed to devote myself specially to insects.

2   "When do you wish to begin?" he asked.

3   "Now," I replied.

4   This seemed to please him, and with an energetic "Very well!" he reached from a shelf a huge jar of specimens in yellow alcohol. "Take this fish," he said, "and look at it; we call it a haemulon; by and by I will ask what you have seen."

5   With that he left me, but in a moment returned with explicit instructions as to the care of the object entrusted to me.

6   "No man is fit to be a naturalist," said he, "who does not know how to take care of specimens."

7   I was to keep the fish before me in a tin tray, and occasionally moisten the surface with alcohol from the jar, always taking care to replace the stopper tightly. Those were not the days of ground-glass stoppers and elegantly shaped exhibition jars; all the old students will recall the huge neckless glass bottles with their leaky, wax-besmeared corks, half eaten by insects, and begrimed with cellar dust. Entomology was a cleaner science than ichthyology, but the example of the Professor, who had unhesitatingly plunged to the bottom of the jar to produce the fish, was infectious; and though this alcohol had a "very ancient and fishlike smell," I really dared not show any aversion within these sacred precincts, and treated the alcohol as though it were pure water. Still I was conscious of a passing feeling of disappointment, for gazing at a fish did not commend itself to an ardent entomologist. My friends at home, too, were annoyed when they discovered that no amount of eau-de-Cologne would drown the perfume which haunted me like a shadow.

8   In ten minutes I had seen all that could be seen in that fish, and started in search of the Professor—who had, however, left the Museum; and when I returned, after lingering over some of the odd animals stored in the upper apartment, my specimen was dry all over. I dashed the fluid over the fish as if to resuscitate the beast from a fainting fit, and looked with anxiety for a return of the normal sloppy appearance. This little excitement over, nothing was to be done but to return to a steadfast gaze at my mute companion. Half an hour passed—an hour—another hour; the fish began to look loathsome. I turned it over and around; looked it in the face—ghastly; from behind, beneath, above, sideways, at three-quarters' view—just as ghastly. I was in despair; at an early hour I concluded that lunch was necessary; so, with infinite relief, the fish was carefully replaced in the jar, and for an hour I was free.

9   On my return, I learned that Professor Agassiz had been at the Museum, but had gone, and would not return for several hours. My fellow-students were too busy to be disturbed by continued conversation. Slowly I drew forth that hideous fish, and with a feeling of desperation again looked at it. I might not use a magnifying-glass; instruments of all kinds were interdicted. My two hands, my two eyes, and the fish: it seemed a most limited field. I pushed my finger down its throat to feel how sharp the teeth were. I began to count the scales in the different rows, until I was convinced that was nonsense. At last a happy thought struck me—I would draw the fish; and now with sur-

prise I began to discover new features in the creature. Just then the Professor returned.

10   "That is right," said he; "a pencil is one of the best of eyes. I am glad to notice, too, that you keep your specimen wet, and your bottle corked."

11   With these encouraging words, he added: "Well, what is it like?"

12   He listened attentively to my brief rehearsal of the structure of parts whose names were still unknown to me: the fringed gill-arches and movable operculum; the pores of the head, fleshy lips and lidless eyes; the lateral line, the spinous fins and forked tail; the compressed and arched body. When I finished, he waited as if expecting more, and then, with an air of disappointment:

13   "You have not looked very carefully; why," he continued more earnestly, "you haven't even seen one of the most conspicuous features of the animal, which is plainly before your eyes as the fish itself; look again, look again!" and he left me to my misery.

14   I was piqued; I was mortified. Still more of that wretched fish! But now I set myself to my task with a will, and discovered one new thing after another, until I saw how just the Professor's criticism had been. The afternoon passed quickly; and when, towards its close, the Professor inquired:

15   "Do you see it yet?"

16   "No," I replied, "I am certain I do not, but I see how little I saw before."

17   "That is next best," said he, earnestly, "but I won't hear you now; put away your fish and go home; perhaps you will be ready with a better answer in the morning. I will examine you before you look at the fish."

18   This was disconcerting. Not only must I think of my fish all night, studying, without the object before me, what this unknown but most visible feature might be; but also, without reviewing my discoveries, I must give an exact account of them the next day. I had a bad memory; so I walked home by Charles River in a distracted state, with my two perplexities.

19   The cordial greeting from the Professor the next morning was reassuring; here was a man who seemed to be quite as anxious as I that I should see for myself what he saw.

20   "Do you perhaps mean," I asked, "that the fish has symmetrical sides with paired organs?"

21   His thoroughly pleased "Of course! of course!" repaid the wakeful hours of the previous night. After he had discoursed most happily and

enthusiastically—as he always did—upon the importance of this point, I ventured to ask what I should do next.

22   "Oh, look at your fish!" he said, and left me again to my own devices. In a little more than an hour he returned, and heard my new catalogue.

23   "That is good, that is good!" he repeated; "but that is not all; go on"; and so for three long days he placed that fish before my eyes, forbidding me to look at anything else, or to use any artificial aid. "Look, look, look," was his repeated injunction.

24   This was the best entomological lesson I ever had—a lesson whose influence has extended to the details of every subsequent study; a legacy the Professor had left to me, as he has left it to so many others, of inestimable value which we could not buy, with which we cannot part.

25   A year afterward, some of us were amusing ourselves with chalking outlandish beasts on the Museum blackboard. We drew prancing starfishes; frogs in mortal combat; hydra-headed worms; stately crawfishes, standing on their tails, bearing aloft umbrellas; and grotesque fishes with gaping mouths and staring eyes. The Professor came in shortly after, and was as amused as any at our experiments. He looked at the fishes.

26   "Haemulons, every one of them," he said; "Mr. _____ drew them."

27   True; and to this day, if I attempt a fish, I can draw nothing but haemulons.

28   The fourth day, a second fish of the same group was placed beside the first, and I was bidden to point out the resemblances and differences between the two; another and another followed, until the entire family lay before me, and a whole legion of jars covered the table and surrounding shelves; the odor had become a pleasant perfume; and even now, the sight of an old, six-inch worm-eaten cork brings fragrant memories.

29   The whole group of haemulons was thus brought in review; and, whether engaged upon the dissection of the internal organs, the preparation and examination of the bony framework, or the description of the various parts, Agassiz's training in the method of observing facts and their orderly arrangement was ever accompanied by the urgent exhortation not to be content with them.

30   "Facts are stupid things," he would say, "until brought into connection with some general law."

31   At the end of eight months, it was almost with reluctance that I left these friends and turned to insects; but what I had gained by this outside experience has been of greater value than years of later investigation in my favorite groups.

Understanding Meaning

1. What is the purpose of Scudder's narrative? What is he trying to impress on his reader? What makes this essay more than a simple "first day of school" story?
2. Why did the professor prevent Scudder from using a magnifying glass? What did Professor Agassiz mean when he said "a pencil is one of the best of eyes"?
3. What did Scudder find frustrating about Dr. Agassiz's teaching method?
4. *Critical Thinking:* How effective was Professor Agassiz's nineteenth-century teaching method? By directing a new student to "look again, look again," did he accomplish more than if he had required Scudder to attend a two-hour lecture on the importance of observation? Is close observation a discipline most of us lack? Can you consider detailed observation the first level of critical thinking?

Evaluating Strategy

1. How does Scudder focus his narrative? What details does he leave out?
2. Do his personal reactions to the smell and his frustrations dramatize an extremely passive event? How can a writer create action in a story where the events are mental or emotional?
3. How does Scudder re-create his sense of boredom and frustration?
4. *Other Modes:* How does Scudder use *description* of the fish, the specimen bottles, and the smells to provide readers with a clear impression of the laboratory?

Appreciating Language

1. Review Scudder's narrative. How much scientific language does he use in relating his story? What does this say about his readers?
2. This story has little action. Essentially, it is a story about a man interacting with a dead fish. What words add drama or humor to the narrative?

Connections across the Disciplines

1. Scudder is a scientist writing to a general reader. How do you compare his writing style and vocabulary with Oliver Sacks's (page 81)?
2. *Critical Thinking:* Consider Professor Agassiz's statement, "Facts are stupid things until brought into connection with some general law." What does this say about instructors who teach facts and give multiple-choice tests based on rote memory?

Writing Suggestions

1. Apply Professor Agassiz's technique to a common object you might use every day. Spend five minutes carefully examining a clock radio, your watch, or a can of your favorite soft drink. Then write a brief *description* of what you have observed. List the features you have never noticed before.
2. Professor Agassiz gave his student little direction beyond a simple command. Write an essay relating an experience in which a parent, teacher, superior officer, or boss left you to act on your own. What problems did you encounter? Were you frustrated, afraid, or angry? Was it a learning experience?
3. *Collaborative Writing:* Working with three or four other students, select an object unfamiliar to the group. Allow each member to study the object and make notes. *Compare* your findings, and work to create a single *description* of it. Pay attention to the words you select to create an accurate, objective picture of the object. Notice the details you overlooked that others observed.

NATHAN McCALL

Nathan McCall grew up in Portsmouth, Virginia, where he attended both black and integrated public schools. In 1975 he was convicted of armed robbery and sentenced to eight years in prison. After serving three years, McCall was released and studied journalism at Norfolk State University. He became a reporter for the Virginian Pilot-Ledger Star *and later moved to* The Atlanta Journal-Constitution. *He covered the 1988 Republican National Convention in New Orleans and accompanied Andy Young on a European trade mission. In 1989 he joined the staff of* The Washington Post. *McCall's autobiography* Makes Me Wanna Holler *was published in 1995 and a collection of essays,* What's Going On, *in 1997.*

The Lesson

In this passage of his autobiography, McCall relates his experience as one of the first African-American students bused to a previously all-white public school in Virginia. His goal in this narrative is to share with readers the emotional trauma caused by racial hatred.

1   My harshest introduction to the world of white folks came in September 1966, when my parents sent me to Alford J. Mapp, a white school across town. It was the beginning of my sixth-grade school year, and I was walking down the hall, searching for my new class, when a white boy timed my steps, extended his foot, and tripped me. The boy and his friends nudged each other and laughed as I stumbled into a locker, spilling books and papers everywhere. "Hey, nigger," the boy said. "You dropped something."

2   The word sounded vile coming from his white mouth. When I regained my footing, I tore into that cat and tried to take his head off. Pinning him against a locker, I punched him in the face and kept on punching him until his two buddies jumped in to help him out. While other white students crowded around and cheered them on, we scuffled there in the hall until the bell rang, signaling the start of the next class period. Like combatants in a prizefight, we automatically stopped throwing punches and separated at the sound of the bell. The white boys went their way down the hall, calling me names along the way

and threatening to retaliate. I gathered my papers, straightened my clothes, and reeled toward my next class, dazed, trying to figure out what had just happened to me.

3   My parents sent me to Mapp in 1966 because that was the first year that blacks in Portsmouth were able to attend school wherever they wanted. The U.S. Supreme Court had long before ruled against the notion of separate but equal schools; still, Virginia, one of the states that had resisted desegregation, was slow in putting together a busing plan. Without a plan to ship black students to schools across town, over the years blacks and whites in Portsmouth had simply remained in separate schools. I could have gone to W. E. Waters, a junior high school that had just been built in our neighborhood, but, like many blacks then, my parents figured I could get a better education at the white school across town.

4   I was proud of their decision and held it out teasingly to my brothers as proof that I was the smart one in the family, that I held more academic promise than them. Billy had flunked the second grade, and Dwight and Junnie never showed much interest in books. My less studious brothers would attend their regular, all-black high school, but I was going to a *white* school, which made me feel special.

5   My parents didn't talk with me beforehand about the challenge I would face as one in the first wave of blacks to integrate Mapp. We had all seen TV news footage of police in riot gear escorting black students through hostile, jeering crowds to enroll in all-white high schools and colleges across the country, but for various reasons my parents saw no cause for alarm at Mapp. It was only a junior high school, which seemed far less menacing than the racially torn high schools and college campuses we heard about. Besides, there were no warning signals in Portsmouth to tip off my parents, no public protests by white citizens or high-profile white supremacist politicians like Alabama governor George Wallace threatening to buck the school integration plan.

6   At Mapp, I was the only African-American in most of my classes. When I walked into one room and sat down, the students near me would get up and move away, as if my dark skin were dirty and hideous to them. Nobody talked directly to me. Instead, they shot daggers to each other that were intended for me. "You know, I hate niggers," they would say. "I don't understand why they're always following white people everywhere. We can't seem to get away from them. Why don't they just stay in their own schools?"

7   It wasn't much better dealing with white teachers. They avoided eye contact with me as much as possible and pretended not to see or hear white student hecklers. It was too much for an eleven-year-old to challenge, and I didn't try. Instead, I tried to become invisible. I kept to myself, remained quiet during class discussions, and never asked questions in or after class. I kept my eyes glued to my desk or looked straight ahead to avoid drawing attention to myself. I staggered, numb and withdrawn, through each school day and hurried from my last class, gym, without showering so that I wouldn't miss the only bus headed home. Students who missed the first school bus had to walk through the white neighborhood to the main street to catch the city bus. Mapp was located in a middle-class section of town called Craddock, where the whites were as hateful as the poor whites in Academy Park.

8   The daily bus ride home brought its own set of fears. A group of white boys got on our bus regularly for the sole purpose, it seemed, of picking fights. I was scared to death of them. With older brothers to fight at home, I was confident I could whip any white boy my age and size, but many of the white guys who got on that bus were eighth graders, and they looked like giants to me. Others were older, white, leather-jacket-wearing hoods who I was certain were high school dropouts.

9   When we boarded the bus, blacks automatically moved to the rear, as if Jim Crow laws were still in effect. The white boys would board last, crowd into the aisles, and start making racial slurs when the bus pulled away from school. "I hate the smell of niggers. They sure do stink. Don't you think niggers stink, Larry?"

10   "They sure do, man. They smell bad."

11   Before long, fists flew, girls screamed, and people tussled in the aisles. Few of the black guys on the bus were big and bad enough to beat the tough white boys, who outnumbered us seven to one. I never joined in to help the black guys out. I huddled in the far corner at the rear of the bus, tense, scared as hell, hoping the fighting wouldn't reach that far before the driver broke it up.

12   Children have an enormous capacity to adapt to insanity. I took my lumps in school and tried as much as possible to shrug it off when I went home. Billy, Dwight, and Junnie came home most days full of stories about the fun they were having at pep rallies and football games at their all-black high school. I envied them because I couldn't match their stories with tales of my own about fun times at Mapp. I

savored every minute of my weeknights at home and used weekends to gather the heart to face Mapp again. Monday mornings, I rose and dutifully caught the school bus back to hell.

13 The harassment never let up. Once, when my English teacher left the room, a girl sitting near me drew a picture of a stickman on a piece of paper, colored it black, scribbled my name below it, and passed it around the classroom for others to see. I lost my temper, snatched it from her, and ripped it up. She hit me. I hit her back, then the whole class jumped in. When the teacher returned, I was standing up, punching one guy while another was riding my back and hitting me in the head. The teacher demanded, "What's going on here?"

14 The white kids cried out in unison, "That *black* boy started a fight with us!"

15 Without another word, the teacher sent me to the principal's office and I was dismissed from school. The weeklong suspension alerted my parents that something was wrong. Mama sat me down and tried to talk to me about it. "Why were you fighting in school?"

16 "It wasn't my fault, Mama. That girl drew a picture of me and colored it black."

17 "That's no reason to fight. What's the matter with you? Your grades are falling and now you get into a fight. Don't you like your school?"

18 I tried to explain, then choked up and broke down in tears. Seeing that, my parents sought and got approval to transfer me to the neighborhood school, W. E. Waters.

19 But it wasn't over yet. One day, before the transfer went through, I was sitting on the gym floor with the rest of the student body, watching a school assembly program, when a group of rowdy white upperclassmen began plucking my head and ridiculing me. I got confused. *What should I do?* To turn around and say something to them would start another fight. To get up and leave would require me to wade through a sea of hostile white students to reach the nearest exit. With nowhere to go, I sat there and took the humiliation until I broke. Tears welled in my eyes and started running, uncontrollably, down my face. I sat silently through the remainder of the assembly program with my vision blurred and my spirit broken. That was the only time, then or since, that I've been crushed so completely. When it was over, I collected myself, went to the boys' bathroom, and boohooed some more.

20 There was no greater joy than that last bus ride home from Mapp. I sat near a window and stared out, trying to make sense of those past few

months. Everything that had happened to me was so contrary to all I'd been taught about right and wrong. Before Mapp, every grudge I had ever held against a person could be traced to some specific deed. I couldn't understand someone hating me simply for being black and alive. I wondered, *Where did those white people learn to hate so deeply at such a young age?* I didn't know. But, over time, I learned to hate as blindly and viciously as any of them.

Understanding Meaning

1. Why did McCall's parents send him to a white school?
2. How did the white students respond to his presence?
3. How was McCall treated by the white faculty?
4. What impact did the students' reactions have on the author?
5. Why did McCall envy his brothers, who attended all-black schools?
6. What lesson did McCall learn?
7. *Critical Thinking:* McCall makes the observation that "Children have an enormous capacity to adapt to insanity." Can you think of current incidents or examples from your own life that support this view? Is this a universal phenomenon?

Evaluating Strategy

1. How does McCall blend a series of separate incidents into a single narrative?
2. What objective facts does McCall introduce into the narrative? Why are they important?
3. *Other Modes:* How does McCall use *description* and *comparison* to develop his narrative?

Appreciating Language

1. McCall uses the terms *black* and *African-American* interchangeably. Does this appear inconsistent, or does it simply help the writer avoid repetition?
2. McCall states that the word *nigger* sounded "vile" coming from a white student. Is he suggesting that the race of the user determines the meaning of a word most people view as a term of contempt?
3. *Critical Thinking:* At one point McCall states that he wished to be "invisible." Why does this word have special meaning for African-Americans?

Connections across the Disciplines

1. Consider Carl T. Rowan's account of his black teacher in "Unforgettable Miss Bessie" (page 131). Does McCall's account suggest that many students are better served in black schools with black teachers?
2. How does McCall's experience compare to that of Ramon Pérez (page 62)? Do their experiences give them a sense of being alien?

Writing Suggestions

1. Write a short essay about an incident in which you learned something about your status in society. Think of a time in which people responded to you not as an individual but as a member of a group. Have you ever been seen as one of *them* and labeled by others who have a fear or hatred for people who are different? What occurred, and how did people's reactions make you feel? Choose words carefully to express how the incident made you feel.
2. *Collaborative Writing:* Discuss McCall's narrative with a group of students. Ask members of the group to respond to McCall's "lesson." Work together to write a brief *description* of how children learn to hate others.

MOLLY IVINS

Molly Ivins worked as a reporter for the New York Times *before becoming a columnist for the* Dallas Times Herald. *She has published numerous articles in* Ms., The Nation, The Progressive, Texas Observer, *and other magazines. Many of her pieces were published in her collections,* Molly Ivins Can't Say That, Can She? *(1992) and* Nothin' But Good Times Ahead *(1994). Her witty and often sarcastic commentaries have covered a range of topics, including politics, country music, fashion, religion, and National Football League cheerleaders.*

A Short Story about the Vietnam War Memorial

Ivins is best noted for satiric social commentary. But in this column, published shortly after the Vietnam War Memorial was dedicated, Ivins uses fictional techniques to create a moving narrative. She impresses readers with the memorial's significance by demonstrating the emotions of a single visitor.

1   She had known, ever since she first read about the Vietnam War Memorial, that she would go there someday. Sometime she would be in Washington and would go and see his name and leave again.

2   So silly, all that fuss about the memorial. Whatever else Vietnam was, it was not the kind of war that calls for some *Raising the Flag at Iwo Jima* kind of statue. She was not prepared, though, for the impact of the memorial. To walk down into it in the pale winter sunshine was like the war itself, like going into a dark valley and damned if there was ever any light at the end of the tunnel. Just death. When you get closer to the two walls, the number of names start to stun you. It is terrible, there in the peace and the pale sunshine.

3   The names are listed by date of death. There has never been a time, day or night, drunk or sober, for thirteen years that she could not have told you the date. He was killed on August 13, 1969. It is near the middle of the left wall. She went toward it as though she had known beforehand where it would be. His name is near the bottom. She had to kneel to find it. Stupid clichés. His name leaped out at her. It was like being hit.

4   She stared at it and then reached out and gently ran her fingers over the letters in the cold black marble. The memory of him came back so strong, almost as if he were there on the other side of the stone, she could see his hand reaching out to touch her fingers. It had not hurt for years and suddenly, just for a moment, it hurt again so horribly that it twisted her face and made her gasp and left her with tears running down her face. Then it stopped hurting but she could not stop the tears. Could not stop them running and running down her face.

5   There had been a time, although she had been an otherwise sensible young woman, when she had believed she would never recover from the pain. She did, of course. But she is still determined never to sentimentalize him. He would have hated that. She had thought it was like an amputation, the severing of his life from hers, that you could live on afterward but it would be like having only one leg and one arm. But it was only a wound. It healed. If there is a scar, it is only faintly visible now at odd intervals.

6   He was a biologist, a t.a. at the university getting his Ph.D. They lived together for two years. He left the university to finish his thesis but before he lined up a public school job—teachers were safe in those years—the draft board got him. They had friends who had left the country, they had friends who had gone to prison, they had friends who had gone to Nam. There were no good choices in those years. She thinks now he unconsciously wanted to go even though he often said, said in one of his last letters, that it was a stupid, f---in' war. He felt some form of guilt about a friend of theirs who was killed during the Tet offensive. Hubert Humphrey called Tet a great victory. His compromise was to refuse officer's training school and go as an enlisted man. She had thought then it was a dumb gesture and they had a half-hearted quarrel about it.

7   He had been in Nam less than two months when he was killed, without heroics, during a firefight at night by a single bullet in the brain. No one saw it happen. There are some amazing statistics about money and tonnage from that war. Did you know that there were more tons of bombs dropped on Hanoi during the Christmas bombing of 1972 than in all of World War II? Did you know that the war in Vietnam cost the United States $123.3 billion? She has always wanted to know how much that one bullet cost. Sixty-three cents? $1.20? Someone must know.

8   The other bad part was the brain. Even at this late date, it seems to her that was quite a remarkable mind. Long before she read C. P.

Snow, the ferociously honest young man who wanted to be a great biologist taught her a great deal about the difference between the way scientists think and the way humanists think. Only once has she been glad he was not with her. It was at one of those bizarre hearings about teaching "creation science." He would have gotten furious and been horribly rude. He had no patience with people who did not understand and respect the process of science.

9   She used to attribute his fierce honesty to the fact that he was a Yankee. She is still prone to tell "white" lies to make people feel better, to smooth things over, to prevent hard feelings. Surely there have been dumber things for lovers to quarrel over than the social utility of hypocrisy. But not many.

10   She stood up again, still staring at his name, stood for a long time. She said, "There it is," and turned to go. A man to her left was staring at her. She glared at him. The man had done nothing but make the mistake of seeing her weeping. She said, as though daring him to disagree, "It was a stupid, f---in' war," and stalked past him.

11   She turned again at the top of the slope to make sure where his name is, so whenever she sees a picture of the memorial she can put her finger where his name is. He never said goodbye, literally. Whenever he left he would say, "Take care love." He could say it many different ways. He said it when he left for Vietnam. She stood at the top of the slope and found her hand half-raised in some silly gesture of farewell. She brought it down again. She considered thinking to him, "Hey, take care, love" but it seemed remarkably inappropriate. She walked away and was quite entertaining for the rest of the day, because it was expected of her.

12   She thinks he would have liked the memorial. He would have hated the editorials. He did not sacrifice his life for his country or for a just or noble cause. There just were no good choices in those years and he got killed.

Understanding Meaning

1. What impact did the memorial have on the visitor?
2. What attitude did the woman's lover have toward the war?
3. Why did she view his refusal to attend officers' training school as a "dumb gesture"?
4. What assumptions did the woman make about how the man's loss would affect her?

5. *Critical Thinking:* Ivins remarks that there were "no good choices in those years." Could this apply to soldiers in other wars, perhaps in all wars? Do wars ever provide people with "good choices"?

Evaluating Strategy

1. Does the title suggest that the story is purely fictional? Why should journalists clearly mark imaginative work to avoid allegations of falsification?
2. Ivins does not provide the people with names. What effect does this have? How would the story be different if the woman were called Jane, Kim, Juanita, or Siobhan?
3. *Critical Thinking:* Does a nonfiction writer such as a columnist or social commentator risk compromising his or her position by publishing what appears to be fiction in a newspaper column? Will readers assume that future articles may contain material that is "made up"?

Appreciating Language

1. What words does Ivins use to describe the monument?
2. Ivins compares the woman's grief to an "amputation." How effective is this image in describing an emotion?

Connections across the Disciplines

1. Would Nathan McCall's plight (page 51) of attending either possibly inferior black schools or hostile integrated schools suggest a similar lack of good choices?
2. Does Ivins admire the woman? Are her tone and approach similar to Carl Rowan's in "Unforgettable Miss Bessie" (page 131)?

Writing Suggestions

1. Write a short narrative with a fictional character. Your story may be serious, humorous, or satirical. Develop an unnamed character who embodies a typical student or employee. Have the character engage in a simple act, such as walking to class or answering the telephone at work.
2. Write a dramatic story about a person experiencing something momentous such as facing an angry boss, confronting an unfaithful lover, approaching a clinic to be tested for HIV, or taking a final examination. Focus on the emotions and memories this confrontation evokes.

3. *Collaborative Writing:* Working with a group of students, discuss Ivins's comments about people who have "no good choices." Have each student write a brief narrative or description about a person facing limited options. At a second meeting have each student read his or her paper to the group. Determine which narrative best illustrates the dilemma of choice.

Ramon "Tianguis" Pérez is an undocumented alien and does not release biographical information.

The Fender-Bender

This narrative, taken from Pérez's book Diary of an Undocumented Immigrant, *illustrates how even a minor incident can affect the precarious existence of an undocumented alien. For Pérez, a few pieces of paper stand between a life in America and deportation.*

1 One night after work, I drive Rolando's old car to visit some friends, and then head towards home. At a light, I come to a stop too late, leaving the front end of the car poking into the crosswalk. I shift into reverse, but as I am backing up, I strike the van behind me. Its driver immediately gets out to inspect the damage to his vehicle. He's a tall Anglo-Saxon, dressed in a deep blue work uniform. After looking at his car, he walks up to the window of the car I'm driving.

2 "Your driver's license," he says, a little enraged.

3 "I didn't bring it," I tell him.

4 He scratches his head. He is breathing heavily with fury.

5 "Okay," he says. "You park up ahead while I call a patrolman."

6 The idea of calling the police doesn't sound good to me, but the accident is my fault. So I drive around the corner and park at the curb. I turn off the motor and hit the steering wheel with one fist. I don't have a driver's license. I've never applied for one. Nor do I have with me the identification card that I bought in San Antonio. Without immigration papers, without a driving permit, and having hit another car, I feel as if I'm just one step away from Mexico.

7 I get out of the car. The white man comes over and stands right in front of me. He's almost two feet taller.

8 "If you're going to drive, why don't you carry your license?" he asks in an accusatory tone.

9 "I didn't bring it," I say, for lack of any other defense.

10   I look at the damage to his car. It's minor, only a scratch on the paint and a pimple-sized dent.

11   "I'm sorry," I say. "Tell me how much it will cost to fix, and I'll pay for it; that's no problem." I'm talking to him in English, and he seems to understand.

12   "This car isn't mine," he says. "It belongs to the company I work for. I'm sorry, but I've got to report this to the police, so that I don't have to pay for the damage."

13   "That's no problem," I tell him again. "I can pay for it."

14   After we've exchanged these words, he seems less irritated. But he says he'd prefer for the police to come, so that they can report that the dent wasn't his fault.

15   While we wait, he walks from one side to the other, looking down the avenue this way and that, hoping that the police will appear.

16   Then he goes over to the van to look at the dent.

17   "It's not much," he says. "If it was my car, there wouldn't be any problems, and you could go on."

18   After a few minutes, the long-awaited police car arrives. Only one officer is inside. He's a Chicano, short and of medium complexion, with short, curly hair. On getting out of the car, he walks straight towards the Anglo.

19   The two exchange a few words.

20   "Is that him?" he asks, pointing at me.

21   The Anglo nods his head.

22   Speaking in English, the policeman orders me to stand in front of the car and to put my hands on the hood. He searches me and finds only the car keys and my billfold with a few dollars in it. He asks for my driver's license.

23   "I don't have it," I answered in Spanish.

24   He wrinkles his face into a frown, and casting a glance at the Anglo, shakes his head in disapproval of me.

25   "That's the way these Mexicans are," he says.

26   He turns back towards me, asking for identification. I tell him I don't have that, either.

27   "You're an illegal, eh?" he says.

28   I won't answer.

29   "An illegal," he says to himself.

30   "Where do you live?" he continues. He's still speaking in English.

31   I tell him my address.

32   "Do you have anything with you to prove that you live at that address?" he asks.

33   I think for a minute, then realize that in the glove compartment is a letter that my parents sent to me several weeks earlier.

34   I show him the envelope and he immediately begins to write something in a little book that he carries in his back pocket. He walks to the back of my car and copies the license plate number. Then he goes over to his car and talks into his radio. After he talks, someone answers. Then he asks me for the name of the car's owner.

35   He goes over to where the Anglo is standing. I can't quite hear what they're saying. But when the two of them go over to look at the dent in the van, I hear the cop tell the Anglo that if he wants, he can file charges against me. The Anglo shakes his head and explains what he had earlier explained to me, about only needing for the police to certify that he wasn't responsible for the accident. The Anglo says that he doesn't want to accuse me of anything because the damage is light.

36   "If you want, I can take him to jail," the cop insists.

37   The Anglo turns him down again.

38   "If you'd rather, we can report him to Immigration," the cop continues.

39   Just as at the first, I am now almost sure that I'll be making a forced trip to Tijuana. I find myself searching my memory for my uncle's telephone number, and to my relief, I remember it. I am waiting for the Anglo to say yes, confirming my expectations of the trip. But instead, he says no, and though I remain silent, I feel appreciation for him. I ask myself why the Chicano is determined to harm me. I didn't really expect him to favor me, just because we're of the same ancestry, but on the other hand, once I had admitted my guilt, I expected him to treat me at least fairly. But even against the white man's wishes, he's trying to make matters worse for me. I've known several Chicanos with whom, joking around, I've reminded them that their roots are in Mexico. But very few of them see it that way. Several have told me how when they were children, their parents would take them to vacation in different states of Mexico, but their own feeling, they've said, is, "I am an American citizen!" Finally, the Anglo, with the justifying paper in his hands, says goodbye to the cop, thanks him for his services, gets into his van and drives away.

40   The cop stands in the street in a pensive mood. I imagine that he's trying to think of a way to punish me.

41   "Put the key in the ignition," he orders me.

42   I do as he says.

43   Then he orders me to roll up the windows and lock the doors.

44   "Now, go on, walking," he says.

45   I go off taking slow steps. The cop gets in his patrol car and stays there, waiting. I turn the corner after two blocks and look out for my car, but the cop is still parked beside it. I begin looking for a coat hanger, and after a good while, find one by a curb of the street. I keep walking, keeping about two blocks away from the car. While I walk, I bend the coat hanger into the form I'll need. As if I'd called for it, a speeding car goes past. When it comes to the avenue where my car is parked, it makes a turn. It is going so fast that its wheels screech as it rounds the corner. The cop turns on the blinking lights of his patrol car and leaving black marks on the pavement beneath it, shoots out to chase the speeder. I go up to my car and with my palms force a window open a crack. Then I insert the clothes hanger in the crack and raise the lock lever. It's a simple task, one that I'd already performed. This wasn't the first time that I'd been locked out of a car, though always before, it was because I'd forgotten to remove my keys.

Understanding Meaning

1. How serious is the accident?
2. Why does the van driver insist on calling the police?
3. What makes this incident a dangerous one for Pérez?
4. How does Pérez attempt to prevent the van driver from summoning the police?
5. Pérez answers the Chicano patrolman in Spanish. Was this a mistake? How did the officer treat Pérez?
6. *Critical Thinking:* Pérez implies that Chicanos have been offended when he has alluded to their Mexican roots; they insist on being seen as American citizens. What does this say about assimilation and identity? Does the Chicano officer's comments about Mexicans reveal contempt for immigrants? Have other ethnic groups—Jews, Italians, the Irish—resented the presence of unassimilated new arrivals from their homelands?

Evaluating Strategy

1. Why is a minor incident like a fender bender a better device to explain the plight of the undocumented immigrant than a dramatic one?
2. How does Pérez use dialogue to advance the narrative?

Appreciating Language

1. What words does Pérez use to minimize the damage caused by the accident?
2. What word choices and images stress the importance of paper documents in the lives of aliens?

Connections across the Disciplines

1. Compare Armando Rendón's attitude (page 611) toward his Spanish heritage with that of the Chicanos Pérez describes. How are they different? How common is the issue of embracing or rejecting one's ethnic origins?
2. How does Pérez's situation differ from Nathan McCall's (page 51)?

Writing Suggestions

1. Write a short narrative essay detailing a minor event that provided insight into your life or social conditions. Perhaps you discovered our dependence on energy when your apartment lost power and you could not use your computer, watch television, or even open the garage door to get your car. A simple interaction with a homeless person may have caused you to question your assumptions about the poor.
2. *Collaborative Writing:* Working with a group of students, discuss your views on immigration and undocumented or "illegal" aliens. Take notes and write a brief statement outlining your views. If major differences of opinion exist, split the group into subgroups, and draft pro and con opinion statements.

Richard Preston is a journalist who frequently contributes to The New Yorker. *In 1987 he published a book about astronomy,* First Light, *which won the American Institute of Physics Award. His next book,* American Steel, *examined the Nucor Corporation's plan to build a revolutionary steel mill. In 1994 he published* The Hot Zone *documenting the outbreak and spread of the deadly Ebola virus.*

Ebola River

In this passage from The Hot Zone, *Preston details the initial appearance of the Ebola virus in Sudan. Although written in the third person and focusing on objective observation, Preston's use of factual detail creates a chilling drama.*

1   On July 6, 1976, five hundred miles northwest of Mount Elgon, in southern Sudan, near the fingered edge of the central-African rain forest, a man who is known to Ebola hunters as Yu. G. went into shock and died with blood running from the orifices of his body. He is referred to only by his initials. Mr. Yu. G. was the first identified case, the index case, in an outbreak of an unknown virus.

2   Mr. Yu. G. was a storekeeper in a cotton factory in the town of Nzara. The population of Nzara had grown in recent years—the town had experienced, in its own way, the human population explosion that is occurring throughout the equatorial regions of the earth. The people of that area in southern Sudan are the Zande, a large tribe. The country of the Zande is savanna mixed with riverine forest, beautiful country, where acacia trees cluster along the banks of seasonal rivers. African doves perch in the trees and call their drawn-out calls. The land between the rivers is a sea of elephant grass, which can grow ten feet high. As you head south, toward Zaire, the land rises and forms hills, and the forest begins to spread away from the river and thickens into a closed canopy, and you enter the rain forest. The land around the town of Nzara held rich plantations of teak and fruit trees and cotton. People were poor, but they worked hard and raised large families and kept to their tribal traditions.

3   Mr. Yu. G. was a salaried man. He worked at a desk in a room piled with cotton cloth at the back of the factory. Bats roosted in the ceiling of the room near his desk. If the bats were infected with Ebola, no one has been able to prove it. The virus may have entered the cotton factory by some unknown route—perhaps in insects trapped in the cotton fibers, for example, or in rats that lived in the factory. Or, possibly, the virus had nothing to do with the cotton factory, and Mr. Yu. G. was infected somewhere else. He did not go to a hospital, and died on a cot in his family compound. His family gave him a traditional Zande funeral and left his body under a mound of stones in a clearing of elephant grass. His grave has been visited more than once by doctors from Europe and America, who want to see it and reflect on its meaning, and pay their respects to the index case of what later became known as Ebola Sudan.

4   He is remembered today as a "quiet, unremarkable man." No photograph was taken of him during his lifetime, and no one seems to remember what he looked like. He wasn't well known, even in his hometown. They say that his brother was tall and slender, so perhaps he was, too. He passed through the gates of life unnoticed by anyone except his family and a few of his co-workers. He might have made no difference except for the fact that he was a host.

5   His illness began to copy itself. A few days after he died, two other salaried men who worked at desks near him in the same room broke with bleeding, went into shock, and died with massive hemorrhages from the natural openings of the body. One of the dead men was a popular fellow known as P. G. Unlike the quiet Mr. Yu. G., he had a wide circle of friends, including several mistresses. He spread the agent far and wide in the town. The agent jumped easily from person to person, apparently through touching and sexual contact. It was a fast spreader, and it could live easily in people. It passed through as many as sixteen generations of infection as it jumped from person to person in Sudan. It also killed many of its hosts. While this is not necessarily in the best interest of the virus, if the virus is highly contagious, and can jump fast enough from host to host, then it does not matter, really, what happens to the previous host, because the virus can amplify itself for quite a while, at least until it kills off much of the population of hosts. Most of the fatal cases of Ebola Sudan can be traced back through chains of infection to the quiet Mr. Yu. G. A hot strain radiated out of him and nearly devastated the human population

of southern Sudan. The strain burned through the town of Nzara and reached eastward to the town of Maridi, where there was a hospital.

6   It hit the hospital like a bomb. It savaged patients and snaked like chain lightning out from the hospital through patients' families. Apparently the medical staff had been giving patients injections with dirty needles. The virus jumped quickly through the hospital via the needles, and then it hit the medical staff. A characteristic of a lethal, contagious, and incurable virus is that it quickly gets into the medical people. In some cases, the medical system may intensify the outbreak, like a lens that focuses sunlight on a heap of tinder.

7   The virus transformed the hospital at Maridi into a morgue. As it jumped from bed to bed, killing patients left and right, doctors began to notice signs of mental derangement, psychosis, depersonalization, zombie-like behavior. Some of the dying stripped off their clothes and ran out of the hospital, naked and bleeding, and wandered through the streets of the town, seeking their homes, not seeming to know what had happened or how they had gotten into this condition. There is no doubt that Ebola damages the brain and causes psychotic dementia. It is not easy, however, to separate brain damage from the effects of fear. If you were trapped in a hospital where people were dissolving in their beds, you might try to escape, and if you were a bleeder and frightened, you might take off your clothes, and people might think you had gone mad.

8   The Sudan strain was more than twice as lethal as Marburg virus—its case-fatality rate was 50 percent. That is, fully half of the people who came down with it ended up dying, and quickly. This was the same kind of fatality rate as was seen with the black plague during the Middle Ages. If the Ebola Sudan virus had managed to spread out of central Africa, it might have entered Khartoum in a few weeks, penetrated Cairo a few weeks after that, and from there it would have hopped to Athens, New York, Paris, London, Singapore—it would have gone everywhere on the planet. Yet that never happened, and the crisis in Sudan passed away unnoticed by the world at large. What happened in Sudan could be compared to the secret detonation of an atomic bomb. If the human race came close to a major biological accident, we never knew it.

9   For reasons that are not clear, the outbreak subsided, and the virus vanished. The hospital at Maridi had been the epicenter of the emergence. As the virus ravaged the hospital, the surviving medical staff

panicked and ran off into the bush. It was probably the wisest thing to do and the best thing that could have happened, because it stopped the use of dirty needles and emptied the hospital, which helped break the chain of infection.

10   There was another possible reason why the Ebola Sudan virus vanished. It was exceedingly hot. It killed people so fast that they didn't have much time to infect other people before they died. Furthermore, the virus was not airborne. It was not quite contagious enough to start a full-scale disaster. It traveled in blood, and the bleeding victim did not touch very many other people before dying, and so the virus did not have many chances to jump to a new host. Had people been coughing the virus into the air . . . it would have been a different story. In any case, the Ebola Sudan virus destroyed a few hundred people in central Africa the way a fire consumes a pile of straw—until the blaze burns out at the center and ends in a heap of ash—rather than smoldering around the planet, as AIDS has done, like a fire in a coal mine, impossible to put out. The Ebola virus, in its Sudan incarnation, retreated to the heart of the bush, where undoubtedly it lives to this day, cycling and cycling in some unknown host, able to shift its shape, able to mutate and become a new thing, with the potential to enter the human species in a new form.

Understanding Meaning

1.   What is known about Mr. Yu. G.? What made him important to science?
2.   What effect does the Ebola virus have on people? How does it kill?
3.   How does the virus spread from one person to another?
4.   Why did this outbreak kill only a few hundred people and not spread across the world like AIDS?
5.   *Critical Thinking:* What implications do Ebola and similar viruses have in a world where jet travel would make it easy for a single patient to spread the disease to people thousands of miles from the outbreak?

Evaluating Strategy

1.   How does Preston organize the chain of events? What chronological pattern does he use?
2.   How does Preston assemble scientific facts to create a dramatic story? Can an objective narrative have an emotional impact on readers? Can facts truly "speak for themselves"?

3. In paragraph seven, Preston places his readers into the events by using second person, "If you were trapped in a hospital . . ." What impact does this have? Is this an effective strategy?

Appreciating Language

1. How would you characterize Preston's level of diction? Does the lack of medical terminology weaken the narrative's scientific value? What does it say about the intended audience?
2. Underline those phrases that dramatize the events. How effective are they?
3. What words does Preston use to describe the virus? How does he emphasize its lethality?

Connections across the Disciplines

1. Preston is writing about people threatened by an invisible virus. How does this confrontation differ from the dramas related by Nathan McCall (page 51) and Ramon Pérez (page 62)? Does Preston have to personalize the action of the virus to heighten the narrative's drama?
2. Consider Samuel Scudder's "Take This Fish and Look at It" (page 45). How important is detailed observation in Preston's account?

Writing Suggestions

1. Write a short essay *analyzing* what threats the Ebola and related viruses could pose in the future. What would happen if the virus broke out in a city like New York or Las Vegas?
2. Write a brief factual but dramatic narrative about an event you experienced or witnessed. Select details that create strong impressions, but avoid exaggerating or distorting facts.
3. *Collaborative Writing:* Working with at least three other students, draft a short persuasive letter to the White House, arguing that the military should be equipped to rapidly respond to biomedical disasters. You may use Einstein's letter to President Roosevelt (page 622) as a model. Use Preston's account to support your thesis.

George Orwell was the pen name of Eric Blair (1903–1950), who was born in In-
dia, the son of a British official. Blair graduated from the prestigious Eton school
but joined the Indian Imperial Police instead of attending a university. After four
years of service in Burma, he left to pursue a writing career. His first book,
Down and Out in Paris and London, *explored the plight of the poor and home-*
less during the Depression. His later books included Animal Farm *and* Nineteen
Eighty-Four.

Shooting an Elephant

As you read Orwell's narrative, consider what message about imperialism he was
trying to communicate to his British readers. What is his implied thesis?

1   In Moulmein, in Lower Burma, I was hated by large numbers of
people—the only time in my life that I have been important enough
for this to happen to me. I was sub-divisional police officer of the town,
and in an aimless, petty kind of way anti-European feeling was very
bitter. No one had the guts to raise a riot, but if a European woman
went through the bazaars alone somebody would probably spit betel
juice over her dress. As a police officer I was an obvious target and
was baited whenever it seemed safe to do so. When a nimble Burman
tripped me up on the football field and the referee (another Burman)
looked the other way, the crowd yelled with hideous laughter. This
happened more than once. In the end the sneering yellow faces of
young men that met me everywhere, the insults hooted after me when
I was at a safe distance, got badly on my nerves. The young Buddhist
priests were the worst of all. There were several thousands of them in
the town and none of them seemed to have anything to do except
stand on street corners and jeer at Europeans.

2   All this was perplexing and upsetting. For at that time I had already made up my mind that imperialism was an evil thing and the
sooner I chucked up my job and got out of it the better. Theoretically—
and secretly, of course—I was all for the Burmese and all against their

oppressors, the British. As for the job I was doing, I hated it more bitterly than I can perhaps make clear. In a job like that you see the dirty work of Empire at close quarters. The wretched prisoners huddling in the stinking cages of the lock-ups, the grey, cowed faces of the long-term convicts, the scarred buttocks of the men who had been flogged with bamboos—all these oppressed me with an intolerable sense of guilt. But I could get nothing into perspective. I was young and ill-educated and I had had to think out my problems in the utter silence that is imposed on every Englishman in the East. I did not even know that the British Empire is dying, still less did I know that it is a great deal better than the younger empires that are going to supplant it. All I knew was that I was stuck between my hatred of the empire I served and my rage against the evil-spirited little beasts who tried to make my job impossible. With one part of my mind I thought of the British Raj as an unbreakable tyranny, as something clamped down, in *saecula saeculorum*, upon the will of prostrate peoples; with another part I thought that the greatest joy in the world would be to drive a bayonet into a Buddhist priest's guts. Feelings like these are the normal by-products of imperialism; ask any Anglo-Indian official, if you can catch him off duty.

3   One day something happened which in a roundabout way was enlightening. It was a tiny incident in itself, but it gave me a better glimpse than I had had before of the real nature of imperialism—the real motives for which despotic governments act. Early one morning the sub-inspector at a police station the other end of the town rang me up on the phone and said that an elephant was ravaging the bazzar. Would I please come and do something about it? I did not know what I could do, but I wanted to see what was happening and I got on to a pony and started out. I took my rifle, an old .44 Winchester and much too small to kill an elephant, but I thought the noise might be useful *in terrorem*. Various Burmans stopped me on the way and told me about the elephant's doings. It was not, of course, a wild elephant, but a tame one which had gone "must." It had been chained up as tame elephants always are when their attack of "must" is due, but on the previous night it had broken its chain and escaped. Its mahout, the only person who could manage it when it was in that state, had set out in pursuit, but he had taken the wrong direction and was now twelve hours' journey away, and in the morning the elephant had suddenly reappeared in the town. The Burmese population had no weapons and were quite

helpless against it. It had already destroyed somebody's bamboo hut, killed a cow and raided some fruit-stalls and devoured the stock; also it had met the municipal rubbish van, and, when the driver jumped out and took to his heels, had turned the van over and inflicted violence upon it.

4   The Burmese sub-inspector and some Indian constables were waiting for me in the quarter where the elephant had been seen. It was a very poor quarter, a labyrinth of squalid bamboo huts, thatched with palm-leaf, winding all over a steep hillside. I remember that it was a cloudy stuffy morning at the beginning of the rains. We began questioning the people as to where the elephant had gone, and, as usual, failed to get any definite information. That is invariably the case in the East; a story always sounds clear enough at a distance, but the nearer you get to the scene of events the vaguer it becomes. Some of the people said that the elephant had gone in one direction, some said that he had gone in another, some professed not even to have heard of any elephant. I had almost made up my mind that the whole story was a pack of lies, when we heard yells a little distance away. There was a loud, scandalised cry of "Go away, child! Go away this instant!" and an old woman with a switch in her hand came round the corner of a hut, violently shooing away a crowd of naked children. Some more women followed, clicking their tongues and exclaiming; evidently there was something there that the children ought not to have seen. I rounded the hut and saw a man's dead body sprawling in the mud. He was an Indian, a black Dravidian coolie, almost naked, and he could not have been dead many minutes. The people said that the elephant had come suddenly upon him round the corner of the hut, caught him with its trunk, put its foot on his back and ground him into the earth. This was the rainy season and the ground was soft, and his face had scored a trench a foot deep and a couple of yards long. He was lying on his belly with arms crucified and head sharply twisted to one side. His face was coated with mud, the eyes wide open, the teeth bared and grinning with an expression of unendurable agony. (Never tell me, by the way, that the dead look peaceful. Most of the corpses I have seen looked devilish.) The friction of the great beast's foot had stripped the skin from his back as neatly as one skins a rabbit. As soon as I saw the dead man I sent an orderly to a friend's house nearby to borrow an elephant rifle. I had already sent back the pony, not wanting it to go mad with fright and throw me if it smelled the elephant.

5 The orderly came back in a few minutes with a rifle and five cartridges, and meanwhile some Burmans had arrived and told us that the elephant was in the paddy fields below, only a few hundred yards away. As I started forward practically the whole population of the quarter flocked out of their houses and followed me. They had seen the rifle and were all shouting excitedly that I was going to shoot the elephant. They had not shown much interest in the elephant when he was merely ravaging their homes, but it was different now that he was going to be shot. It was a bit of fun to them, as it would be to an English crowd; besides, they wanted the meat. It made me vaguely uneasy. I had no intention of shooting the elephant—I had merely sent for the rifle to defend myself if necessary—and it is always unnerving to have a crowd following you. I marched down the hill, looking and feeling a fool, with the rifle over my shoulder and an ever-growing army of people jostling at my heels. At the bottom, when you got away from the huts, there was a metalled road and beyond that a miry waste of paddy fields a thousand yards across, not yet ploughed but soggy from the first rains and dotted with coarse grass. The elephant was standing eighty yards from the road, his left side towards us. He took not the slightest notice of the crowd's approach. He was tearing up bunches of grass, beating them against his knees to clean them and stuffing them into his mouth.

6 I had halted on the road. As soon as I saw the elephant I knew with perfect certainty that I ought not to shoot him. It is a serious matter to shoot a working elephant—it is comparable to destroying a huge and costly piece of machinery—and obviously one ought not to do it if it can possibly be avoided. And at that distance, peacefully eating, the elephant looked no more dangerous than a cow. I thought then and I think now that his attack of "must" was already passing off; in which case he would merely wander harmlessly about until the mahout came back and caught him. Moreover, I did not in the least want to shoot him. I decided that I would watch him for a little while to make sure that he did not turn savage again, and then go home.

7 But at that moment I glanced round at the crowd that had followed me. It was an immense crowd, two thousand at the least and growing every minute. It blocked the road for a long distance on either side. I looked at the sea of yellow faces above the garish clothes—faces all happy and excited over this bit of fun, all certain that the elephant was going to be shot. They were watching me as they would watch a

conjuror about to perform a trick. They did not like me, but with the magical rifle in my hands I was momentarily worth watching. And suddenly I realised that I should have to shoot the elephant after all. The people expected it of me and I had got to do it; I could feel their two thousand wills pressing me forward, irresistibly. And it was at this moment, as I stood there with the rifle in my hands, that I first grasped the hollowness, the futility of the white man's dominion in the East. Here was I, the white man with his gun, standing in front of the unarmed native crowd—seemingly the leading actor of the piece; but in reality I was only an absurd puppet pushed to and fro by the will of those yellow faces behind. I perceived in this moment that when the white man turns tyrant it is his own freedom that he destroys. He becomes a sort of hollow, posing dummy, the conventionalised figure of a sahib. For it is the condition of his rule that he shall spend his life in trying to impress the "natives" and so in every crisis he has got to do what the "natives" expect of him. He wears a mask, and his face grows to fit it. I had got to shoot the elephant. I had committed myself to doing it when I sent for the rifle. A sahib has got to act like a sahib; he has got to appear resolute, to know his own mind and do definite things. To come all that way, rifle in hand, with two thousand people marching at my heels, and then to trail feebly away, having done nothing—no, that was impossible. The crowd would laugh at me. And my whole life, every white man's life in the East, was one long struggle not to be laughed at.

8   But I did not want to shoot the elephant. I watched him beating his bunch of grass against his knees, with that preoccupied grandmotherly air that elephants have. It seemed to me that it would be murder to shoot him. At that age I was not squeamish about killing animals, but I had never shot an elephant and never wanted to. (Somehow it always seems worse to kill a *large* animal.) Besides, there was the beast's owner to be considered. Alive, the elephant was worth at least a hundred pounds; dead, he would only be worth the value of his tusks—five pounds, possibly. But I had got to act quickly. I turned to some experienced-looking Burmans who had been there when we arrived, and asked them how the elephant had been behaving. They all said the same thing: he took no notice of you if you left him alone, but he might charge if you went too close to him.

9   It was perfectly clear to me what I ought to do. I ought to walk up to within, say, twenty-five yards of the elephant and test his behaviour. If he charged I could shoot, if he took no notice of me it would be safe

to leave him until the mahout came back. But also I knew that I was going to do no such thing. I was a poor shot with a rifle and the ground was soft mud into which one would sink at every step. If the elephant charged and I missed him, I should have about as much chance as a toad under a steam-roller. But even then I was not thinking particularly of my own skin, only the watchful yellow faces behind. For at that moment, with the crowd watching me, I was not afraid in the ordinary sense, as I would have been if I had been alone. A white man mustn't be frightened in front of "natives"; and so, in general, he isn't frightened. The sole thought in my mind was that if anything went wrong those two thousand Burmans would see me pursued, caught, trampled on and reduced to a grinning corpse like that Indian up the hill. And if that happened it was quite probable that some of them would laugh. That would never do. There was only one alternative. I shoved the cartridges into the magazine and lay down on the road to get a better aim.

10   The crowd grew very still, and a deep, low, happy sigh, as of people who see the theatre curtain go up at last, breathed from innumerable throats. They were going to have their bit of fun after all. The rifle was a beautiful German thing with cross-hair sights. I did not then know that in shooting an elephant one should shoot to cut an imaginary bar running from ear-hole to ear-hole. I ought therefore, as the elephant was sideways on, to have aimed straight at his ear-hole; actually I aimed several inches in front of this, thinking the brain would be further forward.

11   When I pulled the trigger I did not hear the bang or feel the kick— one never does when a shot goes home—but heard the devilish roar of glee that went up from the crowd. In that instant, in too short a time, one would have thought, even for the bullet to get there, a mysterious, terrible change had come over the elephant. He neither stirred nor fell, but every line of his body had altered. He looked suddenly stricken, shrunken, immensely old, as though the frightful impact of the bullet had paralysed him without knocking him down. At last, after what seemed a long time—it might have been five seconds, I dare say—he sagged flabbily to his knees. His mouth slobbered. An enormous senility seemed to have settled upon him. One could have imagined him thousands of years old. I fired again into the same spot. At the second shot he did not collapse but climbed with desperate slowness to his feet and stood weakly upright, with legs sagging and head drooping. I fired a third time. That was the shot that did for him. You could see the agony of it jolt his whole body and knock the last remnant of

strength from his legs. But in falling he seemed for a moment to rise, for as his hind legs collapsed beneath him he seemed to tower upwards like a huge rock toppling, his trunk reaching skyward like a tree. He trumpeted, for the first and only time. And then down he came, his belly towards me, with a crash that seemed to shake the ground even where I lay.

12   I got up. The Burmans were already racing past me across the mud. It was obvious that the elephant would never rise again, but he was not dead. He was breathing very rhythmically with long rattling gasps, his great mound of a side painfully rising and falling. His mouth was wide open—I could see far down into caverns of pale pink throat. I waited a long time for him to die, but his breathing did not weaken. Finally I fired my two remaining shots into the spot where I thought his heart must be. The thick blood welled out of him like red velvet, but still he did not die. His body did not even jerk when the shots hit him, the tortured breathing continued without a pause. He was dying, very slowly and in great agony, but in some world remote from me where not even a bullet could damage him further. I felt that I had got to put an end to that dreadful noise. It seemed dreadful to see the great beast lying there, powerless to move and yet powerless to die, and not even to be able to finish him. I went back for my small rifle and poured shot after shot into his heart and down his throat. They seemed to make no impression. The tortured gasps continued as steadily as the ticking of a clock.

13   In the end I could not stand it any longer and went away. I heard later that it took him half an hour to die. Burmans were arriving with dahs and baskets even before I left, and I was told they had stripped his body almost to the bones by the afternoon.

14   Afterwards, of course, there were endless discussions about the shooting of the elephant. The owner was furious, but he was only an Indian and could do nothing. Besides, legally I had done the right thing, for a mad elephant has to be killed, like a mad dog, if its owner fails to control it. Among the Europeans opinion was divided. The older men said I was right, the younger men said it was a damn shame to shoot an elephant for killing a coolie, because an elephant was worth more than any damn Coringhee coolie. And afterwards I was very glad that the coolie had been killed; it put me legally in the right and it gave me a sufficient pretext for shooting the elephant. I often wondered whether any of the others grasped that I had done it solely to avoid looking a fool.

Understanding Meaning

1. What is Orwell's goal in relating this incident? What does this event symbolize?
2. What role does Orwell play in the narrative? How does his behavior as a police officer conflict with his personal views?
3. What are Orwell's attitudes toward the Burmese?
4. Orwell's readers were primarily British. What was he trying to impress upon them?
5. *Critical Thinking:* Consider Orwell's statement, "With one part of my mind I thought of the British Raj as an unbreakable tyranny . . . with another part I thought that the greatest joy in the world would be to drive a bayonet into a Buddhist priest's guts." What does this admission reveal?

Evaluating Strategy

1. Orwell opens the essay with the statement, "I was hated by large numbers of people." What impact does this have on readers? Does it accomplish more than simply attracting attention?
2. How does Orwell balance his role between narrator and participant?
3. *Other Modes:* Where does Orwell use *description*, *comparison*, *analysis*, and *persuasion* within his narrative?

Appreciating Language

1. What metaphors does Orwell use in telling the story?
2. Underline the figurative language Orwell uses on page 78 to describe the labored death of the elephant. What images does he use to create a sense of horror?
3. Orwell calls the Burmese "natives," "coolies," and "Burmans." He describes their huts as "squalid" and the rice paddies as a "miry waste." What does this suggest about his view of Asia?

Connections across the Disciplines

1. How does Orwell's first-person narrative about an event differ from Richard Preston's third-person account? How does the writer's presence in the drama affect the focus of the essay?
2. Review Yi-Fu Tuan's "Chinese Space, American Space" (page 245) and William Ouchi's "Japanese and American Workers: Two States of Mind"

(page 267). What do these essays reveal about the differences between Asians and Europeans? Can they shed light on the conflict Orwell encountered?

Writing Suggestions

1. *Critical Thinking:* Orwell relates an incident in which his role conflicted with his personal beliefs. Write a brief narrative about an event which placed you in a similar situation. Have your roles as parent, employee, manager, student, or friend caused you to act against your values? Have you ever been compelled to lie on behalf of others? In relating the story, clearly distinguish between the actions you took and your better judgment.

2. *Collaborative Writing:* Work with other students to create a short statement analyzing Orwell's message about political power and the nature of abusive governments. Have each member write a draft then work together to combine ideas into a single statement. If there are major differences, develop a comparison or division paper to contrast or list opinions.

OLIVER SACKS

Oliver Sacks (1933–) was born in London and studied in Oxford before coming to the United States to complete his education. A professor of neurology, he has written several accounts of his patients who suffer from baffling and often disturbing neurological disorders. His 1974 book Awakenings *told the stories of patients recovering from comas and served as the basis of a motion picture. This section, taken from a book of the same title, tells the story of Dr. P., who developed prosopagnosia, an inability to connect perceptions with understanding.*

The Man Who Mistook His Wife for a Hat

In this "tale"—a term he uses to describe his patients' histories—Sacks first describes a set of odd symptoms exhibited by a professor of music. He then recalls his own astonishment as the highly educated artist found it difficult to identify common objects. As you read notice how Sacks uses comparison, analysis, definition, *and* cause and effect *to develop his narrative.*

1   Dr. P. was a musician of distinction, well-known for many years as a singer, and then, at the local School of Music, as a teacher. It was here, in relation to his students, that certain strange problems were first observed. Sometimes a student would present himself, and Dr. P. would not recognise him; or, specifically, would not recognise his face. The moment the student spoke, he would be recognised by his voice. Such incidents multiplied, causing embarrassment, perplexity, fear—and, sometimes, comedy. For not only did Dr. P. increasingly fail to see faces, but he saw faces when there were no faces to see: genially, Magoo-like, when in the street he might pat the heads of water hydrants and parking meters, taking these to be the heads of children; he would amiably address carved knobs on the furniture and be astounded when they did not reply. At first these odd mistakes were laughed off as jokes, not least by Dr. P. himself. Had he not always had a quirky sense of humour and been given to Zen-like paradoxes and jests? His musical powers were as dazzling as ever; he did not feel ill— he had never felt better; and the mistakes were so ludicrous—and so

ingenious—that they could hardly be serious or betoken anything serious. The notion of there being "something the matter" did not emerge until some three years later, when diabetes developed. Well aware that diabetes could affect his eyes, Dr. P. consulted an ophthalmologist, who took a careful history and examined his eyes closely. "There's nothing the matter with your eyes," the doctor concluded. "But there is trouble with the visual parts of your brain. You don't need my help, you must see a neurologist." And so, as a result of this referral, Dr. P. came to me.

2   It was obvious within a few seconds of meeting him that there was no trace of dementia in the ordinary sense. He was a man of great cultivation and charm who talked well and fluently, with imagination and humour. I couldn't think why he had been referred to our clinic.

3   And yet there *was* something a bit odd. He faced me as he spoke, was oriented towards me, and yet there was something the matter—it was difficult to formulate. He faced me with his *ears*, I came to think, but not with his eyes. These, instead of looking, gazing, at me, "taking me in," in the normal way, made sudden strange fixations—on my nose, on my right ear, down to my chin, up to my right eye—as if noting (even studying) these individual features, but not seeing my whole face, its changing expressions, "me," as a whole. I am not sure that I fully realised this at the time—there was just a teasing strangeness, some failure in the normal interplay of gaze and expression. He saw me, he *scanned* me, and yet . . .

4   "What seems to be the matter?" I asked him at length.

5   "Nothing that I know of," he replied with a smile, "but people seem to think there's something wrong with my eyes."

6   "But *you* don't recognise any visual problems?"

7   "No, not directly, but I occasionally make mistakes."

8   I left the room briefly to talk with his wife. When I came back, Dr. P. was sitting placidly by the window, attentive, listening rather than looking out. "Traffic," he said, "street sounds, distant trains—they make a sort of symphony, do they not? You know Honegger's *Pacific 234*?"

9   What a lovely man, I thought to myself. How can there be anything seriously the matter? Would he permit me to examine him?

10   "Yes, of course, Dr. Sacks."

11   I stilled my disquiet, his perhaps, too, in the soothing routine of a neurological exam—muscle strength, coordination, reflexes, tone. . . . It was while examining his reflexes—a trifle abnormal on the left

side—that the first bizarre experience occurred. I had taken off his left shoe and scratched the sole of his foot with a key—a frivolous-seeming but essential test of a reflex—and then, excusing myself to screw my ophthalmoscope together, left him to put on the shoe himself. To my surprise, a minute later, he had not done this.

12   "Can I help?" I asked.

13   "Help what? Help whom?"

14   "Help you put on your shoe."

15   "Ach," he said, "I had forgotten the shoe," adding, *sotto voce*, "The shoe? The shoe?" He seemed baffled.

16   "Your shoe," I repeated. "Perhaps you'd put it on."

17   He continued to look downwards, though not at the shoe, with an intense but misplaced concentration. Finally his gaze settled on his foot: "That is my shoe, yes?"

18   Did I mis-hear? Did he mis-see?

19   "My eyes," he explained, and put a hand to his foot. "*This* is my shoe, no?"

20   "No, it is not. That is your foot. *There* is your shoe."

21   "Ah! I thought that was my foot."

22   Was he joking? Was he mad? Was he blind? If this was one of his "strange mistakes," it was the strangest mistake I had ever come across.

23   I helped him on with his shoe (his foot), to avoid further complication. Dr. P. himself seemed untroubled, indifferent, maybe amused. I resumed my examination. His visual acuity was good: he had no difficulty seeing a pin on the floor, though sometimes he missed it if it was placed to his left.

24   He saw all right, but what did he see? I opened out a copy of the *National Geographic Magazine* and asked him to describe some pictures in it.

25   His responses here were very curious. His eyes would dart from one thing to another, picking up tiny features, individual features, as they had done with my face. A striking brightness, a colour, a shape would arrest his attention and elicit comment—but in no case did he get the scene-as-a-whole. He failed to see the whole, seeing only details, which he spotted like blips on a radar screen. He never entered into relation with the picture as a whole—never faced, so to speak, *its* physiognomy. He had no sense whatever of a landscape or scene.

26   I showed him the cover, an unbroken expanse of Sahara dunes.

27   "What do you see here?" I asked.

28   "I see a river," he said. "And a little guest-house with its terrace on the water. People are dining out on the terrace. I see coloured parasols here and there." He was looking, if it was "looking," right off the cover into mid-air and confabulating nonexistent features, as if the absence of features in the actual picture had driven him to imagine the river and the terrace and the coloured parasols.

29   I must have looked aghast, but he seemed to think he had done rather well. There was a hint of a smile on his face. He also appeared to have decided that the examination was over and started to look around for his hat. He reached out his hand and took hold of his wife's head, tried to lift if off, to put it on. He had apparently mistaken his wife for a hat! His wife looked as if she was used to such things.

30   I could make no sense of what had occurred in terms of conventional neurology (or neuropsychology). In some ways he seemed perfectly preserved, and in others absolutely, incomprehensibly devastated. How could he, on the one hand, mistake his wife for a hat and, on the other, function, as apparently he still did, as a teacher at the Music School?

31   I had to think, to see him again—and to see him in his own familiar habitat, at home.

32   A few days later I called on Dr. P. and his wife at home, with the score of the *Dichterliebe* in my briefcase (I knew he liked Schumann), and a variety of odd objects for the testing of perception. Mrs. P. showed me into a lofty apartment, which recalled fin-de-siècle Berlin. A magnificent old Bösendorfer stood in state in the centre of the room, and all around it were music stands, instruments, scores. . . . There were books, there were paintings, but the music was central. Dr. P. came in, a little bowed, and, distracted, advanced with outstretched hands to the grandfather clock, but, hearing my voice, corrected himself, and shook hands with me. We exchanged greetings and chatted a little of current concerts and performances. Diffidently, I asked him if he would sing.

33   "The *Dichterliebe!*" he exclaimed. "But I can no longer read music. You will play them, yes?"

34   I said I would try. On that wonderful old piano even my playing sounded right, and Dr. P. was an aged but infinitely mellow Fischer-Dieskau, combining a perfect ear and voice with the most incisive musical intelligence. It was clear that the Music School was not keeping him on out of charity.

35   Dr. P.'s temporal lobes were obviously intact: he had a wonderful musical cortex. What, I wondered, was going on in his parietal and occipital lobes, especially in those areas where visual processing occurred? I carry the Platonic solids in my neurological kit and decided to start with these.

36   "What is this?" I asked, drawing out the first one.

37   "A cube, of course."

38   "Now this?" I asked, brandishing another.

39   He asked if he might examine it, which he did swiftly and systematically: "A dodecahedron, of course. And don't bother with the others—I'll get the icosahedron, too."

40   Abstract shapes clearly presented no problems. What about faces? I took out a pack of cards. All of these he identified instantly, including the jacks, queens, kings, and the joker. But these, after all, are stylised designs, and it was impossible to tell whether he saw faces or merely patterns. I decided I would show him a volume of cartoons which I had in my briefcase. Here, again, for the most part, he did well. Churchill's cigar, Schnozzle's nose: as soon as he had picked out a key feature he could identify the face. But cartoons, again, are formal and schematic. It remained to be seen how he would do with real faces, realistically represented.

41   I turned on the television, keeping the sound off, and found an early Bette Davis film. A love scene was in progress. Dr. P. failed to identify the actress—but this could have been because she had never entered his world. What was more striking was that he failed to identify the expressions on her face or her partner's, though in the course of a single torrid scene these passed from sultry yearning through passion, surprise, disgust, and fury to a melting reconciliation. Dr. P. could make nothing of any of this. He was very unclear as to what was going on, or who was who or even what sex they were. His comments on the scene were positively Martian.

42   It was just possible that some of his difficulties were associated with the unreality of a celluloid, Hollywood world; and it occurred to me that he might be more successful in identifying faces from his own life. On the walls of the apartment there were photographs of his family, his colleagues, his pupils, himself. I gathered a pile of these together and, with some misgivings, presented them to him. What had been funny, or farcical, in relation to the movie, was tragic in relation to real life. By and large, he recognised nobody: neither his family, nor

his colleagues, nor his pupils, nor himself. He recognised a portrait of Einstein because he picked up the characteristic hair and moustache; and the same thing happened with one or two other people. "Ach, Paul!" he said, when shown a portrait of his brother. "That square jaw, those big teeth—I would know Paul anywhere!" But was it Paul he recognised, or one or two of his features, on the basis of which he could make a reasonable guess as to the subject's identity? In the absence of obvious "markers," he was utterly lost. But it was not merely the cognition, the *gnosis*, at fault; there was something radically wrong with the whole way he proceeded. For he approached these faces— even of those near and dear—as if they were abstract puzzles or tests. He did not relate to them, he did not behold. No face was familiar to him, seen as a "thou," being just identified as a set of features, an "it." Thus, there was formal, but no trace of personal, gnosis. And with this went his indifference, or blindness, to expression. A face, to us, is a person looking out—we see, as it were, the person through his *persona*, his face. But for Dr. P. there was no *persona* in this sense—no outward *persona*, and no person within.

43   I had stopped at a florist on my way to his apartment and bought myself an extravagant red rose for my buttonhole. Now I removed this and handed it to him. He took it like a botanist or morphologist given a specimen, not like a person given a flower.

44   "About six inches in length," he commented. "A convoluted red form with a linear green attachment."

45   "Yes," I said encouragingly, "and what do you think it *is*, Dr. P.?"

46   "Not easy to say." He seemed perplexed. "It lacks the simple symmetry of the Platonic solids, although it may have a higher symmetry of its own. . . . I think this could be an inflorescence or flower."

47   "Could be?" I queried.

48   "Could be," he confirmed.

49   "Smell it," I suggested, and he again looked somewhat puzzled, as if I had asked him to smell a higher symmetry. But he complied courteously, and took it to his nose. Now, suddenly, he came to life.

50   "Beautiful!" he exclaimed. "An early rose. What a heavenly smell!" He started to hum *"Die Rose, die Lillie . . ."* Reality, it seemed, might be conveyed by smell, not by sight.

51   I tried one final test. It was still a cold day, in early spring, and I had thrown my coat and gloves on the sofa.

52   "What is this?" I asked, holding up a glove.

53   "May I examine it?" he asked, and, taking it from me, he proceeded to examine it as he had examined the geometrical shapes.

54   "A continuous surface," he announced at last, "infolded on itself. It appears to have"—he hesitated—"five outpouchings, if this is the word."

55   "Yes," I said cautiously. "You have given me a description. Now tell me what it is."

56   "A container of some sort?"

57   "Yes," I said, "and what would it contain?"

58   "It would contain its contents!" said Dr. P., with a laugh. "There are many possibilities. It could be a change purse, for example, for coins of five sizes. It could . . . "

59   I interrupted the barmy flow. "Does it not look familiar? Do you think it might contain, might fit, a part of your body?"

60   No light of recognition dawned on his face.[1]

61   No child would have the power to see and speak of "a continuous surface . . . infolded on itself," but any child, any infant, would immediately know a glove as a glove, see it as familiar, as going with a hand. Dr. P. didn't. He saw nothing as familiar. Visually, he was lost in a world of lifeless abstractions. Indeed, he did not have a real visual world, as he did not have a real visual self. He could speak about things, but did not see them face-to-face. Hughlings Jackson, discussing patients with aphasia and left-hemisphere lesions, says they have lost "abstract" and "propositional" thought—and compares them with dogs (or, rather, he compares dogs to patients with aphasia). Dr. P., on the other hand, functioned precisely as a machine functions. It wasn't merely that he displayed the same indifference to the visual world as a computer but—even more strikingly—he construed the world as a computer construes it, by means of key features and schematic relationships. The scheme might be identified—in an "identi-kit" way—without the reality being grasped at all.

62   The testing I had done so far told me nothing about Dr. P.'s inner world. Was it possible that his visual memory and imagination were still intact? I asked him to imagine entering one of our local squares from the north side, to walk through it, in imagination or in memory,

---

[1] Later, by accident, he got it on, and exclaimed, "My God, it's a glove!" This was reminiscent of Kurt Goldstein's patient "Lanuti," who could only recognise objects by trying to use them in action.

and tell me the buildings he might pass as he walked. He listed the buildings on his right side, but none of those on his left. I then asked him to imagine entering the square from the south. Again he mentioned only those buildings that were on the right side, although these were the very buildings he had omitted before. Those he had "seen" internally before were not mentioned now; presumably, they were no longer "seen." It was evident that his difficulties with leftness, his visual field deficits, were as much internal as external, bisecting his visual memory and imagination.

63   What, at a higher level, of his internal visualisation? Thinking of the almost hallucinatory intensity with which Tolstoy visualises and animates his characters, I questioned Dr. P. about *Anna Karenina*. He could remember incidents without difficulty, had an undiminished grasp of the plot, but completely omitted visual characteristics, visual narrative, and scenes. He remembered the words of the characters but not their faces; and though, when asked, he could quote, with his remarkable and almost verbatim memory, the original visual descriptions, these were, it became apparent, quite empty for him and lacked sensorial, imaginal, or emotional reality. Thus, there was an internal agnosia as well.[2]

64   But this was only the case, it became clear, with certain sorts of visualisation. The visualisation of faces and scenes, of visual narrative and drama—this was profoundly impaired, almost absent. But the visualisation of *schemata* was preserved, perhaps enhanced. Thus, when I engaged him in a game of mental chess, he had no difficulty visualising the chessboard or the moves—indeed, no difficulty in beating me soundly.

65   Luria said of Zazetsky that he had entirely lost his capacity to play games but that his "vivid imagination" was unimpaired. Zazetsky and Dr. P. lived in worlds which were mirror images of each other. But the saddest difference between them was that Zazetsky, as Luria said, "fought to regain his lost faculties with the indomitable tenacity of the damned," whereas Dr. P. was not fighting, did not know what was lost,

---

[2] I have often wondered about Helen Keller's visual descriptions, whether these, for all their eloquence, are somehow empty as well? Or whether, by the transference of images from the tactile to the visual, or, yet more extraordinarily, from the verbal and the metaphorical to the sensorial and the visual, she *did* achieve a power of visual imagery, even though her visual cortex had never been stimulated, directly, by the eyes? But in Dr. P.'s case it is precisely the cortex that was damaged, the organic prerequisite of all pictorial imagery. Interestingly and typically he no longer dreamed pictorially—the "message" of the dream being conveyed in nonvisual terms.

did not indeed know that anything was lost. But who was more tragic, or who was more damned—the man who knew it, or the man who did not?

66 When the examination was over, Mrs. P. called us to the table, where there was coffee and a delicious spread of little cakes. Hungrily, hummingly, Dr. P. started on the cakes. Swiftly, fluently, unthinkingly, melodiously, he pulled the plates towards him and took this and that in a great gurgling stream, an edible song of food, until, suddenly, there came an interruption: a loud, peremptory rat-tat-tat at the door. Startled, taken aback, arrested by the interruption, Dr. P. stopped eating and sat frozen, motionless, at the table, with an indifferent, blind bewilderment on his face. He saw, but no longer saw, the table; no longer perceived it as a table laden with cakes. His wife poured him some coffee: the smell titillated his nose and brought him back to reality. The melody of eating resumed.

67 How does he do anything? I wondered to myself. What happens when he's dressing, goes to the lavatory, has a bath? I followed his wife into the kitchen and asked her how, for instance, he managed to dress himself. "It's just like the eating," she explained. "I put his usual clothes out, in all the usual places, and he dresses without difficulty, singing to himself. He does everything singing to himself. But if he is interrupted and loses the thread, he comes to a complete stop, doesn't know his clothes—or his own body. He sings all the time—eating songs, dressing songs, bathing songs, everything. He can't do anything unless he makes it a song."

68 While we were talking my attention was caught by the pictures on the walls.

69 "Yes," Mrs. P. said, "he was a gifted painter as well as a singer. The School exhibited his pictures every year."

70 I strolled past them curiously—they were in chronological order. All his earlier work was naturalistic and realistic, with vivid mood and atmosphere, but finely detailed and concrete. Then, years later, they became less vivid, less concrete, less realistic and naturalistic, but far more abstract, even geometrical and cubist. Finally, in the last paintings, the canvasses became nonsense, or nonsense to me—mere chaotic lines and blotches of paint. I commented on this to Mrs. P.

71 "Ach, you doctors, you're such Philistines!" she exclaimed. "Can you not see *artistic development*—how he renounced the realism of his earlier years, and advanced into abstract, nonrepresentational art?"

72 "No, that's not it," I said to myself (but forbore to say it to poor Mrs. P.). He had indeed moved from realism to nonrepresentation to

the abstract, yet this was not the artist, but the pathology, advancing—advancing towards a profound visual agnosia, in which all powers of representation and imagery, all sense of the concrete, all sense of reality, were being destroyed. This wall of paintings was a tragic pathological exhibit, which belonged to neurology, not art.

73   And yet, I wondered, was she not partly right? For there is often a struggle, and sometimes, even more interestingly, a collusion between the powers of pathology and creation. Perhaps, in his cubist period, there might have been both artistic and pathological development, colluding to engender an original form; for as he lost the concrete, so he might have gained in the abstract, developing a greater sensitivity to all the structural elements of line, boundary, contour—an almost Picasso-like power to see, and equally depict, those abstract organisations embedded in, and normally lost in, the concrete. . . . Though in the final pictures, I feared, there was only chaos and agnosia.

74   We returned to the great music room, with the Bösendorfer in the centre, and Dr. P. humming the last torte.

75   "Well, Dr. Sacks," he said to me. "You find me an interesting case, I perceive. Can you tell me what you find wrong, make recommendations?"

76   "I can't tell you what I find wrong," I replied, "but I'll say what I find right. You are a wonderful musician, and music is your life. What I would prescribe, in a case such as yours, is a life which consists entirely of music. Music has been the centre, now make it the whole, of your life."

77   This was four years ago—I never saw him again, but I often wondered about how he apprehended the world, given his strange loss of image, visuality, and the perfect preservation of a great musicality. I think that music, for him, had taken the place of image. He had no body-image, he had body-music: this is why he could move and act as fluently as he did, but came to a total confused stop if the "inner music" stopped. And equally with the outside, the world . . .[3]

78   In *The World as Representation and Will*, Schopenhauer speaks of music as "pure will." How fascinated he would have been by Dr. P., a man who had wholly lost the world as representation, but wholly preserved it as music or will.

---

[3] Thus, as I learned later from his wife, though he could not recognise his students if they sat still, if they were merely "images," he might suddenly recognise them if they *moved*. "That's Karl," he would cry. "I know his movements, his body-music."

79 And this, mercifully, held to the end—for despite the gradual advance of his disease (a massive tumor or degenerative process in the visual parts of his brain) Dr. P. lived and taught music to the last days of his life.

Understanding Meaning

1. How does Sacks *describe* Dr. P.'s initial symptoms? What led Dr. P. to seek medical help?
2. What is prosopagnosia? How does Sacks demonstrate its effects?
3. What is Sacks trying to tell readers about how the brain connects perceptions to meaning? Does he use the plight of one patient to demonstrate how our brains operate normally?
4. What did the glove test reveal about Dr. P.'s condition?
5. How does Sacks explain how a person who failed to distinguish his hat from his wife or his shoe from his foot could continue to teach a complex subject like music?
6. *Critical Thinking:* On page 85 Sacks presented "with some misgivings" family pictures for Dr. P. to identify. Why was he reluctant to administer this test? Does this suggest that even doctors, like family members, prefer to deny the seriousness of a patient's condition?

Evaluating Strategy

1. Sacks organizes his writing in a format standard to scientific and medical discourse. He *describes* symptoms, and then provides an *analysis*. Is this method easy for general readers to follow?
2. What role does Sacks play in the narrative?
3. *Other Modes:* What parts of the narrative include *description, comparison, analysis, definition,* and *cause and effect?* What does the use of these modes reveal about the scientific methods Sacks employs to examine a patient and determine his condition?

Appreciating Language

1. What reaction did you have to Sacks's level of language? Did you find his use of scientific terminology a barrier to meaning, or could you understand much of it through context?
2. Look up the words *dementia, parietal lobe, ophthalmologist, gnosis,* and *persona.*

3. Can a reader understand the *thesis* of Sacks's narrative without knowing the definitions of *ophthalmoscope, fin-de-siècle,* or *empirical?*
4. In explaining some of Dr. P.'s baffling observations, Sacks describes them as being "Martian." How does this metaphor help a general reader grasp the effect of this disorder?

Connections across the Disciplines

1. How does Sacks's role as doctor compare to the role George Orwell plays in "Shooting an Elephant" (page 72)? Do they both strive to objectively observe their subjects?
2. What role does close observation play in the narrative? How does Sacks embody the "look again, look again" approach described by Samuel Scudder (page 45)?

Writing Suggestions

1. Write a few paragraphs relating an incident in which you observed or encountered someone's puzzling behavior. Use detailed observations to share with readers the actions and statements you found intriguing, bizarre, or frightening.
2. *Critical Writing:* Sacks tells his patient he cannot find out what is wrong and urges him to accept what is right and make music the whole of his life. Did Sacks fail as a physician because he could not "cure" Dr. P.? Write a short paper in response to the assertion that people expect too much from doctors.
3. *Collaborative Writing:* Work with other students to generate a one-paragraph *definition* of prosopagnosia based on the information provided in Sacks's article. Read the paragraph aloud to the group, and have each member comment on its accuracy.

FEDERAL BUREAU OF INVESTIGATION

At 12:30 P.M. on November 22, 1963, President John F. Kennedy was assassinated in Dallas, Texas. An hour and a half later a twenty-four-year-old man named Lee Harvey Oswald was arrested following a scuffle in a movie theater. Oswald was suspected of murdering the president and a Dallas police officer. Witnesses reported seeing Oswald taking a long package into the Texas School Book Depository, the building where he was employed, overlooking the site of the assassination. In the early hours of November 23, Oswald was charged with murder and interrogated by Federal Bureau of Investigation (FBI) agents.

Interrogation of Lee Harvey Oswald

This FBI report records statements made by Lee Harvey Oswald in response to questions and summarizes his account of his movements on November 22. Notice that the writer uses simple, direct language free of figurative expressions or personal responses to create an objective, fact-driven account.[1]

1   LEE HARVEY OSWALD was interviewed by Captain J. W. FRITZ, Homicide and Robbery Bureau, Dallas Police Department. OSWALD was advised of the identity of SA JAMES W. BOOKHOUT, and his capacity as a Special Agent of the Federal Bureau of Investigation. He was informed of his right to an attorney, that any statement he might make could be used against him in a court of law, and that any statement which he might make must be free and voluntary. He furnished the following information in the presence of T. J. NULLY, U.S. Secret Service; DAVID B. GRANT, Secret Service; ROBERT I. NASH, United States Marshall; and Detectives BILLY L. SENKEL and FAY M. TURNER of the Homicide and Robbery Bureau, Dallas Police Department.

---

[1] This document contains neither recommendations nor conclusions of the FBI. It was recorded by Special Agent James W. Bookhout in Dallas, Texas on November 23, 1963 and dictated on November 24, 1963.

2   Following his departure from the Texas School Book Depository, he boarded a city bus to his residence and obtained transfer upon departure from the bus. He stated that officers at the time of arresting him took his transfer out of his pocket.

3   OSWALD advised that he had only one post office box which was at Dallas, Texas. He denied bringing any package to work on the morning of November 22, 1963. He stated that he was not in the process of fixing up his apartment and he denied telling WESLEY FRAZIER that the purpose of his visit to Irving, Texas, on the night of November 21, 1963, was to obtain some curtain rods from MRS. RUTH PAINE.

4   OSWALD stated that it was not exactly true as recently stated by him that he rode a bus from his place of employment to his residence on November 22, 1963. He stated actually he did board a city bus at his place of employment but that after about a block or two, due to traffic congestion, he left the bus and rode a city cab to his apartment on North Beckley. He recalled that at the time of getting into the cab, some lady looked in and asked the driver to call her a cab. He stated that he might have made some remarks to the cab driver merely for the purpose of passing the time of day at that time. He recalled that his fare was approximately 85 cents. He stated that after arriving at his apartment, he changed his shirt and trousers because they were dirty. He described his dirty clothes as being a reddish colored, long sleeved, shirt with a button-down collar and gray colored trousers. He indicated that he had placed these articles of clothing in the lower drawer of his dresser.

5   OSWALD stated that on November 22, 1963, he had eaten lunch in the lunch room at the Texas School Book Depository, alone, but recalled possibly two Negro employees walking through the room during this period. He stated possibly one of these employees was called "Junior" and the other was a short individual whose name he could not recall but whom he would be able to recognize. He stated that his lunch had consisted of a cheese sandwich and an apple which he had obtained at MRS. RUTH PAINE'S residence in Irving, Texas, upon his leaving for work that morning.

6   OSWALD stated that MRS. PAINE receives no pay for keeping his wife and children at her residence. He stated that their presence in MRS. PAINE'S residence is a good arrangement for her because of her language interest, indicating that his wife speaks Russian and MRS. PAINE is interested in the Russian language.

7   OSWALD denied having kept a rifle in MRS. PAINE'S garage at Irving, Texas, but stated that he did have certain articles stored in her

garage, consisting of two sea bags, a couple of suitcases, and several boxes of kitchen articles and also kept his clothes at MRS. PAINE'S residence. He stated that all of the articles in MRS. PAINE'S garage had been brought there about September, 1963, from New Orleans, Louisiana.

8   OSWALD stated that he has had no visitors at his apartment on North Beckley.

9   OSWALD stated that he has no receipts for purchase of any guns and has never ordered any guns and does not own a rifle nor has he ever possessed a rifle.

10   OSWALD denied that he is a member of the Communist Party.

11   OSWALD stated that he purchased a pistol, which was taken off him by police officers November 22, 1963, about six months ago. He declined to state where he had purchased it.

12   OSWALD stated that he arrived about July, 1962, from USSR and was interviewed by the FBI at Fort Worth, Texas. He stated that he felt they overstepped their bounds and had used various tactics in interviewing him.

13   He further complained that on interview of RUTH PAINE by the FBI regarding his wife, that he felt that his wife was intimidated.

14   OSWALD stated that he desired to contact Attorney ABT, New York City, indicating that ABT was the attorney who had defended the Smith Act case about 1949–1950. He stated that he does not know Attorney ABT personally. Captain FRITZ advised OSWALD that arrangements would be immediately made whereby he could call Attorney ABT.

15   OSWALD stated that prior to coming to Dallas from New Orleans he had resided at a furnished apartment at 4706 Magazine Street, New Orleans, Louisiana. While in New Orleans, he had been employed by WILLIAM B. RILEY Company, 640 Magazine Street, New Orleans.

16   OSWALD stated that he has nothing against President JOHN F. KENNEDY personally; however in view of the present charges against him, he did not desire to discuss this phase further.

17   OSWALD stated that he could not agree to take a polygraph examination without the advice of counsel. He added that in the past he has refused to take polygraph examinations.

18   OSWALD stated that he is a member of the American Civil Liberties Union and added that MRS. RUTH PAINE was also a member of same.

19   With regard to Selective Service card in the possession of OSWALD bearing photograph of OSWALD and the name of ALEX

JAMES HIDELL, OSWALD admitted that he carried this Selective Service card but declined to state that he wrote the signature of ALEX J. HIDELL appearing on same. He further declined to state the purpose of carrying same or any use he has made of same.

20   OSWALD stated that an address book in his possession contains the names of various Russian immigrants residing in Dallas, Texas, whom he has visited with.

21   OSWALD denied shooting President JOHN F. KENNEDY on November 22, 1963, and added that he did not know that Governor JOHN CONNALLY had been shot and denied any knowledge concerning this incident.

Understanding Meaning

1. What is the writer's goal in this narrative?
2. Does the writer seek to imply Oswald's guilt in any way? What attitude, if any, does the writer project toward his subject?
3. *Critical Thinking: Analyze* this report in light of your own knowledge of the Kennedy assassination. How is looking at an actual document different from reading a narrative written by a historian or journalist?

Evaluating Strategy

1. How does the writer structure the narrative?
2. What does the agent do to create as much objectivity as possible?
3. *Other Modes:* Where does the agent use *description* in his report to create a picture of Lee Harvey Oswald? How objective is it?
4. *Critical Thinking:* How is writing an internal document to a specific reader different from addressing a general audience in a book or magazine article?

Appreciating Language

1. At first glance this report appears to break all the "rules" of good writing. It is flat, colorless, and repetitive. Why is this kind of writing acceptable in this context? Why would the use of lively, colorful imagery defeat the purpose of the report?
2. *Critical Thinking:* Examine this report the way a prospective defense attorney might, looking for evidence of prejudice against the accused. Can you find any examples?

Connections across the Disciplines

1. In "The Man Who Mistook His Wife for a Hat" (page 81) a professional records observations about his subject. Would Sacks' notes or academic reports to colleagues likely read much like this one?
2. How does the text of this report by a law enforcement officer differ from the observations made by George Orwell in "Shooting an Elephant" (page 72)?

Writing Suggestions

1. Imagine you are writing a highly factual novel based on the Kennedy assassination. Rewrite a passage from this report using dialogue, gestures, descriptions. Add the agent's tone of voice, describe Oswald's facial expression, tell readers about the furniture in the room, and create a sense of tension, fatigue, or anger.
2. *Collaborative Writing:* Working with three or four students, write a purely objective report of the incident Nathan McCall describes during the assembly in "The Lesson" (page 51). Imagine your report will be read by the school board and several attorneys. Eliminate McCall's personal reflections, and state simply and directly what occurred in objective terms. Read the text aloud, and ask group members to identify statements that are subjective or make judgments without proof.

Walter Lord (1917–) was born in Baltimore and studied history at Princeton University. He entered Yale Law School, but his studies were interrupted by World War II. After serving with the Office of Strategic Services, he returned to law school. He served as editor in chief of a business information service but soon turned to writing history. He tracked down and interviewed the sixty-three living survivors of the Titanic and studied the ship's records to produce A Night to Remember, a minute-by-minute account of the doomed luxury liner. Lord's style of blending fact with tense human drama made his book a best seller. His later books include Day of Infamy, about the Japanese attack on Pearl Harbor, and Incredible Victory, which tells the story of the Battle of Midway.

The Reconstructed Logbook
of the *Titanic*

A Night to Remember *tells the dramatic story of the famous liner that sank on its maiden voyage in 1912. Considered "unsinkable" by its builders, the* Titanic *had only twenty lifeboats for its 2,207 passengers. Rescuers located 705 survivors, many of them picked up in half-empty boats. To assist readers in following the chronology of events, Lord placed a reconstructed logbook of the ship in the appendix of his book.*

1 *April 10, 1912*

12 noon	Leaves Southampton dock; narrowly escapes collision with American liner *New York*.
7:00 P.M.	Stops at Cherbourg for passengers.
9:00 P.M.	Leaves Cherbourg for Queenstown.

April 11, 1912

12:30 P.M.	Stops at Queenstown for passengers and mail. One crewman deserts.
2:00 P.M.	Leaves Queenstown for New York, carrying 1316 passengers and 891 crew.

April 14, 1912

9:00 A.M.	*Caronia* reports ice Latitude 42°N from Longitude 49° to 51° W.
10 1:42 P.M.	*Baltic* reports ice Latitude 41°51′N from Longitude 49°52′W.
1:45 P.M.	*Amerika* reports ice Latitude 41°27′N, Longitude 50°8′W.

7:00 P.M.	Temperature 43°.
7:30 P.M.	Temperature 39°.
7:30 P.M.	*Californian* reports ice Latitude 42°3′N, Longitude 49°9′W.
9:00 P.M.	Temperature 33°.
9:30 P.M.	Second Officer Lightoller warns carpenter and engine room to watch fresh water supply—may freeze up; warns crow's-nest to watch for ice.
9:40 P.M.	*Mesaba* reports ice Latitude 42°N to 41°25′N, Longitude 49° to 50°30′W.
10:00 P.M.	Temperature 32°.
10:30 P.M.	Temperature of sea down to 31°.
11:00 P.M.	*Californian* warns of ice, but cut off before she gives location.
11:40 P.M.	Collides with iceberg Latitude 41°46′N, Longitude 50°14′W.

April 15, 1912

12:05 A.M.	Orders given to uncover the boats, muster the crew and passengers.
12:15 A.M.	First wireless call for help.
12:45 A.M.	First rocket fired.
12:45 A.M.	First boat, No. 7, lowered.
1:40 A.M.	Last rocket fired.
2:05 A.M.	Last boat, Collapsible D, lowered.
2:10 A.M.	Last wireless signals sent.
2:18 A.M.	Lights fail.
2:20 A.M.	Ship founders.
3:30 A.M.	*Carpathia's* rockets sighted by boats.
4:10 A.M.	First boat, No. 2, picked up by *Carpathia*.
8:30 A.M.	Last boat, No. 12, picked up.
8:50 A.M.	*Carpathia* heads for New York with 705 survivors.

Understanding Meaning

1. What is the goal of presenting events in a timeline?
2. How does this log help readers to follow events in a complex story such as a disaster involving hundreds of people?
3. Why would this log be valuable to a board of inquiry investigating the disaster?
4. *Critical Thinking:* According to the log, it took forty minutes to launch the first lifeboat. Although the crew had more than two and one-half hours to evacuate the ship, fifteen hundred people were lost. Do these facts alone raise suspicion of incompetence?

Evaluating Strategy

1. Can such a log as this distort events by emphasizing time relationships instead of causal relationships?
2. How does a writer deal with events that do not have a clear time reference?

Appreciating Language

1. Why is word choice important in brief notations such as those in a log?
2. Can you locate any words that are not objective?

Connections across the Disciplines

1. How is Lord's timeline similar to the FBI report on Lee Harvey Oswald?
2. Would a timeline assist readers in understanding narratives such as Richard Preston's "Ebola River" (page 67)? Why or why not?

Writing Suggestions

1. Reconstruct a log of the actions you took yesterday. Consider the problems that arise in attempting to explain events that did not occur in a specific time frame.
2. *Collaborative Writing:* Working with a group of students, read the log and discuss your impressions. Should a luxury liner be able to safely evacuate its passengers in two hours? Write a paragraph summarizing your group's discussion.

STRATEGIES FOR WRITING NARRATION

1. **Determine your purpose.** Does your narrative have a goal beyond simply telling a story? What details or evidence do readers need to accept your point of view?
2. **Define your role.** As a narrator you can write in first person, either as the major participant in or a witness to events. You can use third person for greater objectivity, inserting personal opinions if desired.
3. **Consider your audience.** What are your readers' needs and expectations? How much background material will you have to supply? Which events will the audience find most impressive?
4. **Review the discipline or writing situation.** If you are writing a narrative report as an employee or agent of an organization, study samples to determine how you should present your story.
5. **Identify the beginning and end of your narrative.** You may find it helpful to place background information in a separate foreword or introduction and limit comments on the ending to an afterword. This can allow the body of the paper to focus on a specific chain of events.
6. **Select a chronological pattern.** After reviewing the context of the narrative, determine which pattern would be most effective for your purpose—using a straight chronology, opening with a mid- or turning point, or presenting the final events first.
7. **Make use of transitional statements.** To prevent readers from becoming confused, make clear transitional statements to move the narrative. Statements such as "later that day" or "two weeks later" can help readers follow the passage of time. Clear transitions are important if you alter chronological order with flashbacks and flash-forwards.

SUGGESTED TOPICS FOR WRITING NARRATION

General Assignments

Write a narrative on any of the following topics. Your narrative may contain passages making use of other modes, such as definition or comparison. Choose your narrative structure carefully, and avoid including minor details that add little to the story line. Use flashbacks and flash-forwards carefully. Transitional statements, paragraphing, and line breaks can help clarify changes in the chronology.

1. Your first job interview
2. Moving into your first dorm room or apartment

3. The events that led you to take a major action—quit a job, end a relationship, or join an organization
4. A sporting event you played in or observed—you may wish to limit the narrative to a single play.
5. A first date
6. An event that placed you in danger
7. An experience that led you to change your opinion about a friend or family member
8. A typical day at school or your job
9. The worst day of your college career
10. An accident or medical emergency—focus on creating a clear, minute-by-minute chronology.

Writing in Context

1. Imagine you are participating in an experiment. Psychologists ask you to write a journal recording your experiences in college. Specifically, the researchers are interested in measuring stressors students face—deadlines, lack of sleep, conflicts with jobs, financial pressures. Write a diary for a week, detailing instances when you experience stress. Be as objective as possible.
2. Write a letter to a friend relating the events of a typical day in college. Select details your friend will find humorous or interesting.
3. Preserve on paper a favorite story told by your grandparents or other relatives. Include background details and identify characters.
4. You are accused of committing a crime last Tuesday. To establish an alibi, create a detailed log to the best of your recollection of the day's events and your movements.

STUDENT PAPER: NARRATION

This paper was written in response to the following assignment:

*Write a 350–500-word narrative essay based on personal experience or ob-
servation. Limit your topic, select details, and use figurative language to re-
create the sights, sounds, smells, and moods you experienced.*

Spare Change

1   As I stepped off the San Diego Trolley, I knew that I was going to em-
bark on a great adventure. Tijuana. As I neared the entrance to cross the
border there was a priest with a plastic bowl and a picture of some kids.
The caption on the picture said, "feed Tijuana's homeless children."
Yeah, right, I thought to myself, just another scam, this guy probably
isn't even a priest.

2   Tijuana. Just the name of the city brings back a distinct smell. A
smell that you will only know if you have been there. It only takes one
time and you can relate to what I am saying. A smell that will permeate
my olfactory senses forever. A thousand different scents compounded
into one. The smell of fast food, sweat, sewage, and tears.

3   As you cross the border the first thing that hits you is the smell I
mentioned earlier. Then you witness the first of many human suffer-
ings you will encounter. The man with no legs begging for money, the
woman with her children huddled around her with an old grease
stained wax cup hovering in the air waving at you with the eyes of
poverty, the children dressed in Salvation Army hand-me-downs, ripped
pants and mismatched shoes surrounding you, begging for money. Their
hands searching your pockets for change, a wallet, anything that will
get them food for the night.

4   Once I got past the few blocks of human suffering and handed out
all I could, I wandered upon a busy little plaza. This place is reasonably
clean and clear of trash, you hear the deafening sounds of the music
from the nearby clubs, and see dozens of young drunken Americans
stumbling around. A lot of tourists are carrying what seems like five
bags each and a distressed look, the kind you get when you have been
shopping all day long. The children, a score of them holding out these
little packs of colored Chiclets, a local gum, sold to you at any price you

can haggle them down to. It's pretty pathetic that you should feel the need to haggle over the price of gum with a child, but this is Tijuana. Americans and tourists have come from all over the world to haggle here. That is just the way it is, the way it always will be.

5   As I continued my journey, I reached a bridge. The bridge was horrible. Along the sides there was trash and rubbish. Towards the midspan of the bridge, I experienced one of the most touching moments of my life, one of those happy ones where you don't know if you should shed a tear from happiness or out of despair. There was this little child playing the accordion and another one playing a guitar. He was singing a Spanish song, well actually it sounded like he was screaming as his compadre was strumming the guitar. He had a little cup in front of him, and I threw a coin into it. He just smiled and kept singing. I turned around and left, but this time as I passed the priest I filled his plastic bowl with the rest of my money.

Questions for Review and Revision

1. This student was assigned a 350–500-word narrative in a composition class. How successfully does this paper meet this goal?
2. How does the student open and close the narrative? Does the opening grab attention? Does the conclusion make a powerful statement?
3. What devices does the student use to advance the chronology?
4. Most writers focus on visual details. This student includes the senses of sound and smell as well. How effective is this approach?
5. The narrative switches from first person ("I") to second person ("you")— should this be corrected? How does it affect the focus of the narrative?
6. Read the paper aloud. What changes would you make? Can you detect passages that would benefit from revision or rewording?

Writing Suggestions

1. Using this essay as a model, write a short narrative about a trip that exposed you to another culture. Try to recapture the sights, sounds, smells that characterized the experience.
2. *Collaborative Writing:* Ask a group of students to assign a grade to this essay then explain their evaluations. What strengths and weaknesses does the group identify?

NARRATION CHECKLIST

Before submitting your paper, review these points.

1. Does your narrative have a clear focus?

2. Can your readers clearly follow the chronology of events?

3. Do you write in a consistent tense? Does your narrative contain illogical shifts from past to present?

4. Does the narrative flow evenly, or is it cluttered with unnecessary detail?

5. Does your narrative maintain a consistent point of view? Do you switch from first to third person without reason?

6. Does your narrative suit your purpose, reader, and discourse community?

 WebTutor

See www.harcourtcollege.com/english/sundance for information on writing narration.

3

DESCRIPTION

WHAT IS DESCRIPTION?

Description captures the essence of a person, place, object, or condition through sensory details. Nearly all writing requires description. Before you can narrate events, compare, classify, or analyze, you must provide readers with a clear picture of your subject. Dramatists open plays with set and character descriptions. Homicide detectives begin reports with descriptions of crime scenes. Before proposing expanding an airport, the writers of a government study must first describe congestion in the existing facility.

The way writers select and present details depends on context. Carl T. Rowan's article "Unforgettable Miss Bessie" (page 131), published in *Reader's Digest,* describes an influential teacher to a general audience reading for human interest:

> She was only about five feet tall and probably never weighed more than 110 pounds, but Miss Bessie was a towering presence in the classroom. She was the only woman tough enough to make me read *Beowulf* and think for a few foolish days that I liked it. From 1938 to 1942, when I attended Bernard High School in McMinnville, Tenn., she taught me English, history, civics—and a lot more than I realized.

Rowan's description includes details about the teacher's height and weight, the courses she taught, and the name of the school. But Rowan's focus is her "presence" and the impact she had in shaping his life. Writing in the first person, Rowan places himself in the essay to build rapport with his readers.

This intimate portrait contrasts sharply with the description of Lee Harvey Oswald included in an FBI report:

> OSWALD was advised questions were intended to obtain his complete physical description and background. Upon repetition of the question as to his present employment, he furnished same without further discussion.

Race	White
Sex	Male
Date of Birth	October 18, 1939
Place of Birth	New Orleans, Louisiana
Height	5'9"
Weight	140
Hair	Medium brown, worn medium length, needs haircut
Eyes	Blue-gray

Aside from noting that Oswald needed a haircut, the FBI agent never offers personal impressions and presents his observations in cold, factual statements. Unlike Rowan, who is writing to a general audience reading for entertainment, the FBI agent is preparing a report for a specialized reader who will use this information in a criminal investigation. The writer's statements will be scrutinized by investigators and attorneys. The introduction of any personal impressions or colorful phrases would be unprofessional and subject to challenge.

The differences between the descriptions of Miss Bessie and Lee Harvey Oswald illustrate the differences between *objective* and *subjective* description.

Objective and Subjective Description

The purpose of *objective* description is to inform readers by accurate reporting of factual details. Its language attempts to provide photographic realism of what people, places, things, and conditions are like. Research papers, business and government reports, and newspaper accounts of current events are objective. Objective description is effective when the writer's purpose is to present readers with information required to make an evaluation or decision. In many instances, it does not attempt to arouse a reader's interest since it is often written in response to reader demand.

Objective description focuses on facts and observable detail. *The New Illustrated Columbia Encyclopedia*, for example, offers readers this description of Chicago:

> The second largest city in the country and the heart of a metropolitan area of almost 7 million people, it is the commercial, financial, industrial, and cultural center for a vast region and a great midcontinental shipping port. It is a port of entry; a major Great Lakes port, located at the junction of the St. Lawrence Seaway with the Mississippi River system; the busiest air center in the country; and an important rail and highway hub.

In contrast to objective description, *subjective* description creates impressions through sensory details and imagery. Short stories, novels, essays, and opinion pieces use highly personal sensory details to create an individual sense of the subject. Instead of photographic realism, subjective description paints scenes, creates moods, or generates emotional responses. Providing accurate information is less important than giving readers a "feel" for the subject. In a subjective description of a car, the color, shape, ride, and the memories it evokes for the writer are more important than facts about horsepower, base price, and fuel efficiency.

Attempting to capture his view of Chicago, John Rechy compares the city to an expectant mother:

> You get the impression that once Chicago was like a constantly pregnant woman, uneasy in her pregnancy because she has miscarried so often. After its rise as a frontier town, plush bigtime madams, adventurers, and soon the titanic rise of the millionaires, the city's subsequent soaring population—all gave more than a hint that Chicago might easily become America's First City. But that title went unquestionably to New York. Brazenly, its skyscrapers, twice as tall as any in the Midwest city, symbolically invaded the sky. Chicago, in squat self-consciousness, bowed out. It became the Second City . . .

Rechy uses imagery and unconventional syntax to create a highly personalized view of the city. In the context of this essay written for a literary magazine, impression is more important than accuracy. Exact number and date statistics are irrelevant to his purpose. The writer's purpose in subjective description is to share a vision, not provide information.

Many writers blend the realism of objective description with the impressionistic details of subjective description to create striking portraits, such as Russell Miller's depiction of Chicago's State Street:

> Summer 1983. State Street, "that great street," is a dirty, desolate, and depressing street for most of its length. It runs straight and potholed from the Chicago city line, up through the black ghettos of the South Side, an aching wasteland of derelict factories pitted with broken windows, instant slum apartment blocks, vandalized playgrounds encased in chain-linked fencing, and vacant lots where weeds sprout gamely from the rubble and from the rusting hulks of abandoned automobiles. Those shops that remain open are protected by barricades of steel mesh. One or two men occupy every doorway, staring sullenly onto the street, heedless of the taunting cluster of skyscrapers to the north.

In this passage, details such as "vandalized playgrounds" are interwoven with expressions granting human emotions to inanimate objects, so wastelands are "aching" and skyscrapers "taunting." Blended descriptions such as this one are useful in strengthening subjective views with factual details. This style of writing is used by journalists and freelance authors writing to audiences who may be reading for both enjoyment and information.

Whether objective or subjective, all descriptive writing communicates through detail—through a careful selection and clear presentation of facts or impressions that serve the writer's purpose and impress readers.

The Language of Description

Words have power. The impact descriptive writing makes depends on *diction*, the writer's choice of words. Whether your description is objective, subjective, or a blend, the words you select should be accurate, appropriate, and effective. In choosing words, consider your purpose, readers, and discipline.

Use Words Precisely

Many words are easily confused. Should a patient's heart rate be monitored "continually"—meaning at regular intervals such as once an hour, or "continuously"—meaning without interruption? Is the city council planning to "adapt" or "adopt" a handgun ban? Some of the numerous pairs of frequently misused words follow:

allusion An indirect reference
illusion A false or imaginary impression

infer To interpret
imply To suggest

conscience A sense of moral or ethical conduct
conscious To be awake or aware of something

principle Basic law, rule, or concept
principal Something or someone important, as in school principal

When writing, consult a dictionary or review the usage section of a handbook to ensure you are using the correct word.

Use Concrete Words

Concrete words are direct and understandable. They communicate more information and make clearer impressions than vague, abstract words:

ABSTRACT	CONCRETE
motor vehicle	pickup truck
modest suburban home	three-bedroom colonial
human resources contingent	employees
protective headgear	helmet
residential rental unit	apartment

Eliminate Unnecessary Words

Avoid cluttering your description with words that add little or no meaning:

WORDY	IMPROVED
at this point in time	now
few in number	few
consensus of opinion	consensus
strike situation	strike
thunderstorm activity	thunderstorms
winter months	winter

Avoid Diluted Verbs

Verbs convey action. Do not dilute their meaning by turning them into wordy phrases that weaken their impact and obscure the action they describe:

DILUTED VERB	IMPROVED
achieve purification	purify
render an examination of	examine
are found to be in agreement	agree
conduct an analysis	analyze

Avoid Clichés and Inflated Phrases

Description uses figurative language such as *similes* (comparisons using *like* or *as*) and *metaphors* (direct comparisons). To be effective, figurative language should create fresh and appropriate impressions. Avoid *clichés* (overly used expressions) and inflated phrases that distort through exaggeration:

CLICHE/INFLATED	IMPROVED
crack of dawn	dawn
pretty as a picture	attractive

straight from the shoulder	direct
as plain as day	obvious
terrible disaster	disaster
in the whole world today	today

Understand the Roles of Denotation and Connotation

All words *denote* or indicate a particular meaning. The words *home, residence*, and *domicile* all refer to where a person lives. Each has the same basic meaning or denotation, but the word *home* evokes personal associations of family, friends, and favorite belongings. *Domicile*, on the other hand, has a legalistic and official sound devoid of personal associations.

Connotations are implied or suggested meanings. Connotations often reflect the writer's purpose and opinion. A resort cabin can be described as a "rustic cottage" or a "seedy shack" depending on a person's point of view. The person who spends little money and shops for bargains can be praised for being "frugal" or ridiculed for being "cheap."

The following pairs of words have the same basic meaning or denotation, but their connotations create different impressions:

young	inexperienced
traditional	old-fashioned
brave	reckless
casual	sloppy
the homeless	bums
residential care facility	nursing home
unintended landing	plane crash

Connotations shape meaning and, in many contexts, can be used to express opinion and influence readers. Depending on your point of view, graffiti can be seen as a "prank" or an "act of vandalism."

Be Conscious of Ethical Issues with Connotation   Words can be selected to dramatize or minimize an event or situation. This raises ethical issues. Because words like *accident* and *explosion* might alarm the public, nuclear regulations substitute the terms *event* and *rapid disassembly*. When the space shuttle *Challenger* exploded in midair, the National Aeronautics and Space Administration (NASA) referred to a "major malfunction." Writers in all disciplines have to weigh the moral implications of the words they choose.

STRATEGIES FOR READING DESCRIPTIONS

While reading the descriptions in this chapter, keep these questions in mind.

Meaning

1. What is the author's goal—to inform, enlighten, share personal observations, or provide information demanded by others? What is the writer's role? Is he or she writing from a personal or professional perspective?
2. What is the intended audience—general or specific readers? How much knowledge does the author assume his or her readers have? Are technical terms defined? Does the description appear to have a special focus?
3. What is the nature of the discipline, discourse community, or writing situation? Is the description objective or subjective? Does the original source of the description (newsmagazine, scientific journal, or government document) reveal something about context?

Strategy

1. What details does the writer select? Does he or she seem to ignore or minimize some details?
2. Does the description seek to establish a dominant impression? Which details support this impression?
3. How are details organized? Does the author use a particular method of grouping observations?

Language

1. What level of language does the writer employ? Are technical terms used without explanation?
2. Does the language include connotations that shade reader reaction to the subject?

*Truman Capote (1924–1985) was born in New Orleans and first gained promi-
nence as a writer of short stories. At age twenty-four he produced his first novel,*
Other Voices, Other Rooms, *which achieved international attention. His other
works include* Breakfast at Tiffany's *and* A Tree of Night. *In 1965 he published*
In Cold Blood, *which became an immediate best seller. Based on extensive research and interviews,* In Cold Blood *told the story of a 1959 mass murder of
a Kansas farm family and the fate of the killers. Although nonfiction, Capote's
book read much like a novel.* In Cold Blood *helped shape a new school of journalism that uses the stylistic touches of fiction to relate wholly factual events.*

Out There

The opening pages of In Cold Blood *describe the small town of Holcomb, Kansas,
where the murders occurred. Capote spent a great deal of time in Holcomb and describes it almost as if it had been his own hometown.*

1   The village of Holcomb stands on the high wheat plains of western
Kansas, a lonesome area that other Kansans call "out there." Some
seventy miles east of the Colorado border, the countryside, with its
hard blue skies and desert-clear air, has an atmosphere that is rather
more Far Western than Middle West. The local accent is barbed with a
prairie twang, a ranch-hand nasalness, and the men, many of them,
wear narrow frontier trousers, Stetsons, and high-heeled boots with
pointed toes. The land is flat, and the views are awesomely extensive;
horses, herds of cattle, a white cluster of grain elevators rising as grace-
fully as Greek temples are visible long before a traveler reaches them.

2   Holcomb, too, can be seen from great distances. Not that there is
much to see—simply an aimless congregation of buildings divided in
the center by the main-line tracks of the Santa Fe Railroad, a haphaz-
ard hamlet bounded on the south by a brown stretch of the Arkansas
(pronounced "Ar-kan-sas") River, on the north by a highway, Route
50, and on the east and west by prairie lands and wheat fields. After
rain, or when snowfalls thaw, the streets, unnamed, unshaded, un-
paved, turn from the thickest dust into the direst mud. At one end of

the town stands a stark old stucco structure, the roof of which supports an electric sign—DANCE—but the dancing has ceased and the advertisement has been dark for several years. Nearby is another building with an irrelevant sign, this one in flaking gold on a dirty window—HOLCOMB BANK. The bank closed in 1933, and its former counting rooms have been converted into apartments. It is one of the town's two "apartment houses," the second being a ramshackle mansion known, because a good part of the local school's faculty lives there, as the Teacherage. But the majority of Holcomb's homes are one-story frame affairs, with front porches.

3   Down by the depot, the postmistress, a gaunt woman who wears a rawhide jacket and denims and cowboy boots, presides over a falling-apart post office. The depot itself, with its peeling sulphur-colored paint, is equally melancholy; the Chief, the Super Chief, the El Capitan go by every day, but these celebrated expresses never pause there. No passenger trains do—only an occasional freight. Up on the highway, there are two filling stations, one of which doubles as a meagerly supplied grocery store, while the other does extra duty as a café—Hartman's Café, where Mrs. Hartman, the proprietress, dispenses sandwiches, coffee, soft drinks, and 3.2 beer. (Holcomb, like all the rest of Kansas, is "dry.")

4   And that, really, is all. Unless you include, as one must, the Holcomb School, a good-looking establishment, which reveals a circumstance that the appearance of the community otherwise camouflages: that the parents who send their children to this modern and ably staffed "consolidated" school—the grades go from kindergarten through senior high, and a fleet of buses transport the students, of which there are usually around three hundred and sixty, from as far as sixteen miles away—are, in general, a prosperous people. Farm ranchers, most of them, they are outdoor folk of very varied stock—German, Irish, Norwegian, Mexican, Japanese. They raise cattle and sheep, grow wheat, milo, grass seed, and sugar beets. Farming is always a chancy business, but in western Kansas its practitioners consider themselves "born gamblers," for they must contend with an extremely shallow precipitation (the annual average is eighteen inches) and anguishing irrigation problems. However, the last seven years have been years of droughtless beneficence. The farm ranchers in Finney County, of which Holcomb is a part, have done well; money has been made not from farming alone but also from the exploitation of plentiful natural-

gas resources, and its acquisition is reflected in the new school, the comfortable interiors of the farmhouses, the steep and swollen grain elevators.

5   Until one morning in mid-November of 1959, few Americans—in fact, few Kansans—had ever heard of Holcomb. Like the waters of the river, like the motorists on the highway, and like the yellow trains streaking down the Santa Fe tracks, drama, in the shape of exceptional happenings, had never stopped there. The inhabitants of the village, numbering two hundred and seventy, were satisfied that this should be so, quite content to exist inside ordinary life—to work, to hunt, to watch television, to attend school socials, choir practice, meetings of the 4-H Club. But then, in the earliest hours of that morning in November, a Sunday morning, certain foreign sounds impinged on the normal nightly Holcomb noises—on the keening hysteria of coyotes, the dry scrape of scuttling tumbleweed, the racing, receding wail of locomotive whistles. At the time not a soul in sleeping Holcomb heard them—four shotgun blasts that, all told, ended six human lives. But afterward the townspeople, theretofore sufficiently unfearful of each other to seldom trouble to lock their doors, found fantasy re-creating them over and again—those somber explosions that stimulated fires of mistrust in the glare of which many old neighbors viewed each other strangely, and as strangers.

Understanding Meaning

1. How much of Capote's description can be considered objective, and how much appears subjective?
2. Capote includes a great deal of factual detail—names of highways, the number of students in the high school, and Holcomb's population. What do these facts add to the description?
3. What does Capote attempt to capture in his description of Holcomb?

Evaluating Strategy

1. *Critical Thinking:* A key goal in the opening of any book is to get people's attention and motivate them to continue reading. How does Capote generate interest in describing a nondescript town?
2. What responses do the closing lines in this section of the story create?

Appreciating Language

1. How does the language of Capote's description differ from that of an encyclopedia or newspaper article?
2. *In Cold Blood* has sold millions of copies. What elements in Capote's style make his story about a crime in a small Kansas town so popular? What phrases strike you as being colorful or interesting?

Connections across the Disciplines

1. How does Capote's description of a small town compare with Luis Alberto Urrea's "Border Story" (page 118)? What attitudes do the writers have toward their subjects? What "feel" do they give the landscapes they describe?
2. Does Edward Abbey's "The First Morning" (page 143) suggest a different view of nature and open spaces than Capote's "Out There"?

Writing Ideas

1. Rewrite a recent article from the local newspaper, adding subjective details to arouse human interest for a national audience. Include details about your community to give readers a feel for the location.
2. Using Capote's description of Holcomb as a resource, write a purely objective, one-paragraph description of the town. Include as much factual detail as possible.

Luis Alberto Urrea was born in Tijuana to a Mexican father and American mother. He grew up in San Diego and attended the University of California. After graduation and a brief career as a movie extra, Urrea worked with a volunteer organization that provides food, clothing, and medical supplies to the poor of northern Mexico. In 1982 he taught writing at Harvard. His most recent novel, In Search of Snow, *was published in 1994, and he published a collection of poems,* Ghost Sickness, *in 1997.*

Border Story

In this description of the Mexican-American border from Across the Wire: Life and Hard Times on the Mexican Border *(1993), Urrea uses the device of second person to place his reader in the scene. By making "you," the "illegal," he seeks to dramatize and humanize the plight of the poor seeking a new life in the United States.*

1   At night, the Border Patrol helicopters swoop and churn in the air all along the line. You can sit in the Mexican hills and watch them herd humans on the dusty slopes across the valley. They look like science fiction crafts, their hard-focused lights raking the ground as they fly.

2   Borderlands locals are so jaded by the sight of nightly people-hunting that it doesn't even register in their minds. But take a stranger to the border, and she will *see* the spectacle: monstrous Dodge trucks speeding into and out of the landscape; uniformed men patrolling with flashlights, guns, and dogs; spotlights; running figures; lines of people hurried onto buses by armed guards; and the endless clatter of the helicopters with their harsh white beams. A Dutch woman once told me it seemed altogether "un-American."

3   But the Mexicans keep on coming—and the Guatemalans, the Salvadorans, the Panamanians, the Colombians. The seven-mile stretch of Interstate 5 nearest the Mexican border is, at times, so congested with Latin American pedestrians that it resembles a town square.

4   They stick to the center island. Running down the length of the island is a cement wall. If the "illegals" (currently, "undocumented workers"; formerly, "wetbacks") are walking north and a Border Patrol

vehicle happens along, they simply hop over the wall and trot south. The officer will have to drive up to the 805 interchange, or Dairy Mart Road, swing over the overpasses, then drive south. Depending on where this pursuit begins, his detour could entail five to ten miles of driving. When the officer finally reaches the group, they hop over the wall and trot north. Furthermore, because freeway arrests would endanger traffic, the Border Patrol has effectively thrown up its hands in surrender.

5   It seems jolly on the page. But imagine poverty, violence, natural disasters, or political fear driving you away from everything you know. Imagine how bad things get to make you leave behind your family, your friends, your lovers; your home, as humble as it might be; your church, say. Let's take it further—you've said good-bye to the graveyard, the dog, the goat, the mountains where you first hunted, your grade school, your state, your favorite spot on the river where you fished and took time to think.

6   Then you come hundreds—or thousands—of miles across territory utterly unknown to you. (Chances are, you have never traveled farther than a hundred miles in your life.) You have walked, run, hidden in the backs of trucks, spent part of your precious money on bus fare. There is no AAA or Travelers Aid Society available to you. Various features of your journey north might include police corruption; violence in the forms of beatings, rape, murder, torture, road accidents; theft; incarceration. Additionally, you might experience loneliness, fear, exhaustion, sorrow, cold, heat, diarrhea, thirst, hunger. There is no medical attention available to you. There isn't even Kotex.

7   Weeks or months later, you arrive in Tijuana. Along with other immigrants, you gravitate to the bad parts of town because there is nowhere for you to go in the glittery sections where the *gringos* flock. You stay in a run-down little hotel in the red-light district, or behind the bus terminal. Or you find your way to the garbage dumps, where you throw together a small cardboard nest and claim a few feet of dirt for yourself. The garbage-pickers working this dump might allow you to squat, or they might come and rob you or burn you out for breaking some local rule you cannot possibly know beforehand. Sometimes the dump is controlled by a syndicate, and goon squads might come to you within a day. They want money, and if you can't pay, you must leave or suffer the consequences.

8   In town, you face endless victimization if you aren't streetwise. The police come after you, street thugs come after you, petty criminals

come after you; strangers try your door at night as you sleep. Many shady men offer to guide you across the border, and each one wants all your money now, and promises to meet you at a prearranged spot. Some of your fellow travelers end their journeys right here—relieved of their savings and left to wait on a dark corner until they realize they are going nowhere.

9   If you are not Mexican, and can't pass as *tijuanense*, a local, the tough guys find you out. Salvadorans and Guatemalans are routinely beaten up and robbed. Sometimes they are disfigured. Indians—Chinantecas, Mixtecas, Guasaves, Zapotecas, Mayas—are insulted and pushed around; often they are lucky—they are merely ignored. They use this to their advantage. Often they don't dream of crossing into the United States: a Mexican tribal person would never be able to blend in, and they know it. To them, the garbage dumps and street vending and begging in Tijuana are a vast improvement over their former lives. As Doña Paula, a Chinanteca friend of mine who lives at the Tijuana garbage dump, told me, "This is the garbage dump. Take all you need. There's plenty here for *everyone!*"

10   If you are a woman, the men come after you. You lock yourself in your room, and when you must leave it to use the pestilential public bathroom at the end of your floor, you hurry, and you check every corner. Sometimes the lights are out in the toilet room. Sometimes men listen at the door. They call you "good-looking" and "bitch" and "*mamacita*," and they make kissing sounds at you when you pass.

11   You're in the worst part of town, but you can comfort yourself—at least there are no death squads here. There are no torturers here, or bandit land barons riding into your house. This is the last barrier, you think, between you and the United States—*los Yunaites Estaites*.

12   You still face police corruption, violence, jail. You now also have a wide variety of new options available to you: drugs, prostitution, white slavery, crime. Tijuana is not easy on newcomers. It is a city that has always thrived on taking advantage of a sucker. And the innocent are the ultimate suckers in the Borderlands.

Understanding Meaning

1. Urrea has called the border a "battlefield." How does his description illustrate this view?
2. What problems do the undocumented aliens face in their attempt to cross the border?

3. How are non-Mexican refugees treated in Tijuana?
4. What is the plight of refugee women on the border?
5. *Critical Thinking:* Urrea quotes a Dutch woman who used the term "un-American" to describe the border patrols. What is un-American about fences and helicopter patrols? Does this response to immigration clash with the Statue of Liberty's promise to welcome the tired and poor?

Evaluating Strategy

1. How effective is the use of the second person? Does it really put "you" in the scene? Does it help dramatize the plight of people many readers might choose to ignore?
2. What details does Urrea use to dramatize conditions along the border?

Appreciating Language

1. Throughout the description, Urrea uses lists—"beatings, rape, murder, torture, road accidents. . . ." How effective are they? Can listing words become tedious?
2. Select the words that create the most powerful images of the border. Why do they make strong impressions?

Connections across the Disciplines

1. How does Urrea's attempt to introduce his reader to the border compare with Truman Capote's description of Holcomb (page 114)?
2. Do the poverty and violence immigrants face in Mexico suggest a reason why some of their descendants, such as the Chicano police officer in "The Fender-Bender" (page 62), reject their heritage?

Writing Suggestions

1. Write an essay describing a place that highlights a social problem. Select a location of which you have personal knowledge, and try to convey the conditions residents face through lists of details.
2. *Collaborative Writing:* Ask a group of fellow students to respond to Urrea's account. Consider the issues his description of the border raises. Ask members to suggest how conditions could be improved, and then draft a short *persuasion* essay outlining your ideas.

Joan Didion (1934–) was born in Sacramento and attended the University of California at Berkeley. After graduating in 1956, Didion became an associate editor for Vogue. *Didion achieved prominence in the 1960s for articles commenting on American life and society. Her novels* Play It As It Lays *and* A Book of Common Prayer *were published in the 1970s. She also has written nonfiction accounts of her travels to Central America. Her book* Miami *examines problems faced by Florida's Cuban population. She has collaborated with her husband John Gregory Dunne on a number of screenplays, including* A Star Is Born *and* True Confessions.

Marrying Absurd

Written in 1967, "Marrying Absurd" remains one of Didion's most anthologized essays. As you read her description of the Las Vegas wedding chapels, determine her thesis.

1   To be married in Las Vegas, Clark County, Nevada, a bride must swear that she is eighteen or has parental permission and a bridegroom that he is twenty-one or has parental permission. Someone must put up five dollars for the license. (On Sundays and holidays, fifteen dollars. The Clark County Courthouse issues marriage licenses at any time of the day or night except between noon and one in the afternoon, between eight and nine in the evening, and between four and five in the morning.) Nothing else is required. The State of Nevada, alone among these United States, demands neither a premarital blood test nor a waiting period before or after the issuance of a marriage license. Driving in across the Mojave from Los Angeles, one sees the signs way out on the desert, looming up from that moonscape of rattlesnakes and mesquite, even before the Las Vegas lights appear like a mirage on the horizon: "GETTING MARRIED? Free License Information First Strip Exit." Perhaps the Las Vegas wedding industry achieved its peak operational efficiency between 9:00 p.m. and midnight of August 26, 1965, an otherwise unremarkable Thursday which happened

to be, by Presidential order, the last day on which anyone could improve his draft status merely by getting married. One hundred and seventy-one couples were pronounced man and wife in the name of Clark County and the State of Nevada that night, sixty-seven of them by a single justice of the peace, Mr. James A. Brennan. Mr. Brennan did one wedding at the Dunes and the other sixty-six in his office, and charged each couple eight dollars. One bride lent her veil to six others. "I got it down from five to three minutes," Mr. Brennan said later of his feat. "I could've married them *en masse*, but they're people, not cattle. People expect more when they get married."

2   What people who get married in Las Vegas actually do expect— what, in the largest sense, their "expectations" are—strikes one as a curious and self-contradictory business. Las Vegas is the most extreme and allegorical of American settlements, bizarre and beautiful in its venality and in its devotion to immediate gratification, a place the tone of which is set by mobsters and call girls and ladies' room attendants with amyl nitrite poppers in their uniform pockets. Almost everyone notes that there is no "time" in Las Vegas, no night and no day and no past and no future (no Las Vegas casino, however, has taken the obliteration of the ordinary time sense quite so far as Harold's Club in Reno, which for a while issued, at odd intervals in the day and night, mimeographed "bulletins" carrying news from the world outside); neither is there any logical sense of where one is. One is standing on a highway in the middle of a vast hostile desert looking at an eighty-foot sign which blinks "STARDUST" or "CAESAR'S PALACE." Yes, but what does that explain? This geographical implausibility reinforces the sense that what happens there has no connection with "real" life; Nevada cities like Reno and Carson are ranch towns, Western towns, places behind which there is some historical imperative. But Las Vegas seems to exist only in the eye of the beholder. All of which makes it an extraordinarily stimulating and interesting place, but an odd one in which to want to wear a candlelight satin Priscilla of Boston wedding dress with Chantilly lace insets, tapered sleeves and a detachable modified train.

3   And yet the Las Vegas wedding business seems to appeal to precisely that impulse. "Sincere and Dignified Since 1954," one wedding chapel advertises. There are nineteen such wedding chapels in Las Vegas, intensely competitive, each offering better, faster, and, by implication, more sincere services than the next: Our Photos Best Anywhere, Your Wedding on A Phonograph Record, Candlelight with Your Ceremony, Honeymoon Accommodations, Free Transportation from

Your Motel to Courthouse to Chapel and Return to Motel, Religious or Civil Ceremonies, Dressing Rooms, Flowers, Rings, Announcements, Witnesses Available, and Ample Parking. All of these services, like most others in Las Vegas (sauna baths, payroll-check cashing, chinchilla coats for sale or rent) are offered twenty-four hours a day, seven days a week, presumably on the premise that marriage, like craps, is a game to be played when the table seems hot.

4   But what strikes one most about the Strip chapels, with their wishing wells and stained-glass paper windows and their artificial bouvardia, is that so much of their business is by no means a matter of simple convenience, of late-night liaisons between show girls and baby Crosbys. Of course there is some of that. (One night about eleven o'clock in Las Vegas I watched a bride in an orange minidress and masses of flame-colored hair stumble from a Strip chapel on the arm of her bridegroom, who looked the part of the expendable nephew in movies like *Miami Syndicate*. "I gotta get the kids," the bride whimpered. "I gotta pick up the sitter, I gotta get to the midnight show." "What you gotta get," the bridegroom said, opening the door of a Cadillac Coupe de Ville and watching her crumple on the seat, "is sober.") But Las Vegas seems to offer something other than "convenience"; it is merchandising "niceness," the facsimile of proper ritual, to children who do not know how else to find it, how to make the arrangements, how to do it "right." All day and evening long on the Strip, one sees actual wedding parties, waiting under the harsh lights at a crosswalk, standing uneasily in the parking lot of the Frontier while the photographer hired by The Little Church of the West ("Wedding Place of the Stars") certifies the occasion, takes the picture: the bride in a veil and white satin pumps, the bridegroom usually in a white dinner jacket, and even an attendant or two, a sister or a best friend in hot-pink *peau de soie*, a flirtation veil, a carnation nosegay. "When I Fall in Love It Will Be Forever," the organist plays, and then a few bars of *Lohengrin*. The mother cries; the stepfather, awkward in his role, invites the chapel hostess to join them for a drink at the Sands. The hostess declines with a professional smile; she has already transferred her interest to the group waiting outside. One bride out, another in, and again the sign goes up on the chapel door: "One moment please—Wedding."

5   I sat next to one such wedding party in a Strip restaurant the last time I was in Las Vegas. The marriage had just taken place; the bride still wore her dress, the mother her corsage. A bored waiter poured out a few swallows of pink champagne ("on the house") for everyone but the bride, who was too young to be served. "You'll need something

with more kick than that," the bride's father said with heavy jocularity to his new son-in-law; the ritual jokes about the wedding night had a certain Panglossian character, since the bride was clearly several months pregnant. Another round of pink champagne, this time not on the house, and the bride began to cry. "It was just as nice," she sobbed, "as I hoped and dreamed it would be."

Understanding Meaning

1. What is Didion's purpose? Why does she consider these weddings "absurd"?
2. To whom does this essay seem directed? Which readers would share Didion's views? How would owners of the wedding chapel industry respond to her description?
3. What do the Las Vegas wedding chapels suggest about marriage in America?
4. *Critical Thinking:* Does the slickness of these ceremonies necessarily indicate anything negative about the couples who choose to marry in Las Vegas chapels? Why or why not? Do they suggest a kind of desperation to achieve the elaborate beauty of traditional weddings quickly and cheaply? Why?

Evaluating Strategy

1. How effective are the opening and closing of the essay? What is the impact of the young bride's remarks in the last line?
2. *Critical Thinking:* How does Didion develop her thesis? How much is stated and how much is implied?
3. *Other Modes:* Locate where Didion uses *narration* and *comparison* to develop her description. How do the brief narrations add action to the essay?

Appreciating Language

1. Underline those words that establish Didion's view of Las Vegas. What connotations do they have?
2. Didion selects wording used in various advertisements. How does including these words and phrases allow Las Vegas to represent itself? Why is this an effective device?
3. What does the word "absurd" in the title suggest? What other words might apply to Didion's description?

Connections across the Disciplines

1. Compare Didion's tone and style with Truman Capote's (page 114) and Luis Alberto Urrea's (page 118). What does each author's choice of words reveal about his or her attitudes toward the places described?
2. How do the slick wedding chapels with their promise of instant happiness relate to the observations made in John Ciardi's "What Is Happiness?" (page 192)?

Writing Suggestions

1. If you have visited Las Vegas, write a description of some aspect of the city that struck you as being the most memorable.
2. Write a description of a wedding you have attended. Choose words carefully so they capture both factual details and your personal observations.
3. *Collaborative Writing:* Work with a group of students to create a short description of a place with which you are all familiar. Decide on the tone or attitude you wish to create for readers—respectful, humorous, or sarcastic. Have each member write a draft then read them aloud. Select the best words and images from the different drafts to create a master copy.

José Antonio Burciaga (1940–1996) grew up in a synagogue in El Paso, where his father worked as a custodian. Burciaga served in the U.S. Air Force and then attended the University of Texas, where he earned a fine arts degree. Pursuing both art and literature, Burciaga was also active in Chicano affairs. His artwork was first exhibited in 1974. Two years later he published a collection of poetry called Restless Serpents, *followed by a variety of other publications.*

My Ecumenical Father

This essay, which first appeared in Drink Cultura, *describes Burciaga's father, a man who maintained his ties to Mexican culture while taking pride in his American citizenship and developing a fierce devotion to the Jewish faith.*

1   ¡Feliz Navidad! Merry Christmas! Happy Hanukkah! As a child, my season's greetings were tricultural—Mexicano, Anglo and Jewish.

2   Our devoutly Catholic parents raised three sons and three daughters in the basement of a Jewish synagogue, Congregation B'nai Zion in El Paso, Texas. José Cruz Burciaga was the custodian and *shabbat goy.* A shabbat goy is Yiddish for a Gentile who, on the Sabbath, performs certain tasks forbidden to Jews under orthodox law.

3   Every year around Christmas time, my father would take the menorah out and polish it. The eight-branched candleholder symbolizes Hanukkah, the commemoration of the first recorded war of liberation in that part of the world.

4   In 164 B.C., the Jewish nation rebelled against Antiochus IV Epiphanes, who had attempted to introduce pagan idols into the temples. When the temple was reconquered by the Jews, there was only one day's supply of oil for the Eternal Light in the temple. By a miracle, the oil lasted eight days.

5   My father was not only in charge of the menorah but for 10 years he also made sure the Eternal Light remained lit.

6   As children we were made aware of the differences and joys of Hanukkah, Christmas and Navidad. We were taught to respect each

celebration, even if they conflicted. For example, the Christmas carols taught in school. We learned the song about the twelve days of Christmas, though I never understood what the hell a partridge was doing in a pear tree in the middle of December.

7   We also learned a German song about a boy named Tom and a bomb—*O Tannenbaum*. We even learned a song in the obscure language of Latin, called "Adeste Fideles," which reminded me of, *Ahh! d'este fideo*, a Mexican pasta soup. Though 75% of our class was Mexican-American, we never sang a Christmas song in *Español*. Spanish was forbidden.

8   So our mother—a former teacher—taught us "Silent Night" in Spanish: *Noche de paz, noche de amor:* It was so much more poetic and inspirational.

9   While the rest of El Paso celebrated Christmas, Congregation B'nai Zion celebrated Hanukkah. We picked up Yiddish and learned a Hebrew prayer of thanksgiving. My brothers and I would help my father hang the Hanukkah decorations.

10   At night, after the services, the whole family would rush across the border to Juarez and celebrate the *posadas*, which takes place for nine days before Christmas. They are a communal re-enactment of Joseph and Mary's search for shelter, just before Jesus was born.

11   To the posadas we took candles and candy left over from the Hanukkah celebrations. The next day we'd be back at St. Patrick's School singing, "I'm dreaming of a white Christmas."

12   One day I stopped dreaming of the white Christmases depicted on greeting cards. An old immigrant from Israel taught me Jesus was born in desert country just like that of the West Texas town of El Paso.

13   On Christmas Eve, my father would dress like Santa Claus and deliver gifts to his children, nephews, godchildren and the little kids in orphanages. The next day, minus his disguise, he would take us to Juarez, where we delivered gifts to the poor in the streets.

14   My father never forgot his childhood poverty and forever sought to help the less fortunate. He taught us to measure wealth not in money but in terms of love, spirit, charity and culture.

15   We were taught to respect the Jewish faith and culture. On the Day of Atonement, when the whole congregation fasted, my mother did not cook, lest the food odors distract. The respect was mutual. No one ever complained about the large picture of Jesus in our living room.

16   Through my father, leftover food from B'nai B'rith luncheons, Bar Mitzvahs and Bat Mitzvahs, found its way to Catholic or Baptist churches or orphanages. Floral arrangements in the temple that

surrounded a Jewish wedding *huppah* canopy many times found a second home at the altar of St. Patrick's Cathedral or San Juan Convent School. Surplus furniture, including old temple pews, found their way to a missionary Baptist Church in *El Segundo Barrio.*

17   It was not uncommon to come home from school at lunch time and find an uncle priest, an aunt nun and a Baptist minister visiting our home at the same time that the Rabbi would knock on our door. It was just as natural to find the president of B'nai Zion eating beans and tortillas in our kitchen.

18   My father literally risked his life for the Jewish faith. Twice he was assaulted by burglars who broke in at night. Once he was stabbed in the hand. Another time he stayed up all night guarding the sacred Torahs after anti-Semites threatened the congregation. He never philosophized about his ecumenism, he just lived it.

19   Cruz, as most called him, was a man of great humor, a hot temper and a passion for dance. He lived the Mexican Revolution and rode the rails during the Depression. One of his proudest moments came when he became a U.S. citizen.

20   September 23, 1985, sixteen months after my mother passed away, my father followed. Like his life, his death was also ecumenical. The funeral was held at Our Lady of Peace, where a priest said the mass in English. My cousins played mandolin and sang in Spanish. The president of B'nai Zion Congregation said a prayer in Hebrew. Members of the congregation sat with Catholics and Baptists.

21   Observing Jewish custom, the cortege passed by the synagogue one last time. Fittingly, father was laid to rest on the Sabbath. At the cemetery, in a very Mexican tradition, my brothers, sisters and I each kissed a handful of dirt and threw it on the casket.

22   I once had the opportunity to describe father's life to the late, great Jewish American writer Bernard Malamud. His only comment was, "Only in America!"

Understanding Meaning

1.   What is a *shabbat goy?*
2.   How did the author's family show respect to the congregation?
3.   How did the author's family manage to blend respect for several cultures?
4.   Burciaga points out that though he learned German and Latin songs in school, he was not allowed to sing in Spanish. What does this reveal about the educational system?

5. Why is the description of his father's funeral central to Burciaga's story?
6. *Critical Thinking:* What values does the ecumenical father represent? Are these values rare in our society? What lesson could this essay teach?

Evaluating Strategy

1. Would Bernard Malamud's comment, "Only in America," make a good title for this essay? Why or why not?
2. Burciaga offers an explanation of Hanukkah. What does this suggest about his intended audience?
3. *Other Modes:* Can this *description* be seen as an extended *definition* of *ecumenical?*

Appreciating Language

1. How did Burciaga's father define "wealth"?
2. Read through Burciaga's description and highlight his use of non-English words and phrases. How does he define them? What impact do all these unfamiliar words have?

Connections across the Disciplines

1. How does Burciaga's multicultural upbringing differ from the childhood described by Nathan McCall (page 51)?
2. How does Burciaga's description of a person he admired compare to that of Carl T. Rowan's account of Miss Bessie (page 131)? Do they use similar techniques? How do they bring their characters to life? What details do they include?

Writing Suggestions

1. Burciaga builds his description largely through details about his father's actions and behavior. Write a few paragraphs describing a person you know well. Try to capture what you consider the person's principal attributes by describing actions that reveal their values.
2. *Collaborative Writing:* Discuss this essay with a group of other students. What do readers find most striking about this Mexican immigrant? Are his attitudes valuable to society? Is multiculturalism a trend today? Have each member write a few paragraphs explaining the significance of this essay. Read the responses aloud, and work to blend as many as possible in a short *analysis* of this essay.

CARL T. ROWAN

Carl T. Rowan (1925–) was born in Tennessee and received degrees from Ober-lin College and the University of Minnesota. He worked for years as a columnist for the Minneapolis Tribune *and the* Chicago Sun Times, *expressing his views on a variety of issues, especially race relations. Rowan also served as the direc-tor of the United States Information Agency and was the ambassador to Finland.*

Unforgettable Miss Bessie

This article describing a schoolteacher originally appeared in Reader's Digest, *where Rowan serves as an editor. Rowan's account is personal, and much of his description focuses on the impact this teacher had on him and other disadvantaged students.*

1 She was only about five feet tall and probably never weighed more than 110 pounds, but Miss Bessie was a towering presence in the class-room. She was the only woman tough enough to make me read *Beowulf* and think for a few foolish days that I liked it. From 1938 to 1942, when I attended Bernard High School in McMinnville, Tenn., she taught me English, history, civics—and a lot more than I realized.

2 I shall never forget the day she scolded me into reading *Beowulf*.

3 "But Miss Bessie," I complained, "I ain't much interested in it."

4 Her large brown eyes became daggerish slits. "Boy," she said, "how dare you say 'ain't' to me! I've taught you better than that."

5 "Miss Bessie," I pleaded, "I'm trying to make first-string end on the football team, and if I go around saying 'it isn't' and 'they aren't,' the guys are gonna laugh me off the squad."

6 "Boy," she responded, "you'll play football because you have guts. But do you know what *really* takes guts? Refusing to lower your stan-dards to those of the crowd. It takes guts to say you've got to live and be somebody fifty years after all the football games are over."

7 I started saying "it isn't" and "they aren't," and I still made first-string end—and class valedictorian—without losing my buddies' respect.

8 During her remarkable 44-year career, Mrs. Bessie Taylor Gwynn taught hundreds of economically deprived black youngsters—includ-ing my mother, my brother, my sisters and me. I remember her now

with gratitude and affection—especially in this era when Americans are so wrought-up about a "rising tide of mediocrity" in public education and the problems of finding competent, caring teachers. Miss Bessie was an example of an informed, dedicated teacher, a blessing to children and an asset to the nation.

9   Born in 1895, in poverty, she grew up in Athens, Ala., where there was no public school for blacks. She attended Trinity School, a private institution for blacks run by the American Missionary Association, and in 1911 graduated from the Normal School (a "super" high school) at Fisk University in Nashville. Mrs. Gwynn, the essence of pride and privacy, never talked about her years in Athens; only in the months before her death did she reveal that she had never attended Fisk University itself because she could not afford the four-year course.

10   At Normal School she learned a lot about Shakespeare, but most of all about the profound importance of education—especially, for a people trying to move up from slavery. "What you put in your head, boy," she once said, "can never be pulled out by the Ku Klux Klan, the Congress or anybody."

11   Miss Bessie's bearing of dignity told anyone who met her that she was "educated" in the best sense of the word. There was never a discipline problem in her classes. We didn't dare mess with a woman who knew about the Battle of Hastings, the Magna Carta and the Bill of Rights—and who could also play the piano.

12   This frail-looking woman could make sense of Shakespeare, Milton, Voltaire, and bring to life Booker T. Washington and W. E. B. DuBois. Believing that it was important to know who the officials were that spent taxpayers' money and made public policy, she made us memorize the names of everyone on the Supreme Court and in the President's Cabinet. It could be embarrassing to be unprepared when Miss Bessie said, "Get up and tell the class who Frances Perkins is and what you think about her."

13   Miss Bessie knew that my family, like so many others during the Depression, couldn't afford to subscribe to a newspaper. She knew we didn't even own a radio. Still, she prodded me to "look out for your future and find some way to keep up with what's going on in the world." So I became a delivery boy for the Chattanooga *Times*. I rarely made a dollar a week, but I got to read a newspaper every day.

14   Miss Bessie noticed things that had nothing to do with schoolwork, but were vital to a youngster's development. Once a few classmates made fun of my frayed, hand-me-down overcoat, calling me "Strings."

As I was leaving school, Miss Bessie patted me on the back of that old overcoat and said, "Carl, never fret about what you *don't* have. Just make the most of what you *do* have—a brain."

15   Among the things that I did not have was electricity in the little frame house that my father had built for $400 with his World War I bonus. But because of her inspiration, I spent many hours squinting beside a kerosene lamp reading Shakespeare and Thoreau, Samuel Pepys and William Cullen Bryant.

16   No one in my family had ever graduated from high school, so there was no tradition of commitment to learning for me to lean on. Like millions of youngsters in today's ghettos and barrios, I needed the push and stimulation of a teacher who truly cared. Miss Bessie gave plenty of both, as she immersed me in a wonderful world of similes, metaphors and even onomatopoeia. She led me to believe that I could write sonnets as well as Shakespeare, or iambic-pentameter verse to put Alexander Pope to shame.

17   In those days the McMinnville school system was rigidly "Jim Crow," and poor black children had to struggle to put anything in their heads. Our high school was only slightly larger than the once-typical little red schoolhouse, and its library was outrageously inadequate—so small, I like to say, that if two students were in it and one wanted to turn a page, the other one had to step outside.

18   Negroes, as we were called then, were not allowed in the town library, except to mop floors or dust tables. But through one of those secret Old South arrangements between whites of conscience and blacks of stature, Miss Bessie kept getting books smuggled out of the white library. That is how she introduced me to the Brontës, Byron, Coleridge, Keats and Tennyson. "If you don't read, you can't write, and if you can't write, you might as well stop dreaming," Miss Bessie once told me.

19   So I read whatever Miss Bessie told me to, and tried to remember the things she insisted that I store away. Forty-five years later, I can still recite her "truths to live by," such as Henry Wadsworth Longfellow's lines from "The Ladder of St. Augustine":

20   The heights by great men reached and kept
Were not attained by sudden flight.
But they, while their companions slept,
Were toiling upward in the night.

21   Years later, her inspiration, prodding, anger, cajoling and almost osmotic infusion of learning finally led to that lovely day when Miss Bessie dropped me a note saying, "I'm so proud to read your column in the Nashville *Tennessean*."

22   Miss Bessie was a spry 80 when I went back to McMinnville and visited her in a senior citizens' apartment building. Pointing out proudly that her building was racially integrated, she reached for two glasses and a pint of bourbon. I was momentarily shocked, because it would have been scandalous in the 1930s and '40s for word to get out that a teacher drank, and nobody had ever raised a rumor that Miss Bessie did.

23   I felt a new sense of equality as she lifted her glass to mine. Then she revealed a softness and compassion that I had never known as a student.

24   "I've never forgotten that examination day," she said, "when Buster Martin held up seven fingers, obviously asking you for help with question number seven, 'Name a common carrier.' I can still picture you looking at your exam paper and humming a few bars of 'Chattanooga Choo Choo.' I was so tickled, I couldn't punish either of you."

25   Miss Bessie was telling me, with bourbon-laced grace, that I never fooled her for a moment.

26   When Miss Bessie died in 1980, at age 85, hundreds of her former students mourned. They knew the measure of a great teacher: love and motivation. Her wisdom and influence had rippled out across generations.

27   Some of her students who might normally have been doomed to poverty went on to become doctors, dentists and college professors. Many, guided by Miss Bessie's example, became public-school teachers.

28   "The memory of Miss Bessie and how she conducted her classroom did more for me than anything I learned in college," recalls Gladys Wood of Knoxville, Tenn., a highly respected English teacher who spent 43 years in the state's school system. "So many times, when I faced a difficult classroom problem, I asked myself, *How would Miss Bessie deal with this?* And I'd remember that she would handle it with laughter and love."

29   No child can get all the necessary support at home, and millions of poor children get *no* support at all. This is what makes a wise, educated, warm-hearted teacher like Miss Bessie so vital to the minds, hearts and souls of this country's children.

Understanding Meaning

1. What is Rowan's purpose in describing Miss Bessie? What makes this teacher significant to a middle-aged man?
2. What qualities of Miss Bessie does Rowan admire?
3. Does Rowan offer Miss Bessie as a role model? How does he demonstrate that she is an "asset to the nation"?

Evaluating Strategy

1. Rowan opens his essay with a physical description of Miss Bessie. Why are these details important to his purpose?
2. Why would this article appeal to readers of *Reader's Digest?* What values does it reinforce?
3. *Critical Thinking:* Would some people object to Rowan's article as being sentimental? Why or why not? Does this article suggest simple solutions to complex problems? Would a Miss Bessie be able to succeed in a modern urban high school?

Appreciating Language

1. Study the words Rowan uses in describing Miss Bessie. Which words have the most impact?
2. Rowan includes dialogue in his article. What do you notice about Miss Bessie's language? What does this add to the description?

Connections across the Disciplines

1. Consider William Raspberry's article "The Handicap of Definition" (page 51). Would Miss Bessie be a figure that resists such a handicap?
2. *Critical Thinking:* Compare Rowan's experience in a black high school with Nathan McCall's experience in "The Lesson" (page 310). Do African-American students from disadvantaged communities benefit from integration or from participation in black schools with black teachers like Miss Bessie?

Writing Suggestions

1. Write a brief description of a teacher, employer, or coworker who greatly influenced your development. Provide specific examples of the lessons you learned.

2. *Collaborative Writing:* Working with three or four other students, discuss Miss Bessie's statement, "What you put in your head, boy, can never be pulled out by the Ku Klux Klan, the Congress or anybody." Use this quote as the headline of a poster urging people to read. Keep your message short. Read it aloud to hear how it sounds.

Navarre Scott Momaday (1934–) was born in Oklahoma and graduated from the University of New Mexico in 1958. He received a doctorate in English from Stanford University. Momaday is a literature professor, poet, artist, and frequent contributor to The New Yorker. *A Native American, he has published a collection of Kiowa folktales and edited* American Indian Authors. *His other books have included* The Gourd Dancer, *an illustrated children's book, and* House Made of Dawn, *a novel that received a Pulitzer Prize.*

The Way to Rainy Mountain

This essay first appeared in The Reporter. *Momaday later revised it and used it as an introduction to a book of the same title.*

1   A single knoll rises out of the plain in Oklahoma, north and west of the Wichita Range. For my people, the Kiowas, it is an old landmark, and they gave it the name Rainy Mountain. The hardest weather in the world is there. Winter brings blizzards, hot tornadic winds arise in the spring, and in summer the prairie is an anvil's edge. The grass turns brittle and brown, and it cracks beneath your feet. There are green belts along the rivers and creeks, linear groves of hickory and pecan, willow and witch hazel. At a distance in July or August the steaming foliage seems almost to writhe in fire. Great green-and-yellow grasshoppers are everywhere in the tall grass, popping up like corn to sting the flesh, and tortoises crawl about on the red earth, going nowhere in the plenty of time. Loneliness is an aspect of the land. All things in the plain are isolate; there is no confusion of objects in the eye, but *one* hill or *one* tree or *one* man. To look upon that landscape in the early morning, with the sun at your back, is to lose the sense of proportion. Your imagination comes to life, and this, you think, is where Creation was begun.

2   I returned to Rainy Mountain in July. My grandmother had died in the spring, and I wanted to be at her grave. She had lived to be very old and at last infirm. Her only living daughter was with her when she died, and I was told that in death her face was that of a child.

3   I like to think of her as a child. When she was born, the Kiowas were living that last great moment of their history. For more than a hundred years they had controlled the open range from the Smoky Hill River to the Red, from the headwaters of the Canadian to the fork of the Arkansas and Cimarron. In alliance with the Comanches, they had ruled the whole of the southern Plains. War was their sacred business, and they were among the finest horsemen the world has ever known. But warfare for the Kiowas was preeminently a matter of disposition rather than of survival, and they never understood the grim, unrelenting advance of the U.S. Cavalry. When at last, divided and ill-provisioned, they were driven onto the Staked Plains in the cold rains of autumn, they fell into panic. In Palo Duro Canyon they abandoned their crucial stores to pillage and had nothing then but their lives. In order to save themselves, they surrendered to the soldiers at Fort Sill and were imprisoned in the old stone corral that now stands as a military museum. My grandmother was spared the humiliation of those high gray walls by eight or ten years, but she must have known from birth the affliction of defeat, the dark brooding of old warriors.

4   Her name was Aho, and she belonged to the last culture to evolve in North America. Her forebears came down from the high country in western Montana nearly three centuries ago. They were a mountain people, a mysterious tribe of hunters whose language has never been positively classified in any major group. In the late seventeenth century they began a long migration to the south and east. It was a long journey toward the dawn, and it led to a golden age. Along the way the Kiowas were befriended by the Crows, who gave them the culture and religion of the Plains. They acquired horses, and their ancient nomadic spirit was suddenly free of the ground. They acquired Tai-me, the sacred Sun Dance doll, from that moment the object and symbol of their worship, and so shared in the divinity of the sun. Not least, they acquired the sense of destiny, therefore courage and pride. When they entered upon the southern Plains, they had been transformed. No longer were they slaves to the simple necessity of survival; they were a lordly and dangerous society of fighters and thieves, hunters and priests of the sun. According to their origin myth, they entered the world through a hollow log. From one point of view, their migration was the fruit of an old prophecy, for indeed they emerged from a sunless world.

5   Although my grandmother lived out her long life in the shadow of Rainy Mountain, the immense landscape of the continental interior

lay like memory in her blood. She could tell of the Crows, whom she had never seen, and of the Black Hills, where she had never been. I wanted to see in reality what she had seen more perfectly in the mind's eye, and traveled fifteen hundred miles to begin my pilgrimage.

6   Yellowstone, it seemed to me, was the top of the world, a region of deep lakes and dark timber, canyons and waterfalls. But, beautiful as it is, one might have the sense of confinement there. The skyline in all directions is close at hand, the high wall of the woods and deep cleavages of shade. There is a perfect freedom in the mountains, but it belongs to the eagle and the elk, the badger and the bear. The Kiowas reckoned their stature by the distance they could see, and they were bent and blind in the wilderness.

7   Descending eastward, the highland meadows are a stairway to the plain. In July the inland slope of the Rockies is luxuriant with flax and buckwheat, stonecrop and larkspur. The earth unfolds and the limit of the land recedes. Clusters of trees and animals grazing far in the distance cause the vision to reach away and wonder to build upon the mind. The sun follows a longer course in the day, and the sky is immense beyond all comparison. The great billowing clouds that sail upon it are shadows that move upon the grain like water, dividing light. Farther down, in the land of the Crows and Blackfeet, the plain is yellow. Sweet clover takes hold of the hills and bends upon itself to cover and seal the soil. There the Kiowas paused on their way; they had come to the place where they must change their lives. The sun is at home in the plains. Precisely there does it have the certain character of a god. When the Kiowas came to the land of the Crows, they could see the dark lees of the hills at dawn across the Bighorn River, the profusion of light on the grain shelves, the oldest deity ranging after the solstices. Not yet would they veer southward to the caldron of the land that lay below; they must wean their blood from the northern winter and hold the mountains a while longer in their view. They bore Taime in procession to the east.

8   A dark mist lay over the Black Hills, and the land was like iron. At the top of a ridge I caught sight of Devil's Tower upthrust against the gray sky as if in the birth of time the core of the earth had broken through its crust and the motion of the world was begun. There are things in nature that engender an awful quiet in the heart of man; Devil's Tower is one of them. Two centuries ago, because they could not do otherwise, the Kiowas made a legend at the base of the rock. My grandmother said:

9   Eight children were there at play, seven sisters and their brother. Suddenly the boy was struck dumb; he trembled and began to run upon his hands and feet. His fingers became claws, and his body was covered with fur. Directly there was a bear where the boy had been. The sisters were terrified; they ran, and the bear after them. They came to the stump of a great tree, and the tree spoke to them. It bade them climb upon it, and as they did so, it began to rise into the air. The bear came to kill them, but they were just beyond its reach. It reared against the tree and scored the bark all around with its claws. The seven sisters were borne into the sky, and they became the stars of the Big Dipper.

10   From that moment, and so long as the legend lives, the Kiowas have kinsmen in the night sky. Whatever they were in the mountains, they could be no more. However tenuous their well-being, however much they had suffered and would suffer again, they had found a way out of the wilderness.

11   My grandmother had a reverence for the sun, a holy regard that now is all but gone out of mankind. There was a wariness in her, and an ancient awe. She was a Christian in her later years, but she had come a long way about, and she never forgot her birthright. As a child she had been to the Sun Dances; she had taken part in those annual rites, and by them she had learned the restoration of her people in the presence of Tai-me. She was about seven when the last Kiowa Sun Dance was held in 1887 on the Washita River above Rainy Mountain Creek. The buffalo were gone. In order to consummate the ancient sacrifice—to impale the head of a buffalo bull upon the medicine tree—a delegation of old men journeyed into Texas, there to beg and barter for an animal from the Goodnight herd. She was ten when the Kiowas came together for the last time as a living Sun Dance culture. They could find no buffalo; they had to hang an old hide from the sacred tree. Before the dance could begin, a company of soldiers rode out from Fort Sill under orders to disperse the tribe. Forbidden without cause the essential act of their faith, having seen the wild herds slaughtered and left to rot upon the ground, the Kiowas backed away forever from the medicine tree. That was July 20, 1890, at the great bend of the Washita. My grandmother was there. Without bitterness, and for as long as she lived, she bore a vision of deicide.

12   Now that I can have her only in memory, I see my grandmother in the several postures that were peculiar to her: standing at the wood stove on a winter morning and turning meat in a great iron skillet; sitting at the south window, bent above her beadwork, and afterwards,

when her vision had failed, looking down for a long time into the fold of her hands; going out upon a cane, very slowly as she did when the weight of age came upon her; praying. I remember her most often at prayer. She made long, rambling prayers out of suffering and hope, having seen many things. I was never sure that I had the right to hear, so exclusive were they of all mere custom and company. The last time I saw her she prayed standing by the side of her bed at night, naked to the waist, the light of a kerosene lamp moving upon her dark skin. Her long, black hair, always drawn and braided in the day, lay upon her shoulders and against her breasts like a shawl. I do not speak Kiowa, and I never understood her prayers, but there was something inherently sad in the sound, some merest hesitation upon the syllables of sorrow. She began in a high and descending pitch, exhausting her breath to silence; then again and again—and always the same intensity of effort, of something that is, and is not, like urgency in the human voice. Transported so in the dancing light among the shadows of her room, she seemed beyond the reach of time. But that was illusion; I think I knew then that I should not see her again.

Understanding Meaning

1. How does Momaday describe Rainy Mountain? How do its physical characteristics differ from its importance to the Kiowas?
2. How does Momaday describe his grandmother? What were the dominant features of her life and her home?
3. What is the significance of the Kiowa legend about the seven sisters?
4. *Other Modes:* How does Momaday use *narration* and *comparison* to develop his description?
5. *Critical Thinking:* Momaday states that he did not speak his grandmother's language and did not understand her prayers. Does this loss of an ancestral language by a man interested in his past illustrate Jamaica Kincaid's observation that Americans are "impatient with memory"?

Evaluating Strategy

1. Most descriptions focus on visual images. How does Momaday use sounds to describe his subject?
2. How does Momaday introduce historical background into a highly personal essay? What transitions does he use?

Appreciating Language

1. Momaday discusses his grandmother's reverence for the sun. What connotation does the word *sun* have?
2. Focus on Momaday's word choices. How does he refer to the beliefs of the ancient Native Americans? What do his connotations reveal about his attitudes toward their faith?

Connections across the Disciplines

1. How does Momaday's role as tribal member returning home compare to Armando Rendón's discovery of his roots in "Kiss of Death" (page 611)? Does a difference exist between immigrant and Native American cultures? Is one harder to maintain or preserve?
2. How does Momaday's description of people and places compare with Truman Capote's in "Out There" (page 114)? Do they pay similar attention to detail? Are their attitudes different? Does one writer seem more of an outsider?

Writing Suggestions

1. Write an essay describing an ancestral figure in your own past. Choose a relative, family friend, or neighbor who embodied a sense of your family, community, or culture. Choose words carefully to share with readers your attitudes toward this person.
2. *Collaborative Writing:* Discuss the role of grandparents in current society with several students. Select observations you agree on, and write a few paragraphs presenting your main points. Has the role of grandparents changed? On the one hand, are they discredited because our society emphasizes youth? On the other hand, are they often more influential since many take an active role in raising grandchildren?

Edward Abbey (1927–1989) was born in Pennsylvania and first traveled to the West in 1948 to attend the University of New Mexico. Initially impressed with the romance of the cowboy, he later became concerned about the use of public lands and the environmental damage caused by development. Abbey worked as a park ranger for fifteen years. In 1968 he published Desert Solitaire, *which he called "not a travel guide but an elegy." His later works include* The Monkey Wrench Gang, Abbey's Road, *and* Down by the River.

The First Morning

Abbey opens this essay from Desert Solitaire *with a bold assertion: "This is the most beautiful place on earth." Abbey uses rich imagery and sensory details to get his reader to share his awe for a landscape empty of people.*

1   This is the most beautiful place on earth.

2   There are many such places. Every man, every woman, carries in heart and mind the image of the ideal place, the right place, the one true home, known or unknown, actual or visionary. A houseboat in Kashmir, a view down Atlantic Avenue in Brooklyn, a gray gothic farmhouse two stories high at the end of a red dog road in the Allegheny Mountains, a cabin on the shore of a blue lake in spruce and fir country, a greasy alley near the Hoboken waterfront, or even, possibly, for those of a less demanding sensibility, the world to be seen from a comfortable apartment high in the tender, velvety smog of Manhattan, Chicago, Paris, Tokyo, Rio or Rome—there's no limit to the human capacity for the homing sentiment. Theologians, sky pilots, astronauts have even felt the appeal of home calling to them from up above, in the cold black outback of interstellar space.

3   For myself I'll take Moab, Utah. I don't mean the town itself, of course, but the country which surrounds it—the canyonlands. The slickrock desert. The red dust and the burnt cliffs and the lonely sky—all that which lies beyond the end of the roads.

4   The choice became apparent to me this morning when I stepped out of a Park Service housetrailer—my caravan—to watch for the first

time in my life the sun come up over the hoodoo stone of Arches National Monument.

5   I wasn't able to see much of it last night. After driving all day from Albuquerque—450 miles—I reached Moab after dark in cold, windy, clouded weather. At park headquarters north of town I met the superintendent and the chief ranger, the only permanent employees, except for one maintenance man, in this particular unit of America's national park system. After coffee they gave me a key to the housetrailer and directions on how to reach it; I am required to live and work not at headquarters but at this one-man station some twenty miles back in the interior, on my own. The way I wanted it, naturally, or I'd never have asked for the job.

6   Leaving the headquarters area and the lights of Moab, I drove twelve miles farther north on the highway until I came to a dirt road on the right, where a small wooden sign pointed the way: Arches National Monument Eight Miles. I left the pavement, turned east into the howling wilderness. Wind roaring out of the northwest, black clouds across the stars—all I could see were clumps of brush and scattered junipers along the roadside. Then another modest signboard:

7   WARNING: QUICKSAND
DO NOT CROSS WASH
WHEN WATER IS RUNNING

8   The wash looked perfectly dry in my headlights. I drove down, across, up the other side and on into the night. Glimpses of weird humps of pale rock on either side, like petrified elephants, dinosaurs, stone-age hobgoblins. Now and then something alive scurried across the road: kangaroo mice, a jackrabbit, an animal that looked like a cross between a raccoon and a squirrel—the ringtail cat. Farther on a pair of mule deer started from the brush and bounded obliquely through the beams of my lights, raising puffs of dust which the wind, moving faster than my pickup truck, caught and carried ahead of me out of sight into the dark. The road, narrow and rocky, twisted sharply left and right, dipped in and out of tight ravines, climbing by degrees toward a summit which I would see only in the light of the coming day.

9   Snow was swirling through the air when I crossed the unfenced line and passed the boundary marker of the park. A quarter-mile beyond I found the ranger station—a wide place in the road, an informa-

tional display under a lean-to shelter, and fifty yards away the little tin government housetrailer where I would be living for the next six months.

10   A cold night, a cold wind, the snow falling like confetti. In the lights of the truck I unlocked the housetrailer, got out bedroll and baggage and moved in. By flashlight I found the bed, unrolled my sleeping bag, pulled off my boots and crawled in and went to sleep at once. The last I knew was the shaking of the trailer in the wind and the sound, from inside, of hungry mice scampering around with the good news that their long lean lonesome winter was over—their friend and provider had finally arrived.

11   This morning I awake before sunrise, stick my head out of the sack, peer through a frosty window at a scene dim and vague with flowing mists, dark fantastic shapes looming beyond. An unlikely landscape.

12   I get up, moving about in long underwear and socks, stooping carefully under the low ceiling and the lower doorways of the house-trailer, a machine for living built so efficiently and compactly there's hardly room for a man to breathe. An iron lung it is, with windows and venetian blinds.

13   The mice are silent, watching me from their hiding places, but the wind is still blowing and outside the ground is covered with snow. Cold as a tomb, a jail, a cave; I lie down on the dusty floor, on the cold linoleum sprinkled with mouse turds, and light the pilot on the butane heater. Once this thing gets going the place warms up fast, in a dense unhealthy way, with a layer of heat under the ceiling where my head is and nothing but frigid air from the knees down. But we've got all the indispensable conveniences: gas cookstove, gas refrigerator, hot water heater, sink with running water (if the pipes aren't frozen), storage cabinets and shelves, everything within arm's reach of everything else. The gas comes from two steel bottles in a shed outside; the water comes by gravity flow from a tank buried in a hill close by. Quite luxurious for the wilds. There's even a shower stall and a flush toilet with a dead rat in the bowl. Pretty soft. My poor mother raised five children without any of these luxuries and might be doing without them yet if it hadn't been for Hitler, war and general prosperity.

14   Time to get dressed, get out and have a look at the lay of the land, fix a breakfast. I try to pull on my boots but they're stiff as iron from the cold. I light a burner on the stove and hold the boots upside down

above the flame until they are malleable enough to force my feet into. I put on a coat and step outside. In the center of the world, God's navel, Abbey's country, the red wasteland.

15   The sun is not yet in sight but signs of the advent are plain to see. Lavender clouds sail like a fleet of ships across the pale green dawn; each cloud, planed flat on the wind, has a base of fiery gold. Southeast, twenty miles by line of sight, stand the peaks of the Sierra La Sal, twelve to thirteen thousand feet above sea level, all covered with snow and rosy in the morning sunlight. The air is dry and clear as well as cold; the last fogbanks left over from last night's storm are scudding away like ghosts, fading into nothing before the wind and the sunrise.

16   The view is open and perfect in all directions except to the west where the ground rises and the skyline is only a few hundred yards away. Looking toward the mountains I can see the dark gorge of the Colorado River five or six miles away, carved through the sandstone mesa, though nothing of the river itself down inside the gorge. Southward, on the far side of the river, lies the Moab valley between thousand-foot walls of rock, with the town of Moab somewhere on the valley floor, too small to be seen from here. Beyond the Moab valley is more canyon and tableland stretching away to the Blue Mountains fifty miles south. On the north and northwest I see the Roan Cliffs and the Book Cliffs, the two-level face of the Uinta Plateau. Along the foot of those cliffs, maybe thirty miles off, invisible from where I stand, runs U.S. 6-50, a major east-west artery of commerce, traffic and rubbish, and the main line of the Denver-Rio Grande Railroad. To the east, under the spreading sunrise, are more mesas, more canyons, league on league of red cliff and arid tablelands, extending through purple haze over the bulging curve of the planet to the ranges of Colorado—a sea of desert.

17   Within this vast perimeter, in the middle ground and foreground of the picture, a rather personal demesne, are the 33,000 acres of Arches National Monument of which I am now sole inhabitant, usufructuary, observer and custodian.

18   What are the Arches? From my place in front of the housetrailer I can see several of the hundred or more of them which have been discovered in the park. These are natural arches, holes in the rock, windows in stone, no two alike, as varied in form as in dimension. They range in size from holes just big enough to walk through to openings large enough to contain the dome of the Capitol building in Washington, D.C. Some resemble jug handles or flying buttresses,

others natural bridges but with this technical distinction: a natural bridge spans a watercourse—a natural arch does not. The arches were formed through hundreds of thousands of years by the weathering of the huge sandstone walls, or fins, in which they are found. Not the work of a cosmic hand, nor sculptured by sand-bearing winds, as many people prefer to believe, the arches came into being and continue to come into being through the modest wedging action of rainwater, melting snow, frost, and ice, aided by gravity. In color they shade from off-white through buff, pink, brown and red, tones which also change with the time of day and the moods of the light, the weather, the sky.

19   Standing there, gaping at this monstrous and inhuman spectacle of rock and cloud and sky and space, I feel a ridiculous greed and possessiveness come over me. I want to know it all, possess it all, embrace the entire scene intimately, deeply, totally, as a man desires a beautiful woman. An insane wish? Perhaps not—at least there's nothing else, no one human, to dispute possession with me.

20   The snow-covered ground glimmers with a dull blue light, reflecting the sky and the approaching sunrise. Leading away from me the narrow dirt road, an alluring and primitive track into nowhere, meanders down the slope and toward the heart of the labyrinth of naked stone. Near the first group of arches, looming over a bend in the road, is a balanced rock about fifty feet high, mounted on a pedestal of equal height; it looks like a head from Easter Island, a stone god or a petrified ogre.

21   Like a god, like an ogre? The personification of the natural is exactly the tendency I wish to suppress in myself, to eliminate for good. I am here not only to evade for a while the clamor and filth and confusion of the cultural apparatus but also to confront, immediately and directly if it's possible, the bare bones of existence, the elemental and fundamental, the bedrock which sustains us. I want to be able to look at and into a juniper tree, a piece of quartz, a vulture, a spider, and see it as it is in itself, devoid of all humanly ascribed qualities, anti-Kantian, even the categories of scientific description. To meet God or Medusa face to face, even if it means risking everything human in myself. I dream of a hard and brutal mysticism in which the naked self merges with a nonhuman world and yet somehow survives still intact, individual, separate. Paradox and bedrock.

22   Well—the sun will be up in a few minutes and I haven't even begun to make coffee. I take more baggage from my pickup, the grub box and cooking gear, go back in the trailer and start breakfast. Simply

breathing, in a place like this, arouses the appetite. The orange juice is frozen, the milk slushy with ice. Still chilly enough inside the trailer to turn my breath to vapor. When the first rays of the sun strike the cliffs I fill a mug with steaming coffee and sit in the doorway facing the sunrise, hungry for the warmth.

23 Suddenly it comes, the flaming globe, blazing on the pinnacles and minarets and balanced rocks, on the canyon walls and through the windows in the sandstone fins. We greet each other, sun and I, across the black void of ninety-three million miles. The snow glitters between us, acres of diamonds almost painful to look at. Within an hour all the snow exposed to the sunlight will be gone and the rock will be damp and steaming. Within minutes, even as I watch, melting snow begins to drip from the branches of a juniper nearby; drops of water streak slowly down the side of the trailerhouse.

24 I am not alone after all. Three ravens are wheeling near the balanced rock, squawking at each other and at the dawn. I'm sure they're as delighted by the return of the sun as I am and I wish I knew the language. I'd sooner exchange ideas with the birds on earth than learn to carry on intergalactic communications with some obscure race of humanoids on a satellite planet from the world of Betelgeuse. First things first. The ravens cry out in husky voices, blue-black wings flapping against the golden sky. Over my shoulder comes the sizzle and smell of frying bacon.

25 That's the way it was this morning.

Understanding Meaning

1. What does Abbey mean by the "one true home"?
2. How would you *define* Abbey's concept of a "homing sentiment"?
3. How comfortable is Abbey's home? Does this conflict with our usual concept of the ideal home? What makes this place more of a home to Abbey than a suite at a resort hotel?
4. What are the most striking features of this location? What draws Abbey to this spot? Why is it the "most beautiful place on earth" in his eyes?
5. How does Abbey respond to his environment? What reactions does he wish to suppress?
6. *Critical Thinking:* How does Abbey's solitary confrontation with "inhuman" nature alter his perceptions and his sense of self? Does something draw people to experience or contemplate the desert, a mountain, or the sea in isolation? Can one achieve greater insights away from civilization?

Evaluating Strategy

1. How effective is the opening statement? Does a bold statement arouse attention, or can it appear too cliché?
2. How does Abbey view his role in nature?
3. *Other Modes:* Locate places where Abbey uses *narration* and *comparison* in creating a description of his favorite place. Is his real goal to describe or to tell a story?

Appreciating Language

1. Abbey uses words such as "iron lung," "tomb," "jail," and "cave" to describe his trailer. What is his intent in using these connotations? Would the essay have a different focus if he sentimentalized his home as a "snug cabin"? Would it alter the role of nature in the essay?
2. What words does Abbey use to describe the arches? Would his language impress an urban reader?

Connections across the Disciplines

1. Does Abbey share a similar view of nature with Gretel Ehrlich (page 197)? Do they share a sense of awe?
2. *Critical Thinking:* N. Scott Momaday (page 137) returns to a remote region associated with his cultural heritage. Abbey travels to a landscape with no personal associations. How do their responses to nature differ?

Writing Suggestions

1. Write a short essay describing your "most beautiful place on earth." Review Abbey's opening paragraph, in which he states that even a waterfront alley in Hoboken can be beautiful. If you choose an unconventional location, use imagery to explain why you find beauty here. You may wish to focus as much on your own feelings as on the place itself.
2. *Collaborative Writing:* Discuss Abbey's essay with a group of students. Ask members to agree or disagree with this statement:

   Abbey's love of nature implies a dislike of human beings. He seems to suggest that people are inherently dangerous to the environment as if they were alien creatures and not inhabitants of the same planet as the ravens he wishes he could speak to. Something is disturbing about someone who craves isolation, as if he alone can appreciate the natural world.

Record comments and develop a common reaction to this suggestion. If members disagree, they may develop group pro and con statements.

BLENDING THE MODES

E. B. WHITE

Elwyn Brooks White (1899–1985) was born in Mount Vernon, New York, and attended Cornell University. He was a regular contributor to the New Yorker *and* Harper's *magazine for fifty years. His articles achieved a reputation for their wit and style. White assisted Edmund Strunk in revising his popular book on writing,* Elements of Style. *He also gained popularity as a writer of children's literature. His books* Stuart Little *and* Charlotte's Web *have become classics.*

Once More to the Lake

First published in Harper's *in 1941, "Once More to the Lake" describes White's nostalgic return to a boyhood vacation spot. As you read the essay, notice how White uses comparison and narration in developing his description.*

August 1941

1   One summer, along about 1904, my father rented a camp on a lake in Maine and took us all there for the month of August. We all got ringworm from some kittens and had to rub Pond's Extract on our arms and legs night and morning, and my father rolled over in a canoe with all his clothes on; but outside of that the vacation was a success and from then on none of us ever thought there was any place in the world like that lake in Maine. We returned summer after summer—always on August 1 for one month. I have since become a salt-water man, but sometimes in summer there are days when the restlessness of the tides and the fearful cold of the sea water and the incessant wind that blows across the afternoon and into the evening make me wish for the placidity of a lake in the woods. A few weeks ago this feeling got so strong I bought myself a couple of bass hooks and a spinner and returned to the lake where we used to go, for a week's fishing and to revisit old haunts.

2   I took along my son, who had never had any fresh water up his nose and who had seen lily pads only from train windows. On the journey over to the lake I began to wonder what it would be like. I wondered how time would have marred this unique, this holy spot—the coves and streams, the hills that the sun set behind, the camps and the paths

behind the camps. I was sure that the tarred road would have found it out, and I wondered in what other ways it would be desolated. It is strange how much you can remember about places like that once you allow your mind to return into the grooves that lead back. You remember one thing, and that suddenly reminds you of another thing. I guess I remembered clearest of all the early mornings, when the lake was cool and motionless, remembered how the bedroom smelled of the lumber it was made of and of the wet woods whose scent entered through the screen. The partitions in the camp were thin and did not extend clear to the top of the rooms, and as I was always the first up I would dress softly so as not to wake the others, and sneak out into the sweet outdoors and start out in the canoe, keeping close along the shore in the long shadows of the pines. I remembered being very careful never to rub my paddle against the gunwale for fear of disturbing the stillness of the cathedral.

3   The lake had never been what you would call a wild lake. There were cottages sprinkled around the shores, and it was in farming country although the shores of the lake were quite heavily wooded. Some of the cottages were owned by nearby farmers, and you would live at the shore and eat your meals at the farmhouse. That's what our family did. But although it wasn't wild, it was a fairly large and undisturbed lake and there were places in it that, to a child at least, seemed infinitely remote and primeval.

4   I was right about the tar: it led to within half a mile of the shore. But when I got back there, with my boy, and we settled into a camp near a farmhouse and into the kind of summertime I had known, I could tell that it was going to be pretty much the same as it had been before—I knew it, lying in bed the first morning, smelling the bedroom and hearing the boy sneak quietly out and go off along the shore in a boat. I began to sustain the illusion that he was I, and therefore, by simple transposition, that I was my father. This sensation persisted, kept cropping up all the time we were there. It was not an entirely new feeling, but in this setting it grew much stronger. I seemed to be living a dual existence. I would be in the middle of some simple act, I would be picking up a bait box or laying down a table fork, or I would be saying something, and suddenly it would be not I but my father who was saying the words or making the gesture. It gave me a creepy sensation.

5   We went fishing the first morning. I felt the same damp moss covering the worms in the bait can, and saw the dragonfly alight on the tip of my rod as it hovered a few inches from the surface of the water. It

was the arrival of this fly that convinced me beyond any doubt that everything was as it always had been, that the years were a mirage and that there had been no years. The small waves were the same, chucking the rowboat under the chin as we fished at anchor, and the boat was the same boat, the same color green and the ribs broken in the same places, and under the floorboards the same fresh-water leavings and débris—the dead hellgrammite, the wisps of moss, the rusty discarded fish-hook, the dried blood from yesterday's catch. We stared silently at the tips of our rods, at the dragonflies that came and went. I lowered the tip of mine into the water, tentatively, pensively dislodging the fly, which darted two feet away, poised, darted two feet back, and came to rest again a little farther up the rod. There had been no years between the ducking of this dragonfly and the other one—the one that was part of memory. I looked at the boy, who was silently watching his fly, and it was my hands that held his rod, my eyes watching. I felt dizzy and didn't know which rod I was at the end of.

6   We caught two bass, hauling them in briskly as though they were mackerel, pulling them over the side of the boat in a businesslike manner without any landing net, and stunning them with a blow on the back of the head. When we got back for a swim before lunch, the lake was exactly where we had left it, the same number of inches from the dock, and there was only the merest suggestion of a breeze. This seemed an utterly enchanted sea, this lake you could leave to its own devices for a few hours and come back to, and find it had not stirred, this constant and trustworthy body of water. In the shallows, the dark, water-soaked sticks and twigs, smooth and old, were undulating in clusters on the bottom against the clean ribbed sand, and the track of the mussel was plain. A school of minnows swam by, each minnow with its small individual shadow, doubling the attendance, so clear and sharp in the sunlight. Some of the other campers were in swimming, along the shore, one of them with a cake of soap, and the water felt thin and clear and unsubstantial. Over the years there had been this person with the cake of soap, this cultist, and here he was. There had been no years.

7   Up to the farmhouse to dinner through the teeming, dusty field, the road under our sneakers was only a two-track road. The middle track was missing, the one with the marks of the hooves and the splotches of dried, flaky manure. There had always been three tracks to choose from in choosing which track to walk in; now the choice was narrowed down to two. For a moment I missed terribly the middle alternative.

But the way led past the tennis court, and something about the way it lay there in the sun reassured me; the tape had loosened along the backline, the alleys were green with plantains and other weeds, and the net (installed in June and removed in September) sagged in the dry noon, and the whole place steamed with midday heat and hunger and emptiness. There was a choice of pie for dessert, and one was blueberry and one was apple, and the waitresses were the same country girls, there having been no passage of time, only the illusion of it as in a dropped curtain—the waitresses were still fifteen; their hair had been washed, that was the only difference—they had been to the movies and seen the pretty girls with the clean hair.

8   Summertime, oh summertime, pattern of life indelible, the fade-proof lake, the woods unshatterable, the pasture with the sweetfern and the juniper forever and ever, summer without end; this was the background, and the life along the shore was the design, their tiny docks with the flagpole and the American flag floating against the white clouds in the blue sky, the little paths over the roots of the trees leading from camp to camp and the paths leading back to the outhouses and the can of lime for sprinkling, and at the souvenir counters at the store the miniature birch-bark canoes and the postcards that showed things looking a little better than they looked. This was the American family at play, escaping the city heat, wondering whether the newcomers in the camp at the head of the cove were "common" or "nice," wondering whether it was true that the people who drove up for Sunday dinner at the farmhouse were turned away because there wasn't enough chicken.

9   It seemed to me, as I kept remembering all this, that those times and those summers had been infinitely precious and worth saving. There had been jollity and peace and goodness. The arriving (at the beginning of August) had been so big a business in itself, at the railway station the farm wagon drawn up, the first smell of the pine-laden air, the first glimpse of the smiling farmer, and the great importance of the trunks and your father's enormous authority in such matters, and the feel of the wagon under you for the long ten-mile haul, and at the top of the last long hill catching the first view of the lake after eleven months of not seeing this cherished body of water. The shouts and cries of the other campers when they saw you, and the trunks to be unpacked, to give up their rich burden. (Arriving was less exciting nowadays, when you sneaked up in your car and parked it under a tree

near the camp and took out the bags and in five minutes it was all over, no fuss, no loud wonderful fuss about trunks.)

10   Peace and goodness and jollity. The only thing that was wrong now, really, was the sound of the place, an unfamiliar nervous sound of the outboard motors. This was the note that jarred, the one thing that would sometimes break the illusion and set the years moving. In those other summertimes all the motors were inboard; and when they were at a little distance, the noise they made was a sedative, an ingredient of summer sleep. They were one-cylinder and two-cylinder engines, and some were make-and-break and some were jump-spark, but they all made a sleepy sound across the lake. The one-lungers throbbed and fluttered, and the twin-cylinder ones purred and purred, and that was a quiet sound, too. But now the campers all had outboards. In the daytime, in the hot mornings, these motors made a petulant, irritable sound; at night, in the still evening when the afterglow lit the water, they whined about one's ears like mosquitoes. My boy loved our rented outboard, and his great desire was to achieve single-handed mastery over it, and authority, and he soon learned the trick of choking it a little (but not too much), and the adjustment of the needle valve. Watching him I would remember the things you could do with the old one-cylinder engine with the heavy flywheel, how you could have it eating out of your hand if you got really close to it spiritually. Motor-boats in those days didn't have clutches, and you would make a landing by shutting off the motor at the proper time and coasting in with a dead rudder. But there was a way of reversing them, if you learned the trick, by cutting the switch and putting it on again exactly on the final dying revolution of the flywheel, so that it would kick back against the compression and begin reversing. Approaching a dock in a strong following breeze, it was difficult to slow up sufficiently by the ordinary coasting method, and if a boy felt he had complete mastery over his motor, he was tempted to keep it running beyond its time and then reverse it a few feet from the dock. It took a cool nerve, because if you threw the switch a twentieth of a second too soon you would catch the flywheel when it still had speed enough to go up past center, and the boat would leap ahead, charging bull-fashion at the dock.

11   We had a good week at camp. The bass were biting well and the sun shone endlessly, day after day. We would be tired at night and lie down in the accumulated heat of the little bedrooms after the long hot day and the breeze would stir almost imperceptibly outside and the

smell of the swamp drift in through the rusty screens. Sleep would come easily and in the morning the red squirrel would be on the roof, tapping out his gay routine. I kept remembering everything, lying in bed in the mornings—the small steamboat that had a long rounded stem like the lip of a Ubangi, and how quietly she ran on the moonlight sails, when the older boys played their mandolins and the girls sang and we ate doughnuts dipped in sugar, and how sweet the music was on the water in the shining night, and what it had felt like to think about girls then. After breakfast we would go up to the store and the things were in the same place—the minnows in a bottle, the plugs and spinners disarranged and pawed over by the youngsters from the boys' camp, the Fig Newtons and the Beeman's gum. Outside, the road was tarred and cars stood in front of the store. Inside, all was just as it had always been, except there was more Coca-Cola and not so much Moxie and root beer and birch beer and sarsaparilla. We would walk out with the bottle of pop apiece and sometimes the pop would backfire up our noses and hurt. We explored the streams, quietly, where the turtles slid off the sunny logs and dug their way into the soft bottom; and we lay on the town wharf and fed worms to the tame bass. Everywhere we went I had trouble making out which I was, the one walking at my side, the one walking in my pants.

12   One afternoon while we were there at that lake a thunderstorm came up. It was like the revival of an old melodrama that I had seen long ago with childish awe. The second-act climax of the drama of the electrical disturbance over a lake in America had not changed in any important respect. This was the big scene, still the big scene. The whole thing was so familiar, the first feeling of oppression and heat and a general air around camp of not wanting to go very far away. In mid-afternoon (it was all the same) a curious darkening of the sky, and a lull in everything that had made life tick; and then the way the boats suddenly swung the other way at their moorings with the coming of a breeze out of the new quarter, and the premonitory rumble. Then the kettle drum, then the snare, then the bass drum and cymbals, then the crackling light against the dark, and the gods grinning and licking their chops in the hills. Afterward the calm, the rain steadily rustling in the calm lake, the return of light and hope and spirits, and the campers running out in joy and relief to go swimming in the rain, their bright cries perpetuating the deathless joke about how they were getting simply drenched, and the children screaming with delight at the new sensation of bathing in the rain, and the joke about getting drenched

linking the generations in a strong indestructible chain. And the comedian who waded in carrying an umbrella.

13   When the others went swimming my son said he was going in, too. He pulled his dripping trunks from the line where they had hung all through the shower and wrung them out. Languidly, and with no thought of going in, I watched him, his hard little body, skinny and bare, saw him wince slightly as he pulled up around his vitals the small, soggy, icy garment. As he buckled the swollen belt, suddenly my groin felt the chill of death.

Understanding Meaning

1.   What is White's purpose in describing the resort? What lessons or observations does this journey reveal to him?
2.   What are the key features of the lake? How much of it had changed in forty years?
3.   White comments in the last line that he "felt the chill of death." How does viewing his son give White a sense of his mortality?
4.   *Critical Thinking*: What role does time play in this description? What is White saying about the passage of time, the passage of life? How does watching a child grow affect a parent?

Evaluating Strategy

1.   How does White use his son as a device for recalling his own youth?
2.   Descriptions of places can become tedious lists of geographical details. How does White create action and bring the lake to life?
3.   Writers usually rely on visual details to develop a description of a place. Locate places where White uses other sensory impressions. How effective are they?
4.   *Other Modes*: Locate passages where White uses *comparison* and *narration*. How do they develop the essay? Could you classify this essay as *narration*?

Appreciating Language

1.   White uses figurative language associated with non-natural objects to describe the lake. For instance, he describes the lake as having the "stillness of a cathedral" and uses references to musical instruments—"the kettle drum, then the snare, then the bass drum and cymbals"—to capture the sound of a storm. What do these word choices suggest about his audience?

2. White uses brand names throughout his essay. What effect do references to Moxie, Fig Newtons, and Coca-Cola have?

Connections across the Disciplines

1. How does White's attitude toward the lake compare to Abbey's view of the desert in "The First Morning" (page 143)? Do they have a similiar view of nature?
2. Review John Ciardi's essay "What Is Happiness?" (page 192). Does White's journey to a boyhood retreat suggest an attempt to find happiness in the security of the past?

Writing Suggestions

1. Write an essay describing a place you revisited after a considerable lapse of time. Comment on what has and has not changed. Use as many sensory details as you can.
2. *Collaborative Writing:* Work with a group of students who share a common memory of a historical event or recent campus incident. Have each member write a brief narrative. Read each paper aloud to see how people recall and interpret events differently.

WRITING BEYOND THE CLASSROOM

FRANK PILIPP AND CHARLES SHULL

Abstracts are brief summaries describing articles and reports. The fields of chemistry, biology, law, medicine, literature, and psychology each have specialized abstracts that serve as a valuable source to students and researchers. Most abstracts are now available on computer. This abstract describes an article analyzing how the subject of AIDS has been treated by TV movies. Other abstracts describe articles on everything from solar power to plastic surgery. As you review this entry, consider how abstracts can help students locate sources for research papers and skim current scholarship. See page 343 for the full article.

TV Movies of the First Decade of AIDS (Abstract)

1 Database: Expanded Academic Index
Subject: AIDS (disease) in motion pictures

2 TV movies of the first decade of AIDS. (American Values and Images)

3 Journal of Popular Film and Television, Spring 1993 v21 n1 p19(8).

4 Author: Frank Pilipp and Charles Shull

5 Abstract: The decade of 1983–1993 has produced several full-length feature films which respond to the AIDS epidemic. Three of them, 'As Is,' 'Andre's Mother,' and 'An Early Frost' undoubtedly portray the virus as non-partisan when it comes to gender, color, or sexual orientation, although they fail to destroy the image of AIDS as being a purely homosexual disease. The disease instead is viewed as punishment inflicted on the main characters and their families for their violation of middle-class norms and values.

6 Subjects: Gays—Portrayals, depictions, etc.
Motion pictures—Criticism, interpretation, etc.
AIDS (disease) in motion pictures—Criticism, interpretation, etc.

7   Features: illustration; photograph

8   AN: 14558418

Understanding Meaning

1. What information is contained in the abstract? How helpful would it be if you were researching the way television has responded to AIDS?
2. Is the abstract objective?

Evaluating Strategy

1. What problems does an abstract writer have in reducing an eight-page article to a single paragraph?
2. Should an abstract writer inject subjective opinion?

Appreciating Language

1. How objective is the language of the abstract?
2. Should an abstract be devoid of figurative language?

Connections across the Disciplines

1. At the library locate abstracts in your field and review summaries of several articles. How would they be helpful in doing research?
2. Read the full article (page 343). How successfully does this abstract summarize Pilipp and Shull's article?

Writing Suggestions

1. Select one of the articles in this book and draft an abstract. Try to capture the writer's thesis and main support in a single paragraph.
2. *Collaborative Writing:* Discuss this abstract with a number of students who have read the full article. How effective is this summary? What points do students feel have been omitted?

Want ads describe the ideal candidate for a job opening. This ad, which appeared in the New Orleans Times-Picayune, *presents a job description for a sales representative.*

3M Pharmaceutical Sales Representative Want Ad

3M **Sales Representative**
Pharmaceutical Products
3M Pharmaceuticals has an immediate need for an experienced sales professional to represent our products to physicians, pharmacies, hospitals and managed care facilities. These products include prescription medications related to the treatment of arthritic, cardiovascular and pulmonary conditions. This position will be based in New Orleans and will require overnight travel.

We prefer a college degree and 2+ years successful outside sales experience. Medical sales experience is preferred. Excellent communications and interpersonal skills are required. We provide base salary plus bonus, company car, complete business expenses and an attractive benefits package.

For confidential consideration, send <u>two (2)</u> copies of your resume to the below address by August 16, 1994. Candidates selected for consideration will be notified by September 2, 1994. No telephone inquiries or employment agency referrals please.

NAS REPLY SERVICE
Dept #7MP1089   One Appletree Square   Minneapolis, MN 55425
We Are An Equal Opportunity Employer M/F/D/V

Understanding Meaning

1. What are the requirements for this position?
2. What does this ad suggest about the reader 3M hopes to reach?
3. *Critical Thinking:* What are the limits of any want ad? Can a job be fully described in a few paragraphs? Why can't employers address all their interests and concerns?

Evaluating Strategy

1. Why does the ad first describe the job and then list the requirements?
2. Why is it important for an employer to promise applicants "confidential consideration"?

Appreciating Language

1. What words does the ad use to describe the ideal candidate?
2. Some ads promise applicants "huge commissions" and demand "hard charging" people. What does the absence of this kind of language suggest about this employer?

Connections across the Disciplines

1. Study want ads in your local newspaper. What common words stand out? How do employers describe the positions and the desired candidates? Do you see trends in the job market?

Writing Suggestions

1. Write a want ad for a job you once had. Try to model yours after ones you have seen in the newspaper. Keep your ad as short as possible.
2. *Collaborative Writing:* Work with a group of students and write a want ad together. Imagine you are hiring a part-time employee to act as secretary for your writing group. Determine the skills needed, the major duties, and how the ad should be worded. If members have differences of opinion, craft more than one ad, and ask other students to choose the most effective ad.

Monica Ramos was born in New Orleans and worked as a nurse before entering advertising sales. Although she has never sold pharmaceuticals, she prepared this résumé to apply for the position advertised by 3M (page 161). Given her sales ability and experience working in a hospital, Ramos feels she is qualified for the position. Notice that her résumé uses bulleted lists of specific accomplishments to provide details that are easily read or skimmed.

The Résumé of Monica Ramos

1

MONICA RAMOS
1455 Josephine Street #12
New Orleans, Louisiana 70118
(504) 524-6580

2 OBJECTIVE   Pharmaceutical Sales

3 OVERVIEW   Three years experience in outside sales. Proven ability to secure new accounts in competitive markets. Five years experience in cardiac and pulmonary patient care. Knowledgeable in cardiac medications. Skilled in communicating with physicians and hospital staff.

4 EXPERIENCE   CRESCENT CITY MAGAZINE,
   1993–Present New Orleans, LA
                 Account representative selling advertising space in upscale magazine with 50,000 circulation.
                 * Developed 300 active accounts including hospitals, nursing homes, HMO's, clinics, and drug stores.
                 * Personally developed restaurant/ entertainment section, selling ads to

100 area restaurants worth $200,000 annually.
* Consistently rank in top 3 of 15 sales reps.
* Generated 65 new accounts in first three months.
* Directly assisted vice president of Charity Hospital in design of four-page insert.

5   1989–1993   TULANE UNIVERSITY MEDICAL CENTER, New Orleans, LA
Nurse in 25-bed intensive care unit specializing in critical cardiac and pulmonary care.
* Worked directly with physicians, cardiologists, and cardiovascular surgeons.
* Administered full range of cardiac medications.
* Attended in-service seminars presented by pharmaceutical representatives.
* Represented hospital on regional and state planning committees.

6   EDUCATION   LOUISIANA STATE UNIVERSITY MEDICAL CENTER—NEW ORLEANS
B.S. Nursing, 1989

7   SALES   SALES MANAGEMENT INSTITUTE, New Orleans, LA
    TRAINING
    1994–1995   * Attended seminars on networking, presentation skills, and closing strategies.

8   VOLUNTEER   GREATER NEW ORLEANS YWCA
    WORK   Conduct cardiac health/stress management workshops

9   References Available on Request

Understanding Meaning

1. Compare this résumé to the 3M want ad (page 161). Does it address the employer's needs?
2. What skills and experiences does Monica Ramos highlight? What are her important attributes?

Evaluating Strategy

1. One study revealed that the average executive devotes nine seconds to each résumé on initial screening. Does this résumé communicate its main points in a few seconds? Would it make a reader stop skimming and start reading?
2. How is the information arranged? Is it clear and easy to follow?

Appreciating Language

1. What is the tone of the résumé? How do the words portray the applicant?
2. What device does Monica Ramos use to convey a sense of action?

Connections across the Disciplines

1. Review this résumé after reading the article "Resumes That Rate a Second Look" (page 471). How does this résumé rate?

Writing Suggestions

1. Write your own résumé, either a current one or one as if you were prepared to graduate this semester.
2. *Collaborative Writing:* Meet with a group of students and have each member supply a résumé. Discuss the merits of each résumé you review. Talk about problems you have encountered. Take notes to improve your own résumé. Your library or placement office may offer guides and computer programs to help you develop your résumé.

STRATEGIES FOR WRITING DESCRIPTION

1. **Determine your purpose.** What is your goal—to entertain a general audience or to provide information to colleagues, employees, superiors, or customers? What are the most important details needed to support your purpose?

2. **Define your role.** If you are expressing personal opinion, you are free to add subjective elements to your writing. You may wish to include yourself in the piece of writing by making personal references and writing in the first person. If you are writing as a representative of a larger body, objective language is usually more appropriate.

3. **Consider your audience.** Which type of description would best suit your readers—subjective impressions or objective facts? What needs and expectations does your audience have? What details, facts, statistics, or descriptions will influence readers the most?

4. **Review the discipline or writing situation.** Determine if you should use technical or specialized terminology. If you are writing for a profession, academic discipline, government agency, or corporation, use standard methods of developing ideas.

5. **Select details.** Having determined the context, select details that emphasize your purpose, impress your audience, and follow any guidelines in your discipline. Descriptions should have focus. Eliminate details that may be interesting in themselves but do not serve your purpose.

6. **Organize details in an effective manner.** Good description is more than a collection of details. To be effective, your writing should be logically organized. You may organize details spatially by describing a house room by room or a city neighborhood by neighborhood. You may organize details in order of importance. If you use objective and subjective description, these details can alternate or be placed in separate sections.

7. **Avoid unnecessary detail or mechanical organization.** Descriptions have focus. A description of your apartment does not have to list every piece of furniture. Explain how each room is decorated, or provide dimensions. In general avoid writing descriptions that draw unnecessary attention to mechanical arrangements:

> *On the left-hand wall* is a bookcase. *To the right of the bookcase* is a stereo. *Around the corner of the stereo* stands an antique aquarium filled with tropical fish. *Above the aquarium* is a large seascape painting. Model ships line the window sill. A cabinet *to the right of the window* is filled with seashells.

8. **Allow details to create a dominant impression.** A subjective description of a room can focus on a single theme:

Although I live hundreds of miles from the ocean, my apartment has a seagoing motif. Beneath a sweeping seascape, a large antique aquarium dominates the living room, its colorful tropical fish flashing among rocks and shells I collected in Florida. Miniature schooners, windjammers, and ketches line the windowsill. The ornate glass cabinet intended for china houses my prize collection of Hawaiian seashells.

SUGGESTED TOPICS FOR DESCRIPTIVE WRITING

General Assignments

Write a description on any of the following topics. Your description may contain passages demonstrating other modes, such as comparison or cause and effect. Select details carefully. Determine whether your description should rely on factual, objective support or subjective impressions. In choosing diction, be aware of the impact of connotation.

- Your first apartment
- The people who gather in a place you frequent—a coffee shop, store, tavern, library, or student union
- Your boss or professor
- The most desirable/least desirable place to live in your community
- The most dangerous situation you have faced
- The type of man/woman you find attractive
- The type of relationship you find most desirable
- The most serious environmental problem in your area
- The most interesting or most unconventional person you have met in the past year
- The best/worst party you have attended

Writing in Context

1. Imagine that your college has asked you to write a description of the campus for a brochure designed to recruit students. Your depiction should be easy to read and create a favorable impression.
2. Assume you write a column for an alternative campus newspaper. Develop a sarcastic description of the campus, the college administration, the faculty, or the student body.

3. Write an open letter to the student body of your high school describing what college life is like.
4. Imagine you are trying to sell your car. Write two brief ads, one designed for a campus flyer and the other for a newspaper.

STUDENT PAPER: DESCRIPTION

This is the second version of a descriptive paper a student wrote in response to an assignment calling for "a brief description of a person, place, or thing." In the first draft, the student attempted to provide an overall view of New Orleans' French Quarter. Dissatisfied with its superficiality, he decided to concentrate on a single feature of the city.

CITIES OF THE DEAD

1   From the freeway the tombs look like a collection of children's playhouses. The white mausoleums mimic spired churches, porticoed mansions, neo-classic banks, Greek temples. The more elaborate tombs are arranged in neat rows and are adorned with flowers. Humbler tombs, resembling concrete dog houses, are jammed haphazardly together like lost luggage.

2   Few graveyards are as famous as New Orleans' above-ground cemeteries. In the 1700s the city's earliest settlers buried their dead along the banks of the Mississippi. As the population grew, the city selected a plot of land near Rampart Street as a burial ground. The traditional practice of burying the dead caused problems in Louisiana's tropical climate and watery soil. The water table was so high that grave diggers frequently struck water after two feet. Coffins bobbed to the surface and had to be sunk. Decaying bodies posed a major health threat, especially in summer. As a result, the dead had to be interred above ground in "vaults."

3   Unlike tombs in other cities, the vaults of New Orleans are reusable. Following a burial, the coffin is sealed in the vault until the body decomposes. Later the remaining bones are removed and placed in a lower crypt, leaving space for a new coffin. This way a single vault can serve a family for generations. Many civic organizations offered their mem-

bers a cheaper alternative to the family vault by building attached tombs. Often several stories tall, these "apartment buildings" provided rows of tombs called "ovens."

4   Those resting in the three cemeteries, St. Louis Nos. one, two, and three, reflect the city's colorful history. Among the bankers and former mayors lie the remains of Dominique You, a pirate; the chess player Paul Morphy; and Alexander Milne, a noted philanthropist.

5   But perhaps the most famous and mysterious tomb belongs to Marie Laveau, still revered by many as the Voodoo Queen. Loyal followers of Marie Laveau enact elaborate graveyard rituals to curry favor. Seeking her blessing, they turn around three times, tap the slab of the tomb three times, and make a cross with the edge of a brick kept atop the tomb. Visitors leave flowers and light votive candles, while others place "hoodoo money"—two pennies or a dime and a penny—in the flower holders flanking the tomb of one of the most famous residents in the City of the Dead.

Questions for Review and Revision

1. How effective is the title?
2. The student describes the tombs by comparing them to Greek temples and dog houses. How effective is this device? Would the essay benefit from including more of the tombs' physical details?
3. What method does the student use to organize the essay? How important are paragraph breaks?
4. How effective is the ending? Would you like to see a more developed conclusion?
5. Throughout the essay the student places specialized terms like "ovens" and "hoodoo money" in quotation marks. How effective are his definitions? Are they clearly stated?
6. Read the paper aloud. What revisions would you make?

Writing Suggestions

1. Write a brief description of a feature unique to your hometown. Is there a piece of local history that visitors overlook or find puzzling? Present as many sensory details as possible.

2. *Collaborative Writing:* Discuss this essay with a group of students. Have each member volunteer opinions on its strengths and weaknesses. Do members suggest revisions or a need for added detail?

DESCRIPTION CHECKLIST

Before submitting your paper, review these points.

1. Have you limited your topic?

2. Do your supporting details suit your context? Should they be objective, subjective, or a blend?

3. Is your description focused and clearly organized, or is it only a random list of facts and observations?

4. Have you avoided including unnecessary details and awkward constructions?

5. Does sensory detail include more than sight? Can you add impressions of taste, touch, sound, or smell?

6. Do you avoid overly general terms and focus on specific impressions? Have you created dominant impressions?

7. Do you *show* rather than *tell*? Can you add action to your description to keep it from being static?

8. Do you keep a consistent point of view?

9. READ YOUR PAPER ALOUD. How does it sound? Do any sections need expansion? Are there irrelevant details to be deleted or awkward expressions to be revised?

WebTutor

See www.harcourtcollege.com/english/sundance for information on writing description.

4

DEFINITION

ESTABLISHING MEANING

WHAT IS DEFINITION?

Effective communication requires that writers and readers have a shared language. Words and ideas must be *defined* clearly to eliminate confusion and misinterpretation. Definitions limit or explain the meaning of a term or concept. As a college student you have probably devoted much of your time to learning new words and their definitions. Fields such as chemistry, psychology, sociology, economics, law, and anatomy have technical terms that must be mastered in order to communicate within the discipline.

Clearly stated definitions play a critical role in professional and business writing. In order to prevent confusion, conflict, and litigation, many union contracts, insurance policies, sales agreements, and leases include definitions so all parties will share a common understanding of important terms. Government documents and business proposals contain glossaries to familiarize readers with new or abstract terms. Failing to understand a definition can be costly. A tenant who does not understand a landlord's definition of "excessive noise" may face eviction. The car buyer who misinterprets the manufacturer's definition of "normal use" can void his or her warranty.

The term *definition* leads most people to think of a dictionary. But defining entails more than looking something up. Definitions are not always precise or universally accepted. Distinctly different types of definitions exist. To be an effective writer in college and your future profession, it is important to appreciate the range of definitions:

- **Standard definitions** are universally accepted and rarely subject to change. Words such as *tibia, dolphin, uranium, felony, turbine,* and *rifle* have exact meanings that are understood and shared by scholars, professionals, and the general public. Doctors, nurses, paramedics, and football coaches, for example, all recognize *tibia* as a specific bone in the body. Though different state legislatures might disagree on which specific crime constitutes a *felony,* they all accept its general concept.
- **Regulatory definitions** are officially designated terms and are subject to change. The National Football League, Internal Revenue Service (IRS), Federal Aviation Administration, and Federal Communications Commission, school boards, labor organizations, the Catholic Church, and insurance companies issue definitions to guide policy, control operations, and make decisions. The IRS definition of *deductible meal allowance* can change yearly. One health insurance company may pay for a liver transplant while another carrier refuses, defining the procedure *experimental.* Regulatory definitions may be universally accepted, but they can change or be limited to a specific region or discipline. The building codes of New York and San Francisco may have varying definitions of what buildings are *structurally sound.* The medical definition of *insanity* varies greatly from the court-accepted, legal definition.
- **Evolving definitions** reflect changes in community attitudes, social values, governmental policy, and scientific research. In the nineteenth century corporal punishment was a routine feature of public school discipline. Today the same actions would be defined as *child abuse.* The term *date rape* defines incidents that generations ago would not be viewed as criminal assaults. Decades ago medical and psychology texts defined *homosexuality* as a mental disorder. Evolving definitions track social change and rarely shift as abruptly as regulatory definitions.
- **Qualifying definitions** limit meanings of words or concepts that are abstract or subject to dispute. How does one define an *alcoholic?* At what point do doctors label a patient *obese* or *senile?* Which young people are labeled *juvenile delinquents?* How does one define *genius?* In some fields organizations provide definitions. The American Medical Association may offer a definition of *alcoholism.* But unlike a regulatory term, physicians and researchers are free to dispute it and apply a different meaning altogether. Some definitions are hotly debated. Researchers, politicians, and social commentators continually argue whether drug addiction and alcoholism should be defined as a *disability,* which would entitle people to receive benefits.
- **Cultural definitions** are shaped by the history, values, and attitudes of a national, ethnic, or religious group. Just as evolving definitions alter over time, cultural definitions differ from group to group. In some countries it is customary to offer cash gifts to officials as a *tribute.* In the United States the

same action would be defined as an illegal *bribe*. People around the world embrace *freedom* but define it very differently. For most Americans *freedom* is defined in personal terms, meaning freedom of individual movement and expression. In other countries, people may define *freedom* in national terms, as protecting the independence and security of their homeland even if it means censorship and restricted personal liberties.

- **Personal definitions** are used by writers to express individual interpretations of words or ideas. Your concept of a good parent would be a personal definition. A writer can frame an entire essay in terms of a personal definition, such as John Ciardi's "What Is Happiness?" (page 192), or simply establish a series of personal definitions at the outset of a narrative or persuasive paper. Writers often use personal definition as a method of stating their opinions.

Methods of Definition

Definitions can be established using a number of techniques:

1. **Defining through synonyms** is the simplest method of providing meaning for a word. Glossaries and dictionaries customarily define technical terms or foreign words with synonyms. *Costal* refers to *ribs*. A *siesta* can be translated as a *nap*. A *casement* can be explained as a *window*.
2. **Defining by description** provides details about a word or subject and gives readers a sense of what it might look, feel, taste, smell, or sound like. Defining a *costrel* as *a small flask with a loop or loops that is suspended from a belt* provides readers with a clear picture. Descriptive definitions also can demonstrate how something operates. An *airbag* can be defined as *a rapidly inflated cushion designed to protect automobile passengers in a collision*.
3. **Defining by example** provides specific illustrations to establish meaning. A *felony* can be defined as *a serious crime such as murder, rape, or burglary*. Examples can establish meaning through identification. Telling a fourth-grade class that an *adjective is a word that modifies a noun* will not be as effective as providing examples children can easily recognize—*red, fast, tall, silly, old-fashioned, hot*. Complex or abstract concepts are easier to comprehend if defined by example. Income tax instructions include numerous examples to define what is and is not deductible.
4. **Defining by comparison** uses analogies readers can understand to provide meaning to something less familiar. A television reporter covering a space mission defined NASA terminology using comparisons viewers would readily understand. To explain the term *power down*, she remarked that the astronauts were *conserving power by turning off nonessential electrical*

devices, much like switching off the radio and windshield wipers on a car. Because they can oversimplify complex ideas, comparative definitions must be used carefully.

5. **Extended definitions** qualify or limit the meaning of abstract, disputed, or highly complex words or concepts. Words such as *sin, love,* and *racism* cannot be adequately explained through synonyms, brief descriptions, or examples. A full description may require several paragraphs. The *yucca* can be defined as a *spear-leafed desert plant,* but, to explain its significance to the Navajo, Terry Tempest Williams writes an entire essay (page 203).

The Purpose of Definition

Definitions generally serve to establish meaning, to provide a common or shared understanding. But they also can be persuasive. Evolving definitions frequently indicate a break with past beliefs and suggest alternative interpretations. The first psychiatrists who defined *homosexuality* in terms of *sexual orientation* rather than as *deviancy, mental disorder,* or *sexual perversion* were clearly trying to persuade their readers to change their attitudes. In "Deafness as Culture" (page 212) Edward Dolnick explains that many deaf people prefer to define themselves as members of a distinct *culture* rather than as people sharing a *handicap.*

To transform public attitudes, writers frequently urge readers to redefine something, to change their perceptions and see striking a child as *abuse* instead of *spanking* or to accept graffiti as *street art* and not *vandalism.* Definitions can play a critical role in shaping opinions and making arguments. Drug addicts, for instance, can be defined in legalistic terms and viewed as *criminals* who should be imprisoned or depicted in medical terms as *sufferers* needing treatment.

Definition in Context

The way writers define subjects depends greatly on context. In defining *depression* for a marketing brochure, a psychotherapist directs an explanation to prospective clients:

> Depression is an internal state—a feeling of sadness, loss, "the blues," deep disappointment. *When it is more severe, you may have feelings of irritability, touchiness, guilt, self-reproach, loss of self-esteem, worthlessness, hopelessness, helplessness, and even thoughts of death and suicide.*

The definition is addressed to the reader, using the word "you," and focuses on personal "feelings" stated in general terms. In contrast, Jessica Kuper's *Encyclopedia of Psychology* offers a definition for mental health professionals:

> *Depression* is a term used to describe a mood, a symptom, and syndromes of affective disorders. As a mood, it refers to a transient state of feeling sad, blue, forlorn, cheerless, unhappy, and/or down. As a symptom, it refers to a complaint that often accompanies a group of biopsychosocial problems. In contrast, the depressive syndromes include a wide spectrum of psychobiological dysfunctions that vary in frequency, severity, and duration.

The inclusion of words such as "affective disorders" and "biopsychosocial" indicate that this definition is intended for a specialized audience familiar with technical terms.

STRATEGIES FOR READING DEFINITIONS

In reading the definition entries in this chapter, keep these questions in mind.

Meaning

1. Which type of definition is the author developing—standard, regulatory, evolving, qualifying, cultural, or personal?
2. What is the author's purpose—to provide a definition to establish common ground, to explain a complex issue, or to persuade readers to alter their opinions?
3. What audience is the writer addressing—a general reader or a specialist? Does the audience need to know the definitions in order to base decisions or guide future actions?
4. What is the nature of the discipline or writing situation? Is the writer working within a strictly regulated profession or the general marketplace of ideas?

Strategy

1. How does the writer define the word, object, or concept—through synonyms, descriptions, examples, or comparisons?

2. Is the definition limited to a specific incident or context, or can it be applied generally? Is the writer defining a particular person or a personality trait that could be shared by millions?

3. Does the writer supply personal examples, or does he or she rely on official sources to establish the definition?

Language

1. What role do word choice and connotation play in establishing the definition?

2. What do the tone and level of language reveal about the writer's purpose and intended audience?

Eileen Simpson is a psychotherapist who struggled for years to overcome dyslexia, a reading disorder that affects more than 20 million Americans. She is the author of several books, including Poets in Their Youth, *a memoir of her marriage to the poet John Berryman. Other books based on her personal experiences explored problems of children growing up without parents. This section comes from her 1979 book* Reversals: A Personal Account of Victory over Dyslexia.

Dyslexia

Simpson provides a standard definition of an existing term by examining its Greek and Latin roots and then demonstrates the effects dyslexia has on its victims. Notice that she supplies examples to help readers fully appreciate the implications of a widely misunderstood disorder.

1   Dyslexia (from the Greek, *dys,* faulty + *lexis,* speech, cognate with the Latin *legere,* to read), developmental or specific dyslexia as it's technically called, the disorder I suffered from, is the inability of otherwise normal children to read. Children whose intelligence is below average, whose vision or hearing is defective, who have not had proper schooling, or who are too emotionally disturbed or brain-damaged to profit from it belong in other diagnostic categories. They, too, may be unable to learn to read, but they cannot properly be called dyslexics.

2   For more than seventy years the essential nature of the affliction has been hotly disputed by psychologists, neurologists, and educators. It is generally agreed, however, that it is the result of a neurophysiological flaw in the brain's ability to process language. It is probably inherited, although some experts are reluctant to say this because they fear people will equate "inherited" with "untreatable." Treatable it certainly is: not a disease to be cured, but a malfunction that requires retraining.

3   Reading is the most complex skill a child entering school is asked to develop. What makes it complex, in part, is that letters are less constant than objects. A car seen from a distance, close to, from above, or below, or in a mirror still looks like a car even though the optical image

changes. The letters of the alphabet are more whimsical. Take the letter *b*. Turned upside down it becomes a *p*. Looked at in a mirror, it becomes a *d*. Capitalized, it becomes something quite different, a *B*. The *M* upside down is a *W*. The *E* flipped over becomes Ǝ. This reversed *E* is familiar to mothers of normal children who have just begun to go to school. The earliest examples of art work they bring home often have I LOVƎ YOU written on them.

4   Dyslexics differ from other children in that they read, spell, and write letters upside down and turned around far more frequently and for a much longer time. In what seems like a capricious manner, they also add letters, syllables, and words, or, just as capriciously, delete them. With palindromic words (was-saw, on-no), it is the order of the letters rather than the orientation they change. The new word makes sense, but not the sense intended. Then there are other words where the changed order— "sorty" for story—does not make sense at all.

5   The inability to recognize that g, *g*, and *G* are the same letter, the inability to maintain the orientation of the letters, to retain the order in which they appear, and to follow a line of text without jumping above or below it—all the results of the flaw—can make of an orderly page of words a dish of alphabet soup.

6   Also essential for reading is the ability to store words in memory and to retrieve them. This very particular kind of memory dyslexics lack. So, too, do they lack the ability to hear what the eye sees, and to see what they hear. If the eye sees "off," the ear must hear "off" and not "of," or "for." If the ear hears "saw," the eye must see that it looks like "saw" on the page and not "was." Lacking these skills, a sentence or paragraph becomes a coded message to which the dyslexic can't find the key.

7   It is only a slight exaggeration to say that those who learned to read without difficulty can best understand the labor reading is for a dyslexic by turning a page of text upside down and trying to decipher it.

8   While the literature is replete with illustrations of the way these children write and spell, there are surprisingly few examples of how they read. One, used for propaganda purposes to alert the public to the vulnerability of dyslexics in a literate society, is a sign warning that behind it are guard dogs trained to kill. The dyslexic reads:

9
Wurring
Guard God
Patoly

for

10
Warning
Guard Dog
Patrol

and, of course, remains ignorant of the danger.

11   Looking for a more commonplace example, and hoping to recapture the way I must have read in fourth grade, I recently observed dyslexic children at the Educational Therapy Clinic in Princeton, through the courtesy of Elizabeth Travers, the director. The first child I saw, eight-year-old Anna (whose red hair and brown eyes reminded me of myself at that age), had just come to the Clinic and was learning the alphabet. Given the story of "Little Red Riding Hood," which is at the second grade level, she began confidently enough, repeating the title from memory, then came to a dead stop. With much coaxing throughout, she read as follows:

12   Grandma you a top. Grandma [looks over at picture of Red Riding Hood]. Red Riding Hood [long pause, presses index finger into the paper. Looks at me for help. I urge: Go ahead] the a [puts head close to the page, nose almost touching] on Grandma

for

13   Once upon a time there was a little girl who had a red coat with a red hood. Etc.

14   "Grandma" was obviously a memory from having heard the story read aloud. Had I needed a reminder of how maddening my silences must have been to Miss Henderson, and how much patience is required to teach these children, Anna, who took almost ten minutes to read these few lines, furnished it. The main difference between Anna and me at that age is that Anna clearly felt no need to invent. She was perplexed, but not anxious, and seemed to have infinite tolerance for her long silences.

15   Toby, a nine-year-old boy with superior intelligence, had a year of tutoring behind him and could have managed "Little Red Riding Hood" with ease. His text was taken from the *Reader's Digest's Reading Skill Builder*, Grade IV. He read:

16   A kangaroo likes as if he had but truck together warm. His saw neck and head do not . . . [Here Toby sighed with fatigue] seem to feel happy back. They and tried and so every a tiger Moses and shoots from lonesome day and shouts and long shore animals. And each farm play with five friends . . .

17   He broke off with the complaint, "This is too hard. Do I have to read any more?"

18   His text was:

19   A kangaroo looks as if he had been put together wrong. His small neck and head do not seem to fit with his heavy back legs and thick tail. Soft eyes, a twinkly little nose and short front legs seem strange on such a large strong animal. And each front paw has five fingers, like a man's hand.

20   An English expert gives the following bizarre example of an adult dyslexic's performance:

21   An the bee-what in the tel mother of the biothodoodoo to the majoram or that emidrate eni eni Krastrei, mestriet to Ketra lotombreidi to ra from treido as that.

22   His text, taken from a college catalogue the examiner happened to have close at hand, was:

23   It shall be in the power of the college to examine or not every licentiate, previous to his admission to the fellowship, as they shall think fit.

24   That evening when I read aloud to Auntie for the first time, I probably began as Toby did, my memory of the classroom lesson keeping me close to the text. When memory ran out, and Auntie did not correct my errors, I began to invent. When she still didn't stop me, I may well have begun to improvise in the manner of this patient— anything to keep going and keep up the myth that I was reading—until Auntie brought the "gibberish" to a halt.

Understanding Meaning

1. What basic definition does Simpson provide? What misinterpretation does she note can occur if a condition is considered "inherited"?

2. How does Simpson summarize controversies in the field of research? What do scientists from different disciplines agree on?
3. What is the implication to dyslexics and their parents that dyslexia is "not a disease to be cured, but a malfunction that requires retraining"?
4. *Critical Thinking:* How can this disorder affect a child's development if it is not detected?

Evaluating Strategy

1. Why is it effective to provide an etymology of the word *dyslexia* at the opening? Does this help satisfy reader curiosity about a term many people have heard but do not fully understand?
2. How does Simpson's introduction of personal experience affect the definition? Does this add a human dimension to her definition, or does it detract from its objectivity? Would the inclusion of personal experience be appropriate in a textbook?
3. Do the examples of dyslexic reading dramatize the effects of this disorder? Would an explanation alone suffice to impress readers with the crippling effects of a reading disorder?
4. *Other Modes:* How does Simpson use *description* and *narration* to develop her definition? What role can stories or case studies provide readers seeking to understand a complex subject?

Appreciating Language

1. Simpson is defining a complex disorder. How does her language indicate that she is seeking to address a general audience? Would the vocabulary differ in a definition written for psychology students?
2. Simpson cites an example of a dyslexic reading a warning sign as "propaganda." Does the use of this word weaken her argument that dyslexia is a serious condition? Why or why not?
3. How does Simpson define the term "palindromic"?

Connections across the Disciplines

1. Simpson describes a disorder from the standpoint of a patient. How does her account differ from Oliver Sacks's account as a physician (page 81)?
2. *Compare* this article about a reading disorder with Edward Dolnick's commentary about deafness (page 212). What do they say about how people with disorders *define* themselves and how they function in a society designed by people with different abilities?

Writing Suggestions

1. Write a concisely worded definition of dyslexia in your own words.
2. *Critical Writing:* Write an essay expressing your view on how dyslexics should be graded in college. Should students with dyslexia be allowed more time on essay tests, be offered special tutorial services, or be given alternative assignments and examinations? Can students with disabilities be accommodated while maintaining academic standards?
3. *Collaborative Writing:* Working with several other students, craft a brief explanation of dyslexia to be incorporated into a brochure for parents of children with learning impairments. Keep your audience in mind, and avoid making negative comments that might upset parents.

JANICE CASTRO, DAN COOK, AND CRISTINA GARCIA

Janice Castro (1949–) is a journalist who became Time *magazine's first health-policy reporter. In 1994 she published* The American Way of Health: How Medicine is Changing and What it Means to You. *In addition to writing about medicine, she has published articles on topics ranging from pension plans to home-shopping. This essay appeared as part of a* Time *cover story about Hispanics.*

SPANGLISH

In this essay the writers invent a term to define a blend of English and Spanish spoken by a growing number of Americans. As you read their article, notice how they use description, example, *and* comparison *to develop their definition.*

1 In Manhattan a first-grader greets her visiting grandparents, happily exclaiming, "Come here, *siéntate*!" Her bemused grandfather, who does not speak Spanish, nevertheless knows she is asking him to sit down. A Miami personnel officer understands what a job applicant means when he says, "*Quiero un* part time." Nor do drivers miss a beat reading a billboard alongside a Los Angeles street advertising CERVEZA—SIX PACK!

2 This free-form blend of Spanish and English, known as Spanglish, is common linguistic currency wherever concentrations of Hispanic Americans are found in the U.S. In Los Angeles, where 55% of the city's 3 million inhabitants speak Spanish, Spanglish is as much a part of daily life as sunglasses. Unlike the broken-English efforts of earlier immigrants from Europe, Asia and other regions, Spanglish has become a widely accepted conversational mode used casually—even playfully—by Spanish-speaking immigrants and native-born Americans alike.

3 Consisting of one part Hispanicized English, one part Americanized Spanish and more than a little fractured syntax, Spanglish is a bit like a Robin Williams comedy routine: a crackling line of cross-cultural

patter straight from the melting pot. Often it enters Anglo homes and families through the children, who pick it up at school or at play with their young Hispanic contemporaries. In other cases, it comes from watching TV; many an Anglo child watching *Sesame Street* has learned *uno dos tres* almost as quickly as one two three.

4   Spanglish takes a variety of forms, from the Southern California Anglos who bid farewell with the utterly silly *"hasta la* bye-bye" to the Cuban-American drivers in Miami who *parquean* their *carros*. Some Spanglish sentences are mostly Spanish, with a quick detour for an English word or two. A Latino friend may cut short a conversation by glancing at his watch and excusing himself with the explanation that he must *"ir al* supermarket."

5   Many of the English words transplanted in this way are simply handier than their Spanish counterparts. No matter how distasteful the subject, for example, it is still easier to say "income tax" than *impuesto sobre la renta*. At the same time, many Spanish-speaking immigrants have adopted such terms as VCR, microwave and dishwasher for what they view as largely American phenomena. Still other English words convey a cultural context that is not implicit in the Spanish. A friend who invites you to a *lonche* most likely has in mind the brisk American custom of "doing lunch" rather than the languorous afternoon break traditionally implied by *almuerzo*.

6   Mainstream Americans exposed to similar hybrids of German, Chinese or Hindi might be mystified. But even Anglos who speak little or no Spanish are somewhat familiar with Spanglish. Living among them, for one thing, are 19 million Hispanics. In addition, more American high school and university students sign up for Spanish than for any other foreign language.

7   Only in the past ten years, though, has Spanglish begun to turn into a national slang. Its popularity has grown with the explosive increases in U.S. immigration from Latin American countries. English has increasingly collided with Spanish in retail stores, offices and classrooms, in pop music and on street corners. Anglos whose ancestors picked up such Spanish words as *rancho, bronco, tornado* and *incommunicado*, for instance, now freely use such Spanish words as *gracias, bueno, amigo* and *por favor*.

8   Among Latinos, Spanglish conversations often flow more easily from Spanish into several sentences of English and back.

9   Spanglish is a sort of code for Latinos: the speakers know Spanish, but their hybrid language reflects the American culture in which they live. Many lean to shorter, clipped phrases in place of the longer, more

graceful expressions their parents used. Says Leonel de la Cuesta, an assistant professor of modern languages at Florida International University in Miami: "In the U.S., time is money, and that is showing up in Spanglish as an economy of language." Conversational examples: *taipiar* (type) and *winshi-wiper* (windshield wiper) replace *escribir a máquina* and *limpiaparabrisas.*

10   Major advertisers, eager to tap the estimated $134 billion in spending power wielded by Spanish-speaking Americans, have ventured into Spanglish to promote their products. In some cases, attempts to sprinkle Spanish through commercials have produced embarrassing gaffes. A Braniff airlines ad that sought to tell Spanish-speaking audiences they could settle back *en* (in) luxuriant *cuero* (leather) seats, for example, inadvertently said they could fly without clothes (*encuero*). A fractured translation of the Miller Lite slogan told readers the beer was "Filling, and less delicious." Similar blunders are often made by Anglos trying to impress Spanish-speaking pals. But if Latinos are amused by mangled Spanglish, they also recognize these goofs as a sort of friendly acceptance. As they might put it, *no problema.*

Understanding Meaning

1.   What is Spanglish? Can you define it in a single sentence?
2.   How does the concept of "Spanglish" differ from "broken English"?
3.   Who uses Spanglish? What does it indicate about the growing Hispanic influence in the United States?
4.   *Critical Thinking:* Many Americans advocate "English only" and oppose bilingual education. What does the emergence of Spanglish reveal about the status of English in America? Is there any danger that immigrants will fail to master English?

Evaluating Strategy

1.   How do the authors use examples to create their definition?
2.   How do the authors organize details to build a coherent essay?
3.   How effective are the opening and closing paragraphs?

Appreciating Language

1.   What do the tone and style of the essay suggest about the authors' attitude toward their subject?

2. *Critical Thinking:* The writers call Spanglish "slang." What is slang to you? Would you consider it an appropriate label for Spanglish?

Connections across the Disciplines

1. How does defining an invented term like *Spanglish* differ from defining an established concept like dyslexia? How does this article differ from Eileen Simpson's (page 177)?
2. Review Amy Tan's "The Language of Discretion" (page 274). Tan suggests that languages do not always offer clear word-for-word or idea-to-idea translations. Does Spanglish do more than blend words? Does it blend cultural outlooks and perceptions as well?

Writing Suggestions

1. Invent a word to represent something you have observed and support your definition with details. You might define "blind datism" or "recycling phobia" or "cable television withdrawal."
2. *Collaborative Writing:* Ask three or four students to identify a special kind of language they have encountered. Discuss samples and list examples, then write a short definition of "campus-ese," "first-date euphemisms," parent-ese," or "online slang," for example.

JONATHAN RITTER

Jonathan Ritter (1965–) is a technical writer. After completing his studies at the University of Alberta, Ritter worked as a consultant, computer salesman, and engineer in Canada and Australia. Ritter now edits a community newspaper and develops software programs. Among his greatest interests is the role computers play in shaping society.

THE WORLD VIEW OF A COMPUTER HACKER

As you read this article, consider what definition you would ascribe to a computer hacker. Can some hackers be deemed "terrorists," "blackmailers," or "vandals"?

1 The dawn of the electronic age has brought a new breed of individual to life: the computer hacker. A distant cousin of the weekend hobbyist or casual enthusiast, the hacker regards computers and their employment as the single most defining element of his being. He derives both physical and spiritual fulfillment from their use.

2 Viewing *data* as weapons and *programs* as their delivery system, the hacker considers himself a privateer of the modern era. He likens his computer to a vessel, a battleship for him to cruise the world's computer networks, assailing the weak and subverting the unsuspecting. To his prying fingers, no data base is sacred. He is the underdog, a David against an army of Goliaths, and he fantasizes about bringing big corporations and, indeed, entire governments, to their knees.

3 Periodically having to detach himself for such things as going to work or gathering food, the computer hacker is decisively in his element when perched in front of a computer terminal in his basement or attic. Once he has dispensed with his dinner of Alphabits and cheese toast, secured a plentiful supply of Coke and cleaned the previous night's tobacco dust from his screen, the hacker will ready himself for another night's computing session. Consoled by the soothing hum of his machine's cooling fan, he will bask momentarily in the warm glow

of the monitor before easing forward, after a few minutes of quiet concentration, to quickly, but gently and with precision, tap out a string of keystrokes. He has targeted his prey.

4   The computer hacker is not a social animal. He struggles with small talk and has difficulty communicating with technically uninformed people, and his introversion confines him to a tightly knit circle of friends. Arriving unescorted at a party, he will drift about making perfunctory conversation before gravitating to the basement (or garage) to happily chat away in technobabble with two or three like-minded people. At the party's breakup, he will offer genuine thanks to the host, not so much for the Chivas, but for the chance to meet a fellow developer of self-propagating, autonomous computer programs. A sporadic user of alcohol, the computer hacker breaks his prolonged dry spells with feverish bouts of whisky drinking with other hackers, who invariably spend the evening contriving a plot to destabilize the overseas currency market.

5   The computer hacker's bizarre fixations and peculiar habits are telling signs of his breed. He will, for example, operate all of his computers with the covers removed, partly because he relishes the sight of raw electronics, and partly because he is regularly installing and removing components. He will speak lustily of the "techno-aroma" of new equipment and will regularly place his nose next to the cooling fan to inhale the scents of jet-moulded plastic metal and printed circuit boards. An amorous relationship exists between the hacker and his computers. He can often be found slinking away from a late-night computing session, physically drained and smoking a cigarette.

6   The hacker will often display perplexing and astonishing behavior when associating with mainstream society. When planning to move from one dumpy apartment to another, for instance, the hacker will ask the landlord questions about reliable power and "clean" telephone lines, and his eyes will expertly scan the dwelling for an abundance of AC outlets. In a consumer-electronics shop, the "candy store" for the hacker, he will do such things as program VCRs and ask to look *inside* television sets. He typically knows exactly what he wants before he shops, having studied the 600-page *Computer Shopper's Guide* and memorized product evaluations from *Byte Magazine*. Fluent in at least three computer languages, the hacker commonly leaves people bewildered by his speech. He does this unintentionally, absentmindedly forgetting to include English in his conversation.

7   Friends and family who seek advice or help from the hacker frequently regret the decision. Humour is often of a vocational nature to

the hacker, who is likely to regard as extremely funny the suggestions to a co-worker that she look "behind the desk" for a missing computer file, or that perhaps a document that didn't get printed is somehow "stuck in the cable."

8   The hacker's preferences, predictably, reflect his personality. He regards Radio Shack as a store for amateurs and any equipment not meeting U.S. military specifications as "Fisher Price playthings." He spends an inordinate amount of his income on gadgetry, keeps a spare computer around just in case, and is interested in cellular car phones only for the possibility of using them with his laptop computer.

9   To the hacker, a job is only a source of income [with] which he is able to purchase more computing implements. He will usually disguise himself as a white-collar worker and function as a support or development person, burrowing himself away in a back office to work on obscure projects unknown and incomprehensible to most of his co-workers. The anonymity of his circumstances is deliberate, as he loathes the idea of a more public position and does not like people to know of his extracurricular activities. He derides IBM for setting the industry standard—stiffened white shirt, plain tie and dark blazer—and will habitually show up for work wearing the same corduroy jacket, pop-stained tie, untucked shirt and beltless trousers. When the temperature drops, he will simply add layers of mismatched clothing as needed.

10   His company's computer system is almost certainly regarded with disdain, as it rarely matches the power and flexibility of his home system(s). When his management refuses to authorize the purchase of the computer equipment he has asked for, he contemptuously, but briefly, considers sabotaging the company's computer network, or at least crippling it enough to justify his requisition.

11   Politically, the hacker is attracted to the Reform Party, solely because of its promise to pour millions into lengthening the information highway. Conversely, he is suspicious of the NDP for its "Luddite thinking," and instinctively would never vote for a party whose literature was printed on cheap, dot-matrix printers. Bill Clinton gets praise from the hacker for advertising himself as the first president who can be reached by electronic mail.

12   The computer hacker can be seen as a manifestation of a society surrounded and enthralled by technology. He is awed by its magnitude, inspired by its possibilities and anxious about its future. He can be likened to his ancestors 10,000 years ago, who rubbed two sticks together and changed the course of the world forever.

Understanding Meaning

1. How does Ritter define hackers? Are they misfits in your view?
2. What role does ego or professional pride play in the world of computer hackers?
3. What attitude does Ritter have toward hackers?
4. *Critical Thinking:* At one point Ritter calls hackers "a distant cousin of the weekend hobbyist" but later states they spend evenings plotting to "destabilize the overseas currency market." Do you see a conflict between these views? Is the hacker harmless or threatening? Do you see hackers as potential "techno-terrorists"?

Evaluating Strategy

1. What methods does Ritter use to define the world of the hacker?
2. Ritter never mentions the damage hackers have inflicted and could continue to inflict on individuals, corporations, and governments. Is this a serious omission? What does it reveal about his attitude?

Appreciating Language

1. Examine the words Ritter uses to describe hackers. What connotations do they have?
2. How would you characterize Ritter's tone?
3. *Critical Thinking:* Ritter uses the male pronoun "he" throughout the article. Do you see this as an oversight or as a deliberate choice to emphasize his view that hackers are exclusively men?

Connections across the Disciplines

1. Consider the points Carl Sagan makes in his article "Why We Need to Understand Science" (page 589). Do you think many Americans are unable to comprehend how computer hackers could affect society?
2. Review Louis Mizell Jr.'s article, "Who's Listening to Your Cell Phone Calls?" (page 337). What do Ritter and Mizell reveal about how technology can be used by criminals? Do you think most people are aware of how vulnerable they are?

Writing Suggestions

1. Define a personality type you have observed—the male chauvinist, the compulsive shopper, the smoker, the party animal. Your essay should include numerous examples and may be serious or humorous in tone.
2. *Collaborative Writing:* Discuss hackers with several students and write a counter-definition, highlighting the threat hackers can pose to national security, personal privacy, and law enforcement.

JOHN CIARDI

John Ciardi (1916–1986) was a poet, literary critic, and translator. After teaching at Harvard, Rutgers, and the University of Kansas, he left academics to pursue a full-time literary career. As poetry editor for the Saturday Review *for two decades, he attempted to make poetry accessible to a wide audience. Ciardi's most ambitious work was a translation of Dante Alighieri's work, which took him sixteen years. As a poet, critic, and professor, Ciardi was a student of language. For many years he was a guest commentator on National Public Radio, where he offered listeners interesting and amusing anecdotes about the origins and histories of everyday words.*

What Is Happiness?

In this essay, which first appeared in Saturday Review, *Ciardi tries to define the elusive concept of happiness. In developing his definition, Ciardi analyzes the role of advertising and the nature of materialism in American life.*

1   The right to pursue happiness is issued to Americans with their birth certificates, but no one seems quite sure which way it ran. It may be we are issued a hunting license but offered no game. Jonathan Swift seemed to think so when he attacked the idea of happiness as "the possession of being well-deceived," the felicity of being "a fool among knaves." For Swift saw society as Vanity Fair, the land of false goals.

2   It is, of course, un-American to think in terms of fools and knaves. We do, however, seem to be dedicated to the idea of buying our way to happiness. We shall all have made it to Heaven when we possess enough.

3   And at the same time the forces of American commercialism are hugely dedicated to making us deliberately unhappy. Advertising is one of our major industries, and advertising exists not to satisfy desires but to create them—and to create them faster than any man's budget can satisfy them. For that matter, our whole economy is based on a dedicated insatiability. We are taught that to possess is to be happy, and then we are made to want. We are even told it is our duty to want. It was only a few years ago, to cite a single example, that car dealers

across the country were flying banners that read "You Auto Buy Now." They were calling upon Americans, as an act approaching patriotism, to buy at once, with money they did not have, automobiles they did not really need, and which they would be required to grow tired of by the time the next year's models were released.

4 Or look at any of the women's magazines. There, as Bernard De-Voto once pointed out, advertising begins as poetry in the front pages and ends as pharmacopoeia and therapy in the back pages. The poetry of the front matter is the dream of perfect beauty. This is the baby skin that must be hers. These, the flawless teeth. This, the perfumed breath she must exhale. This, the sixteen-year-old figure she must display at forty, at fifty, at sixty, and forever.

5 Once past the vaguely uplifting fiction and feature articles, the reader finds the other face of the dream in the back matter. This is the harness into which Mother must strap herself in order to display that perfect figure. These, the chin straps she must sleep in. This is the salve that restores all, this is her laxative, these are the tablets that melt away fat, these are the hormones of perpetual youth, these are the stockings that hide varicose veins.

6 Obviously no half-sane person can be completely persuaded either by such poetry or by such pharmacopoeia and orthopedics. Yet someone is obviously trying to buy the dream as offered and spending billions every year in the attempt. Clearly the happiness-market is not running out of customers, but what is it trying to buy?

7 The idea "happiness," to be sure, will not sit still for easy definition: The best one can do is to try to set some extremes to the idea and then work in toward the middle. To think of happiness as acquisitive and competitive will do to set the materialistic extreme. To think of it as the idea one senses in, say, a holy man of India will do to set the spiritual extreme. That holy man's idea of happiness is in needing nothing from outside himself. In wanting nothing, he lacks nothing. He sits immobile, rapt in contemplation, free even of his own body. Or nearly free of it. If devout admirers bring him food he eats it; if not, he starves indifferently. Why be concerned? What is physical is an illusion to him. Contemplation is his joy and he achieves it through a fantastically demanding discipline, the accomplishment of which is itself a joy within him.

8 Is he a happy man? Perhaps his happiness is only another sort of illusion. But who can take it from him? And who will dare say it is more illusory than happiness on the installment plan?

9   But, perhaps because I am Western, I doubt such catatonic happiness, as I doubt the dreams of the happiness-market. What is certain is that his way of happiness would be torture to almost any Western man. Yet these extremes will still serve to frame the area within which all of us must find some sort of balance. Thoreau—a creature of both Eastern and Western thought—had his own firm sense of that balance. His aim was to save on the low levels in order to spend on the high.

10   Possession for its own sake or in competition with the rest of the neighborhood would have been Thoreau's idea of the low levels. The active discipline of heightening one's perception of what is enduring in nature would have been his idea of the high. What he saved from the low was time and effort he could spend on the high. Thoreau certainly disapproved of starvation, but he would put into feeding himself only as much effort as would keep him functioning for more important efforts.

11   Effort is the gist of it. There is no happiness except as we take on life-engaging difficulties. Short of the impossible, as Yeats put it, the satisfactions we get from a lifetime depend on how high we choose our difficulties. Robert Frost was thinking in something like the same terms when he spoke of "The pleasure of taking pains." The mortal flaw in the advertised version of happiness is in the fact that it purports to be effortless.

12   We demand difficulty even in our games. We demand it because without difficulty there can be no game. A game is a way of making something hard for the fun of it. The rules of the game are an arbitrary imposition of difficulty. When the spoilsport ruins the fun, he always does so by refusing to play by the rules. It is easier to win at chess if you are free, at your pleasure, to change the wholly arbitrary rules, but the fun is in winning within the rules. No difficulty, no fun.

13   The buyers and sellers at the happiness-market seem too often to have lost their sense of the pleasure of difficulty. Heaven knows what they are playing, but it seems a dull game. And the Indian holy man seems dull to us, I suppose, because he seems to be refusing to play anything at all. The Western weakness may be in the illusion that happiness can be bought. Perhaps the Eastern weakness is in the idea that there is such a thing as perfect (and therefore static) happiness.

14   Happiness is never more than partial. There are no pure states of mankind. Whatever else happiness may be, it is neither in having nor in being, but in becoming. What the Founding Fathers declared for us as an inherent right, we should do well to remember, was not happi-

ness but the *pursuit* of happiness. What they might have underlined, could they have foreseen the happiness-market, is the cardinal fact that happiness is in the pursuit itself, in the meaningful pursuit of what is life-engaging and life-revealing, which is to say, in the idea of *becoming*. A nation is not measured by what it possesses or wants to possess, but by what it wants to become.

15   By all means let the happiness-market sell us minor satisfactions and even minor follies so long as we keep them in scale and buy them out of spiritual change. I am no customer for either puritanism or asceticism. But drop any real spiritual capital at those bazaars, and what you come home to will be your own poorhouse.

Understanding Meaning

1. How does the view "whoever dies with the most toys wins" fit with Ciardi's thoughts on materialism?
2. What seems to be Ciardi's purpose in this essay? How much of this definition is *persuasive?* What does he mean by the comment that "a nation is not measured by what it possesses or wants to possess, but by what it wants to become"?
3. How does Ciardi *compare* the Eastern mystic's concept of happiness with that of most Americans? Can happiness be achieved by being free of possessions or by owning them all?
4. How does advertising exploit the public hunger for happiness? Does advertising suggest, in Ciardi's view, that happiness can be purchased instead of earned?
5. *Critical Thinking:* Although he criticizes what he calls "the happiness-market," Ciardi does not condemn it. However, he advises readers to be cautious consumers. What does he warn readers against? What does he mean by his comment about dropping "any real spiritual capital"?

Evaluating Strategy

1. Ciardi admits that happiness is not easy to define, noting "the best one can do is to try to set some extremes to the idea and then work in toward the middle." Is this an effective method of defining abstract or elusive concepts?
2. Throughout the essay, Ciardi quotes Swift, Bernard DeVoto, and Frost. Is this an effective way of working toward the definition of a difficult subject? Does this add credibility to Ciardi's view?

3. *Other Modes:* How does Ciardi use *comparison* and *analysis* to develop his definition?

Appreciating Language

1. Ciardi uses simple but abstract words—*happiness, possessions, dream, illusion.* How does he define these terms and give them personal meaning?
2. How does Ciardi paraphrase the language of advertising to reveal its appeals to consumers?

Connections across the Disciplines

1. How does Juliet B. Schor's article "Addicted to Plastic: The Overspent American" (page 306) relate to Ciardi's observation that people seek happiness in materialism and consumption?
2. How might Ciardi respond to the wedding chapel marriages described by Joan Didion in "Marrying Absurd" (page 122)?

Writing Suggestions

1. Use Ciardi's technique of setting extremes and then working toward the middle to define an elusive or complex subject such as love, friendship, success, wealth, or beauty in a short essay.
2. *Critical Writing:* Write an essay based on Ciardi's observation that the founding fathers did not promise a right to happiness but a right to the *pursuit* of happiness. Do Americans today seem to believe they have a *right* to happiness? Discuss whether Americans feel cheated if they are not happy and whether this partly explains the epidemic of drug abuse and violence.
3. *Collaborative Writing:* Discuss Ciardi's essay with a group of students, and then write a few paragraphs reflecting the group's viewpoint on happiness. You may wish to address a single observation made by Ciardi, such as the partial nature of happiness or the idea that it must derive from a challenge met.

GRETEL EHRLICH

Gretel Ehrlich (1946–) was born in Santa Barbara, California, and studied at the University of California, Los Angeles, film school and the New School of Social Research in New York. Ehrlich first visited Wyoming in 1976 to produce a film and made the state her home. She married a rancher and now lives near the Bighorn Mountains. She has published several books set in Wyoming, including Heart Mountain, *a novel about the internment camps established to house Japanese Americans during World War II. Her work has earned her several awards, including a Guggenheim Fellowship in 1989.*

A Storm, the Cornfield, and Elk

This essay, which appeared in her collection The Solace of Open Places, *provides a personal definition of autumn. Like much of her work, the essay explores the relationship between people and places and the role of nature in shaping our lives.*

1   Last week a bank of clouds lowered itself down summer's green ladder and let loose with a storm. A heavy snow can act like fists: Trees are pummeled, hay- and grainfields are flattened, splayed out like deer beds; field corn, jackknifed and bleached blond by the freeze, is bedraggled by the brawl. All night we heard groans and crashes of cottonwood trunks snapping. "I slept under the damned kitchen table," one rancher told me. "I've already had one of them trees come through my roof." Along the highway electric lines were looped to the ground like dropped reins.

2   As the storm blows east toward the Dakotas, the blue of the sky intensifies. It inks dry washes and broad grasslands with quiet. In their most complete gesture of restraint, cottonwoods, willows, and wild rose engorge themselves with every hue of ruddiness—russet, puce, umber, gold, musteline—whose spectral repletion we know also to be an agony, riding oncoming waves of cold.

3   The French call the autumn leaf *feuille morte.* When the leaves are finally corrupted by frost they rain down into themselves until the tree, disowning itself, goes bald.

4   All through autumn we hear a double voice: One says everything is ripe; the other says everything is dying. The paradox is exquisite. We feel what the Japanese call "aware"—an almost untranslatable word meaning something like "beauty tinged with sadness." Some days we have to shoulder against a marauding melancholy. Dreams have a hallucinatory effect: in one, a man who is dying watches from inside a huge cocoon while stud colts run through deep mud, their balls bursting open, their seed spilling into the black ground. My reading brings me this thought from the mad Zen priest Ikkyu: "Remember that under the skin you fondle lie the bones, waiting to reveal themselves." But another day, I ride in the mountains. Against rimrock, tall aspens have the graceful bearing of giraffes, and another small grove, not yet turned, gives off a virginal limelight that transpierces everything heavy.

5   Fall is the end of a rancher's year. Third and fourth cuttings of hay are stacked; cattle and sheep are gathered, weaned, and shipped; yearlings bulls and horse colts are sold. "We always like this time of year, but it's a lot more fun when the cattle prices are up!" a third-generation rancher tells me.

6   This week I help round up their cows and calves on the Big Horns. The storm system that brought three feet of snow at the beginning of the month now brings intense and continual rain. Riding for cows resembles a wild game of touch football played on skis: Cows and cowboys bang into each other, or else, as the calves run back, the horse just slides. Twice today my buckskin falls with me, crushing my leg against a steep sidehill, but the mud and snow, now trampled into a gruel, is so deep it's almost impossible to get bruised.

7   When the cattle are finally gathered, we wean the calves from the cows in portable corrals by the road. Here, black mud reaches our shins. The stock dogs have to swim in order to move. Once, while trying to dodge a cow, my feet stuck, and losing both boots in the effort to get out of the way, I had to climb the fence barefooted. Weaning is noisy; cows don't hide their grief. As calves are loaded into semis and stock trucks, their mothers—five or six hundred of them at a time—crowd around the sorting alleys with outstretched necks, their squared-off faces all opened in a collective bellowing.

8   On the way home a neighboring rancher who trails his steers down the mountain highway loses one as they ride through town. There's a high-speed chase across lawns and flower beds, around the general store and the fire station. Going at a full lope, the steer ducks behind the fire truck just as Mike tries to rope him. "Missing something?" a

friend yells out her window as the second loop sails like a burning hoop to the ground.

9   "That's nothing," one onlooker remarks. "When we brought our cattle through Kaycee one year, the minister opened the church door to see what all the noise was about and one old cow just ran in past him. He had a hell of a time getting her out."

10   In the valley, harvest is on but it's soggy. The pinto bean crops are sprouting, and the sugar beets are balled up with mud so that one is indistinguishable from the other. Now I can only think of mud as being sweet. At night the moon makes a brief appearance between storms and laces mud with a confectionary light. Farmers whose last cutting of hay is still on the ground turn windrows to dry as if they were limp, bedridden bodies. The hay that has already been baled is damp, and after four inches of rain (in a county where there's never more than eight inches a year) mold eats its way to the top again.

11   The morning sky looks like cheese. Its cobalt wheel has been cut down and all the richness of the season is at our feet. The quick-blanch of frost stings autumn's rouge into a skin that is tawny. At dawn, mowed hay meadows are the color of pumpkins, and the willows, leafless now, are pink and silver batons conducting inaudible river music. When I dress for the day, my body, white and suddenly numb, looks like dead coral.

12   After breakfast there are autumn chores to finish. We grease head gates on irrigation ditches, roll up tarp dams, pull horseshoes, and truck horses to their winter pasture. The harvest moon gives way to the hunter's moon. Elk, deer, and moose hunters repopulate the mountains now that the livestock is gone. One young hunting guide has already been hurt. While he was alone at camp, his horse kicked him in the spleen. Immobilized, he scratched an SOS with the sharp point of a bullet on a piece of leather he cut from his chaps. "Hurt bad. In pain. Bring doctor with painkiller," it read. Then he tied the note to the horse's halter and threw rocks at the horse until it trotted out of camp. When the horse wandered into a ranch yard down the mountain, the note was quickly discovered and a doctor was helicoptered to camp. Amid orgiastic gunfire, sometimes lives are saved.

13   October lifts over our heads whatever river noise is left. Long carrier waves of clouds seem to emanate from hidden reefs. There's a logjam of them around the mountains, and the horizon appears to drop seven thousand feet. Though the rain has stopped, the road ruts are

filled to the brim. I saw a frog jump cheerfully into one of them. Once in a while the mist clears and we can see the dark edge of a canyon or an island of vertical rimrock in the white bulk of snow. Up there, bull elk have been fighting all fall over harems. They charge with antlered heads, scraping the last of the life-giving velvet off, until one bull wins and trots into the private timber to mount his prize, standing almost humanly erect on hind legs while holding a cow elk's hips with his hooves.

14   In the fall, my life, too, is timbered, an unaccountably libidinous place: damp, overripe, and fading. The sky's congestion allows the eye's iris to open wider. The cornfield in front of me is torn parchment paper, as brittle as bougainvillea leaves whose tropical color has somehow climbed these northern stalks. I zigzag through the rows as if they were city streets. Now I want to lie down in the muddy furrows, under the frictional sawing of stalks, under corncobs which look like erections, and out of whose loose husks sprays of bronze silk dangle down.

15   Autumn teaches us that fruition is also death; that ripeness is a form of decay. The willows, having stood for so long near water, begin to rust. Leaves are verbs that conjugate the seasons.

16   Today the sky is a wafer. Placed on my tongue, it is a wholeness that has already disintegrated; placed under the tongue, it makes my heart beat strongly enough to stretch myself over the winter brilliances to come. Now I feel the tenderness to which this season rots. Its defenselessness can no longer be corrupted. Death is its purity, its sweet mud. The string of storms that came across Wyoming like elephants tied tail to trunk falters now and bleeds into a stillness.

17   There is neither sun, nor wind, nor snow falling. The hunters are gone; snow geese waddle in grainfields. Already, the elk have started moving out of the mountains toward sheltered feed-grounds. Their great antlers will soon fall off like chandeliers shaken from ballroom ceilings. With them the light of these autumn days, bathed in what Tennyson called "a mockery of sunshine," will go completely out.

Understanding Meaning

1. Why does Ehrlich see autumn as a season of paradox?
2. What does the opening paragraph reveal about the power of nature?
3. What does fall symbolize to the rancher?

4. What is the significance of the story of the hunting guide who uses the horse that nearly killed him to carry his message to summon help? What does it reveal about the interaction of people and the natural world?
5. *Critical Thinking:* Can this essay be seen as a commentary about death? Is Ehrlich's purpose to define autumn as a time of death so her readers will accept it as something natural?

Evaluating Strategy

1. What figurative language does Ehrlich use to develop her essay about autumn?
2. How does Ehrlich use quotations and dialogue to introduce ideas in her essay?
3. What methods does Ehrlich employ to arrange her thoughts on the nature of autumn?
4. *Other Modes:* How does Ehrlich use *comparison* and *narration* to develop her essay?

Appreciating Language

1. Ehrlich compares elements of the natural world with artificial objects such as paper and chandeliers. How effective are these similes and metaphors in explaining nature to a largely urban audience?
2. Underline the most striking images you find in the essay. What makes them memorable? How do they help define Ehrlich's perception of autumn?

Connections across the Disciplines

1. How does Ehrlich's view of people's interaction with nature compare to that of Terry Tempest Williams's in her essay "Yucca" (page 203)?
2. How does Ehrlich's role of observer compare to that of George Orwell's in his essay "Shooting an Elephant" (page 72)?

Writing Suggestions

1. Write a brief essay that defines the human significance of a natural event. You might write about tornadoes, floods, blizzards, the change of seasons, the migration of wildlife, or shooting stars. What lessons about life, the fragility of civilization, or our perceptions of reality can nature teach us?

2. *Collaborative Writing:* Working with a group of students, select a season or a natural event that is common in your location. Have each member suggest an idea of what this season or event teaches. Compare ideas and try to combine them in a single brief essay.

Terry Tempest Williams (1955–) was born in Utah, where her ancestors had lived for more than a century and a half. She received degrees in English and science education from the University of Utah, where she now teaches in a women's studies program. Williams also serves as Naturalist-in-Residence at the Utah Museum of Natural History in Salt Lake City. Her concern for nature is evident in her writing, which includes children's books, short stories about Utah, and several nonfiction books blending natural history and personal experience.

Yucca

This essay from Pieces of White Shell: A Journey to Navajoland *provides a personal definition of a plant, emphasizing its importance to the Navajo people of the Southwest. Notice how Williams blends several modes to demonstrate the significance of a common desert plant.*

1   One night the stars pulled me into a dream. A basket sat before me, coiled: around and around and around and around. It was striped with persimmon. I should not touch it. This much I knew. I knelt down closely and saw a woman's long black hair curled between stitches. I picked up a sprig of salt bush and rattled it above the hair strand. Suddenly, the woven bowl began to pulsate, writhe, until a snake uncoiled herself slowly. This is what I heard:

2
> Sha-woman, Sha-woman, hiss
> Sha-woman, Sha-woman, hiss
> Tongue, rattle, hiss
> Tongue, rattle, hiss
> Sha-woman, Sha-woman, hiss

3   She stopped. She raised her head and blew upward. I watched the breezes pull her vertically until she became a white desert torch. Yucca.

4   In the Navajo account of yucca's birth, Tracking Bear was a monster from whom there was no escape. He lived in a cave in the mountains. Monster Slayer, pursued by Tracking Bear, climbed a sheer wall. As he did so he grasped a fruit of the yucca in his left hand, and in his right a twig of hard oak. The monster feared these medicine rattles. Monster Slayer killed Tracking Bear and cut off his claws and large canine teeth, taking the gall and windpipe as trophies. He then cut the head into three pieces: One became the broad-leaved yucca, one the narrow-leaved yucca, and one the mescal.

5   And so yucca appears evenly spaced across the land. They stand as sentinels with their flowering stalks rising from vegetative swords. They are shields for creatures who live near. Sundown strikes yucca. Desert candles flame.

6   I remember peering into a yucca flower at dusk and seeing a tiny moth scraping pollen from within. The little white-robed pilgrim rolled the pollen into a tight ball and carried it to another blossom. There I watched her pierce the ovary wall with her long ovipositor and lay a clutch of eggs among the ovules, much as a farmer in the spring scatters seeds along his furrows. She packed the sticky mass of pollen through the openings of the stigma. Moth larvae and seeds would now develop simultaneously, with the larvae feeding on developing yucca. She walked to the edge of the petals. With her last bit of strength, she glided into the darkness, carried away by grace. The larvae would eventually gnaw their way through the ovary wall and lower themselves to the ground to pupate until the yuccas bloomed again. Circles. Cycles. Yucca and moth.

7   Perhaps the moth was on her way to pollinate the Navajo mind as well, for yucca and Navajo are relatives. Yucca is the single most important noncultivated plant to Indian peoples in the Southwest. It has been plaited into baskets, woven into mats, and wrapped around bundles. Early peoples walked with yucca bound around their feet. Sandals. Imagine the care extended to plants when they mean your survival.

8   In days of painted language, yucca leaves were soaked in warm water to soften. They were then beaten against the rocks for further pliancy. Fibers finely peeled—like corn silk, only stronger—were twisted into cordage with organic tension. This same process can be tried today with patience.

9   The children know yucca, *tsá-ászi'*, intimately. On the banks of the San Juan River we stood in a circle with yucca at the center.

10   "What is this?" I asked.

11   "Yucca!" they sang out in unison.

12   "And what story does it tell?"

13   I heard as many responses as there are yucca blossoms. But one common strand connecting their stories was soap.

14   "We call it soapweed because there's soap under there. . . . "

15   "Yes?"

16   "Yes. You find the root under here—they pointed to the body of the plant—cut off a piece, and slice it into four strips. Then you pound it with your hands and add warm water until it lathers up."

17   "Then what do you do?"

18   "We wash our hair with the suds."

19   Before I knew what was happening, two boys pulled the plant out from the sand. They cut off the root, sliced it into four strips, placed it on the sandstone, and began pounding it with a rock—just as they had said. It worked: The root was frothing with suds.

20   The boys didn't stop there. They moved to a desert pothole that was holding rainwater. Loren bent over the basin as Bryan washed his hair. The rest of the children gathered. This was a familiar sight and they laughed.

21   "Loren, you better watch out—tomorrow you'll come to school with hair hanging down your back!"

22   The lore of yucca supports this teasing. The Navajo say a yucca shampoo will make your hair long, shiny, and black. If there are doubts as to yucca magic, just look at the children.

23   On another occasion, the children warned me against using yucca.

24   "Why not?" I asked. My curiosity was up.

25   "Because it might give you warts." A wave of giggles rushed over them.

26   But on this day, things were different. After the boys had finished their demonstration, they handed me a fresh section of the root.

27   "Try it."

28   The girls disappeared and returned with a brush they had made from a bunch of rice grass. They began combing my hair. I sat toward the wind, unable to speak.

29   The ritual of bathing with yucca suds is woven into the Navajo Way. It has been said that the mound of earth upon which the basket for water and suds is placed commemorates the visit of two children to Changing Woman's home, where they witnessed her rejuvenation. Blessed yucca suds have the power to transform—to change the

30 profane to sacred, the doubtful to controlled, the contaminated to the purified.

31 One of the Navajo ceremonies associated with yucca washings is *Kinaaldá*, Changing Woman's puberty rites. *Kinaaldá* is part of the Blessing Way, a Navajo rite that maintains harmony for the people by attracting the goodness and power of benevolent Holy People. Most Navajo use the word *kinaaldá* to refer to the "first menses," alluding to the ceremonial rather than the physical event.

32 *Kinaaldá* ushers the adolescent Navajo girl into womanhood and invokes blessings upon her, ensuring her health, prosperity, and well-being. It is a festive occasion where the accounts of Changing Woman and her *Kinaaldá* are retold and reenacted.

33 The *Kinaaldá* started when White Shell Woman first menstruated. Nine days after her *Kinaaldá*, Changing Woman gave birth to twin boys: Monster Slayer and Child-of-the-waters. They were placed on the earth to kill the monsters. As soon as they had done this, their mother, Changing Woman, who was then living at Governador Knob, left and went to her home in the west, where she lives today.

34 After she moved to her home in the west, she created the Navajo people. When she had done this, she told these human beings to go to their original home, which was Navajo country. Before they left, she said, "After this, all the girls born to you will have periods at certain times when they become women. When the time comes, you must set a day and fix the girl up to be *Kinaaldá;* you must have these songs sung and do whatever else needs to be done at that time. After this period, a girl is a woman and will start having children."

35 That is what Changing Woman told the people she made in the west. She told them to go to their own country and do this.

36 And so *Kinaaldá* continues. A *Kinaaldá* may last anywhere from three to five days depending on the circumstances. Today, many families cannot afford this ceremony as it has become too expensive to hire a medicine man and provide food for friends and family. Even so, many young Navajo women have participated in this celebration. Traditionally, the singer or medicine man conducting the ceremony asks the mentoring woman, usually the girl's mother or aunt, to set out the basket containing the yucca roots. This is done usually before dawn of the last day of the ceremony. The roots have been carefully unearthed with two rocks found close by to aid in the crushing. The older woman ritualistically shreds the roots and pulverizes them. She then pours

water into the basket, creating yucca suds so that the girl can bathe her hair. But first, the woman washes all the girl's jewelry—beads, bracelets, rings, and concha belt—and sets them on a blanket to dry. Then the girl kneels before the water, unfastens her hair tie, and begins to wash her hair with the same lather. The woman helps her, making certain she receives a good shampoo. All during the washing ritual "Songs of Dawn" are being sung and a ritual cake is being prepared.

37   The older woman takes the basket of soapweed water, *táláwosh*, to the west and empties it in a northerly direction. As soon as the singing stops, the young woman in *Kinaaldá* wrings out her hair and begins her last run to the east before dawn. Younger sisters and friends may follow her.

38   The breeze coming from her as she runs
The breeze coming from her as she runs
The breeze coming from her as she runs is beautiful.

39   The breeze coming from her as she runs
The breeze coming from her as she runs
The breeze coming from her as she runs is beautiful.

40   How many times have Navajo hands asked for the release of this root from the earth? How many times have these beaten roots been rubbed between flesh in warm water until heavy lather appeared? This source of soap, containing the compound saponin, has bathed skeins of yarn and skeins of hair, leaving both to glisten in desert sunlight.

41   Yucca is also edible. The children call yucca fruit "Navajo bananas." When boiled, it tastes much like summer squash, slightly sweet but with a twist of bitterness. But most of the yucca fruit is left in the heat to dry and wither. I have cut into its flesh many times and found exquisite symmetry. Six windows—once panes for seeds—become a chartreuse kaleidoscope.

42   The children look through yucca and see each other playing the ball and stick game, traditionally known as the "moccasin game."

43   "You play the game like this," they said. "You make a ball out of the yucca root with your hands, then everyone takes off their shoes and lines them up on either side of the yucca. One side takes the ball

and hides it inside one of the shoes. The other team has to guess which shoe it's in. If they guess right it's their turn to hide the ball, but if they're wrong, the other side gets to cut off a yucca leaf. The side with the most yucca sticks at the end of the game wins."

44   Another story is told. A long, long time ago all creatures on earth, including insects, spoke as human beings. The Animal People gathered around the yucca and said, "Let's have a shoe game." A great hoopla rose from the crowd as everyone showed his favor for such an event.

45   "But how will we keep score?" asked a small beast.

46   "We will use the blades of yucca as counters," spoke another. And one hundred and two yucca sticks were pulled. A ball from the root of yucca was shaped, along with a stick for pointing.

47   "We will have the shoe game at a place called Tse´yaa Hodilhil," they said. And everyone ran, jumped, flew and crawled to the designated site.

48   Gopher dug two shallow furrows on either side. Four moccasins were placed in each groove and then covered with sand. Then it was asked among the herds, swarms, and flocks, "What shall we bet?"

49   A great stirring occurred in the animal assemblage as everyone offered opinions. Finally, all the diurnal beings said, "We will bet the earth to have continual sunlight."

50   The nocturnal beings stepped forward and said, "We will bet the sky to have perpetual darkness."

51   And so the bets were placed between day and night.

52   There were many, many Animal People on both sides. The diurnal creatures on the south, the nocturnal creatures on the north. Anticipation for the contest grew like midsummer corn.

53   The game began with one side hiding the ball in one of the four moccasins, then covering the moccasins up with sand. The other side began guessing with the indicator stick which shoe the ball was in. They were given three chances. If they guessed correctly it became their turn to hide the ball. If they were fooled, the opponents took a yucca counter. Back and forth, back and forth it went, with lots of laughter and singing.

54   The Animal People became so immersed in the shoe game that no one realized morning had come. They continued to play throughout the day and into the night placing their bets high, with neither side ever quite winning all one hundred and two yucca sticks.

55   They did things then just as people do today. Once they started something, they would not stop. The wager between day and night still continues.

56   The shoe game is played by Navajos with delight. Some call it Navajo gambling. But those who know the stories say it keeps Sun and Moon in balance.

57   After all the children have shared their own versions of the game, they are quick to tell you that "you must only play this game in winter." A botanist will tell you winter is the dormant season for yucca. Earth wisdom.

58   I brought out my pouch and took a slice, a circle of yucca. It had been aged by Sun. Once supple, now shriveled. Bitter, hard. What could this be? I mused over the possibilities. If I were home, it could be cucumber, zucchini, even eggplant. But here it could be peyote or datura, any number of powerful medicines. Where could they take me? I closed my eyes and slipped the yucca slice into my mouth. From a far-off place I could smell the smoke of piñyon.

59   Yucca. Plants. Navajo. Plants yield their secrets to those who know them. They can weep the colors of chokecherry tears, purplish-brown, into a weaver's hands. They can be backbones for baskets holding the blessings of *Kinaaldá*. Cedar bark and sage can purify; Indian paintbrush soothes an ailing stomach. Juniper ash water creates blue cornmeal. Petals of larkspur are sprinkled in ceremony. Native plants are a repository. They hold our health. A Navajo medicine man relies on plants as we rely on pharmacies.

60   Edward S. Ayensu, director of the Office of Biological Conservation at the Smithsonian Institution, tells a story about an African herbalist who told his students to pay attention to the natural world, to listen and observe the behavior of animals such as lizards, snakes, birds, rodents, and insects.

61   To stress his point, the herbalist narrated a fight between two chameleons. As Ayensu describes it:

62   At the climax of the fight one of the chameleons passed out. The other quickly dashed into a thicket and came back with a piece of a leaf in its mouth. It forcibly pushed the leaf into the mouth of the unconscious lizard. In a matter of two or three minutes the defeated chameleon shook its body and took off.

63   The specific plant that saved the life of the chameleon was not dis-
closed to me. When I insisted on knowing, the teacher smiled and said,
"This is a trade secret. It is a plant that can spring a dying person to life.
Unless you became one of us I cannot tell you."

64   This is earth medicine, and it is all around us, delivered into the
hands that trust it. What do we know?

65   Yucca. The desert torch burns and returns its ashes to crimson
sand. A snake slithers across the way and recoils itself under a slickrock slab. This is what I heard:

66 Sha-woman, Sha-woman, hiss
Sha-woman, Sha-woman, hiss
Tongue, rattle, hiss
Tongue, rattle, hiss
Sha-woman, Sha-woman, hiss

67 Silence. A basket sits before me, coiled: around and around and
around and around. It is striped with persimmon.

Understanding Meaning

1. What are the principal characteristics of the yucca plant?
2. How was the yucca plant created, according to Navajo legend?
3. Why is the plant so important to the Native Americans of the Southwest?
4. What traditions do the children reenact?
5. What special role does the yucca plant play in the lives of Navajo women?
6. *Critical Thinking:* Williams makes the statement that "yucca and Navajo
    are relatives." Could a similar essay define the importance of the potato
    to the prefamine Irish or rice to the Chinese? Can American urban civi-
    lization be defined by oil or electricity?

Evaluating Strategy

1. Williams opens the essay with a dream. How does this help introduce the
    spiritual importance of yucca to the Navajo?
2. What role does Williams play in the essay? How does she use dialogue?

3. Near the end of her essay, Williams introduces comments by an official of the Smithsonian Institution. Is the inclusion of outside scientific authorities essential to her essay?
4. *Other Modes:* How does Williams blend *narration* and *description* in creating a definition of the yucca plant?

Appreciating Language

1. Underline the metaphors Williams uses to describe the yucca plant. How do they aid in creating a definition?
2. Look up the terms *nocturnal* and *diurnal.*

Connections across the Disciplines

1. How does Williams's role in the essay compare with that of Gretel Ehrlich's in "A Storm, the Cornfield, and Elk" (page 197)?
2. Does Williams's detailed observation of the yucca follow Dr. Agassiz's admonition to "look again, look again" in Samuel Scudder's essay "Take This Fish and Look at It" (page 45)?

Writing Suggestions

1. Write a brief essay defining an element central to the lives of a group of people. You might define a computer as the heart of a small business or coffee as the lifeblood of students during exam week. Provide details to illustrate the significance of this object or substance.
2. *Collaborative Writing:* Working with several students, ask each to select an item that is central to a group they know. If the yucca plant defines the Navajo, what would define students on your campus—soda, pizza, computer disks, sweatshirts? Ask each member of the group to supply a brief definition.

EDWARD DOLNICK

Edward Dolnick wrote this article for the September 1993 issue of The Atlantic Monthly, *a magazine specializing in the arts and public affairs. In this article he discusses how numerous deaf people refuse to see deafness as a "disability" but define it as a "culture."*

Deafness as Culture

Edward Dolnick uses several modes to develop his essay about deafness. The act of defining can be persuasive, altering public perceptions and social policy. Notice how comparison, cause and effect, description, and narration play important roles in the article.

1   In 1773, on a tour of Scotland and the Hebrides Islands, Samuel Johnson visited a school for deaf children. Impressed by the students but daunted by their predicament, he proclaimed deafness "one of the most desperate of human calamities." More than a century later Helen Keller reflected on her own life and declared that deafness was a far greater hardship than blindness. "Blindness cuts people off from things," she observed. "Deafness cuts people off from people."

2   For millennia deafness was considered so catastrophic that very few ventured to ease its burdens. Isolation in a kind of permanent solitary confinement was deemed inevitable; a deaf person, even in the midst of urban hubbub, was considered as unreachable as a fairy-tale princess locked in a tower. The first attempts to educate deaf children came only in the sixteenth century. As late as 1749 the French Academy of Sciences appointed a commission to determine whether deaf people were "capable of reasoning." Today no one would presume to ignore the deaf or exclude them from full participation in society. But acknowledging their rights is one thing, coming to grips with their plight another. Deafness is still seen as a dreadful fate.

3   Lately, though, the deaf community has begun to speak for itself. To the surprise and bewilderment of outsiders, its message is utterly contrary to the wisdom of centuries: Deaf people, far from groaning

under a heavy yoke, are not handicapped at all. Deafness is not a disability. Instead, many deaf people now proclaim, they are a subculture like any other. They are simply a linguistic minority (speaking American Sign Language) and are no more in need of a cure for their condition than are Haitians or Hispanics.

4   That view is vehemently held. "The term 'disabled' describes those who are blind or physically handicapped," the deaf linguists Carol Padden and Tom Humphries write, "not Deaf people." (The uppercase *D* is significant: It serves as a succinct proclamation that the deaf share a culture rather than merely a medical condition.) So strong is the feeling of cultural solidarity that many deaf parents cheer on discovering that their baby is deaf. Pondering such a scene, a hearing person can experience a kind of vertigo. The surprise is not simply the unfamiliarity of the views; it is that, as in a surrealist painting, jarring notions are presented as if they were commonplaces.

5   The embrace of what looks indisputably like hardship is what, in particular, strikes the hearing world as perverse, and deaf leaders have learned to brace themselves for the inevitable question. "No!" Roslyn Rosen says, by shaking her head vehemently, she *wouldn't* prefer to be able to hear. Rosen, the president of the National Association of the Deaf, is deaf, the daughter of deaf parents, and the mother of deaf children. "I'm happy with who I am," she says through an interpreter, "and I don't want to be 'fixed.' Would an Italian-American rather be a WASP? In our society everyone agrees that whites have an easier time than blacks. But do you think a black person would undergo operations to become white?"

6   The view that deafness is akin to ethnicity is far from unanimously held. "The world of deafness often seems Balkanized, with a warlord ruling every mountaintop," writes Henry Kisor, the book editor for the *Chicago Sun-Times* and deaf himself. But the "deaf culture" camp—Kisor calls it the "New Orthodoxy"—is in the ascendancy, and its proponents invoke watchwords that still carry echoes of earlier civil-rights struggles. "Pride," "heritage," "identity," and similar words are thick in the air.

7   Rhetoric aside, however, the current controversy is disorientingly unfamiliar, because the deaf are a group unlike any ethnic minority: 90 percent of all deaf children are born to hearing parents. Many people never meet a deaf person unless one is born to them. Then parent and child belong to different cultures, as they would in an adoption across racial lines. And deaf children acquire a sense of cultural identity from

their peers rather than their parents, as homosexuals do. But the crucial issue is that hearing parent and deaf child don't share a means of communication. Deaf children cannot grasp their parents' spoken language, and hearing parents are unlikely to know sign language. Communication is not a gift automatically bestowed in infancy but an acquisition gained only by laborious effort.

8   This gulf has many consequences. Hearing people tend to make the mistake of considering deafness to be an affliction that we are familiar with, as if being deaf were more or less like being hard of hearing. Even those of us with sharp hearing are, after all, occasionally unable to make out a mumbled remark at the dinner table, or a whispered question from a toddler, or a snatch of dialogue in a movie theater.

9   To get a hint of blindness, you can try making your way down an unfamiliar hall in the dark, late at night. But clamping on a pair of earmuffs conveys nothing essential about deafness, because the earmuffs can't block out a lifetime's experience of having heard language. That experience makes hearing people ineradicably different. Because antibiotics have tamed many of the childhood diseases that once caused permanent loss of hearing, more than 90 percent of all deaf children in the United States today were born deaf or lost their hearing before they had learned English. The challenge that faces them—recognizing that other peoples' mysterious lip movements *are* language, and then learning to speak that language—is immeasurably greater than that facing an adult who must cope with a gradual hearing loss.

10   Learning to speak is so hard for people deaf from infancy because they are trying, without any direct feedback, to mimic sounds they have never heard. (Children who learn to speak and then go deaf fare better, because they retain some memory of sound.) One mother of a deaf child describes the challenge as comparable to learning to speak Japanese from within a soundproof glass booth. And even if a deaf person does learn to speak, understanding someone else's speech remains maddeningly difficult. Countless words look alike on the lips, though they sound quite different. "Mama" is indistinguishable from "papa," "cat" from "hat," "no new taxes" from "go to Texas." Context and guesswork are crucial, and conversation becomes a kind of fast and ongoing crossword puzzle.

11   "Speechreading is EXHAUSTING. I hate having to depend on it," writes Cheryl Heppner, a deaf woman who is the executive director of the Northern Virginia Resource Center for Deaf and Hard of

Hearing Persons. Despite her complaint, Heppner is a speech-reading virtuoso. She made it through public school and Pennsylvania State University without the help of interpreters, and she says she has never met a person with better speech-reading skills. But "even with peak conditions," she explains, "good lighting, high energy level, and a person who articulates well, I'm still guessing at half of what I see on the lips." When we met in her office, our conversation ground to a halt every sentence or two, as if we were travelers without a common language who had been thrown together in a train compartment. I had great difficulty making out Heppner's soft, high-pitched speech, and far more often than not my questions and comments met only with her mouthed "Sorry." In frustration we resorted to typing on her computer.

12   For the average deaf person, lip-reading is even less rewarding. In tests using simple sentences, deaf people recognize perhaps three or four words in every ten. Ironically, the greatest aid to lip-reading is knowing how words sound. One British study found, for example, that the average deaf person with a decade of practice was no better at lip-reading than a hearing person picked off the street.

13   Unsurprisingly, the deaf score poorly on tests of English skills. The average deaf sixteen-year-old reads at the level of a hearing eight-year-old. When deaf students eventually leave school, three in four are unable to read a newspaper. Only two deaf children in a hundred (compared with forty in a hundred among the general population) go on to college. Many deaf students write English as if it were a foreign language. One former professor at Gallaudet, the elite Washington, D.C., university for the deaf, sometimes shows acquaintances a letter written by a student. The quality of the writing, he says, is typical. "As soon as you had lend me $15," the letter begins, "I felt I must write you to let you know how relievable I am in your aid."

14   Small wonder that many of the deaf eagerly turn to American Sign Language, invariably described as "the natural language of the deaf." Deaf children of deaf parents learn ASL as easily as hearing children learn a spoken language. At the same age that hearing babies begin talking, deaf babies of parents who sign begin "babbling" nonsense signs with their fingers. Soon, and without having to be formally taught, they have command of a rich and varied language, as expressive as English but as different from it as Urdu or Hungarian.

15   At the heart of the idea that deafness is cultural, in fact, is the deaf community's proprietary pride in ASL. Even among the hearing the discovery of ASL's riches has sometimes had a profound impact. The

most prominent ally of the deaf-culture movement, for example, is the Northeastern University linguist Harlan Lane, whose interest in the deaf came about through his study of ASL. When he first saw people signing to one another, Lane recalls, he was stunned to realize that "language could be expressed just as well by the hands and face as by the tongue and throat, even though the very definition of language we had learned as students was that it was something spoken and heard." For a linguist, Lane says, "this was astonishing, thrilling. I felt like Balboa seeing the Pacific."

16 Until the 1960s critics had dismissed signing as a poor substitute for language, a mere semaphoring of stripped-down messages ("I see the ball"). Then linguists demonstrated that ASL is in fact a full-fledged language, with grammar and puns and poems, and dignified it with a name. Anything that can be said can be said in ASL. In the view of the neurologist and essayist Oliver Sacks, it is "a language equally suitable for making love or speeches, for flirtation or mathematics."

17 ASL is the everyday language of perhaps half a million Americans. A shared language makes for a shared identity. With the deaf as with other groups, this identity is a prickly combination of pride in one's own ways and wariness of outsiders. "If I happened to strike up a relationship with a hearing person," says MJ Bienvenu, a deaf activist speaking through an interpreter, "I'd have considerable trepidation about my [deaf] parents' reaction. They'd ask, 'What's the matter? Aren't your own people good enough for you?' and they'd warn, 'They'll take advantage of you. You don't know what they're going to do behind your back.'"

18 Blind men and women often marry sighted people, but 90 percent of deaf people who marry take deaf spouses. When social scientists ask people who are blind or in wheelchairs if they wish they could see or walk, they say yes instantly. Only the deaf answer the equivalent question no. The essence of deafness, they explain, is not the lack of hearing but the community and culture based on ASL. Deaf culture represents not a denial but an affirmation.

19 Spokespeople for deaf pride present their case as self-evident and commonsensical. Why should anyone expect deaf people to deny their roots when every other cultural group proudly celebrates its traditions and history? Why stigmatize the speakers of a particular language as disabled? "When Gorbachev visited the U.S., he used an interpreter to talk to the President," says Bienvenu, who is one of the

directors of an organization called The Bicultural Center. "Was Gorbachev disabled?"

UNEASY ALLIES

20   Despite the claims made in its name, though, the idea that deafness is akin to ethnicity is hardly straightforward. On the contrary, it is an idea with profound and surprising implications, though these are rarely explored. When the deaf were in the news in 1988, for instance, protesting the choice of a hearing person as president of Gallaudet, the press assumed that the story was about disabled people asserting their rights, and treated it the same as if students at a university for the blind had demanded a blind president.

21   The first surprise in the cultural view of deafness is that it rejects the assumption that medical treatment means progress and is welcome. Since deafness is not a deprivation, the argument runs, talk of cures and breakthroughs and technological wizardry is both inappropriate and offensive—as if doctors and newspapers joyously announced advances in genetic engineering that might someday make it possible to turn black skin white.

22   Last fall, for example, *60 Minutes* produced a story on a bright, lively little girl named Caitlin Parton. "We don't remember ever meeting [anyone] who captivated us quite as much as this seven-year-old charmer," it began. Caitlin is deaf, and *60 Minutes* showed how a new device called a cochlear implant had transformed her life. Before surgeons implanted a wire in Caitlin's inner ear and a tiny receiver under her skin, she couldn't hear voices or barking dogs or honking cars. With the implant she can hear ordinary conversation, she can speak almost perfectly, and she is thriving in school. *60 Minutes* presented the story as a welcome break from its usual round of scandal and exposé. Who could resist a delightful child and a happy ending?

23   Activists in the deaf community were outraged. Implants, they thundered in letters to *60 Minutes*, are "child abuse" and "pathological" and "genocide." The mildest criticism was that Caitlin's success was a fluke that would tempt parents into entertaining similar but doomed hopes for their own children. "There should have been parades all across America," Caitlin's father lamented months later. "This is a miracle of biblical proportions, making the deaf hear. But we keep

hearing what a terrible thing this is, how it's like Zyklon B, how it has to be stopped."

24   The anger should have been easy to anticipate. The magazine *Deaf Life,* for example, runs a question-and-answer column called "For Hearing People Only." In response to a reader's question well before *60 Minutes* came along, the editors wrote, "An implant is the ultimate invasion of the ear, the ultimate denial of deafness, the ultimate refusal to let deaf children be Deaf. . . . Parents who choose to have their children implanted, are in effect saying, 'I don't respect the Deaf community, and I certainly don't want my child to be part of it. I want him/her to be part of the hearing world, not the Deaf world.'"

25   The roots of such hostility run far deeper than the specific fear that cochlear implants in children are unproved and risky. More generally, the objection is that from the moment parents suspect their child is deaf, they turn for expert advice to doctors and audiologists and speech therapists rather than to the true experts, deaf people. Harlan Lane points to one survey that found that 86 percent of deaf adults said they would not want a cochlear implant even if it were free. "There are many prostheses from eyeglasses and artificial limbs to cochlear implants," Lane writes. "Can you name another that we insist on for children in flagrant disregard of the advice of adults with the same 'condition'?"

26   The division between the deaf community and the medical one seems to separate two natural allies. Even more surprising is a second split, between deaf people and advocates for the disabled. In this case, though, the two sides remain uneasy partners, bound as if in a bad marriage. The deaf community knows that whatever its qualms, it cannot afford to cut itself off from the larger, savvier, wealthier disability lobby.

27   Historically, advocates for every disabled group have directed their fiercest fire at policies that exclude their group. No matter the good intentions, no matter the logistical hurdles, they have insisted, separate is not equal. Thus buildings, buses, classes, must be accessible to all; special accommodations for the disabled are not a satisfactory substitute. All this has become part of conventional wisdom. Today, under the general heading of "mainstreaming," it is enshrined in law and unchallenged as a premise of enlightened thought.

28   Except among the deaf. Their objection is that even well-meaning attempts to integrate deaf people into hearing society may actually imprison them in a zone of silence. Jostled by a crowd but unable to

communicate, they are effectively alone. The problem is especially acute in schools, where mainstreaming has led to the decline of residential schools for the disabled and the deaf and the integration of many such students into ordinary public schools. Since deafness is rare, affecting one child in a thousand, deaf students are thinly scattered. As a result, half of all deaf children in public school have either no deaf classmates at all or very few.

29   "Mainstreaming deaf children in regular public-school programs," the prominent deaf educator Leo Jacobs writes, will produce "a new generation of educational failures" and "frustrated and unfulfilled adults." Another deaf spokesman, Mervin Garretson, is even harsher. The danger of mainstreaming, he contends, is that deaf children could be "educationally, vocationally, and emotionally mutilated."

THE CASE FOR ASL

30 In his brilliant and polemical book *The Mask of Benevolence*, Harlan Lane, the chief theoretician of the deaf-culture movement, makes his case seem as clear-cut as a proposition in formal logic. Deaf children are biologically equipped to do everything but hear, he argues; spoken language turns on the ability to hear; therefore spoken language is a poor choice for deaf children. For good measure, Lane throws in a corollary: Since an alternative language, ASL, is both available and easy for the deaf to learn, ASL is a better choice for a first language. QED.

31   For the parents of a deaf child, though, matters are far from simple. (Lane is childless.) Parents have crucial decisions to make, and they don't have the luxury of time. Children who learn a language late are at a lifelong disadvantage. Deafness is, in one scholar's summary, "a curable, or rather a preventable, form of mental retardation."

32   Osmond and Deborah Crosby's daughter was born in July of 1988. "Dorothy Jane Crosby," the birth announcement began. "Stanford class of 2009, track, academic all-American, B.S. in pre-astronautics, Cum Laude. 2008 Olympics (decathlon), Miss Florida, Senate hopeful."

33   "You can chuckle about that announcement," Oz Crosby says now, "but we all have expectations for our kids. That card was a message from my unconscious—these are the kinds of things I'd like to see, that would make me proud, in my child. And the first thing that happened after DJ's deafness was diagnosed was that I felt that child had

died. That's something you hear a lot from parents, and it's that blunt and that real."

34   Crosby, fifty, is tall and athletic, with blond hair and a small, neat moustache. A timber executive who now lives in the suburbs of Washington, D.C., he is a serious and intelligent man who had scarcely given deafness a thought before it invaded his household. Then he plunged into the deafness literature and began keeping a journal of his own.

35   He found that every path was pocked with hazards. The course that sounds simplest, keeping the child at home with her parents and teaching her English, can prove fantastically difficult. Even basic communication is a constant challenge. In a memoir called *Deaf Like Me*, a man named Thomas Spradley tells of raising a deaf daughter, Lynn. One Saturday morning shortly after Lynn had begun school, Spradley and his wife, Louise, found her outdoors, waiting for the school bus. Lynn stood at the end of the driveway, scanning the street every few seconds. After half an hour she gave up and came indoors. For weeks Lynn repeated the same futile wait every Saturday and Sunday, until her parents finally managed to convey the concept of "weekday" and "weekend." Words like "car" and "shoes" were easy; abstractions and relationships were not. The Spradleys knew Lynn loved her grandparents, for instance, but they had no idea if she knew who those devoted elderly people were. When Lynn once had to undergo a spinal tap, her parents could not explain what the painful test was for.

36   As much trouble as Thomas and Louise Spradley had in talking with their daughter, she was just as frustrated in trying to communicate with them. "How do you tell Mommy that you don't like your cereal with that much milk on it?" Spradley writes. "How do you ask Daddy to swing you upside down when all he seems to understand is that you want to be held? How do you tell them that you want to go to other people's houses like [her older brother]? How do you make them understand you want the same kind of Kool-Aid that you had two weeks ago at your cousin's house and just now remembered? How do you say, 'I forgot what I wanted'?"

37   Making matters more frustrating still, no one seems able to tell parents how successful their child will be in speaking and understanding English. "I'd ask, 'What's the future for us?'" Crosby says, "and they'd say, 'Every deaf child is different.'" Though given to measured, even pedantic, phrasing, Crosby grows angry as he recalls the scene. "It seemed like such a cop-out. I wanted to grab them by the throat and shout, 'Here's the bloody audiogram. How's she going to talk?'"

38   The truth, Crosby has reluctantly come to concede, is that only a few generalizations are possible. Children who are born deaf or who lose their hearing before learning to speak have a far harder time than those deafened later. Children with a profound hearing loss have a harder time than children with a mild loss. Children who cannot detect high-pitched sounds have problems different from those of children who cannot detect low pitches. Finally, and unaccountably, some deaf children just happen to have an easier time with spoken English than others.

39   Hence few overall statistics are available. Those few are not encouraging. In one study, for example, teachers of the deaf, evaluating their own pupils, judged the speech of two thirds of them to be hard to understand or unintelligible. Timothy Jaech, the superintendent of the Wisconsin School for the Deaf, writes, "The vast majority of deaf children will never develop intelligible speech for the general public." Jaech, who is deaf, speaks and reads lips. "To gamble 12 to 15 years of a deaf child's life is almost immoral," he says. "[My sister] and I were among the lucky ones. What of the other 99 percent?"

40   Still, it is indisputable that many profoundly deaf adults participate fully and successfully in the hearing world, as lawyers and engineers and in dozens of other roles. Do these examples show what parents might expect for their own child? Or are they inspiring but irrelevant tales that have as little bearing on the typical deaf child as Michael Jordan's success has on the future of a ten-year-old dreaming of NBA glory?

41   The case for ASL has problems of its own. ASL is certainly easier for the deaf child to learn, but what of the rest of the family? How can parents say anything meaningful to their child in a foreign language they have only begun to study? Moreover, many hearing parents point out, even if deaf culture is rich and vital, it is indisputably not the majority culture. Since spoken language is the ticket to the larger world, isn't giving a child ASL as a first language a bit risky?

42   The choices are agonizing. "I understand now how people choosing a cancer therapy for their child must feel," Crosby says, "You can't afford to be wrong." To illustrate the dilemma, Crosby wrote what he calls a parable:

43   Suppose that your one-year-old, who has been slow to walk, has just been diagnosed with a rare disorder of the nervous system. The prognosis is

44   for great difficulty in muscular control of the arms and legs due to tremors and impaired nerve pathways. With the help of special braces, physical therapy, and lots of training, she will be able to walk slowly, climb stairs haltingly, and use her hands awkwardly. In general, she will be able to do most of the things other kids do, although not as easily, smoothly, or quickly. Some children respond to this therapy better than others, but all can get around on their legs after a fashion. Even though they will never run or play sports, they will have complete mobility at a deliberate, shuffling pace.

45   There *is* an alternative, however. If her legs are amputated right away, the tremors will cease, and the remaining nerve pathways will strengthen. She will be able to use a wheelchair with ease. She can even be a wheelchair athlete, "running" marathons, playing basketball, etc., if she desires. Anywhere a wheelchair can go is readily available to her. There is easy access to a world that is geographically smaller. On the other hand, she can't climb simple stairs, hike trails slowly, or even use public transportation without special assistance.

46   "Now, Mr. and Mrs. Solomon," Crosby concluded, "which life do *you* choose for your child?"

CUED SPEECH

47   Crosby and his wife have chosen a compromise, a controversial technique called cued speech, in which spoken English is accompanied by hand signals that enable a deaf person to distinguish between words that look alike on the lips. The aim is to remove the guesswork from lip-reading by using eight hand shapes in different positions near the face to indicate that the word being spoken is, say, "bat" rather than "pan."

48   The technique, which is spread by a tiny but zealous group of parents with deaf children, has several advantages. It's easy to learn, for one thing, taking only twenty or so hours of study. A parent who sets out to learn American Sign Language, in contrast, must devote months or years to the project, as he would have to do in order to learn any foreign language. And since cued speech is, essentially, English, parents can bypass the stilted, often useless phrases of the beginning language student. Instead of stumbling over "*la plume de ma tante,*" they can talk to their deaf child from the beginning about any subject in the world.

49   Moreover, because cued speech is simply English transliterated, rather than a new language, nothing has to be lost in translation. A deaf child who learns cued speech learns English, along with its slang and jargon and idioms and jokes, as his native language. "It's a way to embrace English, the language your whole country runs on, instead of trying to pretend it doesn't exist," says Judy Weiss, a woman in Washington, D.C., who has used cued speech with her son since he lost his hearing as a ten-month-old.

50   This method, which was invented at Gallaudet in 1965–1966, is nonetheless out of favor with the deaf community. It's seen as a slap at ASL and as just a new version of the despised "oralism," in which deaf students were forced for hour upon hour to try to pronounce English words they had never heard. But the proponents of cued speech insist that these objections are political and unfounded. They point to a handful of small studies that conclude that deaf children who learn cued speech read as well as hearing students, and they mention a small group of highly successful deaf students who rely on cuing. Perhaps the most accomplished of all is a Wellesley undergraduate named Stasie Jones. Raised in France by an American mother and a British father, she speaks French and English and is now studying Russian and Spanish.

51   But the system is no godsend. "The trap I see a lot of cuing families fall into," Crosby says, "is to say, 'Johnny understands everything we say, we understand everything he says, he's getting As at school— what's the problem?' The problem is, Johnny can't talk to someone he meets on the street and Johnny can't order a hamburger at McDonald's."

TOTAL COMMUNICATION

52   Cued speech is used only in a relative handful of schools. By far the most common method of teaching the deaf today is called "total communication." The idea is that teachers use any and all means of communication with their students—speech, writing, ASL, fingerspelling. Total communication was instituted in the 1970s as a reaction to a century of oralism, in which signing was forbidden and the aim was to teach the deaf child to speak and lip-read.

53   Oralism still has zealous adherents, but today it is used mainly with hard-of-hearing students and only rarely with deaf ones. Its dominance began with the Congress of Milan, an international meeting of educators in 1880, which affirmed "the incontestable superiority of speech over sign" and voted to banish sign language from deaf education. The ban, notorious to this day among the deaf, was effective. In 1867 every American school for the deaf taught in ASL; by 1907 not a single one did.

54   When total communication came along, the two rival camps in deaf education accepted it warily. Those who favored English reasoned that at least teachers would be speaking to their students; those who preferred ASL were pleased that teachers would be signing. Today hardly anyone is pleased, and one of the few points of agreement in the present debate is that deaf education is distressingly bad. The Commission on Education of the Deaf, for example, which reported to the President and Congress in 1988, began its account, "The present status of education for persons who are deaf in the United States is unsatisfactory. Unacceptably so. This is [our] primary and inescapable conclusion."

55   The explanation for these dreary findings, depending on who is carrying out the analysis, is either that deafness is so debilitating that poor results are inevitable or that something is wrong with current teaching methods. Total communication, its critics contend, is unworkable. No teacher can speak in English and simultaneously sign the same message in ASL, which has a completely different grammar and word order. "In practice," Harlan Lane writes, "'total communication' merely means that the teacher may accompany his spoken English with some signs from American Sign Language, if he knows a few. While the teacher is speaking, he occasionally 'shouts' a sign— that is, signs a prominent noun or verb if he knows it, in the wrong order and without using the complex grammar of ASL."

56   Lane and his allies support an approach called bilingual-bicultural. In this new and still rare program (so new that few measures of its success or failure are available) students are taught in ASL and eventually build on that knowledge to learn English as a second language. Since learning to speak is so difficult and time-consuming, the emphasis in English courses is on reading and writing rather than on speaking.

57   Neither this new approach nor any other single method may prove right for everyone. Take Cheryl Heppner, the director of the Northern Virginia Resource Center. She was deafened by meningitis as a second-grader, long after she had become expert in English. Today

Heppner is a great admirer of ASL, which she learned as an adult, but she says nonetheless that classes taught in ASL would not have been best for her. "Why should they have stripped English away from me?" she asks. "I already had to learn to cope with deafness."

58   The objections of many hearing parents to the bilingual scheme are far more strenuous. ASL is not simply a different language, they note, but a language without a written form. Partly as a consequence, deaf culture has a marked anti-book bias. (Lane himself confesses that he is "really frustrated" that so few deaf people have read his eloquent but lengthy accounts of deaf culture.) "If you give your child, as a first language, a language that has no written form," Oz Crosby says, "and if that language on average does not lead to good reading skills, then you're giving that child a life in which she reads at a third- to fifth-grade level. She will be in danger of being exploited, because low-end jobs are all that will be available to her."

59   Two deep and related fears lie at the heart of the resentment of the bilingual approach. First, many hearing parents suspect that bilingualism is a Trojan horse. Once ASL has been smuggled in, they fear, talk of English as a second language will dry up. Second, and more important, they resent the implication that deaf adults know better than a deaf child's own parents what is best for her. This is more than parental paranoia. Lane has written, for instance, that "most hearing parents make a botch of having a Deaf child."

60   Deaf leaders do their best to defuse such fears. "We don't say that hearing parents aren't qualified to make decisions about their deaf children," says Roslyn Rosen, of the National Association of the Deaf. "We say that they need to have contact with deaf people if they're going to make educated decisions. The way the system works now is that the first people the parents see are doctors and audiologists, who see deafness as a pathology. What we need are partnerships between hearing parents and the deaf community, so that parents can meet deaf people who are doing well."

61   Even deaf adults who don't identify with deaf culture often feel that they have important but untapped expertise on growing up deaf. "There is a strong feeling of community, and deaf people feel ownership of deaf children," Cheryl Heppner says. "I admit it. I feel it too. I really struggle in not wanting to interfere with a parent's right to parent and at the same time dealing with my own feelings and knowing that they have to accept that the child can never be one hundred percent theirs."

62   Such concessions rouse dark fears in hearing parents. Time and
again their talk turns to laments about "giving up" or "losing" or
"turning over" their child to the deaf community. Even Oz Crosby,
who strives to be open-minded, observes that "sometimes Deaf Culture looks like the Moonies to me: 'Your child will be happy, just don't
expect to see her anymore, she's too busy being happy.'"

63   These fears crystallize around the issue of residential schools for
the deaf, which have far different associations for deaf and hearing families. Hearing parents think of residential schools and conjure up the
bleakest scenes in Dickens or the angriest images in a Frederick Wise-
man documentary, with their child stuck away in a human warehouse.
But among the deaf, residential schools have tremendous support.
Here deaf children will not "drown in the mainstream," as Lane puts
it, but will instead flourish among their peers. The schools provide a
lifesaving chance to escape from isolation into community.

64   Patrick Graybill, a prominent figure in the deaf community and
a former member of the National Theatre of the Deaf, attended a
residential school in Kansas starting at age five. His enthusiastic memories of those years are typical. "I was really happy at school," he says,
through an interpreter. "I saw my first plays there, and I knew that's
what I wanted to do when I grew up. There were deaf adults I looked
up to, and a good support system."

65   The classes were by no means uniformly excellent. "The emphasis was on English, and we were hit if we were caught talking with our
hands. The speech teacher couldn't sign, and I used to hate having to
touch her throat and neck, to learn the sounds to make, and smelling
her breath." But pedagogy wasn't the point. "ASL was allowed in the
dormitories," Graybill says, "and that's where we learned Deaf culture. Now I see kids in public schools, and some accept themselves as
Deaf people, but others have a problem with it. We knew who we
were, but I'm afraid they'll be lost between two worlds, because they
can't speak well enough to be understood by hearing people and
they're ashamed to use ASL."

66   Residential schools play such an important role in deaf culture that
when two deaf adults meet, they tell each other not only their names
but also the names of the schools they attended. "These schools were
the place where their culture was transmitted to them," Lane says. "If
they had hearing parents, they weren't going to find out how to be deaf
in their homes or in the local schools. This was where it happened,

and frequently it's where they found their spouses, too. The schools are what Israel is to the Jews, the land of a minority without a land."

67   The world of the deaf is heterogeneous, and the fault lines that run through it are twisted and tricky. Now politics has worsened the strains. Frances Parsons, for example, is a much honored Gallaudet professor who, though deaf herself, has denounced "the extremists fanatically hawking ASL and Deafism." Such views have brought her hate mail and denunciatory posters and, once, a punch in the neck. Parsons sees her attackers as cultists and propagandists; they call her and her allies traitors and Uncle Toms.

68   Much of the dispute has to do with who is authentically deaf. Parsons is suspect because she speaks and has hearing parents. To be the deaf child of deaf parents has cachet, because this is as deaf as one can be. (The four student leaders of the 1988 Gallaudet protest were all "deaf of deaf.") To use ASL is "better" than to use a manual language that mimics English grammar and arranges ASL signs in English word order. "Those born deaf deride those who become deaf at six years or twelve years or later," the Gallaudet psychologist Larry Stewart observed last year in a bitter essay titled "Debunking the Bilingual-Bicultural Snow Job in the American Deaf Community." "ASL-users who do not use lip movements scorn those who sign with mouthed English, or, the other way around. Residential school graduates turn up their nose at mainstream graduates, or the reverse. And so it goes; a once cohesive community now splintered apart by ideology."

69   Still, there is some common ground and even room for optimism. Captioning on television is universally welcomed; so are TTYs, keyboard devices that allow the deaf to use the telephone, provided the person called also has a TTY. In most states phone companies provide a free "relay" service, in which an operator with a TTY serves as a link between a deaf person with a TTY and a hearing person without one.

70   "Things are getting better," Roslyn Rosen says. "When I check into a hotel, because of the Americans With Disabilities Act, I expect the TV in the room will have captions, there'll be a TTY, the phone and the fire alarm will have flashing lights, and all that. And soon there will be TV-phones, which will be a wonderful boon for people who use sign language."

71   What's the difference between these technologies, which Rosen welcomes, and such a device as the cochlear implant, which she

denounces? "An implant," she says, "alters *me*. The critical point is, it changes me instead of changing the environment. Therefore the problem is seen as belonging to the deaf person, and *that's* a problem."

72

To an outsider, this sounds a bit forced. Do eyeglasses, say, belong to one moral category and eye surgery to another? A more useful distinction may be between approaches that allow deaf people to participate in the world and those that leave them stranded on the sidelines. "Part of the odyssey I've made," Cheryl Heppner says, "is in realizing that deafness is a disability, but it's a disability that is unique." It is unique in that a deaf person, unaided and independent, can travel wherever he wants, whenever he wants. The question is whether he will be able to communicate with anyone when he gets there.

Understanding Meaning

1. Dolnick opens his essay with a *narrative* outlining the historical view of deafness. What was the traditional definition of deafness?
2. What definition do many deaf advocates rebel against? If deafness is not a "disability" or a "handicap," what is it? Does a common language define a culture?
3. Dolnick *compares* blindness to deafness. Sighted people can wear a blindfold, he points out, and realize what obstacles the blind encounter. But why does wearing earmuffs and blocking out all sounds fail to approximate deafness in hearing people?
4. Dolnick states that "many deaf parents cheer on discovering that their baby is deaf." What does this reveal? Discuss whether it signifies a dramatic gulf between the hearing and deaf communities.
5. *Critical Thinking:* How do you respond to the idea that performing surgery to make a deaf child hear is akin to bleaching the skin of an African American child? Is this a rational comparison?

Evaluating Strategy

1. *Other Modes:* How does Dolnick use the *narrative* of the Crosby family to develop his essay?
2. *Other Modes:* How does Dolnick use *division* to explain the different methods of teaching deaf children to communicate? Where does he use *classification* to demonstrate the range of hearing impairment?
3. Dolnick uses quotes and interviews throughout the essay. Is this an effective technique in discussing a complex and controversial issue? Is it

best to let people speak for themselves instead of paraphrasing their views? Does this help a writer maintain objectivity?

Appreciating Language

1. In discussing a controversial issue, Dolnick must choose words that are loaded with meaning. "Disability" and "culture" have clear connotations. Can one make an objective definition when forced to choose words that might contain subjective meanings to the reader?
2. How does Dolnick's word choice reflect his views on deafness? What words does he use to *describe* advocates who define deafness as a culture and not a handicap?
3. Why do people capitalize *deaf?* What is implied by the use of "the Deaf"?
4. How does Dolnick define the terms "total communication," "bicultural," and "cued speech"?

Connections across the Disciplines

1. Relate Dolnick's article to Amy Tan's "The Language of Discretion" (page 274). How does language, in any form, determine culture?
2. Consider Eileen Simpson's article about dyslexia (page 177). She describes coping skills dyslexics use to function. At what point do people who share a coping process become a "community" or a "culture"?

Writing Suggestions

1. Write an essay outlining your definition of *culture.* Include examples to support your view.
2. *Critical Writing:* Write an essay responding to this writing prompt: "If medical technology develops methods of curing deafness at birth, a valuable culture and unique language will be lost." Agree or disagree with this point of view.
3. *Collaborative Writing:* Ask other students about their own experience and knowledge of deaf people. Then write a brief *analysis* of how society has attempted to accommodate the needs of the deaf. Consider this point: Since many deaf people do not consider English their language, do closed-captioned television programs and related efforts really address the needs of the deaf?

Two Definitions of Depression

Definition is a critical feature of all professional writing. Professionals need common standards in order to communicate and operate efficiently. The way definitions are expressed depends on the writer's goal, the audience, and the discipline.

This definition is taken from a specialized encyclopedia designed for mental health professionals. As a standard reference, it seeks to establish a common understanding of terms for people who must diagnose and treat patients with psychological problems.

DEPRESSION

The Concept of Depression

1   *Depression* is a term used to describe a mood, a symptom, and syndromes of affective disorders. As a mood, it refers to a transient state of feeling sad, blue, forlorn, cheerless, unhappy, and/or down. As a symptom, it refers to a complaint that often accompanies a group of biopsychosocial problems. In contrast, the depressive syndromes include a wide spectrum of psychobiological dysfunctions that vary in frequency, severity, and duration. Normal depression is a transient period of sadness and fatigue that generally occurs in response to identifiable stressful life events. The moods associated with normal depression vary in length but generally do not exceed 7 to 10 days. If the problems continue for a longer period and if the symptoms grow in complexity and severity, clinical levels of depression may be present. Clinical depression generally involves sleep disorders, eating disorders, anergia, hopelessness, and despair. Sometimes problems assume psychotic proportions, and the depressed individual may attempt suicide and/or may experience hallucinations, delusions, and serious psychological and motor retardation.

DON D. ROSENBERG

This definition, written by a practicing psychologist, appeared in a brochure distributed in the waiting room of a Milwaukee mental health clinic. It is directed to the general public and seeks to explain the nature of depression to people seeking help from psychological problems they may have difficulty understanding.

WHAT IS DEPRESSION?

1 Depression is <u>an internal state—a feeling of sadness, loss, "the blues,"</u> <u>deep disappointment</u>. *When it is more severe, you may have feelings of irritability, touchiness, guilt, self-reproach, loss of self-esteem, worthlessness, hopelessness, helplessness, and even thoughts of death and suicide.* It may include such other feelings as <u>tearfulness, being sensitive and easily</u> <u>hurt, loss of interests, loss of sexual drive, loss of control in life, feeling</u> <u>drained and depleted, anger at yourself, and loss of the ability to feel</u> <u>pleasure.</u>

2 It may be accompanied by *physical symptoms* similar to the sense of profound loss, including:

3 * *loss of appetite*, often with weight loss, but sometimes we find increased eating
 * *insomnia or early morning waking*, often 2–4 times per night, nearly every day, but sometimes we see a need to sleep excessively
 * moving and speaking slows down, but sometimes we see *agitation*
 * *fatigue or loss of energy* nearly every day
 * *loss of concentration*, foggy and indecisive
 * sometimes it includes anxious and headachy feelings and also *frequent crying*

4 Besides the <u>physical sensations</u> and <u>emotions of depression</u>, depressed people may *withdraw, may brood or ruminate about problems*, have trouble remembering things, wonder if they would be better off dead, and become very concerned about bodily symptoms and pains. They may be grouchy, sulking, restless, and unwilling to interact with family and friends.

Understanding Meaning

1. *The Encyclopedia of Psychology* is a reference text for mental health students and professionals. What is the purpose of this definition? How does

it differ from the clinic's brochure's definition, aimed at the general public?

2. What role does definition play in the treatment of any disorder? How is addressing professionals different from addressing potential patients?
3. Which are the objective statements in both definitions? Do both definitions agree on the basic elements of depression?
4. How does the brochure address its readers differently from the encyclopedia?
5. *Other Modes:* What *persuasive* elements are used in the brochure?

Evaluating Strategy

1. The brochure by Don Rosenberg uses italics, underlining, and asterisks for highlighting. What functions do these have? Discuss their suitability.
2. How does the brochure direct its message to the public and potential patients?

Appreciating Language

1. Does the purpose of the definition dictate the tone of the language in these two examples? Does the encyclopedia's *description* focus on objective, observable symptoms? Does the brochure seem to focus on feelings and emotions?
2. Would the language of the encyclopedia appear cold and unfeeling to a patient seeking help with depression?

Writing Suggestions

1. Take a definition from the glossary section of a textbook, and write a version for a general audience of clients, consumers, or students.
2. Using information from the encyclopedia and brochure, write a definition of depression targeted to college students. Describe symptoms in terms students will readily identify.
3. *Collaborative Writing:* Discuss a common problem or issue with fellow students: job insecurity, lack of sleep, stressful family relationships, child care, or the fear of crime. Select a term you often overhear, and provide a clear definition for it. Have each member of the group list features of this term. Try to incorporate objective elements. Write the definition in two versions: one designed for an "official" publication such as the college catalog or textbook, the other for an informal handout.

STRATEGIES FOR WRITING DEFINITIONS

1. **Determine your purpose.** Does your definition seek to provide a common language to prevent confusion, or does it seek to persuade readers by altering their perceptions?
2. **Define your role.** Your definition can be based on personal observation and opinion or standard principles and methods followed in a specific discipline or profession.
3. **Consider your audience.** What knowledge base do your readers have? Your definition should offer recognizable examples in language they will understand. Determine what uses your audience has for this definition. Will readers have to base decisions on your definition?
4. **Make extended definitions relevant.** Extended definitions depend on examples, illustrations, and narratives. The items you include to explain your topic should be relevant and understandable to your audience.
5. **Review special needs of the discipline or writing situation.** Each discipline can have a distinct history, research methodology, and set of concerns. Make sure your definition respects any special interests and addresses special needs.
6. **Use or refer to existing definitions.** Instead of attempting to create your own definition, you can adopt an existing one. If you accept the American Psychological Association's definition of *obsession*, you can simply restate the definition for readers. In using existing definitions, acknowledge their sources. If you disagree with an existing or official definition, restate it and then demonstrate how your interpretation differs.

SUGGESTED TOPICS FOR WRITING DEFINITIONS
General Assignments

Write a definition on any of the following topics. Your definition will probably contain other modes, such as description, comparison, and narration. Choose your terminology carefully, and avoid using words with misleading connotations. When defining complex and abstract concepts, consider using John Ciardi's method of defining extremes and then working toward the middle.

- A successful professional in your career. Define a good defense attorney, computer programmer, nurse, or teacher.
- A good relationship

- Pornography. Provide a personal definition including examples and social impact.
- Addiction
- The perfect career
- An educated person
- A healthy lifestyle
- The level of insanity at which a person should not be held criminally liable for his or her actions
- Racism
- Self-respect

Writing in Context

1. Imagine you have been asked to write a brief brochure about college life to be distributed to disadvantaged high school students. The principal stresses that she fears many of her students lack independent study skills and the discipline needed to succeed in college. Define the characteristics of a good college student, stressing hard work.

2. You have been asked to participate in a panel on sexual harassment. In preparation, provide two definitions of sexual harassment: one expressing attitudes, feelings, and statements you have observed and heard from males on campus, the other from females. Try to be as objective as possible, and state any differences fairly.

STUDENT PAPER: DEFINITION

This is a working draft of a paper written in response to the following assignment:

Invent a definition for a social issue or problem you have experienced. You may support your definition with factual research or personal observation. Make sure your paper clearly defines the subject and not simply describes it.

DISNEYLAND DADS

1   Like half the members of my generation, I am the product of what used to be called a "broken home." My parents divorced when I was eight. I lived with my mother and saw my father on alternate weekends and two weeks during the summer.

2   My father, like many of *his* generation, was a classic Disneyland Dad. The Disneyland Dad is usually found at malls, little league fields, upscale pizza restaurants and ice cream parlors. He is usually accompanied by a child busily eating food forbidden by Mom, wearing new clothes, or playing with expensive toys. The Disneyland Dad dispenses cash like an ATM and provides an endless supply of quarters for arcade games. Whether they are motivated by guilt, frustration, or an inability to parent, Disneyland Dads substitute material items for fatherly advice, guidance, and discipline.

3   While my mother furnished the hands-on, day to day parenting, my father remained distant. My mother monitored my eating habits, my friends, my grades, even the programs I watched on television. But without daily contact with my mother, my father found it difficult to make decisions about my upbringing. He was afraid of contradicting Mom. So he showered me with gifts and trips. He expanded my wardrobe, gave me my first pieces of real jewelry, introduced me to Broadway shows, and took me to Disneyland — but he did not help me with school, teach me about the job market, give me insight into boys, or allow me to be nothing more than a spoiled consumer.

4   As I grew older, my relationship with my father became strained. Weekends with him were spent shopping, going to movies, playing tennis, and horseback riding — activities I loved, but activities that limited opportunities for anything but casual conversation.

5   Like most of my friends, I came to view my father as more of an uncle than a parent. He was a beloved family figure, someone who could be counted on for some extra cash, new clothes, a pizza. And like most of my friends, I was troubled by the gulf that widened between my father and myself. I talked, argued, and made up with my mother as I went through my teens. Both of us changed over the years. But my father remained the same — the generous but distant Disneyland Dad.

6   The Disneyland Dad is a neglected figure. While books and daytime talk shows focus on the plight of single moms, few people offer advice to the fathers. Men in our society are judged by success and conditioned to dispense tokens of their achievement to their children. We kids of divorce *want* all the things the Disneyland Dad can offer, but we really *need* his attention, his guidance, his experience, his mentoring. Someone has to help Disneyland Dads become fathers.

Questions for Review and Revision

1. What tone does the term "Disneyland Dad" have? Is it suitable for a serious essay? What connotations does it suggest?
2. Does this student really "define" or merely "describe" Disneyland Dads?
3. Does the paper include enough details to outline the qualities of a Disneyland Dad?
4. The student uses italics to highlight certain words. Do you find this an effective technique?
5. *Other Modes:* Where does the student use *narration* and *comparison* to develop the essay? Does the final paragraph state a *persuasive argument?*
6. Read the paper aloud. Can you detect awkward or vague passages that would benefit from revision?

Writing Suggestions

1. Invent a term that defines a personality type, and illustrate it using a parent, friend, or coworker as an example.
2. *Collaborative Writing:* Discuss this paper with several students, and collect ideas for a process paper that offers tips to teenage children on how to communicate with a Disneyland Dad.

DEFINITION CHECKLIST

Before submitting your paper, review these points.

1.   Is your purpose clear—to inform or persuade?

2.   Do you avoid defining a word with the same word, such as "a diffusion pump diffuses"?

3.   Is your level of technical or professional language suited to your audience?

4.   Does your definition provide enough information and examples so that readers can restate your thesis in their own words?

5.   Are there existing definitions you can use for reference or contrast?

6.   Do extended definitions contain illustrations, narratives, or comparisons that readers may either not recognize or misinterpret?

7.   Do you state the essence of your definition in a short summary statement that readers can remember or highlight for future reference?

 WebTutor

See www.harcourtcollege.com/english/sundance
for information on writing definitions.

5

Comparison and Contrast

INDICATING SIMILARITIES
AND DIFFERENCES

WHAT IS COMPARISON AND CONTRAST?

Comparison and contrast answers the question: How are things alike or different? What distinguishes a gasoline engine from a diesel engine? Is it cheaper to buy or lease a car? What separates a misdemeanor from a felony? How does a bacterial infection differ from a viral one? What did Malcolm X and Martin Luther King Jr. have in common? Do men and women approach mathematics differently? All of these questions can be answered by comparing similarities and contrasting differences.

You have probably encountered essay questions that require comparison and contrast responses:

Compare the industrial output of the North and South at the outbreak of the Civil War. Which side was better equipped to prosecute a protracted conflict?

How do the rules of evidence differ in criminal and civil proceedings?

Which arrangement offers business owners greater protection of personal assets—full or limited partnerships?

Contrast Freud's dream theory with Jung's concept of the unconscious.

At the end of *The Great Gatsby*, Nick Carraway decides to return to the West because he is too "squeamish" for the East. What differences did Fitzgerald see between the East and West?

Outline the principal differences between warm- and cold-blooded animals.

Comparison and contrast writing is commonly used to organize re-search papers. You might compare two short stories by Edgar Allan Poe in an English course, explain the differences among methods of depreciation in accounting, or contrast conflicting theories of child-hood development for psychology. Comparison and contrast writing is also used by engineers to explain the fuel efficiency of different en-gines, by real estate developers to explore potential building sites, and by social workers to determine the best method of delivering medical services to the homeless.

The Purposes of Comparison and Contrast

Writers use comparison and contrast for two purposes:

1. **To draw distinctions among related subjects.** In many instances com-parison is used to eliminate confusion. Many people, for instance, mistake an *optician*, who makes and sells eyeglasses, for an *optometrist*, who per-forms eye examinations and prescribes lenses. Comparison can pair extended definitions to show readers the difference, for example, between air-cooled and water-cooled engines, African and Indian elephants, or cross-country and downhill skiing. When drawing distinctions, writers explain differences between similar subjects but do not choose one over the other. William Zinsser's essay "The Transaction" (page 248) con-trasts the ways two writers work without endorsing either writer's method. The basic goal of drawing distinctions is to *inform readers of similarities and differences*.
2. **To recommend a choice between two things.** Television commercials compare competing products. Political campaign brochures urge voters to support a candidate over his or her rival. Articles in medical journals argue that one drug is more effective than another. Business proposals rec-ommend one computer program or one security service over competitors. Government studies assert that one air-quality standard is preferable to another. In "A Tale of Two Sitcoms" (page 259), Steven Stark recom-mends *Home Improvement* as "a better reflection of who we are" than *Seinfeld*, despite its lesser success with critics. The basic purpose of stat-ing recommendations is to *persuade readers to make a choice*.

Organizing Comparison and Contrast Papers

When developing a paper using comparison and contrast, you must be sure your subjects share enough common points for meaningful discussion. You can compare two sports cars, two action adventure films, or two diets. But comparing a sports car to a station wagon, an action film to a comedy, or a diet to plastic surgery is not likely to generate more than superficial observations. The entries in this chapter focus on related subjects, such as the ways two writers work or the backgrounds of two Civil War generals.

In addition, comparisons have to be carefully limited, especially when comparing broad or complex subjects. For contrasting the differences between American and Chinese cultures, Yi-Fu Tuan (page 245) limits the essay to demonstrating the different ways Americans and Chinese view space and place. By exploring this limited topic in depth, Yi-Fu Tuan reveals more about Chinese culture in a page or two than a twenty-page essay would that attempts to cover religion, politics, economics, history, and marriage customs. If you are comparing two presidents, you might focus your comparison on their relations with the press, the way they handled crises, or their trade policies.

Perhaps the most frustrating problem students face while writing comparison and contrast papers is organizing ideas. Without careful planning, you may find yourself awkwardly switching back and forth between subjects. Your reader may have difficulty following your train of thought and may confuse one subject with another. Whether drawing distinctions or making recommendations, writers use two methods of organizing comparison and contrast.

Subject by Subject

The *subject-by-subject* method divides the paper into two sections. Writers state all the information about topic A and then discuss topic B. Usually, the actual comparisons are drawn in the second part of the paper, where B is discussed in relation to A. In a short paper about two types of life insurance, the writer first explains "whole life" insurance and then discusses "term" insurance and draws distinctions between the two types. Since the purpose is to make distinctions, the conclusion does not offer a recommendation:

WHOLE LIFE AND TERM INSURANCE

Most life insurance companies offer a variety of life insurance products, investments, and financial services. Two of the most common policies provided are whole life and term insurance.

Whole life insurance is the oldest and most traditional form of life insurance. Life insurance became popular in the nineteenth century as a way of protecting the buyer's dependents in the event of premature death. A purchaser would select a policy amount to be paid to his or her beneficiaries after his or her death. Payments called premiums were made on a yearly, quarterly, or monthly basis. As the policyholder paid premiums, the policy gained cash value. Part of the payment earned interest like money in a bank account. Insurance served as an investment tool, allowing people to save for retirement and giving them access to guaranteed loans. For a low interest fee, insurance holders could borrow against the cash value of their policies.

Term insurance, introduced in the twentieth century, serves the same basic purpose as whole life insurance, protecting the insured's dependents. Unlike whole life, however, no cash value accrues. In a sense the policyholder is "renting" insurance, buying only a death benefit. The advantage of term insurance is its low cost. Because there is no money set aside for investment, the premiums are lower. This allows a person to afford a larger policy. A term policy for $100,000 could be cheaper than a whole life policy for $50,000.

The type of insurance a person needs depends on his or her income, family situation, investment goals, savings, and obligations. Most investment counselors agree, however, that anyone with a spouse or children should have some form of life insurance protection.

Advantages and Disadvantages   The subject-by-subject method is best suited to short papers. A twenty-page report organized in this fashion would read much like two ten-page papers fastened together. It would be difficult for readers to remember enough of the first subject to appreciate how it differs from the second. This method, however, allows writers to compare abstract subjects with ease, especially when a subject has individual features the other does not share.

Point by Point

The *point-by-point* method organizes the comparison of A and B on a number of specific points. Following an introduction, A and B are discussed in a series of comparisons. Hotels, for example, have a number of common points: location, appearance, atmosphere, and room rates. In the following paper, the writer groups comments about the two hotels in each paragraph. For the recommendation, the writer states a clear preference in the opening and concluding paragraphs:

ST. GREGORY AND FITZPATRICK HOTELS

Campus organizations and academic conventions visiting the city hold special events in either the St. Gregory or Fitzpatrick. Both are large convention hotels, but for many reasons the St. Gregory is more desirable.

Opened in 1892, the St. Gregory is the oldest surviving hotel in the city. The Fitzpatrick is the newest, having opened just last spring. The St. Gregory has a commanding view of State Street. The Fitzpatrick is part of the $200 million Riverfront Centre.

The chief attraction of the St. Gregory is its famed domed lobby ornamented with carved mahogany and elaborate brass and marble fittings. Admiral Dewey was presented with the key to the city here following his victory in Manila Bay in 1898. In contrast, the sleek Fitzpatrick is noted for its sweeping thirty-story atrium. The open lobby is banked with massive video screens.

The main lounge of the St. Gregory is the Pump Room, a plush, turn-of-the-century Irish bar decorated with gilt-framed paintings of the Emerald Isle. The Fitzpatrick features two bars. Homerun, a sports bar, is popular with local students and young professionals. The Exchange is a smaller, quieter bar that is a favorite of visiting executives. Copies, fax machines, and computers are available in the nearby executive center.

Both hotels offer a range of room rates. The cheapest rooms at the St. Gregory are $95 a night. Though small, they are comfortable. The Fitzpatrick has only a dozen single traveler rooms for $125. Double rooms at the St. Gregory range from $175 to $250, depending on size and decor. All Fitzpatrick double rooms are identical and cost $195. In addition to convention rates, the St. Gregory offers 20 percent student discounts. The Fitzpatrick does not offer student discounts.

Both hotels provide excellent convention services. Since most professors and academic delegates have access to university computers and fax machines, they prefer the historic elegance of the St. Gregory. Students especially appreciate discount rates and the availability of public transport to the university.

Advantages and Disadvantages   The point-by-point method is useful in organizing longer and more technical papers. The specific facts, statistics, and quotes about A and B appear side by side. Readers of a long report about two hotels organized in a subject-by-subject manner would be easily frustrated because instead of seeing room rates compared in the same paragraph, they might have to flip back a dozen pages. Point-by-point organization is helpful when addressing multiple readers who may be interested in only a portion of the paper. However, point-by-point papers about abstract subjects such as two films or two novels might be difficult to organize because many important details about one subject may have nothing in common with the other subject.

As you read the essays in this chapter, you may note that many writers blend both methods to develop their comparisons.

STRATEGIES FOR READING COMPARISON AND CONTRAST

When reading the comparison and contrast entries in this chapter, keep these questions in mind.

Meaning

1. What is the writer's goal—to draw distinctions or to recommend a choice?
2. What details does the writer present about each subject?
3. Who is the intended audience? Is the essay directed to a general or a specific reader?
4. Is the comparison valid? Is the writer comparing two subjects in a fair manner? Have any points been overlooked?
5. Does the author have an apparent bias?
6. If the comparison makes a recommendation, does the selection seem valid? What makes the chosen subject superior to the others? What evidence is offered?

Strategy

1. What is the basic pattern of the comparison—subject by subject or point by point? Do variations occur?
2. Does the author use a device to narrow the topic or to advance the comparison?
3. Does the writer make use of visual aids? Are they effective?

Language

1. Does the writer use connotations that ascribe positive or negative qualities to one or both of the items? How does the author describe the two subjects?

2. What do the diction, level of language, and use of technical terms reveal about the intended audience?
3. If suggesting a choice, how does the writer use language to highlight its desirability?

Yi-Fu Tuan (1930–) was born in China and later moved to the United States. Now a geography professor in Madison, Wisconsin, he has studied the cultural differences between America and his native country. He states that he writes "from a single perspective—namely that of experience." In this article published in Harper's, he compares the way people in two cultures view their environments.

Chinese Space,
American Space

Cultures as diverse as America's and China's have many points of difference. In attempting to provide insight into their differences in a brief essay, Yi-Fu Tuan focuses on the concept of space and location. Americans, he asserts, are less rooted to place and are future oriented. The Chinese, savoring tradition, are deeply tied to specific locations.

1   Americans have a sense of space, not of place. Go to an American home in exurbia, and almost the first thing you do is drift toward the picture window. How curious that the first compliment you pay your host inside his house is to say how lovely it is outside his house! He is pleased that you should admire his vistas. The distant horizon is not merely a line separating earth from sky, it is a symbol of the future. The American is not rooted in his place, however lovely: his eyes are drawn by the expanding space to a point on the horizon, which is his future.

2   By contrast, consider the traditional Chinese home. Blank walls enclose it. Step behind the spirit wall and you are in a courtyard with perhaps a miniature garden around a corner. Once inside his private compound you are wrapped in an ambiance of calm beauty, an ordered world of buildings, pavement, rock, and decorative vegetation. But you have no distant view: nowhere does space open out before you. Raw nature in such a home is experienced only as weather, and the only open space is the sky above. The Chinese is rooted in his place. When he has to leave, it is not for the promised land on the terrestrial

horizon, but for another world altogether along the vertical, religious axis of his imagination.

3   The Chinese tie to place is deeply felt. Wanderlust is an alien sentiment. The Taoist classic *Tao Te Ching* captures the ideal of rootedness in place with these words: "Though there may be another country in the neighborhood so close that they are within sight of each other and the crowing of cocks and barking of dogs in one place can be heard in the other, yet there is no traffic between them; and throughout their lives the two peoples have nothing to do with each other." In theory if not in practice, farmers have ranked high in Chinese society. The reason is not only that they are engaged in a "root" industry of producing food but that, unlike pecuniary merchants, they are tied to the land and do not abandon their country when it is in danger.

4   Nostalgia is a recurrent theme in Chinese poetry. An American reader of translated Chinese poems may well be taken aback—even put off—by the frequency, as well as the sentimentality, of the lament for home. To understand the strength of this sentiment, we need to know that the Chinese desire for stability and rootedness in place is prompted by the constant threat of war, exile, and the natural disasters of flood and drought. Forcible removal makes the Chinese keenly aware of their loss. By contrast, Americans move, for the most part, voluntarily. Their nostalgia for home town is really longing for a childhood to which they cannot return: in the meantime the future beckons and the future is "out there," in open space. When we criticize American rootlessness, we tend to forget that it is a result of ideals we admire, namely, social mobility and optimism about the future. When we admire Chinese rootedness, we forget that the word "place" means both a location in space and position in society: to be tied to place is also to be bound to one's station in life, with little hope of betterment. Space symbolizes hope; place, achievement and stability.

Understanding Meaning

1. How does the author see a difference between "space" and "place"?
2. What do the traditional designs of American and Chinese homes reveal about cultural differences?
3. Why do the Chinese honor farmers?
4. What historical forces have shaped the Chinese desire for "rootedness"? How is American history different?

5. What negative aspects does Yi-Fu Tuan see in the Chinese sense of place?

Evaluating Strategy

1. The writer really devotes only a single paragraph to describing American concepts of space. Why? Is the essay out of balance? Discuss whether or not a comparison paper should devote half its space to each topic.
2. Is the author objective? Is it possible for a writer to discuss cultures without inserting a measure of bias?

Appreciating Language

1. What words does Yi-Fu Tuan use in describing the two cultures? Do they seem to differ in connotation?
2. Does the word *rootlessness* suggest something negative to most people? How does Yi-Fu Tuan define it?
3. Look up the word *wanderlust*. How does a German term fit in an essay comparing American and Chinese cultures?

Connections across the Disciplines

1. Compare this article with those of Amy Tan (page 274) and William Ouchi (page 267). What do they reveal about the differences between Asian and Western cultures?
2. Does Edward Abbey's "First Morning" (page 143) express what Yi-Fu Tuan would define as an American attitude toward space and place?

Writing Suggestions

1. If you have lived in or visited another country or region within the United States, write a brief essay outlining how it differs from your home. Just as Yi-Fu Tuan used the concept of space to focus a short article, you may wish to limit your comparison to discussing eating habits, dress, attitudes to work, music, or dating practices.
2. *Collaborative Writing:* Ask a group of students about their attitudes toward rootlessness and place. Determine how often students have moved in their lives. How many have spent their entire lives in a single house or apartment? Write a few paragraphs outlining the attitudes expressed by the group.

WILLIAM ZINSSER

William Zinsser (1922–) was born in New York City and graduated from Princeton in 1944. He was a feature writer, drama editor, and film critic for the New York Herald Tribune. He wrote columns for Life *and the* New York Times. *In the 1970s Zinsser taught English at Yale. For seven years he served as general editor for the Book-of-the-Month Club. Zinsser has written many books on a variety of subjects, including jazz and baseball. But he is best known by college students for his books and articles on writing and study skills. His book* On Writing Well: An Informal Guide to Writing Nonfiction *and an article "College Pressures" have become standard reading for a generation of freshmen.*

The Transaction

This article uses the point-by-point method to compare Zinsser's writing style with that of a popular writer. Zinsser organizes his article using interviewer questions as a device to contrast the responses of the two writers.

1   A school in Connecticut once held "a day devoted to the arts," and I was asked if I would come and talk about writing as a vocation. When I arrived I found that a second speaker had been invited—Dr. Brock (as I'll call him), a surgeon who had recently begun to write and had sold some stories to magazines. He was going to talk about writing as an avocation. That made us a panel, and we sat down to face a crowd of students, teachers and parents, all eager to learn the secrets of our glamorous work.

2   Dr. Brock was dressed in a bright red jacket, looking vaguely bohemian, as authors are supposed to look, and the first question went to him. What was it like to be a writer?

3   He said it was tremendous fun. Coming home from an arduous day at the hospital, he would go straight to his yellow pad and write his tensions away. The words just flowed. It was easy. I then said that writing wasn't easy and it wasn't fun. It was hard and lonely, and the words seldom just flowed.

4   Next Dr. Brock was asked if it was important to rewrite. Absolutely not, he said. "Let it all hang out," and whatever form the

sentences take will reflect the writer at his most natural. I then said that rewriting is the essence of writing. I pointed out that professional writers rewrite their sentences repeatedly and then rewrite what they have rewritten. I mentioned that E. B. White and James Thurber rewrote their pieces eight or nine times.

5   "What do you do on days when it isn't going well?" Dr. Brock was asked. He said he just stopped writing and put the work aside for a day when it would go better. I then said that the professional writer must establish a daily schedule and stick to it. I said that writing is a craft, not an art, and that the man who runs away from his craft because he lacks inspiration is fooling himself. He is also going broke.

6   "What if you're feeling depressed or unhappy?" a student asked. "Won't that affect your writing?"

7   Probably it will, Dr. Brock replied. Go fishing. Take a walk. Probably it won't, I said. If your job is to write every day, you learn to do it like any other job.

8   A student asked if we found it useful to circulate in the literary world. Dr. Brock said he was greatly enjoying his new life as a man of letters, and he told several stories of being taken to lunch by his publisher and his agent at Manhattan restaurants where writers and editors gather. I said that professional writers are solitary drudges who seldom see other writers.

9   "Do you put symbolism in your writing?" a student asked me.

10   "Not if I can help it," I replied. I have an unbroken record of missing the deeper meaning in any story, play or movie, and as for dance and mime, I have never had any idea of what is being conveyed.

11   "I *love* symbols!" Dr. Brock exclaimed, and he described with gusto the joys of weaving them through his work.

12   So the morning went, and it was a revelation to all of us. At the end Dr. Brock told me he was enormously interested in my answers—it had never occurred to him that writing could be hard. I told him I was just as interested in *his* answers—it had never occurred to me that writing could be easy. (Maybe I should take up surgery on the side.)

13   As for the students, anyone might think we left them bewildered. But in fact we probably gave them a broader glimpse of the writing process than if only one of us had talked. For there isn't any "right" way to do such intensely personal work. There are all kinds of writers and all kinds of methods, and any method that helps you to say what you want to say is the right method for you.

14   Some people write by day, others by night. Some people need silence, others turn on the radio. Some write by hand, some by typewriter or word processor, some by talking into a tape recorder. Some people write their first draft in one long burst and then revise; others can't write the second paragraph until they have fiddled endlessly with the first.

15   But all of them are vulnerable and all of them are tense. They are driven by a compulsion to put some part of themselves on paper, and yet they don't just write what comes naturally. They sit down to commit an act of literature, and the self who emerges on paper is far stiffer than the person who sat down to write. The problem is to find the real man or woman behind all the tension.

16   Ultimately the product that any writer has to sell is not the subject being written about, but who he or she is. I often find myself reading with interest about a topic I never thought would interest me—some scientific quest, perhaps. What holds me is the enthusiasm of the writer for his field. How was he drawn into it? What emotional baggage did he bring along? How did it change his life? It's not necessary to want to spend a year alone at Walden Pond to become deeply involved with a writer who did.

17   This is the personal transaction that's at the heart of good non-fiction writing. Out of it come two of the most important qualities that this book will go in search of: humanity and warmth. Good writing has an aliveness that keeps the reader reading from one paragraph to the next, and it's not a question of gimmicks to "personalize" the author. It's a question of using the English language in a way that will achieve the greatest strength and the least clutter.

18   Can such principles be taught? Maybe not. But most of them can be learned.

Understanding Meaning

1. What is the "transaction" suggested by the title?
2. What is the purpose of this comparison? What is Zinsser trying to say about the writing process?
3. Is Zinsser, who no doubt considers himself a "professional" writer, suggesting that his work is superior to the surgeon's? Is the surgeon an amateur?

4. Zinsser states that "ultimately the product that any writer has to sell is not his subject, but who he or she is." Do you agree with this assessment?
5. *Critical Thinking:* After reading this article, review your own writing habits. Can this article assist you to master techniques Zinsser admits cannot be "taught" but can be "learned"?

Evaluating Strategy

1. How effective is the device of using interviewer questions to organize the comparison? Does it put the professional writer and surgeon on an equal footing?
2. Zinsser describes the "Bohemian" dress of the doctor and his enthusiasm for entering literary circles. What does this suggest about Zinsser's attitude?
3. Is the comparison the heart of the essay or simply a device introducing Zinsser's comments about writing?

Appreciating Language

1. What language does Zinsser use to describe the surgeon? What impact does this have on the reader?
2. Zinsser calls writing "hard and lonely" and writers "solitary drudges." What was he attempting to express to the audience?

Connections across the Disciplines

1. Compare this essay with Peter Elbow's "Desperation Writing" (page 461). What do these writers suggest about the writing process?
2. Review Samuel Scudder's essay "Take This Fish and Look at It" (page 45). Is Zinsser, like Professor Agassiz, arguing that his profession demands hard work?

Writing Suggestions

1. Write a brief essay comparing two methods of accomplishing similar tasks: cooking, dieting, exercising, studying for exams, playing a sport, parenting, or managing employees.
2. *Collaborative Writing:* Have a number of students write a few paragraphs about their own writing practices. Remind the group to write honestly, to

describe how they really write. Have each member read his or her statement to the group, and then discuss how writing styles could be improved to overcome common problems. Have one member of the group record the suggestions.

Bruce Catton (1899–1978) grew up listening to stories of Civil War veterans. His own college career was interrupted by service in the First World War. Catton went to work as a reporter for the Cleveland Plain Dealer *and later served as information director for several government agencies. His interest in history, especially the Civil War, never flagged. In 1953 his book* A Stillness at Appomattox *became a best-seller, and Catton received a Pulitzer Prize. He wrote several other books about the Civil War and edited* American Heritage *magazine for two decades.*

Grant and Lee

Perhaps no other essay is as widely anthologized as a sample of comparison writing than Catton's "Grant and Lee," which first appeared in a collection, The American Story. *Directed to a general audience, the essay seeks to contrast the two most famous generals of the Civil War.*

1   When Ulysses S. Grant and Robert E. Lee met in the parlor of a modest house at Appomattox Court House, Virginia, on April 9, 1865, to work out the terms for the surrender of Lee's Army of Northern Virginia, a great chapter in American life came to a close, and a great new chapter began.

2   These men were bringing the Civil War to its virtual finish. To be sure, other armies had yet to surrender, and for a few days the fugitive Confederate government would struggle desperately and vainly, trying to find some way to go on living now that its chief support was gone. But in effect it was all over when Grant and Lee signed the papers. And the little room where they wrote out the terms was the scene of one of the poignant, dramatic contrasts in American history.

3   They were two strong men, these oddly different generals, and they represented the strengths of two conflicting currents that, through them, had come into final collision.

4   Back of Robert E. Lee was the notion that the old aristocratic concept might somehow survive and be dominant in American life.

5   Lee was tidewater Virginia, and in his background were family, culture, and tradition . . . the age of chivalry transplanted to a New World which was making its own legends and its own myths. He embodied a way of life that had come down through the age of knighthood and the English country squire. America was a land that was beginning all over again, dedicated to nothing much more complicated than the rather hazy belief that all men had equal rights and should have an equal chance in the world. In such a land Lee stood for the feeling that it was somehow of advantage to human society to have a pronounced inequality in the social structure. There should be a leisure class, backed by ownership of land; in turn, society itself should be keyed to the land as the chief source of wealth and influence. It would bring forth (according to this ideal) a class of men with a strong sense of obligation to the community; men who lived not to gain advantage for themselves, but to meet the solemn obligations which had been laid on them by the very fact that they were privileged. From them the country would get its leadership; to them it could look for the higher values—of thought, of conduct, of personal deportment—to give it strength and virtue.

6   Lee embodied the noblest elements of this aristocratic ideal. Through him, the landed nobility justified itself. For four years, the Southern states had fought a desperate war to uphold the ideals for which Lee stood. In the end, it almost seemed as if the Confederacy fought for Lee; as if he himself was the Confederacy . . . the best thing that the way of life for which the Confederacy stood could ever have to offer. He had passed into legend before Appomattox. Thousands of tired, underfed, poorly clothed Confederate soldiers, long since past the simple enthusiasm of the early days of the struggle, somehow considered Lee the symbol of everything for which they had been willing to die. But they could not quite put this feeling into words. If the Lost Cause, sanctified by so much heroism and so many deaths, had a living justification, its justification was General Lee.

7   Grant, the son of a tanner on the Western frontier, was everything Lee was not. He had come up the hard way and embodied nothing in particular except the eternal toughness and sinewy fiber of the men who grew up beyond the mountains. He was one of a body of men who owed reverence and obeisance to no one, who were self-reliant to a fault, who cared hardly anything for the past but who had a sharp eye for the future.

8   These frontier men were the precise opposite of the tidewater aristocrats. Back of them, in the great surge that had taken people over the Alleghenies and into the opening Western country, there was a deep, implicit dissatisfaction with a past that had settled into grooves. They stood for democracy, not from any reasoned conclusion about the proper ordering of human society, but simply because they had grown up in the middle of democracy and knew how it worked. Their society might have privileges, but they would be privileges each man had won for himself. Forms and patterns meant nothing. No man was born to anything, except perhaps to a chance to show how far he could rise. Life was competition.

9   Yet along with this feeling had come a deep sense of belonging to a national community. The Westerner who developed a farm, opened a shop, or set up in business as a trader, could hope to prosper only as his own community prospered—and his community ran from the Atlantic to the Pacific and from Canada down to Mexico. If the land was settled, with towns and highways and accessible markets, he could better himself. He saw his fate in terms of the nation's own destiny. As its horizons expanded, so did his. He had, in other words, an acute dollars-and-cents stake in the continued growth and development of his country.

10   And that, perhaps, is where the contrast between Grant and Lee becomes most striking. The Virginia aristocrat, inevitably, saw himself in relation to his own region. He lived in a static society which could endure almost anything except change. Instinctively, his first loyalty would go to the locality in which that society existed. He would fight to the limit of endurance to defend it, because in defending it he was defending everything that gave his own life its deepest meaning.

11   The Westerner, on the other hand, would fight with an equal tenacity for the broader concept of society. He fought so because everything he lived by was tied to growth, expansion, and a constantly widening horizon. What he lived by would survive or fall with the nation itself. He could not possibly stand by unmoved in the face of an attempt to destroy the Union. He would combat it with everything he had, because he could only see it as an effort to cut the ground out from under his feet.

12   So Grant and Lee were in complete contrast, representing two diametrically opposed elements in American life. Grant was the modern man emerging; beyond him, ready to come on the stage, was the great

age of steel and machinery, of crowded cities and a restless burgeoning vitality. Lee might have ridden down from the old age of chivalry, lance in hand, silken banner fluttering over his head. Each man was the perfect champion of his cause, drawing both his strengths and his weaknesses from the people he led.

13   Yet it was not all contrast, after all. Different as they were—in background, in personality, in underlying aspiration—these two great soldiers had much in common. Under everything else, they were marvelous fighters. Furthermore, their fighting qualities were really very much alike.

14   Each man had, to begin with, the great virtue of utter tenacity and fidelity. Grant fought his way down the Mississippi Valley in spite of acute personal discouragement and profound military handicaps. Lee hung on in the trenches at Petersburg after hope itself had died. In each man there was an indomitable quality . . . the born fighter's refusal to give up as long as he can still remain on his feet and lift his two fists.

15   Daring and resourcefulness they had, too; the ability to think faster and move faster than the enemy. These were the qualities which gave Lee the dazzling campaigns of Second Manassas and Chancellorsville and won Vicksburg for Grant.

16   Lastly, and perhaps greatest of all, there was the ability, at the end, to turn quickly from war to peace once the fighting was over. Out of the way these two men behaved at Appomattox came the possibility of a peace of reconciliation. It was a possibility not wholly realized, in the years to come, but which did, in the end, help the two sections to become one nation again . . . after a war whose bitterness might have seemed to make such a reunion wholly impossible. No part of either man's life became him more than the part he played in their brief meeting in the McLean house at Appomattox. Their behavior there put all succeeding generations of Americans in their debt. Two great Americans, Grant and Lee—very different, yet under everything very much alike. Their encounter at Appomattox was one of the great moments of American history.

Understanding Meaning

1.   What does Catton see as the most striking differences between the two generals?
2.   How did Grant and Lee differ in background and sense of allegiance?

3. What were the historical forces that shaped the two men?
4. What areas of similarity between the two does Catton detect?
5. *Critical Thinking:* Essentially Catton is telling the story of a confrontation between victor and vanquished, yet his account does not seem to depict the men as winner and loser. Catton does not dwell on what made Grant victorious or on the causes for Lee's defeat. What does this reveal about Catton's purpose?

Evaluating Strategy

1. How does Catton organize his comparison? Is this an effective method?
2. The Civil War was, in part, a battle over slavery. Catton does not mention this issue. Does his account appear to be ethically neutral, suggesting that neither the Union nor the Confederacy were morally superior in their war aims?

Appreciating Language

1. Does Catton appear to be neutral in his descriptions of the two men? What similes or metaphors does he use? Is the language balanced or biased?
2. What do the tone, level of language, and word choice suggest about Catton's intended audience?

Connections across the Disciplines

1. Catton uses words such as "nobility" and "virtue" to describe Robert E. Lee. How might an African-American writer such as Cornel West respond to Catton's depiction of Lee's "daring" and "resourcefulness" as a defender of the Confederacy?
2. Compare Catton's discussion of two individuals with William Ouchi's comparison of two kinds of people in the essay "Japanese and American Workers: Two States of Mind" (page 267). What are the similarities? Do comparisons risk simplification and stereotyping?

Writing Suggestions

1. Write an essay comparing two people in the same profession you have known. Compare two teachers, two bosses, two landlords, or two coworkers. Try to focus on their personalities rather than appearance. You may

limit your discussion to a specific attitude, situation, or activity. For example, compare how two teachers dealt with troublesome students, how two bosses motivated employees, or how two landlords maintained their properties.

2. *Collaborative Writing:* Work with a group of students to write a short dramatic scene based on Catton's essay. Use set descriptions to establish the locale, and invent dialogue. Discuss with members of the group how Lee and Grant might have sounded. What words would they have chosen? How would their vocabulary indicate their different backgrounds and personalities?

STEVEN D. STARK

Steven D. Stark (1952–) graduated from Yale Law School and worked as an aide to Jimmy Carter before becoming a journalist. He has written a column for The Boston Globe *and lectured at Harvard Law School. His articles have appeared in* The New York Times, The Atlantic Monthly, *and* The Los Angeles Times. *Stark is a regular commentator on popular culture for National Public Radio. In 1997 he published* Glued to the Set: The 60 Television Shows That Made Us Who We Are Today.

A TALE OF TWO SITCOMS

In this section from his recent book, Stark compares two popular television programs— Home Improvement *and* Seinfeld. *As you read the essay, notice how Stark organizes his commentary.*

1   The popular shows of a decade are usually a lot alike. In many ways *Dallas* and *Dynasty* were indistinguishable, and it would take Wyatt Earp himself to discern great differences between *Wagon Train* and *Gunsmoke*. In the late seventies, *Happy Days, Laverne and Shirley*, and *Three's Company* often seemed to form one long seamless web.

2   Yet sometimes, in eras of cultural conflict or confusion, no one type of show can accurately capture the public mood. In the early 1970s, for example, *All in the Family* made a hero of a conservative traditionalist while *The Mary Tyler Moore Show* romanticized the life of a single career woman blazing new ground. In their own ways, both shows reflected their time and both were popular—often with the same viewers.

3   In much the same fashion, popular programming in the nineties offered a contrast, as it struggled with an emerging question which had no clear answer: What does it mean to be a man in a postfeminist age? Two very different situation comedies which hit Number 1 in that decade tried to provide an answer. On the one hand, there was ABC's *Home Improvement*—the top-rated show for the 1993–94 season. And then, there was NBC's *Seinfeld*—which hit Number 1 the following season.

4   Even the reaction to both shows provided a sharp contrast. Critics regularly lavished *Seinfeld* with praise for its postmodern plots; its

technical innovations were hailed as breakthroughs; and the show was always an Emmy contender in several categories. Novelist Jay McInerney went so far in a 1996 issue of *TV Guide* to ask, "Is *Seinfeld* the Best Comedy Ever?" By comparison, *Home Improvement* was perhaps the quietest Number 1 in TV history, eliciting few critical comments and winning little more than a slew of (what else?) People's Choice awards, in which the public does the voting.

5   There were indeed surface similarities between the two shows. Both starred male comedians, who took their standup nightclub acts and transformed them for television. Both comedians wrote best-selling books once they hit it big, and both shows featured subplots about television itself. Both presented memorable supporting players, like Kramer of *Seinfeld*, or next-door neighbor Wilson of *Home Improvement*, whose full face is never shown over his fence. Both ran in prime time and in syndication over roughly the same period with similar ratings— though the one time *Seinfeld* was matched directly against *Home Improvement* in 1992–93, *Seinfeld* got plastered in the ratings.

6   Yet the differences between the shows were more revealing. *Home Improvement* was set in suburban Detroit, in the white-bread heartland. Though actually filmed in L.A., *Seinfeld* was a New York show which roughly approximated the lifestyles of influential New York critics and Madison Avenue types. *Home Improvement* was solidly suburban middle class; *Seinfeld* was a portrait of life in yuppie Upper Manhattan.

7   *Home Improvement* was a rather traditional family sitcom about a wife, three kids, and a bumbling Dad; the *Seinfeld* family of friends featured no children and no workplace either, at least in the traditional sense. With its "morality tale" quality, *Home Improvement* was cousin of *Leave It to Beaver* and *My Three Sons*—an anachronism in an era when wisecracking shows like *Friends* or *Murphy Brown* dispensed with nuclear families altogether.

8   By contrast, *Seinfeld* was closer to Jack Benny, or even Milton Berle. That was a remarkable turnaround for a medium which for much of its bland and homogeneous entertainment life took single Jews like Seinfeld, changed their names, converted them to Christianity, married them off to attractive WASP housewives, and moved them to the suburbs. New York *Newsday* once called *Seinfeld* "the most fully realized schlemiel in the history of television."

9   What encouraged programmers to take these chances was the way that cable television had atomized the viewing audience. Because of cable competition, network television was not the mass medium in

1995 that it was in 1975; it took far fewer viewers to make a hit. *Seinfeld* won the 1994–95 ratings race with a rating that two decades earlier wouldn't have even placed the show in the Top Twenty-five. Such a disintegration of the network audience meant that the networks no longer had to program for as large a mass to make money, and shows like *Seinfeld*—which appealed to upscale viewers—often were the results. By 1995, half the sitcoms on TV seemed to feature singles living in cities like New York, if only because these series appealed to viewers similarly situated who, in turn, appealed to advertisers because they have lots of discretionary income.

10   Yet even though television was finally acknowledging the nation's diversity, that didn't mean that shows like *Seinfeld* were realistic national self-portraits either. After all, the more that television sitcoms have moved in the direction of "realism," the less authentic they have often become. For all the praise that *All in the Family* received, Archie Bunker was a parody; even the witty comedy of *Mary Tyler Moore* hardly reflected a workplace anyone could recognize with honest assurance. Similarly, no one—not even an Upper East Sider—has hours every day to spend chatting with friends in a diner. Yet critics were fond of praising the realism of *Seinfeld*. "Men probably laughed louder than women at the episode in which Elaine discovered that her nipple was exposed on her Christmas card photo," wrote McInerney. "This stuff happens to all of us." Oh, really?

11   *Seinfeld* did have considerable strengths, however. The show was genuinely funny, a rare treat on prime-time television. Some of the series episodes, like the one on the "soup Nazi" or on losing a car in a parking lot, were inspired, and the supporting cast of Elaine, Kramer, and George was exceptional. "It's about nothing, everything else is about something; this, it's about nothing," said George in pitching his and Jerry's sitcom proposal to a network, as *Seinfeld* became a show within a show. Already, some of its lines have become pop culture classics: "I'm Cosmo Kramer, the Assman!"; "Not that there's anything wrong with that"; and "Master of your Domain."

12   *Seinfeld* was also a hit because it appealed to men more than did many other sitcoms, as it reflected a new adolescent sensibility sweeping America in the 1990s. Along with the comedy of David Letterman, the cartoon series *Beavis and Butt-Head*, megamovies like *Jurassic Park*, and syndicated radio talkmeisters Howard Stern and Don Imus, *Seinfeld* often echoed the world of 11-to-15-year-old boys. The radio style of Stern and Imus, for example, was that of the narcissistic class cutup

in seventh grade: Both sat in a playhouse-like radio studio with a bunch of guys and horsed around for hours talking about sex, sports, and politics, all while laughing at their own loutish, subversive jokes.

13   *Seinfeld* shared a similar sensibility, albeit softened somewhat for television. Like a group of 14-year-olds, the men on *Seinfeld* seemed not to hold regular jobs, the better to devote time to "the gang." (One woman, Elaine, was allowed to tag along with the boys, much like those younger sisters who are permitted to hang out with their brothers.) Not only was every man in *Seinfeld*'s gang unmarried and pushing forty-something, but it also was difficult to imagine any having a real relationship with any woman but his mother. Note how much more often parents of adult children appeared here than on other shows.

14   Or compare *Seinfeld* to its predecessor in its NBC Thursday night time slot, *Cheers.* If the men on that show didn't spend much time at work either, they did hang out in a traditional domain of adults—the tavern—and the hero, Sam Malone, spent many of his waking hours chasing women. Seinfeld, by contrast, was better known for sitting in a restaurant eating french fries with his pals. One of the most celebrated risqué *Seinfeld* episodes was about (what else?) masturbation, while others dealt with urinating in the shower or on couches. That's usually big stuff in the seventh grade, but not much beyond.

15   The *Seinfeld* evocation of early male adolescence did reflect deeper cultural strains. This country has always venerated "bad boys," from Huck Finn to Holden Caulfield. Moreover, many psychologists consider that preteen stage of life, when one is acutely aware of being powerless, as the time when individuals are most subversive of the society at-large. That sentiment fit a nineties cultural mood as America became full of the defiant, oppositional anger that often characterizes the early adolescent—witness the tearing down of public figures with the ready help of the tabloid press, and the flocking to antiestablishment talk radio whereon humor grew more derisive by the day. In a similar vein, one could imagine the whole *Seinfeld* cast of perpetual adolescents on the Clinton White House staff working with George Stephanopolous or Craig Livingstone. Yet boys will be boys: Maybe that's why much of the country viewed the Clinton administration's missteps as benignly as they viewed George Costanza's.

16   Because this country has always had tendencies that remind observers of a 14-year-old-boy, no one would blame *Seinfeld* alone for society's failure to grow up and take care of its real children; its current ambivalence about paternal authority; or its vulgarity and exhibitionist

inclinations. Yet the show definitely played a role, along with its cultural cousins. In much the same way that *Roseanne* had domesticated tabloid television for the masses, *Seinfeld* did the same for sophomoric talk radio, as embodied by fellow Manhattanites Stern and Imus.

17   By contrast, *Home Improvement* had the gentle ring of mainstream truth. It's no accident that 14-to-30-year-olds in a *TV Guide* poll voted Jill and Tim the TV parents most like their own. Naturally, that state of affairs sometimes drew the critics' ire. "'*Home Improvement*' is a reactionary return, after 'Roseanne' and 'Married with Children' and all those Census Bureau reports, to the semi-extinct idea of a nuclear family whose members actually like each other," wrote Chuck Eddy in a review of the show for *millenium pop*.

18   Unlike *Seinfeld, Home Improvement* was about grown-ups. Take the premiere episode: Tim (the Toolman) Taylor, host of a cable show called *Tool Time*, wants to rewire his dishwasher to make it more powerful but ends up breaking it. When he goes to comfort his wife after she doesn't get a job, he inadvertently ends up making her feel worse. In just such a fashion *Home Improvement* was built around that preoccupation central to the zeitgeist of the nineties: If television once told us *Father Knows Best*, this show proved what it meant to be the best father and husband in an age of feminism and embattled male identity.

19   When Matt Williams and David McFadzean were developing the idea for this show, they were both reading the work of noted linguist Deborah Tannen on male-female communication. "Her book deals with the fact that men and women speak different languages," Williams once remembered. "That right there is the piston that drives this television series. Jill and Tim will never do the same thing the same way, and both sides are valid." On another occasion, Williams noted:

> The biggest challenge for us is to take absurd situations, or extreme points of view or actions, and root them in some kind of truth. . . . If we do our job correctly, those are the things the audience will never think twice about, because we've rooted them in some kind of behavioral truth.

20   And so the show went in the 1990s, quietly drawing better in rural than urban areas, yet still doing well among professionals. Like Jerry Seinfeld, Tim Allen's persona became a new cultural icon—the postfeminist handyman. His was a sitcom prototype with the qualities that many Americans in the 1990s held dear—low-key, predictable, intelligent but not particularly well-educated, with a little dirt under his

fingernails. If he'd been a politician in the nineties, he would have had little in common with Bill Clinton or Newt Gingrich—Washington insiders and policy preachers to the core. (Colin Powell would be another story.) For different reasons, Taylor also would have had little to talk about with Seinfeld, who never would have tuned in to *Tool Time*, much less own a hammer. (Like many Manhattanites, Seinfeld always seemed to prefer the movies to television anyway.)

21   Here, then, were two conflicting strains in the American character: *Seinfeld*, a popular urban show about eccentric individualism and the flight from adulthood, versus *Home Improvement*, a popular suburban show about commitment and ultimately about family. The forces which create "the buzz" in this country—the press, the public relations establishment, and Madison Avenue—simply loved *Seinfeld*, which tells us as much about their makeup and tastes as about the show itself. We also had our *Seinfeld*-esque White House.

22   The guess here, however, is that *Home Improvement* was still a better reflection of who we are, despite major social changes over decades. In the not-so-grand tradition of television, viewers still feel more comfortable with the Cleavers, the Andersons, and the Bradys than they do with the *Seinfeld* alternative. Viewers want happy, traditional families, even when they realize that a TV family and setting is idealized—or perhaps *especially* when they realize it. The perfect man for the nineties? It's OK to have that fling with the "bad boy"—who, after all, has always been part of the greater American family. But when it's time to settle down, he isn't the guy you're going to want to bring into your living rooms and bedrooms, night after night.

Understanding Meaning

1.   What similarities does Stark see between *Home Improvement* and *Seinfeld?* Why were their differences more revealing?
2.   How did the expansion of cable television affect the ratings of network programs?
3.   In Stark's view, what was the appeal of *Seinfeld* and *Home Improvement?* Did they appeal to different audiences or different attitudes within the same viewers?
4.   How did *Seinfeld* and *Home Improvement* differ from previous sitcoms?
5.   *Critical Thinking:* Traditional sitcoms focused on family situations. In the 1990s, programs like *Murphy Brown, Friends,* and *Seinfeld* featured non-family groups of friends, neighbors, and coworkers. How does this reflect social changes and demographic trends?

Evaluating Strategy

1. What method does Stark use in organizing his essay? What role do paragraph breaks play in signaling transitions?
2. Stark concludes his comparison, stating, "The guess here, however, is that *Home Improvement* was still a better reflection of who we are. . . ." Should his choice be more strongly worded? Does using the word "guess" appear to weaken the merit of his judgment?
3. Does Stark provide enough details about the two programs for readers unfamiliar with *Home Improvement* or *Seinfeld* to grasp their essential character?

Appreciating Language

1. Does Stark's choice of words in describing the programs reveal any preference or bias, favoring one show over the other?
2. *Critical Thinking:* Stark repeatedly comments on the "adolescent" nature of *Seinfeld* and its unmarried characters. Does this imply a bias, suggesting immaturity? Would another writer celebrate the characters' youth and freedom?

Connections across the Disciplines

1. "TV Movies in the First Decade of AIDS" (page 343) analyzes the way in which television confronted a controversial social issue. Can sitcoms address serious issues as well? Can you think of any examples?
2. *Critical Thinking:* The key figure in many family sitcoms—*Home Improvement, Father Knows Best, Leave it to Beaver, The Brady Bunch, Family Matters*—is often the father. In "Fatherless America" (page 598) David Blankenhorn argues that children growing up without fathers are denied essential benefits and privileges. What values or qualities do sitcom fathers exhibit? Do they represent an ideal? Do many fatherless children grow up seeing television characters as surrogate fathers?

Writing Suggestions

1. Using this essay as a model, compare two popular soap operas, talk shows, or dramas. Outline both their similarities and their differences. Highlight reasons for their popularity, and describe their viewers.
2. Magazines, like television shows, often bear striking similarities. Examine issues of related magazines such as *Time* and *Newsweek* or *Cosmopolitan*

and *Redbook*. Write an essay comparing the two magazines, focusing on what distinguishes them. Can you develop a profile of their intended readers? Do the magazines seem to target the same or different audiences? Review the advertisements as well as the articles.

3. *Collaborative Writing:* Discuss current sitcoms with a group of students, and develop a cause and effect essay detailing the impact you feel these programs have on young people. If members of the group disagree, consider writing contrasting statements.

WILLIAM OUCHI

William Ouchi (1943–) was born in Hawaii and educated at Williams College, Stanford, and the University of Chicago. A specialist in organizational behavior, he has written several books widely studied by executives and government administrators. In 1981 he published Theory Z: How American Business Can Meet the Japanese Challenge. *Appearing at a time when many American corporations felt threatened by Japanese imports, the book became a best-seller. Theory Z was developed in response to two contrasting views espoused by Douglas McGregor. According to Theory X, people hate work and need to be directed and motivated. Theory Y assumed people gain satisfaction from work and require the freedom to direct themselves. Ouchi's Theory Z, based on Japanese management practices, stresses the importance of involving workers in the process.*

Japanese and American Workers: Two States of Mind

In this essay from Theory Z, *Ouchi not only contrasts different business practices but different cultures. The incentives that work so well for American workers fail to motivate and in fact discourage Asian employees.*

1　Perhaps the most difficult aspect of the Japanese for Westerners to comprehend is the strong orientation to collective values, particularly a collective sense of responsibility. Let me illustrate with an anecdote about a visit to a new factory in Japan owned and operated by an American electronics company. The American company, a particularly creative firm, frequently attracts attention within the business community for its novel approaches to planning, organizational design, and management systems. As a consequence of this corporate style, the parent company determined to make a thorough study of Japanese workers and to design a plant that would combine the best of East and West. In their study they discovered that Japanese firms almost never make use of individual work incentives, such as piecework or even individual performance appraisal tied to salary increases. They concluded that rewarding individual achievement and individual ability is always a good thing.

2   In the final assembly area of their new plant long lines of young Japanese women wired together electronic products on a piece-rate system: The more you wired, the more you got paid. About two months after opening, the head foreladies approached the plant manager. "Honorable plant manager," they said humbly as they bowed, "we are embarrassed to be so forward, but we must speak to you because all of the girls have threatened to quit work this Friday." (To have this happen, of course, would be a great disaster for all concerned.) "Why," they wanted to know, "can't our plant have the same compensation system as other Japanese companies? When you hire a new girl, her starting wage should be fixed by her age. An eighteen-year-old should be paid more than a sixteen-year-old. Every year on her birthday, she should receive an automatic increase in pay. The idea that any one of us can be more productive than another must be wrong, because none of us in final assembly could make a thing unless all of the other people in the plant had done their jobs right first. To single one person out as being more productive is wrong and is also personally humiliating to us." The company changed its compensation system to the Japanese model.

3   Another American company in Japan had installed a suggestion system much as we have in the United States. Individual workers were encouraged to place suggestions to improve productivity into special boxes. For an accepted idea the individual received a bonus amounting to some fraction of the productivity savings realized from his or her suggestion. After a period of six months, not a single suggestion had been submitted. The American managers were puzzled. They had heard many stories of the inventiveness, the commitment, and the loyalty of Japanese workers, yet not one suggestion to improve productivity had appeared.

4   The managers approached some of the workers and asked why the suggestion system had not been used. The answer: "No one can come up with a work improvement idea alone. We work together, and any ideas that one of us may have are actually developed by watching others and talking to others. If one of us was singled out for being responsible for such an idea, it would embarrass all of us." The company changed to a group suggestion system, in which workers collectively submitted suggestions. Bonuses were paid to groups which would save bonus money until the end of the year for a party at a restaurant or, if there was enough money, for family vacations together. The suggestions and productivity improvements rained down on the plant.

5   One can interpret these examples in two quite different ways. Perhaps the Japanese commitment to collective values is an anachronism that does not fit with modern industrialism but brings economic success despite that collectivism. Collectivism seems to be inimical to the kind of maverick creativity exemplified in Benjamin Franklin, Thomas Edison, and John D. Rockefeller. Collectivism does not seem to provide the individual incentive to excel which has made a great success of American enterprise. Entirely apart from its economic effects, collectivism implies a loss of individuality, a loss of the freedom to be different, to hold fundamentally different values from others.

6   The second interpretation of the examples is that the Japanese collectivism is economically efficient. It causes people to work well together and to encourage one another to better efforts. Industrial life requires interdependence of one person on another. But a less obvious but far-reaching implication of the Japanese collectivism for economic performance has to do with accountability.

7   In the Japanese mind, collectivism is neither a corporate or individual goal to strive for nor a slogan to pursue. Rather, the nature of things operates so that nothing of consequence occurs as a result of individual effort. Everything important in life happens as a result of teamwork or collective effort. Therefore, to attempt to assign individual credit or blame to results is unfounded. A Japanese professor of accounting, a brilliant scholar trained at Carnegie-Mellon University who teaches now in Tokyo, remarked that the status of accounting systems in Japanese industry is primitive compared to those in the United States. Profit centers, transfer prices, and computerized information systems are barely known even in the largest Japanese companies, whereas they are a commonplace in even small United States organizations. Though not at all surprised at the difference in accounting systems, I was not at all sure that the Japanese were primitive. In fact, I thought their system a good deal more efficient than ours.

8   Most American companies have basically two accounting systems. One system summarizes the overall financial state to inform stockholders, bankers, and other outsiders. That system is not of interest here. The other system, called the managerial or cost accounting system, exists for an entirely different reason. It measures in detail all of the particulars of transactions between departments, divisions, and key individuals in the organization, for the purpose of untangling the interdependencies between people. When, for example, two departments share one truck for deliveries, the cost accounting system charges each

department for part of the cost of maintaining the truck and driver, so that at the end of the year, the performance of each department can be individually assessed, and the better department's manager can receive a larger raise. Of course, all of this information processing costs money, and furthermore may lead to arguments between the departments over whether the costs charged to each are fair.

9   In a Japanese company a short-run assessment of individual performance is not wanted, so the company can save the considerable expense of collecting and processing all of that information. Companies still keep track of which department uses a truck how often and for what purposes, but like-minded people can interpret some simple numbers for themselves and adjust their behavior accordingly. Those insisting upon clear and precise measurement for the purpose of advancing individual interests must have an elaborate information system. Industrial life, however, is essentially integrated and interdependent. No one builds an automobile alone, no one carries through a banking transaction alone. In a sense the Japanese value of collectivism fits naturally into an industrial setting, whereas the Western individualism provides constant conflicts. The image that comes to mind is of Chaplin's silent film *Modern Times* in which the apparently insignificant hero played by Chaplin successfully fights against the unfeeling machinery of industry. Modern industrial life can be aggravating, even hostile, or natural: All depends on the fit between our culture and our technology.

10   The *shinkansen* or "bullet train" speeds across the rural areas of Japan giving a quick view of cluster after cluster of farmhouses surrounded by rice paddies. This particular pattern did not develop purely by chance, but as a consequence of the technology peculiar to the growing of rice, the staple of the Japanese diet. The growing of rice requires construction and maintenance of an irrigation system, something that takes many hands to build. More importantly, the planting and the harvesting of rice can only be done efficiently with the cooperation of twenty or more people. The "bottom line" is that a single family working alone cannot produce enough rice to survive, but a dozen families working together can produce a surplus. Thus the Japanese have had to develop the capacity to work together in harmony, no matter what the forces of disagreement or social disintegration, in order to survive.

11   Japan is a nation built entirely on the tips of giant, suboceanic volcanoes. Little of the land is flat and suitable for agriculture. Terraced

hillsides make use of every available square foot of arable land. Small homes built very close together further conserve the land. Japan also suffers from natural disasters such as earthquakes and hurricanes. Traditionally homes are made of light construction materials, so a house falling down during a disaster will not crush its occupants and also could be quickly and inexpensively rebuilt. During the feudal period until the Meiji restoration of 1868, each feudal lord sought to restrain his subjects from moving from one village to the next for fear that a neighboring lord might amass enough peasants with which to produce a large agricultural surplus, hire an army and pose a threat. Apparently bridges were not commonly built across rivers and streams until the late nineteenth century, since bridges increased mobility between villages.

12   Taken all together, this characteristic style of living paints the picture of a nation of people who are homogeneous with respect to race, history, language, religion, and culture. For centuries and generations these people have lived in the same village next door to the same neighbors. Living in close proximity and in dwellings which gave very little privacy, the Japanese survived through their capacity to work together in harmony. In this situation, it was inevitable that the one most central social value which emerged, the one value without which the society could not continue, was that an individual does not matter.

13   To the Western soul this is a chilling picture of society. Subordinating individual tastes to the harmony of the group and knowing that individual needs can never take precedence over the interests of all is repellent to the Western citizen. But a frequent theme of Western philosophers and sociologists is that individual freedom exists only when people willingly subordinate their self-interests to the social interest. A society composed entirely of self-interested individuals is a society in which each person is at war with the other, a society which has no freedom. This issue, constantly at the heart of understanding society, comes up in every century, and in every society, whether the writer be Plato, Hobbes, or B. F. Skinner. The question of understanding which contemporary institutions lie at the heart of the conflict between automatism and totalitarianism remains. In some ages, the kinship group, the central social institution, mediated between these opposing forces to preserve the balance in which freedom was realized; in other times the church or the government was most critical. Perhaps our present age puts the work organization as the central institution.

14   In order to complete the comparison of Japanese and American living situations, consider a flight over the United States. Looking out

of the window high over the state of Kansas, we see a pattern of a single farmhouse surrounded by fields, followed by another single homestead surrounded by fields. In the early 1800s in the state of Kansas there were no automobiles. Your nearest neighbor was perhaps two miles distant; the winters were long, and the snow was deep. Inevitably, the central social values were self-reliance and independence. Those were the realities of that place and age that children had to learn to value.

15   The key to the industrial revolution was discovering that non-human forms of energy substituted for human forms could increase the wealth of a nation beyond anyone's wildest dreams. But there was a catch. To realize this great wealth, non-human energy needed huge complexes called factories with hundreds, even thousands of workers collected into one factory. Moreover, several factories in one central place made the generation of energy more efficient. Almost overnight, the Western world was transformed from a rural and agricultural country to an urban and industrial state. Our technological advance seems to no longer fit our social structure: In a sense, the Japanese can better cope with modern industrialism. While Americans still busily protect our rather extreme form of individualism, the Japanese hold their individualism in check and emphasize cooperation.

Understanding Meaning

1. What are the essential differences between American and Japanese workers according to Ouchi?
2. What historical forces have shaped the American and Japanese attitudes toward self-identity and community?
3. When you think of success, do you think of individuals or groups? Is it natural for most Americans to think of successful men and women rather than institutions or corporations? Explain your answer.
4. Why do the "primitive" accounting methods used by Japanese corporations seem to work so well?
5. *Critical Thinking:* Ouchi states that Western individualism creates many conflicts in an industrialized society. Discuss whether the American insistence on individuality and resistance to conformity causes needless social and psychological stress. Would Americans lose a sense of themselves if they identified with a corporation or institution?

Evaluating Strategy

1. How effective is Ouchi's analogy of Japanese and American farms in highlighting cultural differences?
2. How does Ouchi organize his comparison? What devices does he use?
3. *Other Modes:* Where does Ouchi use *narration* and *cause and effect* to develop his comparison?

Appreciating Language

1. What words does Ouchi use to describe Japanese and American cultures, values, and attitudes? Is his language neutral, or does it have an implied bias?
2. Ouchi holds a doctoral degree and is accustomed to addressing scholars and executives. What do his word choice and level of diction reveal about the readers he hoped to reach in this essay?

Connections across the Disciplines

1. Having read Ouchi's descriptions of Japanese workers, review Kenna and Lacy's "Communications Styles: United States and Taiwan" (page 290). Would this chart help an American conduct business in Japan as well? Why or why not?
2. Compare this essay in the context of Yi-Fu Tuan's essay about Chinese space (page 245). Although Chinese and Japanese cultures are unique, do you see that they share similar differences between Asian and Western concepts of individual identity?

Writing Suggestions

1. Write a short essay about your own sense of individuality and your career goals. How much personal expression do you expect or desire in your work?
2. *Collaborative Writing:* After reading Ouchi's essay, discuss the issue of individual success with a group of students. Would Americans accept a more collective management system? Does the success of individual workers create conflict in the workplace? Have members reflect on their own job experiences. Have one member of the group take notes of the discussion and then draft a short paper outlining the views of the group.

Amy Tan (1952–) was born in San Francisco to parents born in China. Visiting China at the age of thirty-five, she reported feeling an instant bond with the culture of her parents. A freelance writer, Tan has written several articles about the nature of immigrant cultures and the roles of women in Asian and Asian American society. Her novel The Joy Luck Club, *published in 1989, became a best-seller and later a motion picture. This novel, like her later novels* The Kitchen God's Wife *and* A Hundred Secret Senses, *explores the relationships between Chinese women and their Chinese American daughters.*

The Language of Discretion

In this essay, first published in The State of the Language, *edited by Christopher Ricks and Leonard Michaels, Tan compares two languages as well as two cultures. As you read this article, consider how languages do more than simply transmit different words or expressions. Consider how language differences complicate the process of translation.*

1   At a recent family dinner in San Francisco, my mother whispered to me: "Sau-sau [Brother's Wife] pretends too hard to be polite. Why bother? In the end, she always takes everything."

2   My mother thinks like a *waixiao*, an expatriate, temporarily away from China since 1949, no longer patient with ritual courtesies. As if to prove her point, she reached across the table to offer my elderly aunt from Beijing the last scallop from the Happy Family seafood dish.

3   Sau-sau scowled. *"B'yao, zhen b'yao!"* (I don't want it, really I don't!) she cried, patting her plump stomach.

4   "Take it! Take it!" scolded my mother in Chinese.

5   "Full, I'm already full," Sau-sau protested weakly, eyeing the beloved scallop.

6   "Ai!" exclaimed my mother, completely exasperated. "Nobody else wants it. If you don't take it, it will only rot!"

7   At this point, Sau-sau sighed, acting as if she were doing my mother a big favor by taking the wretched scrap off her hands.

8   My mother turned to her brother, a high-ranking communist official who was visiting her in California for the first time: "In America a

Chinese person could starve to death. If you say you don't want it, they won't ask you again forever."

9   My uncle nodded and said he understood fully: Americans take things quickly because they have no time to be polite.

10 I thought about this misunderstanding again—of social contexts failing in translation—when a friend sent me an article from the *New York Times Magazine* (24 April 1988). The article, on changes in New York's Chinatown, made passing reference to the inherent ambivalence of the Chinese language.

11 Chinese people are so "discreet and modest," the article stated, there aren't even words for "yes" and "no."

12 That's not true, I thought, although I can see why an outsider might think that. I continued reading.

13 If one is Chinese, the article went on to say, "One compromises, one doesn't hazard a loss of face by an overemphatic response."

14 My throat seized. Why do people keep saying these things? As if we truly were those little dolls sold in Chinatown tourist shops, heads bobbing up and down in complacent agreement to anything said!

15 I worry about the effect of one-dimensional statements on the unwary and guileless. When they read about this so-called vocabulary deficit, do they also conclude that Chinese people evolved into a mild-mannered lot because the language only allowed them to hobble forth with minced words?

16 Something enormous is always lost in translation. Something insidious seeps into the gaps, especially when amateur linguists continue to compare, one-for-one, language differences and then put forth notions wide open to misinterpretation: that Chinese people have no direct linguistic means to make decisions, assert or deny, affirm or negate, just say no to drug dealers, or behave properly on the witness stand when told, "Please answer yes or no."

17 Yet one can argue, with the help of renowned linguists, that the Chinese are indeed up a creek without "yes" and "no." Take any number of variations on the old language-and-reality theory stated years ago by Edward Sapir: "Human beings are very much at the mercy of the particular language which has become the medium for their society. . . . The fact of the matter is that the 'real world' is to a large extent built upon the language habits of the group."[1]

---

[1] Edward Sapir, *Selected Writings*, ed. D. G. Mandelbaum (Berkeley and Los Angeles, 1949).

18   This notion was further bolstered by the famous Sapir-Whorf hypothesis, which roughly states that one's perception of the world and how one functions in it depend a great deal on the language used. As Sapir, Whorf, and new carriers of the banner would have us believe, language shapes our thinking, channels us along certain patterns embedded in words, syntactic structures, and intonation patterns. Language has become the peg and the shelf that enables us to sort out and categorize the world. In English, we see "cats" and "dogs"; what if the language had also specified *glatz*, meaning "animals that leave fur on the sofa," and *glotz*, meaning "animals that leave fur and drool on the sofa"? How would language, the enabler, have changed our perceptions with slight vocabulary variations?

19   And if this were the case—of language being the master of destined thought—think of the opportunities lost from failure to evolve two little words, *yes* and *no*, the simplest of opposites! Ghenghis Khan could have been sent back to Mongolia. Opium wars might have been averted. The Cultural Revolution could have been sidestepped.

20   There are still many, from serious linguists to pop psychology cultists, who view language and reality as inextricably tied, one being the consequence of the other. We have traversed the range from the Sapir-Whorf hypothesis to EST and neurolinguistic programming, which tell us "you are what you say."

21   I too have been intrigued by the theories. I can summarize, albeit badly, ages-old empirical evidence: of Eskimos and their infinite ways to say "snow," their ability to *see* the differences in snowflake configurations, thanks to the richness of their vocabulary, while non-Eskimo speakers like myself founder in "snow," "more snow," and "lots more where that came from."

22   I too have experienced dramatic cognitive awakenings via the word. Once I added "mauve" to my vocabulary I began to see it everywhere. When I learned how to pronounce *prix fixe*, I ate French food at prices better than the easier-to-say *á la carte* choices.

23   But just how seriously are we supposed to take this?

24   Sapir said something else about language and reality. It is the part that often gets left behind in the dot-dot-dots of quotes: " . . . No two languages are ever sufficiently similar to be considered as representing the same social reality. The worlds in which different societies live are distinct worlds, not merely the same world with different labels attached."

25   When I first read this, I thought, Here at last is validity for the dilemmas I felt growing up in a bicultural, bilingual family! As any

child of immigrant parents knows, there's a special kind of double bind attached to knowing two languages. My parents, for example, spoke to me in both Chinese and English; I spoke back to them in English.

26   "Amy-ah!" they'd call me.

27   "What?" I'd mumble back.

28   "Do not question us when we call," they scolded me in Chinese. "It is not respectful."

29   "What do you mean?"

30   "Ai! Didn't we just tell you not to question?"

31   To this day, I wonder which parts of my behavior were shaped by Chinese, which by English. I am tempted to think, for example, that if I am of two minds on some matter it is due to the richness of my linguistic experiences, not to any personal tendencies toward wishy-washiness. But which mind says what?

32   Was it perhaps patience—developed through years of deciphering my mother's fractured English—that had me listening politely while a woman announced over the phone that I had won one of five valuable prizes? Was it respect—pounded in by the Chinese imperative to ac-cept convoluted explanations—that had me agreeing that I might find it worthwhile to drive seventy-five miles to view a time-share resort? Could I have been at a loss for words when asked, "Wouldn't you like to win a Hawaiian cruise or perhaps a fabulous Star of India designed exclusively by Cartier and Van Arpels?"

33   And when this same woman called back a week later, this time complaining that I had missed my appointment, obviously it was my type A language that kicked into gear and interrupted her. Certainly, my blunt denial—"Frankly I'm not interested"—was as American as apple pie. And when she said, "But it's in Morgan Hill," and I shouted, "Read my lips. I don't care if it's Timbuktu," you can be sure I said it with the precise intonation expressing both cynicism and disgust.

34   It's dangerous business, this sorting out of language and behavior. Which one is English? Which is Chinese? The categories manifest themselves: passive and aggressive, tentative and assertive, indirect and direct. And I realize they are just variations of the same theme: that Chinese people are discreet and modest.

35   Reject them all!

36   If my reaction is overly strident, it is because I cannot come across as too emphatic. I grew up listening to the same lines over and over again, like so many rote expressions repeated in an English phrase-book. And I too almost came to believe them.

37   Yet if I consider my upbringing more carefully, I find there was nothing discreet about the Chinese language I grew up with. My parents made everything abundantly clear. Nothing wishy-washy in their demands, no compromises accepted: "Of course you will become a famous neurosurgeon," they told me. "And yes, a concert pianist on the side."

38   In fact, now that I remember, it seems that the more emphatic outbursts always spilled over into Chinese: "Not that way! You must wash rice so not a single grain spills out."

39   I do not believe that my parents—both immigrants from mainland China—are an exception to the modest-and-discreet rule. I have only to look at the number of Chinese engineering students skewing minority ratios at Berkeley, MIT, and Yale. Certainly they were not raised by passive mothers and fathers who said, "It is up to you, my daughter. Writer, welfare recipient, masseuse, or molecular engineer—you decide."

40   And my American mind says, See, those engineering students weren't able to say no to their parents' demands. But then my Chinese mind remembers: Ah, but those parents all wanted their sons and daughters to be *pre-med*.

41   Having listened to both Chinese and English, I also tend to be suspicious of any comparisons between the two languages. Typically, one language—that of the person doing the comparing—is often used as the standard, the benchmark for a logical form of expression. And so the language being compared is always in danger of being judged deficient or superfluous, simplistic or unnecessarily complex, melodious or cacophonous. English speakers point out that Chinese is extremely difficult because it relies on variations in tone barely discernible to the human ear. By the same token, Chinese speakers tell me English is extremely difficult because it is inconsistent, a language of too many broken rules, of Mickey Mice and Donald Ducks.

42   Even more dangerous to my mind is the temptation to compare both language and behavior *in translation*. To listen to my mother speak English, one might think she has no concept of past or future tense, that she doesn't see the difference between singular and plural, that she is gender blind because she calls my husband "she." If one were not careful, one might also generalize that, based on the way my mother talks, all Chinese people take a circumlocutory route to get to the point. It is, in fact, my mother's idiosyncratic behavior to ramble a bit.

43   Sapir was right about differences between two languages and their realities. I can illustrate why word-for-word translation is not enough to translate meaning and intent. I once received a letter from China which I read to non–Chinese speaking friends. The letter, originally written in Chinese, had been translated by my brother-in-law in Beijing. One portion described the time when my uncle at age ten discovered his widowed mother (my grandmother) had remarried—as a number three concubine, the ultimate disgrace for an honorable family. The translated version of my uncle's letter read in part:

44   In 1925, I met my mother in Shanghai. When she came to me, I didn't have greeting to her as if seeing nothing. She pull me to a corner secretly and asked me why didn't have greeting to her. I couldn't control myself and cried, "Ma! Why did you leave us? People told me: one day you ate a beancake yourself. Your sister-in-law found it and sweared at you, called your names. So . . . is it true?" She clasped my hand and answered immediately, "It's not true, don't say what like this." After this time, there was a few chance to meet her.

45   "What!" cried my friends. "Was eating a beancake so terrible?"

46   Of course not. The beancake was simply a euphemism; a ten-year-old boy did not dare question his mother on something as shocking as concubinage. Eating a beancake was his equivalent for committing this selfish act, something inconsiderate of all family members, hence, my grandmother's despairing response to what seemed like a ludicrous charge of gluttony. And sure enough, she was banished from the family, and my uncle saw her only a few times before her death.

47   While the above may fuel people's argument that Chinese is indeed a language of extreme discretion, it does not mean that Chinese people speak in secrets and riddles. The contexts are fully understood. It is only to those on the *outside* that the language seems cryptic, the behavior inscrutable.

48   I am, evidently, one of the outsiders. My nephew in Shanghai, who recently started taking English lessons, has been writing me letters in English. I had told him I was a fiction writer, and so in one letter he wrote, "Congratulate to you on your writing. Perhaps one day I should like to read it." I took it in the same vein as "Perhaps one day we can get together for lunch." I sent back a cheery note. A month went by and another letter arrived from Shanghai. "Last one perhaps I hadn't writing distinctly," he said. "In the future, you'll send a copy of your works for me."

49   I try to explain to my English-speaking friends that Chinese language use is more *strategic* in manner, whereas English tends to be more direct; an American business executive may say, "Let's make a deal," and the Chinese manager may reply, "Is your son interested in learning about your widget business?" Each to his or her own purpose, each with his or her own linguistic path. But I hesitate to add more to the pile of generalizations, because no matter how many examples I provide and explain, I fear that it appears defensive and only reinforces the image: that Chinese people are "discreet and modest"—and it takes an American to explain what they really mean.

50   Why am I complaining? The description seems harmless enough (after all, the *New York Times Magazine* writer did not say "slippery and evasive"). It is precisely the bland, easy acceptability of the phrase that worries me.

51   I worry that the dominant society may see Chinese people from a limited—and limiting—perspective. I worry that seemingly benign stereotypes may be part of the reason there are few Chinese in top management positions, in mainstream political roles. I worry about the power of language: that if one says anything enough times—in *any* language—it might become true.

52   Could this be why Chinese friends of my parents' generation are willing to accept the generalization?

53   "Why are you complaining?" one of them said to me. "If people think we are modest and polite, let them think that. Wouldn't Americans be pleased to admit they are thought of as polite?"

54   And I do believe anyone would take the description as a compliment—at first. But after a while, it annoys, as if the only things that people heard one say were phatic remarks: "I'm so pleased to meet you. I've heard many wonderful things about you. For me? You shouldn't have!"

55   These remarks are not representative of new ideas, honest emotions, or considered thought. They are what is said from the polite distance of social contexts: of greetings, farewells, wedding thank-you notes, convenient excuses, and the like.

56   It makes me wonder, though. How many anthropologists, how many sociologists, how many travel journalists have documented so-called "natural interactions" in foreign lands, all observed with spiral notebook in hand? How many other cases are there of the long-lost primitive tribe, people who turned out to be sophisticated enough to put on the stone-age show that ethnologists had come to see?

57   And how many tourists fresh off the bus have wandered into Chinatown expecting the self-effacing shopkeeper to admit under duress that the goods are not worth the price asked? I have witnessed it.

58   "I don't know," the tourist said to the shopkeeper, a Cantonese woman in her fifties. "It doesn't look genuine to me. I'll give you three dollars."

59   "You don't like my price, go somewhere else," said the shopkeeper.

60   "You are not a nice person," cried the shocked tourist, "not a nice person at all!"

61   "Who say I have to be nice," snapped the shopkeeper.

62   "So how does one say 'yes' and 'no' in Chinese?" ask my friends a bit warily.

63   And here I do agree in part with the *New York Times Magazine* article. There is no one word for "yes" or "no"—but not out of necessity to be discreet. If anything, I would say the Chinese equivalent of answering "yes" or "no" is dis*crete*, that is, specific to what is asked.

64   Ask a Chinese person if he or she has eaten, and he or she might say *chrle* (eaten already) or perhaps *meiyou* (have not).

65   Ask, "So you had insurance at the time of the accident?" and the response would be *dwei* (correct) or *meiyou* (did not have).

66   Ask, "Have you stopped beating your wife?" and the answer refers directly to the proposition being asserted or denied: stopped already, still have not, never beat, have no wife.

67   What could be clearer?

68   As for those who are still wondering how to translate the language of discretion, I offer this personal example.

69   My aunt and uncle were about to return to Beijing after a three-month visit to the United States. On their last night I announced I wanted to take them out to dinner.

70   "Are you hungry?" I asked in Chinese.

71   "Not hungry," said my uncle promptly, the same response he once gave me ten minutes before he suffered a low-blood-sugar attack.

72   "Not too hungry," said my aunt. "Perhaps you're hungry?"

73   "A little," I admitted.

74   "We can eat, we can eat," they both consented.

75   "What kind of food?" I asked.

76   "Oh, doesn't matter. Anything will do. Nothing fancy, just some simple food is fine."

77   "Do you like Japanese food? We haven't had that yet," I suggested.

78   They looked at each other.

79   "We can eat it," said my uncle bravely, this survivor of the Long March.

80   "We have eaten it before," added my aunt. "Raw fish."

81   "Oh, you don't like it"? I said. "Don't be polite. We can go somewhere else."

82   "We are not being polite. We can eat it," my aunt insisted.

83   So I drove them to Japantown and we walked past several restaurants featuring colorful plastic displays of sushi.

84   "Not this one, not this one either," I continued to say, as if searching for a Japanese restaurant similar to the last. "Here it is," I finally said, turning into a restaurant famous for its Chinese fish dishes from Shandong.

85   "Oh, Chinese food!" cried my aunt, obviously relieved.

86   My uncle patted my arm. "You think Chinese."

87   "It's your last night here in America," I said. "So don't be polite. Act like an American."

88   And that night we ate a banquet.

Understanding Meaning

1. What is Tan's thesis about language differences?
2. What does the opening narrative reveal about the nature of Chinese language and culture? How would a typical American family behave and speak differently?
3. Tan quotes a linguist named Sapir who states, "Human beings are very much at the mercy of the particular language which has become the medium for their society." Does Tan agree with this assumption?
4. *Critical Thinking:* Tan speaks two languages. Does she seem to reflect two distinct mindsets, two different ways of looking at and responding to the world around her? Do immigrants face making a choice, or can they continue maintaining a dual vision? Is this clash or blend of identity lost on succeeding generations?

Evaluating Strategy

1. How effective is the opening scene? Does Tan follow the standard writer's admonition to "show; don't tell"?
2. How successfully does Tan weave personal experience and observations with more scholarly commentary on linguistics?

3. Why is dialogue so important in this essay?
4. *Other Modes:* How does Tan use *description, narration,* and *cause and effect* in constructing her comparison?

Appreciating Language

1. Analyze Tan's use of Chinese words in the essay. How effective is it? Do you get a sense of how Chinese and English differ?
2. How much linguistic terminology does Tan use?

Connections across the Disciplines

1. Read Kesaya E. Noda's "Growing Up Asian in America" (page 397). How are cultural differences perceived by the children of immigrants—those with no direct contact with Asian society? How important is language in forming a cultural identity?
2. How does reading Yi-Fu Tuan's "Chinese Space, American Space" (page 245) assist you in understanding some of the issues raised by Tan's essay?

Writing Suggestions

1. Write a brief narrative or description of your own interactions with some-one or some group of people who spoke a different language. Focus on word choices and behaviors you may have found mystifying, troubling, or humorous.
2. *Collaborative Writing:* Work with a group of students, and consider how Americans use English. What cultural features do you believe stand out? Consider Tan's closing statement: "So don't be polite. Act like an Ameri-can." Do Americans live up to their stereotype of being brash, loud, impolite? Record remarks, and then write a short description detailing observations made by the group.

BLENDING THE MODES

RENE DENFELD

Rene Denfeld (1967–) is a journalist and amateur boxer. In 1995 she became the first woman to win the Tacoma Golden Gloves tournament. That same year she published her first book, The New Victorians: A Young Woman's Challenge to the Old Feminist Order. *In 1997 her book* Kill the Body, The Head Will Fall: A Closer Look at Women, Violence, and Aggression *appeared. Both books question what Denfeld considers the basic assumptions of traditional feminism.*

The New Victorians

As you read Denfeld's essay, notice how she uses comparison to persuade readers to accept her criticism of feminism. Consider your own attitudes toward feminism and your knowledge of the Victorians.

1   It is said that Victorians placed women on a pedestal. They did—in fiction. In reality, this pedestal was a prison for the many middle- to upper-class women taught to revel in it: a dainty life indoors, a worship of illness, and an utter lack of recourse when abused by men. And this pedestal was a crushing weight to the lower-class working women who were most harmed by moral crusades such as those against prostitution, which were consistently used to take legal rights away from poor women. As the moral saviors of humanity, women were held to a much higher standard than men—and punished when they could not achieve it.

2   In pushing their varied causes, today's feminists promote a similar vision of womanhood. Discussing the dramatic redefinitions of rape by current feminists, journalist Stephanie Gutmann wrote for the July 1990 *Reason* magazine: "An almost Victorian denial of complicity—of woman's emotional stake in the sexual relationship—is a big feature of the date rape *oeuvre*. Man is entirely predatory; woman is entirely passive, a hapless victim, there by accident." Author Cathy Young, looking at similar sweeping definitions of sexual harassment, questioned this victim-centered view in the January 25, 1993, *New York Forum*:

"This new, hypersensitive woman is remarkably similar to the Victorian lady fainting at any mention of sex. . . . Once upon a time, this view of women as dainty creatures with chaste ears was considered *anti-feminist*."

3   Today it is not—at least not by feminist leaders. Today's feminists are remarkably similar to Victorians in significant ways, and not only in their vision of sexuality. This is clear through an examination of several different causes and trends in today's movement that, if anything, are a complete reversal of the movement's progress during the seventies.

4   This is the New Victorianism. And this is why women of my generation are abandoning the women's movement.

5   One of the most powerful trends in New Victorianism is what can be called the feminist antiphallic campaign. Today's feminists have created an overarching theory that blames male sexuality for the world's woes. In short, they believe that heterosexual intercourse—as an inherently invasive and oppressive act—is the root cause of all oppression. This theory is espoused by such influential feminist writers as Adrienne Rich and Cheryl Clarke, taught to women's studies students, and promoted in organizations such as local chapters of NOW. It is behind much of the antimale sentiment in the movement, and at its logical end it calls for separatism—the cessation of all intercourse between women and men, whether social or sexual. By naming the "institution" of heterosexuality as oppressive, current feminists promote the Victorian view that relationships between the sexes are by nature unequal and will always remain so.

6   In light of the evils of heterosexual sex, a powerful school of feminist thought teaches that only lesbian relationships are acceptable for enlightened feminists. This topic is often shrouded in silence because feminist leaders consistently condemn as homophobic those who would discuss it. But it is true in groups such as NOW, and it is also true in women's studies literature and magazines. The June/July 1991 San Francisco NOW *Times* summed up this cause succinctly: "Embracing lesbianism, or lesbian-feminist theory, is pivotal to the feminist movement, which works to change society through the elimination of gender-defined roles . . . heterosexism and male supremacy reinforce one another in maintaining our oppression. Both must be eliminated for any woman to be free."

7   This antimale sentiment has led to what amounts to victim mythology, a set of beliefs that promote women as the helpless victims of

masculine oppression. This bleak and uninviting—certainly not empowering—view of the sexes has crept into much feminist activism and theory. It is the basis of Faludi's thesis, when she names nearly every aspect of culture as part of an ambiguous yet devastatingly orchestrated war against women—a war in which men have consistently won and, since they are so conniving, will probably always win. And it has reached its apex in today's antirape movement.

8   Using a handful of extreme statistics from flawed surveys, today's feminists are pushing the idea that men are constantly out to rape women—and that women will constantly be raped. Sexual assault has been redefined to include whistling, touching, and sexual humor. "Other forms of sexual assault include unwanted sexual comments, jokes, and gestures," declares just one among numerous college acquaintance rape pamphlets. Even consensual sex has come to be considered rape, as it was in the nineteenth century. "Perhaps the wrong of rape has proven so difficult to articulate because the unquestionable starting point has been that rape is definable as distinct from intercourse," students attending "A History of Feminist Thought" at Duke University learn from an essay by Catharine MacKinnon, "when for women it is difficult to distinguish them under conditions of male dominance."

9   Fitting hand in glove with this view is the feminist fight against pornography. Stamping out sexually oriented expression is considered a top priority for many of today's feminists. This goal is enthusiastically supported by leaders such as Robin Morgan and given mainstream credibility by others such as Gloria Steinem. It has become an issue for organizations such as NOW, and the fight extends to other countries, including England and Germany. Young women, particularly on campuses, are told that to be a good feminist they must support the censorship of all varieties of sexual material—from *Playboy* to even lesbian erotic literature—because such material will inevitably cause violence against women. By blaming sexual material for sexual violence, current feminists invoke the Victorian-era belief that sexuality is inherently evil and any display of it must be squashed.

10   The antiphallic campaign's attack on heterosexuality, victim mythology's sweeping redefinitions of rape, and the effort to censor sexual material combine to create a repressive sexual morality that judges women's personal lives according to strict Victorianesque standards. We are told what is proper for us to read, whom we can sleep with, and even when we are violated. While some aspects of current feminism

have arisen out of a desire to apply a quick fix to complex problems—such as believing that banning sexual material will stop rape, though rape existed long before *Playboy*—at their heart these are simply recycled old morals that preach shame and repression. Introductory women's studies students at the University of Utah, for example, are told that enjoying sex is shameful: "Internalizing the devaluation of self is fundamental in being the screwed one, the slut, the whore, celebrating it, not rebelling one bit, female complicity does not even have the dignity or the insight of world-class misogyny. . . ." Yes, it is the twentieth century, and the writer is feminist leader Andrea Dworkin. And it would seem that, once again, women who would dare enjoy sex are no more than complicit whores and sluts.

11   The feminist sexual-purity crusades would have appalled our mothers as they fought for liberation in the sixties and seventies. It appalls their daughters, as well.

12   But these are not the only causes in feminism to ape the moral order of the nineteenth century. A new focus on spiritual and moral purity has pervaded the feminist movement. Major feminist schools of thought extoll an ideal of womanhood that rivals the best efforts of the Victorians to restrict our public role to nothing more than that of the shining example.

13   One of these is the growing feminist infatuation with goddess worship. Extrapolating freely from a few prehistoric artifacts, New Victorians have created a romanticized historical period where women not only ruled societies but were revered as deities. Ignoring all evidence that life at the time was not exactly Disneyland, feminists teach that these matriarchies were utopias. "Life was celebrated in all rituals, there were no blood sacrifices, or violence. Cultures were nurturing, non-violent, dependent upon each other and therefore respectful of each other's needs," asserts a NOW flyer entitled "Goddess cultural beliefs," which was handed out to women at a 1993 International Women's Day conference. "There were no weapons of violence, no fortifications surrounding goddess communities and no warfare." Only by returning to the worship of the goddess, this school of though contends, can women find a spiritual balance and truly become feminists. . . .

14   The feminist utopian vision is based on the belief that women are morally, ethically, and spiritually different from men—and, by extension, superior to them. From leading authors such as Carol Gilligan, who makes sweeping claims that women have a different "moral" voice

from men, one that makes us less violent and more caring, to feminist commentators in the 1992 elections who were often far more critical of female candidates than male (a situation that analysts believe contributed to Geraldine Ferraro's defeat in New York's Democratic U.S. Senate primaries), this view permeates feminist thought. In pushing this vision, feminists have abandoned the idea that women and men should be treated equally, endorsing the Victorian view of women as the guardians of morality, alone responsible for a more decent place. . . .

15 From male bashing to goddess worship, each leading feminist cause today alienates women. Many heterosexual women—as well as gay—balk at the adoption of lesbianism as a purely political action, large numbers of liberal women are turned off by the campaign to censor sexual material; and many religious women find the conversation tactics of the feminist spiritualists appalling. All of these trends have distanced huge blocs of potential activists from the movement. Independently, each do enough damage to the movement.

16 Combined, they have almost killed feminism. It is their collective force that has redefined the meaning of feminism for women of all ages. And it is their sum total that has caused women of my generation to abandon the movement, leaving it without troops and without a future.

17 This is the danger of New Victorianism. This feminist promotion of repressive sexual morality and spiritual passivity promulgates the vision of an ideal woman, sexually pure and helpless yet somehow morally superior to men and all male-influenced institutions. The leading causes in feminism today are all morally driven. The influential voices are entirely passive, speaking always in the language of victim mythology or inner transformation.

18 And so the women's movement has come to duplicate Victorianism in all its repressive glory: the woman revered on the pedestal, charged with keeping society's moral order yet politically powerless—perpetually martyred.

Understanding Meaning

1. How does Denfeld describe Victorian attitudes and values? What do they have in common with modern feminist beliefs, in her view?
2. What are the principal elements of what Denfeld calls "the New Victorianism"?

3. Why are young women, according to Denfeld, leaving the feminist movement?
4. What is wrong, in Denfeld's view, with feminist views of history?
5. *Critical Thinking:* Can a writer criticize feminism without appearing to criticize women's rights or minimize problems such as sexism, sexual harassment, etc? What can a writer do to anticipate reader responses?

Evaluating Strategy

1. How effective is Denfeld's comparison between feminists and Victorians? Does it depend on readers having a set view of the Victorians?
2. How does Denfeld organize her essay? What role do paragraph breaks play in making transitions?
3. *Other Modes:* How does Denfeld use *argument and persuasion, description,* and *cause and effect* in developing her essay?

Appreciating Language

1. What connotations does Denfeld bring to her description of feminists?
2. *Critical Thinking:* What connotations does the word "Victorian" have to you? What images does it conjure up in your mind? Do readers have to have a shared definition in order to understand the connection Denfeld makes?

Connections across the Disciplines

1. Gloria Steinem is a leader of what Denfeld calls the "old feminist order." Read Steinem's "Words and Change" (page 514), and see if you can locate any statements that would characterize her as a "New Victorian."
2. Read "Why More Women Are Going to Prison" (page 522). Does Gammage's article support or refute Denfeld's observations about women and violence?

Writing Suggestions

1. Write a persuasive essay in which you use a positive or negative comparison.
2. *Collaborative Writing:* Work with a group of students, and discuss Denfeld's essay. Select one point, and measure attitudes within the group. Develop pro and con points, and write a brief paper.

WRITING BEYOND THE CLASSROOM

PEGGY KENNA AND SONDRA LACY

Peggy Kenna and Sondra Lacy are communications specialists based in Arizona who work with foreign-born employees. In addition, they provide cross-cultural training to executives conducting international business. Kenna is a speech and language pathologist who specializes in accent modification. Kenna and Lacy have collaborated on a series of fifty-page booklets that compare American and foreign business organizations, habits, behaviors, and negotiating styles. Widely sold in airports, these booklets give Americans tips on doing business overseas.

Communication Styles: United States and Taiwan

This section from Business Taiwan *contrasts American and Taiwanese styles of communicating. In designing their booklets for quick skimming, Kenna and Lacy use charts to highlight cultural differences.*

UNITED STATES	TAIWAN
• *Frank*	• *Subtle*
Americans tend to be very straightforward and un-reserved. The people of Taiwan often find them abrupt and not interested enough in human relationships.	Frankness is not appreciated by the people of Taiwan. They particularly dislike unqualified negative statements.
• *Face saving less important*	• *Face saving important*

To Americans accuracy is important but errors are toler-ated. Admitting mistakes is seen as a sign of maturity. They believe you learn from failure and therefore encour-age some risk taking.
 	
    Americans believe criticism can be objective and not per-sonal, however, all criticism should be done with tact.
	The Chinese do not like to be put in the position of having to admit a mistake or failure. They also do not like to tell you when they don't understand your point.
	
	    You also should not admit too readily when you don't know something as it can cause you to lose face.

8 | UNITED STATES | TAIWAN

9

• Direct eye contact

• Avoid direct eye contact

10 Direct eye contact is very important to Americans since they need to see the nonverbal cues the speaker is giving. Nonverbal cues are a very important part of the American English language. Americans use intermittent eye contact when they are speaking but fairly steady eye contact when they are listening.

Holding the gaze of another person is considered rude.

11

• Direct and to the point

• Indirect and ambiguous

12 Americans prefer people to say what they mean. Because of this they tend to sometimes miss subtle nonverbal cues. Americans are uncomfortable with ambiguousness and don't like to have to "fill in the blanks." They also tend to

13 discuss problems directly.

People in Taiwan dislike saying "no." They may not tell you when they don't understand. They often hedge their answers if they know you won't like the answer. If they say something like, "We'll think about it," they may mean they aren't interested.

They dislike discussing problems directly and will often go around the issue which can be frustrating for Americans.

14 The Chinese language (Mandarin) is so concise that the listener needs to use much imagination to "fill in the gaps."

15

• "Yes" means agreement

• "Yes" means "I hear"

16 Americans look for clues such as nodding of the head, a verbal "yes" or "uh huh" in order to determine if their arguments are succeeding.

People in Taiwan do not judge information given to them so they do not indicate agreement or disagreement; they only nod or say "yes" to indicate they are listening to you.

The people of Taiwan believe politeness is more important than frankness so they will not directly tell you "no." The closest they will come to "no" is "maybe."

Understanding Meaning

1. What appear to be the major differences between American and Taiwanese methods of communicating?
2. Why is it important for Americans to be sensitive about making direct eye contact with Taiwanese?
3. How do Americans and Taiwanese accept failure?
4. *Critical Thinking:* Why would this booklet be valuable to Americans visiting Taiwan on business? Does such a brief, to-the-point guide risk relying on stereotypes?

Evaluating Strategy

1. How easy is this document to read and review? How accessible would the information be if it were written in standard paragraphs?
2. What does the directness of the document reveal about the intended audience? Would it be suitable for a college classroom?

Appreciating Language

1. What language do the writers use in describing the Taiwanese? Do they attempt to be neutral, or does their word choice favor one nationality over another?
2. Kenna and Lacy suggest that many Taiwanese find Americans to be "abrupt." Is this a good word choice? Does the guide express common prejudices?

Connections across the Disciplines

1. Compare Kenna and Lacy's observations with those stated in Yi-Fu Tuan's "Chinese Space, American Space" (page 245) and William Ouchi's "Japanese and American Workers" (page 267). Do these authors make similar observations about American attitudes and behaviors?
2. Review Amy Tan's article "The Language of Discretion" (page 274). How do her insights into the differences between English and Chinese explain differences in communication styles?

Writing Suggestions

1. Using William Ouchi's article about Japanese and American workers (page 267), write a chart similar to Kenna and Lacy's outlining national

differences in work habits and attitudes. Demonstrate how Japanese and American workers differ on issues of leadership, individuality, communications, and attitudes toward success.
2. Develop a chart outlining the differences between two groups of students, workers, professors, or employers you have known. Suggest to readers how to best communicate with each group.

STRATEGIES FOR WRITING COMPARISON AND CONTRAST

1. **Determine your purpose.** Is your goal to explain differences between two topics or to recommend one over the other? Do you want readers to be informed, or do you wish them to make a choice?
2. **Consider your audience.** Before you can compare two items, you may have to explain background information. Before comparing two treatments for arthritis, it may be necessary to explain the nature of the disease and to define basic terminology.
3. **Determine which method would best suit your topic.** A short, nontechnical paper might be best organized using the subject-by-subject method. Longer works with facts and statistics that should be placed side by side are better developed using the point-by-point method.
4. **Make use of transitional statements.** To prevent confusion in writing comparison, use transitional statements carefully. You may wish to invent labels or titles to clearly distinguish the different subjects you are examining.
5. **Use visual aids to guide your readers.** Careful paragraphing, page breaks, bold or italic headings, and charts can help readers follow your comparison and prevent confusion.

SUGGESTED TOPICS FOR COMPARISON AND CONTRAST WRITING

General Assignments

Write a comparative paper on one of the following topics. You may use either subject-by-subject or point-by-point methods of organization. Clearly determine your purpose. Is your goal to inform or recommend?

- High school versus college
- Your best and worst jobs
- Male and female student attitudes on dating/marriage/career/parenting
- The two most influential teachers you have known
- Two popular situation comedies
- Two computer programs you have worked with
- Your best and worst college courses
- Your parents' values and your own

- Two campus political organizations
- Two popular entertainers

Writing in Context

1. Imagine you have been asked by a British newsmagazine to write an article explaining the pro-and-con attitudes Americans have about a controversial topic such as gun control, capital punishment, or affirmative action. Your article should be balanced and objective and provide background information rather than express an opinion.
2. Write the text for a brief pamphlet directed to high school seniors comparing high school and college. You may wish to use a chartlike format.
3. Write a letter to a friend comparing the best and worst aspects of your college, dorm room, community, or job.
4. Examine a magazine on cars, computers, or entertainment. Write a letter to the editor comparing the magazine's best and worst features.
5. Compare two popular student clubs or restaurants for a review in the campus newspaper. Direct your comments to students interested in inexpensive entertainment.

STUDENT PAPER: COMPARISON AND CONTRAST

This is a draft of a comparison paper a student wrote after reading several articles comparing different cultures. In addition to fulfilling a composition assignment, she considered using these ideas for a talk or display for an upcoming Saint Patrick's Day celebration.

Parallel States: Israel and Ireland

1   Despite obvious historical and cultural differences, Israel and Ireland share striking similarities. Both are small — each has a population of about five million — yet significant nations. Israel is a narrow sliver of desert on the Mediterranean, a Middle Eastern country with negligible oil reserves. Ireland, an island on the fringe of Europe, is a neutral nation which played marginal roles in World War II and the Cold War.

2   Yet these nations have greater profiles than their larger and more powerful neighbors, largely because they represent homelands to vast

Diaspora populations. More Jews live in America than Israel; more Irish live in America than Ireland. American Jews and Irish were significant supporters of the Zionist and Republican movements that helped establish the modern independent states.

3   Their recent emergence as sovereign states indicates a shared legacy of oppression and occupation. Although both the Jews and the Irish have cultures thousands of years old, Israel and Ireland did not achieve full independence until after the Second World War. Israel was recognized by the United Nations in 1948. Though partitioned in 1922, Ireland was not officially declared a republic until 1949, ending eight hundred years of British influence.

4   Since their creation, Israel and Ireland have endured decades of violence and terrorism. Both nations have labored to maintain democratic rights while preserving security for their citizenry.

5   Both nations have dual identities. On one hand, both Israel and Ireland were founded as Western-style Parliamentary democracies. Yet both are religious states. Israel is the Jewish homeland. Ireland is a Catholic nation. The religious authorities — the Catholic bishops and orthodox rabbis — believe citizens should accept their views on marriage, divorce, abortion, censorship, and civil customs. Secular forces, who view the religious orthodoxies as tradition-bound and male dominated, champion diversity and tolerance. Issues such as the role of women and gay rights evoke similar debates in Israel and Ireland as both nations struggle to reconcile their political and religious traditions.

6   In recent years both nations have engaged in a peace process to resolve long standing conflicts in contested areas. In both Northern Ireland and the West Bank the populations are split by religious, political, and cultural differences.

7   Recently the President of the United States, prompted by the large number of Jews and Irish in America, played a pivotal role in stimulating stalled peace talks. Negotiations in both regions were difficult to conduct because Israeli and Northern Irish politicians did not wish to recognize leaders of terrorist organizations.

8   By first inviting Yasser Arrafat and Gerry Adams to the White House, Bill Clinton helped transform their public images from terrorists to legitimate leaders so that other democratic leaders could negotiate with them without appearing to endorse violence.

9   Despite ongoing tensions in both regions, Israel and Ireland enjoy expanding tourism, particularly from millions of American Jews and Irish who enjoy visiting homelands that represent their heritage.

Questions for Review and Revision

1. Is the thesis of this essay too general? Does the paper provide genuine insights or merely list obvious observations? Would it be better to fully develop a single issue, such as the role of religion in the two countries?
2. Would a revised introduction and conclusion provide greater focus?
3. What audience does the student seem to address?
4. *Critical Thinking:* To be effective, does a comparison paper have to accomplish more than merely list similarities? Should there be a greater purpose?
5. How effectively does the student organize the comparison? What role does paragraph structure play?
6. Read the paper aloud. Do you detect any passages that could be revised to reduce wordiness and repetition?

Writing Suggestions

1. Write a 500-word essay comparing two nations, cities, or neighborhoods. Stress similarities of which most readers would be unaware.
2. *Collaborative Writing:* Discuss this paper with a group of students. Ask each member to suggest possible changes. Do they find common areas needing improvement?

COMPARISON AND CONTRAST CHECKLIST

Before submitting your paper, review these points.

1. Are your subjects closely related enough to make a valid comparison?

2. Have you identified the key points of both subjects?

3. Have you selected the best method of organizing your paper?

4. Is the comparison easy to follow? Are transitions clear?

5. Does the comparison meet reader needs and expectations?

6. Have you defined terms or provided background information necessary for readers to fully appreciate the comparison?

7. Is your thesis clearly stated and located where it will have the greatest impact?

 WebTutor

See www.harcourtcollege.com/english/sundance for information on writing comparison and contrast.

6

Analysis

MAKING EVALUATIONS

WHAT IS ANALYSIS?

Analysis moves beyond description and narration to make judgments or evaluations about persons, places, objects, ideas, or situations. A movie reviewer *describes* a new film and then *analyzes* it—critiquing the plot, acting, special effects, and social message. A historian *narrates* an event and then *evaluates* its lasting significance. Marketing executives *summarize* sales reports to *judge* the results of their advertising campaign. A psychiatrist *examines* a patient and then *diagnoses* the individual's mental condition.

Analysis often seeks to answer questions. Does aspirin prevent heart attacks? What are Vicki Shimi's chances for being elected governor? Is General Motors' new minivan fuel efficient? Does America have too many lawyers? Is addiction a disease? How effective were the poverty programs launched in the 1960s? What is the best way to remove asbestos from a public school? Is a defendant mentally competent to stand trial? Is the central figure of *Death of a Salesman*, Willy Loman, a victim of society or of his own delusions? The answers to all these questions require a careful gathering of information, critical thinking, and a clear presentation of the writer's thesis.

Analysis entails more than expressing an opinion or creating an impression. In an analytical paper, you cannot simply write, "I hated *A Streetcar Named Desire* because it was stupid," or "Welfare programs waste taxpayers' money." You must base your positions on observations and evidence. Why is the play stupid? What facts demonstrate that welfare programs are wasteful? When asked to write analytical papers, students often supply description and narration, summarizing a short story or describing a social problem. To keep your paper analytical, you can use the journalists' "five W's"—*Who? What? When? Where? Why?*—to develop your thesis. By answering questions, you are forced to find evidence and provide answers instead of simply retelling a story or describing a situation.

Subjective and Objective Analysis

The way writers develop analytical writing depends greatly on context. In many situations, writers rely wholly on personal observation and experience. Film critics, political columnists, book reviewers, fashion consultants, and social commentators tend to write subjective analysis. *Subjective analysis* is based on close observation and careful interpretation. The writer's points are supported by examples and illustrations he or she has chosen rather than by research. Subjective analysis is informed opinion. In a newspaper column, "The Handicap of Definition" (page 310), William Raspberry analyzes the negative impact of the popular definition of "blackness" accepted by many African American children:

> What we have here is a tragically limited definition of blackness, and it isn't only white people who buy it.
> Think of all the ways black children can put one another down with charges of "whiteness." For many of these children, hard study and hard work are "white." Trying to please a teacher might be criticized as acting "white." Speaking correct English is "white." Scrimping today in the interest of tomorrow's goals is "white." Educational toys and games are "white."
> An incredible array of habits and attitudes that are conducive to success in business, in academia, in the nonentertainment professions are likely to be thought of as somehow "white." Even economic success, unless it involves such "black" undertakings as numbers banking, is defined as "white."
> And the results are devastating.

After analyzing how children label activities as being "black" or "white," Raspberry explains how limited definitions lead to limited opportunities. Raspberry's article, written for a general audience, makes conclusions, although it provides no independent research such as surveys or interviews.

Objective analysis begins with close observations but seeks to answer questions through factual research. In objective analysis, the writer needs more than personal experience and anecdotal examples to support a position. In "Addicted to Plastic: The Overspent American" (page 306), Juliet B. Schor cites statistics documenting the increase in credit card debt:

> The rise in indebtedness is in large part due to credit cards. Between 1990 and 1996, credit card debt doubled. Credit cards, with interest rates reaching nearly 20 percent, are a remarkably lucrative part of the loan business. Debtors pay an average of $1,000 a year in interest and fees alone. And the companies look increasingly like "credit pushers," soliciting heavily and beyond their traditional creditworthy base. Using subtle tactics to encourage borrowing, the recent onslaught has led consumers to hold more cards, to borrow more, and to fork over an increasing fraction of their incomes to the companies. If you don't borrow, the company may cancel your card, since it isn't making money on you.

Objective analysis is not limited to facts and statistics. Writers can balance numbers with interviews, personal examples, and anecdotal accounts. To dramatize the human cost of credit indebtedness, Schor details the plight of an individual consumer:

> Donna Schudson began accumulating her balances while she was in college, entering what she calls a debt cycle. "I wanted to drive a nice car, and so I went into debt for one. Then I got a credit card to 'establish credit' when I was twenty. Since my wages mainly went to my car and related expenses, I used my credit card for expenditures." Originally she thought that after graduation she would make a lot of money and pay everything off. But "once I got my job after college I needed a newer car, my own apartment, furnishings for the apartment, etc. I never stopped to pay off past debt. Little by little it kept piling up." Working her way up in a financial services company, she was eventually earning $47,000 a year but had accumulated credit card debts of $19,000 plus a $10,000 loan on her car.

The blending of statistics and personal interviews strengthens her analysis because her conclusions are drawn from more than one source of information.

The way writers develop their analytical writing is often influenced by their readers and their discipline. A widely respected restaurant critic will review a new cafe in wholly personal and subjective terms. But an engineer analyzing the structure of a hurricane-damaged bridge will use standard tests and procedures and will only provide conclusions clearly supported by scientific findings and observable detail. Kimberly Crawford, an attorney, analyzes the admissibility of surreptitious recordings of suspects by strictly studying Supreme Court rulings. Suppose the police arrest a man suspected of a bank robbery and place him in a cell with an officer posing as a fellow criminal. The officer engages the suspect in conversation, leading him to boast of his robbery. Could a recording of this admission be admitted as evidence in court, even though the Fifth Amendment of the Constitution protects citizens from self-incrimination? Crawford provides this analysis of the Constitution's guarantee against self-incrimination:

> To be successful, a challenge to the admissibility of surreptitiously recorded conversations based on the fifth amendment self-incrimination clause would have to establish that the conversations in question were the product of unlawful custodial interrogation. Because statements made to individuals not known to the defendant as government actors do not normally amount to interrogation for purposes of the fifth amendment, this challenge is destined to fail.

Crawford is writing strictly as a legal analyst of the Constitution. A defense attorney concerned with defendant rights or an ethicist might analyze this issue in moral rather than legal terms.

Detailed Observation

Analysis requires close observation, critical thinking, and in some instances outside research. If you have not read Samuel Scudder's "Take This Fish and Look at It" (page 45), you might wish to review it. This essay demonstrates the value of close observation. Good analysis cannot rely on first impressions. Before you can analyze a short story or a poem, you will have to read the work several times. If you are thinking of evaluating how women are depicted in television commercials, you may wish to videotape two or three evenings' worth of commercials and watch them several times rather than relying on memory. The more you observe about your subject, the more likely you will move from superficial observation to detecting details you may have previously overlooked.

CRITICAL THINKING FOR WRITING ANALYSIS

Analytical writing can be challenging. Even the best writers often fall into common traps called *logical fallacies* and make errors in judgment. Following these guidelines can help you improve your analytical writing skills:

1. **Ask questions to avoid summarizing.** The most common error students make is mistaking summary or description for analysis. Asking questions such as *why?* or *who?* can help you avoid simply retelling the plot of a story rather than analyzing it. For example, before starting to write an analysis of Hemingway's short story "Hills Like White Elephants," you might develop questions. Answering a question such as "Who is the stronger character, the man or the woman?" will guide you toward evaluating the story rather than supplying a two-page summary.

2. **Limit the scope of your analysis.** Unless you are willing to devote months to research, it would be difficult to gather sufficient material to fully analyze a subject such as day-care centers. You might restrict your topic to day-care centers in one neighborhood or focus commentary on a single issue such as licensing requirements.

3. **Evaluate sources for bias.** If you were analyzing the use of animals in medical research, you would not want to base your judgments solely on information from an animal rights group. When evaluating controversial subjects, you may be unable to obtain objective information, but you can achieve a measure of balance by examining data provided by organizations with opposing viewpoints.

4. **Apply common standards.** Analyzing data from different sources will be accurate only if all the sources have the same standards and definitions. If you were analyzing juvenile delinquency, you might face a problem if each study examined has a different definition of just who is a delinquent.

5. **Distinguish between opinion and fact.** Opinions are judgments or inferences, not facts. Facts are reliable pieces of information that can be verified by studying other sources:

   OPINION: John Smith is an alcoholic.
   FACT: John Smith drinks two martinis at lunch and frequents nightclubs on weekends.

   The factual statement relies on observation. The judgment of alcoholism is based on limited evidence and probably requires more support.

6. **Avoid hasty generalizations.** Generalizations should be based on adequate information, not a few instances that you may find dramatic or

interesting. The fact that two friends had purses stolen in the Student Union last week and that your car was broken into this morning does not mean the college is in the grip of a crime wave. You would have to examine several months of police reports to determine if an actual increase in campus crime has occurred.

7. **Consider alternative interpretations.** Facts do not always indicate what they imply at first glance. A rise in reported cases of child abuse may not indicate increasing violence against children but instead better reporting. If a school has a low retention rate, does that indicate it is failing to address the needs of students or that it instead maintains such rigorous standards that only the best students graduate?

8. **Avoid "filtering" data.** If you begin with a preconceived thesis, you may consciously or unconsciously select evidence that supports your view and omit evidence that contradicts it. Good analysis is objective; it does not consist of simply collecting facts to support a previously held conviction.

9. **Do not assume that parts represent the whole.** Just because one or more patients respond favorably to a new drug does not mean that it will cure all people suffering from the same disease. In the extreme, because individual men and women die does not mean the human race will eventually become extinct.

10. **Do not assume that the whole represents each part.** If fifty percent of students on campus receive financial aid, it does not mean you can assume that half the English majors receive aid. The student population in any given department may be less or more than the college average.

11. **Avoid reasoning on false analogies.** Analogy or comparison essays often provide weak evidence because they overlook that no two situations are exactly alike. Avoid assuming, for example, that results from a study conducted in Japan provide valid evidence for researchers in the United States. Because airbags have been proven to save lives in car accidents does not mean they should be installed in airplanes.

STRATEGIES FOR READING ANALYSIS

As you read the analysis entries in this chapter, keep the following questions in mind.

MEANING

1. What is the author's purpose—to provide a personal opinion or an evaluation based on standard research methods?

2. What discipline is the writer operating in? What kinds of evidence and what analytical methods are presented?
3. Does the writer present sources for his or her information?
4. What does the original source of the entry indicate about the intended audience and discipline?
5. What is the most significant conclusion the author draws?

Strategy

1. Does the writer rely on close observation, surveys, statistics, or expert testimony?
2. How were the data collected? Does the writer cite sources and supply footnotes?
3. Did the writer consider alternative interpretations?
4. Does the entry appear to be biased? Does the writer present facts to support a preconceived theory?
5. Does the writer avoid the logical fallacies?

Language

1. Do the author's choice of words and use of connotations indicate bias?
2. What language does the writer use in discussing people or organizations that hold different beliefs?
3. Are standard terms defined?

JULIET B. SCHOR

Juliet B. Schor is an economist who has served as an associate professor at Harvard University. She has edited several books, including Financial Openness and National Autonomy: Opportunities and Constraints *and* Golden Age of Capitalism: Reinterpreting the Postwar Experience. *In 1991 she published* The Overworked American: The Unexpected Decline of Leisure. *Her recent book* The Overspent American *describes the crippling effect of consumer debt.*

Addicted to Plastic:
The Overspent American

In this section from The Overspent American, *Schor analyzes the impact of credit cards. As you read her essay, consider how many offers for credit cards you receive in the mail.*

1   Not everyone earns before buying. Most of what we purchase we finance through borrowing. The earning comes later. Nearly all Americans borrow to buy their homes, and most automobiles are bought on time. Add to this the credit card balances, finance company loans, department store debts, and debts to individuals, and you begin to get an idea of the pervasiveness of household debt (about $5.5 trillion in late 1997). We "sign and travel" for vacations, charge the wife's birthday present, and put the health club membership on plastic. About one-third of the nation's population describe themselves as either heavily or moderately in financial debt, one-third report being slightly in debt, and only one-third report no financial (that is, excluding home mortgage) debts at all. As I write these words, the fraction of Americans' disposable income that goes toward debt servicing continues to rise; it has now reached 18 percent. The total amount of debt held by the average household has increased relentlessly for decades, and it now equals just about what that household makes in any given year.

2   The rise in indebtedness is in large part due to credit cards. Between 1990 and 1996, credit card debt doubled. Credit cards, with interest rates reaching nearly 20 percent, are a remarkably lucrative part

of the loan business. Debtors pay an average of $1,000 a year in interest and fees alone. And the companies look increasingly like "credit pushers," soliciting heavily and beyond their traditional creditworthy base. Using subtle tactics to encourage borrowing, the recent onslaught has led consumers to hold more cards, to borrow more, and to fork over an increasing fraction of their incomes to the companies. If you don't borrow, the company may cancel your card, since it isn't making money on you.

3   A significant number of spending downshifters are ex-credit card debtors. Donna Schudson began accumulating her balances while she was in college, entering what she calls a debt cycle. "I wanted to drive a nice car, and so I went into debt for one. Then I got a credit card to 'establish credit' when I was twenty. Since my wages mainly went to my car and related expenses, I used my credit card for expenditures." Originally she thought that after graduation she would make a lot of money and pay everything off. But "once I got my job after college I needed a newer car, my own apartment, furnishings for the apartment, etc. I never stopped to pay off past debt. Little by little it kept piling up." Working her way up in a financial services company, she was eventually earning $47,000 a year but had accumulated credit card debts of $19,000 plus a $10,000 loan on her car.

4   The credit card–spending link has become almost Pavlovian. Researcher Richard Feinberg placed some Mastercard signs and logos in the corner of his lab, with instructions to subjects that they were for another experiment and should be ignored. Apparently that's no longer possible. In comparison to a control group, those who saw the red and yellow logo spent more during the experiment. Credit card tips tend to be higher than with cash, and people report feeling looser with their money when they use plastic. The painlessness of spending with plastic makes it hard for many people to control.

5   Rich Moroni, a downshifter who eventually exchanged his job as a bad-debt collector for a more satisfying one as a consumer credit counselor, believes there's an underlying structural problem. "The bottom line for most people is they just simply don't think about what kind of money they make and what kind of lifestyle they're living. And they do want to be richer. They want to look richer than they are. If you have five credit cards, that actually makes it very easy to look richer than you are. And then add merchandisers and advertisers to that, and it's a formula for disaster for a lot of people."

6   At Telecom, debt emerged as a prominent feature of life. Only 11 percent of employees reported having no consumer debt, excluding mortgages. The average level of nonmortgage consumer debt was $13,700. About two-thirds of these respondents carry persistent credit card balances, and 14 percent pay only the minimum due each month. They identified debt as the single most important factor keeping their noses to the grindstone. Of the 68 percent of the sample who said, "I would like to reduce my working hours but feel that I just cannot afford it at this time," more than half named debt as the reason. Among those who said they would like to live a simpler life, debt outpaced all other reasons as the main barrier to doing so.

Understanding Meaning

1. How pervasive is consumer debt?
2. What implications does this amount of debt have on consumers and the general economy?
3. Are many Americans trapped in what one consumer calls the "debt cycle"? How does this affect their peace of mind and their quality of life?
4. *Critical Thinking:* What causes people to overspend? Do credit cards lead people you know to purchase items they cannot afford? Do many people buy items without considering how much they will pay in interest?

Evaluating Strategy

1. Schor blends statistics with personal examples. Would her essay be as effective if her analysis was based only on numbers? What does the testimony of a single consumer provide?
2. Would Schor's essay be more effective if her thesis were clearly stated in a single sentence?

Appreciating Language

1. What does Schor's level of diction reveal about her intended audience? Are there any terms the average reader would not comprehend?
2. Schor uses the term "Pavlovian" in paragraph four. How would you define this term? Would it baffle many readers?

Connections across the Disciplines

1. Refer to John Ciardi's "What Is Happiness?" (page 192). How does over-spending relate to his comments about material pleasures? Are many Americans trapped into trying to live beyond their means as a way of achieving happiness?
2. In "A Tale of Two Sitcoms" (page 259), Steven Stark notes that advertisers liked *Seinfeld* because its viewers included young single professionals with large discretionary incomes. Are young people targeted by advertisers and induced to spend, live beyond their means, or measure their lives by what they own?

Writing Suggestions

1. Examine a number of credit card commercials, and write a short paper analyzing their motivational appeals. What do they promise consumers? Are the interest rates clearly stated?
2. *Collaborative Writing:* Discuss credit cards with a group of students, and draft a short set of instructions to guide consumers in their proper use. How can people avoid getting into debt?

WILLIAM RASPBERRY

William Raspberry was born in Mississippi and began his journalism career as a photographer and reporter for the Indianapolis Recorder *in 1956. In 1962 he began working for the* Washington Post. *He received the Capital Press Club's Journalist of the Year Award in 1965 for his coverage of the Watts riot in Los Angeles. In 1971 Raspberry began an urban affairs column for the* Washington Post *that has been nationally syndicated since 1977. William Raspberry was awarded the Pulitzer Prize for Distinguished Commentary in 1994.*

The Handicap of Definition

In this Washington Post *article Raspberry analyzes the effect that the definition of "blackness" has on African-American children. Typically, stereotypes are viewed as limiting definitions imposed on people. Raspberry suggests that in many instances young African-Americans accept negative stereotypes that limit their opportunities.*

1   I know all about bad schools, mean politicians, economic deprivation and racism. Still, it occurs to me that one of the heaviest burdens black Americans—and black children in particular—have to bear is the handicap of definition: the question of what it means to be black.

2   Let me explain quickly what I mean. If a basketball fan says that the Boston Celtics' Larry Bird plays "black," the fan intends it—and Bird probably accepts it—as a compliment. Tell pop singer Tom Jones he moves "black" and he might grin in appreciation. Say to Teena Marie or the Average White Band that they sound "black" and they'll thank you.

3   But name one pursuit, aside from athletics, entertainment or sexual performance, in which a white practitioner will feel complimented to be told he does it "black." Tell a white broadcaster he talks "black" and he'll sign up for diction lessons. Tell a white reporter he writes "black" and he'll take a writing course. Tell a white lawyer he reasons "black" and he might sue you for slander.

4   What we have here is a tragically limited definition of blackness, and it isn't only white people who buy it.

5   Think of all the ways black children can put one another down with charges of "whiteness." For many of these children, hard study and hard work are "white." Trying to please a teacher might be criticized as acting "white." Speaking correct English is "white." Scrimping today in the interest of tomorrow's goals is "white." Educational toys and games are "white."

6   An incredible array of habits and attitudes that are conducive to success in business, in academia, in the nonentertainment professions are likely to be thought of as somehow "white." Even economic success, unless it involves such "black" undertakings as numbers banking, is defined as "white."

7   And the results are devastating. I wouldn't deny that blacks often are better entertainers and athletes. My point is the harm that comes from too narrow a definition of what is black.

8   One reason black youngsters tend to do better at basketball, for instance, is that they assume they can learn to do it well, and so they practice constantly to prove themselves right.

9   Wouldn't it be wonderful if we could infect black children with the notion that excellence in math is "black" rather than white, or possibly Chinese? Wouldn't it be of enormous value if we could create the myth that morality, strong families, determination, courage and love of learning are traits brought by slaves from Mother Africa and therefore quintessentially black?

10   There is no doubt in my mind that most black youngsters could develop their mathematical reasoning, their elocution and their attitudes the way they develop their jump shots and their dance steps: by the combination of sustained, enthusiastic practice and the unquestioned belief that they can do it.

11   In one sense, what I am talking about is the importance of developing positive ethnic traditions. Maybe Jews have an innate talent for communication; maybe the Chinese are born with a gift for mathematical reasoning; maybe blacks are naturally blessed with athletic grace. I doubt it. What is at work, I suspect, is assumption, inculcated early in their lives, that this is a thing our people do well.

12   Unfortunately, many of the things about which blacks make this assumption are things that do not contribute to their career success— except for that handful of the truly gifted who can make it as entertainers and athletes. And many of the things we concede to whites are the things that are essential to economic security.

13   So it is with a number of assumptions black youngsters make about what it is to be a "man": physical aggressiveness, sexual prowess, the refusal to submit to authority. The prisons are full of people who, by this perverted definition, are unmistakably men.

14   But the real problem is not so much that the things defined as "black" are negative. The problem is that the definition is much too narrow.

15   Somehow, we have to make our children understand that they are intelligent, competent people, capable of doing whatever they put their minds to and making it in the American mainstream, not just in a black subculture.

16   What we seem to be doing, instead, is raising up yet another generation of young blacks who will be failures—by definition.

Understanding Meaning

1. What kind of analysis does Raspberry provide?
2. What do readers expect in a personal column? What standards for gathering and studying data do they require?
3. According to the author, how does the definition of "blackness," internalized by many young African-Americans, affect the development of many children?
4. *Critical Thinking:* Does Raspberry ignore other definitions of "blackness" encountered by African-American children, such as black literature they read in school and black politicians they see on television? If so, does it affect his thesis?

Evaluating Strategy

1. Raspberry opens his essay by briefly referring to other burdens hampering the success of African-American children. Why is this important?
2. What evidence does Raspberry provide readers to support his views?
3. *Other Modes:* How does Raspberry *define* popular concepts of "blackness"? How does he use *comparison* to other ethnic groups to illustrate how definitions shape people's self-concept?

Appreciating Language

1. How does Raspberry use connotations to shape his analysis?

2. Raspberry talks of an idea to "infect" black children and create a "myth" that morality is a "black" value. What is the impact of this language?

Connections across the Disciplines

1. How did Miss Bessie, Carl Rowan's teacher, help African-American children overcome negative stereotypes (page 131)?
2. Review Edward Dolnick's article about deafness as culture (page 212). Should deaf children define themselves as members of a cultural minority or as victims of a disease?

Writing Suggestions

1. Look back on your own childhood, and write a brief essay describing how you came to define yourself. Analyze how it helped or hindered your development.
2. Write an essay analyzing how stereotyped attitudes have led women, the elderly, the disabled, or others to define themselves.
3. *Collaborative Writing:* Working in a group of students, write your own lists of behaviors defined as "black," "white," "Asian," "male," or "female." Discuss these definitions, and then draft a short analysis of your views and experiences.

MICHAEL ZIELENZIGER

Michael Zielenziger is a reporter for the Knight-Ridder/Tribune News Service. Based in Tokyo, he has published numerous articles on Asian economic and political affairs. In addition, he has commented on a wide variety of social and cultural issues, ranging from Japanese wedding customs to Tokyo nightlife.

Black Is Beautiful: Tokyo Style

As you read this article, consider the media images of African Americans distributed throughout the world. Does popular culture provide realistic representations of blacks and other minorities?

1 TOKYO — They're bouncing to hip-hop music at health clubs, boogying all night to rhythm and blues at the Soul Train Cafe. Women are curling their hair into Afro style haircuts—called "wafferu" (waffle) hair—while their boyfriends are growing goatees or taking to tanning rooms to darken their complexion.

2 Suddenly black is very, very beautiful for some of Tokyo's trendiest youth.

3 From dance parties in Roppongi to cutting-edge videos on television, from rising demand for porkpie hats to a rush for "gangsta" fashion, a new focus on African-American music and culture is giving voice to a strain of rebelliousness in young Japanese, confronting the most serious economic stagnation in 50 years.

4 "When I listen to this music, I don't have to think," explained Takako Yamamoto, 20, as she danced with a boyfriend at a Tokyo soul club. "I don't have to deal with work or stress. I can just be free. Black people and black music are totally cool."

5 "It's a way of telling people you don't want to be part of the large corporate lifestyle," said Minako Suzuki Wilder, who admires the new black scene. "A lot of people in their 20s are not into working at old-fashioned companies, so they get into the black music and the hip-hop dancing, getting frizzy hair or an Afro haircut."

6   "It's new to us and it seems fun. People like the way the music helps you work out your stress."

7   Strains of black culture have long existed in Japan, often carried here by African-American soldiers who decide to stay on. Jazz bars permeated in the 1950s and black baseball players often have become popular.

8   But now a new generation of black culture has entered the Japanese mainstream.

9   The most obvious sign: the appearance last month of a new beer called "Dunk," whose name alone connotes the German word "dunkel," for dark beer, with allusions to basketball players jamming the ball through the hoop.

10   Dunk advertisements, which now plaster Tokyo's subways, employ three sequined-studded, sashaying Motown-style singers and a Japanese entertainer, Masayuki Suzuki, most noted for his efforts to look African-American. During the 1980s, Suzuki dressed in blackface and white gloves to belt out soul songs for a group known as "Shanels."

11   "We didn't need to have a focus group to see whether black is cool," said Kiyoshi Oguri, marketing researcher for Asahi Brewery, manufacturers of Dunk. "But when we see black people playing ball on TV, not only basketball but also on entertainment programs, we could see that would be the right focus for us. We didn't intentionally focus on black culture, but certainly there is a recognition that black is cool.

12   "We knew that black things were 'kakko-ii' (cool). It's hard to explain the reason that it's 'kakko-ii,' but we know it is there."

13   However, observers note that because the relatively insulated Japanese have not been exposed to African-American culture, they tend to go wild over stereotypes.

14   "They may be interested in the trappings, but really their interest in African-American culture is completely superficial," said Kako Kawachi, who teaches women's and African-American studies at the prestigious Waseda University.

15   She dismisses the black fashion trend as a fad that has not brought new students into her classes.

16   "It's very shallow," she said.

17   Still, the surge in interest in things black is creating opportunities for African-Americans in Japan.

18   "Really, it's paradise over here," said Thomas Paul, a hip-hop dance

instructor and promoter, who earns nearly $4,000 a month teaching spin moves and twists at a health club. "People think we're really exotic, and most are really open to learning about the real hip-hop scene. A lot of folks come to check out my class just to experience real black culture."

19   His classes are a sea of twisting arms and sweat-drenched T-shirts as 20- and 30-year old Japanese, predominately women, try to mimic Paul's dance-steps and twirls. "Twist! 'Mawatte!' (Turn!) 'Tatte!' (Stand!)," Paul shouts at his students as they attempt to master his complex choreography.

20   While there aren't many blacks in Japan, those who land here find themselves among the most exotic, erotic and sought-after foreigners ever to set foot in this homogeneous and somewhat insulated island nation.

21   "You can feel the difference in the air," said jazz saxophone star Branford Marsalis, who recently concluded a three-week tour of Japan with his quartet. "When I first came to Japan eight years ago, people stared at you and thought you were strange. They really kept their distance and were sort of standoffish.

22   "But now, people are totally into what we are doing," he explained after a set at Tokyo's Blue Note jazz cafe. "They really listen to the music, and after the shows, the people really want to meet and talk to you.

23   "The attitude has completely changed, and it's really great."

24   In a nation that consciously encourages its young people to forge cohesive group identity, Japan always has produced its share of rebels who shun the corporate blue suits. Twenty-something "greasers" with slicked-back, duck-tail haircuts and leather jackets regularly dance on the weekends in Yoyogi Park. The Varsity shop sells cheerleader costumes. Reggae bars and salsa clubs beckoned the affluent and adventurous seeking a good time.

25   But the black trend, researchers say, signifies a clear disenchantment with the rigidity and lack of individual expression in Japan.

26   "In Japanese society, you don't have many options; society is quite inflexible," said Akiko Togawa, a market researcher for Dentsu Eye. "Most young Japanese don't see any successful entrepreneurs around them in Japan.

27   "So when they see black people who have made it, despite the discrimination in America, they see people who have successfully asserted their individual identity. So in a way, it's a revolt against traditional Japanese culture."

28   Valerie Koehn, a Tokyo-based designer and writer, says the re-
bellious quality of hip-hop and rap music is what is generating more
interest in African-Americans and their culture. "It's the young people
saying 'We don't care what our parents did or what society demands of
us. We don't have to do that.' It's totally in your face."

29   Toshiaki Koike, 34, an executive with a debt-ridden construction
company, says he prefers going to black music bars because "there's
more energy. Times aren't good right now," he said, over the strains of
a rap song at the Soul Train Cafe. "But here I can get great energy from
the music."

30   His friend Yamamoto said she really likes rap music and would
love to meet more African-Americans. But, as Kawachi, the black studies professor, indicated, this new fascination with black people might
be more style than substance and does not necessarily mean all cultural biases have been conquered.

31   "I don't think I'd want to date one," Yamamoto said of African-
Americans. "I'd be a little afraid."

Understanding Meaning

1. Why do young Japanese embrace hip-hop music and "gangsta" fashion?
    What does it represent to them? Why is black "cool"?
2. How have Japanese attitudes toward African-Americans changed in the
    last decade?
3. What images of African-Americans seem to have been exported to Japan?
4. How did Japan's recent recession influence the popularity of black
    culture?
5. *Critical Thinking:* American movies and television programs are viewed
    worldwide. Are people in other countries likely to develop distorted im-
    ages of America?

Evaluating Strategy

1. Zielenziger includes numerous quotations in his essay. How effectively
    does he organize them?
2. Do the comments by Kako Kawachi, who dismisses the Japanese interest
    in black culture as a shallow fad, form an implied thesis?
3. How effective is the last quotation? What impact does it have on readers?
    What does it reveal about Japanese attitudes toward African-Americans?

Appreciating Language

1. This is a news article, which is written to be skimmed rather than read. How do word choice, sentence structure, and paragraph length affect its readability?
2. What do Japanese words like "wafferu" for "waffle" and "kako-ii" for "cool" suggest about the influence of English in Japan?

Connections across the Disciplines

1. Carl Rowan (page 131) argues that limited definitions of blackness have harmed African-American youth. How have definitions of blackness influenced the Japanese? What does the woman's statement that she would be "afraid" of dating an African-American reveal?
2. In "Spanglish," Janice Castro (page 183) discusses the confluence of Hispanic and American cultures. Is there a different interchange when the introduction of a new culture into an established one is based on media images rather than immigration?

Writing Suggestions

1. Write a brief essay outlining your view of the Japanese, based solely on their media image. How are the Japanese represented in movies and television programs? What are the positive and negative stereotypes?
2. *Collaborative Writing:* Discuss this article with a group of students. Note members' observations and reactions. Work together to draft a short statement analyzing the way in which American popular culture influences world opinion.

JOEL CONNELLY

Joel Connelly is the national correspondent for the Seattle Post Intelligencer. *In 1990 he wrote this essay for a special nature issue of* Aperture, *a photography magazine. Connelly analyzes the way environmentalists came to understand the power of visual images and use the media to project their concerns to the American public through photographs and videotapes.*

A Growing Awareness: Environmental Groups and the Media

In this essay Connelly provides several examples of how environmentalists have used dramatic images to influence the public and conduct what he calls "visual lobbying."

1   A half century ago, Mao Zedong taught his followers that political power grows out of the barrel of a gun. In the world of the 1990s, however, political and societal change flow through the lens of a camera. Environmentalists learned this lesson long ago. These days the "green lobby" packs political clout in many countries. In its infancy, however, the movement found that the only way to save species and preserve wild places was to arouse the public with visual images. Some of these images, both the brutal and the beautiful, will remain in our memories for a long time.

2   A pioneer in the use of visual images to alert the public to environmental threats was Dr. Fred Darvill, a Mt. Vernon, Washington, family doctor. Darvill was among the first to display images of sublime places followed by the horrors that awaited them. Over twenty years ago, Darvill flew to New York armed only with a painting of Image Lake, a 10,000-foot-high tarn in Washington's Glacier Peak Wilderness Area, some slides, and three shares in the Kennecott Copper Company. He was bound for the annual meeting of the multinational mining company, which proposed to build a half-mile-wide open-pit copper mine in the wilderness area. Kennecott had the legal right to

do so, in the form of a mining claim that predated the Wilderness Act. Darvill set out to test the company's will. "The Sierra Club had alerted the wire services," he recalls. "I showed the painting of Image Lake, and explained what a mine would do in the area. I mentioned that it would be so big it could be seen through a telescope from the moon."

3   The presentation received nationwide publicity. It also attracted the eye of David Brower, then executive director of the Sierra Club and a man who pioneered the use of visual images in conservation battles. A full-page ad appeared in the *New York Times* under the heading: "AN OPEN PIT LARGE ENOUGH THAT IT CAN BE SEEN FROM THE MOON." Readers were presented with a picture of alpine glory beside one of a gouged-out open-pit mine in Utah.

4   In the end Kennecott never touched the wilderness. Brower would later deploy the same sorts of imagery—in a style described by John McPhee as "Early Paul Revere"—to stop two planned dams in the Grand Canyon. Above a canyon sunset picture was the classic headline: "WOULD YOU FLOOD THE SISTINE CHAPEL SO TOURISTS COULD GET CLOSER TO THE CEILING?" The Sierra Club lost its tax-exempt status, but the Grand Canyon was saved. Congressman Morris Udall of Arizona later paid grudging tribute to Brower's genius for capturing public attention, and for stopping an unwise project that Udall at the time had supported.

5   A prime goal of conservationists, according to Brock Evans of the National Audubon Society, has been to nationalize and even internationalize key battles. "Visual images are the key for us," says Evans. "They've kept ancient forests standing and oil rigs out of the Arctic Refuge." Cameras connect the global village. Viewers thousands of miles away can watch pictures of thousand-year-old Sitka spruce trees falling under a logger's chain saw. They can see oil-covered otters being lifted from Prince William Sound. They can feel the fear of those on a Greenpeace Zodiac boat as Soviet whalers fire a harpoon over its bow to mortally wound one of the world's largest marine mammals. Such pictures can generate thousands of words in citizen anger, enough to sway Congress or force the new president of Brazil to name an environmentalist to his cabinet.

6   When the Exxon *Valdez* fouled Prince William Sound, it disrupted a slick campaign aimed at persuading Congress to allow oil drilling in Alaska's Arctic National Wildlife Refuge. Oil lobbyists had effectively argued the necessity of reducing dependence on foreign petroleum.

Environmentalists had been unable to sway the public with pretty pictures of caribou. But images of oil-soaked beaches, birds, and seals triggered outrage. Alaska Senator Ted Stevens put it best: The Exxon *Valdez* spill had set drilling back at least two years. Asked when it would resurface, he replied: "When the oil spill is no longer news."

7 Direct action has proven a potent way to focus the camera on environmental events. "The Fox" was its prophet. This anonymous ecological saboteur stalked Chicago in the late 1960s. He never showed his face, but publicized his deeds with calls to TV stations and explained his outrage to columnist Mike Royko. Refineries found their outfalls plugged. Banners were hung from smokestacks. The Fox even invaded the executive offices of a steel company to dump smelly effluent on its carpets.

8 Over twenty years later, the Fox is frequently copied. Greenpeace protestors recently decorated a stack at the Longview Fiber Company pulp mill in Washington, on the Columbia River. When the press arrived, the activists were ready with documentation of dioxin dumping into one of North America's great rivers.

9 Direct action is sometimes condemned by mainstream environmentalists who stress action through Congress and the courts. But confrontations can purchase time. In rain forests along the Northwest coast, the radical environmental group Earth First has plunked down protesters in ancient trees marked for logging. When hauled down and arrested, they've given such names as "Doug Fir" and "Bobcat." These tree-ins have generated nationwide attention and slowed the pace of logging.

10 A daring, filmed protest can focus attention on activities that some might wish to remain unnoticed. The Greenpeace Foundation was formed in Vancouver, British Columbia, in 1971, an outgrowth of protests aimed at planned U.S. nuclear tests in Alaska's Aleutian Islands. In 1973 Greenpeace began stalking bigger game—atmospheric nuclear tests being conducted by the French. Greenpeace vessels were boarded by the French navy, and crew members beaten. But the protesters kept sailing into test zones, and kept arguing that radiation posed a danger to peoples of the South Pacific. In 1986 French commandos sank a Greenpeace ship as it prepared to sail from a New Zealand harbor. One crew member was killed. The resulting uproar strained French relations with New Zealand, drove the French defense minister to resign, and cast France in the role of international outlaw.

11   Greenpeace has chosen the camera lens as its weapon for a variety of environmental crusades. "We go to the scene of a crime and bring back images of what's going on," says Alan Reichman, ocean ecology director for Greenpeace International. "In that way we mobilize public concern and pressure. We're not talking abstractions and descriptions. We're showing a factory ship which cuts up whales. We're showing marine mammals trapped in nets. We're showing what comes out of pulp mills." Reichman has helped create memorable images. He was part of a flotilla of Zodiac boats that tried to stop a supertanker test run up the Strait of Juan de Fuca between British Columbia and Washington. Airborne photographers had a field day as the tiny craft buzzed around the 185,000-ton oil ship. A maneuverability test by the U.S. Coast Guard was turned into a political confrontation over whether to permit supertankers in sensitive West Coast estuaries.

12   A Greenpeace photo service makes pictures available to news sources, and engages in visual lobbying on Capitol Hill. Members of Congress, aides, and press gathered in a Longworth Building office last year to watch films of dolphins and birds entangled in the thick mesh of driftnet fishing lines. The seventy-mile-long driftnets are set on the North Pacific by Japanese and Taiwanese fishermen, supposedly to catch tuna and squid. In real life, they snare thousands of birds, marine mammals, and salmon. Congress has since pressed a reluctant Bush administration to support a worldwide ban on driftnet fishing.

13   The media savvy of such groups as Greenpeace has reached the environmental mainstream. The Natural Resources Defense Council has generally stayed far removed from visual imagery: Its battles have been fought in court, notably with suits that have forced the U.S. Department of Energy to abide by the nation's environmental laws in operating its nuclear weapons plants. On February 26, 1989, though, NRDC entered the court of public opinion. It gave CBS's *60 Minutes* a study entitled "Intolerable Risk: Pesticides in Our Children's Food." One of the pesticides in the report was daminozide (trade name Alar), a chemical sprayed on apples to improve their color, crispness, and shelf life. In its study, NRDC predicted that Alar might cause one case of cancer for every 4,200 preschool children—a rate of risk 240 times the standard considered acceptable by the Environmental Protection Agency.

14   Although written by scientists, "Intolerable Risk" translated well to the TV screen. *60 Minutes* focused on Alar. Americans saw apples being sprayed in fields. They watched those apples going into baby food. And a day later, Oscar-winning actress (and parent) Meryl Streep

went before a Senate hearing to argue the case for a ban on Alar. During the week following the *60 Minutes* report, apple sales fell 14 percent, and industry losses were estimated at over $100 million. A few months later, Uniroyal Chemical, Inc., announced it was taking the product off the market.

15   The media determines what is seen, and often what is saved. Photographs taken in a remote corner of northwest Wyoming helped create Yellowstone National Park over a century ago. Pictures can also lift politicians' sights up from ledger sheets. The U.S. Forest Service urged a veto of 1976 legislation creating a 393,000-acre Alpine Lakes Wilderness Area in Washington, arguing that it would cost too much to acquire private lands. Washington Governor Dan Evans, an avid backpacker, carried a picture book into an Oval Office meeting with President Gerald Ford. Evans turned to photos of the Enchantment Lakes region and told of guiding his three young sons over rugged, 7,800-foot Aasgard Pass during a violent storm. "Dan, we've got to save it," said Ford. He signed the bill.

16   As a writer I hate to admit it, but the camera's lens can be more powerful than the writer's pen. A physical confrontation convinced me. The state had let a logging contract on one of the few stands of old-growth trees left on Whidbey Island in Washington's scenic Puget Sound. Island environmentalists vowed to block the logging. I stood at the end of a narrow logging track with Mark Anderson, a young photographer with KING-TV in Seattle. A logging rig rumbled into view; protesters sat down in its path, and Anderson began filming. The truck stopped. After much waving of arms, the loggers retreated. A few hours later, KING carried an unforgettable film of trucks and bodies. It followed up with a film of the undisturbed forest. Birds chirped and sunlight wafted through 500-year-old trees. Anderson grew up in a logging town and knew the difference between a natural scene and a "working forest." Logging plans were promptly suspended.

17   The lawyering over Whidbey's forest was long and tedious. Not long ago, however, I enjoyed a walk among those same ancient trees, now—thanks at least in part to the powerful images presented by KING-TV and others—part of South Whidbey State Park.

Understanding Meaning

1.   Why does Connelly assert that power now comes not from the barrel of a gun but from the lens of a camera?

2.   How have environmentalists used visual images to achieve their goals?

3. What gives visual images their power, according to Connelly? How does a picture or video create a "global village"?

4. How do scenes of oil spills, dying whales, and ravaged forests affect the public?

5. What does Connelly mean by "direct action"? What examples does he provide?

6. *Critical Thinking:* Would your reaction to the use of images to influence public opinion be different if the subject were not the environment but abortion, busing, or gun control? Would you view the selected presentation of media images as something sinister if used to promote a cause you opposed? Is Connelly, after all, simply writing about *propaganda?*

Evaluating Strategy

1. What is Connelly's method of analysis? What standards does he use? Does he supply enough evidence?

2. *Other Modes:* What role does *narration* play in Connelly's essay?

Appreciating Language

1. What does Connelly mean by "global village"?

2. What meaning does "working forest" suggest?

3. *Critical Thinking:* Underline the words Connelly uses to describe "direct action" taken by environmentalists. What do the connotations of his words suggest? Do you detect a bias?

Connections across the Disciplines

1. Michael Zielenziger's "Black Is Beautiful: Tokyo Style" (page 314) documents the influence media images can have. How does this support Connelly's view that visual images can be used to influence policymakers as well as the public?

2. Does Connelly's article suggest a lack of critical thinking on the part of politicians, corporate executives, and the public? Are people too easily influenced by images? Examine the examples cited by Darrell Huff in "How to Lie with Statistics" (page 326). Is a similar article needed titled "How to Lie with Pictures"?

Writing Suggestions

1. Select a photo or image that greatly affected you. Perhaps it was a television commercial, a news report about a famine, or an illustration in one of your textbooks. Describe the image in a short essay, and then analyze why you found it so powerful.

2. *Collaborative Writing:* Discuss this essay with a group of students. Ask members of the group to provide examples of photographs or films they found moving or disturbing. Consider if pictures can lie through distortion or omission. Work together and develop a list of questions people should ask themselves before being moved to action by a photograph.

DARRELL HUFF

Darrell Huff was born in 1913 and received his B.A. and M.A. at the State University of Iowa in the 1930s. He published hundreds of articles in popular magazines and served as editor of Better Homes and Gardens *for several years. "How to Lie with Statistics" appeared in* Harper's *in 1950. His analysis of how statistics are misused remains a useful primer on what he calls "the secret language of statistics," which is used to "sensationalize, inflate, confuse, and oversimplify."*

How to Lie with Statistics

Perhaps no other evidence is more misinterpreted or misunderstood than statistics. People often hear and repeat statistics without knowing their source or their true meaning. As you read Huff's article, consider why appreciating statistics is an important element of critical thinking.

1   "The average Yaleman, Class of '24," *Time* magazine reported last year after reading something in the New York *Sun*, a newspaper published in those days, "makes $25,111 a year."

2   Well, good for him!

3   But, come to think of it, what does this improbably precise and salubrious figure mean? Is it, as it appears to be, evidence that if you send your boy to Yale you won't have to work in your old age and neither will he? Is this average a mean or is it a median? What kind of sample is it based on? You could lump one Texas oilman with two hundred hungry freelance writers and report *their* average income as $25,000-odd a year. The arithmetic is impeccable, the figure is convincingly precise, and the amount of meaning there is in it you could put in your eye.

4   In just such ways is the secret language of statistics, so appealing in a fact-minded culture, being used to sensationalize, inflate, confuse, and oversimplify. Statistical terms are necessary in reporting the mass data of social and economic trends, business conditions, "opinion" polls, this year's census. But without writers who use the words with honesty and understanding and readers who know what they mean, the result can only be semantic nonsense.

5   In popular writing on scientific research, the abused statistic is almost crowding out the picture of the white-jacketed hero laboring

overtime without time-and-a-half in an ill-lit laboratory. Like the "little dash of powder, little pot of paint," statistics are making many an important fact "look like what she ain't." Here are some of the ways it is done.

6   *The sample with the built-in bias.* Our Yale men—or Yalemen, as they say in the Time-Life building—belong to this flourishing group. The exaggerated estimate of their income is not based on all members of the class nor on a random or representative sample of them. At least two interesting categories of 1924-model Yale men have been excluded.

7   First there are those whose present addresses are unknown to their classmates. Wouldn't you bet that these lost sheep are earning less than the boys from prominent families and the others who can be handily reached from a Wall Street office?

8   There are those who chucked the questionnaire into the nearest wastebasket. Maybe they didn't answer because they were not making enough money to brag about. Like the fellow who found a note clipped to his first pay check suggesting that he consider the amount of his salary confidential: "Don't worry," he told the boss. "I'm just as ashamed of it as you are."

9   Omitted from our sample then are just the two groups most likely to depress the average. The $25,111 figure is beginning to account for itself. It may indeed be a true figure for those of the Class of '24 whose addresses are known and who are willing to stand up and tell how much they earn. But even that requires a possibly dangerous assumption that the gentlemen are telling the truth.

10   To be dependable to any useful degree at all, a sampling study must use a representative sample (which can lead to trouble too) or a truly random one. If *all* the Class of '24 is included, that's all right. If every tenth name on a complete list is used, that is all right too, and so is drawing an adequate number of names out of a hat. The test is this: Does every name in the group have an equal chance to be in the sample?

11   You'll recall that ignoring this requirement was what produced the *Literary Digest's* famed fiasco. When names for polling were taken only from telephone books and subscription lists, people who did not have telephones or *Literary Digest* subscriptions had no chance to be in the sample. They possibly did not mind this underprivilege a bit, but their absence was in the end very hard on the magazine that relied on the figures.

12   This leads to a moral: You can prove about anything you want to by letting your sample bias itself. As a consumer of statistical data—a

reader, for example, of a news magazine—remember that no statistical conclusion can rise above the quality of the sample it is based upon. In the absence of information about the procedures behind it, you are not warranted in giving any credence at all to the result.

13   *The truncated, or gee-whiz, graph.* If you want to show some statistical information quickly and clearly, draw a picture of it. Graphic presentation is the thing today. If you don't mind misleading the hasty looker, or if you quite clearly *want* to deceive him, you can save some space by chopping the bottom off many kinds of graphs.

14   Suppose you are showing the upward trend of national income month by month for a year. The total rise, as in one recent year, is 7 per cent. It looks like this:

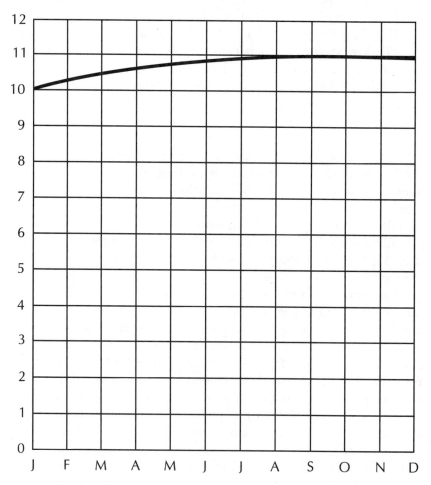

15 That is clear enough. Anybody can see that the trend is slightly upward. You are showing a 7 per cent increase and that is exactly what it looks like.

16   But it lacks schmaltz. So you chop off the bottom, this way:

17 The figures are the same. It is the same graph and nothing has been falsified—except the impression that it gives. Anyone looking at it can just feel prosperity throbbing in the arteries of the country. It is a subtler equivalent of editing "National income rose 7 per cent" into " . . . climbed a whopping 7 per cent."

18   It is vastly more effective, however, because of that illusion of objectivity.

19   *The souped-up graph.* Sometimes truncating is not enough. The trifling rise in something or other still looks almost as insignificant as it is. You can make that 7 per cent look livelier than 100 per cent ordinarily does. Simply change the proportion between the ordinate and the abscissa. There's no rule against it, and it does give your graph a prettier shape.

20   But it exaggerates, to say the least, something awful [see page 336].

21   *The well-chosen average.* I live near a country neighborhood for which I can report an average income of $15,000. I could also report it as $3,500.

22   If I should want to sell real estate hereabouts to people having a high snobbery content, the first figure would be handy. The second figure, however, is the one to use in an argument against raising taxes, or the local bus fare.

23   Both are legitimate averages, legally arrived at. Yet it is obvious that at least one of them must be as misleading as an out-and-out lie. The $15,000-figure is a mean, the arithmetic average of the incomes of all the families in the community. The smaller figure is a median; it

might be called the income of the average family in the group. It indicates that half the families have less than $3,500 a year and half have more.

24   Here is where some of the confusion about averages comes from. Many human characteristics have the grace to fall into what is called the "normal" distribution. If you draw a picture of it, you get a curve that is shaped like a bell. Mean and median fall at about the same point, so it doesn't make very much difference which you use.

25   But some things refuse to follow this neat curve. Income is one of them. Incomes for most large areas will range from under $1,000 a year to upward of $50,000. Almost everybody will be under $10,000, way over on the left-hand side of that curve.

26   One of the things that made the income figure for the "average Yaleman" meaningless is that we are not told whether it is a mean or a median. It is not that one type of average is invariably better than the other; it depends upon what you are talking about. But neither gives you any real information—and either may be highly misleading—unless you know which of those two kinds of average it is.

27   In the country neighborhood I mentioned, almost everyone has less than the average—the mean, that is—of $10,500. These people are all small farmers, except for a trio of millionaire week-enders who bring up the mean enormously.

28   You can be pretty sure that when an income average is given in the form of a mean nearly everybody has less than that.

29   *The insignificant difference or the elusive error.* Your two children Peter and Linda (we might as well give them modish names while we're about it) take intelligence tests. Peter's IQ, you learn, is 98 and Linda's is 101. Aha! Linda is your brighter child.

30   Is she? An intelligence test is, or purports to be, a sampling of intellect. An IQ, like other products of sampling, is a figure with a statistical error, which expresses the precision or reliability of the figure. The size of this probable error can be calculated. For their test the makers of the much-used Revised Stanford-Binet have found it to be about 3 per cent. So Peter's indicated IQ of 98 really means only that there is an even chance that it falls between 95 and 101. There is an equal probability that it falls somewhere else—below 95 or above 101. Similarly, Linda's has no better than a fifty-fifty chance of being within the fairly sizeable range of 98 to 104.

31   You can work out some comparisons from that. One is that there is rather better than one chance in four that Peter, with his lower IQ rating, is really at least three points smarter than Linda. A statistician doesn't like to consider a difference significant unless you can hand him odds a lot longer than that.

32   Ignoring the error in a sampling study leads to all kinds of silly conclusions. There are magazine editors to whom readership surveys are gospel; with a 40 per cent readership reported for one article and a 35 per cent for another, they demand more like the first. I've seen even smaller differences given tremendous weight, because statistics are a mystery and numbers are impressive. The same thing goes for market surveys and so-called public-opinion polls. The rule is that you cannot make a valid comparison between two such figures unless you

know the deviations. And unless the difference between the figures is many times greater than the probable error of each, you have only a guess that the one appearing greater really is.

33   Otherwise you are like the man choosing a camp site from a report of mean temperature alone. One place in California with a mean annual temperature of 61 is San Nicolas Island on the south coast, where it always stays in the comfortable range between 47 and 87. Another with a mean of 61 is in the inland desert, where the thermometer hops around from 15 to 104. The deviation from the mean marks the difference, and you can freeze or roast if you ignore it.

34   *The one-dimensional picture.* Suppose you have just two or three figures to compare—say the average weekly wage of carpenters in the United States and another country. The sums might be $60 and $30. An ordinary bar chart makes the difference graphic.

35   That is an honest picture. It looks good for American carpenters, but perhaps it does not have quite the oomph you are after. Can't you make that difference appear overwhelming and at the same time give it what I am afraid is known as eye-appeal? Of course you can. Following tradition, you represent these sums by pictures of money bags. If the $30 bag is one inch high, you draw the $60 bag two inches high. That's in proportion, isn't it? The catch is, of course, that the American's money bag, being twice as tall as that of the $30 man, covers an area on your page four times as great. And since your two-dimensional

picture represents an object that would in fact have three dimensions, the money bags actually would differ much more than that. The volumes of any two similar solids vary as the cubes of their heights. If the unfortunate foreigner's bag holds $30 worth of dimes, the American's would hold not $60 but a neat $240.

36   You didn't say that, though, did you? And you can't be blamed, you're only doing it the way practically everybody else does.

37   *The ever-impressive decimal.* For a spurious air of precision that will lend all kinds of weight to the most disreputable statistics, consider the decimal.

38   Ask a hundred citizens how many hours they slept last night. Come out with a total of, say, 781.3. Your data are far from precise to begin with. Most people will miss their guess by fifteen minutes or more and some will recall five sleepless minutes as half a night of tossing insomnia.

39   But go ahead, do your arithmetic, announce that people sleep an average of 7.813 hours a night. You will sound as if you knew precisely what you are talking about. If you were foolish enough to say 7.8 (or "almost 8") hours it would sound like what it was—an approximation.

40   *The semi-attached figure.* If you can't prove what you want to prove, demonstrate something else and pretend that they are the same thing. In the daze that follows the collision of statistics with the human mind, hardly anybody will notice the difference. The semi-attached

figure is a durable device guaranteed to stand you in good stead. It always has.

41   If you can't prove that your nostrum cures colds, publish a sworn laboratory report that the stuff killed 31,108 germs in a test tube in eleven seconds. There may be no connection at all between assorted germs in a test tube and the whatever-it-is that produces colds, but people aren't going to reason that sharply, especially while sniffling.

42   Maybe that one is too obvious and people are beginning to catch on. Here is a trickier version.

43   Let us say that in a period when race prejudice is growing it is to your advantage to "prove" otherwise. You will not find it a difficult assignment.

44   Ask that usual cross section of the population if they think Negroes have as good a chance as white people to get jobs. Ask again a few months later. As Princeton's Office of Public Opinion Research has found out, people who are most unsympathetic to Negroes are the ones most likely to answer yes to this question.

45   As prejudice increases in a country, the percentage of affirmative answers you will get to this question will become larger. What looks on the face of it like growing opportunity for Negroes actually is mounting prejudice and nothing else. You have achieved something rather remarkable: the worse things get, the better your survey makes them look.

46   *The unwarranted assumption, or* post hoc *rides again.* The interrelation of cause and effect, so often obscure anyway, can be most neatly hidden in statistical data.

47   Somebody once went to a good deal of trouble to find out if cigarette smokers make lower college grades than non-smokers. They did. This naturally pleased many people, and they made much of it.

48   The unwarranted assumption, of course, was that smoking had produced dull minds. It seemed vaguely reasonable on the face of it, so it was quite widely accepted. But it really proved nothing of the sort, any more than it proved that poor grades drive students to the solace of tobacco. Maybe the relationship worked in one direction, maybe in the other. And maybe all this is only an indication that the sociable sort of fellow who is likely to take his books less than seriously is also likely to sit around and smoke many cigarettes.

49   Permitting statistical treatment to befog causal relationships is little better than superstition. It is like the conviction among the people of the Hebrides that body lice produce good health. Observation over

the centuries had taught them that people in good health had lice and sick people often did not. *Ergo,* lice made a man healthy. Everybody should have them.

50   Scantier evidence, treated statistically at the expense of common sense, has made many a medical fortune and many a medical article in magazines, including professional ones. More sophisticated observers finally got things straightened out in the Hebrides. As it turned out, almost everybody in those circles had lice most of the time. But when a man took a fever (quite possibly carried to him by those same lice) and his body became hot, the lice left.

51   Here you have cause and effect not only reversed, but intermingled.

52   There you have a primer in some ways to use statistics to deceive. A well-wrapped statistic is better than Hitler's "big lie": it misleads, yet it can't be pinned onto you.

53   Is this little list altogether too much like a manual for swindlers? Perhaps I can justify it in the manner of the retired burglar whose published reminiscences amounted to a graduate course in how to pick a lock and muffle a footfall: The crooks already know these tricks. Honest men must learn them in self-defense.

Understanding Meaning

1. Why do statistics impress people? What is their appeal in advertising?
2. What are the principal methods used to create misleading statistics?
3. Is Huff suggesting that advertisers deliberately lie, or is he suggesting that advertisers often do not understand the meaning of their own numbers?
4. Armed with computers, many people love to construct elaborate graphs to include in their reports. What does Huff's article reveal about the reliability of many visual aids?
5. *Critical Thinking:* What are the implications of Huff's observation that "A well-wrapped statistic is better than Hitler's 'big lie': it misleads, yet it can't be pinned onto you"? Can you think of examples of falsely stated statistics that have been used to influence the public?

Evaluating Strategy

1. What impact does the title have?
2. How effective are Huff's examples in communicating complex ideas to a general audience?

3. How does Huff try to maintain reader interest while explaining a topic many readers find abstract, boring, or intimidating?

Appreciating Language

1. What does Huff's choice of words suggest about the tone he is trying to establish?
2. What changes in language would you suggest making if the article were to be rewritten for inclusion in a textbook?

Connections across the Disciplines

1. Consider the lesson Samuel Scudder learned about close observation in "Take This Fish and Look at It" (page 45). Does Huff's article provide another lesson in critical thinking?
2. Consider recent statistics you have heard used in commercials or by politicians. Were any sources provided? Could you evaluate their validity?

Writing Suggestions

1. Select a statistic you have heard people cite. Write a brief essay analyzing why the statistic is popular. Do statistics that support a cause serve the same purpose as a slogan on a bumper sticker by providing a shorthand argument?
2. Imagine you plan to publish this article as a brochure for distribution. Write a brief analysis of the audience that would benefit most from its contents.
3. *Collaborative Writing:* Working with a group of students, use this writing exercise to learn more about statistics:

   Imagine that a school district has 1,000 teachers earning an average of $30,000 a year. After a bitter dispute, the school board agrees to provide teachers with a five percent raise. Discuss the impact of the following newspaper headlines:

   Teachers Get 5% Pay Hike
   Teachers Get $1,500 Raise
   Teachers Get $31.5 Million

   Write a short analysis of how presenting numbers in different forms can influence readers. Which statistic do members of the group feel to be the most accurate?

LOUIS R. MIZELL JR.

Louis R. Mizell Jr. was a special agent and intelligence officer for the U. S. State Department. He is now president of Mizell and Company, an international firm specializing in crime prevention. Mizell frequently appears on television commenting on home and personal security issues. He has published a series of books on personal safety. In 1998 he published Invasion of Privacy, *analyzing how modern technology has compromised personal privacy and security.*

Who's Listening to Your Cell Phone Calls?

Before reading this passage from Invasion of Privacy, *consider how often you have used or have seen friends use a cell phone. Do people assume their conversations are private?*

1 More than forty million cellular phones are currently in use in the United States, and the numbers are dramatically increasing each year.

2 On any given day, thousands of eavesdroppers intercept, record, and listen to conversations made from cellular and so-called cordless phones. These eavesdroppers include curious neighbors, business competitors, stalkers, journalists, private investigators, and even espionage agents.

3 In California, spies for hire cruise the highways of Hollywood and the Silicon Valley, hoping to steal valuable trade secrets from executives talking on their car phones. Armed with radio scanners, tabloid reporters in New York monitor conversations of the rich, famous, and infamous, hoping to get a front-page scoop. In Florida, a ham operator monitoring the poolside conversations of a prominent lawyer got incredible inside information on three divorce cases.

4 Cellular telephone conversations can be easily monitored by anyone with a radio scanner, but it is a violation of state and federal law to do so intentionally. A 1993 law made it illegal to make or sell radio scanners that pick up cellular calls, but the law didn't make it illegal to own the old scanners. Furthermore, it is rather easy, although

illegal, to modify a legal police scanner so that it will pick up cellular conversations.

5   The problem is that there are hundreds of thousands of the old radio scanners in circulation and an equal number of people who don't care about the law. "How are they going to catch me and how are they going to prove it?" said one ham operator who listens to his neighbors' cellular conversations "just for the fun of it."

6   In truth, only a very small percentage of the people who have been monitored ever learn that their calls were intercepted. An even smaller percentage of the perpetrators are ever caught. Curious kooks, corporate snoops, and spies for hire who use intercepted information are usually smart enough not to publicize where they got it.

7   "I really couldn't care less if someone listens to my conversations," said a schoolteacher from Indiana. "I'm not discussing my love life or national security." One of the biggest problems concerning privacy and portable phones is that most people do not realize how even innocent information can be used by criminals and other opportunists. Another problem is that just because you don't care if someone is listening to your conversation, the person you are talking to might care very much.

8   Burglars are known to monitor the calls of people discussing evening or weekend plans. Knowing that the occupants are going to be away, the burglars enter their homes.

9   Doctors and lawyers frequently discuss everyday business on cellular phones. In one case, a doctor was notified that a VIP patient had tested positive for AIDS. The information was intercepted, and before long, the VIP's medical status was common knowledge. In another case, a lawyer from Ohio reviewed a client's prenuptial agreement with a second lawyer who was using a cellular telephone. A teenage neighbor of the second lawyer intercepted the conversation. "Before long, the whole damn neighborhood knew about our secret wedding and my financial situation," said the angry groom-to-be.

10   Stalking, or inappropriate pursuit, has become a dangerous epidemic in the United States and is evolving into one of the most insidious threats to personal privacy. Many researchers estimate that more than two hundred thousand women, men, and children are currently being harassed, threatened, and endangered by stalkers.

11   Stalking may begin with an innocuous contact and then, through misinterpretation or delusion, the pursuer escalates to harassment, surveillance, threats, and sometimes murder.

12   I have been involved in seven cases and am aware of many more in which stalkers intercepted cellular phone conversations and used the intelligence to harass their targets.

13   A jobless and toothless forty-one-year-old man, hooked on amphetamines, became infatuated with a fifteen-year-old girl whom he first noticed at a state swimming competition. "He's really scary and keeps showing up wherever I go," explained the frightened swimmer. "It's like he always knows where I'm going to be."

14   The young lady had good reason to be scared; the man had a long history of bizarre and criminal behavior. On one occasion, he burglarized a home and fell asleep in a teenage girl's bed. The horrified family called the police who arrested the man and confiscated handcuffs and a number of stolen house keys.

15   Released on good behavior, the "nonviolent" criminal was once again free to victimize others. We can't prove what his ultimate plans were concerning our fifteen-year-old client, but we did prove that he had a scanner in his car and had recorded the swimmer's mother as she talked on various cell phones, including a car phone. Two of the taped conversations informed the stalker where his target would be. "I've got to pick my daughter up at McDonald's at 4:30," she mentioned to one friend. "The swim team is celebrating at the Hyatt tonight," she told her neighbor. Needless to say, the stalker showed up at both locations.

16   Eavesdropping on cellular phones is only one of the issues that worry privacy advocates. There is also concern that cellular phones will be used by police and sophisticated criminals to locate the caller.

17   Unbeknownst to most consumers, cellular phones are portable homing devices that allow police and others to pinpoint the caller's position. Police have used this tool to locate a wide range of criminals and kidnap victims. Privacy advocates worry that police will abuse this tool to spy on innocent citizens

18   When a cellular phone is switched to the On position, it emits a low-power signal to the network to announce which cell site it is in. A cell site is a zone served by a single relay station and is generally several square miles in size. When a caller moves out of one cell site, the call is automatically switched to a different cell site.

19   By using a technique called triangulation, police are able to get a directional fix on the cellular signal and pinpoint the phone's cell site or location. This is the technique police used to locate the car owned by the slain father of basketball great Michael Jordan. Triangulation techniques have also been used by intelligence agencies to locate enemy

radio sites and by ocean search-and-rescue teams to pinpoint the location of vessels.

20   There are dozens of cases in which triangulation techniques have assisted law enforcement worldwide.

21   When the Los Angeles police needed to locate O. J. Simpson during the now-famous highway chase, they received court-ordered help from a mobile phone company and were able to locate the Ford Bronco by tracing its cellular phone radio signal. In Colombia, ruthless drug boss Pablo Escobar was finally located and shot dead by police after they traced his mobile telephone's radio signal. Police in the United States located fugitive lawyer Nicholas Bissell, Jr., in Nevada on November 26, 1996, after tracing calls he made on his cellular telephone. Bissell was running from the law after being convicted of fraud, embezzlement, and abuse of power.

22   Another advantage of cellular tracing from a law enforcement perspective is that cellular phones can tell police not only where a suspect is going but also where he has been.

23   A federal drug informant is accused of booby-trapping a briefcase in an unsuccessful attempt to kill a U. S. prosecutor. Using the informant's cellular phone records, prosecutors showed that he was in the same town on the same day where the would-be assassination kit was purchased.

24   Unlike hard-line telephones that most people have in their homes, customers pay for each local cellular call. The billing record for each cellular call shows the cell site from which it was made.

25   Privacy advocates recognize that cellular call tracing can be a great tool for law enforcement, but they argue that the bad will outweigh the good if police abuse their powers.

26   "Police have no right to know my location just because they reason that I might be relevant to some investigation," explained a law-abiding political science professor. "I want to make sure police cannot track and follow a person using a mobile phone unless they obtain a full wiretap warrant." At present, police only need a simple subpoena, which is easier to obtain than a wiretap warrant, to legally intercept cell phone signals.

27   "I bet the good professor would change his mind real quickly if his daughter were kidnapped," countered a police captain. "We don't have the time, the resources, or the inclination to snoop on law-abiding citizens. . . . We only use cellular tools to catch criminals," he protested.

"Shouldn't we be more worried about the way rapists and burglars invade our privacy and less worried about taking crime-fighting weapons from the police?"

Understanding Meaning

1. Why are cell phones easy to monitor? What makes them different from traditional telephones?
2. Why have laws banning police scanners that can pick up cell calls failed to curb illegal monitoring?
3. How can even innocent calls expose people to risk?
4. How do cell phones work as homing devices? How can police use them to track people's movements?
5. *Critical Thinking:* Can anyone be sure that his or her legal, medical, or financial records are secure? Even if you never use a cell phone, can you be sure that conversations by your lawyer, doctor, or broker are not being monitored?

Evaluating Strategy

1. How effective is the evidence Mizell presents? Do you find it convincing? Do you think it will change people's use of cell phones?
2. *Other Modes:* How does Mizell use *narration* and *cause and effect* in developing his analysis?

Appreciating Language

1. Mizell uses words like "kook" in his essay. Does the use of slang make the essay easy to read, or does it detract from the seriousness of the subject?
2. Mizell's book is targeted to a wide audience. Do you find his style readable? Can you easily remember facts and details? Would the use of technical or legal terminology lend the article greater authority?

Connections across the Disciplines

1. Refer to Kimberly Crawford's article about recording suspects' conversations (page 366). How can society balance concerns for privacy with the need for police departments to investigate crime?

2. Review television commercials or print advertisements for cell phones. Do manufacturers explain how easily these devices can be monitored? Should cell phones come with clearer warnings?

Writing Suggestions

1. Write an essay analyzing how technology—cell phones, e-mail, computers, the Internet, security video cameras—have robbed citizens of their privacy. Is there any way to protect people from stalkers and hackers who might monitor phone calls or illegally access computer files and post the information on a Web page?
2. *Collaborative Writing:* Working with a group of students, review Mizell's article, and write a short process paper instructing consumers in cell phone use. Remind people to avoid discussing sensitive issues or providing information that could be used by burglars or stalkers.

FRANK PILIPP
AND CHARLES SHULL

Frank Pilipp is an associate professor of German at the Georgia Institute of Technology. He has conducted research in modern European literature and film and is the author of The Novels of Martin Walser: A Critical Introduction. *Charles Shull is an associate professor of sociology at Lynchburg College in Virginia, where he teaches courses about AIDS. He served as president of an AIDS support group and assisted people with HIV. Pilipp and Shull collaborated to write an analysis of how movies made for television have treated the epidemic and its victims.*

TV Movies of the First Decade of AIDS

First published in the Journal of Popular Film and Television *in 1993, Pilipp and Shull's article analyzes the messages about AIDS contained in four television movies that appeared between 1985 and 1991.*

1　Among the media of popular culture, television, over the past decade, has hesitantly become a mouthpiece for reporting and responding to the AIDS epidemic.[1] In addition to documentary and news-related coverage, a small array of fictional accounts, that is full-length feature films spawned by the disease, have constituted a general, albeit basic, chronicle of the multi-faceted dimensions of the epidemic. As a set, these movies both challenge *and* reinforce a number of basic values and stereotypes linked to nurturing, caretaking, parenting, and sexuality. Consequently, these movies generate an imagery of the first AIDS decade as multifarious and, perhaps, as confusing as the epidemic itself. Contrasting the presentations of the gay male AIDS protagonists and their families in the films *An Early Frost* (1985), *As Is* (1986), *Andre's Mother* (1990), and *Our Sons* (1991) should not only show the degree to which the AIDS epidemic has been a cultural catalyst and influenced American society but also how cultural values predetermine public and personal perceptions of such an issue as AIDS.

2　These films present the views of the AIDS issue[2] through images of those who are either "inside" or "outside" the social worlds of gay men and/or of AIDS. This division reflects the parallel worlds of the "gay"/"straight" and AIDS involved/non-involved experiential worlds of contemporary American society. The films illustrate the tensions generated when a terminal illness forces strangers to acknowledge the experiences of the other; to confront, accept, and interact with a social (or medical) world alien to them. The walls that divide these worlds have been built by the dynamics of fear: families fearing and rejecting those who are gay and/or AIDS infected and gay men fearing rejection by their families. That insider/outsider dichotomy has also been identified as the worlds of the *immune* and the *implicated*.[3] In a compelling manner, Goldstein illustrates how popular culture and the arts have reacted differently to the AIDS epidemic. He indicates that although the treatment or representation of AIDS in the arts reflects the insider perspective of the implicated, often the traumatized view of the artist himself, popular culture represents the unassailable refuge of the immune, the unaffected, and presumably non-infected, outside platform of the broad masses. Unquestionably this premise is well argued, though we must disagree with Goldstein's view that "TV movies about AIDS shy away from gay male protagonists" and that "the typical protagonist is a young, virtuous, and vulnerable woman" (28–29). Although this holds true for most of those films of the '80s that deal with terminal diseases in general[4] (which are generically indebted to the AIDS epidemic), the films to be discussed here all introduce single, white, professionally successful, gay, male protagonists experiencing AIDS.

3   On the other hand, Goldstein aptly comments:

4   In television, where demography is destiny, the person with AIDS is rarely an innocent everyman. . . . Adult males are usually represented as transgressors whose behavior places others in jeopardy; infected women are usually exempt from blame, but rendered nearly as helpless as their children. In these prime-time masques, it is not the person with AIDS who is victimized but those threatened or affected by the disease. Family and community occupy center stage, and the issue is not survival but cohesion: how to deal with a breach in the safety net. (21)

5   He suggests that in order to appeal to rather than appall the populace, television must resort to cautious and sensible treatment of the AIDS threat for, as one critic comments, "the social stigma surrounding homosexuality and intravenous drug use create a distance that precludes

automatic sympathy."[5] Therefore TV movies redirect primary emphasis away from the anxieties, self-reproaches, and fears of the HIV-infected (or the world of homosexuals) and toward the reactions of those around him. Only secondarily do these movies focus on the AIDS epidemic as experienced by gay men—in fact, modes of contraction (or prevention for that matter) are mostly silenced and sex and drug use are not discussed.[6]

6   Unlike the independent theatrical releases *Parting Glances* (1986) and *Longtime Companion* (1990), the movies made for commercial television lack any direct presentation of the linkage of their protagonists, usually gay couples, with other members of the gay community.[7] *Parting Glances* and *Longtime Companion*, however, are documentary-style investigations of the impact of the AIDS epidemic *specifically* upon the gay male community. Set in New York City, these two movies examine the issue through distinctly different approaches. Both of these movies must be seen from the point of view of the respective temporal context (i.e., knowledge about and impact of the AIDS crisis in 1986 vs. 1990). Both are rich with interwoven subtle and complex motifs presenting issues of the lives of gay men and of gay men dealing with AIDS during the 1980s.

7   *Parting Glances* uses a micro-level lens, limiting the action to a period of twenty-four hours. Within that time, the impact of the epidemic is presented as a force that is a presence, a given that pervades and invades reality in the lives of the characters. Good-byes must be said; caretaking must be carried out; relationships must be resolved. Each must deal with the possibility of the death of friends and relationships. *Longtime Companion* reverses the view and, using a macro-level approach, scans across the first decade of the crisis, presenting the multi-faceted AIDS experiences and responses of gay men during those years. The viewer is shown how the disease reorganizes the lives of a network of friends. Friends die alone; partners take care of partners; some become AIDS activists; and each must deal with personal feelings about dying and death. Although the two movies apply a direct and exclusive approach in their focus on the gay community, their intentions do not seem notably different from that of those films made for television. Both force the viewer to confront (1) the social world of gay men; (2) the multiple dimensions of the destructiveness of AIDS; and (3) the complications of unresolved relationships.

8   *An Early Frost* is the first of the AIDS films made for TV, starring Aidan Quinn as the infected Michael, Gena Rowlands as his caring

mother, and Ben Gazzara as the prejudiced father. An eminently successful Ivy League law school graduate, Michael inhabits a luxurious
house in Chicago with his lover, Peter. Diagnosed as having AIDS,
Michael ejects Peter when Peter confesses infidelity during their two-
year relationship and resorts to the support of his (Michael's) family in
suburbia. His return forces his parents to deal with a double-barrelled
issue: their son's sexuality and his terminal disease. They are facing a
diseased stranger. Additionally, the son now must break down the
false image of himself that he has worked to maintain for his parents
and that has helped the denial pattern of his parents to continue.
Michael is the only "closeted" gay man in these films. Contrary to
him, his lover, Peter, is said to be open to his parents/family. Michael's
fear of disclosing himself is validated by his father's reaction of pure
repulsion and hatred, perceiving it as a family shame having to call "a
homosexual [with] this disease" his son and he relegates Michael to
"his own kind." The father asks "How can a son of mine become a
stranger?" This is a hollow question since it is unclear whether he is
saying that his son is a stranger because he (Michael) is gay or because
he (Michael) had not been honest with his parents. It is not entirely
clear whether he is questioning Michael's sexuality, his own lack of
perception, or his son's not telling him the truth.

9   Michael's revelations force both father and mother to realize that
they do not know their son as an adult; they merely remember him as
a child/teenager playing Chopin and running track. They have allowed him privacy as an adult but that choice means not having to ask
too many questions about his life in the city.[8] After Michael's disclo-
sures the film illustrates how the protagonist's "otherness" shatters the
harmony of this representative middle-class family and meticulously
traces the path as one by one family members and friends accept his
strangeness. The film's strategy is such that it repeatedly pits two characters against each other in all possible (relevant) constellations in order to expound the views on the AIDS/gay-issue from various outsider
perspectives. These views are shown both by the reactions of family members who know nothing about the disease, and even by the
rescue squad who refuse to transport Michael to the hospital. The
mother's fear and confusion is balanced by her unflagging understanding and love and her resolute demand for information from his doctor
and for her husband's acceptance of Michael. Her reaction forms a
sharp contrast with his pregnant sister's fear of possible transmission to
her small son and unborn child and his father's fear when Michael

moves to kiss his mother. Within the family only Michael's totally reasonable grandmother offers nothing but love and support pronouncing the film's message: "It's a disease, not a disgrace."

10   Two scenes reflect that Michael as a gay man knew about AIDS but was able to stand outside until his own illness transformed him into an insider. When Michael's doctor explains to him that someone can be a "carrier of the disease without actually showing the symptoms himself," Michael responds "You mean you can pass it on without actually getting it?"[9] Michael's anger at Peter's infidelity is an all too understandable reaction to the breaking of the safety bond that protected them from what was happening to others.

11   As an insider Michael comes into contact with the larger world of AIDS when he joins a hospital AIDS support group: mostly young— by inference, gay—white men, but also including a heterosexual male infected through a prostitute, and a black male. There he is exposed to their fears and the humiliating reactions of others to their illness. Only the blackest of humors displayed by a fellow-patient, Victor (John Glover in a superb performance), grants the viewer temporary comic relief. Representing the popular stereotype of the effeminate, flamboyant homosexual man, this character is easy to laugh at, and to discount without taking him seriously as a man or acknowledging his sexuality. Yet the viewer is forced to acknowledge the humanness of Victor as he is seen dictating his will to Michael. When Michael sees Victor's belongings in a trash can after Victor's death, both Michael and the viewer are shown the deadly physical and social power of the disease as well as a forecast of Michael's future. The insider gay male messages also focus on the problem of accepting one's sexual orientation as part of one's individual identity and being accepted by others. Peter, who is open to his family, has criticized Michael for never admitting his homosexuality to his parents: "When are they going to find out who you really are? After you're dead?" Michael's difficulty becomes evident in a hospital conversation with his mother about his being gay. His statement "I haven't been unhappy" certainly is not a very strong self-affirmation.

12   The fear of the outsiders' reaction to Michael's "coming out" is one dynamic that drives this movie. Faced with the panicky reactions of those around him, most notably his father's, and in order to rid the latter of the burden of society's disapproval, while at the same time not wanting to burden Peter with his sickness, Michael attempts suicide. After Michael is rescued by his father, the ensuing, violently

verbose altercation between father and son allows the father to break through his own fears and to demand that Michael fight, because the father does not want to see his life's work destroyed. Although this patriarchal reasoning is probably based on material values (the life-long struggle of the hard-working petit bourgeois may serve as an explanation for the prejudices rampant in this social class), the film's ending celebrates reconciliations all around. Sister and father have fully accepted Michael's fate. Yet Michael, the "contaminated stranger," has to leave the restored family order (reinforced by the final image of the parents in an endearing embrace) and return to "his own kind," to the world of gay men and AIDS where his family does not belong. Although he has gained acceptance within the social microcosm of his familial circle, he has to "win that case" alone. He is still the "other," the outcast who represents a threat, but an outsider who enjoys universal familial sympathy.

13   In *As Is*, Robert Carradine plays Rich, a gay man in New York City newly diagnosed as having AIDS. Structurally far less complex than *An Early Frost*, this film, adapted from the play of the same title, shows Rich returning to Saul (Jonathan Hadary), his lover of many years. Rich's new lover has left him; his catering business is gone; his health insurance company is trying to get out of covering his illness; he is nearly broke. In this film the viewer is shown the double insider experience from the narrow focus of two gay men struggling against the onslaught of the disease. Together the two recall friends who are sick or have already died of AIDS; remember their life together; and, ultimately, move apprehensively to face the future. Assuring Rich of his unconditional acceptance ("as is"), Saul finally succeeds in dissuading Rich from his intentions to commit suicide. The film ends on a didactic note when a hospice worker (Colleen Dewhurst), whose function as a narrative framing device has been adopted from the play, states that she is "angry with God" and that for the HIV infected "(i)t's a long way to finding acceptance."

14   This second film, like the first, "reads" much like a popular introduction to AIDS, presenting again the typical symptoms (persistent cough, weight-loss, night sweats, seizures, recurrent flu, swollen glands) and admitting medicine's ignorance and inability to cope with the problem. Like Peter in *An Early Frost*, Saul also has to face the possibility of being infected and getting sick. Contrary to the first film, *As Is* dispels popular misconceptions such as that the disease can be contracted through mere physical contact or by air. *As Is* also draws more attention

to the diversity of AIDS victims. For example, among the patients of an AIDS crisis center we hear the story of a pregnant woman who contracted AIDS from her husband who "shot up." Nevertheless, the film seems to suggest that the disease originated in the gay male, thus reaffirming the social stigma imposed on homosexuality. Indeed homosexuality is shown to be accepted only by homosexuals, first and foremost by the loyal Saul or by minorities, such as Saul's Jewish father, whom we never meet, and Rich's actress friend, Lilly.

15   Outsider responses are minimal in this film as the parents of the two protagonists remain off-stage or are assumed to be dead. However, the open-minded approval of Saul's family is contrasted with the conservative and fearful attitude of Rich's brother (whose name is never used). Aware of but not entirely accepting Rich's life (he can never remember Saul's name), the brother is the only immediate family member to visit Rich in the hospital. He enters the room appearing frightened and ridiculous in gown and mask. Rich has become the doubly threatening "other" who represents a threat to his brother's outside, untainted rural—south Jersey—environment. Yet, in the end, brotherly love overrides fear and, breaking through his reservations—"Richie, you're my brother!"—the two characters finally embrace.

16   *Andre's Mother*, a film adapted from a play by Terrence McNally, displays an unmistakable staginess with its monologues and its oftentimes too brisk dialogues. The two central figures are Cal (Richard Thomas), the lover of the deceased Andre, and Andre's mother (Sada Thompson) who still has not accepted her late son's social-sexual identity.[10] The tension of the film is created by Cal's fight for that acceptance from Andre's mother. The events portrayed center on Andre's memorial service. There, for one last time, the characters attest to their attachment to the admired, beloved, almost worshipped friend. The outsider AIDS dimension in this film is illustrated by Andre's mother, who does not understand the releasing of the memorial balloons in Central Park as a symbol of a final "letting go," a ceremony that has become part of many AIDS memorials. Cal's behavior toward her shows the inside perspective of someone who has lived through months of caretaking of a loved one during the illness. His own need for resolution and closure of his anger and pain may explain his demands upon the mother who has remained an outsider to her son's being gay and to his disease.

17   Cal introduces the final scene when he attempts resolution of that tension by forcing acknowledgement of what caused Andre's death:

"Andre died of AIDS." When he cries "I didn't kill him!" and reveals that he is HIV-negative, he hopes to get the mother to accept and share his love for the deceased Andre. In a vehement tirade of anger and tears about the walls of denial—"how many of us . . . don't want to disappoint our mothers?"—he demands her approval. Indeed, her aversion surprisingly turns to hesitant affection (she returns Cal's embrace) and Cal earns her acceptance. In this scene the musical score, "L'amero, Saro Costante" from Mozart's "Il Re Pastore" underscores the theme of loyalty and commitment but also contributes to the stylized ambiance of this film that never manages to convincingly develop the motivation for the title character's change or Cal's obsessive behavior. In sum, this short film deals with the two main characters resolving tensions: coming to terms with the "other" and making peace with themselves. Again, attitudes about gay men are reflected in the clashing views of two families. Cal's sister and father are shown as accepting Cal's sexuality, although the latter indicates minimal understanding, "a lack of imagination on my part"; Cal's mother and Andre's father are shown as rejecting it. Andre's mother is moving towards acceptance only as the film ends.

18   Although the stage of physical deterioration of the AIDS victim was intimated in *As Is* and briefly illustrated in *Early Frost*, the TV movie *Our Sons* is more graphic in revealing the suffering of the AIDS victim. Here the central protagonist, twenty-eight-year-old Donald (Zeljko Ivanek), previously a successful architect in San Diego, is near death. In a fairly simple plot, his lover, James (Hugh Grant), enlists his own mother, Audrey (Julie Andrews), to help in reuniting Donald and his mother, Lou-Anne (Ann-Margaret), before death occurs. Audrey, a successful, liberal and open-minded, upper-class executive business woman, has to travel to Fayetteville, Arkansas, to confront the waitress Lou-Anne, who is presented as typifying the prejudices and ignorance of the lower-middle class in small-town America. Her frighteningly immature view that "homosexuality is an offense against God, man, and nature" seems like a learned prejudice. She is embittered that her son is "one of them," "a queer," and it takes all of Audrey's persuasive powers to induce her to return with her to visit the dying Donald. When she (all too quickly and quite predictably) overcomes her reluctance and visits Donald, she is controlled and unemotional, still blaming her son. The movie suggests that Lou-Anne's anger and denial begins to break only when Audrey makes the central statement, "Our sons are two of us" (as opposed to two of *them*). Those words seem to

work wonders. Lou-Anne hastens to cleanse herself of the past by swimming nude in Audrey's pool; seeks reconciliation with Donald at his bedside in a touching, albeit somewhat pathetic scene; and stays with James and Donald until the end. The movie ends with Donald's coffin being carried onto the plane on which Lou-Anne takes off—into a cliché-glorious California sunset. Dedicated to all the United States AIDS victims, the movie, similar to *As Is*, pleads for emancipation from "centuries of rules and revulsions."[11]

19   This film, too, centers on the issue of overcoming prejudices about homosexuality by presenting the conflicting perspectives of the two single parents. Both mothers have already confronted the issues of their sons' homosexuality, which led to two distinctly different reactions. Lou-Anne drove Donald away so that she would not have to know anything about him and his life while Audrey accepted James's gay life-style. But that acceptance is revealed as having been superficial and non-confrontational. Audrey has always refrained from prying into her son's personal life and has chosen to ignore his homosexuality because, as James says, "(w)e know what we want to know." In parallel fashion, Donald has created a life without any family connection while James has never breached the wall of privacy and non-interference that he and his mother maintain. Just as both mothers have chosen not to know their sons as adult men, the sons have not forced their mothers to know. The crisis of the disease forces the walls to be broken.

20   This film minimally deals with the AIDS insider-outsider dichotomy. Here the mothers represent only slightly different AIDS knowledge patterns, probably reflecting education levels more than anything else. Lou-Anne is fearful of even touching Donald and Audrey is surprised when James says that he and Donald have "been to twenty different funerals in the past eighteen months"; the sons are insiders, the mothers outsiders. Audrey's contact with Donald and James forces her to deal with her son as a gay man and with the possibility that he might also become sick and die. Part of this mother-son dynamic is her belated questioning about his HIV status and urging him to be tested. The fact that James has not been tested reflects an insider AIDS issue that troubles many gay men. That choice requires a personal confrontation with the possibility of being anti-body positive, of having to deal with the probability of impending disease and death. James must break through his own very honest fear. He is able to face this when he and his mother begin to deal with each other as concerned adults.

21   Throughout these four films certain messages, images, and stereotypes are presented about AIDS and gay men. As for demographics, two images of the city are presented: one as a refuge for gay men where they can be free, anonymous, and create their lives as gay men, and another as a location of the AIDS infected.[12] On the other hand, in the rural, suburban settings where there are few gay men, the disease is perceived as an alien phenomenon. Naturally, this reinforces the classic American "city" myth. In reality, gay men do live in rural-suburban America and, even when the earliest of these films was released, most rural-suburban areas had their own indigenous AIDS populations. Bigotry, prejudice, and fear of gay men and AIDS have no geographical boundaries. On a medical level, mixed images of medical professionals illustrate the experiences of many AIDS patients. Some doctors (although not portrayed in these films) are still AIDS-phobic, although most others are both concerned and overworked. And, as these films indicate, some rescue squads, nurses, and other staff members have refused to treat AIDS patients, whereas most others have proven to be deeply compassionate in working with their patients.

22   As to the familial issues of acceptance, we can discern interesting generational and gender combination patterns. The two grandmothers presented in these films (both played by Sylvia Sidney) are accepting characters. In *An Early Frost* she reacts more to the disease issue than to the fact of having a gay grandson. In *Andre's Mother*, it is—ironically—the grandmother who accepts her grandson as he is. She is also a catalyst pushing her daughter to break through the wall of denial. Similarly, the two sisters presented in the movies both know about and accept their brothers being gay, although Michael's pregnant sister (*An Early Frost*) withdraws in fear because of AIDS. The mothers in the films have difficulties accepting their sons as men bonding with other men. Four mothers, two of them on camera, have known about and rejected their sons. However, the stereotypical female gender roles of nurturing and defending ultimately help all of them to overcome their fears. We only *hear* of cases in which this does not happen, e.g., the family that disowned its son who had AIDS (Victor in *An Early Frost*). That, on the other hand, is used by Michael's mother to reaffirm that this "is not going to happen to *our* son."

23   Men tend to have greater difficulties with acceptance than women. Grandfathers and brothers are absent in these films—with one nameless exception in *As Is*. Even Michael's brother-in-law (*An Early Frost*),

who knows Michael is gay, is absent after Michael's return to his family and Cal's future brother-in-law (*Andre's Mother*), who is said to be supportive, is off camera. Like their wives, the fathers of the HIV-infected protagonists, as far as they are introduced, reflect minimal variation of the male parent struggling to accept his gay son. Michael's father in *An Early Frost* rejects but shifts towards more acceptance when his son agrees to fight the disease—like a man. In *Andre's Mother*, Cal's father accepts his son although Andre's father turns his back on his son completely. The absence of the other five fathers, for whatever reason, seems to emphasize the difficulties in presenting male parent acceptance of the gay son to viewers. Overall, the parental generation is shown struggling (presumably because of their own unfulfilled wishes for their sons) with acceptance.

24   Three variations of gay male interaction with the "straight world" occur in these films: There is the son who is open and accepted by his family (Peter, Saul, Cal, James, the lovers of the HIV-infected protagonists); the son who is open but not accepted or discussed (Rich, Andre, and Donald); and the son who lives in hiding from his family (Michael). An interesting pattern is that those gay men who are neither open to nor accepted by their families are the men stricken with AIDS. Those who are open to their families are uninfected[13] and are shown as supportive, nurturing, caretaking, and constant companions who are willing to sacrifice their energies and emotions for their partners. They choose, even insist on remaining with their partners, reaffirming the positive force of parental acceptance overcoming all stereotypes and fears. These caring characters present an interesting variation on the stereotype of gay men. Their model of personal and social responsibility may be the beginning of a new gay male image in film. On the other hand, however, all of the other characters who are shown as nurturers are women, which may one more time reinforce the general stereotype of gay men not really being "men."

25   In all the films a certain blame seems to be imputed to the biased parent, who perhaps did not provide sufficient understanding, openness, warmth, and security for the son to breed the right "virtues." Because of this, the parent becomes partly responsible for the son's exodus to a life in an environment harboring "sin" and disease, away and separate from the mainstream, conservative middle-class values. The flight of the sons can be perceived as an escape from these values, from a world in which they are strangers. Their homosexuality and

infection contaminate their identities and they become, much like Kafka's Gregor Samsa, estranged, almost metamorphosized (physically in some films) into a socially unacceptable "other." Usually, the family is unable to provide that much needed ultimate support for its sons; this can only be rendered by the respective lover, their "own kind." And, as in Samsa's case, sometimes only their deaths can restore the former identities as respectable sons and citizens.

26   Although scattered comments in these films mark the HIV virus as blind to gender, race, or sexual orientation, this does not necessarily neutralize the false image of AIDS as a purely homosexual disease. In these films the virus is often seen as a punishment inflicted on the protagonists and their families for their breach with middle-class norms and values. By contrast, it is most striking that if the son's openness is reciprocated by the family's approval, he does not experience HIV infection. The conclusion lies at hand: Unflagging adherence to the solid values of parental or companion love and honesty, constancy and exclusiveness in love relationships, or simply, "doing the right thing" precludes contraction. Although this exhortation to middle-class conformism would weaken the otherwise socio-critical and emancipatory impact with regard to the implicated, these values are presented as larger than the issues that make the characters strangers to each other. These values and behaviors are shown to heal the wounds caused by that strangeness. Throughout these movies the terror of the destruction of AIDS leads most of the characters of both worlds to be involved with each other, to resolve tensions about sexuality or fear of rejection, to break the walls between them. Ultimately, however, and despite parental and sibling love overriding stereotypes and fears, the movies seem to suggest that these walls should have never been built.

NOTES

1.   For a detailed synopsis see Timothy E. Cook and David Colby, "The Mass-Mediated Epidemic: The Politics of AIDS on the Nightly Network News," in *AIDS: The Making of a Chronic Disease*, ed. Elizabeth Fee and Daniel M. Fox (Berkeley and Los Angeles: University of California Press, 1992) 84–122.

2.   The term AIDS will be used here to refer both to the condition of infection with the human immunosuppressive virus (HIV infection) and to the condition of anyone experiencing the multiple disease pattern referred to as acquired immune depressive syndrome (AIDS).

3. Richard Goldstein, "The Implicated and the Immune: Responses to AIDS in the Arts and Popular Culture," in *A Disease of Society: Cultural and Institutional Responses to AIDS*, ed. Dorothy Nelkin, et al. (Cambridge: Cambridge UP, 1991) 17–42. Goldstein's dichotomy is somewhat simplified because it does not deal with the complexities that this epidemic has engendered, i.e., what happens when the disease process forces the two groups into a confrontation, which is precisely the central conflict of the films discussed here.

4. Unlike the independent, and mostly made-for-television "AIDS movies," the films in this category are all star-studded, major Hollywood productions and have been enormous box office hits—for example *Terms of Endearment* (1983), *Beaches* (1988), *Steel Magnolias* (1989), *Silence Like Glass* (1990), *Dying Young* (1991; the only film with a male victim), or *The Doctor* (1991). These films usually appeal to the whole gamut of emotions in the spectator, ranging from flighty and frivolous comedy to the tear-jerking drama of the young and innocent protagonist's slow decease. The audience strongly identifies with the "heroines" of these films, whereas in the "AIDS movies" the HIV-infected protagonist does not necessarily serve as a figure of identification.

5. Don Shewey, "In Memory of My Feelings," *Film Comment*, vol. 24, May/June 1990: 12.

6. Contrary to this squeamish treatment indigenous to American culture, the German film *A Virus Knows No Morals* (1986), a cynical black comedy by Rosa von Praunheim (Holger Mischwitzki), employs a casual directness and explicitness in its depiction of the world of gays.

7. Vice-versa, in *Parting Glances* the parents are all "off stage" and there is no indication of their acceptance or rejection, and *Longtime Companion* makes no mention of parents of any of the gay male protagonists.

8. In an earlier bantering table conversation, the parents question Michael about relationships to which Michael ambiguously jokes about not being celibate and the conversation is dropped. The parents are satisfied and Michael has successfully fended off any probing into his personal life.

9. This is a reflection of the lack of medical knowledge in 1985 about the incubation period of the virus. Justifiably scared that he may have been the transmitter, Peter refuses to be checked himself. In fact, any further discussion of the disquieting issue of "finding out" is strictly avoided.

10. Her somewhat dubious rationale is that approving of her son would mean "too terrible a criticism" of herself.

11. These words are uttered by James. Incidentally, it is somewhat surprising that when Audrey hears about Donald she does not immediately ask her son James about his own health, but rather the issue of finding out is saved for the end.

12. However, as Cal in *Andre's Mother* indicates, the choice of many gays to live in the "dreadful, anonymous city" is simply to spare their family the disappointment.

13. What is not mentioned, however, is that they may have to face infection in the future, depending on what transmission-risk behaviors they shared with their partners. Another issue glossed over is that Cal's negative HIV result does not guarantee that he will not later test positive. And finally, throughout these films no mention is made of transmission prevention or of safe sex techniques.

Understanding Meaning

1. What general impressions do the authors have about the films they describe?
2. How have commercial television movies about AIDS dealt with homosexuality? How have they differed from independently produced, theatrical releases?
3. Do Pilipp and Shull see these films educating the public or reinforcing common stereotypes about people with AIDS?
4. According to Pilipp and Shull's analysis, do television films present scientifically accurate information about the disease?
5. How are images of the city and the suburb presented in these films? What do they suggest about American values?
6. What seems to be the common message apparent in most of these television dramas about AIDS?
7. *Critical Thinking:* Commercial television is, after all, an entertainment medium. Can a movie made for television seriously address complex and controversial topics? Does the need to present characters people can identify with lead to a "good guys" and "bad guys" formula? Are stereotypes bound to emerge?

Evaluating Strategy

1. How do the authors provide readers with enough information about four films without turning the article into a series of plot summaries?
2. What analytical methods do the authors use? How important is detailed observation in their analysis?
3. How do the authors use direct quotes from characters in the films to dramatize their points? Is this an effective device?

Appreciating Language

1. This article appeared in a journal dedicated to film and television. Does it have technical terms that many readers would find confusing or unfamiliar?
2. How do the authors describe the attitudes expressed by characters in the films? Does their choice of words reveal a bias?
3. What do the authors mean by "the worlds of the *immune* and the *implicated*"?

Connections across the Disciplines

1. Joel Connelly (page 319) asserts that visual images have tremendous power to influence people's attitudes and social policy. Do Pilipp and Shull sense that the values implied in television movies will have lasting influence on the American public?
2. Edward Dolnick's "Deafness as Culture" (page 212) reveals that many deaf people resent being viewed as disabled. How might gay advocates respond to the way homosexuals are defined in the films Pilipp and Shull discuss?

Writing Suggestions

1. Select a recent made-for-television film, and write a short analysis of the social messages it seems to advocate. Do television films seek to reinforce widely held values or to challenge them?
2. *Collaborative Writing:* Discuss Pilipp and Shull's conclusions with a group of students. What opinions do members of the group have about the way television has treated people with AIDS? Has the media responded with intelligence and compassion or simply exploited the public's fears? Write a brief paper outlining the views of the group.

RICHARD RODRIQUEZ AND LAUREN GREENFIELD

Richard Rodriquez (1944–) was born in San Francisco of Mexican parents. Though he grew up in a non-English speaking family, he embraced English and attended Stanford, Columbia, and Berkeley. He received a doctorate in English and was awarded a Fulbright fellowship to study English in London. Rodriquez is best known for Hunger of Memory, *a collection of essays examining the immigrant experience. Since the book's publication in 1982, Rodriquez has become a noted journalist and frequent commentator on public television. Lauren Greenfield is a Los Angeles photographer who spent four years taking pictures and conducting interviews for her book* Fast Forward: Growing Up in the Shadow of Hollywood.

Growing Up Old in L.A.

As you read this analysis of young people in Los Angeles, consider if their attitudes reflect a regional or national attitude toward youth, image, money, and values. Notice how the writers use comparison, cause and effect, *and* narration.

1   America's greatest contribution to the world of ideas is adolescence. European novels often begin with a first indelible memory—a golden poplar, or Mama standing in the kitchen. American novels begin at the moment of rebellion, the moment of appetite for distance, the moonless night Tom Sawyer pries open the back-bedroom window, shinnies down the drainpipe, drops to the ground, and runs.

2   America invented a space—a deferment, a patch of asphalt between childhood and adulthood, between the child's ties to family and the adult's re-creation of family. Within this space, within this boredom, American teenagers are supposed to innovate, to improvise, to rebel, to turn around three times before they harden into adults.

3   If you want to see the broadcasting center, the trademark capital of adolescence, come to Los Angeles. The great postwar, postmodern, suburban city in Dolby sound was built by restless people who intended to give their kids an unending spring.

4   There are times in Los Angeles—our most American of American cities—when teenagers seem the oldest people around. Many seem barely children at all—they are tough and cynical as ancients, beyond laughter in a city that idolizes them. Their glance, when it meets ours, is unblinking.

5   At a wedding in Brentwood, I watch the 17-year-old daughter of my thrice-divorced friend give her mother away. The mother is dewy with liquid blush. The dry-eyed daughter has seen it all before.

6   I know children in Los Angeles who carry knives and guns because the walk to and from school is more dangerous than their teachers or parents realize. One teenager stays home to watch her younger sister, who is being pursued by a teenage stalker. The girls have not told their parents because they say they do not know how their parents would react.

7   Have adults become the innocents?

8   Adults live in fear of the young. It's a movie script, a boffo science-fiction thriller that has never been filmed but that might well star Jean-Claude Van Damme or Sylvester Stallone.

9   A friend of mine, a heavyweight amateur wrestler, wonders if it's safe for us to have dinner at a Venice Beach restaurant. (There are, he says, 12-year-old gangsters who prowl the neighborhood with guns.)

10   Some of the richest people in town have figured out how to sell the idea of American adolescence to the world. The children with the most interesting dilemma are the children of 90210. What does adolescence mean when your father is a record producer who drives to work in a Jeep to audition rap groups? What do you do when your father— who has a drug habit and is nowhere around in the years when you are growing up—is an internationally recognizable 50-foot face on the movie screen?

11   On the other hand: What can it feel like to grow up a teenager in South Central when your mama is on crack and you are responsible for her five kids? Teenagers who never had reliable parents or knew intimacy are having babies. There are teenagers in East L.A. who (literally) spend their young lives searching for family—"blood"—in some gang that promises what they never had.

12   It is every teenager's dream to "get big." In L.A. you can be very big, indeed. Fame is a billboard along Sunset Boulevard. Mexican-American gangstas pass the Southern California night by writing crypto-nonsense on sides of buildings, because the biggest lesson they

have taken from the city is that advertisement is existence. Los Angeles is a horizontal city of separate freeway exits, separate malls, suburb fleeing suburb. Parents keep moving their children away from what they suppose is the diseased inner city. But there is no possibility of a healthy suburb radiant from a corrupt center. No man is an island entire of itself. Didn't we learn that in high school?

13   The children of East L.A. live in the same city as Madonna and Harvard-educated screenwriters who use cocaine for inspiration, selling a believably tarnished vision of the world to children of the crack mothers in Compton.

14   And look: There's always a TV in the houses of Watts. And it is always on. In the suburbs, white kids watch black rappers on MTV. Suburbanites use TV to watch the mayhem of the inner city. But on the TV in the inner city, they watch the rest of us. The bejeweled pimp in his gold BMW parodies the Beverly Hills matron on Rodeo Drive.

15   Elsewhere in America, we like to tell ourselves that Los Angeles is the exception. The truth is that, for all its eccentricity, Los Angeles tells us great deal about adolescence in rural Kansas. And postmodern L.A. is linked to colonial Boston. Today's gangsta with a tattooed tear on his face is kin to young men fighting Old Man Europe's wars in the trenches of 1914 or 1941, to the young rebels who overthrew Old Man England rather than submit to another curfew, and to Judy Garland, who will always be a stage-struck teenager.

16   The earliest Americans imagined that they had fled the past— motherland, fatherland—and had come upon land that was without history or meaning. By implication, the earliest Americans imagined themselves adolescent, orphans. Their task was self-creation, without benefit or burden of family. The myth that we must each create our own meaning has passed down through American generations.

17   Young Meriwether Lewis heads out for the territory. He writes to his widowed mother, "I . . . hope therefore you will not suffer yourself to indulge any anxiety for my safety. . . ." The ellipsis is adolescence: estrangement, embarrassment, self-absorption, determination. The adolescent body plumps and furs, bleeds and craves to be known for itself. In some parts of the world, puberty is a secret, a shameful biological event, proof that you have inevitably joined the community of your gender. In America, puberty is the signal to rebel.

18   American teenagers invent their own tongue, meant to be indecipherable to adult hearing. Every generation of adolescents does it.

Adults are left wondering what they mean: Scrilla. Juking. Woop, woop, woop.

19   "Children grow up too quickly," American parents sigh. And yet nothing troubles an American parent so much as the teenager who won't leave home. Several times in this century, American teenagers have been obliged to leave home to fight overseas. Nineteen-year-old fathers vowed to their unborn children that never again would the youth of the world be wasted by the Potentates of Winter.

20   My generation, the baby boom generation, was the refoliation of the world. We were the children of mothers who learned how to drive, dyed their hair, used Maybelline, and decorated their houses for Christmas against the knowledge that winter holds sway in the world. Fathers, having returned from blackened theaters of war, used FHA loans to move into tract houses that had no genealogy. In such suburbs, disillusioned parents intended to ensure their children's optimism.

21   Prolonged adolescence became the point of us—so much the point of me that I couldn't give it up. One night, in the 1950s, I watched Mary Martin, a middle-aged actress, play an enchanted boy so persuasively that her rendition of "I Won't Grow Up" nurtured my adolescent suspicions of anyone over the age of 30.

22   My generation became the first in human history (only hyperbole can suggest our prophetic sense of ourselves) that imagined we might never grow old.

23   Jill, a friend of mine whose fame was an orange bikini, whose face has fallen, whose breasts have fallen, whose hair is gray, is telling me about her son who has just gone to New York and has found there the most wonderful possibilities. My friend's eyes fill with tears. She fumbles in her handbag for the pack of cigarettes she had just sworn off.

24   What's wrong?

25   "Dammit," she says, "I'm a geezer."

26   From my generation arose a culture for which America has become notorious. We transformed youth into a lifestyle, a political manifesto, an aesthetic, a religion. My generation turned adolescence into a commodity that could be sold worldwide by 45-year-old executives at Nike or Warner Bros. To that extent, we control youth.

27   But is it unreasonable for a child to expect that Mick Jagger or Michael Jackson will grow up, thicken, settle, and slow—relinquish adolescence to a new generation?

28   At the Senior Ball, teenagers in the ballroom of the Beverly Hills Hotel, beautiful teenagers in black tie and gowns, try very hard not to look like teenagers. But on the other hand, it is very important not to look like one's parents.

29   The balancing trick of American adolescence is to stand in-between—neither to be a child nor an adult.

30   Where are you going to college?

31   The question intrudes on the ball like a gong from some great clock. It is midnight, Cinderella. Adolescence must come to an end. Life is governed by inevitabilities and consequences—a thought never communicated in America's rock-and-roll lyrics.

32   American storytellers do better with the beginning of the story than the conclusion. We do not know how to mark the end of adolescence. Mark Twain brings Huck Finn back to Missouri, to Hannibal, and forces his young hero to bend toward inevitability. But Huck yearns, forever, "to light out for the territory . . . because Aunt Sally she's going to adopt me and civilize me, and I can't stand it."

33   And then comes the least convincing conclusion ever written in all of American literature: THE END. YOURS TRULY, HUCK FINN.

· · ·

34   From the forthcoming book *Fast Forward: Growing Up in the Shadow of Hollywood* by Lauren Greenfield:

35   "My mom does embarrass me because sometimes when we go somewhere together and she dresses in these outfits I guess they are in style but like too in style. . . . and they are really embarrassing. . . . My friends think that my mom is really young." BRANDON, 13

36   "I put a picture of the Playboy Playmate Stephanie on my wall because I think she's hot. The Barbie Twins are pretty good looking, also. My mom got the pictures for me, actually. She knows I like that. When we moved in, my room was pretty dull. She wanted me to decorate it. We had this subscription to *Playboy* and we had like a million of them. You can send in an application for *Playboy* and they just give it to you. . . . Me and my brother did this when he was about 12 and I was 9. We had the *Playboy* channel from when I was like 6 to when I was about 10. We would lock our door. . . . We watched it every night." ARI, 13

37   "The glamorous Hollywood, the TV and movie industry—it affects kids. Who I know, who you know, how rich you are, what your dad does, what your mom does, does he work, does she work, what you have, what I have, what movies he has produced, what movie he is

producing. Money affects kids in many ways. I mean, it's ruined a lot of kids I know. And not to brag—I feel it has ruined me. Expensive watches, expensive glasses, shoes, knives, dresses. Wearing a Rolex watch to school. Or just buying a $200 pair of shoes or a $200 jacket or Doc Martens. I mean, I know a person who has a soccer field and an indoor basketball court." ADAM, 13

38   "Kids should have no knowledge of the stuff that people talk about in most music today. But you can't lock 'em up in a closet and keep them away from it, because it's everywhere, you know, everywhere you go. Music is life. Everybody listens to music. It seems like everything is going downhill. The lyrics, they're only going to get worse. Pretty soon, everything is going to blow up. I'm not blaming it all just on music, either, because it's not just the music. But it does play a role in society. If the music changes, then life will change. That's how I feel. . . . There has to be someplace out there, though, where it's not like that." OZZIE, 17

39   "My mom says my life is like the story Eloise. It's about a little girl, just like me, who lives in a big hotel and is very good friends with all the staff. I am good friends with a lot of the staff. When you come to the door of the hotel, there are, like, 80 people welcoming you and talking to you. Every time you pass by one of the staff, they go, 'Good day.' It's part of their job to say that. . . . My nanny, Yolanda, is almost like our family. She plays with us. Gladys and Marcella are our housekeepers, and Renee—he kind of, like, washes the cars and stuff like that. My mom didn't want to lose them and give away their jobs, so now they are with us. . . ." EMILY, 10

40   "Everyone thinks they are a gang member. The trend now is for the white girls to go out with the black guys who are in gangs or crews or whatever. All the styles that everyone wears come from the black neighborhoods, like South Central Los Angeles. So that's why when you wear baggy pants or whatever you are considered wanting to be black. I don't think there are gangbangers in the Beverly scene. There are just crew members—these little guys who have so much money who run around tagging on walls and stuff. A crew is like a small gang—except they don't gangbang or anything." ALISON (A PSEUDONYM), 13

41   "Where I live, it's a pretty rough neighborhood. It's very odd to see a limo around here. A limo is a sign of status, you know, that you have money. And so, living in this neighborhood and knowing that nobody here has that kind of money, it's a sight people like to see—but

they also like to talk about it. For the day, you want to feel that you are well-to-do and that you are able to get all that, even if you are not able to and you just barely get it. I spent close to $600. I worked hard to get the money so that the prom would be at least halfway decent for me. . . . It took me about two years to raise that much for the prom."
ENRIQUE, 17

Understanding Meaning

1. Why do the authors consider adolescence an American idea? How is the time between childhood and adulthood in this country different from that in other cultures?
2. Do Americans yearn for eternal adolescence? Is there a denial of age, a reluctance to accept the responsibilities of adulthood?
3. What role does Hollywood have in shaping young people's values? What expectations do Hollywood images foster?
4. Why do many young people resort to violence?
5. *Critical Thinking:* How do television images affect young people's racial attitudes? In a highly segregated society, do whites learn about blacks by watching rap videos, and do blacks learn about whites by viewing *Beverly Hills 90210?*

Evaluating Strategy

1. How do the authors use interviews? When should writers summarize testimony, and when should they use direct quotations? Can a writer use too many quotations?
2. Within the essay the writers pose questions. How effective is this device?
3. *Other Modes:* Identify passages in which the writers use *comparison*, *cause and effect*, and *narration*.

Appreciating Language

1. How would you characterize the tone and style of the essay? What attitude toward the young people of Los Angeles is reflected by the writers' choice of words?
2. How would you define "postmodern"?

Connections across the Disciplines

1. Review Michael Zielenziger's "Black Is Beautiful: Tokyo Style" (page 314). Both Japanese and white American youth are influenced by African-American music, dance, and fashion. Is this interest superficial, or does it reflect a deeper desire to appreciate and understand another culture?

2. How do John Ciardi's comments on the search for happiness (page 192) relate to the observations made in this essay?

Writing Suggestions

1. Write an essay about your own adolescence, comparing it to the experiences, values, and attitudes outlined by Rodriquez and Greenfield. Were your friends like the teenagers presented in this article? Did anyone you know rent a limo for a prom or have a parent marry for a third time?

2. *Collaborative Writing:* Discuss this essay with a group of students. Have each member comment on the young people described in the article, indicating whether or not they see them as representative of young people in their community. Have someone take notes, then work together to assemble the group's observations. Do these L.A. teens reflect the views of most American young people? Write a brief essay expressing the views of the group. You may organize the paper using *comparison*, *division*, or *cause and effect*.

WRITING BEYOND THE CLASSROOM

KIMBERLY A. CRAWFORD, J.D.

Kimberly A. Crawford is an attorney specializing in criminal law and a legal instructor at the FBI Academy. In this article written for law enforcement officers, she analyzes the constitutionality of secretly recording suspects' conversations to gather evidence. Her article appeared in the FBI Law Enforcement Bulletin *in 1993.*

Surreptitious Recording of Suspects' Conversations

Crawford's analysis focuses on the legality, not the morality or political implications, of using secret recordings to gather evidence about suspects. She addresses the needs of her audience, law enforcement professionals seeking direction on which investigative techniques they can legally use.

1   Whether in a prison cell, interrogation room, or the back seat of a police car, suspects left seemingly unattended with a co-conspirator, friend, or total stranger often seize the opportunity to discuss or lament their current predicament. Very often, incriminating statements are made. Law enforcement officers who put themselves in a position to hear and record suspects' conversations, either by planting a listening device or by posing as a co-conspirator, friend, or stranger, are apt to obtain very valuable incriminating evidence.

2   Of course, in any subsequent prosecution, the government is likely to be confronted with a vehement constitutional and statutory attack to the admissibility of such damaging evidence. Specifically, the defense is likely to argue that the surreptitious recording of the suspects' conversations violated rights guaranteed by the fourth, fifth, and sixth amendments to the U.S. Constitution, as well as certain protections afforded individuals under Title III of the Omnibus Crime Control and Safe Streets Act[1] (hereinafter title III).

3   This article discusses the validity of these constitutional and statutory challenges. It then provides a review of court decisions that have dealt with the admissibility of such surreptitiously recorded conversations and related issues.

FIFTH AMENDMENT—
SELF-INCRIMINATION CLAUSE CHALLENGE

4 To be successful, a challenge to the admissibility of surreptitiously recorded conversations based on the fifth amendment self-incrimination
clause would have to establish that the conversations in question were
the product of unlawful custodial interrogation. Because statements
made to individuals not known to the defendant as government actors do not normally amount to interrogation for purposes of the fifth
amendment, this challenge is destined to fail.

5 The fifth amendment to the U.S. Constitution provides in part
that "no person . . . shall be compelled in any criminal case to be a witness against himself. . . . "[2] Over two decades ago, the U.S. Supreme
Court in *Miranda* v. *Arizona*[3] held that custodial interrogation of an individual creates a psychologically compelling atmosphere that works
against this fifth amendment protection.[4] In other words, the Court in
Miranda believed that an individual in custody undergoing police interrogation would feel compelled to respond to police questioning.
This compulsion, which is a byproduct of most custodial interrogation,
directly conflicts with every individual's fifth amendment protection
against self-incrimination.

6 Accordingly, the Court developed the now-familiar *Miranda* warnings as a means to reduce the compulsion attendant in custodial interrogation. The *Miranda* rule requires that these warnings be given to
individuals in custody prior to the initiation of interrogation. This rule,
however, is not absolute.[5]

7 *Stanley* v. *Wainwright*[6] is one of the original cases to deal with a fifth
amendment challenge to the admissibility of surreptitiously recorded
suspect conversations. In *Stanley,* two robbery suspects were arrested
and placed in the back seat of a police car. Unbeknownst to the suspects, one of the arresting officers had activated a tape recorder on the
front seat of the car before leaving the suspects unattended for a short
period of time. During that time, the suspects engaged in a conversation that later proved to be extremely incriminating.

8 On appeal, the defense argued that the recording violated the
rule in *Miranda,* because the suspects were in custody at the time
the recording was made and placing of the suspects alone in the vehicle with the activated recorder was interrogation for purposes of *Miranda.* The Court of Appeals for the Fifth Circuit, however, summarily

dismissed this argument and found that the statements were spontaneously made and not the product of interrogation.

9   The Supreme Court later validated the rationale in *Stanley* with its decision in *Illinois* v. *Perkins*.[7] Although *Perkins* did not deal specifically with the issue of surreptitious recordings, the Court's analysis of *Miranda* is applicable to situations in which suspects' conversations with either private individuals or undercover government actors are recorded.

10   In *Perkins,* police placed an informant and an undercover officer in a cell block with Lloyd Perkins, a suspected murderer incarcerated on an unrelated charge of aggravated assault. While planning a prison break, the undercover officer asked Perkins whether he had ever "done" anyone. In response, Perkins described at length the details of a murder-for-hire he had committed.

11   When Perkins was subsequently charged with the murder, he argued successfully to have the statements that he made in prison suppressed, because no *Miranda* warnings had been given prior to his conversation with the informant and undercover officer. On review, however, the Supreme Court reversed the order of suppression.

12   Rejecting Perkins' argument, the Supreme Court recognized that there are limitations to the rule announced in *Miranda.* The Court expressly declined to accept the notion that "*Miranda* warnings are required whenever a suspect is in custody in a technical sense and converses with someone who happens to be a government agent."[8] Rather, the Court concluded that not every custodial interrogation creates the psychologically compelling atmosphere that *Miranda* was designed to protect against. When the compulsion is lacking, so is the need for *Miranda* warnings.

13   The Court in *Perkins* found the facts at issue to be a clear example of a custodial interrogation that created no compulsion. Pointing out that compulsion is "determined from the perspective of the suspect,"[9] the Court noted that Perkins had no reason to believe that either the informant or the undercover officer had any official power over him, and therefore, he had no reason to feel any compulsion. On the contrary, Perkins bragged about his role in the murder in an effort to impress those he believed to be his fellow inmates. *Miranda* was not designed to protect individuals from themselves.

14   Applying this rationale to the surreptitious recording of suspects' conversations while they are in the back seat of a police car, a prison

cell, or an interrogation room, it is clear that *Miranda* warnings are unnecessary if the suspect is conversing with someone who either is, or is presumed by the suspect to be, a private individual. Because suspects in this situation would have no reason to believe that the person to whom they are speaking has any official power over them, they have no reason to feel the compulsion that *Miranda* was designed to protect against.

SIXTH AMENDMENT— RIGHT-TO-COUNSEL CHALLENGE

15 Because of its limited application, a successful challenge to the admissibility of surreptitiously recorded suspect conversations based on the sixth amendment right to counsel will require the convergence of certain factors. Specifically, the defense must be able to establish that the suspect's right to counsel had attached and that the government took deliberate steps to elicit information from the suspect about a crime with which the suspect had been previously charged.

Right to Counsel Attaches at Critical Stage

16 The sixth amendment to the U.S. Constitution guarantees that "[i]n all criminal prosecutions, the accused shall . . . have the Assistance of Counsel for his defense."[10] The U.S. Supreme Court has interpreted the sixth amendment as guaranteeing not merely the right to counsel but, more importantly, the right to the *effective assistance* of counsel.[11] To be effective, an attorney must be permitted to form a relationship with the accused some time prior to trial,[12] and the government cannot needlessly interfere with that relationship.[13]

17 Although the right to counsel would be meaningless if the suspect and attorney were not permitted to form a relationship some time prior to trial, the Supreme Court has held that it is not necessary to allow this relationship to form simply because the individual becomes a suspect in a case.[14] Instead, the Court has found that the sixth amendment guarantee of the effective assistance of counsel is satisfied if the attorney and suspect are permitted to form their relationship once the prosecution has reached a critical stage.[15] The Court has defined

the critical stage as the filing of formal charges (i.e., an indictment or information) or the initiation of adversarial judicial proceedings.[16]

18   Thus, a necessary first step in a successful sixth amendment challenge to the admissibility of a surreptitiously recorded conversation is to establish that the right to counsel had attached at the time of the recording. If the suspect was neither formally charged nor subjected to adversarial judicial proceedings at the time the recorded conversation took place, the sixth amendment challenge will fail.

Deliberate Elicitation by the Government

19   If successful in establishing that the suspect's right to counsel had attached at the time a surreptitious recording took place, the defense will also have to prove that the conversation in question was the result of deliberate elicitation on the part of the government. The Supreme Court has determined that simply placing suspects in situations where they are likely to incriminate themselves does not, in and of itself, constitute a sixth amendment violation.[17] Rather, there must be some deliberate attempt on the part of the government to elicit information from the suspect.[18] It is the act of deliberate elicitation that creates the sixth amendment violation.

20   In *Kuhlmann* v. *Wilson*,[19] the Supreme Court held that placing an informant in a cell with a formally charged suspect in an effort to gain incriminating statements did not amount to deliberate elicitation on the part of the government. In doing so, the Court made the following statement:

21   'Since the Sixth Amendment is not violated whenever—by luck or happenstance—the State obtains incriminating statements from the accused after the right to counsel has attached,' a defendant does not make out a violation of that right simply by showing that an informant, either through prior arrangement or voluntarily, reported his incriminating statements to the police. Rather, the defendant must demonstrate that the police and their informant took some action, *beyond merely listening*, that was designed deliberately to elicit incriminating remarks.[20] (emphasis added)

22   As a result of the Supreme Court's decision in *Kuhlmann*, the mere placing of a recorder in a prison cell, interrogation room, or police

vehicle will not constitute deliberate elicitation by the government. Instead, to raise a successful sixth amendment challenge, the defense has to show that someone acting on behalf of the government went beyond the role of a mere passive listener (often referred to by the courts as a "listening post") and actively pursued incriminating statements from the suspect.

Right to Counsel Is Crime-Specific

23 Even if it can be established that the government deliberately elicited and recorded incriminating conversations from a suspect after the right to counsel had attached, a sixth amendment challenge to the admissibility of those recordings will not succeed if the conversations in question pertained to crimes with which the suspect had not yet been charged at the time of the recording. Because the sixth amendment is crime-specific, a suspect only has the right to the assistance of counsel with respect to the crimes formally charged against him.[21] Consequently, the surreptitious recording of a conversation with a formally charged suspect that pertains to some unrelated, uncharged offense, will not violate the sixth amendment, regardless of whether there is deliberate elicitation on the part of the government.

FOURTH AMENDMENT— RIGHT-TO-PRIVACY CHALLENGE

24 Another constitutional attack waged against the admissibility of surreptitiously recorded conversations is the claim that monitoring and recording these conversations violates the suspects' fourth amendment right of privacy. However, if the recorded conversations take place in government space, whether it be a prison cell, interrogation room, or back seat of a police car, the fourth amendment challenge is bound to fail unless law enforcement officers give suspects specific assurances that their conversations will be private.

25 The fourth amendment to the U.S. Constitution guarantees the right of the people to be secure from unreasonable searches and seizures.[22] As it is used in the fourth amendment, the term "search" includes any governmental action that intrudes into an area where

there is an expectation of privacy that is both subjectively and objectively reasonable.[23] To be objectively reasonable, an expectation of privacy must be one that society as a whole is willing to recognize and protect.[24]

26   Thus, to be successful, a fourth amendment challenge to the surreptitious recording of suspects' conversations would have to establish that the suspects expected their conversations to be private and that society as a whole recognizes those expectations as reasonable. Although sometimes willing to accept suspects' assertions that they believed their conversations were private,[25] courts generally reject the notion that the suspects' beliefs were objectively reasonable.

27   For example, in *Ahmad A.* v. *Superior Court*,[26] the California Court of Appeals confronted a fourth amendment challenge to the admissibility of a surreptitiously recorded conversation between the defendant and his mother. The defendant, a juvenile arrested for murder, asked to speak with his mother when advised of his constitutional rights. The defendant and his mother were thereafter permitted to converse in an interrogation room with the door closed. During the surreptitiously recorded conversation that ensued, the defendant admitted his part in the murder.

28   Reviewing the defendant's subsequent fourth amendment challenge, the California court noted that at the time the mother and her son were permitted to meet in the interrogation room, "no representations or inquiries were made as to privacy or confidentiality."[27] Finding the age-old truism "Walls have ears" to be applicable, the court held that any subjective expectation that the defendant had regarding the privacy of his conversation was not objectively reasonable.

29   Several Federal and State courts have adhered to the rationale announced in *Ahmad A.* and have concluded that any expectation of privacy a suspect may foster in a conversation occurring in government space is objectively unreasonable.[28] While some courts predicate their conclusion on an arrest having taken place, thereby reducing the suspects' expectations of privacy,[29] other courts have taken the position that the lack of an expectation of privacy in government space is not dependent on an arrest.[30]

30   This latter position is demonstrated by the holding of the U.S. Court of Appeals for the 11th Circuit in *United States* v. *McKinnon*.[31] In *McKinnon*, law enforcement officers stopped the vehicle in which the defendant was riding for failing to abide traffic laws. Once stopped,

the driver of the vehicle was asked to submit to a sobriety test. After successfully completing the test, officers asked the driver whether they could search his vehicle for drugs. Upon receiving consent, the officers invited the driver and defendant to sit in the back seat of the police car until the search was completed.

31   Accepting the officers' invitation, defendant and the driver sat in the police car and engaged in an incriminating conversation that was surreptitiously recorded. Cocaine was found during the search of the vehicle, and both the defendant and driver were subsequently arrested. Following their arrest, the defendant and driver were again placed, seemingly unattended, in the back seat of the police car, where they once again engaged in an incriminating conversation.

32   Conceding the admissibility of the post-arrest statements, the defendant argued that prior to arrest, he had an expectation of privacy in his conversation that was violated by the surreptitious recording. The court, however, found "no persuasive distinction between pre-arrest and post-arrest situation"[32] and refused to suppress the recordings. In support of its decision, the court in *McKinnon* cited several cases in which surreptitious recordings of conversations were found to be admissible against visitors and guests of arrestees and other individuals not under formal arrest at the time of the recorded conversations.[33]

Specific Assurances

33   Although courts generally find no reasonable expectation of privacy in suspects' conversations occurring in government space, specific assurances offered by officers that such conversations will be private may generate a valid fourth amendment claim. As previously noted, in the case of *Ahmad A.*, the court was particularly impressed by the fact that "no representations or inquiries were made as to privacy or confidentiality."[34]

34   A reasonable inference to be drawn from this case is that the resulting expectations would have been reasonable, had there been some representations or inquiries regarding privacy that were met with assurances. This inference is supported by the case of *People* v. *Hammons*,[35] in which a California court found that law enforcement officers' actions had fostered the suspects' expectations of privacy, and therefore, the expectations were reasonable.[36]

35   Consequently, when placing suspects together with co-conspirators, friends, or strangers for the purpose of surreptitiously recording a conversation, law enforcement officers should be careful not to give the suspects any specific assurances that their conversations will be private. To do so would likely create a reasonable expectation of privacy in their subsequent conversations that would be protected by the fourth amendment.

TITLE III—STATUTORY CHALLENGE

36   The only statutory attack based on Federal law likely to be raised regarding the surreptitious recording of suspects' conversations is that the recording violates Title III of the Omnibus Crime Control and Safe Streets Act.[37] Because title III protects only oral conversations in which there is a reasonable expectation of privacy, such challenges are resolved by reference to fourth amendment analysis.

37   To be protected under title III, oral communications must be "uttered by a person exhibiting an expectation that such communication is not subject to interception under circumstances justifying such expectation."[38] In other words, the statute only affords protection to oral conversations uttered under conditions indicating that there was a reasonable expectation of privacy. Consequently, the warrantless surreptitious recording of suspects' oral conversations does not violate title III where the suspects lack a fourth amendment expectation of privacy in those conversations.[39]

CONCLUSION

38   The surreptitious recording of suspects' conversations is an effective investigative technique that, if done properly, can withstand both constitutional and statutory challenges. Law enforcement officers contemplating the use of this technique should keep the following points in mind:

39   1.   Because the technique does not amount to "interrogation" for purposes of *Miranda*, it is not necessary to advise suspects of their constitutional rights and obtain a waiver prior to using this technique.

40   2.   To avoid a sixth amendment problem, this technique should not be used
          following the filing of formal charges or the initial appearance in court,
          unless the conversation does not involve a government actor, the conver-
          sation involves a government actor who has assumed the role of a "listen-
          ing post," or the conversation pertains to a crime other than the one with
          which the suspect has been charged.
41   3.   To avoid both fourth amendment and title III concerns, suspects should
          not be given any specific assurances that their conversations are private.

42   In addition, State and local law enforcement officers should consult
     with their legal advisors prior to using this investigative technique.
     This will ensure compliance with State statutes or local policies that
     may be more restrictive than the Federal law discussed in this article.

ENDNOTES

1.   18 U.S.C. §§ 2510 *et seq*. Defendants may also claim that the surreptitious record-
     ing of their conversations violated State eavesdropping statutes. Although many
     State eavesdropping statutes closely follow title III, law enforcement officers
     should consult their State statute before using this technique, because some
     State laws are more restrictive than title III.
2.   U.S. Const. amend. V.
3.   394 U.S. 436 (1966).
4.   *Id*. at 467.
5.   *See, e.g., Berkemer* v. *McCarty*, 468 U.S. 420 (1984), wherein the Supreme Court
     held *Miranda* inapplicable to traffic stops. *See also, New York* v. *Quarles*, 467 U.S.
     649 (1984), which recognizes a public safety exception to *Miranda*.
6.   604 F.2d 379 (5th Cir. 1979), *cert. denied*, 100 S.Ct. 3019.
7.   110 S.Ct. 2394 (1990).
8.   *Id*. at 2397.
9.   *Id*. in *Perkins*, the Supreme Court used the words coercion and compulsion inter-
     changeably.
10. U.S. Const. amend. VI.
11. *Cuyler* v. *Sullivan*, 100 S.Ct. 1708 (1980).
12. *United States* v. *Wade*, 338 U.S. 218 (1967).
13. In *Weatherford* v. *Bursey*, 429 U.S. 545 (1977), the Supreme Court held that some
     interference with the right to counsel may be justified.
14. *United States* v. *Gouveia*, 104 S.Ct. 2292 (1984).
15. *Massiah* v. *United States*, 377 U.S. 201 (1964).
16. *Id*.
17. *Kuhlmann* v. *Wilson*, 106 S.Ct. 2616 (1986).
18. *Id*.
19. *Id*.

20. *Id.* at 2630.
21. *Hoffa* v. *United States*, 377 U.S. 201 (1964).
22. U.S. Const. amend. IV.
23. *Katz* v. *United States*, 389 U.S. 347 (1967).
24. *Oliver* v. *United States*, 104 S.Ct. 1735 (1984).
25. Most courts reject this notion as well. In *United States* v. *Harrelson*, 754 F.2d 1153 (5th Cir. 1985), *cert. denied*, 106 S.Ct. 277 (1985), the Court found that "one who expects privacy under the circumstances of a prison visit is, if not actually foolish, exceptionally naive." *Id.* at 1169.
26. 263 Cal. Rptr. 747 (Cal.App. 2 Dist. 1989), *cert. denied*, 11 S.Ct. 102 (1991).
27. *Id.* at 751.
28. *See, e.g., United States* v. *McKinnon*, 985 F.2d 525 (11th Cir. 1993) *cert. pending* (filed 1/7/93 No. 92-8963); *United States* v. *Harrelson*, 754 F.2d 1153 (5th Cir. 1985), *cert. denied*, 106 S.Ct. 277 (1985); *United States* v. *Sallee*, (unreported; 1991 WL 352613 N.D. Ill. 1991); *State* v. *McAdams*, 559 So.2d 601 (Fla.App. 5th Dist. 1990); *People* v. *Marland*, 355 N.W. 2d 378 (Mich.App. 1984).
29. *See, e.g., Brown* v. *State*, 349 So.2d 1196 (Fla.App. 4th Dist. 1977), *cert. denied*, 98 S.Ct. 1271 (1978).
30. *See, e.g., United States* v. *McKinnon*, 985 F.2d 525 (11th Cir. 1993), *cert. pending* (filed 1/7/93 No. 92-8963); and *State* v. *Hussey*, 469 So.2d 346 (La. Ct. App. 2d Cir. 1985), reconsideration denied, 477 So.2d 700 (La. 1985).
31. 985 F.2d 525 (11th Cir. 1993).
32. *Id.* at 528.
33. *Id.*
34. 263 Cal Rptr. 747 (Cal.App. 2 Dist. 1989), *cert. denied*, 111 S.Ct. 102 (1991).
35. 5 Cal. Rptr.2d 317 (Cal.App. 1st Dist. 1991).
36. *See also, State* v. *Calhoun*, 479 So.2d 241 (Fla.App. 4th Dist. 1985).
37. U.S.C. §§ 2510 *et seq.*
38. 18 U.S.C. § 2510(2).
39. *See, e.g., United States* v. *Harrelson*, 754 F.2d 1153 (1985), *cert. denied*, 106 S.Ct. 277 (1986).

Understanding Meaning

1. What is the purpose of Crawford's analysis? Why does her audience need this information?
2. How does she analyze the Fourth, Fifth, and Sixth Amendments?
3. What rights do criminals have in custody? Do they surrender all pretense of privacy when they are arrested?
4. *Critical Thinking:* Does the surreptitious recording of suspects' conversations threaten privacy and democracy or protect it? Would you approve of using this technique to gather evidence that would establish the guilt of a child molester or a terrorist? Should the technique be used to secure evidence against people accused of "victimless" crimes?

Evaluating Strategy

1. Does citing specific cases help readers understand what is constitutional and what is not?
2. How is Crawford's analysis organized?
3. Crawford concludes the article with a list of suggestions. What does this imply about the needs of her readers?

Appreciating Language

1. How much legal terminology does the writer use? What does this reveal about her audience?
2. What language does Crawford use to describe suspects? What does this suggest about suspects?

Connections across the Disciplines

1. How does Crawford's professional role as attorney shape her writing? Compare her article to the one written by physician Oliver Sacks (page 81). What similarities do you see?
2. Compare this article with the FBI report on Lee Harvey Oswald (page 93). What do these entries reveal about writing in law enforcement?

Writing Suggestions

1. Write a short essay analyzing your view of secretly recording suspects' conversations. Should police officers advise suspects that anything they say in private may be held against them? Is surreptitious recording a violation of people's rights? How would you feel if the person who admitted killing a friend of yours was acquitted because his or her statements could not be entered into evidence?
2. *Collaborative Writing:* Working with a group of students, consider the following scenario. A student suspects his or her lover of being unfaithful and installs a recording device in the lover's apartment that transmits clear evidence that this person is engaging in unsafe practices with multiple partners. Discuss the ethics of this situation. Have a member of the group record responses, and as a group review the list and each write a brief analysis. Does a consensus exist? Do the responses indicate gender differences?

STRATEGIES FOR WRITING ANALYSIS

1. **Determine your purpose.** Does your analysis seek to explain the parts of a complex object, issue, condition, or situation, or does it seek to identify a reason, a cause, or a solution to a problem? Persuasive analysis requires greater attention to context.

2. **Define your role.** Are you expressing personal opinion supported by facts and examples of your own choosing, or are you following the dictates of a specific discipline? When writing in a professional role, use standard methods and tools of analysis. If you use unconventional methods, explain your rationale, and be prepared for criticism.

3. **Consider your audience.** In addition to evaluating your readers' knowledge base, you should consider their perceptual world. Are your readers likely to be receptive or hostile to your conclusions? What kind of evidence will most impress them?

4. **Limit your subject.** Analysis requires close study, and an ill-defined topic likely will lead to confusion.

5. **Gather appropriate sources, data, and information.** The strength of your analysis will depend on the quantity and quality of the information you examine. Avoid making judgments on limited data. Evaluate the sources of your data for possible flaws, oversights, or bias.

6. **Be open to alternative interpretations.** Do not make general statements based on data without entertaining alternative interpretations. Consider possible data you may have overlooked.

7. **Apply the rules of critical thinking, and avoid the logical fallacies (review page 507).**

SUGGESTED TOPICS FOR WRITING ANALYSIS

General Assignments

Write an analysis on any of the following topics. Your analysis will require careful thinking, observation, and possibly outside research. Remember to avoid the logical fallacies and to qualify your remarks.

- Affordable student housing (Define "affordable" in your area.)
- Current movies (Use the newspaper listings as a source.)
- Status of women in your college's faculty and administration
- The principal problem facing fellow students

- The political climate on your campus
- The popularity of a current fad or celebrity
- Your generation's attitude toward the Vietnam War, the Civil Rights movement, or any other historical event
- Gender differences
- The effect of divorce on children
- America's role in international affairs

Writing in Context

1. Assume you have been asked by the campus newspaper to analyze how students feel about abortion, gun control, or another controversial issue. Design a method to gather and analyze data. Indicate what methods you would use, such as focus groups, surveys, or personal interviews.
2. Analyze the image of women, the elderly, black males, businessmen, or any other group presented in popular television shows. Include as many examples as possible in your analysis.
3. Analyze editions of the largest newspaper in your area to determine the amount of attention given to international events versus domestic news. Explain your research methods—the number of editions reviewed and the methods of measurement (number of articles or amount of space).

STUDENT PAPER: ANALYSIS

This paper was written in response to the following assignment:

Analyze the meaning or significance of a common personal trait, event, social phenomenon, prevailing attitude, or widespread problem. Support your thesis with examples, and provide readers with a clear description of your subject.

Nostalgia: Why We Need and Love the Past

1   I met my current girlfriend at a '70s party. That night the usual Irish decor of O'Donoghue's Pub was obscured by posters of Farrah Fawcett and Burt Reynolds. Men in white suits and girls in disco dresses bounced and twirled to the whining voices of the Bee-Gees and the moans of Donna Summer. Winners of the dance competition received timely prizes — eight-track tapes, lava lamps, mood rings, and Studio 54 T-shirts.

2   Twenty-five years ago my parents, new hires at rival law firms, met at a '50s party. It was the 1970s and my Mom, who normally tried to look like Jaclyn Smith (the brunette on "Charlie's Angels"), cut a striking figure in her poodle skirt and saddle shoes. A fading Polaroid shows her leaning against my Dad in his teen angel leather jacket, his hair greased up into an early Elvis do.

3   Nostalgia is not new. Snapshots my grandfather took in England during World War II show a group of B-17 pilots partying in riding boots and silk scarves, imitating the pilots of the First World War. No doubt in 1917 doughboys tried to impress French girls by impersonating Teddy Roosevelt's Rough Riders.

4   Why this appeal of the past? Why does every generation seem to find a previous era more interesting, more glamorous, more adventurous, more fun? In part, there is simply the desire to be young again. The forty-fifty somethings look back twenty years to a time when they were young, attractive, and idealistic — a time when their lives were new and their options open. To the teens and twenty-somethings this former era offers safety.

5   In the past we can play and feel secure. We can look back on the Seventies, the Fifties, even the Thirties because we survived them. We find previous decades "simpler" and "better" because they existed before current problems. The 1970s seem simpler and more innocent because AIDS, cyberstalking, and crack were unknown. We forget, however, that the Seventies meant Cold War, Watergate, inflation, mass unemployment, and gas lines. Back in the Seventies, people like my parents could escape the malaise of the Carter era by dressing up like Fifties teens and dancing to do-wop music. No doubt, in their eagerness to find the perfect skirt, locate the right nail polish, and fix their hair to look like Annette Funicello's they forgot that the simpler and nicer era of the Fifties meant segregation, sexual hypocrisy, air raid drills, McCarthyism, and war in Korea.

6   Nostalgia — that longing for the past — has deleterious elements. It can trivialize problems and distort our view of history. It can mar our ability to think critically. Looking back on the Sixties, certain figures like Martin Luther King Jr. and John F. Kennedy emerge as icons. We forget they were controversial in their time and that intelligent men and women of good will opposed them. The complexity of Vietnam and

the Civil Rights marches are blurred because we can look back and easily see in hindsight the right course the nation should have taken.

7   What we really look for in nostalgia is peace and direction. In the past we can side with the winners, forgetting how stressful and fearful those times were. The Seventies parties evoke a time when all sexually transmitted diseases were curable with a penicillin shot, when feminism meant reading *Fear of Flying*, and people assumed racism would evaporate in a decade or two because the Love Boat was integrated. In reliving that era and trying to dance like younger and thinner Travoltas, we forget that the crowds who jammed the discos then lived in an era when imports were filling the parking lots, factories were closing, and experts predicted America was doomed to become a second-class nation owned by Japanese bankers and Arab sheiks.

8   Maybe I am reading too much into nostalgia, seeing a harmless pastime as some kind of brain-deadening addiction. I just hope that in our desire to find the perfect costume, remember who won the Academy Award in 1978, or which team won the most Super Bowls in the Eighties we learn a little something about our past. Maybe in looking back and dressing up, we can think about the progress women and minorities have made. We might even imagine what it was like to write without computers, conduct research without the Internet, and live without cable TV.

Questions for Review and Revision

1.   What does the student see as the principal reasons people enjoy pretending to be in another era?
2.   How does the student open the paper? Does the opening quickly demonstrate the writer's subject?
3.   How is the essay organized? How effective is the paragraph structure?
4.   *Critical Thinking:* Could this student provide a more in-depth analysis of nostalgia? Does this paper do more than simply describe nostalgia? Can you think of other ideas this essay might explore?
5.   Do you see any paragraphs that could be deleted or should be expanded?
6.   Read the paper aloud. How effectively does the choice of words establish the writer's tone and style?

Writing Suggestions

1. Write an essay analyzing a current fad, trend, or common behavior. Include key details, and suggest the cause or significance of your subject.
2. *Collaborative Writing:* Discuss this essay with a group of students, and work together to develop a statement on nostalgia. What current examples of nostalgia can your group identify? Do you see nostalgia as a harmless pastime or something with negative implications?

ANALYSIS CHECKLIST

Before submitting your paper, review these points.

1. Is the topic clearly limited?

2. Is your approach appropriate for the writing context?

3. Do you present enough evidence?

4. Have you evaluated sources for inaccuracy or bias?

5. Have you avoided errors in logic?

6. Are your research methods clearly explained?

7. Do you clearly present the results of your analysis?

8. Have you considered alternative interpretations?

 WebTutor

See www.harcourtcollege.com/english/sundance
for information on writing analysis.

7

DIVISION AND CLASSIFICATION

SEPARATING INTO PARTS AND RATING CATEGORIES

WHAT ARE DIVISION AND CLASSIFICATION?

Division helps readers understand complex subjects by separating them into parts. *Classification*, often used to aid decision making, rates subjects by placing them on a scale of different categories.

Division

If you enter a hospital, you will probably see signs directing you to different departments: cardiology, radiology, psychiatry, and pediatrics. Hospitals are divided into specific services. Universities consist of separate colleges, such as business and liberal arts. American literature can be divided into courses by historical era (nineteenth- and twentieth-century American writers), by genre (American poetry and American drama), or by special interest (women's literature and science fiction). Corporations place personnel into different departments: design, production, maintenance, marketing, sales, and accounting.

Division makes complicated subjects easier to comprehend and work with. For example, the human body is overwhelmingly intricate. In order to understand how it functions, medical disciplines divide it into systems: digestive, respiratory, nervous, muscular-skeletal, reproductive, and others. By studying individual systems, medical students come to a fuller understanding of how the whole body operates. Crime is such a vast social problem that writers discuss it in terms of traditional divisions—robbery, car theft, homicide, and fraud—or invent their own categories, dividing crime by causes: power, greed, identity, and revenge. People use the term *depression* to express everything from minor disappointment to suicidal despair. In order to inform patients about the variety of depressive illnesses, a mental health brochure divides the disorder into specific types:

> **Bereavement**—a 2–8 week process of grieving with sad and empty feelings after the death of someone important to you. May linger for much longer after loss of parent, child, or partner, but tends to gradually improve over time. You should observe steady readjustment to your changed world and resumption of social activities and pleasures.
>
> **Adjustment Reaction**—a period of up to 6 months after a major stressful event during which depressed mood, or hopeless feelings are more intense than normal and interfere with daily social and school or work activities. Like BEREAVEMENT, it is often helped by brief crisis therapy or family therapy.
>
> **Major Depression**—depressed mood or loss of interests with a variety of the symptoms and feelings of depression discussed earlier, lasting at least 2 weeks. Major depression ranges from mild cases with few symptoms to severe cases (known as *"clinical depression"*) marked by a persistent bleak outlook which may lead to thoughts of escape through suicide. Depression may begin to lift after several weeks or may become chronic, lasting 2 years or more.

In this case division presents readers with a series of definitions. Division writing can also organize a set of narratives, descriptions, processes, or persuasive arguments.

Critical Thinking for Writing Division

Dividing any subject can be challenging. Would it make more sense to explain American politics to a foreign visitor in terms of political parties or specific issues? Would you group used cars by year, by price, or by model? When division writing, follow these guidelines:

1. **Avoid oversimplifying your subject.** You have no doubt seen magazine articles announcing three kinds of bosses, four types of marriages, or five methods of childrearing. Writers often invent descriptive or humorous labels, warning you to avoid "the toxic controller" or advising you how to

negotiate with the "whiny wimp." Although these divisions can be amusing and insightful, they can trivialize or oversimplify a subject. Not all people or situations can neatly fit into three or four types. *When discussing complex topics, inform readers of possible exceptions to your categories.*

2. **Select a method of division that includes all parts of the whole.** If you divide college students into four types, for example, make sure everyone on campus is included in one of the groups. Eliminate potential gaps. You cannot simply divide students into Protestants, Catholics, and Jews if some are agnostics or Muslims. Every member or part of the whole must be accounted for.

3. **Make sure individual parts fit only one category.** If you were to divide businesses by geographical region—North, South, East, and West—how would you handle a company with operations on both coasts? If items can fit in more than one category, your method of division is not suited to your subject. It might be better to discuss businesses in terms of their gross sales, products, or size rather than location.

4. **Avoid categories that include too many differences.** If you were examining people of different ages, it could make sense to write about people in groups from age thirty to forty or fifty to sixty. But a category of age sixty to seventy would include both working and retired people, both those still paying into Social Security and those receiving benefits. It might be more accurate to break this group into people who are age sixty to sixty-five and those who are older than sixty-five.

Classification

Like division, classification breaks a complex subject into parts. But for classification, the categories are ranked or rated according to a single standard. In medicine, for example, burns are classified first-, second-, and third-degree based on the amount of tissue damage. Teachers grade tests according to the number of correct answers. Insurance companies set rates based on their clients' history of loss. Motion pictures are judged G, PG, PG13, R, NC17, and X based on depictions of sex and violence.

Perhaps no more serious an incident occurs in society than when an individual causes the death of another. In addressing this issue, the law identifies a range of situations in which a fatality occurs and ranks them from the most to least objectionable:

Felonious homicide. The wrongful killing of a human being, of any age or either sex, without justification or excuse in law; of which offense there are two degrees, manslaughter and murder.

Homicide by misadventure. The accidental killing of another, where the slayer is doing a lawful act, unaccompanied by any criminally careless or reckless conduct. . . .

Homicide by necessity. A species of justifiable homicide, because it arises from some unavoidable necessity, without any will, intention, or desire, and without any inadvertence or negligence in the party killing, and therefore without any shadow of blame.

Classification helps people to make decisions and to direct actions. Classifications can set prices, establish salaries, and in some cases save lives. The importance of classification is demonstrated by the use of triage in emergency medicine. When a hospital is flooded with accident victims, doctors place patients into three categories: those who will die with or without immediate medical attention, those who will survive without emergency care, and those who will survive only if treated without delay. The last group is given priority to ensure that doctors do not waste time on the dying or those with minor injuries.

Critical Thinking for Writing Classification

As with division writing, classification requires careful planning. To avoid common problems, follow these guidelines:

1. **Avoid confusing division with classification.** Perhaps the most frequent mistake students make in classification writing papers is simply dividing a subject into parts. *Classification not only divides a subject into parts but also rates the parts on a scale.*
2. **Establish a clearly defined standard of measurement.** To successfully teach writing, for example, an English professor must provide students with a clear understanding of what distinguishes an A paper from a B paper. Even if you are making up your own categories, each one should be clearly defined so readers understand what distinguishes one from the other.
3. **Do not mix standards.** You can classify automobiles, for instance, from the cheapest to the most expensive, from the safest to the most dangerous, or from the most fuel efficient to the least fuel efficient. But you cannot write a classification essay that rates cars as being safe, fuel efficient, or expensive since many cars could be both expensive and fuel efficient.
4. **Arrange categories in order.** Organize the categories so they follow a ladderlike pattern, such as judging items from the best to the worst, the cheapest to the most expensive, or the newest to the oldest.

5. **Provide enough categories to include all parts of the whole.** If you were to classify cars as being either American or foreign, how would you account for Toyotas produced in the United States or Chryslers assembled in Mexico?

STRATEGIES FOR READING DIVISION AND CLASSIFICATION

As you read the division and classification entries in this chapter, keep the following questions in mind.

Meaning

1. What is the writer trying to explain by dividing or classifying his or her topic? Does the division or classification help you understand the subject better than a simple description would?
2. Do the divisions risk oversimplifying the subject?
3. Do the classification essays have a clearly defined standard?
4. Do the standards seem fair? Do they adequately measure what they claim to evaluate?

Strategy

1. How does the writer introduce or set up the division or classification?
2. How does the author use definitions and examples to create distinct categories?
3. Does the writer use standard divisions and classifications accepted by a particular discipline or profession, or does he or she invent new ones?
4. Does the writer use division or classification to explain a topic, or is it used as a device to recommend one item over another?

Language

1. What does the level of language reveal about the writer's discipline and intended audience?
2. What words does the author use to describe or define standards of classification? Do you detect a bias?

RUSSELL BAKER

Russell Baker (1925–) was born in Virginia and raised in New Jersey and Mary-land. After serving in World War II, he attended Johns Hopkins University. After graduating in 1947, Baker became a reporter for a Baltimore newspaper. In the 1950s he joined the staff of The New York Times *and covered the White House and the State Department. In 1962 he began writing "Observer," a column which now appears in hundreds of newspapers. In the 1980s he published two autobio-graphical books,* Growing Up *and* The Good Times. *Many of his columns ap-peared in the collection* There's a Country in My Cellar *in 1990.*

The Plot Against People

In this humorous piece, Baker invents three categories of common objects we en-counter. As you read the essay, notice how Baker uses definition, description, *and* example.

1   Inanimate objects are classified into three major categories—those that don't work, those that break down and those that get lost.

2   The goal of all inanimate objects is to resist man and ultimately to defeat him, and the three major classifications are based on the method each object uses to achieve its purpose. As a general rule, any object capable of breaking down at the moment when it is needed most will do so. The automobile is typical of the category.

3   With the cunning typical of its breed, the automobile never breaks down while entering a filling station with a large staff of idle mechan-ics. It waits until it reaches a downtown intersection in the middle of the rush hour, or until it is fully loaded with family and luggage on the Ohio Turnpike.

4   Thus it creates maximum misery, inconvenience, frustration and ir-ritability among its human cargo, thereby reducing its owner's life span.

5   Washing machines, garbage disposals, lawn mowers, light bulbs, automatic laundry dryers, water pipes, furnaces, electrical fuses, tele-vision tubes, hose nozzles, tape recorders, slide projectors—all are in league with the automobile to take their turn at breaking down when-ever life threatens to flow smoothly for their human enemies.

6   Many inanimate objects, of course, find it extremely difficult to break down. Pliers, for example, and gloves and keys are almost totally incapable of breaking down. Therefore, they have had to evolve a different technique for resisting man.

7   They get lost. Science has still not solved the mystery of how they do it, and no man has ever caught one of them in the act of getting lost. The most plausible theory is that they have developed a secret method of locomotion which they are able to conceal the instant a human eye falls upon them.

8   It is not uncommon for a pair of pliers to climb all the way from the cellar to the attic in its single-minded determination to raise its owner's blood pressure. Keys have been known to burrow three feet under mattresses. Women's purses, despite their great weight, frequently travel through six or seven rooms to find a hiding space under a couch.

9   Scientists have been struck by the fact that things that break down virtually never get lost, while things that get lost hardly ever break down.

10   A furnace, for example, will invariably break down at the depth of the first winter cold wave, but it will never get lost. A woman's purse, which after all does have some inherent capacity for breaking down, hardly ever does; it almost invariably chooses to get lost.

11   Some persons believe this constitutes evidence that inanimate objects are not entirely hostile to man, and that a negotiated peace is possible. After all, they point out, a furnace could infuriate a man even more thoroughly by getting lost than by breaking down, just as a glove could upset him far more by breaking down than by getting lost.

12   Not everyone agrees, however, that this indicates a conciliatory attitude among inanimate objects. Many say it merely proves that furnaces, gloves and pliers are incredibly stupid.

13   The third class of objects—those that don't work—is the most curious of all. These include such objects as barometers, car clocks, cigarette lighters, flashlights and toy train locomotives. It is inaccurate, of course, to say that they never work. They work once, usually for the first few hours after being brought home, and then quit. Thereafter, they never work again.

14   In fact, it is widely assumed that they are built for the purpose of not working. Some people have reached advanced ages without ever seeing some of these objects—barometers, for example—in working order.

15   Science is utterly baffled by the entire category. There are many theories about it. The most interesting holds that the things that don't

work have attained the highest state possible for an inanimate object, the state to which things that break down and things that get lost can still only aspire.

16   They have truly defeated man by conditioning him never to expect anything of them, and in return they have given man the only peace he receives from inanimate society. He does not expect his barometer to work, his electric locomotive to run, his cigarette lighter to light or his flashlight to illuminate, and when they don't, it does not raise his blood pressure.

17   He cannot attain that peace with furnaces and keys and cars and women's purses as long as he demands that they work for their keep.

Understanding Meaning

1. What is Baker's purpose?
2. How have objects "defeated" people?
3. Are there objects that you frankly do not expect to work?
4. *Critical Thinking:* Humor is often based on acute observation. What is Baker saying about the lives of Americans, who often measure their success or happiness by the number of objects they possess? Do all the things we yearn to have truly enrich or merely complicate our lives?

Evaluating Strategy

1. Why is the essay's introduction important? Is it effective in setting up the body of the essay?
2. How important are the examples Baker uses to define each category? Can readers relate to these?
3. Baker creates three categories. Would the humor of the essay wear thin if he invented four, five, or six categories? Is there a limit to audience attention when reading for entertainment?

Appreciating Language

1. Baker uses the third person to describe people's experiences with objects. Would a first person approach, emphasizing his personal encounters with things, have the same effect?
2. *Critical Thinking:* Throughout this 1968 essay Baker uses male references—"man" and "he." Would a modern editor insist on non-sexist language? Would you suggest making changes? Why or why not?

Connections across the Disciplines

1. Compare this essay to Martin Luther King Jr.'s "The Ways of Meeting Oppression" (page 401) and Meg Greenfield's "Why Nothing Is 'Wrong' Anymore" (page 406). How do the authors organize their essays? What transitional devices do they use to separate each item?
2. Both John Ciardi (page 192) and Juliet B. Schor (page 306) describe a consumer-driven society in which people overspend to acquire material objects and to achieve status and happiness. Does Baker indicate that these "washing machines, garbage disposals, and lawn mowers" only frustrate us? Consider the happiness Edward Abbey (page 143) senses as he contemplates the empty desert, a landscape free of consumer goods.

Writing Suggestions

1. Write a short essay, using Baker's as a model, to humorously classify college courses, professors, local restaurants, garages, or stores. Define each type clearly, and illustrate with examples.
2. *Collaborative Writing:* Discuss Baker's essay with a group of students, and work together to create a short, humorous, updated version that includes CD's, computers, e-mail, answering machines, and VCR's.

Mary Mebane (1933–) received a doctorate in English from the University of North Carolina. She teaches English at the University of South Carolina at Columbia. Mebane is the author of a play, Take a Sad Song, *and two autobiographical books,* Mary *and* Mary Wayfarer. *In 1982 she received a National Endowment for the Arts Creative Writing Fellowship. Much of her work has focused on the experience of African-Americans in the South.*

Black Wasn't Beautiful

This section from Mebane's autobiography Mary *(1981) details the four options that dark-complexioned African-American women faced in the segregated South. Attending a black college in the 1950s, Mebane encountered a rigid system of discrimination in which lighter-skinned African-Americans considered themselves superior to those with darker skin.*

1   In the fall of 1951 during my first week at North Carolina College, a black school in Durham, the chairman's wife, who was indistinguishable from a white woman, stopped me one day in the hall. She wanted to see me, she said.

2   When I went to her office, she greeted me with a big smile. "You know," she said, "you made the highest mark on the verbal part of the examination." She was referring to the examination that the entire freshman class took upon entering the college. In spite of her smile, her eyes and tone of voice were saying, "How could this black-skinned girl score higher on the verbal than some of the students who've had more advantages than she? It must be some sort of fluke." I felt it, but I managed to smile my thanks and back off. For here at North Carolina College, social class and color were the primary criteria used in deciding status. The faculty assumed light-skinned students were more intelligent, and they were always a bit nonplussed when a dark-skinned student did well, especially if she was a girl.

3   I don't know whether African men recently transported to the New World considered themselves handsome or, more important, whether they considered African women beautiful in comparison with native

American Indian women or immigrant European women. But one thing I know for sure: By the twentieth century, really black skin on a woman was considered ugly in this country. In the 1950s this was particularly true among those who were exposed to college. Black skin was to be disguised at all costs. Since a black face is rather hard to disguise, many women took refuge in ludicrous makeup.

4   I observed all through elementary and high school, in various entertainments, the girls were placed on the stage in order of color. And very black ones didn't get into the front row. If they were past caramel-brown, to the back row they would go. Nobody questioned the justice of this—neither the students nor the teachers.

5   Oddly enough, the lighter-skinned black male did not seem to feel so much prejudice toward the black black woman. It was no accident, I felt, that Mr. Harrison, the eighth-grade teacher, who was reddish-yellow himself, once protested to the science and math teacher about the fact that he always assigned sweeping duties to Doris and Ruby, two black black girls. Mr. Harrison said to them one day in the other teacher's presence, "You must be some bad girls. Every day I come down here you all are sweeping." The science and math teacher got the point and didn't ask them to sweep any more. Uneducated black males, too, sometimes related very well to the black black woman. They had been less indoctrinated by the white society around them.

6   Because of the stigma attached to having dark skin, a black black woman had to do many things to find a place for herself. One possibility was to attach herself to a light-skinned woman, hoping that some of the magic would rub off on her. A second was to make herself sexually available, hoping thereby to attract a mate. Third, she could resign herself to a more chaste life-style—either (for the professional woman) teaching and work in established churches or (for the uneducated woman) domestic work and zealous service in "holy and sanctified" churches.

7   Lucy had chosen the first route. Lucy was short, skinny, short-haired and black black, and thus unacceptable. So she made her choice. She selected Patricia, the lightest-skinned girl in the school, as her friend and followed her around. Patricia and her friends barely tolerated Lucy, but Lucy smiled and doggedly hung on, hoping that those who noticed Patricia might notice her also. Though I felt shame for her behavior, even then I understood.

8   A fourth avenue open to the black black woman is excellence in a career. Since in the South the field most accessible to such women is

education, a great many of them prepared to become teachers. But here, too, the black black woman had problems. Grades weren't given to her lightly in school, nor were promotions on the job. She had to pass examinations with flying colors or be left behind. She had to be overqualified for a job because otherwise she didn't stand a chance of getting it—and she was competing only with other blacks.

9 The black woman's training would pay off in the 1970s. With the arrival of integration, the black black woman would find, paradoxically enough, that her skin color in an integrated situation was not the handicap it had been in an all-black situation. But it wasn't until the middle and late 1960s, when the post-1945 generation of black males arrived in college that I noticed any change in the situation at all. *He* wore an Afro and *she* wore an Afro, and sometimes the only way you could tell them apart was when his Afro was taller than hers. Black had become beautiful. It was then that the dread I felt at dealing with the college-educated black male began to ease. Even now, though, when I have occasion to engage in any transaction with a college-educated black man, I gauge his age. If I guess he was born after 1945, I feel confident that the transaction will turn out all right. If he probably was born before 1945, my stomach tightens, I find myself taking shallow breaths, and I try to state my business and escape as soon as possible.

10 When the grades from the first quarter at North Carolina College came out, I had the highest average in the freshman class. The chairman's wife called me into her office again. We did a replay of the same scene we had played during the first week of the term. She complimented me on my grades. Then she reached into a drawer and pulled out a copy of the freshman English final examination. She asked me to take the exam over again.

11 At first I couldn't believe what she was saying. I had taken the course under another teacher; and it was so incredible to her that I should have made the highest score in the class that she was trying to test me again personally. For a few moments I knew rage so intense that I wanted to take my fists and start punching her. I have seldom hated anyone so deeply. I handed the examination back to her and walked out.

Understanding Meaning

1. What caused the African American community to discriminate against those with dark skin?

2. What evidence of discrimination does Mebane offer?
3. Briefly describe the four options dark-skinned women faced.
4. How did gender affect people's attitudes toward dark-skinned women?
5. What changes occurred in the 1970s?
6. *Critical Thinking:* What other examples of discrimination *within* a group can you think of? Have some members of ethnic groups attempted to distance themselves from those seen as less desirable by mainstream society, hence the conflict, for example, between "lace curtain Irish" and "shanty Irish"? Do women discriminate against other women they see as less attractive, less respectable, too traditional, or too radical?

Evaluating Strategy

1. Mebane begins and ends the piece with a narrative. How effective is this device?
2. *Other Modes:* Where does Mebane use *comparison* and *contrast* within her essay?

Appreciating Language

1. How does Mebane describe the differences among African-Americans?
2. What does her word choice reveal about her attitudes toward those who discriminated against her?

Connections across the Disciplines

1. Compare Mebane's account of discrimination *within* the black community with Nathan McCall's essay (page 51), which discusses black-white racial conflict. How did these experiences shape the writers' attitudes? How did they respond to discrimination?
2. Martin Luther King Jr.'s essay (page 401) suggests three ways oppressed people respond to their condition. Does this essay suggest a fourth way? Do oppressed people often build a separate society mirroring the values of their oppressors?

Writing Suggestions

1. Write an essay describing a situation in which you were unfairly classified because of your race, age, appearance, or occupation.

2. *Collaborative Writing:* Discuss Mebane's essay with a small group of students. How often is discrimination internalized? Have members of the group offer examples they have witnessed or experienced. After taking notes, work together to write a brief division or classification paper stating the reasons for this behavior.

KESAYA E. NODA

Although born in the United States, Kesaya Noda has always been viewed as an alien. "A third-generation German-American," she notes, "is an American. A third-generation Japanese-American is a Japanese-American." Seen as being Japanese, Japanese American, or simply Asian, Noda came to question the ways she is perceived by other Americans.

Growing Up Asian in America

In this essay from 1989, Kesaya Noda uses division to answer the question "How is one to know and define oneself?" In this instance, Noda employs division to help her select one of several possible identities.

1 Sometimes when I was growing up, my identity seemed to hurtle toward me and paste itself right to my face. I felt that way, encountering the stereotypes of my race perpetuated by non-Japanese people (primarily white) who may or may not have had contact with other Japanese in America. "You don't like cheese, do you?" someone would ask. "I know your people don't like cheese." Sometimes questions came making allusions to history. That was another aspect of the identity. Events that had happened quite apart from the me who stood silent in that moment connected my face with an incomprehensible past. "Your parents were in California? Were they in those camps during the war?" And sometimes there were phrases or nicknames: "Lotus Blossom." I was sometimes addressed or referred to as racially Japanese, sometimes as Japanese-American, and sometimes as an Asian woman. Confusions and distortions abounded.

2 How is one to know and define oneself? From the inside—within a context that is self-defined, from a grounding in community and a connection with culture and history that are comfortably accepted? Or from the outside—in terms of messages received from the media and people who are often ignorant? Even as an adult I can still see two sides of my face and past. I can see from the inside out, in freedom. And I can see from the outside in, driven by the old voices of childhood and lost in anger and fear.

I AM RACIALLY JAPANESE

3   A voice from my childhood says: "You are other. You are less than. You are unalterably alien." This voice has its own history. We have indeed been seen as other and alien since the early years of our arrival in the United States. The very first immigrants were welcomed and sought as laborers to replace the dwindling numbers of Chinese, whose influx had been cut off by the Chinese Exclusion Act of 1882. The Japanese fell natural heir to the same anti-Asian prejudice that had arisen against the Chinese. As soon as they began striking for better wages, they were no longer welcomed.

4   I can see myself today as a person historically defined by law and custom as being forever alien. Being neither "free white," nor "African," our people in California were deemed "aliens, ineligible for citizenship," no matter how long they intended to stay here. Aliens ineligible for citizenship were prohibited from owning, buying, or leasing land. They did not and could not belong here. The voice in me remembers that I am always a *Japanese*-American in the eyes of many. A third-generation German-American is an American. A third-generation Japanese-American is a Japanese-American. Being Japanese means being a danger to the country during the war and knowing how to use chopsticks. I wear this history on my face.

5   I move to the other side. I see a different light and claim a different context. My race is a line that stretches across ocean and time to link me to the shrine where my grandmother was raised. Two high, white banners lift in the wind at the top of the stone steps leading to the shrine. It is time for the summer festival. Black characters are written against the sky as boldly as the clouds, as lightly as kites, as sharply as the big black crows I used to see above the fields in New Hampshire. At festival time there is liquor and food, rituals, discipline, and abandonment. There is music and drunkenness and invocation. There is hope. Another season has come. Another season has gone.

6   I am racially Japanese. I have a certain claim to this crazy place where the prayers intoned by a neighboring Shinto priest (standing in for my grandmother's nephew who is sick) are drowned out by the rehearsals for the pop singing contest in which most of the villagers will compete later that night. The village elders, the priest, and I stand respectfully upon the immaculate, shining wooden floor of the outer shrine, bowing our heads before the hidden powers. During the patchy intervals when I can hear him, I notice the priest has a stutter. His

voice flutters up to my ears only occasionally because two men and a woman are singing gustily into a microphone in the compound, testing the sound system. A prerecorded tape of guitars, samisens, and drums accompanies them. Rock music and Shinto prayers. That night, to loud applause and cheers, a young man is given the award for the most *netsuretsu*—passionate, burning—rendition of a song. We roar our approval of the reward. Never mind that his voice had wandered and slid, now slightly above, now slightly below the given line of the melody. Netsuretsu. Netsuretsu.

7   In the morning, my grandmother's sister kneels at the foot of the stone stairs to offer her morning prayers. She is too crippled to climb the stairs, so each morning she kneels here upon the path. She shuts her eyes for a few seconds, her motions as matter of fact as when she washes rice. I linger longer than she does, so reluctant to leave, savoring the connection I feel with my grandmother in America, the past, and the power that lives and shines in the morning sun.

Understanding Meaning

1. What confusion did Noda encounter as a child?
2. Are the comments about cheese, her parents' possible internment during World War II, or being nicknamed "Lotus Blossom" intentionally hostile? Would people of other ethnic groups have more troubling, more wounding experiences to relate?
3. Why does her childhood voice tell her "You are other. You are less than" and not "You are other. You are different from"? What does this reveal about her self-esteem?
4. *Critical Thinking:* At what point do people become "Americans"? Teddy Roosevelt once declared that "no hyphenated Americans" must exist—no Irish-Americans, German-Americans, or Italian-Americans. Can this apply to Asian Americans and African Americans (with or without hyphens)?

Evaluating Strategy

1. How does Noda separate the different identities she has confronted?
2. *Other Modes:* Where does Noda use *description* and *comparison* to develop her essay?
3. *Critical Thinking:* Is division an effective method of making a decision? By separating and identifying different options, does a danger of overlooking possible alternatives arise?

Appreciating Language

1. Noda uses the Japanese word *netsuretsu*. What does this add to the essay? What does it demonstrate?
2. What language does Noda use to describe Japanese traditions and festivals? What images stand out?

Connections across the Disciplines

1. How does Noda's sense of alternative identities contrast with the choices Mary Mebane describes African-American women faced in the 1950s (page 392)?
2. How does Noda's perception of being Japanese contrast to the views of ethnic identity expressed by Armando Rendón (page 611) and Barbara Ehrenreich (page 617)?

Writing Suggestions

1. Write a short essay about the way people identified you as you were growing up. Were you seen as black or Jewish, the minister's daughter, a rich kid, or fat? How did these perceptions affect your self-awareness and self-esteem?
2. *Collaborative Writing:* Discuss Noda's essay with a group of students. Does every ethnic group have negative associations to some people? Can any ethnic group be viewed as being totally free of prejudice? Record the views of your group, and write a brief division paper, outlining the principal observations raised in the discussion.

Martin Luther King Jr. (1929–1968) was a leading figure in the Civil Rights movement in the 1950s and 1960s. A noted minister, King blended his deeply felt religious values and his sense of political and social justice. He created the Southern Christian Leadership Conference, organized many demonstrations, and lobbied for voting rights. In 1964 he received the Nobel Peace Prize. He was assassinated in 1968.

The Ways of Meeting Oppression

In this section from his 1958 book Stride toward Freedom, *King classifies three ways oppressed people have responded to oppression. King uses classification to rate which response is the most effective and concludes his comments persuading readers to accept his choice.*

1   Oppressed people deal with their oppression in three characteristic ways. One way is acquiescence: The oppressed resign themselves to their doom. They tacitly adjust themselves to oppression, and thereby become conditioned to it. In every movement toward freedom some of the oppressed prefer to remain oppressed. Almost 2,800 years ago Moses set out to lead the children of Israel from the slavery of Egypt to the freedom of the promised land. He soon discovered that slaves do not always welcome their deliverers. They become accustomed to being slaves. They would rather bear those ills they have, as Shakespeare pointed out, than flee to others that they know not of. They prefer the "fleshpots of Egypt" to the ordeals of emancipation.

2   There is such a thing as the freedom of exhaustion. Some people are so worn down by the yoke of oppression that they give up. A few years ago in the slum areas of Atlanta, a Negro guitarist used to sing almost daily: "Been down so long that down don't bother me." This is the type of negative freedom and resignation that often engulfs the life of the oppressed.

3   But this is not the way out. To accept passively an unjust system is to cooperate with that system; thereby the oppressed become as evil

as the oppressor. Noncooperation with evil is as much a moral obligation as is cooperation with good. The oppressed must never allow the conscience of the oppressor to slumber. Religion reminds every man that he is his brother's keeper. To accept injustice or segregation passively is to say to the oppressor that his actions are morally right. It is a way of allowing his conscience to fall asleep. At this moment the oppressed fails to be his brother's keeper. So acquiescence—while often the easier way—is not the moral way. It is the way of the coward. The Negro cannot win the respect of his oppressor by acquiescing; he merely increases the oppressor's arrogance and contempt. Acquiescence is interpreted as proof of the Negro's inferiority. The Negro cannot win the respect of the white people of the South or the peoples of the world if he is willing to sell the future of his children for his personal and immediate comfort and safety.

4   A second way that oppressed people sometimes deal with oppression is to resort to physical violence and corroding hatred. Violence often brings about momentary results. Nations have frequently won their independence in battle. But in spite of temporary victories, violence never brings permanent peace. It solves no social problem; it merely creates new and more complicated ones.

5   Violence as a way of achieving racial injustice is both impractical and immoral. It is impractical because it is a descending spiral ending in destruction for all. The old law of an eye for an eye leaves everybody blind. It is immoral because it seeks to humiliate the opponent rather than win his understanding; it seeks to annihilate rather than to convert. Violence is immoral because it thrives on hatred rather than love. It destroys community and makes brotherhood impossible. It leaves society in monologue rather than dialogue. Violence ends by defeating itself. It creates bitterness in the survivors and brutality in the destroyers. A voice echoes through time saying to every potential Peter, "Put up your sword."* History is cluttered with the wreckage of nations that failed to follow this command.

6   If the American Negro and other victims of oppression succumb to the temptation of using violence in the struggle for freedom, future generations will be the recipients of a desolate night of bitterness, and our chief legacy to them will be an endless reign of meaningless chaos. Violence is not the way.

---

*The apostle Peter had drawn his sword to defend Christ from arrest. The voice was Christ's, who surrendered himself for trial and crucifixion (John 18:11).

7   The third way open to oppressed people in their quest for freedom is the way of nonviolent resistance. Like the synthesis in Hegelian philosophy, the principle of nonviolent resistance seeks to reconcile the truths of two opposites—the acquiescence and violence—while avoiding the extremes and immoralities of both. The nonviolent resister agrees with the person who acquiesces that one should not be physically aggressive toward his opponent; but he balances the equation by agreeing with the person of violence that evil must be resisted. He avoids the nonresistance of the former and the violent resistance of the latter. With nonviolent resistance, no individual or group need submit to any wrong, nor need anyone resort to violence in order to right a wrong.

8   It seems to me that this is the method that must guide the actions of the Negro in the present crisis in race relations. Through nonviolent resistance the Negro will be able to rise to the noble height of opposing the unjust system while loving the perpetrators of the system. The Negro must work passionately and unrelentingly for full stature as a citizen, but he must not use inferior methods to gain it. He must never come to terms with falsehood, malice, hate, or destruction.

9   Nonviolent resistance makes it possible for the Negro to remain in the South and struggle for his rights. The Negro's problem will not be solved by running away. He cannot listen to the glib suggestion of those who would urge him to migrate en masse to other sections of the country. By grasping his great opportunity in the South he can make a lasting contribution to the moral strength of the nation and set a sublime example of courage for generations yet unborn.

10   By nonviolent resistance, the Negro can also enlist all men of good will in his struggle for equality. The problem is not a purely racial one, with Negroes set against whites. In the end, it is not a struggle between people at all, but a tension between justice and injustice. Nonviolent resistance is not aimed against oppressors but against oppression. Under its banner consciences, not racial groups, are enlisted.

Understanding Meaning

1. Briefly describe the three ways people respond to oppression, according to King. Do you know of a fourth or fifth way? Do people, for instance, respond to oppression by blaming each other?

2. Humility is a Christian value. How does King, a minister, argue that humble acceptance of injustice is immoral?

3. King admits that nations have won freedom through violence, but why does he reject it for African-Americans?
4. *Critical Thinking:* King defines the third way as a blend or synthesis of the first two. Why does he argue that this last manner is the most successful? What are its advantages?

Evaluating Strategy

1. Why does King use classification to suggest a solution instead of writing a direct persuasive argument?
2. How does King use his religious values as a way of arguing the desirability of his choice?
3. What transition statements does King use to direct his readers?

Appreciating Language

1. How does King define the difference between "acquiescence" and "non-violent resistance"?
2. What do King's use of biblical analogies and reference to Hegelian philosophy reveal about his intended audience?

Connections across the Disciplines

1. In attempting to define happiness, John Ciardi (page 192) suggests the best way is to define the outer boundaries and work toward the center. Does King use this device in classifying or ranking responses to oppression?
2. Read Leonce Gaiter's "The Revolt of the Black Bourgeoisie" (page 583). Does this article suggest the situation of African-Americans has changed since King wrote *Stride toward Freedom?*

Writing Suggestions

1. Use King's essay as a model to write your own classification paper revealing the way people generally respond to a common issue or problem—the death of a loved one, the loss of a job, the discovery that a partner has been unfaithful, or being victimized. Rank the responses from the least effective to the most effective.

2. *Collaborative Writing:* Discuss King's classification with a group of students. How many people suffering oppression appear to be following his "third way"? Have a member of the group take notes, then work together to draft a short paper dividing or classifying, if possible, your group's responses.

MEG GREENFIELD

Meg Greenfield (1930–1999) was born in Seattle, began working for the Reporter *in 1957, and served as the magazine's Washington editor for three years. In 1968 she joined the* Washington Post *as editorial writer, becoming editor of the newspaper's editorial page in 1979. She has also written a column for* Newsweek. *In 1978 Meg Greenfield received a Pulitzer Prize for her editorial writing.*

Why Nothing Is "Wrong" Anymore

In this essay from a 1996 Newsweek, *Greenfield comments on the fact that few people seem willing to condemn antisocial behavior as morally wrong. To illustrate her point, Greenfield creates various categories to catalog people's responses to "negative" behavior.*

1   There has been an awful lot of talk about sin, crime, and plain old antisocial behavior this summer—drugs and pornography at home, terror and brutality abroad. Maybe it's just the heat; or maybe these categories of conduct (sin, crime, etc.) are really on the rise. What strikes me is our curiously deficient, not to say defective, way of talking about them. We don't seem to have a word anymore for "wrong" in the moral sense, as in, for example, "theft is wrong."

2   Let me quickly qualify. There is surely no shortage of people condemning other people on such grounds, especially their political opponents or characters they just don't care for. Name-calling is still very much in vogue. But where the concept of wrong is really important— as a guide to one's own behavior or that of one's own side in some dispute—it is missing; and this is as true of those on the religious right who are going around pronouncing great masses of us sinners as it is of their principal antagonists, those on the secular left who can forgive or "understand" just about anything so long as it has not been perpetrated by a right-winger.

3   There is a fairly awesome literature that attempts to explain how we have changed as a people with the advent of psychiatry, the weakening of religious institutions and so forth, but you don't need to address these matters to take note of a simple fact. As a guide and a standard to

live by, you don't hear so much about "right and wrong" these days. The very notion is considered politically, not to say personally, embarrassing, since it has such a repressive, Neanderthal ring to it. So we have developed a broad range of alternatives to "right and wrong." I'll name a few.

4   **Right and stupid:** This is the one you use when your candidate gets caught stealing, or, for that matter, when anyone on your side does something reprehensible. "It was really so dumb of him"—head must shake here—"I just can't understand it." Bad is dumb, breathtakingly dumb and therefore unfathomable; so, conveniently enough, the effort to fathom it might just as well be called off. This one had a big play during Watergate and has had mini-revivals ever since whenever congressmen and senators investigating administration crimes turn out to be guilty of something similar themselves.

5   **Right and not necessarily unconstitutional:** I don't know at quite what point along the way we came to this one, the avoidance of admitting that something is wrong by pointing out that it is not specifically or even inferentially prohibited by the Constitution or, for that matter, mentioned by name in the criminal code or the Ten Commandments. The various parties that prevail in civil-liberty and civil-rights disputes before the Supreme Court have gotten quite good at making this spurious connection: It is legally permissible, therefore it is morally acceptable, possibly even good. But both as individuals and as a society we do things every day that we know to be wrong even though they may not fall within the class of legally punishable acts or tickets to eternal damnation.

6   **Right and sick:** Crime or lesser wrongdoing defined as physical and/or psychological disorder—this one has been around for ages now and as long ago as 1957 was made the butt of a great joke in the "Gee Officer Krupke!" song in "West Side Story." Still, I think no one could have foreseen the degree to which an originally reasonable and humane assumption (that some of what once was regarded as wrongdoing is committed by people acting out of ailment rather than moral choice) would be seized upon and exploited to exonerate every kind of misfeasance. This route is a particular favorite of caught-out office-holders who, when there is at last no other recourse, hold a press conference, announce that they are "sick" in some wise and throw themselves

and their generally stunned families on our mercy. At which point it becomes gross to pick on them; instead we are exhorted to admire them for their "courage."

7   **Right and only to be expected:** You could call this the tit-for-tat school; it is related to the argument that holds moral wrongdoing to be evidence of sickness, but it is much more pervasive and insidious these days. In fact it is probably the most popular dodge, being used to justify, or at least avoid owning up to, every kind of lapse: The other guy, or sometimes just plain circumstance, "asked for it." For instance, I think most of us could agree that setting fire to live people, no matter what their political offense, is—dare I say it?—wrong. Yet if it is done by those for whom we have sympathy in a conflict, there is a tendency to extenuate or disbelieve it, receiving it less as evidence of wrongdoing on our side than as evidence of the severity of the provocation or as enemy-supplied disinformation. Thus the hesitation of many in the antiapartheid movement to confront the brutality of so-called "necklacing," and thus the immediate leap of Sen. Jesse Helms to the defense of the Chilean government after the horrifying incineration of protesters there.

8   **Right and complex:** This one hardly takes a moment to describe; you know it well. "Complex" is the new "controversial," a word used as "controversial" was for so long to flag trouble of some unspecified, dismaying sort that the speaker doesn't want to have to step up to. "Well, you know, it's very complex. . . ." I still can't get this one out of my own vocabulary.

9   In addition to these various sophistries, we also have created a rash of "ethics committees" in our government, of course, whose function seems to be to dither around writing rules that allow people who have clearly done wrong—and should have known it and probably did—to get away because the rules don't cover their offense (see Right and not necessarily unconstitutional). But we don't need any more committees or artful dodges for that matter. As I listen to the moral arguments swirling about us this summer I become ever more persuaded that our real problem is this: The "still, small voice" of conscience has become far too small—and utterly still.

Understanding Meaning

1. What does Greenfield see as "defective" about the way people now describe antisocial behavior?
2. Why do people seem unwilling to use terms like "right" and "wrong"?
3. What do the alternatives to right and wrong Greenfield describes have in common?
4. When do people dismiss or excuse activities they would normally condemn as immoral or illegal?
5. How common is it for people to blame their behavior on an illness or personality disorder? Have we become a nation of victims?
6. *Critical Thinking:* Consider the adage "To understand all is to forgive all." In seeking to understand criminals, for instance, do we find ourselves excusing their behavior? Can you think of recent instances in which people accused of terrible crimes have been presented as victims themselves?

Evaluating Strategy

1. Greenfield opens her essay with a general description of the societal condition. Would a specific example or narrative dramatize her point more clearly?
2. What method does Greenfield use to divide her subject?

Appreciating Language

1. How does your dictionary define *wrong?* What does the term imply?
2. What are the connotations of the words people use in place of "wrong"?
3. What does "necklacing" mean? Does use of this euphemism make a horrible practice acceptable to contemplate?

Connections across the Disciplines

1. William Raspberry (page 310) suggests that accepting limited definitions can cripple people's options. Does defining antisocial behavior as less than immoral or as wrong make society less humane, less safe, and less livable?
2. Gloria Steinem's essay (page 514) reveals how the women's movement has changed our language. What social forces have led us to abandon the word *wrong?*

Writing Suggestions

1. Write an essay classifying your own views of antisocial behavior. Your classification may include brief definitions, descriptions, and narratives.

2. *Collaborative Writing:* Work with a group of students, and discuss Greenfield's essay. Do members of your group share her concern? In a diverse culture are all citizens expected to follow common standards of behavior? Take notes on comments made by the group, and write a few paragraphs classifying or dividing the group's opinions.

JAMES AUSTIN

Dr. James Austin (1925–) graduated from Harvard Medical School and is a specialist in neurology. He devoted more than twenty years to research on the brain. While serving as professor and chairman of the Department of Neurology at the University of Colorado Medical School, he received the American Association of Neuropathologists Prize. Austin has also earned a reputation as a writer with an ability to make complicated scientific issues understandable to general readers.

Four Kinds of Chance

James Austin has written widely on the role of chance or luck in scientific discovery. In this article, written for the Saturday Review *(1974), he classifies the four kinds of chance that occur in scientific research. Luck, he explains, is not as simple as drawing a winning hand in poker. As you read the article, consider how many of the varieties of chance you have experienced.*

1   What is chance? Dictionaries define it as something fortuitous that happens unpredictably without discernable human intention. Chance is unintentional and capricious, but we needn't conclude that chance is immune from human intervention. Indeed, chance plays several distinct roles when humans react creatively with one another and with their environment.

2   We can readily distinguish four varieties of chance if we consider that they each involve a different kind of motor activity and a special kind of sensory receptivity. The varieties of chance also involve distinctive personality traits and differ in the way one particular individual influences them.

3   Chance I is the pure blind luck that comes with no effort on our part. If, for example, you are sitting at a bridge table of four, it's "in the cards" for you to receive a hand of all 13 spades, but it will come up only once in every 6.3 trillion deals. You will ultimately draw this lucky hand—with no intervention on your part—but it does involve a longer wait than most of us have time for.

4   Chance II evokes the kind of luck Charles Kettering had in mind when he said: "Keep on going and the chances are you will stumble on

something, perhaps when you are least expecting it. I have never heard of anyone stumbling on something sitting down."

5   In the sense referred to here, Chance II is not passive, but springs from an energetic, generalized motor activity. A certain basal level of action "stirs up the pot," brings in random ideas that will collide and stick together in fresh combinations, lets chance operate. When someone, *anyone*, does swing into motion and keeps on going, he will increase the number of collisions between events. When a few events are linked together, they can then be exploited to have a fortuitous outcome, but many others, of course, cannot. Kettering was right. Press on. Something will turn up. We may term this the Kettering Principle.

6   In the two previous examples, a unique role of the individual person was either lacking or minimal. Accordingly, as we move on to Chance III, we see blind luck, but in camouflage. Chance presents the clue, the opportunity exists, but it would be missed except by that one person uniquely equipped to observe it, visualize it conceptually, and fully grasp its significance. Chance III involves a special receptivity and discernment unique to the recipient. Louis Pasteur characterized it for all time when he said: "Chance favors only the prepared mind."

7   Pasteur himself had it in full measure. But the classic example of his principle occurred in 1928, when Alexander Fleming's mind instantly fused at least five elements into a conceptually unified nexus. His mental sequences went something like this: (1) I see that a mold has fallen by accident into my culture dish; (2) the staphylococcal colonies residing near it failed to grow; (3) the mold must have secreted something that killed the bacteria; (4) I recall a similar experience once before; (5) if I could separate this new "something" from the mold, it could be used to kill staphylococci that cause human infections.

8   Actually, Fleming's mind was exceptionally well prepared for the penicillin mold. Six years earlier, while he was suffering from a cold, his own nasal drippings had found their way into a culture dish, for reasons not made entirely clear. He noted that nearby bacteria were killed, and astutely followed up the lead. His observations led him to discover a bactericidal enzyme present in nasal mucus and tears, called lysozyme. Lysozyme proved too weak to be of medical use, but imagine how receptive Fleming's mind was to the penicillin mold when it later happened on the scene!

9   One word evokes the quality of the operations involved in the first three kinds of chance. It is *serendipity*. The term describes the facility for encountering unexpected good luck, as the result of: accident

(Chance I), general exploratory behavior (Chance II), or sagacity (Chance III). The word itself was coined by the Englishman-of-letters Horace Walpole, in 1754. He used it with reference to the legendary tales of the Three Princes of Serendip (Ceylon), who quite unexpectedly encountered many instances of good fortune on their travels. In today's parlance, we have usually watered down *serendipity* to mean the good luck that comes solely by accident. We think of it as a result, not an ability. We have tended to lose sight of the element of sagacity, by which term Walpole wished to emphasize that some distinctive personal receptivity is involved.

10   There remains a fourth element in good luck, an unintentional but subtle personal prompting of it. The English Prime Minister Benjamin Disraeli summed up the principle underlying Chance IV when he noted that "we make our fortunes and we call them fate." Disraeli, a politician of considerable practical experience, appreciated that we each shape our own destiny, at least to some degree. One might restate the principle as follows: *Chance favors the individualized action.*

11   In Chance IV the kind of luck is peculiar to one person, and like a personal hobby, it takes on a distinctive individual flavor. This form of chance is one-man-made, and it is as personal as a signature. . . . Chance IV has an elusive, almost miragelike, quality. Like a mirage, it is difficult to get a firm grip on, for it tends to recede as we pursue it and advance as we step back. But we still accept a mirage when we see it, because we vaguely understand the basis for the phenomenon. A strongly heated layer of air, less dense than usual, lies next to the earth, and it bends the light rays as they pass through. The resulting image may be magnified as if by a telescopic lens in the atmosphere, and real objects, ordinarily hidden far out of sight over the horizon, are brought forward and revealed to the eye. What happens in a mirage then, and in this form of chance, not only appears farfetched but indeed is farfetched.

12   About a century ago, a striking example of Chance IV took place in the Spanish cave of Altamira.[1] There, one day in 1879, Don Marcelino de Sautuola was engaged in his hobby of archaeology, searching Altamira for bones and stones. With him was his daughter, Maria, who had asked him if she could come along to the cave that day. The indulgent father had said she could. Naturally enough, he first looked

---

[1] The cave had first been discovered some years before by an enterprising hunting dog in search of game. Curiously, in 1932 the French cave of Lascaux was discovered by still another dog.

where he had always found heavy objects before, on the *floor* of the cave. But Maria, unhampered by any such preconceptions, looked not only at the floor but also all around the cave with the open-eyed wonder of a child! She looked up, exclaimed, and then he looked up, to see incredible works of art on the cave ceiling! The magnificent colored bison and other animals they saw at Altamira, painted more than 15,000 years ago, might lead one to call it "the Sistine Chapel of Prehistory." Passionately pursuing his interest in archaeology, de Sautuola, to his surprise, discovered man's first paintings. In quest of science, he happened upon Art.

13   Yes, a dog did "discover" the cave, and the initial receptivity was his daughter's, but the pivotal reason for the cave paintings' discovery hinged on a long sequence of prior events originating in de Sautuola himself. For when we dig into the background of this amateur excavator, we find he was an exceptional person. Few Spaniards were out probing into caves 100 years ago. The fact that he—not someone else—decided to dig that day in the cave of Altamira was the culmination of his passionate interest in his hobby. Here was a rare man whose avocation had been to educate himself from scratch, as it were, in the science of archaeology and cave exploration. This was no simple passive recognizer of blind luck when it came his way, but a man whose unique interests served as an active creative thrust—someone whose own actions and personality would focus the events that led circuitously but inexorably to the discovery of man's first paintings.

14   Then, too, there is a more subtle manner. How do you give full weight to the personal interests that imbue your child with your own curiosity, that inspire her to ask to join you in your own musty hobby, and that then lead you to agree to her request at the critical moment? For many reasons, at Altamira, more than the special receptivity of Chance III was required—this was a different domain, that of the personality and its actions.

15   A century ago no one had the remotest idea our caveman ancestors were highly creative artists. Weren't their talents rather minor and limited to crude flint chippings? But the paintings at Altamira, like a mirage, would quickly magnify this diminutive view, bring up into full focus a distant, hidden era of man's prehistory, reveal sentient minds and well-developed aesthetic sensibilities to which men of any age might aspire. And like a mirage, the events at Altamira grew out of de Sautuola's heated personal quest and out of the invisible forces of chance we know exist yet cannot touch. Accordingly, one may intro-

duce the term *altamirage* to identify the quality underlying Chance IV. Let us define it as the facility for encountering unexpected good luck as the result of highly individualized action. Altamirage goes well beyond the boundaries of serendipity in its emphasis on the role of personal action in chance.

16   Chance IV is favored by distinctive, if not eccentric, hobbies, personal life-styles, and modes of behavior peculiar to one individual, usually invested with some passion. The farther apart these personal activities are from the area under investigation, the more novel and unexpected will be the creative product of the encounter.

Understanding Meaning

1.   What are the four categories of chance?
2.   What is meant by "blind" or "dumb" luck? Give some examples from your own life.
3.   What is the Kettering Principle? Would Edison's famous trial-and-error experiments to discover a filament for the incandescent lightbulb fit this kind of chance?
4.   How does the Pasteur principle differ from the Kettering Principle?
5.   How did the dog's discovery of a cave differ from "blind luck" or Chance I?
6.   *Critical Thinking:* How often have you discovered things by chance? What role has chance played in your career and education? Does understanding Austin's four kinds of chance enhance your ability to be "lucky" in the future? Can you "make your own kind of luck"?

Evaluating Strategy

1.   What principle does Austin use to divide chance into four categories?
2.   What examples does Austin use to illustrate each type? Are they accessible by a general audience?
3.   Would a chart aid in explaining the four types of chance?
4.   *Other Modes:* How does Austin make use of *definition* and *narration* in developing his classification essay?

Appreciating Language

1.   How much technical language does Austin include?
2.   *Critical Thinking:* Is part of Austin's task in this article to invent new terms to create categories of chance? Do most of our words for chance—"luck," "fortune," "lot"—all suggest the same meaning?

Connections across the Disciplines

1. Relate this article to Carl Sagan's "Why We Need to Understand Science" (page 589) and Darrell Huff's "How to Lie with Statistics" (page 326). Do all these articles suggest a prevailing lack of critical thinking skills?
2. Would any of Austin's types of chance favor scientists researching a problem such as the Ebola virus (page 67)? Why or why not?

Writing Suggestions

1. List a number of instances in your life you considered lucky. Using Austin's four categories, write a paper categorizing your experiences. Have you ever gotten past Chance I?
2. *Collaborative Writing:* Discuss the role of chance with a group of students. Do many people use the idea of chance to dismiss the accomplishments of others? Do people use luck as an excuse for not trying? Talk about these issues, and then collaborate on a short paper suggesting how Austin's concept of chance should be taught to children.

JOHN HOLT

John Holt (1923–1985) was the author of several books about children and education, including How Children Fail *and* How Children Learn. *Having taught in grade and high schools for fourteen years, Holt became a critic of the American educational system. He created and edited* Growing Without Schooling, *a magazine dedicated to home schooling.*

Three Kinds of Discipline

In this section from his book Freedom and Beyond *(1972), Holt classifies three types of discipline that occur in children's lives. Most people assume discipline only comes from authority figures, such as parents and teachers. Holt reveals that discipline also comes from a child's environment.*

1   A child, in growing up, may meet and learn from three different kinds of disciplines. The first and most important is what we might call the Discipline of Nature or of Reality. When he is trying to do something real, if he does the wrong thing or doesn't do the right one, he doesn't get the result he wants. If he doesn't pile one block right on top of another, or tries to build on a slanting surface, his tower falls down. If he hits the wrong key, he hears the wrong note. If he doesn't hit the nail squarely on the head, it bends, and he has to pull it out and start with another. If he doesn't measure properly what he is trying to build, it won't open, close, fit, stand up, fly, float, whistle, or do whatever he wants it to do. If he closes his eyes when he swings, he doesn't hit the ball. A child meets this kind of discipline every time he tries to *do* something, which is why it is so important in school to give children more chances to do things, instead of just reading or listening to someone talk (or pretending to). This discipline is a good teacher. The learner never has to wait long for his answer; it usually comes quickly, often instantly. Also it is clear, and very often points toward the needed correction; from what happened he can not only see that what he did was wrong, but also why, and what he needs to do instead. Finally, and most important, the giver of the answer, call it Nature, is impersonal, impartial, and indifferent. She does not give opinions, or make judgments; she cannot be wheedled, bullied, or fooled; she does not get

angry or disappointed; she does not praise or blame; she does not remember past failures or hold grudges; with her one always gets a fresh
start, this time is the one that counts.

2   The next discipline we might call the Discipline of Culture, of Society, of What People Really Do. Man is a social, a cultural animal.
Children sense around them this culture, this network of agreements,
customs, habits, and rules binding the adults together. They want to
understand it and be a part of it. They watch very carefully what people
around them are doing and want to do the same. They want to do
right, unless they become convinced they can't do right. Thus children rarely misbehave seriously in church, but sit as quietly as they
can. The example of all those grownups is contagious. Some mysterious ritual is going on, and children, who like rituals, want to be part of
it. In the same way, the little children that I see at concerts or operas,
though they may fidget a little, or perhaps take a nap now and then,
rarely make any disturbance. With all those grownups sitting there,
neither moving nor talking, it is the most natural thing in the world to
imitate them. Children who live among adults who are habitually courteous to each other, and to them, will soon learn to be courteous. Children who live surrounded by people who speak a certain way will
speak that way, however much we may try to tell them that speaking
that way is bad or wrong.

3   The third discipline is the one most people mean when they speak
of discipline—the Discipline of Superior Force, of sergeant to private,
of "you do what I tell you or I'll make you wish you had." There is
bound to be some of this in a child's life. Living as we do surrounded
by things that can hurt children, or that children can hurt, we cannot
avoid it. We can't afford to let a small child find out from experience
the danger of playing in a busy street, or of fooling with the pots on the
top of a stove, or of eating up the pills in the medicine cabinet. So,
along with other precautions, we say to him, "Don't play in the street,
or touch things on the stove, or go into the medicine cabinet, or I'll
punish you." Between him and the danger too great for him to imagine we put a lesser danger, but one he can imagine and maybe therefore wants to avoid. He can have no idea of what it would be like to be
hit by a car, but he can imagine being shouted at, or spanked, or sent
to his room. He avoids these substitutes for the greater danger until he
can understand it and avoid it for its own sake. But we ought to use
this discipline only when it is necessary to protect the life, health,
safety, or well-being of people or other living creatures, or to prevent

destruction of things that people care about. We ought not to assume too long, as we usually do, that a child cannot understand the real nature of the danger from which we want to protect him. The sooner he avoids the danger, not to escape our punishment, but as a matter of good sense, the better. He can learn that faster than we think. In Mexico, for example, where people drive their cars with a good deal of spirit, I saw many children no older than five or four walking unattended on the streets. They understood about cars, they knew what to do. A child whose life is full of the threat and fear of punishment is locked into babyhood. There is no way for him to grow up, to learn to take responsibility for his life and acts. Most important of all, we should not assume that having to yield to the threat of our superior force is good for the child's character. It is never good for *anyone's* character. To bow to superior force makes us feel impotent and cowardly for not having had the strength or courage to resist. Worse, it makes us resentful and vengeful. We can hardly wait to make someone pay for our humiliation, yield to us as we were once made to yield. No, if we cannot always avoid using the discipline of Superior Force, we should at least use it as seldom as we can.

4   There are places where all three disciplines overlap. Any very demanding human activity combines in it the disciplines of Superior Force, of Culture, and of Nature. The novice will be told, "Do it this way, never mind asking why, just do it that way, that is the way we always do it." But it probably *is* just the way they always do it, and usually for the very good reason that it is a way that has been found to work. Think, for example, of ballet training. The student in a class is told to do this exercise, or that; to stand so; to do this or that with his head, arms, shoulders, abdomen, hips, legs, feet. He is constantly corrected. There is no argument. But behind these seemingly autocratic demands by the teacher lie many decades of custom and tradition, and behind that, the necessities of dancing itself. You cannot make the moves of classical ballet unless over many years you have acquired, and renewed every day, the needed strength and suppleness in scores of muscles and joints. Nor can you do the difficult motions, making them look easy, unless you have learned hundreds of easier ones first. Dance teachers may not always agree on all the details of teaching these strengths and skills. But no novice could learn them all by himself. You could not go for a night or two to watch the ballet and then, without any other knowledge at all, teach yourself how to do it. In the same way, you would be unlikely to learn any complicated and difficult

human activity without drawing heavily on the experience of those who know it better. But the point is that the authority of these experts or teachers stems from, grows out of their greater competence and experience, the fact that what they do *works*, not the fact that they happen to be the teacher and as such have the power to kick a student out of the class. And the further point is that children are always and everywhere attracted to that competence, and ready and eager to submit themselves to a discipline that grows out of it. We hear constantly that children will never do anything unless compelled to by bribes or threats. But in their private lives, or in extracurricular activities in school, in sports, music, drama, art, running a newspaper, and so on, they often submit themselves willingly and wholeheartedly to very intense disciplines, simply because they want to learn to do a given thing well. Our Little-Napoleon football coaches, of whom we have too many and hear far too much, blind us to the fact that millions of children work hard every year getting better at sports and games without coaches barking and yelling at them.

Understanding Meaning

1. What lessons in discipline do children learn from experience?
2. How does Holt *define* discipline? Is learning about limits of experience in the physical world, such as the effect of gravity, a kind of discipline?
3. Does Holt's Discipline of Culture indicate that parents should make sure their children participate in adult activities, such as attending concerts and religious services?
4. What is Holt's opinion of parental authority and direction? When does he feel that strict discipline is justified?
5. *Critical Thinking:* What does Holt's view of discipline reveal about his attitude toward children? How much discipline can children learn on their own? Is strict discipline from parents and teachers effective? Would some people view Holt as being permissive?

Evaluating Strategy

1. How does Holt organize his classification?
2. How effective are the titles, which he capitalizes, for defining each type of discipline?
3. *Other Modes:* Where does Holt include *definition* and *narration* in his essay?

Appreciating Language

1. What connotations does the word *discipline* have?
2. How does Holt's word choice reveal his bias toward and against the different types of discipline?

Connections across the Disciplines

1. How does the structure of Holt's essay compare to that of Martin Luther King Jr.'s (page 401)? Are both writers really using classification as a means to persuade readers?
2. Review Mary Mebane's essay (page 392), and analyze the kinds of discipline she faced in childhood.

Writing Suggestions

1. Holt wrote this essay before the tide of school violence and teenage homicide dominated the media. In an era when many public schools require students to wear uniforms and parents are concerned about teenage pregnancy and gangs, would many reject Holt's views? Write an essay expressing your views.
2. *Collaborative Writing:* Working with a group of students, discuss the issue of rearing and disciplining children. Consider your own childhood. If any of the members are parents, ask their honest opinion of Holt's essay. Take notes on the comments, and work together to write a *definition* of good childhood discipline.

BLENDING THE MODES

NORTHROP FRYE

Northrop Frye (1912–1991) was born in Quebec and received a degree in philosophy and English from Victoria College. He studied theology at Emmanuel College in Toronto and was ordained by the United Church of Canada in 1936. Frye obtained a master's degree from Oxford and took a teaching position at Victoria College. Frye published a number of books of literary criticism, including Anatomy of Criticism *(1957),* The Well-Tempered Critic *(1962), and* The Critical Path *(1971).*

Our Three Languages

In this section from The Educated Imagination, *Frye classifies language into three levels of use. Notice how he uses an extended* example *of placing a person on a remote island to illustrate how we use language.*

1   Suppose you're shipwrecked on an uninhabited island in the South Seas. The first thing you do is to take a long look at the world around you, a world of sky and sea and earth and stars and trees and hills. You see this world as objective, as something set over against you and not yourself or related to you in any way. And you notice two things about this objective world. In the first place, it doesn't have any conversation. It's full of animals and plants and insects going on with their own business, but there's nothing that responds to you: it has no morals and no intelligence, or at least none that you can grasp. It may have a shape and a meaning, but it doesn't seem to be a human shape or a human meaning. Even if there's enough to eat and no dangerous animals, you feel lonely and frightened and unwanted in such a world.

2   In the second place, you find that looking at the world, as something set over against you, splits your mind in two. You have an intellect that feels curious about it and wants to study it, and you have feelings or emotions that see it as beautiful or austere or terrible. You know that both these attitudes have some reality, at least for you. If the ship you were wrecked in was a Western ship, you'd probably feel that your intellect tells you more about what's really there in the outer world, and that your emotions tell you more about what's going

on inside you. If your background were Oriental, you'd be more likely to reverse this and say that the beauty or terror was what was really there, and that your instinct to count and classify and measure and pull to pieces was what was inside your mind. But whether your point of view is Western or Eastern, intellect and emotion never get together in your mind as long as you're simply looking at the world. They alternate, and keep you divided between them.

3   The language you use on this level of the mind is the language of consciousness or awareness. It's largely a language of nouns and adjectives. You have to have names for things, and you need qualities like "wet" or "green" or "beautiful" to describe how things seem to you. This is the speculative or contemplative position of the mind, the position in which the arts and sciences begin, although they don't stay there very long. The sciences begin by accepting the facts and the evidence about an outside world without trying to alter them. Science proceeds by accurate measurement and description, and follows the demands of the reason rather than the emotions. What it deals with is there, whether we like it or not. The emotions are unreasonable: for them it's what they like and don't like that comes first. We'd be naturally inclined to think that the arts follow the path of emotion, in contrast to the sciences. Up to a point they do, but there's a complicating factor.

4   That complicating factor is the contrast between "I like this" and "I don't like this." In this Robinson Crusoe life I've assigned you, you may have moods of complete peacefulness and joy, moods when you accept your island and everything around you. You wouldn't have such moods very often, and when you had them, they'd be moods of identification, when you felt that the island was a part of you and you a part of it. That is not the feeling of consciousness or awareness, where you feel split off from everything that's not your perceiving self. Your habitual state of mind is the feeling of separation which goes with being conscious, and the feeling "this is not a part of me" soon becomes "this is not what I want." Notice the word "want": we'll be coming back to it.

5   So you soon realize that there's a difference between the world you're living in and the world you want to live in. The world you want to live in is a human world, not an objective one: it's not an environment but a home; it's not the world you see but the world you build out of what you see. You go to work to build a shelter or plant a garden, and as soon as you start to work you've moved into a different level of

human life. You're not separating only yourself from nature now, but constructing a human world and separating it from the rest of the world. Your intellect and emotions are now both engaged in the same activity, so there's no longer any real distinction between them. As soon as you plant a garden or a crop, you develop the conception of a "weed," the plant you don't want in there. But you can't say that "weed" is either an intellectual or an emotional conception because it's both at once. Further, you go to work because you feel you have to, and because you want something at the end of the work. That means that the important categories of your life are no longer the subject and the object, the watcher and the things being watched: the important categories are what you have to do and what you want to do—in other words, necessity and freedom.

6   One person by himself is not a complete human being, so I'll provide you with another shipwrecked refugee of the opposite sex and an eventual family. Now you're a member of a human society. This human society after a while will transform the island into something with a human shape. What that human shape is, is revealed in the shape of the work you do: the buildings, such as they are, the paths through the woods, the planted crops fenced off against whatever animals want to eat them. These things, these rudiments of city, highway, garden and farm, are the human form of nature, or the form of human nature, whichever you like. This is the area of the applied arts and sciences, and it appears in our society as engineering and agriculture and medicine and architecture. In this area we can never say clearly where the art stops and the science begins, or vice versa.

7   The language you use on this level is the language of practical sense, a language of verbs or words of action and movement. The practical world, however, is a world where actions speak louder than words. In some ways it's a higher level of existence than the speculative level, because it's doing something about the world instead of just looking at it, but in itself it's a much more primitive level. It's the process of adapting to the environment, or rather of transforming the environment in the interests of one species, that goes on among animals and plants as well as human beings. The animals have a good many of our practical skills: some insects make pretty fair architects, and beavers know quite a lot about engineering. In this island, probably, and certainly if you were alone, you'd have about the ranking of a second-rate animal. What makes our practical life really human is a third level of the mind, a level where consciousness and practical skill come together.

8   This third level is a vision or model in your mind of what you want to construct. There's that word "want" again. The actions of man are prompted by desire, and some of these desires are needs, like food and warmth and shelter. One of these needs is sexual, the desire to reproduce and bring more human beings into existence. But there's also a desire to bring a social human form into existence: the form of cities and gardens and farms that we call civilization. Many animals and insects have this social form too, but man knows that he has it: he can compare what he does with what he can imagine being done. So we begin to see where the imagination belongs in the scheme of human affairs. It's the power of constructing possible models of human experience. In the world of the imagination, anything goes that's imaginatively possible, but nothing really happens. If it did happen, it would move out of the world of imagination into the world of action.

9   We have three levels of the mind now, and a language for each of them, which in English-speaking societies means an English for each of them. There's the level of consciousness and awareness, where the most important thing is the difference between me and everything else. The English of this level is the English of ordinary conversation, which is mostly monologue, as you'll soon realize if you do a bit of eavesdropping, or listening to yourself. We can call it the language of self-expression. Then there's the level of social participation, the working or technological language of teachers and preachers and politicians and advertisers and lawyers and journalists and scientists. We've already called this the language of practical sense. Then there's the level of imagination, which produces the literary language of poems and plays and novels. They're not really different languages, of course, but three different reasons for using words.

Understanding Meaning

1. What are the three levels of language we use, according to Frye?
2. What do these levels of language reveal about how we think and how we interact with the world?
3. How does language separate human beings from other animals?
4. *Critical Thinking:* How does this classification of language help you understand the role of language in human thought? At what age do we acquire or use each level? Do some people function at one level more than others in thinking and communicating?

Evaluating Strategy

1. Frye originally delivered this essay as a radio lecture designed for a general audience. Does his use of the deserted island create concrete examples readers can visualize?
2. What methods does Frye use to explain each level? What other modes does he include in this essay?

Appreciating Language

1. Would high school students be able to understand this classification? Are there words requiring definitions or references that are remote? How might you revise it for a tenth-grade English class?
2. What does Frye mean by the "objective" world?

Connections across the Disciplines

1. Relate Frye's essay to Gloria Steinem's "Words and Change" (page 514). Do we really appreciate how language shapes our view of the world and of other people? If our vocabulary is limited, is our ability to express ourselves restricted to simplistic assertions?
2. Examine "Interrogation of Lee Harvey Oswald" (page 93). What level of language did the FBI agent use in this report? Why?

Writing Suggestions

1. Follow up on Frye's example of being shipwrecked on an uninhabited island, and classify the ways personality types would confront their situation—those who would seek immediate escape by fashioning a raft; those who would seek food and shelter; those who might pray; those who would not cope; and so forth.
2. *Collaborative Writing:* Discuss Frye's levels of language with a group of other students, and then work together to write a short process paper explaining how to incorporate his ideas into a unit on critical thinking.

WRITING BEYOND THE CLASSROOM

BLACK'S LAW DICTIONARY

Black's Law Dictionary is a standard reference used by attorneys, paralegals, administrators, and law enforcement personnel. Like any dictionary, it serves to define terms.

Homicide

When reading this entry, which includes a classification, pay attention to the specialized use of language. Note that the authors stress that the word "homicide" is neutral and does not even imply that a crime has been committed. Notice how television and movies have distorted the complexities of this legal issue.

1   **Homicide.** The killing of one human being by the act, procurement, or omission of another. A person is guilty of criminal homicide if he purposely, knowingly, recklessly or negligently causes the death of another human being. Criminal homicide is murder, manslaughter or negligent homicide. Model Penal Code, §210.1; 18 U.S.C.A. §1111 et seq. *See* Manslaughter; Murder.

2   Homicide is not necessarily a crime. It is a necessary ingredient of the crimes of murder and manslaughter, but there are other cases in which homicide may be committed without criminal intent and without criminal consequences, as, where it is done in the lawful execution of a judicial sentence, in self-defense, or as the only possible means of arresting an escaping felon. The term "homicide" is neutral; while it describes the act, it pronounces no judgment on its moral or legal quality. People v. Mahon, 77 Ill.App.3d 413, 395 N.E.2d 950, 958. *See Excusable homicide; Justifiable homicide, below.*

CLASSIFICATION

3   Homicide is ordinarily classified as "justifiable," "excusable," and "felonious." For the definitions of these terms, and of some other compound terms, see *below.*

4   *Culpable homicide.* Described as a crime varying from the very lowest culpability, up to the very verge of murder.

5   *Excusable homicide.* The killing of a human being, either by misadventure or in self-defense. Such homicide consists of a perpetrator's acting in a manner which the law does not prohibit, such as self-defense or accidental homicide. Law v. State, 21 Md.App. 13, 318 A.2d 859, 869. The name itself imports some fault, error, or omission, so trivial, however, that the law excuses it from guilt of felony, though in strictness it judges it deserving of some little degree of punishment. It is of two sorts,—either *per infortunium*, by misadventure, or *se defendendo*, upon a sudden affray. Homicide *per infortunium* is where a man, doing a lawful act, without any intention of hurt, unfortunately kills another; but, if death ensues from any unlawful act, the offense is manslaughter, and not misadventure. Homicide *se defendendo* is where a man kills another upon a sudden affray, merely in his own defense, or in defense of his wife, child, parent, or servant, and not from any vindictive feeling. *See* Self-defense; also *Justifiable homicide, below.*

6   *Felonious homicide.* The wrongful killing of a human being, of any age or either sex, without justification or excuse in law; of which offense there are two degrees, manslaughter and murder.

7   *Homicide by misadventure.* The accidental killing of another, where the slayer is doing a lawful act, unaccompanied by any criminally careless or reckless conduct. The same as "homicide *per infortunium*." *See* Manslaughter.

8   *Homicide by necessity.* A species of justifiable homicide, because it arises from some unavoidable necessity, without any will, intention, or desire, and without any inadvertence or negligence in the party killing, and therefore without any shadow of blame. *See* Self-defense.

9   *Homicide per infortunium.* Homicide by misfortune, or accidental homicide; as where a man doing a lawful act without any intention of hurt, accidentally kills another; a species of excusable homicide. *See* Negligent homicide.

10 *Homicide se defendendo.* Homicide in self-defense; the killing of a person in self-defense upon a sudden affray, where the slayer had no other possible (or, at least, probable) means of escaping from his assailant. A species of excusable homicide. *See* Self-defense.

11 *Justifiable homicide.* Such as is committed intentionally, but without any evil design, and under such circumstances of necessity or duty as render the act proper, and relieve the party from any shadow of blame; as where a

sheriff lawfully executes a sentence of death upon a malefactor, or where the killing takes place in the endeavor to prevent the commission of felony which could not be otherwise avoided, or, as a matter of right, such as self-defense or other causes provided for by statute. *See* Self-defense; also *Excusable homicide, above.*

12 *Negligent homicide.* Criminal homicide constitutes negligent homicide when it is committed negligently. Model Penal Code, §210.4. *See* Negligent homicide; also *Vehicular homicide, below.*

13 *Reckless homicide.* See that title.

14 *Vehicular homicide.* The killing of a human being by the operation of an automobile, airplane, motorboat or other motor vehicle in a manner which creates an unreasonable risk of injury to the person or property of another and which constitutes a material deviation from the standard of care which a reasonable person would observe under the same circumstances.

Understanding Meaning

1. Does it surprise you to learn that homicide may not be a crime? Do most people equate that term with "murder"?
2. What does the law regard as the most serious, most criminal forms of homicide?
3. Provide your own examples of felonious homicide, homicide by misadventure, and homicide by necessity.
4. *Critical Thinking:* What values seem to play a role in determining what is excusable and what is criminal homicide?

Evaluating Strategy

1. How well organized is this entry? Is it easy to follow?
2. How important are the examples used to support the definitions?

Appreciating Language

1. What do the tone, style, and word choice reveal about the intended audience?
2. How might you reword this entry for a general audience?

Connections across the Disciplines

1. How does the writing style of this entry compare to Kimberly Crawford's article written for the *FBI Law Enforcement Journal* (page 366)?
2. How does the style differ from the chart developed for *Communication Styles: United States and Taiwan* (page 290)?

Writing Suggestions

1. Select one of the types of homicide listed in the entry, and provide a fictional example in a brief narrative.
2. *Collaborative Writing:* Discuss the types of homicide listed in the entry with fellow students, and ask members to provide their own version of justifiable homicide. Work together to create a definition.

Textbooks and reference works often use division and classification to explain concepts, processes, objects, or conditions.

Kinds of Sentences

This section from a grammar handbook explains four types of sentences by classifying them according to number of and type of clauses. Independent clauses contain a subject and verb and make a complete statement: I drive to school. *Dependent clauses contain a subject and verb but do not make a complete statement and are not a sentence:* Because I drive to school.

7E   KINDS OF SENTENCES

1   Independent clauses appear alone or in combinations—with other independent clauses or with dependent clauses. One method of classifying sentences is based on the number and kinds of clauses in a single construction. According to this classification system, there are four categories of sentences: simple, compound, complex, and compound-complex.

(1) Simple sentence

2   A **simple sentence** is made up of only one independent clause. The sentence may contain modifiers and compound elements (for example, compound subjects and verbs); but it may not contain more than one subject-predicate structure.

3   Cigarette smoke contains carbon monoxide.
4   For most college students, computers and calculators have become essential.
5   The Rhone flows south through France and then empties into the Mediterranean.

(2) Compound sentence

6   A **compound sentence** is made up of two or more independent clauses. The primary ways to coordinate independent clauses are with commas and coordinating conjunctions *(and, but, or, for, nor, so, yet)* and with semicolons.

7   For centuries, Brittany was an independent state, but now the area is part of France.
8   The restaurant was dark, the air was filled with smoke, and the music was deafening.
9   Socrates wrote nothing; his thoughts are known only through the works of Plato and Xenophon.

(3) Complex sentence

10   A **complex sentence** is made up of one independent clause and one or more dependent clauses—adverb, adjective, or noun.

11   Although most rifle experts have 20/20 vision, pistol experts are often very nearsighted.
12   The game involves three contestants who spin a roulette wheel.
13   Whoever could solve the riddle of the Sphinx would be spared her wrath.

(4) Compound-complex sentence

14   A **compound-complex sentence** is made up of two or more independent clauses and one or more dependent clauses.

15   London's Great Exhibition, which opened in 1851, was designed to show human progress; it brought together in the "Crystal Palace" industrial displays remarkable for their day.
16   Alchemists believed that they could change lesser metals into gold, and although they failed, they helped establish the science of chemistry.
17   The fathom once was the distance that a Viking could encompass in a hug; a gauge was the distance that lay between the wheels of a Roman chariot; an acre was an area that could be plowed in one day by a team of two oxen.

Understanding Meaning

1. Provide an example of each sentence type.
2. How does understanding the four types of sentences help with writing?

Evaluating Strategy

1. How effective is the method of organizing this information?
2. Do the visual effects such as bold print, underscores, numerals, and italics assist readers?
3. *Other Modes:* How are the different sentence types *defined?*

Appreciating Language

1. What does the level of language assume about the readers, who are mostly college students?
2. Are these terms initially misleading? Does "simple" suggest a short or easily read sentence? Would the term "complex sentence" lead you to expect a long, complicated statement?

Connections across the Disciplines

1. Compare this entry to that from *Black's Law Dictionary* (page 427). How important are visual effects in reference books?
2. Compare this explanation with one available in your own grammar book. What are the differences? Is one easier to read than the other?

Writing Suggestions

1. Rewrite this entry for a junior high school audience.
2. Analyze your own use of sentences by reviewing one of your previous papers. How often do you use each type?

STRATEGIES FOR DIVISION AND CLASSIFICATION WRITING

1. **Determine which mode you will use.** Which method will best suit your purpose: dividing your subject into subtopics or measuring subtopics against a common standard?

2. **Select an effective method of division.** If you were writing about improving the public schools, for example, it might be more effective to divide the paper by discipline, discussing how to improve math skills, writing ability, and knowledge of geography rather than improving elementary schools, junior high schools, and high schools.

3. **Avoid divisions that oversimplify or distort meaning.** Your paper should aid in helping readers grasp a complex subject without trivializing or misstating the issues. You may wish to qualify your division and explain to readers that exceptions and situations may exist where the division may not apply.

4. **Avoid overlapping categories.** When writing both division and classification make sure the categories are distinct. Do not separate cars into "domestic, foreign, and antique models" because antique cars would clearly have to belong to the first two groups.

5. **Use a single, clearly defined standard to classify subjects.** Classification relies on a clearly stated standard that is used to measure all the items you discuss. Avoid mixing standards. In some instances you may have to explain or justify why you are using a particular standard.

6. **In classification writing, make sure all topics fit into *one* category.** In a properly written classification paper, every unit should fit only one category. For example, a term paper is either an A− or a B+. In addition, make sure no items are left over that cannot be logically placed.

SUGGESTED TOPICS FOR DIVISION AND CLASSIFICATION WRITING
General Assignments

Write a division essay on any of the following topics. Your division may make use of standard categories or ones you invent. Remember to clearly state the way you are dividing your subject. Each subject or example should be supported with definitions, brief narratives, or descriptions.

- Dates you have had
- Student housing on campus and off
- Baseball, basketball, or football teams
- Popular music
- Careers for women

Write a classification essay on any of the following topics. Make sure to use a single method of rating the subtopics, from best to worst, easiest to hardest, or least desirable to most desirable, for example.

- Jobs you have had
- Student services, including health, police, food, etc.
- Vacation destinations
- Bosses or professors you have known
- Talk shows or news programs

Writing in Context

1. Assume you have been asked by a national magazine to write about students' political attitudes. You may develop your essay by division or classification. You can discuss politics in general terms of liberal and conservative or restrict your comments on students' attitudes toward a particular issue, such as abortion, capital punishment, or health care.
2. Write a humorous paper about campus fashion by dividing students into types. Invent titles or labels for each group, and supply enough details so readers can readily fit the people they meet into one of your categories.

STUDENT PAPER: DIVISION AND CLASSIFICATION

This paper was written in response to the following assignment:

> *Write a 500-word paper classifying people, objects, or issues you have observed on campus. Make sure that you choose meaningful divisions and describe each category fully.*

HISPANICS ON CAMPUS

1   Students, faculty, and administrators tend to refer to "Hispanics" as if all Latino and Latina students belonged to a single homogeneous

group. Actually, there are four distinct groups of Hispanic students. Outsiders may only see slight discrepancies in dress and behavior, but there are profound differences which occasionally border on suspicion and hostility. Their differences are best measured by their attitude toward and their degree of acceptance of mainstream American values and culture.

2   The least assimilated and most alien group of these students are politically active immigrants or children of immigrants. These are the students who sponsored the recent protest against Western Civilization courses. Most of them were born in Mexico or Puerto Rico. English is their second language and a perceived cultural barrier. Because of this, they tend to see European culture as oppressive, an arbitrary hurdle blocking their progress. They are keenly sensitive to negative stereotypes of Hispanics and resent media portrayals of bandits, drug dealers, and gang members.

3   Equally alien to American culture but less politically active are the foreign students from Latin America. Whether they are from Mexico, Chile, or Argentina, they speak excellent English. Many have lived or studied in Europe. As citizens of their native countries, they have no insecurities about their ethnic identities and seem willing to mix socially with Americans, but only if they share the same class values. Unlike the immigrants, they consider themselves linked to European culture. Many speak French and German in addition to Spanish and Italian. Often they seem to feel more at home with foreign students from Europe than either Americans or other Hispanic students.

4   The most assimilated and largest group of Hispanic students are second and third generation Latinos and Latinas. Few speak more than a few Spanish phrases. Many pronounce their names with an Anglo accent, so that they say "Rammer-ez" for Rameriz. They interact with all students and consider themselves Americans. Their parents work for IBM, sell real estate, or own restaurants. These students are not politically active. They use the terms "Chicano," "Latino," and "Spanish" interchangeably. Although many participate in Hispanic cultural activities on campus, they generally avoid political rallies. Only a few consider themselves radical, and some, especially the Cuban-Americans, are extremely conservative.

5   There is a group of Hispanics who are so assimilated into mainstream American culture that I call them invisible. Because of inter-
marriage, many Hispanics have last names like O'Brien, Edelman, and
Kowalski. My father is third generation Irish. While working on an engineering project in Mexico, he met my mother, who ironically had an
Irish grandmother. I was born in San Diego but spent almost every summer in Cancun with my aunt. I speak and write Spanish. I subscribe to
Mexican magazines. I serve on numerous Hispanic organizations. But
because of my blonde hair and my last name, Callaghan, I am frequently viewed as an outsider by Hispanics who don't speak Spanish.

Questions for Review and Revision

1. What's the student's thesis?
2. How does the student define her standard of measurement?
3. What value does this classification have in understanding Hispanic
    students?
4. Is each class of students clearly defined? Can you think of any students
    you know who would not fit in one of the categories?
5. Does the student include enough examples or descriptions to fully ex-
    plain each category of students?
6. Read the essay aloud. Can you detect weak or awkward passages that
    need revision?

Writing Suggestions

1. Using this paper as a model, write a similar classification paper about stu-
    dents on your campus. Classify students by academic performance, school
    spirit, support of athletic teams, or involvement in campus activities or
    politics. Remember to use a single standard or method of evaluation.
2. *Collaborative Writing:* Discuss this essay with other students. Do students
    in other ethnic groups fit a pattern similar to the Hispanics at the writer's
    college? Work together to select a group, and write a short paper that clas-
    sifies them into different types.

DIVISION AND CLASSIFICATION CHECKLIST

Before submitting your paper, review these points.

1. Have you clearly defined your goal—to write a division or classification paper?

2. Do you make meaningful divisions or classifications, or does your paper oversimplify a complex subject?

3. Are your categories clearly defined?

4. Do you avoid overlapping categories?

5. Do you use parallel patterns to develop categories and items?

6. In classification, do you use a single standard of evaluation?

7. Do all the parts of your subject clearly fit into a single category? Are there any items left over?

 WebTutor

See www.harcourtcollege.com/english/sundance
for information on writing division and
classification

8

PROCESS

EXPLAINING HOW THINGS WORK AND GIVING DIRECTIONS

WHAT IS PROCESS?

Process writing shows how things work or how specific tasks are accomplished. The first type of process writing is used to demonstrate how a complex procedure takes place. Biology textbooks describe how the heart operates by separating its actions into a series of steps. This chain-of-events explanation also can illustrate how an engine works, how inflation affects the economy, how the IRS audits an account, or how police respond to a 911 call. Process writing is a directed form of narration that explains how a procedure or event occurs.

The second type of process writing instructs readers how to complete a specific task. Recipes, owners' manuals, textbooks, and home repair articles provide readers with step-by-step directions to bake a cake, rotate tires, set up a stereo system, write a research paper, lose weight, or fix a leaking roof. These instructions are challenging to create because writers may be unable to determine how much background information to provide and may easily forget a critical piece of information.

Explaining How Things Work

Just as division writing seeks to explain an abstract or complex subject by separating it into smaller categories, process writing separates the workings of complicated operations into distinct steps. In her essay "Birth of a TV Show: A Drama All Its Own" (page 445), Elizabeth Kolbert explains the process of how a writer's idea or concept becomes a television program:

> At the start of the season, executives from each of the networks—CBS, NBC, ABC and Fox—listen to hundreds of writers pitch new sitcoms. The fortunate few dozen advance to the next step: writing scripts for the prospective shows. After examining those scripts, the networks narrow their choices to 8 or 10, for which pilot episodes will be filmed. From these pilots, they will eventually make four or five new sitcoms.

In writing explanations such as this, it is important to consider the knowledge base of your readers. You may have to define technical terms; make use of illustrative analogies, such as comparing the heart to a pump; and tell brief narratives so readers will understand the process. Some writers will use an extended analogy, comparing a nuclear power plant to a tea kettle or a computer virus to a brush fire. One of the challenges of explanatory writing can be deciding which details to leave out and where to make separations.

Critical Thinking for Writing Explanations

1. **Study the process carefully.** Note principal features that need emphasis. Identify areas that are commonly confused or might be difficult for readers to understand.
2. **Determine how much background information is needed.** Your readers may require, for example, a basic knowledge of how normal cells divide before being able to comprehend the way cancer cells develop. In some instances, you may have to address common misconceptions. If you were to explain criminal investigation methods, you first might have to point out how actual police operations differ from those depicted on television.
3. **Determine the beginning and end of the process.** In some cases the process may have an obvious beginning and end. Leaves emerge from buds, flower, grow, turn color, and fall off. But the process of a recession may have no clear-cut beginning and no defined end. If you were to write a paper about the process of getting a divorce, would you stop when the final papers are signed or continue to discuss alimony and child visitation rights? When does a divorce end?
4. **Separate the process into logical stages.** Readers will naturally assume all the stages are equally significant unless you indicate their value or im-

portance. Minor points should not be overemphasized by being isolated in separate steps.

5. **Alert readers to possible variations.** If the process is subject to change or alternative forms, present readers with the most common type. Indicate, either in the introduction or in each stage, that exceptions or variations to the pattern of events exist.

6. **Use transitional phrases to link the stages.** Statements such as *at the same time, two hours later,* and *if additional bleeding occurs* help readers follow explanations.

7. **Stress the importance of time relationships.** Process writing creates a slow-motion effect that can be misleading if the chain of events naturally occurs within a short period. You can avoid this confusion by opening with a "real time" description of the process:

> The test car collided with the barrier at thirty-five miles an hour. In less than a tenth of a second the bumper crumpled, sending shock waves through the length of the vehicle as the fenders folded back like a crushed beer can. At the same instant sensors triggered the air bag to deploy with a rapid explosion so that it inflated before the test dummy struck the steering wheel.

The rest of the paper might repeat this process for four or five pages, slowly relating each stage in great detail.

8. **Use images, details, narratives, and examples to enrich the description of each stage.** Give readers a full appreciation of each stage by describing it in details they can grasp. Avoid long strings of nonessential, technical language. Use comparisons and narratives to provide readers with clear pictures of events and situations.

9. **Review the final draft for undefined technical terms.** Use a level of language your readers understand. Include technical terms only when necessary, and define ones your readers may not know or may find confusing.

Giving Directions

Directions are step-by-step instructions guiding readers to accomplish a specific goal or task. Process writing can include advice such as how to buy a house or negotiate a loan. In "Desperation Writing" (page 461), Peter Elbow offers students this initial advice about writing under stress:

> Just write and keep writing. . . . Just write and keep writing. It will probably come in waves. After a flurry, stop and take a brief rest. But don't stop too long. Don't think about what you are writing or what you

have written or else you will overload the circuit again. Keep writing as though you are drugged or drunk. Keep doing this till you feel you have a lot of material that might be useful; or, if necessary, till you can't stand it any more—even if you doubt that there's anything useful there.

Some writers find it more effective to tell people what *not* to do. Negative instructions work best when you are trying to get readers to change their habits or to avoid common mistakes. Fran Martin (page 466), a nurse with extensive experience in medical malpractice trials, offers tips on avoiding four common errors made in charting:

> 1. **Not charting the correct time when events occurred.** Suppose a procedure is charted in several different places, but each entry indicates that it was done at a different time. Lawyers use these times to reconstruct the sequence of events, and inconsistencies like this can make their case—they can easily raise questions about the accuracy of the entire record.

Martin employs numbered steps and italicized topic sentences to highlight major points. She also dramatizes the importance of her advice by citing a case in which a nurse's documentation errors cost a hospital $450,000.

When giving instructions, you may find it helpful to add visual aids such as bold type, capital letters, and underlining, as well as pictures, graphs, and charts. Visual aids are commonly used in documents that must be read quickly or referred to while working. A recipe printed in standard paragraphs instead of lists and numbered steps would be extremely difficult to follow while one is cooking. The instructions for cleaning car battery terminals on page 493 illustrate how directions can be arranged for quick, accurate reading.

Critical Thinking for Writing Directions

1. **Consider your readers carefully.** Determine your readers' current knowledge. They may need background information to understand the process. Readers may also have misconceptions that must be cleared up.
2. **Make sure the directions are self-contained.** A recipe, for example, should list *all* the ingredients, appliances, and instructions needed. *Readers should not be directed to another source for information to complete the process.*
3. **Consider using numbered steps.** Readers find it easier to follow numbered steps and can mark their places if interrupted.

4. **Provide complete instructions.** Do not tell readers to "put the cake in the oven for thirty minutes or until done." Someone baking the cake for the first time has no idea what the cake is supposed to look like at that point—should it be evenly browned, or can the center remain soft? When is it "done"?

5. **Warn readers of possible events they may misinterpret as mistakes.** If, at some point in the process, the mixture readers are working with suddenly changes color or a machine they are operating makes excess noise, they may assume they have made a mistake and stop. If a person assembling a desk discovers the legs are wobbly, he or she may assume the product is defective. If this is normal, if the legs tighten up when the drawers are installed, let readers know what to expect.

6. **Give negative instructions.** Tell readers what not to do, especially if you know people have a tendency to misuse materials, skip difficult steps, or substitute cheaper materials.

7. **Warn readers of any hazards to their safety, health, property, or the environment.** Warnings about dangerous chemicals, fire hazards, and electrical shocks should be clearly stated and placed in large print. *In giving instructions to customers and employees, you are assuming a legal liability.*

STRATEGIES FOR READING PROCESS

As you read the process entries in this chapter, keep these questions in mind.

Meaning

1. What is the writer's goal, to explain or instruct?
2. Is the goal clearly stated?
3. What are the critical steps in the process?
4. What errors should readers avoid?

Strategy

1. What is the nature of the intended audience?
2. How much existing knowledge does the writer assume readers have? Are terms explained?
3. What are the beginning and ending points of the process? Are these clearly defined?

4. How are steps or stages separated? Are the transitions clear?
5. Does the writer use paragraph breaks, numbers, bold type, and other visual prompts? Are these skillfully used?
6. Are instructions easy to follow?
7. Does the writer demonstrate the significance of the process or the value of his or her advice?

Language

1. Are technical terms clearly defined and illustrated?
2. Does the writer use language that creates clear images of what is being explained?

ELIZABETH KOLBERT

Elizabeth Kolbert (1961–) was born in New York City and received a degree in English from Yale University. After college she began working for The New York Times, *eventually heading the newspaper's office in Albany, New York. She has reported on the last two presidential campaigns as well as on the role of media in politics and culture. She also contributes to the* Times's *"Metro Matters" column.*

Birth of a TV Show: A Drama All Its Own

Most readers are familiar only with the finished products of television—the shows that appear on the screen. In this essay, Kolbert explains the behind the scenes process that winnows hundreds of ideas down to the few that eventually become shows.

1   It was supposed to be "Grease" updated for the 1990's and packaged for television. Every week, a bunch of high school students would grapple with—and make wisecracks about—issues of life and love. Occasionally they would break into song.

2   The idea for this musical sitcom belonged to Marta Kauffman and David Crane, who have been writing together for 16 years. A few months ago, they pitched it to a group of high-ranking ABC executives here. The reaction was immediate.

3   "As soon as a couple of words left our mouths, their eyes glazed over," said Ms. Kauffman.

4   "It was like all the blood drained from the room," said Mr. Crane.

THE WINNOWING PROCESS

5   It is now the height of "development season" in the television business, a period that's not really a season, and is only rarely about development. Stretching from early fall through late spring, it is a time when writers like Ms. Kauffman and Mr. Crane watch most of their cherished ideas turned into scrap.

6   At the start of the season, executives from each of the networks—CBS, NBC, ABC and Fox—listen to hundreds of writers pitch new sitcoms. The fortunate few dozen advance to the next step: writing scripts for the prospective shows. After examining those scripts, the networks narrow their choices to 8 or 10, for which pilot episodes will be filmed. From these pilots, they will eventually make four or five new sitcoms.

7   Ideas for dramatic series are winnowed similarly, except that even fewer dramas are made. By the time the networks' fall schedules are fixed, sometime in mid-May, roughly 99 out of 100 of the new series that were proposed will have been relegated to oblivion.

8   From the networks' perspective, the point of development season is to obtain, for the least amount of money, the shows that are most likely to succeed. A network pays nothing for a pitch. It pays anywhere from $50,000 to $100,000 for a script. And it pays up to $1.2 million for a pilot. (The writers and producers don't see all of this money; the cast, the crew and the studios they all work for get a cut.)

9   Over the last few years, the big broadcast networks have lost viewers and dollars to cable channels. So network budgets have shrunk and the number of pilot orders has been cut almost in half. For the people who produce television shows, the stakes and the pressure are now much higher every time they approach a network with an idea or a script or a pilot episode. Even a cherished spot on the fall schedule means little by itself. The networks' new cost-consciousness dictates that new shows are often given just a few weeks (and in the case of CBS's "South of Sunset," only one) to find an audience or be canceled.

10   For writers and producers (and Mr. Crane and Ms. Kauffman are both), development season is a time of unremitting insecurity. Mr. Crane compared the process of vying for a network time slot to entering a beauty pageant and donning a bathing suit.

11   "You feel like Miss New Jersey," he said over lunch the other day at the commissary at Warner Brothers, the studio where the team works.

12   In their not-infrequent encounters with rejection, Ms. Kauffman and Mr. Crane are probably fairly typical of television writers here, except they are a lot more successful at getting their shows on the air.

13   Four years ago, the pair created the popular HBO series "Dream On," which is still in production. (That show, which incorporates nudity and profanity above and beyond "N.Y.P.D. Blue," could not have been made for a broadcast network.)

LOOKING AHEAD TO FALL

14   "Dream On" was followed by "The Powers That Be," which lasted for a season on NBC. Last fall the Crane-Kauffman team, along with a third partner, Kevin Bright, produced "Family Album" on CBS, which got the ax after just six episodes.

15   The set for "Family Album" had barely been dismantled before it was time to start developing ideas for the next fall. Ms. Kauffman, Mr. Crane and Mr. Bright agreed to let a reporter observe the progress of these projects through the scheduling process in May.

16   "Once 'Family Album' was done, we said, 'O.K., what are we going to do next?'" recalled Leslie Moonves, the president of Warner Brothers Television, which has more than 25 other writers working to get pilots on the air. "We do this with all our producers. We analyze what their strengths are, what kind of shows they write. In the meantime, we are gathering acorns at the various networks, trying to get a bidding war going on, trying to get some excitement about them."

17   Because of the success of "Dream On," a comedy about a sex-obsessed man who thinks in film clips, Ms. Kauffman and Mr. Crane are, in Mr. Moonves's words, a "hot commodity." All four networks are eager to work with them, though not necessarily on the shows they want to work on.

18   After several consultations with Warners, Ms. Kauffman and Mr. Crane decided to pitch three sitcoms for the fall: the musical, a show about six people in their 20's making their way in Manhattan and a series about a Staten Island teen-ager with a fertile fantasy life. In an effort to maximize their chances, they examined each network's style—although it might not seem so, people in the industry think the four networks have distinguishable tastes and preferences—and which time slots might be available at each. They decided to pitch the high-school musical to ABC, the teen-age show to Fox and the young-adult show to NBC.

19   "We felt cutting-edge-wise, Fox and NBC probably right now were better for them," Mr. Moonves said.

20   ABC, perhaps still cringing from the response to its last musical venture, "Cop Rock," turned down the show it was pitched. Fox ordered a script. NBC was so eager to work with the pair again that, in an unusual move, it agreed to shoot a pilot, even though no script was in hand.

A NETWORK CONCESSION

21   Explaining the network's concession to Ms. Kauffman and Mr. Crane, Warren Littlefield, the president of NBC Entertainment, said, "You have to make a substantial commitment to be in business with them." If the network eventually decides not to make a pilot episode, it will pay a substantial penalty. (Hundreds of thousands of dollars is typical in such cases.)

22   Ms. Kauffman and Mr. Crane met at Brandeis University, where they both wanted to be actors. After college, they moved to New York and began writing musical comedies together instead. Some of these musicals, including "A . . . My Name Is Alice," and "Upstairs at O'Neal's," ran Off Broadway. Posters for the shows now hang in their shared office at Warner Brothers, above their desks, which face each other.

23   "We actually don't get tired of each other," Ms. Kauffman said of the arrangement.

24   "Annoyed sometimes," Mr. Crane interjected.

25   After all these years of writing together, the two have come to sound alike, and their conversation has the easy, interrupt-each-other quality one expects from a married couple, which they are not. Ms. Kauffman is married to a composer, Michael Skloff, who has written the opening music for some of their television shows.

EXPLORING TEEN-AGERS

26   To prepare for writing the script for the NBC pilot, Ms. Kauffman interviewed several of the twentysomething babysitters who care for her two young children. For the Fox show, she and Mr. Crane rented an armful of teen-age movies, including "Risky Business" and "Say Anything." They started to watch the Fox series "Beverly Hills 90210," trying to discern what it had that attracted so many teen-agers. ("The actors are all very good looking," was Ms. Kauffman's conclusion.)

27   For the last several weeks the pair have been sitting across from each other, doing what television producers must often do: trying to write funny dialogue for two different sets of characters. From the way they talk about the characters—Harry is the lead in the Fox script, Rachel and Monica are important figures in the NBC script—it is

clear they have been spending a lot of time with their creations. "Monica is sick of dating," Ms. Kauffman said knowingly, as if referring to a close friend. "She feels like if she has to eat another Caesar salad, she's going to die."

28   The Fox script was due first, late last month. As the deadline approached, there was a crunch. They weren't satisfied with the opening of the script and decided to rewrite it. The script was too long and had to be cut. On an easel in their office, Ms. Kauffman and Mr. Crane wrote themselves a message in black letters: "Write Faster." After some second thoughts, they crossed out "faster" and replaced it with "better."

CHANGES REQUESTED

29   Fox told the pair recently that it liked the script and wanted to shoot a pilot, but with some changes. The main character will grow up a little—he will be a junior in high school instead of a freshman, as originally planned—and a few family members, including his father, will be dropped. (As to how they will account for the absence of the father, Mr. Crane said, "Ask us in a few weeks.")

30   Pending approval of the script they just sent to NBC, Ms. Kauffman and Mr. Crane are gearing up to shoot two pilots by the end of April. Mr. Crane described their mood as "harried, happy and anxious."

31   Casting is the next step, and much of the shows' future depends on finding the right actors. This is especially true for the Fox show, which requires a dynamic young man for the lead. Ms. Kauffman and Mr. Crane are convinced that somewhere out there, the next Michael J. Fox is waiting. Now all they need to do is find him.

Understanding Meaning

1. What chances do writers have of seeing their ideas become television shows?
2. How has cable television altered the process of network production?
3. What motivates writers to work in a medium that offers so few opportunities for success? How do they cope with rejection?
4. *Critical Thinking:* What does this process reveal about the nature of television? Americans usually despair about the sameness or shallowness of network television. Could the process be altered to include more types of viewer evaluations besides ratings?

Evaluating Strategy

1. How effective is the opening example? Does it make a good introduction to the process?
2. Kolbert uses a single writing team to explain the process. Is this an effective strategy? Does it humanize or "dramatize" a commercial endeavor? Would readers care as much about writers if they remained faceless workers?
3. *Other Modes:* Indicate where Kolbert uses *example*, *narration*, and *comparison* to develop her explanation.

Appreciating Language

1. What tone and style does Kolbert use? What does her choice of words reveal about her attitude toward the writers? Toward television?
2. Note places where Kolbert introduces and defines television terms. How effective are her definitions?

Connections across the Disciplines

1. How do Steven Stark's observations in "A Tale of Two Sitcoms" (page 259) relate to those made by Kolbert?
2. Does this process explain how television confronts controversial social issues? Refer to Pilipp and Shull's "TV Movies in the First Decade of AIDS" (page 343).

Writing Suggestions

1. Using Kolbert's article as a model, write a short essay that explains a process you encountered in a job—the way department stores purchase clothing; the way libraries order new books; the way restaurants plan menus; the way car dealers sell automobiles, and so forth.
2. *Collaborative Writing:* Work with a group of students, and discuss their attitudes about network television. Craft a short essay explaining the ideal process for selecting ideas for new television shows.

ARMOND D. BUDISH

Armond D. Budish is an attorney and consumer-law reporter. He practices law in Ohio, where he writes columns on consumer issues for The Cleveland Plain Dealer. *He has also published articles in* Family Circle *magazine. His book* How to Beat the Catastrophic Costs of Nursing Home Care *was published in 1989, and his latest book is* Avoiding the Medicaid Trap *(1996).*

Fender Benders:
Legal Do's and Don't's

As you read this article, notice how Budish makes use of numbered steps and bold type to make this Family Circle *article easy to skim.*

1   The car ahead of you stops suddenly. You hit the brakes, but you just can't stop in time. Your front bumper meets the rear end of the other car. *Ouch!*

2   There doesn't seem to be any damage, and it must be your lucky day because the driver you hit agrees that it's not worth hassling with insurance claims and risking a premium increase. So after exchanging addresses, you go your separate ways.

3   Imagine your surprise when you open the mail a few weeks later only to discover a letter from your "victim's" lawyer demanding $10,000 to cover car repairs, pain and suffering. Apparently the agreeable gentleman decided to disagree, then went ahead and filed a police report blaming you for the incident and for his damages.

4   When automobiles meet by accident, do you know how to respond? Here are 10 practical tips that can help you avoid costly legal and insurance hassles.

1. Stop! It's the Law.

5   No matter how serious or minor the accident, stop immediately. If possible, don't move your car—especially if someone has been injured. Leaving the cars as they were when the accident occurred helps the police determine what happened. Of course, if your car is blocking traffic or will cause another accident where it is, then move it to the nearest safe location.

6   For every rule there are exceptions, though. If, for example, you are rear-ended at night in an unsafe area, it's wisest to keep on going and notify the police later. There have been cases in which people were robbed or assaulted when they got out of their cars.

2. Zip Loose Lips.

7   Watch what you say after an accident. Although this may sound harsh, even an innocent "I'm sorry" could later be construed as an admission of fault. Also be sure not to accuse the other driver of causing the accident. Since you don't know how a stranger will react to your remarks, you run the risk of making a bad situation worse.

8   Remember, you are not the judge or jury; it's not up to you to decide who is or is not at fault. Even if you think you caused the accident, you might be wrong. For example: Assume you were driving 15 miles over the speed limit. What you probably were not aware of is that the other driver's blood-alcohol level exceeded the legal limits, so he was at least equally at fault.

3. Provide Required Information.

9   If you are involved in an accident, you are required in most states to give your name, address and car registration number to: any person injured in the accident; the owner, driver or passenger in any car that was damaged in the accident; a police officer on the scene. If you don't own the car (say it belongs to a friend or your parents), you should provide the name and address of the owner.

10   You must produce this information even if there are no apparent injuries or damages and even if you didn't cause the accident. Most states don't require you to provide the name of your insurance company, although it's usually a good idea to do so. However, *don't* discuss the amount of your coverage—that might inspire the other person to "realize" his injuries are more serious than he originally thought.

11   What should you do if you hit a parked car and the owner is not around? The law requires you to leave a note with your name, and the other identifying information previously mentioned, in a secure place on the car (such as under the windshield wiper).

4. Get Required Information.

12   You should obtain from the others involved in the accident the same information that you provide them with. However, if the other driver refuses to cooperate, at least get the license number and the make and model of the car to help police track down the owner.

5. Call the Police.

13   It's obvious that if it's a serious accident in which someone is injured, the police should be called immediately. That's both the law and com-

mon sense. But what if the accident seems minor? Say you're stopped, another car taps you in the rear. If it's absolutely clear to both drivers that there is no damage or injury, you each can go your merry way. But that's the exception.

14 Normally, you should call the police to substantiate what occurred. In most cities police officers will come to the scene, even for minor accidents, but if they won't, you and the other driver should go to the station (of the city where the accident occurred) to file a report. Ask to have an officer check out both cars.

15 If you are not at fault, be wary of accepting the other driver's suggestion that you leave the police out of it and arrange a private settlement. When you submit your $500 car-repair estimate several weeks later, you could discover that the other driver has developed "amnesia" and denies being anywhere near the accident. If the police weren't present on the scene, you may not have a legal leg to stand on.

16 Even if you *are* at fault, it's a good idea to involve the police. Why? Because a police officer will note the extent of the other driver's damages in his or her report, limiting your liability. Without police presence the other driver can easily inflate the amount of the damages.

6. Identify Witnesses.

17 Get the names and addresses of any witnesses, in case there's a legal battle some time in the future. Ask bystanders or other motorists who stop whether they saw the accident; if they answer "yes," get their identifying information. It is also helpful to note the names and badge numbers of all police officers on the scene.

7. Go to the Hospital.

18 If there's a chance that you've been injured, go directly to a hospital emergency room or to your doctor. The longer you wait, the more you may jeopardize your health and the more difficult it may be to get reimbursed for your injuries if they turn out to be serious.

8. File a Report.

19 Every driver who is involved in an automobile incident in which injuries occur must fill out an accident report. Even if the property damage is only in the range of $200 to $1,000, most states require that an accident report be filed. You must do this fairly quickly, usually in 1 to 30 days. Forms may be obtained and filed with the local motor vehicle department or police station in the city where the accident occurred.

9. Consider Filing an Insurance Claim.

20 Talk with your insurance agent as soon as possible after an accident. He or she can help you decide if you should file an insurance claim or pay out of your own pocket.

21   For example, let's say you caused an accident and the damages totaled $800. You carry a $250 deductible, leaving you with a possible $550 insurance claim. If you do submit a claim, your insurance rates are likely to go up, an increase that will probably continue for about three years. You should compare that figure to the $550 claim to determine whether to file a claim or to pay the cost yourself. (Also keep in mind that multiple claims sometimes make it harder to renew your coverage.)

10. Don't Be Too Quick to Accept a Settlement.

22   If the other driver is at fault and there's any chance you've been injured, don't rush to accept a settlement from that person's insurance company. You may not know the extent of your injuries for some time, and once you accept a settlement, it's difficult to get an "upgrade." Before settling, consult with a lawyer who handles personal injury cases.

23   When you *haven't* been injured and you receive a fair offer to cover the damage to your car, you can go ahead and accept it.

Understanding Meaning

1.   What problems can motorists run into if they are careless about handling even minor accidents?
2.   What are some of the most important things you should do if involved in a fender bender?
3.   Why should you go to the hospital even if you have what appears to be a minor injury?
4.   *Critical Thinking:* Should this article be printed as a pamphlet and distributed to drivers' education classes? Have you known anyone who has encountered difficulties that could have been avoided if he or she had followed the writer's advice?

Evaluating Strategy

1.   How does Budish arouse reader attention in the opening?
2.   How effective are the numbered steps? Would the article lose impact if printed in standard paragraphs?
3.   How easy is this article to remember? Can you put it down and recall the main points?

Appreciating Language

1.   This article was written for *Family Circle*. Does the level of language appear targeted to a female audience?

2. Why does Budish, who is an attorney, avoid legal terminology?
3. Does Budish's language create concrete images that make strong impressions to dramatize his subject?

Connections across the Disciplines

1. Budish provides tips in numbered points. Could Louis Mizell's article "Who's Listening to Your Cell Phone Calls?" (page 337) be restated in a list of steps instructing consumers on the safe use of cell phones?
2. How does Budish's article relate to Ramon "Tianguis" Perez's "The Fender-Bender" (page 62)?

Writing Suggestions

1. Using this article as a model, provide the general public with a similar list of tips to prevent heart disease, deter muggers, prepare children for school, save money for retirement, or a topic of your choice.
2. *Collaborative Writing:* Work with a group of students to provide tips for new students on campus. Use peer review to make sure you do not overlook details in your student guide.

MARVIN HARRIS

Marvin Harris (1927–) was born in Brooklyn and received degrees from Columbia University. After teaching at Columbia for many years, Harris moved to the University of Florida, where he now is a graduate research professor in anthropology. Harris has conducted research in Harlem, Africa, South America, and Asia. He has published several scholarly works but is best known for books written to general readers such as Cows, Pigs, Wars, and Witches: The Riddles of Culture *and* Cannibals and Kings: The Origins of Cultures. *Much of Harris's work focuses on how people's basic needs for food and shelter influence their culture.*

How Our Skins Got Their Color

In this essay from Our Kind: Who We Are, Where We Came From, Where We Are Going *(1988), Harris explains how human beings developed different skin colors. In reading this account, determine how he addresses a topic laden with controversy.*

1   Most human beings are neither very fair nor very dark, but brown. The extremely fair skin of northern Europeans and their descendants, and the very black skins of central Africans and their descendants, are probably special adaptations. Brown-skinned ancestors may have been shared by modern-day blacks and whites as recently as ten thousand years ago.

2   Human skin owes it color to the presence of particles known as melanin. The primary function of melanin is to protect the upper levels of the skin from being damaged by the sun's ultraviolet rays. This radiation poses a critical problem for our kind because we lack the dense coat of hair that acts as a sunscreen for most mammals. Hairlessness exposes us to two kinds of radiation hazards: ordinary sunburn, with its blisters, rashes, and risk of infection; and skin cancers, including malignant melanoma, one of the deadliest diseases known. Melanin is the body's first line of defense against these afflictions. The more melanin particles, the darker the skin, and the lower the risk of sunburn and all forms of skin cancer. This explains why the highest rates

for skin cancer are found in sun-drenched lands such as Australia, where light-skinned people of European descent spend a good part of their lives outdoors wearing scanty attire. Very dark-skinned people such as heavily pigmented Africans of Zaire seldom get skin cancer, but when they do, they get it on depigmented parts of their bodies— palms and lips.

3   If exposure to solar radiation had nothing but harmful effects, natural selection would have favored inky black as the color for all human populations. But the sun's rays do not present an unmitigated threat. As it falls on the skin, sunshine converts a fatty substance in the epidermis into vitamin D. The blood carries vitamin D from the skin to the intestines (technically making it a hormone rather than a vitamin), where it plays a vital role in the absorption of calcium. In turn, calcium is vital for strong bones. Without it, people fall victim to the crippling diseases rickets and osteomalacia. In women, calcium deficiencies can result in a deformed birth canal, which makes childbirth lethal for both mother and fetus.

4   Vitamin D can be obtained from a few foods, primarily the oils and livers of marine fish. But inland populations must rely on the sun's rays and their own skins for the supply of this crucial substance. The particular color of a human population's skin, therefore, represents in large degree a trade-off between the hazards of too much versus too little solar radiation: acute sunburn and skin cancer on the one hand, and rickets and osteomalacia on the other. It is this trade-off that largely accounts for the preponderance of brown people in the world and for the general tendency for skin color to be darkest among equatorial populations and lightest among populations dwelling at higher latitudes.

5   At middle latitudes, the skin follows a strategy of changing colors with the seasons. Around the Mediterranean basin, for example, exposure to the summer sun brings high risk of cancer but low risk for rickets; the body produces more melanin and people grow darker (i.e., they get suntans). Winter reduces the risk of sunburn and cancer; the body produces less melanin, and the tan wears off.

6   The correlation between skin color and latitude is not perfect because other factors—such as the availability of foods containing vitamin D and calcium, regional cloud cover during the winter, amount of clothing worn, and cultural preferences—may work for or against the predicted relationship. Arctic-dwelling Eskimos, for example, are not as light-skinned as expected, but their habitat and economy afford them a diet that is exceptionally rich in both vitamin D and calcium.

7   Northern Europeans, obliged to wear heavy garments for protection against the long, cold, cloudy winters, were always at risk for rickets and osteomalacia from too little vitamin D and calcium. This risk increased sometime after 6000 B.C., when pioneer cattle herders who did not exploit marine resources began to appear in northern Europe. The risk would have been especially great for the brown-skinned Mediterranean peoples who migrated northward along with the crops and farm animals. Samples of Caucasian skin (infant penile foreskin obtained at the time of circumcision) exposed to sunlight on cloudless days in Boston (42°N) from November through February produced no vitamin D. In Edmonton (52°N) this period extended from October to March. But further south (34°N) sunlight was effective in producing vitamin D in the middle of the winter. Almost all of Europe lies north of 42°N. Fair-skinned, nontanning individuals who could utilize the weakest and briefest doses of sunlight to synthesize vitamin D were strongly favored by natural selection. During the frigid winters, only a small circle of a child's face could be left to peek out at the sun through the heavy clothing, thereby favoring the survival of individuals with translucent patches of pink on their cheeks characteristic of many northern Europeans. . . .

8   If light-skinned individuals on the average had only 2 percent more children survive per generation, the changeover in their skin color could have begun five thousand years ago and reached present levels well before the beginning of the Christian era. But natural selection need not have acted alone. Cultural selection may also have played a role. It seems likely that whenever people consciously or unconsciously had to decide which infants to nourish and which to neglect, the advantage would go to those with lighter skin, experience having shown that such individuals tended to grow up to be taller, stronger, and healthier than their darker siblings. White was beautiful because white was healthy.

9   To account for the evolution of black skin in equatorial latitudes, one has merely to reverse the combined effects of natural and cultural selection. With the sun directly overhead most of the year, and clothing a hindrance to work and survival, vitamin D was never in short supply (and calcium was easily obtained from vegetables). Rickets and osteomalacia were rare. Skin cancer was the main problem, and what nature started, culture amplified. Darker infants were favored by parents because experience showed that they grew up to be freer of disfiguring and lethal malignancies. Black was beautiful because black was healthy.

Understanding Meaning

1. What is Harris's thesis?
2. What is the "natural" color for human skin?
3. What caused people to develop different complexions?
4. What role did sunlight play in human evolution?
5. *Critical Thinking:* What impact could this scientific explanation of skin color have on debates about race and discrimination? Can biological aspects of humanity be separated from social, cultural, political, or psychological attitudes?

Evaluating Strategy

1. How does Harris organize his essay?
2. What research does Harris use to support his views?
3. *Other Modes:* Where does Harris use *narration, comparison,* and *definition* in his explanation?

Appreciating Language

1. How does Harris define *melanin?*
2. Does Harris's selection of words describing color contain connotations that suggest a bias? Is his essay wholly objective? How often does he use words such as *white* and *black?*
3. Would the average newspaper reader be able to understand this essay? What does the level of language suggest about the intended audience?

Connections across the Disciplines

1. Does this article lend more support to the argument made by Carl Sagan in "Why We Need to Understand Science" (page 589)? Can an understanding of science help people cope with social, gender, and cultural conflicts?
2. Would this essay make a good preface to an essay about racial prejudice such as Nathan McCall's "The Lesson" (page 51)?

Writing Suggestions

1. Using this essay for background information, draft a brief explanation about skin color for an elementary school brochure on race relations. Use

easily understood language, and employ comparisons and short narratives to explain scientific principles. Avoid words that may have negative connotations.

2. *Critical Writing:* Write an essay analyzing the effect reading this essay had on you. Did it affect your attitudes toward people of different races? Does the knowledge that all humans probably once shared the same complexion change the way you view yourself?

3. *Collaborative Writing:* Discuss Harris's essay with a group of students. What value does a scientific explanation of skin color have in addressing racial problems? Would it be beneficial to share this information with children? Record members' reactions, and create a short statement about the importance of understanding the origins of skin color. If members disagree, consider developing pro and con responses.

PETER ELBOW

Peter Elbow (1935–) was educated at Williams College, Brandeis, Harvard, and Oxford. A noted director of college writing programs, Elbow started a highly acclaimed "Workshop in Language and Thinking" at Bard College. He has published numerous articles about writing and several books including Writing without Teachers *and* Writing with Power.

Desperation Writing

In this section from Writing without Teachers *(1973), Peter Elbow offers advice to students writing under stress. Facing deadlines, many students feel almost paralyzed, unable to even start an assignment. Elbow presents his recommendations in the form of a process.*

1   I know I am not alone in my recurring twinges of panic that I won't be able to write something when I need to, I won't be able to produce coherent speech or thought. And that lingering doubt is a great hindrance to writing. It's a constant fog or static that clouds the mind. I never got out of its clutches till I discovered that it was possible to write something—not something great or pleasing but at least something usable, workable—when my mind is out of commission. The trick is that you have to do all your cooking out on the table: Your mind is incapable of doing any inside. It means using symbols and pieces of paper not as a crutch but as a wheelchair.

2   The first thing is to admit your condition: Because of some mood or event or whatever, your mind is incapable of anything that could be called thought. It can put out a babbling kind of speech utterance, it can put a simple feeling, perception or sort-of-thought into understandable (though terrible) words. But it is incapable of considering anything in relation to anything else. The moment you try to hold that thought or feeling up against some other to see the relationship, you simply lose the picture—you get nothing but buzzing lines or waving colors.

3   So admit this. Avoid anything more than one feeling, perception, or thought. Simply write as much as possible. Try simply to steer your

mind in the direction or general vicinity of the thing you are trying to write about and start writing and keep writing.

4   Just write and keep writing. (Probably best to write on only one side of the paper in case you should want to cut parts out with scissors—but you probably won't.) Just write and keep writing. It will probably come in waves. After a flurry, stop and take a brief rest. But don't stop too long. Don't think about what you are writing or what you have written or else you will overload the circuit again. Keep writing as though you are drugged or drunk. Keep doing this till you feel you have a lot of material that might be useful; or, if necessary, till you can't stand it any more—even if you doubt that there's anything useful there.

5   Then take a pad of little pieces of paper—or perhaps 3 × 5 cards—and simply start at the beginning of what you were writing, and as you read over what you wrote, every time you come to any thought, feeling, perception, or image that could be gathered up into one sentence or one assertion, do so and write it by itself on a little sheet of paper. In short, you are trying to turn, say, ten or twenty pages of wandering mush into twenty or thirty hard little crab apples. Sometimes there won't be many on a page. But if it seems to you that there are none on a page, you are making a serious error—the same serious error that put you in this comatose state to start with. You are mistaking lousy, stupid, second-rate, wrong, childish, foolish, worthless ideas for no ideas at all. Your job is not to pick out *good* ideas but to pick out ideas. As long as you were conscious, your words will be full of things that could be called feelings, utterances, ideas—things that can be squeezed into one simple sentence. This is your job. Don't ask for too much.

6   After you have done this, take those little slips or cards, read through them a number of times—not struggling with them, simply wandering and mulling through them; perhaps shifting them around and looking through in various sequences. In a sense these are cards you are playing solitaire with, and the rules of this particular game permit shuffling the unused pile.

7   The goal of this procedure with the cards is to get them to distribute themselves in two or three or ten or fifteen different piles on your desk. You can get them to do this almost by themselves if you simply keep reading through them in different orders; certain cards will begin to feel like they go with other cards. I emphasize this passive, thoughtless mode because I want to talk about desperation writing in its pure

state. In practice, almost invariably at some point in the procedure, your sanity begins to return. It is often at this point. You actually are moved to have thoughts or—and the difference between active and passive is crucial here—to *exert* thought; to hold two cards together and *build* or *assert* a relationship. It is a matter of bringing energy to bear.

8 So you may start to be able to do something active with these cards, and begin actually to think. But if not, just allow the cards to find their own piles with each other by feel, by drift, by intuition, by mindlessness.

9 You have now engaged in the two main activities that will permit you to get something cooked out on the table rather than in your brain: writing out into messy words, summing up into single assertions, and even sensing relationships between assertions. You can simply continue to deploy these two activities.

10 If, for example, after the first round of writing, assertion-making, and pile-making, your piles feel as though they are useful and satisfactory for what you are writing—paragraphs or sections or trains of thought—then you can carry on from there. See if you can gather each pile up into a single assertion. When you can, then put the subsidiary assertions of that pile into their best order to fit with that single unifying one. If you *can't* get the pile into one assertion, then take the pile as the basis for doing some more writing out into words. In the course of this writing, you may produce for yourself the single unifying assertion you were looking for; or you may have to go through the cycle of turning the writing into assertions and piles and so forth. Perhaps more than once. The pile may turn out to want to be two or more piles itself; or it may want to become part of a pile you already have. This is natural. This kind of meshing into one configuration, then coming apart, then coming together and meshing into a different configuration—this is growing and cooking. It makes a terrible mess, but if you can't do it in your head, you have to put up with a cluttered desk and a lot of confusion.

11 If, on the other hand, all that writing *didn't* have useful material in it, it means that your writing wasn't loose, drifting, quirky, jerky, associative enough. This time try especially to let things simply remind you of things that are seemingly crazy or unrelated. Follow these odd associations. Make as many metaphors as you can—be as nutty as possible—and explore the metaphors themselves—open them out. You may have all your energy tied up in some area of your experience that you are leaving out. Don't refrain from writing about whatever else is

on your mind: how you feel at the moment, what you are losing your mind over, randomness that intrudes itself on your consciousness, the pattern on the wallpaper, what those people you see out the window have on their minds—though keep coming back to the whateveritis you are supposed to be writing about. Treat it, in short, like ten-minute writing exercises. Your best perceptions and thoughts are always going to be tied up in whatever is really occupying you, and that is also where your energy is. You may end up writing a love poem—or a hate poem—in one of those little piles while the other piles will finally turn into a lab report on data processing or whatever you have to write about. But you couldn't, in your present state of having your head shot off, have written that report without also writing the poem. And the report will have some of the juice of the poem in it and vice versa.

Understanding Meaning

1. What is Elbow's purpose?
2. What problems does Elbow want students to overcome?
3. Do you find this advice helpful? Would you use it?
4. *Critical Thinking:* What does Elbow's essay reveal to you about the writing process? Why is it important to see writing as a process and not merely a product?

Evaluating Strategy

1. Does the opening adequately demonstrate the need for this process?
2. Are the stages or steps clearly defined?
3. How does Elbow signal transitions?

Appreciating Language

1. Elbow writes of ideas that are "lousy" and "stupid" but still have value. What is he trying to indicate to students with these word choices?
2. Judging by the language, what audience, what type of student, is this essay targeted to?

Connections across the Disciplines

1. How do Elbow's comments about writing compare to William Zinsser's (page 248)?
2. How does Elbow's advice differ from Fran Martin's (page 466)?

Writing Suggestions

1. Experiment with the freewriting process Elbow describes. Select a topic, and write nonstop for at least ten minutes. Afterward underline the ideas you came up with while writing.
2. *Collaborative Writing:* Talk about writing with other students. Discuss working methods. Take notes on the tips you feel are helpful. Work with others to craft these into a process essay.

FRAN MARTIN

Fran Martin earned a nursing degree at Wheaton College and completed a doctorate at Florida State University. Martin is the Assistant Professor of maternal-child nursing at the University of Southern Mississippi in Hattiesburg. In addition to her teaching career, Martin often appears in court as an expert witness in medical malpractice cases. In this article, first published in Nursing *in 1994, Martin explains how properly documented charts can protect nurses from litigation.*

Documentation Tips

This article is directed to nurses, though it applies to nearly every professional who must document his or her actions: law enforcement officers, counselors, therapists, maintenance supervisors, and school administrators. As you read the article, notice that Martin stresses what might be called "defensive writing."

1   A nursing student who was reviewing charts for a senior honors class commented to me, "It's amazing how much is left undocumented or unexplained in the record. I had so many questions."

2   Exactly.

3   I often have the same reaction when I read the charts for the cases I consult on. And I think, *If only these nurses had taken the time to completely document the care they claim they'd given, they could have avoided liability.* But, unfortunately, lack of documentation suggests nursing malpractice.

4   Here's what you can do to avoid ending up in the same situation.

TIPS FOR AVOIDING TROUBLE

5   • **Make sure your charting is complete.** Documentation is a pivotal part of a lawsuit—it can be the best way for you to refute charges of malpractice. I've seen four common problem areas.

6   1. *Not charting the correct time when events occurred.* Suppose a procedure is charted in several different places, but each entry indicates that it was

done at a different time. Lawyers use these times to reconstruct the sequence of events, and inconsistencies like this can make their case—they can easily raise questions about the accuracy of the entire record.

7 2. *Failing to record verbal orders or to have them signed.* In an emergency or during a particularly hectic shift, you could overlook this important step. But if you don't record the order and have it signed according to policy and something happens to the patient, the doctor could deny that he gave the order. And without documentation, the jury would wonder whether to believe your word or the doctor's.

8 3. *Charting your actions in advance to save time.* You may be particularly tempted to do this with standing orders for medications, but nothing should be charted until after it's done or administered. You wouldn't want to have to explain how you administered a drug when you were participating in a code at the same time.

9 4. *Charting incorrect data.* You communicate with other health care providers through the chart and, obviously, incorrect data doesn't give an accurate picture of your patient's condition. That could lead to life-threatening errors. It also raises the specter of fraud, which could make your actions appear not just negligent, but also criminal.

10 • *Collect and analyze data from the patient's history and physical, and from laboratory reports.* The doctor may point out pertinent facts, but you're responsible for using your experience to interpret the information you've obtained. In one case I consulted on, a pregnant patient with poor weight gain and uterine growth was 3 weeks overdue. Yet none of her nurses recognized the increased risk of fetal distress.

11 • *Use your data to identify patients at increased risk for complications.* Even if you don't initially think the patient is at risk for complications, you're responsible for monitoring the patient as ordered, watching for trends that signal a developing problem, and calling the doctor if a change occurs. For example, monitoring and recording vital signs shouldn't become meaningless routine. You need to look at what the numbers tell you and act accordingly.

12 • *Don't get into a diagnostic rut.* If you're too focused on the diagnosis, you could be distracted from accurately analyzing your data. I consulted on the case of a woman who died of beta-hemolytic streptococci peritonitis from endometritis after giving birth to her second child. Uninterested in caring for the child, she'd been diagnosed with "poor maternal bonding." Her nurses did an excellent job of documenting this problem. However, they'd overlooked her persistently high heart rate and complaints of pain, with disastrous results.

13 • *Periodically review and revise the policy and procedure manuals.* Lawyers scrutinize hospital and unit policy and procedure manuals to spot

inconsistencies between a nurse's actions and written policy. They also ask experts like me to determine whether these manuals conform to national standards of care. Some of these manuals are frightening—they devote pages to routine things (such as gowning and gloving the doctor for delivery) but ignore serious situations (such as nursing actions for fetal distress). My advice is to ensure that your policy and procedure manuals are complete, current (that is, they reflect changes in nursing practice and technology), and clear to the reader (including any nurses who might float to the unit). If the manuals haven't been updated in years, talk with your nurse-manager—you've got a disaster waiting to happen.

14   Now that I've given you my advice, I'd like to share a case I recently consulted on. It illustrates why these tips are so important.

A CASE IN POINT

15 Patti Bailey was admitted to deliver her third child. During her pregnancy, she'd gained 63 pounds, her blood pressure had risen from 100/70 in her first trimester to 140/80 at term, and an ultrasound done at 22 weeks showed possible placenta previa.

16   Over the next 4 hours, she received 10 units of oxytocin (Pitocin) in 500 ml of 5 percent dextrose in lactated Ringer's solution. Charting during this period was scant—her blood pressure was never recorded, and there were only single notations of the fetal heart rate and how labor was progressing. The nurses failed to record either the baby's reaction to the drug or the nature of Mrs. Bailey's contractions.

17   Suddenly, after complaining of nausea and epigastric pain, Mrs. Bailey suffered a generalized tonic-clonic seizure. Because her condition was so unstable, she couldn't undergo a cesarean section. So her baby girl was delivered by low forceps. Mrs. Bailey developed disseminated intravascular coagulation and required 20 units of whole blood, platelets, and packed red blood cells within 8 hours of delivery.

18   Incredibly, Mrs. Bailey's nurse had essentially documented nothing on the labor or delivery records or the progress notes. And when I reviewed the unit's policy and procedure manuals, I couldn't find a protocol for administering oxytocin and assessing the patient. At the very least, there should have been an oxytocin flow sheet to record vital signs, labor progress, fetal status, and changes in the drug administration rate.

19   Although Mrs. Bailey recovered, her daughter has seizures and is developmentally disabled. Now 15, the daughter can't walk or talk and she has a gastrostomy tube for nutrition. The case was settled out of court for $450,000, with the nurse and hospital responsible for one-third of the amount; the doctor paid the rest.

PRACTICING SAFELY

20   Being named in a lawsuit is unnerving, at the very least. So you need to do your best to practice safely—and to accurately document as proof of your care. If you do, there's a good chance you'll stay out of court.

Understanding Meaning

1.   Why is it important for nurses to carefully document their actions?
2.   What common mistakes do nurses make?
3.   What can happen when nurses fail to report their actions?
4.   *Critical Thinking:* What does Martin's article reveal about how people write outside the classroom? How is this writing different from that taught in most English courses?

Evaluating Strategy

1.   Why does Martin give negative instructions at the opening?
2.   *Other Modes:* How does Martin use *narration* and *analysis* to support her advice?

Appreciating Language

1.   Martin does not define "beta-hemolytic streptococci peritonitis" or "epigastric pain." What does this say about her intended reader?
2.   How much technical language does she use to describe the legal or writing process?

Connections across the Disciplines

1.   How does writing a chart differ, if at all, from writing a résumé? Refer to Anne Weisbord's "Resumes That Rate a Second Look" (page 471). How does the context differ? What are readers' expectations?
2.   How does Martin's advice differ from Peter Elbow's (page 461)?

Writing Suggestions

1. Experiment with charting. Write a chart of your activities throughout a single school day. You might refer to the logbook of the *Titanic* (page 98) as a model. At the end of the day, review your writing. How difficult is it to keep a running journal? Did you forget to record any activities?

2. *Collaborative Writing:* Discuss writing on the job with a group of students. What reports, letters, and memos have they had to write? Discuss whether schools and colleges adequately prepare students for writing "in the real world." Record suggestions and comments, and then collaborate on writing a process paper explaining how English classes could be made more practical.

ANNE WEISBORD

Anne Weisbord has a master's in education and served as director of Career Services at Hahnemann University in Philadelphia before beginning a career as a private career counselor. Widely published, she has appeared on radio and television providing advice on careers, job search strategies, and interviewing. In this article, written for Nurse Extra, *Weisbord tells nurses how to write effective résumés.*

Resumes That Rate a Second Look

Although directed to nurses, Weisbord's advice applies to most professionals. As you read the article, notice how her terse, to-the-point phrases mirror the kind of writing found on most résumés.

1   In today's business and professional environment—in which health-care positions can be eliminated STAT—every nurse should have a resume ready to send to potential employers.

2   The purpose of the resume is to get you a job interview. Employers use resumes to screen out undesirable, or less desirable, candidates. Your resume should summarize your skills and experience, and convince employers of the value they will gain in hiring you. It's an advertisement for yourself, and as with all ads, it should generate interest and motivate the reader.

3   Before you prepare your resume, take a few moments to consider your marketable skills. Identify the strengths and accomplishments that are relevant to the position you are seeking, and present them as succinctly and as clearly as possible. You'll need to organize all of this information in no more than two pages, in an easy-to-read, attractive format. Beyond this, there are really no hard-and-fast rules about writing resumes.

4   Let's look at the standard components of the traditional resume that presents your relevant nursing background in reverse chronological order.

5   1. **Personal identification.** You need include only your name, degree, and your professional certification, address, and phone number. Omit date of birth, marital status, and health; these can be discriminatory factors in hiring.

6   2. **Career objective.** This is optional. If you know *exactly* what you want to do, you can use a phrase that describes the type and level of position you are seeking. An objective might be "Nurse Coordinator in Pediatrics," or "Nurse Manager, ICU." However, if you would consider a variety of positions, skip the objective and use only a summary.

7   3. **Summary.** Describe your background in a few punchy sentences. This is the "hook" that will pique the reader's interest in the rest of the resume.

8   4. **Professional experience.** List names, places, job titles, and dates of employment. Link your experience to your summary or objective. Stress accomplishments, and emphasize responsibilities that will impress the potential employer. Use brief phrases with vivid verbs and nouns to describe the skills essential to each position. Omit obvious duties. Emphasize accomplishments with bullets.

9   As you go back into your work history, present fewer details. When you first became a nurse, you naturally had fewer responsibilities. Devote more space to higher-level, more professional duties.

10 5. **Education.** If you are a recent graduate with little nursing experience, put education before professional experience. Always list the most recent school, degree or certificate program and work backward. Do include honors or academic awards. Don't list high school. If you have a college degree, the employer will assume you earned a high-school diploma.

11 6. **Professional certification(s).** List certifications in reverse chronological order, or organize them according to specialty areas.

12 7. **License(s).** List only the state and title of each professional license. Don't give your license number(s). You will be asked to provide them later in the interview process.

13 8. **Activities.** No one will hire you for a healthcare position based on your interest in golf or coin collecting, but volunteer community involvement shows positive personal characteristics. Be careful about listing political or religious activities. Your reader may have biases against your persuasions.

14   Remember that your resume serves as a first impression of you. To a potential employer, your coffee-stained copy or your misspellings say something about your attention (or lack of attention) to detail, your neatness, and even your attitude. Also, modesty is not an asset in a resume. Toot your own horn!

Understanding Meaning

1. Summarize Weisbord's key points on résumés.
2. What is the purpose of a résumé? Why does this seemingly obvious fact need to be explained? Do many people have misconceptions about résumés?
3. What information does Weisbord suggest omitting? Why?
4. *Critical Thinking:* What is the context of a résumé? How does this document reflect the roles of writer, audience, and discipline?

Evaluating Strategy

1. How effective is the format of Weisbord's article?
2. Weisbord tells readers "there are really no hard-and-fast rules about writing resumes." Why is this important?
3. How does her article mirror the document she is training readers to write?

Appreciating Language

1. How effective are Weisbord's style and choice of words? Is the article readable?
2. How does Weisbord's emphasis on verbs, "*Describe* your background . . ." and "*List* names, places . . ." (italics added), reflect the kind of language found on most résumés?

Connections across the Disciplines

1. Review Monica Ramos's résumé (page 163). Does it follow Weisbord's advice?
2. How does her advice to nurses on writing a résumé differ from Martin's advice on charting (page 466)? Why?

Writing Suggestions

1. If you have not written a résumé already, draft one adopting Weisbord's advice.
2. *Collaborative Writing:* Meet with a group of students, and review each other's résumés. Select the best features you discover, and then write a brief process essay explaining step by step how to create an effective résumé.

EUGENE RAUDSEPP

Eugene Raudsepp is president of Princeton Creative Research Inc., based in New Jersey. An expert on job interviewing techniques, Raudsepp created this article for Machine Design *(1993), a magazine read widely by engineers and industrial managers.*

Seeing Your Way
Past Interview Jitters

This article, directed toward engineers, instructs candidates to use a psychological technique called visualization to improve their performance during job interviews.

1   It is not unusual to experience a mild attack of nerves before a job interview. But there are engineers whose interview jitters are intense enough to be harmful. They have such overwhelming apprehension and fear that they either become tongue-tied or proceed to talk themselves out of the job. Even many capable and articulate engineers act stiff and awkward in interviews, often fidgeting or sitting on the edge of the chair.

2   When we're anxious, we frequently become self-conscious spectators of our own behavior during interviews, observing and judging our every utterance and movement. This makes us not only more anxious and less convincing, but also divides our attention.

3   Excessive self-consciousness is particularly true among engineers who go to interviews with a do-or-die attitude. Trying too hard to succeed increases tension and reduces effectiveness. "The self-imposed pressure of trying to ace an interview can make some people focus too much on how they look and act," says Steven Berglas, a psychiatry instructor at Harvard Medical School. He feels that those who are overly conscious of their grooming, speech, body language, and other interviewing behavior frequently "suppress those elements of their personality that won them the interview in the first place."

4   Perfectionist engineers particularly experience high anxiety during job interviews. Because they have a strong need to do well and

have such inflated expectations of their own performance, any real or imaginary deviation from their self-imposed high, and often unrealistic, standards triggers excessive nervousness and self-critical ruminations. From one slight, innocuous mistake they automatically assume the entire interview will turn out badly.

5   This anticipation often drives them to behaviors and statements that would seem self-sabotage to an innocent bystander.

REDUCING TENSION

6   Although you may feel your blood pressure rise, palms moisten, and stomach tighten before an important interview, you can control these reactions.

7   According to H. Anthony Medley, author of *Sweaty Palms: The Neglected Art of Being Interviewed*, there are four sound reasons why you have nothing to fear but fear itself, and they can help you keep an interview in perspective:

8   1. The interview centers on the subject you know best: yourself.
    2. If you've done your homework, you have a decided advantage: You know more about the interviewer's company than it knows about you.
    3. Interviewers expect job candidates to be a bit nervous.
    4. You have nothing to lose. You didn't have the job offer before the interview, so if you don't have it afterward, you're no worse off.

9   Some interview failures may be inevitable. Most engineers have experienced at least one. The important point is to refrain from exaggerating the importance of an interview situation. Also, if possible, generate several interviews; don't pin your hopes on just one. A winning-at-all-costs attitude seldom wins a job offer.

10   It is detrimental to adopt a confrontational stance with the interviewer. If you feel overly tense or belligerent, it is helpful to pretend that the interviewer is a good friend. A little make-believe can go a long way toward calming hostile feelings.

11   One interesting method of lessening interview stress is suggested by Lawrence Darius, president of Corporate Communication Skills Inc., New York. He is convinced that one of the more effective ways to overcome interview jitters is to separate yourself from your performance. "Just as an actor or actress creates the character in a script, you

must try to create a character for the position you're seeking," he explains. "You probably have an image of the ideal engineer or, better yet, of the perfect candidates for the job. How do they differ from you? How do they walk, talk, and act?"

12   Daralee Schulman, a New York City–based career counselor, teaches her clients to relax before an interview by doing this exercise: "Visualize a serene and beautiful scene, perhaps a moonlit beach, while becoming aware of the rhythm of your breathing. On each breath in, think 'I am' and on each breath out, think 'calm.' Ten repetitions of 'I am calm' breathing done in the reception area before an interview can ease your tension." A "reliving" of a past interview in which you did well boosts your self-confidence, too.

13   A more advanced and exceedingly effective breathing technique is offered by Dan Lang, who conducts stress-reducing workshops in New York. First, exhale totally, imagining that you are relaxing all your tension. Next, close your mouth and place your right thumb on your right nostril so that it is completely closed. Then slowly and deeply inhale and exhale through your left nostril a couple of minutes, or 25 to 30 times. This enables you to tap into the right hemisphere of your brain, particularly the limbic part that governs emotions. You will experience an immediate reduction of fear and anxiety resulting in a more relaxed, in-charge feeling.

THE POWER OF VISUALIZATION

14   Many top athletes experience almost overwhelming stress before important events. However, most of them have learned—through the new sports psychology of visualization—how to manage performance anxiety, improve concentration, and enhance athletic performance.

15   Tennis champion Chris Evert, for example, used to carefully and repeatedly visualize every detail of an upcoming championship match in her mind's eye. She pictured her opponent's style and form, and then visualized how she would counter and respond to every possible maneuver or tactic.

16   Golf great Jack Nicklaus programs his "bio-computer" for success this way: "I never hit a shot, even in practice, without having a sharp, in-focus picture of it in my head. It's like a color movie. First, I 'see' the ball where I want it to finish. I 'see' the ball going there: its path,

trajectory, and shape. The next scene shows me making the kind of swing that will turn the previous image into reality."

17   There are significant emotional parallels between sports and job interviews. Through visualizing your ideal interview performance, you can build confidence and reduce anxiety to manageable levels.

18   Visualization of a successful interview is impressed upon the memory. When the actual event happens, there is complete confidence of success, as if one had done it before with a positive outcome.

Understanding Meaning

1. Does Raudsepp suggest engineers suffer from more anxiety at interviews than other professionals?
2. Describe the process of visualization in your own words. Why does it work?
3. Why does "trying too hard" often defeat a candidate interviewing for a job?
4. What does Raudsepp tell engineers not to do?
5. *Critical Thinking:* Could these techniques aid students facing an oral exam or essay test? Could visualizing your completed paper help in the writing process?

Evaluating Strategy

1. How effective are the examples Raudsepp uses for support?
2. How does Raudsepp reinforce his views with quotes from other authorities? Why is this important in giving advice?

Appreciating Language

1. What kind of language does Raudsepp use in explaining psychological techniques to engineers? How might this article be stated if written for a psychological journal?
2. Do the tone and style of the article help ease a reader's anxiety about facing a job interview? Explain.

Connections across the Disciplines

1. Refer to Anne Weisbord's article about résumé writing (page 471). Would visualization assist a job applicant in highlighting his or her key strengths?

Could reviewing a well-stated résumé help prepare an applicant for an interview by reinforcing his or her accomplishments?

2. Could visualization assist writers? Refer to Peter Elbow's "Desperation Writing" (page 461). Could visualizing the completed document help inspire and guide someone writing under stress?

Writing Suggestions

1. Write a narrative essay about a job interview you have had. At the end provide a brief analysis of your performance. Could it have been better?

2. *Collaborative Writing:* Discuss job interview experiences with a group of students. Ask the members what were the toughest questions they were asked. Have the members suggest possible answers. Collect the comments, and collaborate on a process paper: "How to Handle Tough Questions in a Job Interview."

Liz Grinslade is vice president of MSI Healthcare, a national executive search firm that specializes in locating professionals for health care providers. In this 1993 article published in Healthcare Financial Management, *she tells executives how to evaluate a job opportunity.*

Evaluating a Job Opportunity

Grinslade's advice is directed toward health care professionals but applies to almost anyone considering a job offer. Her article is important because for some people taking the wrong job can do more damage to their careers than not being hired.

1 For financial managers, as well as other job candidates, the decision to accept or reject a position offered during the job hunting process can be a difficult one. However, if eight basic areas are investigated and considered, the decision to accept or reject an offer can be made more easily. During the job interview, the job candidate should try and obtain information that will help answer the following questions:

2 1. Will the work be fulfilling and challenging?
   2. What skills are necessary to be successful at the job? If the skills are not already possessed, can they readily be developed?
   3. Is the facility stable? Is the position stable?
   4. Is the management philosophy acceptable?
   5. Is there good chemistry between the job candidate and the hiring manager and prospective coworkers?
   6. Is the location satisfying?
   7. Will there be opportunities for continuing growth and new challenges?
   8. Is the compensation fair and equitable?

3 The answers to these questions can lead a job candidate to the right decision.

4 *What skills are necessary to be successful at the job? If the skills are not already possessed, can they readily be developed?* The candidate should consider the scope of responsibilities of the position, as well as the expectations of others, including the facility's administrator, board of

directors, and hiring manager. The candidate should try and determine if these expectations are realistic. One way to gather relevant information is to ask what was liked and what was disliked about the performance of the employee previously in the position.

5   Lynn Boltuch, business office director at Mount Sinai Medical Center of Greater Miami, Miami, Florida, suggests that job applicants try to ascertain whether a company is genuinely anxious to hire someone who can make changes to improve operations. Has the company identified specific problems in a department that need to be solved? If the company is seeking a turnaround specialist, will the person hired be given the autonomy, resources, and support needed to make necessary changes? How many layers of management will be involved in making decisions? What are the administrator's overall goals for the position? Are schedules established for implementation of change and does meeting the schedule seem feasible? Are staffing levels adequate?

6   *Is the facility stable? Is the position stable?* Employers expect a job applicant to inquire about a facility's current financial condition. (For independent verification, a Medicare cost report on U.S. healthcare facilities is available for $75 through the Center for Healthcare Industry Performance Studies—CHIPS—in Columbus, Ohio.) If recent financial reports have not been positive, consider the trend. Is the facility's financial position cyclical and approaching an upswing or does an ongoing downslide seem probable? While asking about the financial picture, the job candidate should note not only what the hiring manager says but also the confidence level of his or her response.

7   There are other aspects of stability that should be explored. For instance, the candidate should try to ascertain why the position is open. Has someone been promoted within the system or has there been a "revolving door" of CFOs who could not work with the administrator or the board? What are the market conditions? Are there two other competing hospitals of similar or larger size in the immediate service area? And how tough is the managed care environment?

8   *Is the management philosophy acceptable? Is there good chemistry between the job candidate and the hiring manager and prospective coworkers?* Overall job satisfaction may rest with the answers to these questions. To assess the management philosophy, the candidate should inquire about the priorities for the position and how they should be accomplished. Job candidates should be able to adapt to new ways of doing things and, just as important, organizations should be open to employees' suggestions for change.

9   The job candidate also should ask other staff members, such as the chief operating officer or director of personnel, about the administrator's management style. How does the administrator react in different situations? Is he or she emotional and erratic? Does he or she avoid confrontations at all costs? Boltuch says one factor that determines how well a job candidate will enjoy working with a hiring manager is noting how the manager makes the candidate feel upon entering the office for the first interview. Did the manager make the candidate feel at ease or "on display"?

10   When it comes to evaluating the chemistry between the candidate and the management team and other coworkers, the candidate should make a point of meeting as many people he or she would come in contact with in a position as soon as possible. Meeting off-site is preferable. A lot more can be learned over a casual lunch than in a potential coworker's office. "Gut" feelings should be given strong consideration when evaluating the position.

11   *Is the location satisfying?* If accepting the position means moving to another city, the job candidate should make a list of important considerations, including climate, affordability, quality of school systems, proximity to family and friends, potential cultural and recreational activities, and educational opportunities. The needs of the candidate's spouse should not be forgotten.

12   Cost of living also can be a significant factor to weigh in making a decision. Using the cost-of-living index, produced by the American Chamber of Commerce Researchers Association, the candidate can compare the relative cost of living in a city. The index is updated quarterly and is available at most libraries.

13   *Will there be opportunities for continuing growth and new challenges?* By asking about the organizational structure of a facility, a potential career path can be outlined. Are there higher positions within the company that can be pursued in the future? Have specific situations been mentioned where individuals have been promoted internally? Does the organization provide tuition reimbursement for advanced degrees? Does the organization support/pay for membership in professional associations? In addition to paying for membership, does the organization also allow for time off to attend meetings or serve as a volunteer on committees? All of these factors can indicate the potential for future advancement.

14   *Is the compensation fair and equitable?* The candidate should gather information about competitive salary structures from mentors, human

resource departments, executive recruiters, and professional associations. HFMA periodically surveys and publishes salary data for CFOs and patient accounts managers. But money is only one of many factors to consider.

15   The old "rule of thumb" requiring a certain percentage of increase in compensation to change jobs is no longer valid. Many healthcare financial professionals accept lateral salary moves or even lower salaries to gain valuable experience from a particular position. Opting for a higher salary at the expense of quality of life or job satisfaction can be a poor tradeoff.

Understanding Meaning

1. What key issues should people consider before accepting a job?
2. In their eagerness to accept jobs, what problems can people create for themselves?
3. What questions should an applicant ask about the employer?
4. Why does Grinslade suggest that a high salary is sometimes worth passing over?
5. *Critical Thinking:* Does Grinslade's article suggest that many people, including skilled professionals, are too passive in the job process? Do people fail to interview their potential employers? Are they too trusting? Do you think many people feel they will be perceived as being rude or ungrateful if they seem critical of an organization offering them a job?

Evaluating Strategy

1. How effectively is the article organized? Are points easy to follow?
2. How does Grinslade use transitions?
3. Grinslade offers sources for gaining further information. Do many other writers fail to do this?

Appreciating Language

1. This article is directed to financial managers in the health care industry. Would it require much rewriting to be reprinted in a sales, engineering, or computer magazine?
2. Grinslade uses clichés such as "rule of thumb" and "'gut' feelings." Are these appropriate phrases in this context?

Connections across the Disciplines

1. Review the 3M want ad (page 161) and Monika Ramos's résumé (page 163). What questions should Ramos consider before accepting a job with 3M?

2. Does selecting the right job differ from selecting the right business opportunity? Can any of the points Charles Jamison offers entrepreneurs in "Why My Business Failed" (page 484) assist a job seeker?

Writing Suggestions

1. Have you ever been burned by a job that did not work out? Were you hired only to find that the company was facing bankruptcy or that you would not receive the equipment or resources needed to do the job? Write a narrative essay about your experience.

2. *Collaborative Writing:* Meet with a group of students, and discuss experiences, both good and bad, with job opportunities. Take notes, and write a process essay similar to Grinslade's offering advice on evaluating job offers. You may wish to target your essay to college students seeking part-time or summer jobs.

BLENDING THE MODES

CHARLES N. JAMISON JR.

Charles N. Jamison Jr. became the first African American vice president at Ted Bates Advertising. With ten years' experience in advertising and a doctorate in psychology, Jamison was well-equipped to launch his own ad agency. He teamed up with Kathryn Leary, who also worked at Bates, to create Jamison and Leary. Backed by their former employer and armed with powerful contacts, the team did well. Jamison and Leary landed major accounts such as Bacardi, NYNEX, and the Alvin Ailey dance company. Employing a dozen people, the firm was generating $5 million in billings when it began to fail.

Why My Business Failed

In this "reverse success" story, a talented entrepreneur provides advice to people hoping to achieve success. This article appeared in Black Enterprise *(1994), a magazine aimed at African American executives and business owners. Notice how Jamison uses* narrative, description, cause and effect, *and* analysis *to develop his guidelines.*

1   For nearly five years I ran an advertising agency, Jamison & Associates Advertising Inc. (originally Jamison & Leary Advertising).

2   Starting out, I believed that I knew a lot about making advertising work. I proved to myself that I was right.

3   During our glory years, we did work for such large clients as Bacardi, General Foods, PepsiCo, TIAA-CREF, NYNEX, Dow Jones & Co. Inc., and M&M/MARS, as well as for black clients like *Emerge* magazine, Yaska Shoes Ltd. and the Alvin Ailey American Dance Theater. We did video, television, radio and print. We sold a lot of goods, services and tickets. We even won a CEBA (Communication Excellence in Black Advertising) our second year out.

4   The agency is closed now. A victim of the most recent recession. Bankrupt. Chapter 7. History. Past tense.

5   What I learned, somewhat painfully, was that knowing how to create effective advertising doesn't necessarily mean that you're going to know how to run an advertising business. During a recession, which is what we ran into, it's easy to say that the economic climate is the cause of a business' demise. But there is usually more to the story than the most obvious answer. Along the way, I learned some things that I wish

I had known before I got started. If you're thinking about running a business, I've got 10 tips to consider that may prove helpful to you along the way.

6   1. Be sure to have more than one major backer. When we started the agency, we put all our chips in the same basket. We launched the business as an arm of Bates, our employer at the time.

7   We capitalized on Bates' entry into strategically focused market research. Bates already had a Hispanic ad agency. So, it seemed natural to build a business that offered psychosocial data on African Americans. This information would give Bates clear-cut ways to predict how cultural differences among blacks affect the buying habits of different segments of the market.

8   Ironically, just as our agency was about to turn profitable, Bates dissolved the relationship. The reason was no one's fault and had nothing to do with either side's respect for the other. I still do business with Bates (now Backer Spielvogel & Bates). It was simply that Saatchi and Saatchi, which had purchased Bates, had a different set of business priorities.

9   Despite all this, our agency survived for four more years. But the loss of that early backing definitely affected our ability to weather the financial storms to come.

10   The motto of all this? Never assume that all the business givens will stay that way, and be sure to line up a diverse set of backers early on in starting your firm.

11   2. Sell something people want to buy. When I went into business, I believed that my agency would provide a necessary and potentially profitable service in the marketplace.

12   I spent nearly a decade in large general-market advertising agencies learning how to develop award-winning strategic advertising. I also have a Ph.D. in psychology, where my primary research had been on black culture. Furthermore, I had sole access to a large database on black consumer preferences, attitudes and media behavior.

13   I was convinced that if I had an opportunity to present a story to a client about their product or service, then they would have to give us the business. I had been on enough new-business pitches to know how this works. How could we miss?

14   It didn't work. We made pitch after pitch presenting data to marketing managers about the black consumer presence within their brand products. Instead of giving me the business, they would (a) praise me for giving them better insight into and a more sophisticated understanding of the black consumer market, and (b) tell me that despite this

compelling story, they didn't feel the need to target this consumer base.

15   For instance, one packaged-goods marketing manager told us our presentation made a lot of sense. But when we tried to follow up, we were told that the company had "other priorities."

16   After a while, I realized that I was trying to sell a very good product that, for whatever reason, few people wanted. Sure, I got some business, but nowhere near the amount I had expected.

17   My advice to you is to realize the real potential for what it is you have to offer and adjust your actions and perceptions accordingly. In other words, do the same kind of in-depth research on your marketplace and industry as you would on the clients you want to land.

18   We looked at the tremendous growth in targeted black advertising and assumed we could expand the marketplace even further. What we failed to see was that most of the African-American ad agencies were not growing much. There was a ceiling on the amount of total business out there. Rather than relying solely on breaking new ground with companies that did not yet have carefully targeted black ad campaigns, we should have been trying to take existing business away from other black ad agencies.

19   3. Pick your partner carefully, and be sure you both have a similar approach to doing business. This one should come as no surprise given that my agency changed from a two-person firm into a one-person operation. But what I have to say may be a surprise.

20   Business isn't about making money. Oh yes, that's part of it, but not even the most important part. No, business is about power, decision-making power, control-over-your-destiny power.

21   If you take on a partner or are invited to be one, make sure that you have a clear understanding of the power relationship between you.

22   Those businesses where the power definitions are clear between the partners have a better chance of maximizing those partners' efforts to ensure the survival of the business, instead of continually putting the business through internecine bouts.

23   What happened to me and my partner? We had the same *goals* for the agency, but two radically different *approaches* to running an agency.

24   For example, we had different philosophies about landing new business. My partner believed that to get business one had to socialize and make contacts. It was something she did very well. In contrast, I believed, during the formal presentation process, you had to create a legitimate reason for the company to need your services. This was something I did very well.

25   What we encountered in working together was simply a clash in styles. Plus, we both believed strongly that our individual approach to landing clients was the *right* way.

26   Of course, successful agencies have been built on both approaches to landing new business. But because we had a new business with limited resources, it was difficult to try to take the agency in two different directions at the same time.

27   The problem here is that it's not easy to discover beforehand what control your potential partner really wants over the direction of the business. Ordinary conversation may give you some clues about how each of you views the process of doing business and a feel for one another's goals and values. But coming to a clear understanding of the issues of power and control requires straightforward discussion. You need to be direct with each other *before* you form a partnership.

28   To understand what someone wants out of a business you must really get to know a potential partner. Details about his or her upbringing, family life, social style, fears, expectations, business philosophy and priorities are all key.

29   The success of your venture will require a productive balance of powers—and way of doing things—between the two of you.

30   4. Never stop marketing your business. The breakup in our partnership happened during 1990 and 1991, just before the recession and the really tough times hit. Nonetheless, my partner and I were so distracted dealing with interpersonal issues that we had no time for marketing to new clients.

31   The result was that during the year the partnership was splitting up, I managed to pitch only two pieces of major business, instead of the 12 pitches I had been making before. Needless to say, this had a big impact on total billings.

32   My advice to you: Market, market, market. No matter how well you've done before or how well you're doing now, keep that new business coming in the door.

33   5. Don't hire your friends to work for you. Boy, that sounds cold. But does it sound less cold to lay off, or even worse, fire a friend?

34   When you hire a friend, you are less likely to make strictly business decisions about that person, and any time this happens, you've put yourself in a compromising situation.

35   Objectivity helps an effective boss get his employees to produce great work, but there is nothing objective about friendship. For instance, I should have laid people off at the first stroke of losing business.

But because I had personal ties with some friends I had hired, I kept them on payroll even during tough times.

36   And speaking about being a boss . . .

37   6. Don't be a manager. Be a boss. I was a very good people person when I worked in corporate America. I helped a lot of coworkers get through problems and issues in their lives and they liked working with me. So, naturally, I thought those skills were necessary when I started doing my own thing.

38   Yes. And no.

39   Being a good capitalist means keeping your eyes on the prize. How is what I am doing today going to help the business be more profitable tomorrow than it was yesterday?

40   In any business dealings, there will be distractions that can keep you from focusing on that prize.

41   As a boss with a small business to run, you have no one to fall back on if someone has problems, plus you can't afford the time to support someone emotionally. Trying to be a "good guy" also breaks down your authority, and it wastes energy you could be putting into running your company better.

42   If someone has a personal problem, don't make it your problem. If the problem is affecting productivity and there is a work-related solution to it, implement it. If someone's problems interfere with his or her getting the job done and there is no way that the job can be restructured to provide a solution, replace that person as quickly as possible.

43   7. Charge what you are worth. This primarily concerns those in the service industry where pricing can be somewhat variable.

44   Calculate what your contribution is to your client's bottom line and then charge accordingly. Many people will want your services at reduced fee because they perceive you as hungry or as offering a service that can be derived from other sources. This perception may also be influenced negatively if you are black.

45   If our agency had charged our clients what the value of our services were really worth, we would have been profitable before the tough times hit. You also need to charge a rate that takes into consideration what it costs you to service a particular client. Some accounts required so many agency man hours that we wound up not getting paid for the actual amount of overhead we were investing.

46   In other words, set your fees high enough to reflect what those services really cost you to provide. Be prepared to make a case for why your charges are what they are, and stick to it. Obviously, I am not

suggesting inflexibility. You should make adjustments in what you would charge a *Fortune* 500 company, compared with a mom-and-pop store. But keep in mind, all clients will demand your best work, no matter what price you agree on.

47   8. Turn down bad clients. You won't know whether someone is going to be a good or bad client until you start working with them. However, as soon as you recognize that you've landed a bad client, get rid of them—no matter how much cash you are letting walk out the door.

48   Recognizing them is a lot easier when you're supplying goods and products as opposed to services. In the product industries, a bad client is someone who doesn't pay within 30 days.

49   In the service industry, someone who's paying within 30 days could still create havoc in your business. How? By placing demands on the business that, in the process of fulfilling the work requirements, end up poisoning your work environment.

50   This position can take a variety of forms, but let me mention one example so you get the flavor. We had a packaged-goods client with top executives who had a need for control. Every time we would work on this client's account, these executives would pit one of our staffers against another. Each person who was working on the account would end up getting criticized to another staffer working on the account. The result was that they were demoralizing my people.

51   Everyone in your company can get tangled up in it when there is a client who is consciously trying to manipulate egos.

52   All the usual ways of stopping any intentional miscommunications are done routinely in large companies through written reports. In a small business, few have the time to write "CYA" memos.

53   Why would any client try to undermine your business in this way? The worst clients create trouble so that they either can get more services for free or can justify not paying for services already rendered.

54   If you want to learn from my experience, save yourself the mental anguish. Resign the account and keep your sanity.

55   9. Make sure you save for a rainy day. The advice here is tricky. Once you start a business, you must realize that the business is not you, and that as soon as you bring other people into the venture, it takes on a life all its own. Like any newborn, it has an insatiable appetite and will take all the nurturing you have to offer. That nurturance comes in two forms: capital and psychic energy.

56   You run a significant risk of losing your shirt when you start a business, and it's essential never to forget that. However, as I learned the

hard way, taking all of your personal cash and pouring it into your business is ill-advised, no matter how much you are on the verge of making it. Just as ill-advised is pouring so much of yourself into the enterprise that you have no life outside the office.

57 Therefore, prepare for every contingency, even failure. That's not a defeatist attitude; it's a realistic strategy. Even generals preparing for battle leave themselves a way out so that they can fight again another day. Making sure that you can play the game another day—by having some money put away as well as by keeping your emotional options open—means that a failed business can be thought of as a single chapter in your life, rather than your entire story.

58 10. Know what you want to do with your life the day after. The day after what?

59 The day after you realize that your business is either a success or a failure. If the business is a true success, then for all intents and purposes, it can run without you, which means you'll need something else to do next. If it's a failure, then you don't have to worry about it anymore, which could leave a big hole in your day-to-day life.

60 Either way, you'll have time on your hands. I know because I had prepared no contingency plans in case something happened to my business. As a result of my lack of personal disaster planning, despite all the setbacks, I kept automatically looking for more business for our agency to do, rather than heading out to hunt for a marketing job on someone else's payroll.

61 The moral of this story is: If you know what you want to do the day after, you're giving yourself an alternative that will have meaning over and above what you derive from being associated with your business.

62 Trust me. That's a good idea.

63 These 10 confessions represent the personal knowledge I gained from being an entrepreneur. Now that I know them, I am ready to write a happier ending to the book of my business life. Hopefully, you can learn something from them, too.

Understanding Meaning

1. What appear to have been the chief *causes* for the demise of Jamison & Associates?
2. What lessons did Jamison feel he learned about running a business versus creating advertising?

3. What advice does Jamison offer about selecting partners and employees?
4. Jamison tells readers to "be a boss." What are the elements of a good boss?
5. *Critical Thinking:* Many of Jamison's statements are negative, telling readers what not to do. Does this emphasis on avoiding mistakes suggest that he feels many people who dream of opening their own businesses are naive? What does it take to start and maintain a business? What do people often overlook?

Evaluating Strategy

1. What impact does the title have in a magazine dedicated to success and achievement?
2. How effective is the opening *narration?*
3. How does Jamison use *analysis* to diagnose the forces that caused his business to fail?
4. What would make this article easier to read?

Appreciating Language

1. Jamison uses tips like "save for a rainy day." Does this homey language work in this article?
2. What tone comes across in this essay? Does it convey any sense of bitterness or blame seeking?

Connections across the Disciplines

1. Jamison tells readers to look beyond their business ventures. Whether they succeed or fail, entrepreneurs should, he says, consider their lives beyond their careers. How does this relate to Juliet Schor's "Addicted to Plastic: The Overspent American" (page 312) and John Ciardi's "What Is Happiness?" (page 192)? Do all of these writers suggest that happiness or success cannot be measured solely in dollars?
2. Can you relate the experiences of Charles Jamison to some of the sentiments expressed by Leonce Gaiter's "The Revolt of the Black Bourgeoisie" (page 583)?

Writing Suggestions

1. Write a similar essay in which you offer advice to readers based on a failure you have experienced. Tell readers, for example, how to avoid paying

too much for a car, renting the wrong apartment, losing a lawsuit, or failing a college course.

2. *Collaborative Writing:* Discuss with a number of students the pros and cons of owning a business. Take notes, and then work together to write a set of instructions making use of comparison to demonstrate the advantages and disadvantages of working for yourself instead of someone else.

Auto expert Lucille Treganowan (1930–) operates Transmissions by Lucille, a chain of repair shops in Pittsburgh, Pennsylvania. She also appears on the popular PBS television series Lucille's Car Care Clinic. *In 1996 she published a book on auto repair,* Lucille's Car Care, *written in collaboration with Gina Catanzarite, the producer of her television series.*

Cleaning Battery Terminals

As you read the following instructions from Lucille's Car Care, *think about whether or not you would find it easy to follow them. Do they seem clear and detailed enough for someone who has never performed this procedure before?*

1   Corrosion around the battery terminals affects the way electrical currents are conducted, and if the corrosion is severe it can even prevent the car from starting. Sometimes you'll be able to see a kind of whitish powder develop on the terminals, but most problems are caused by corrosion you *can't* see at the contact surfaces between the terminal and the post.

2   You will need:

3   A ½-inch or ⅝-inch box wrench or an open-end wrench from your tool kit or a small ratchet wrench designed specifically for side terminals. Use a 10M (metric measurements) wrench for imports.

4   screwdriver or battery cable terminal puller

5   battery terminal cleaner brush

6   rag

7   water and baking soda solution

8   petroleum jelly

9   NOTE: *Never* smoke cigarettes or use anything that might spark around a battery. To avoid electrical shock, perform the following procedure in the following sequence:

10   1.   Use the wrench to loosen the nuts on the battery terminals at the end of the cable. Be sure to note which is the negative terminal and which is the

positive terminal. They will be clearly marked, and the positive cable is almost always red.

11 2. Use the battery cable terminal puller to remove the negative terminal. If you do not own this tool, use your fingers to work the cable back and forth until it is loosened, or insert a screwdriver underneath the terminal and gently pry it up.

12 3. Use the battery terminal cleaner brush to scrub the inside of the hole in the terminal. Brush until the surface is shiny like new metal. Then fit the other side of the tool over the battery post and rotate it until the metal shines.

13 4. Dip a rag in the water/baking soda solution and clean the top of the battery, removing metal particles that were brushed off the terminal and posts.

14 5. Repeat Step 2 through 4 with the positive terminal.

15 6. Return the terminals to the proper posts, positive *first*, then negative. Tighten the bolts until you cannot turn the terminal any more.

16 7. Apply a light coating of petroleum jelly to the outside of the terminals to fight future corrosion buildup.

Understanding Meaning

1. Why is it important to make sure that a car's battery terminals are clean?
2. What is the point of the warning note that precedes the numbered list of instructions?
3. Why is it important to note "which is the negative terminal and which is the positive terminal"?
4. Why is the final step to apply petroleum jelly to the cleaned terminals?

Evaluating Strategy

1. Why to you think these instructions begin with a list of items one will need to perform the task? Would they be harder or easier to follow without this opening list?
2. How effectively organized are the instructions? Can they be quickly understood?
3. How do numbered points and typeface variations affect the way you read these instructions?

Appreciating Language

1. What do the level of diction and word choice suggest about the intended audience?
2. Does the author successfully avoid overly technical language that some readers might find difficult?

Writing Suggestions

1. Write a set of instructions on first aid, car or home repair, or campus security to be read in an emergency. Use visual aids and short, direct sentences to communicate in as few words as possible.

2. *Collaborative Writing:* Analyze the effectiveness of these instructions with a group of students. Have members read the instructions, and then close their books. One person should refer to the instructions and quiz the group on the steps. Note how much people remembered, and identify areas that more than one person forgot. Based on your group's experiences, work collaboratively to write a short analysis, suggesting changes for greater readability if needed.

STRATEGIES FOR PROCESS WRITING

1. **Define your goal—to explain or to instruct.** Is your purpose to explain how something takes place, or do you seek to instruct readers how to accomplish a specific task?
2. **Evaluate your audience's existing knowledge.** How much does your audience know about the subject? Do any common misconceptions need to be clarified? What terms should be defined?
3. **Define clear starting and ending points.** When does this process begin? What is the end? Readers must have a clear concept of the beginning and end, especially in instructions.
4. **Separate the process into understandable stages or steps.** To explain a process, it is important to break it down into a chain of separate events that makes the process understandable without distorting it. When giving instructions, do not include too many operations in a single step.
5. **Number steps for clarity in the instructions.** Instructions are easier to follow if organized in numbered steps. If interrupted, readers can easily mark their places and later resume the process without confusion.
6. **Consider using visual aids.** Large print, capital letters, bold or italic type, and underlining can highlight text. Graphs, drawings, diagrams, and other visual aids can be beneficial to reinforce both explanatory writing and instructions.
7. **Measure readability of instructions.** Instructions, especially directions people will have to refer to while working, should communicate at a glance. Short sentences and wide spacing between steps are used in cookbooks and repair manuals so a person working in a kitchen or garage can read the text at a distance.
8. **Test your writing.** Because it is easy to skip steps when explaining a process you are familiar with, it is important to have other people read your writing. Other readers can be objective and easily detect missing information.

SUGGESTED TOPICS FOR PROCESS WRITING
General Assignments

Write a process paper on any of the following topics. Assume you are writing for a general, college-educated audience. You may develop your explanation using narratives, comparisons, and definitions. Explain the process as a clearly stated chain of events. Draw from your own experiences.

- How the university processes student applications
- The operation of an appliance such as a microwave, refrigerator, or washing machine
- The process of a disease or disability
- The way small children learn to talk
- The method your employer used in training
- The stages of childbirth
- How a computer virus "infects" a computer
- The way corporations market a new product
- The way the body loses fat through diet or exercise
- How networks select television programs

Write a process paper giving directions to complete a specific task. You may wish to place your instructions in numbered steps rather than standard paragraphs. Remember to highlight any safety hazards.

- How to protect your computer against viruses
- How to purchase a new or used car at the best price
- How to deter a mugger or attacker
- How to quit smoking
- How to find a job
- How to handle sexual harassment on campus or in a job
- How to prepare for an IRS audit
- How to operate a drill press, microscope, or other piece of industrial or scientific equipment
- How to treat a second-degree burn
- How to teach children the importance of saving money

Writing in Context

1. Imagine you have been selected to write a section for a student handbook instructing freshmen how to register for classes. Write a step-by-step paper giving complete instructions. Give exact room numbers, times, and locations. You may wish to refer to a campus map. When you complete a draft of your paper, review it carefully to see if you have left out any pieces of essential information.
2. Select a process you learned on a job, and write instructions suitable for training a new employee. Consider how your job may have changed. Give trainees the benefit of your experience, and add tips that might not be included in the standard job descriptions. Warn readers, for instance, of common problems that arise.

3. Select a process from one of your textbooks, and rewrite it for a sixth-grade class. Simplify the language, and use analogies sixth graders would understand.

STUDENT PAPER: PROCESS

This paper was written in response to the following assignment:

Write a 500-word process paper providing directions to accomplish a specific task. You may include graphs, charts, diagrams, or numbered steps.

SECURING YOUR HOME

1   Homeowners frequently think of security only when planning a vacation. Leaving home for a week or two, they install additional locks, set timers to trigger lights, purchase sophisticated monitoring systems, alert neighbors, and hope their homes will not be robbed in their absence. But most homes are not burglarized while their owners are thousands of miles away. And most burglaries do not occur in the dead of night. Most houses are robbed before 9 p.m., often while their owners are near or inside the residence. Your house is more likely to be robbed while you are grilling in the backyard or watching a football game than when you are on a cruise or camping trip.

2   Although it is impossible to make any home "burglar proof," there are some actions you can take to protect your home and property:

1. **Document your assets**
   Make a list of your valuables. Photograph or videotape each room in your home. Keep receipts of major purchases. Store these and other records in a safe deposit box so you can prove any losses. Review your insurance policies to see if special items such as furs, artwork, or coin collections are covered.

2. **Identify valuables**
   Engrave computers, televisions, cameras, stereos, and VCR's with your name or an identifying number. Police often discover stolen property but have no way of contacting the owners.

3. **Always lock your doors**

   Nothing attracts a thief more than an open garage or unlatched screen door. Lock up even when you plan to visit a neighbor for "just a minute." That "minute" can easily become half an hour, plenty of time for a burglary to occur. Don't leave doors open if you are going to be upstairs or in the basement.

4. **Install only security systems you will use.**

   Many homeowners invest in expensive, high-tech systems that are so cumbersome they leave them off most of the time. A cheap alarm system used twenty-four hours a day provides more protection than a state of the art system used randomly.

5. **Trim shrubbery around entrances and windows**

   Don't provide camouflage for burglars. Thieves can easily conceal themselves behind foliage while jimmying doors and windows.

6. **Network with neighbors**

   Let neighbors know if you expect deliveries, house guests, or contractors. Thieves have posed as moving crews, casually looting a house and loading a truck while neighbors look on.

7. **Store valuables in attics and basements**

   Thieves are reluctant to venture beyond the ground floor, which usually offers numerous exits in case of detection.

3   Finally, call the police the moment you discover that a burglary has occurred. If you return home and find evidence of a break-in — **do not go inside!** The thieves, who might be armed, could still be on the premises. Go to a neighbor's and call the police. Never attempt to confront a burglar yourself. No personal possession is worth risking death or a disabling injury.

Questions for Review and Revision

1. The student offers seven directions. Would these be easier to recall if emphasized by the subtitle "Seven Tips to Keep Your Home Secure"?
2. What misconceptions does the student address?
3. How important is the final warning?
4. The student writes in the second person, directly addressing the readers. Would the paper be less effective if written in third person?
5. Do the level of language, diction, and tone suit the intended audience?
6. Read the paper aloud. Is this document easy to read and easy to remember? Could revisions increase its clarity?

Writing Suggestions

1. Using this paper as a model, write a set of instructions directed to a general audience about improving the performance of your car, installing a new computer program, planning a trip or a wedding, losing weight, choosing a pet, preparing for a job interview, or another topic of your choice.
2. *Collaborative Writing:* Discuss this paper with other students. Using some of its ideas, work together to write a brief set of instructions on securing a dorm room or an apartment.

PROCESS CHECKLIST

Before submitting your paper, review these points.

1. Is the process clearly defined?

2. Do you supply background information that readers need?

3. Is the information easy to follow? Is the chain of events or the steps logically arranged?

4. Could the text be enhanced by large print, bold or italic type, diagrams, or charts?

5. Are your instructions complete? Do readers know when one step is over and another begins?

6 Do your instructions alert readers to normal changes they might mistake for errors?

7. Are hazards clearly stated?

8. Did you use peer review to test your document?

WebTutor

See www.harcourtcollege.com/english/sundance
for information on writing process

9

CAUSE AND EFFECT

DETERMINING REASONS
AND PREDICTING RESULTS

WHAT IS CAUSE AND EFFECT?

What led to the stock market crash of 1929? Why did the *Hindenburg* explode? What caused the Soviet Union to collapse? How did Microsoft corner the software market? How will budget cuts affect education? Would a handgun ban lower street crime? Can a Supreme Court ruling prevent frivolous law suits? The answers to these questions call for the use of *cause and effect*, writing that either seeks to establish reasons why something occurred or to predict future results.

Historians devote much of their time to determining the causes of events. Did Lenin cause the Russian Revolution, or did the revolution create Lenin? Why did Hitler rise to power? What led to the women's movement of the 1970s? Historians also consider the ramifications of current events and speculate about the future. Will another oil crisis occur? How will a change in American foreign policy affect chances for peace in the Middle East?

Nearly all professions and disciplines engage in cause-and-effect reasoning. Marketers try to determine why a product succeeded. Engineers work to discover why a test engine failed. Medical researchers measure the results of a new drug. City planners predict the effect a major earthquake would have on emergency services. Educators consider if curriculum changes will improve Scholastic Aptitude Test scores. Federal Aviation Administration (FAA) investigators examine wreckage to establish why a plane crashed.

Many of the research papers you will be assigned in college and the letters and reports you write in your future career will be developed using cause and effect. Identifying the reasons why something occurred can be formidable. Determining future outcomes, no matter how much data are examined or how many experiments are conducted, can remain largely guesswork.

Deduction and Induction

Writers often formulate cause-and-effect papers using deduction and induction. *Deduction* is a form of logic in which a *major premise* or general rule is applied to a *minor premise* or specific instance in order to reach a *conclusion*. You may be familiar with this classic example of deduction:

MAJOR PREMISE: All cows are mammals.
MINOR PREMISE: Bessie is a cow.
CONCLUSION: Bessie is a mammal.

This illustration, though famous, fails to show the practical value of deduction. Other examples should give you an idea of how often we use deduction:

MAJOR PREMISE: All full-time students are eligible for financial aid.
MINOR PREMISE: Sandra Lopez is a full-time student.
CONCLUSION: Sandra Lopez is eligible for financial aid.

MAJOR PREMISE: The student health plan is only available to California residents.
MINOR PREMISE: Amy Kwan is a resident of New York.
CONCLUSION: Amy Kwan cannot join the student health plan.

Deduction can be used to solve problems and answer questions: Are dental exams deductible on my income tax? Can I sublet my apartment? Will the college give me a refund if I drop a class in the fourth week? All of these questions form a minor premise. The IRS rules, apartment leases, and college policies you consult for answers serve as major premises.

Deduction can be used to help determine both causes and effects. Was a plane crash caused by a defective part?

MAJOR PREMISE: FAA regulations consider this part defective if three bolts are missing.
MINOR PREMISE: One bolt was missing from this part.
CONCLUSION: This part was not defective.

How will an increase in bus fares affect ridership?

MAJOR PREMISE: Bus ridership declines with fare increases.
MINOR PREMISE: The city authorized a fifty-cent fare increase.
CONCLUSION: Bus ridership will decline.

Problems occur with deductive reasoning if the major and minor premises are not precisely stated. The statement that "All full-time students are eligible for financial aid" might be clearer if it included a definition of who is considered a full-time student: "All students taking twelve credits are eligible for financial aid." Other problems arise if the major premise is subject to interpretation. A warranty for snow tires might refuse to cover "improper use." Is off-road driving considered "improper"? How much damage can be considered "normal wear and tear"? Some major premises may prove to be false or require qualification:

MAJOR PREMISE: Democrats are antibusiness.

Are *all* Democrats antibusiness? What is meant by *antibusiness?*

MAJOR PREMISE: Gun control reduces crime.

Can this be proven? Could a drop in crime in a city that passed gun control be caused by other factors—a decrease in unemployment, a shift in population, or more effective policing?

Induction, unlike deduction, does not open with a major premise. Instead it presents and interprets data and then makes a conclusion:

$$X \quad X \quad X \quad X \quad X$$
$$X \quad X \quad X \quad X$$
$$X \quad X \quad X \quad X \quad X$$
$$X \quad X \quad X \quad X$$
$$X \quad X \quad X$$

X = Data
Inductive Leap → Conclusion

The *X*'s in the diagram could represent stolen cars, the number of computers sold last month, blood tests of patients taking a new fertility drug, satellite photographs, interviews with consumers, or evidence collected at a crime scene. Based on a review of the evidence, a conclusion is drawn: Car thefts are increasing in the suburbs, the new fertility drug damages red blood cells, coastline erosion is worse than last year, the consumers' major complaint is poor service, or the murder suspect is a Caucasian female with O-positive blood and dyed hair.

As these examples illustrate, effective induction requires a large body of valid evidence to achieve reasonable conclusions. Ford Motor Company would have to interview more than a handful of Taurus owners to determine customer satisfaction. Medical researchers must rule out other reasons for damaged red-blood cells. As the diagram notes, the movement from specific details to conclusion requires an *inductive leap*. No matter how much evidence is discovered and examined, no absolute assurance can be made that the conclusion is totally true.

The best demonstration of inductive reasoning takes place in a courtroom. In a criminal case the prosecutor tells members of the jury that if they examine all the evidence they will conclude that the defendant is guilty *beyond a reasonable doubt*. The defense attorney will attempt to raise doubt by providing alternative interpretations and by introducing conflicting evidence. He or she will tell the jury that *reasonable doubt* exists and that not enough evidence has been found to reach a conclusion of guilt.

Establishing Causes

By the 1920s surgeons and physicians began noticing that many of their patients with lung cancer were heavy smokers. An observable association was discovered but not clear proof of a cause-and-effect relationship. Not all lung cancer patients smoked, and millions of smokers were free of the disease. Though scientists were concerned, they had no evidence that smoking *caused* cancer. In fact, throughout the 1930s and 1940s cigarette ads featured endorsements by doctors who claimed the calming effect of nicotine reduced stress and prevented stomach ulcers. It was not until 1964 that researchers assembled enough data to convince the surgeon general of the United States to proclaim cigarette smoking a health hazard.

In some instances causes can be established through investigation and research. Doctors can diagnose an infection as the cause of a fever. Accountants can study financial records to discover why a company lost money. But many controversial issues remain subject to debate for decades. Why are more women being arrested and sentenced to prison? Jeff Gammage (page 522) examined the issue, determining that no single cause can be clearly identified:

> The reasons behind it are complex, overlapping and in many ways unclear. Some authorities believe tougher sentencing laws have ensnared many women who played minor roles in drug organizations. Others say women simply are committing more crimes. There's some evidence that more of today's liberated, assertive women see violence as an acceptable way to solve problems—an attitude particularly prevalent among women who themselves have been victimized.

When evaluating a writer attempting to establish a cause, consider the amount of evidence, the degree of objective analysis, and the willingness to qualify assertions.

Predicting Results

In 1936 the *Literary Digest* predicted that Alf Landon would defeat Franklin Roosevelt in his bid for a second term as president. The editors based their prediction on a detailed telephone survey. By randomly selecting names from phone books and asking people whom they planned to vote for, the surveyors assumed they would get an accurate prediction. Their responses from men and women, government employees and business executives, Italians and Jews, farmers and factory workers, and young and old strongly indicated a preference for Landon. But their research failed to accurately predict the outcome of the election because the survey method did not measure a significant population. In 1936 many Americans could not afford telephones, and these economically deprived voters tended to favor Roosevelt.

Predicting future outcomes can be challenging because evidence may be difficult to collect or may be subject to various interpretations. In addition, numerous unforeseen factors can take place to alter expected events. A school board that determines to close schools because of a declining birth rate may fail to account for an influx of immigrants or the closure of private schools that would place more students into the public system.

In "Swept Away" (page 538), Jodi Jacobson asserts that global warming will dramatically affect the climate in the next century:

> Most scientists now agree that a global warming has begun. Its causes are by now depressingly familiar: Greenhouse gases generated by human activity are accumulating in the atmosphere and trapping the sun's radiant heat. These gases include carbon dioxide and nitrous oxides from the combustion of wood and fossil fuels, chlorofluorocarbons (used as a refrigerant and in industrial applications), and methane (from ruminant animals and rice paddies). Meanwhile, population pressures in the Third World are forcing wholesale forest clearing for fuel, farmland and living space. The result is fewer trees left to recapture the chief greenhouse gas, carbon dioxide.

Jacobson continues to predict that global warming will cause the polar ice caps to melt. The rising oceans will flood cities, consume islands, and devastate low-lying deltas.

Jocelyn Tomkin, on the other hand, dismisses these grim predictions. Tomkin's article "Hot Air" (page 549) cautions that the effects of global warming may not be severe. In fact, no global warming may be happening at all:

> The observational evidence that global warming is actually increasing is very shaky. Some researchers claim to see an increase in global warming of about 0.8 degree since 1860. Although average temperatures since then have increased by this much, it's doubtful that the rise reflects carbon-dioxide-induced global warming.
>
> The large year-to-year fluctuations of average temperature . . . mean that the behavior of average global temperature is somewhat like that of a stock market index. Spotting a "real" temperature trend is like deciding if one is in a bull or a bear market. . . .
>
> Moreover, natural causes, rather than the increase in carbon dioxide, are a more likely explanation of the temperature increase. Most of the rise took place prior to 1940, *before* the main increase in the carbon-dioxide level.

When examining writing that predicts future effects, consider the amount of evidence presented, the recognition of other factors that may affect results, and the use of critical thinking.

CRITICAL THINKING FOR
CAUSE-AND-EFFECT WRITING

When writing cause-and-effect essays, avoid these common traps, many of which are known as logical fallacies.

1. **Avoid mistaking a time relationship for a cause** (post hoc ergo propter hoc). If your brakes fail after taking your car into the dealer for an oil change, does that mean the mechanics are to blame? Can the president take credit for a drop in unemployment six months after signing a labor bill? Because events occur in time, it can be easy to assume an action that precedes another is a cause. The mechanics may have not touched your brakes, which were bound to wear out with or without an oil change. A drop in unemployment could be caused by a decline in interest rates or an upsurge in exports and may have nothing to do with a labor bill. *Do not assume events were caused by preceding events.*

2. **Do not mistake an effect for a cause.** Early physicians saw fever as a cause of disease rather than as an effect or symptom. If you observe that children with poor reading skills watch a lot of television, you might easily assume that television interferes with their reading. In fact excessive viewing could be a symptom. Because they have trouble reading, they watch television.

3. **Do not confuse associations with causes.** For years researchers argued that marijuana use led to heroin addiction. The evidence was clear. Nearly every heroin addict interviewed admitted to starting with marijuana. But since most addicts also drank beer, smoked cigarettes, chewed gum, and attended high school, this association could not alone be considered proof. Associations can be compelling and command attention, but they are not proof of a cause-and-effect relationship.

4. **Anticipate unexpected changes.** Many researchers qualify their predictions with the statement "all things being equal, we can anticipate . . ." But conditions never remain frozen. An increase in sales following a major ad campaign could be caused by a competitor going out of business or a drop in unemployment rather than by television commercials.

5. **Avoid "slippery slope" interpretations.** Do not assume that changes will start a trend that will snowball without restraint. If the government allows euthanasia for the terminally ill, you cannot argue that eventually all the elderly and handicapped will be put to death.

6. **Realize that past performance, though an important factor, cannot predict future results.** During the oil crisis of the 1970s, the price of oil soared from $10 to $40 a barrel. Alarmists predicted financial disaster when Americans would have to pay $50–$100 a barrel for oil to run cars and to

fuel industry. But the dramatic price escalation was short-lived. Price increases spurred exploration for new oil fields and launched conservation efforts. Soon the world was awash in surplus oil, and prices dropped to precrisis levels. *Past trends cannot be assumed to continue into the future.*

STRATEGIES FOR READING CAUSE AND EFFECT

When reading the cause-and-effect entries in this chapter, keep these questions in mind.

Meaning

1. Is the writer seeking to establish a cause or to predict results?
2. What is the source of the evidence? A writer opposed to atomic power citing only studies commissioned by an antinuclear group is not as credible as one who presents data collected by neutral organizations.
3. Are alternative interpretations possible? Does a rise in the number of people receiving food stamps mean an increase in poverty, or does it reflect better government assistance?

Strategy

1. Does the writer mistake a symptom for a cause? A survey revealing that ninety percent of batterers in domestic violence cases are abusing alcohol might lead to a call for more treatment centers. In fact alcohol abuse and domestic violence may both result from unemployment.
2. Does the writer assume past trends will continue into the future?
3. Does the essay rest on unproven assumptions?
4. Does the writer demonstrate skills in critical thinking?
5. Does the author use narratives or comparisons to demonstrate his or her conclusions?

Language

1. Does the author's choice of words indicate bias?
2. How does the writer introduce technical terms? Are definitions supplied?
3. What do the tone and style of the entry suggest about the intended audience?

MICHEL MARRIOTT

Michel Marriott is a journalist who has published numerous articles in News-week and the New York Times. *Marriott has written about computers, the Inter-net, the Million Man March, the popularity of coffee bars, drug addiction, school dress codes, and African politics.*

CyberSoul Not Found

In this Newsweek *article, Marriott explores the reasons why African-Americans have the lowest rate of computer ownership of any ethnic group in the United States. As you read the essay, consider other causes.*

1   For many Americans, the expanding universe of computers lies some-where in the imagination between Buck Rogers and "Mr. Rogers' Neighborhood." Wondrous and neat. But if you happen to be an African-American, the same gadgets may evoke less benign images. Try racially segregated schools, back-of-the-bus seating and town halls buzzing with angry white males.

2   Farfetched? Well, consider this: Blacks spend several billion dol-lars a year on consumer electronics, but relatively few plunk down for computers. As PCs rapidly rewire the ways this country works, plays, learns and communicates, blacks are simply not plugging in to what feels like an alien, unwelcoming place. Certainly economics and edu-cation are also powerful handicaps to computer ownership. The average household income for blacks is $25,409; for whites, it is $40,708. But dollars and diplomas don't fully explain why some black professors let their university-issued computers gather dust. There are other impor-tant causes of this computer gap, reasons that are rooted in African-American history, culture and psychology.

3   Figures drawn from a 1994 study for the National Telecommu-nications and Information Administration found that only 11.1 per-cent of black households had computers, compared with 28.6 percent

of white households. Only 518,000 blacks have modern on-line on ramps—compared with 10.1 million whites. Like millions of Americans, many black people are simply baffled by the digitized mysteries of computers. Technophobia knows no color. But far more often, blacks are reluctant to embrace computers because they think cyberspace is a predominantly white, male domain. When Stafford Battle, coauthor of *The African-American Resource Guide to the Internet*, was giving a recent procomputer talk, he got this response from a black T-shirt vendor: "That's the white man's thing." Battle's retort: "Is this the white man's pencil?" But Battle understands that, in the way cyberspace is marketed to America, little except for the computers' circuits is fully integrated. He says even popular nomenclature is off-putting to many blacks. "They talk about 'surfing the Net.' Well, most black people don't surf. We cruise."

4   **Paranoia:** Young blacks are the hardest sell. To them, computers and computer people are the epitome of white nerdiness. Too much Bill Gates and not enough of MTV's Bill Bellamy. Darnell Yates, 16, goes to high school in New York's South Bronx. He says he has no interest in owning a computer. Yet, like almost all his friends, he wears a pager to keep in touch with friends, and thinks cell phones are "hip and in style." In an increasingly technology-driven society, his generation may be left at the curbside; black advocates say the challenge is as urgent as the need for blacks to conquer literacy a century ago. Eric Easter, editor-in-chief and publisher of *ONE*, a black alternative magazine on the Internet, is hopeful. He says the same kinds of marketing that move sneakers could repackage cyberspace with an urban flava. "If Snoop Doggy Dogg had an e-mail address and Notorious B.I.G. would rap about the Internet," Easter adds, "it would blow up over night." Already, black filmmaker John Singleton has given the decidedly cool rapperactor Ice Cube a computer in his college tale *Higher Learning*. And the upcoming Denzel Washington film, *Virtuosity*, features the actor in a sticky tangle with a computer-generated villain.

5   Computers also evoke a deep-seated fear, perhaps even paranoia, among African-Americans young and old. It's something about the machines' unblinking ability to pry. Some blacks say they don't want computers in their homes because they worry that faceless functionaries might use them to spy, for instance, on the household finances. "There is more concern among blacks about Big Brother," says Gregory Newbold, who has a fast-growing electronic newsletter called *Black On Black Communications*. And in the online world—much criti-

cized for being hostile to women—blacks say they frequently discover that their race or views (or both) make them unwelcome. Gretchen Cook, 26, uses the screen name of Ebony Queen. But even so, she wasn't prepared for the firestorm that awaited her on the Internet. She often defends affirmative action against a "conservative tide," and she once entered a chat room and got flamed: WELFAREQUEEN.

6   Similarly, blacks can feel like interlopers when they venture into computer stores, crammed with software that seldom reflects black images or African-American tastes and habits. While popular CD-ROM discs are transforming computer screens into art museums of European and Euro-American art, few discs feature African or Latin- and African-American art. "Nothing reflects the doggone inner city environment, and that is a mistake," says John J. Oliver Jr., chairman and publisher of the Afro-American newspapers, who has launched parts of his 103-year-old publishing empire into cyberspace.

7   **Log-on hope**: The solution may be the browning of cyberspace. That means more content and services that appeal to nonwhites. Last month's premiere of *NetNoir* on America Online will help close the gap. Now, for the first time, there is a major online site that offers anyone interested in black culture a way to plug into history, news, music, politics and education—from an Afrocentric perspective. Other way stations of African-American interest are cropping up all along the Information Superhighway, including an online service called MelaNet. Since April, Tony Brown, a New York journalist-media entrepreneur, has been on the radio preaching a gospel of racial uplift through better computing. Thursday afternoons, he convenes what he calls his "cyberspace club" on WLIB-AM. The program is a popular collection of interviews with black computer experts and Q&As about CD-ROM drives and Internet home pages. Next month Brown will launch his own online service.

8   There are black converts to be found in cyberspace. Anita Brown, known online as Miss DC, is one of the Net's biggest proponents in her black community. She was a longtime skeptic ("I didn't want Big Brother in my house"). But once her brother, a multimedia director at Pacific Bell, got her started, she was hooked. She's now the online Stuart Smalley—sending out a daily inspiration to a growing ring of cyberfriends. She also markets her business, inspirational T-shirts, on-line. Brown even sends out her own black computer newsletter/road map, called *Welcome to Da Hood*. But enthusiastic invitations like hers are still rare. Will many blacks heed the call? Hope is the log-on.

Understanding Meaning

1. What are the major reasons for African-Americans to avoid computers? Why does Marriott argue that poverty cannot be the main reason?
2. Why does Marriott believe many African-Americans perceive computer use as being "white"?
3. In the author's view, what would cause attitudes toward computers and cyberspace to change? Why have African-Americans quickly acquired other technological developments such as cell phones?
4. *Critical Thinking:* How could African-Americans and other minorities benefit from using the Internet? How could cyberspace overcome barriers many encounter in existing institutions?

Evaluating Strategy

1. How effective is the introduction? Do references to segregated schools and "back-of-the-bus seating" grab attention and dramatize the "whiteness" of cyberspace?
2. *Other Modes:* How does Marriott blend *cause and effect* with *persuasion*?
3. *Critical Thinking: Newsweek* appeals to a largely middle-class, college-educated readership. Would most African-Americans who are likely to read this article already be computer literate? How might they respond to Marriott's view that blacks are fearful of cyberspace?

Appreciating Language

1. Marriott uses the word "paranoia" to describe the way many African Americans respond to computers. What impact does this word have? Does it risk overdramatizing his point?
2. What does Marriott mean by "the browning of cyberspace"? Do most people view cyberspace in racial terms?
3. *Critical Thinking:* Does the language associated with computers alienate minorities? Were computers consciously developed to exclude minorities, or was it merely an incidental result?

Connections across the Disciplines

1. Does this article reveal a further kind of segregation? Refer to Nathan McCall's "The Lesson" (page 51). Could some African-Americans fear that cyberspace will expose them to racist attitudes?

2. Refer to the articles by Charles Jamison (page 484) and Leonce Gaiter (page 583). Do these writers indicate a class difference within the African-American community between those experienced in the exchange of information and those who are excluded?

Writing Suggestions

1. Write a short *narrative* detailing your first experiences in cyberspace or using a computer. What fears did you overcome? Did you encounter any racism or sexism in cyberspace that surprised or offended you?
2. *Collaborative Writing:* Discuss Marriott's observations with a number of students, then work together to write a brief *process* explaining methods of introducing minority children to cyberspace. Think of games and challenges that could make cyberspace inviting and valuable to elementary or middle school students.

Gloria Steinem (1934–) was born in Toledo, Ohio, and graduated from Smith College. In 1968 she helped found New York *magazine. Three years later she played a major role in creating* Ms. *magazine, which she edited until 1987. A contributor to* Vogue, Cosmopolitan, Time, *and* Esquire, *Steinem has published several books, including* Outrageous Acts and Everyday Rebellions.

Words and Change

In this article, taken from the 1995 edition of Outrageous Acts and Everyday Rebellions, *Steinem reveals how feminism has changed the English language.*

1   Think for a minute. Who were you before this wave of feminism began?

2   Trying to remember our way back into past realities, past rooms, past beliefs, is a first step toward measuring the depth of change. New words and phrases are one organic measure of change. They capture transformations of perception and sometimes of reality itself.

3   Now, we have terms like *sexual harassment* and *battered women*. A few years ago, they were just called *life*.

4   Now, we are becoming the men we wanted to marry. Once, women were trained to marry a doctor, not be one.

5   Now, placing *women's* in front of words like *center* or *newspaper, network* or *rock band*, indicates a positive choice. Before feminism, it was a put-down.

6   Now, we've made the revolutionary discovery that children have two parents. Once, even the kindly Dr. Spock held mothers solely responsible for children.

7   In 1972, a NASA official's view of women's function in space was "sexual diversion [on] long-term flights such as Mars." Now, women are simply *astronauts*.

8   *Art* used to be definable as what men created. *Crafts* were made by women and "natives." Only recently have we discovered they are the same, thus bringing craft techniques into art, and art into everyday life.

9   In the seventies, policemen were protesting against the very idea of working with women. Now, females serve in every major city, and the *policeman* has become the *police officer.*

10   Now, some lesbians have kept their jobs and custody of their children, and have even been elected to public office—all without having to lie or hide. A decade ago, *lesbian* was a secret word, and *lesbian mother* was thought to be a contradiction in terms.

11   Much of this newness is in putting accuracy into existing language—for instance, changing *congressmen* to *congresspeople,* or MEN WORKING to PEOPLE WORKING—though even those changes spell major differences in power. But new coinage is also needed to capture new perceptions.

12   Before the current wave of feminism, for instance, we were still discussing *population control,* the enlightened answer to the *population explosion.* Both were negative phrases, the first implying the necessity of an outside force, and the second suggesting endless impersonal breeding. Though feminists were expected to come down on the side of *population control,* one of its underlying assumptions was that women themselves could not possibly be given the power to achieve it. Liberal men who were the population "experts" assumed that women were fulfilled only through motherhood, and so would bear too many babies if given the power to make the choice (unless, of course, they could achieve a higher degree of literacy and education, thus becoming more rational: more like men). On the other hand, very religious or conservative males—who often seemed intent on increasing the numbers of the faithful—treated women as potentially sex-obsessed creatures who would use contraception to avoid childbirth totally, behave sinfully, and thus weaken the patriarchal family and civilization itself.

13   In the seventies, however, feminism transformed the terms of discussion by popularizing *reproductive freedom.* This umbrella term includes safe contraception and abortion, as well as freedom from coerced sterilization (of women or of men) and decent health care during pregnancy and birth. In other words, *reproductive freedom* stated the right of the individual to decide to have or not to have a child. It also allowed the building of new trust and coalitions between white women and women of color, who had rightly suspected that the power implied by *population control* would be directed at some groups more than others.

14   *Reproductive freedom* is simply a way of stating what feminism has been advancing for thousands of years. Witches were freedom fighters

for women because they taught contraception and abortion. The modern contribution is to elevate *reproductive freedom* to a universal human right, at least as basic as freedom of speech. Men who want children must find women willing to bear them; that seems little enough to ask. And governments that want increased rates of population growth must resort to such humane measures as reducing infant mortality, improving health care during pregnancy, sharing the work of child-rearing through child care and equal parenthood, and lengthening people's lives.

15   This reproductive veto power on the part of women is exactly what male supremacists fear most. That's why their authoritarian impulse is so clearly against any sexuality not directed toward childbirth within the patriarchal family. This understanding helped feminists to see why the adversaries of such apparently disparate concerns as contraception and homosexuality are almost always the same. It also helped us to stand together on the side of any consenting, freely chosen sexuality as a rightful form of human expression.

16   In recent years, words like *lover* (whether referring to someone of the same or different gender), *sexual preference*, and *gay rights* have begun to be commonly used. *Homophobia* was invented to describe the irrational fear of sexual expression between people of the same gender, a fear so common in the past that it needed no name. There was also a challenge of such rote phrases as *man-hating lesbian*. As Rita Mae Brown pointed out, it's not lesbians who hate men, but women who depend on men and are thus more likely to be hurt and angry.

17   The feminist spirit has also reclaimed some words with defiance and humor. *Witch, bitch, dyke,* and other formerly pejorative epithets started to turn up in the brave names of feminist groups. A few women artists dubbed their new female imagery *cunt art* in celebration of the discovery that not all sexual symbols were phallic. Humor encouraged the invention of *jockocracy* to describe a certain male obsession with athletics and victory; also *loserism* as a rueful recognition of women's cultural discomfort with anything as "unfeminine" as success. *Supermom* and *Superwoman* were words that relieved us all by identifying the Perfect Wife and Mother, plus the Perfect Career Woman, as humanly impossible goals.

18   The nature of work has been a major area of new understanding, beginning with the word itself. Before feminism, *work* was largely defined as what men did or would do. Thus, a *working woman* was someone who labored outside the home for money, masculine-style. Though

still alarmingly common, the term is being protested, especially by homemakers, who work harder than any other class of workers and are still called people who "don't work." Feminists tend to speak of *work inside the home* or *outside the home,* of *salaried* or *unsalaried workers.* Attributing a financial value to work in the home would go a long way toward making marriage an equal partnership and ending the semantic slavery inherent in the phrase *women who don't work.* It would also begin to untangle the *double-role problem* of millions of women who work both inside and outside the home. Defining human maintenance and home care as a job in itself clarifies that men can and should do it as well as women.

19   In order to reach each other across barriers, feminists have tried to be sensitive to our own linguistically divisive habits: for instance, the racist habit of using images of darkness or blackness as negative (*the dark side of human nature, a black heart, blackmail*) and whiteness as positive (*a white lie, white magic, fair-haired boy*).

20   The difficult efforts to make language more accurate often include the invention of such alternatives as *chairperson* or *spokesperson.* Clearly, only a single-sex organization can have a position of *chairman* or *chairwoman.* An integrated organization needs to have a position that can be occupied by any of its members—thus, *chairperson* or better yet, just *chair.* Given the imbalance of power, however, these gender-free words are sometimes used to neuter women and leave men as the status quo. Thus, a woman might be a *spokesperson,* but a man is still a *spokesman.* Females might become *people,* but men remain *men.*

21   Women sometimes collaborated with our own exclusion by trying to skip to gender-free words too soon. *Humanism* was a special temptation (as in, "Don't be threatened, feminists are really just talking about humanism"). *Androgyny* also raised the hope that female and male cultures could be perfectly blended; but because the female side of the equation has yet to be affirmed, *androgyny* usually tilted toward the male. As a concept, it also raised anxiety levels by conjuring up a unisex or desexed vision, the very opposite of the individuality and freedom that feminism has in mind.

22   *Battered women* is a phrase that named major, long-hidden violence. It helped us to face the fact that the most dangerous place for a woman is in her own home, not in the streets. *Sexual harassment* on the job also exposed a form of intimidation that about a third of all women workers suffer. Naming it allowed women to come forward and legal remedies to be created. By identifying *pornography* (literally, "writing

about female slavery") as the preaching of woman hatred and thus quite different from *erotica*, with its connotation of love and mutuality, there was also the beginning of an understanding that pornography is a major way in which violence and dominance are taught and legitimized.

23   Even *female sexual slavery* (once known by the nineteenth-century racist term *white slavery* because it was the only form of slavery to which whites were also subjected) has been exposed by this wave of feminism. We now know it flourishes in many cities where prostitution and pornography are big business and facts of international life.

24   In response to such realizations of injustice, it's no wonder that *radicalism* began to lose some of its equation with excess or unreasonableness. By exposing the injustice of the sexual caste system and its role as a root of other injustices based on race and class, *radical feminism* laid the groundwork for a common cause among diverse women. And by challenging this masculine-feminine, dominant-passive structure as the chief cause and justification of violence, it also proved that *radicalism* can not only take nonviolent forms, but is the only way to challenge the origins of violence itself.

25   In this wave, words and consciousness have forged ahead, so reality can follow. Measuring the distance between the new and the old evokes the unique part of history that lives in each of us.

UPDATE

26   There are many readers who cannot answer the question, "Who were you before this wave of feminism began?" They were simply born into some degree of feminist consciousness, and their higher expectations, their lack of the female cultural problem of *terminal gratitude*, are necessary for the long path ahead.

27   More women are becoming the men they wanted to marry, but too few men are becoming the women they wanted to marry. That leaves most women with two jobs, one outside the home and one in it, a problem that poor women always had but that is now shared by middle-class women—which means that together, we ought to be able to solve it.

28   In many areas, there is now more recognition of ways that polarized, *either/or* choices, modeled on dividing human nature into "feminine" and "masculine," are disappearing or uniting into *and*, a nonhierarchical, full-circle paradigm. In science, the *new physics* and

chaos theory have blown apart our old linear, mechanistic, and hierarchical assumptions. They have helped us think about *linking,* not *ranking.* Feminist scientists offer us *field dependency:* the understanding that nothing can be studied out of its context. In sexuality, the assumption that a person must be either heterosexual or homosexual has begun to loosen up enough to honor both the ancient tradition of *bisexuality* and the new one of individuals who themselves are *transgender* and cross what once seemed an immutable line. Many groups within the lesbian and gay movement now add these two words to their descriptions. People in couples are more likely to speak of each other as *partner* or *life partner,* a relationship that goes beyond the limited connotation of *lover.* *Homophobic* has been joined by *heterosexist,* a way of describing a person or entity that places heterosexuality at the center, or assumes that all other sexualities are peripheral or nonexistent. *Sexual preference* is frequently replaced by the term *sexual identity,* a way of including both those who feel they were born with a particular sexuality and those who feel they chose it.

29   We're also looking at the way language has allowed the victim to be identified, but not the victimizer. In addition to talking about *how many women have been raped,* for instance, we've begun to talk about *how many men rape.* In addition to talking about *why women don't or can't leave a violent situation,* we're beginning to question *why men are violent.* The term *domestic violence* itself has begun to seem trivializing and inadequate, as if it were a lesser kind of violence. Since violence in the home is actually the training ground for and origin of most other violence, *original violence* is one suggested alternative. In these dozen years, *hate crimes* have finally begun to include crimes against women as well as those directed at people of a particular race, religion, ethnicity, or sexuality. *Terrorism* is now also applied to the bombing of abortion clinics, not just to acts that are perceived as political by a masculine definition.

30   Feminist academics have brought into feminism an imitative group of words. *Deconstruction* is the act of divorcing something from its original context and meaning. Phrases like *the production of women's agency* are substituted for *empowerment; problematize* instead of simply talking about problems and what creates them; and even *feminist praxis* when *feminist practice* would do just as well. Academic and other generalized language often obfuscates, distances, and removes insight and information from readers who need them most—but perhaps this is all necessary to get taken seriously and tenured in an academic world.

31   If there was any doubt about the importance of language, it has been put to rest by an anti-equality right wing that is insisting again on using *unwed mother* and *illegitimate children* instead of *single mother* and *children*. As the representative of the only world religion to have permanent observer status in the United Nations, the Vatican has set out to oppose *reproductive rights* and *reproductive health* as phrases, and even to challenge the use of the word *gender* in the U.N. documents. Clearly, the choice of what words we may use determines what dreams we are able to express.

32   Consider the changes already made or still to come in your own language. They are a good indication of where we are and where we need to go.

Understanding Meaning

1. What change in attitude is Steinem referring to when she states that in the past "*sexual harassment*" and "*battered women*" were just called "*life*"?
2. Was the word "women's" traditionally a "put-down"?
3. What does Steinem mean when she states, "More women are becoming the men they wanted to marry, but too few men are becoming the women they wanted to marry"?
4. How have feminist scientists changed traditional views of the universe? Can this change be attributed to gender or prevailing theories?
5. *Critical Thinking:* Steinem asserts "the choice of what words we may use determines what dreams we are able to express." Do you agree? Does a change in language alter consciousness? Without words to describe issues like sexual harassment, does the problem remain undefined and accepted as just "*life*"?

Evaluating Strategy

1. How important are examples in Steinem's essay? Does she provide enough to convince readers that feminism has affected our language?
2. Do newly termed words and phrases that demean women counter Steinem's thesis? For example, movie reviewers now use the term "chick flick" to describe romantic films that appeal to women. Can you give other examples?
3. How important is the study of connotations in Steinem's essay?

Appreciating Language

1. Consider Steinem's use of the word "feminist." Is this a term that requires definition? Since this article first appeared in *Ms.*, does she seem to feel her readers share her understanding of the term?
2. Steinem defines pornography as "writing about female slavery." Would most people share this view? Is the use of the word "slavery" appropriate?
3. *Critical Thinking:* In focusing on vocabulary, did Steinem miss perhaps the most significant change in our language—the shift from using "he" as a universal pronoun for words like "everyone" or "student"? Does the shift to saying "his or her" suggest a more profound change than the addition of words such as *sexual harassment* and *battered women?*

Connections across the Disciplines

1. Refer to Joel Connelly's article, "A Growing Awareness: Environmental Groups and the Media" (page 319). Do groups influence public opinion through words as well as images?
2. In "The Handicap of Definition" (page 310), William Raspberry argues that numerous African American children accept many positive values as being "white" and therefore alien to them. Have women been socialized to see many attributes or behaviors as being "male"? Can defining endeavors as male or female limit people's options?

Writing Suggestions

1. Write an essay about how words have changed our consciousness of women, ethnic groups, the environment, government, and technology. For instance, how has the connotation of "computer" changed since it now refers to a household appliance and not a mammoth, mysterious machine operated by only corporations and governments?
2. *Collaborative Writing:* Discuss Steinem's article with a group of students. How has the women's movement changed society? Have one student record comments and list the effects of feminism. Develop a short essay highlighting the changes your group considers the most significant.

BLENDING THE MODES

JEFF GAMMAGE

Jeff Gammage is a reporter whose articles for The Philadelphia Inquirer *have covered a wide variety of issues, including crime, AIDS, the environment, sports, agriculture, and Elvis.*

Why More Women Are Going to Prison

As you read Gammage's article, notice where he uses narration, comparison, *and* analysis *in his cause-and-effect essay.*

1   ZION CROSSROADS, VA. — The state's newest prison has plenty of tall, chain-link fences and cinder-block walls. It also has a beauty shop, mammography clinic and children's playroom, where colorful cutouts of Plucky Duck and his Tiny Toons friends dance on the walls.

2   That's so the kids have a cheery place to romp when they come to visit their mothers.

3   The sprawling, $53 million Fluvanna Correctional Center, still permeated by the scents of fresh paint and household cleanser, is Virginia's fifth prison for women, built with a capacity of 1,200—and the hope that it can contain the state's steadily rising number of female criminals.

4   The problem is not peculiar to the Old Dominion, where the female inmate population has nearly doubled since 1990. Nationally, the number of women in state and federal prisons rose an astounding 478 percent from 1980 to 1997, nearly double the rate of men.

5   North Carolina opened its sixth women's prison last year. Texas houses more than 2,400 women for violent crimes alone. Virginia was among the states running out of room, and here, as elsewhere, penologists are scrambling for explanations.

6   "I don't know that I have an answer—I don't know that there is one," said Fluvanna's warden, Patti Leigh Huffman. "And if there is, I know it's not a simple one."

7   Two weeks ago, the first 140 inmates in Huffman's charge were settling into their quarters. The facility sits on the remains of a men's

prison work camp, and staffers were combing the grounds for metal scraps from the demolished camp, collecting anything that could be turned into a weapon.

8   Inmates here will be serving time for crimes ranging from theft to murder. Like their male counterparts, they will have access to a gym and law library. But the Fluvanna prison also houses a cosmetology center, where prisoners can earn state certification as hair stylists, and special units equipped to deal with women's health-care needs.

9   Although there is space for 1,200 inmates, it will house only 900 for the time being, with the extra 300 beds held in reserve. They are unlikely to remain empty for long: The number of women in Virginia's prisons has increased from 925 in 1990 to the present 1,754.

10   "I see the inmate population continuing to grow," Warden Huffman said. "It'll be nice to have those beds, because they'll never be cheaper to build than they were in 1998. And if we never fill them, that'll be fine with me."

11   Nationwide, women still are only a small fraction of the inmate population—about 6 percent. But their numbers are growing faster than those of almost any other demographic group. The 478 percent increase in women in state and federal prisons between 1980 and 1997—from 12,331 to 71,294 inmates—compares with a 260 percent increase among men, from 303,643 to 1,094,152, according to the Justice Department.

12   "It has been an amazing period of growth," said Allen Beck, a researcher with the department's Bureau of Justice Statistics.

13   The reasons behind it are complex, overlapping and in many ways unclear. Some authorities believe tougher sentencing laws have ensnared many women who played minor roles in drug organizations. Others say women simply are committing more crimes. There's some evidence that more of today's liberated, assertive women see violence as an acceptable way to solve problems—an attitude particularly prevalent among women who themselves have been victimized.

14   Violent crimes among young women more than doubled between 1985 and 1994, from 9,000 to 21,000. Many of those women "may be responding to a culture of sexual abuse and physical violence by fighting back—often with knives, guns and other weapons," according to a study by the Center for Women Policy Studies in Washington.

15   When polled, young women who had been physically abused were twice as likely to say it was always acceptable to answer a threat with violence. Many felt brutality was permissible not only if they were struck, but if, for instance, someone spread a rumor about them.

16   "It's a generation that is looking at the world and seeing we have only given them two options: Be a victim or be violent. And they're refusing to be victims," said center president Leslie Wolfe. "More women and girls are responding to violence by committing violence."

17   Yet many researchers see one primary reason for the growth: drugs.

18   A majority of the women who are arrested in the United States are charged with drug offenses or crimes committed to support drug habits, particularly theft and prostitution. More than half test positive for drugs.

19   The women tend to be low-level drug offenders with minor criminal records, rarely the leaders of criminal enterprises, according to research by the Sentencing Project in Washington. But under strict mandatory-sentencing laws, their sentences are likely to be similar to those drawn by major criminals. Women who in the past might have gone free on probation now go to prison, while those who might have been given short sentences now get long ones, the project said.

20   That thesis is borne out by some of the numbers. In New York state in 1982, for instance, 67 women were imprisoned on drug charges. By 1993, there were 1,315.

21   "They are very small cogs in a very large system, not the organizers or backers of illegal drug empires," New York Warden Elaine Lord told a Senate committee. "The glass ceiling seems to operate for women whether we are talking about legitimate or illegitimate business."

22   Race appears to play a role, too. The Sentencing Project found that the number of young, black women under the control of the criminal-justice system—that is, in prison, on parole or on probation—increased 78 percent from 1989 to 1994, double that of black men and white women, nine times that of white men. The number of black women held in state prisons for drug offenses rose from 667 in 1986 to 6,193 in 1991.

23   "It's several things coming together," said Marc Mauer, assistant director of the Sentencing Project. "Drug arrests and prosecutions have disproportionately taken place in inner-city areas. Many low-income women have been caught up in the cycle of drug addiction. . . . On top of that, with the introduction of mandatory sentences in the mid-1980s, your chance of going to prison increased substantially, along with your odds of going for a longer period of time."

24   Traditionally, drug suspects could avoid harsh sentences by cooperating with prosecutors, Mauer said. But women involved in drug operations generally know less than the men running them, and thus

have little information to trade. "She's less culpable, but she gets the harsher sentence," Mauer said.

25   Many researchers say that more women are going to prison simply because they are committing more crimes. From 1987 to 1996, the overall arrest rate for women increased nearly 36 percent, three times the rate of men. Property crimes actually decreased among men but rose among women.

26   Violent crimes by women increased at more than three times the rate for men; the women almost invariably attacked someone they knew, such as a boyfriend, husband or ex-husband.

27   "They may have committed 10 seconds of violence, maybe toward somebody who had it coming," said Jeffrey Dillman, assistant warden of the new Virginia prison. "That was enough to land them here."

28   The community of Zion Crossroads is defined by the Crescent Inn Restaurant and a Texaco gas station, set in the rolling central Virginia woodlands 15 miles east of Charlottesville. The prison is a small, self-contained city of more than 15 buildings on 100 acres. About 40 prisoners will arrive each week until the population reaches 900.

29   If those who come here are like other female prisoners nationwide, most will be members of minority groups, unmarried mothers over age 30 who have at least a high school education. Near six in ten will have grown up in one- or no-parent households. Four of ten will say they have been physically or sexually abused.

30   A comprehensive Justice Department study found that half the women in state prisons were serving time for nonviolent crimes. One in four said they committed their crime to get money for drugs. Nearly four in ten used drugs every day.

31   Warden Huffman estimates that 80 percent of the inmates who will end up at Fluvanna will have abused drugs or alcohol. She hopes they will take advantage of the counseling programs here and alter their lives.

32   "I get a real sense that they do want to 'try'," she said. "I can't change anybody . . . but we can provide the opportunity."

Understanding Meaning

1. How has the arrest and incarceration rate for women increased, compared to that for men in the last decade?
2. What reasons do experts offer to explain the increasing number of women entering the prison system?

3. What special problems or situations do female convicts present to prison authorities?

4. *Critical Thinking:* Gammage quotes an expert who says that because female drug suspects know less about the criminal organizations they work for, they are less able to have charges dropped or sentences reduced by offering the police information. Is this unfair? Should petty criminals receive harsher penalties than their superiors?

Evaluating Strategy

1. What types of evidence does Gammage present to readers? Is there a suitable blend?

2. How does Gammage use quotations? Are they effective?

3. Gammage focuses this report by describing a single women's prison in Virginia. Would the article be as effective if he simply discussed the increase in women inmates in general terms?

4. *Other Modes:* Where does Gammage use *narration, comparison,* and *analysis* in this news report?

Appreciating Language

1. What do the tone and style of this essay reveal about the intended audience? Can this news article be quickly skimmed?

2. *Critical Thinking:* Why is word choice critical in discussing convicts? How could a writer create sympathy or hostility for women imprisoned for committing crime? Are these women "criminals" or "victims"?

Connections across the Disciplines

1. Compare this news article to Michael Zielenziger's "Black Is Beautiful: Tokyo Style" (page 314). Do you see similarities in the level of diction, sentence structure, use of quotations, presentation of facts, and paragraph length? What does this reveal about the style and content of news writing?

2. *Critical Thinking:* Refer to Gloria Steinem's "Words and Change" (page 514) and Rene Denfeld's "The New Victorians" (page 284). As women's roles change in society and more women enter traditional male careers such as law, medicine, banking, and politics, can society expect they will naturally play a larger role in male-dominated criminal enterprises as well?

Writing Suggestions

1. Write a brief essay comparing social attitudes toward male and female ex-convicts. Consider the attitudes of family, friends, fellow students, and co-workers. How would they view a woman who served five years for armed robbery or heroin distribution? Would she be regarded differently than a male ex-offender? Are people more troubled by women who commit crimes? Would a female teenager who stole a car be viewed as more or less troubled than a male car thief?

2. *Collaborative Writing:* Review this article with a group of students, then debate this question: Should judges take a woman's children into consideration when passing sentence? Should, for instance, a woman with young children receive a shorter sentence than one with no children or a male prisoner? Work together, and write an opinion in the form of an editorial. If members disagree, write two opposing arguments.

ALAN M. DERSHOWITZ

Alan Dershowitz (1938–) was born in Brooklyn and graduated from Yale Law School in 1962. He was a law clerk for Supreme Court Justice Arthur Goldberg and joined the faculty of Harvard Law School in 1964. As a defense attorney, he has participated in many high profile cases, representing Claus von Bulow, Mike Tyson, and O. J. Simpson. His recent books include Chutzpah, Contrary to Popular Opinion, The Abuse Excuse, *and* Reasonable Doubts.

The "Abuse Excuse" Is Detrimental to the Justice System

In this essay Alan Dershowitz argues that attorneys and defendants who use abuse as an excuse for violent acts damage the justice system by endorsing vigilante behavior.

1   The "abuse excuse"—the legal tactic by which criminal defendants claim a history of abuse as an excuse for violent retaliation—is quickly becoming a license to kill and maim. More and more defense lawyers are employing this tactic and more and more jurors are buying it. It is a dangerous trend, with serious and widespread implications for the safety and liberty of every American.

2   Among the recent excuses that have been accepted by at least some jurors have been "battered woman syndrome," "abused child syndrome," "rape trauma syndrome," and "urban survival syndrome." This has encouraged lawyers to try other abuse excuses, such as "black rage." For example, the defense lawyer for Colin Ferguson—the black man convicted in March 1995 of killing white commuters on the Long Island Railroad on December 7, 1993—has acknowledged that his black rage variation on the insanity defense "is similar to the utilization of the battered woman's syndrome, the post-traumatic stress syndrome and the child abuse syndrome in other cases to negate criminal accountability."

THE DANGER OF VIGILANTISM

3   On the surface, the abuse excuse affects only the few handfuls of defendants who raise it, and those who are most immediately impacted by an acquittal or reduced charge. But at a deeper level, the abuse excuse is a symptom of a general abdication of responsibility by individuals, families, groups, and even nations. Its widespread acceptance is dangerous to the very tenets of democracy, which presuppose personal accountability for choices and actions. It also endangers our collective safety by legitimating a sense of vigilantism that reflects our frustration over the apparent inability of law enforcement to reduce the rampant violence that engulfs us.

4   At a time of ever-hardening attitudes toward crime and punishment, it may seem anomalous that so many jurors—indeed, so many Americans—appear to be sympathetic to the abuse excuse. But it is not anomalous at all, since the abuse excuse is a modern-day form of vigilantism—a recognition that since official law enforcement does not seem able to prevent or punish abuse, the victim should be entitled to take the law into his or her own hands.

5   In philosophical terms, the claim is that society has broken its "social contract" with the abused victim by not according him or her adequate protection. Because it has broken that social contract, the victim has been returned to a "state of nature" in which "might makes right" and the victim is entitled to invoke the law of the jungle—"kill or be killed." Indeed, these very terms were used in a 1994 Texas case in which one black youth [Daimion Osby] killed two other blacks in a dangerous urban neighborhood. The result was a hung jury.

6   But vigilantism—whether it takes the old-fashioned form of the lynch mob or the new-fashioned form of the abuse victim's killing her sleeping husband—threatens the very fabric of our democracy and sows the seeds of anarchy and autocracy. The abuse excuse is dangerous, therefore, both in its narrow manifestation as a legal defense and in its broader manifestation as an abrogation of societal responsibility.

AFFIRMATIVE ACTION IN THE JUSTICE SYSTEM

7   The other characteristic shared by these defenses is that they are often "politically correct," thus reflecting current trends toward employing

different criteria of culpability when judging disadvantaged groups. In effect, these abuse-excuse defenses, by emphasizing historical discrimination suffered by particular groups, seek to introduce some degree of affirmative action into our criminal-justice system.

8   These abuse-excuse defenses are the daily fare of the proliferating menu of TV and radio talk shows. It is virtually impossible to flip the TV channels during the daytime hours without seeing a bevy of sobbing women and men justifying their failed lives by reference to some past abuse, real or imagined. Personal responsibility does not sell soap as well as sob stories. Jurors who watch this stuff begin to believe it, despite its status as junk science. The very fact that Sally Jessy Raphael and Montel Williams repeat it as if it were gospel tends to legitimate it in the minds of some jurors. They are thus receptive to it in the courtroom, especially when the defendant is portrayed as sympathetic, and his dead victim is unsympathetic. William Kunstler is quick to point to public-opinion polls that show that "two-thirds of blacks and almost half the whites surveyed recognize the validity of our [black rage] theory of Mr. Ferguson's defense."

MOST VICTIMS DO NOT COMMIT VIOLENCE

9   But neither public-opinion polls nor TV talk shows establish the empirical or normative validity of such abuse-excuse defenses. The basic fallacy underlying each of them is that the vast majority of people who have experienced abuses—whether it be sexual, racial, or anything else—do not commit violent crimes. Thus the abuse excuse neither explains nor justifies the violence. A history of abuse is not a psychological or a legal license to kill. It may, in some instances, be relevant at sentencing, but certainly not always.

10   Lest it be thought that the abuse excuse is credited only by radical defense lawyers, lay jurors, and talk-show-watching stay-at-homes, a quotation from the attorney general of the United States illustrates how pervasive this sort of thinking is becoming. In April 1993, Janet Reno was quoted as commenting on urban riots as follows: "An angry young man who lashes out in violence because he never had a childhood might do the right thing," and when the "right thing" is in contradiction with the law, "you try to get the law changed." I wonder if the angry young man's innocent victim agrees that the violence di-

rected against his shop was the "right thing" and that the law protecting his property should be "changed."

11   The worst consequence of these abuse excuses is that they stigmatize all abuse victims with the violence of the very few who have used their victimization as a justification to kill or maim. The vast majority of abuse victims are neither prone to violence nor to making excuses.

Understanding Meaning

1. How does Dershowitz define "the abuse excuse"?
2. Does Dershowitz believe that victims do not have the right to retaliate?
3. Do those who use abuse as an excuse for their violent behavior demean the majority of victims who do not seek revenge?
4. *Critical Thinking:* Does the abuse excuse extend throughout society? Do employees, students, and parents give excuses rather than take responsibility for their actions? Have we become a nation of victims?

Evaluating Strategy

1. What examples does Dershowitz use as illustrations of the abuse excuse?
2. Dershowitz places his thesis at the opening of the essay. Is this effective? Can you think of situations in which it would be better to place the thesis at the conclusion?

Appreciating Language

1. Dershowitz is an attorney. How many legal terms does he use in the essay? What does this reveal about his intended audience?
2. Consider the term "abuse excuse." Is this phrase so glib that it risks trivializing a serious problem?

Connections across the Disciplines

1. How does the abuse excuse relate to Martin Luther King Jr.'s observation (page 401) that people often respond to oppression with violence?
2. Refer to Meg Greenfield's essay "Why Nothing Is Wrong Anymore" (page 406). Does she concur with Dershowitz's view that people seek excuses for their criminal acts?

Writing Suggestions

1. Write an essay expressing your own view of the abuse excuse. Do people seem to dodge or deny responsibility for their actions by making excuses? Has almost every type of criminal or uncivil behavior been excused as the result of some mental or emotional disorder or an abusive past?

2. *Collaborative Writing:* Discuss this essay with a group of students. Have a member record comments of the group. Write an essay expressing your group's view of Dershowitz's essay. If the members disagree, consider writing pro and con statements.

LESLIE ABRAMSON

Leslie Abramson first achieved national attention by defending Erik Menendez, who was accused of conspiring with his brother to murder their wealthy parents. Born in New York, she worked as a public defender for seven years before entering private practice in Los Angeles. Twice named Trial Lawyer of the Year by the Los Angeles Criminal Courts Bar Association, Abramson is a frequent commentator on Court TV. In 1997 she published The Defense is Ready: Life in the Trenches of Criminal Law, *which recounts her experiences as a defense attorney.*

The Abuse Defense Balances the Justice System

In this article, Abramson argues that victims are fully justified in using past abuse as a factor in their defense when charged with a crime of retaliation. As you read her essay, consider how Alan Dershowitz would regard her position.

1   I never learned about "male justice" in school.

2   During my education in the New York City public schools, the City University of New York and the University of California, Los Angeles, School of Law, I was taught the noble fictions of our justice system. I was told that American justice is equal for all. I was instructed that the accused always is presumed innocent until proven guilty, and that the prosecution bears the burden of proving that guilt beyond a reasonable doubt.

3   By the end of my first year of practice I also had learned that much of what I'd been taught was naive. Most important, I discovered that the racism and sexism deforming so many of our institutions also infect the courts, producing a double standard of justice.

4   Much has been written about racism's insidious role in our criminal-justice system. But the recent cases of O.J. Simpson [acquitted of murder in October 1995], Lyle and Erik Menendez [charged with murdering their parents, their trial resulted in hung juries in January 1994], and Lorena Bobbitt [acquitted of maiming her husband in

January 1994] have opened a public debate on how gender bias influences the way we perceive crime, criminal responsibility and justice.

JUSTICE FOR "WRONGED" MEN AND ABUSED WOMEN

5   "Texas justice" was what we criminal lawyers used to call cases in which a man was acquitted after killing his wife and her lover in *flagrante delicto*. It mattered not if the victims were unarmed or asleep when the "wronged" man blew them away in his fit of jealous rage. No one went to the talk shows to decry the "heat of passion" defense employed by men expressing their possessory rights over the women of their choice—including the right to kill. Of course, no such right to kill was expressly provided in the written law, but the unwritten law— what might be called the male bill of rights—was implicitly understood by sympathetic male jurors.

6   The law of macho, of course, does not extend to women and children who kill. They rarely kill, but when they do, they don't do it out of wounded pride or from affronts to their sexuality or in the anger of the rejected. The forces that drive them to act are fear and terror, the motivations of the weak, the oppressed, the tortured and the broken. And they are scorned and ridiculed and hated for it.

7   We guiltily admire the successful barroom brawler, the fastest gun, the aggressive forechecker, the crushing lineman. The law of self-defense as currently codified in most states recognizes this, and is a male version of survival—two physical and emotional equals duking it out or facing off *High Noon* style, pistols at the ready. Burning beds, parents united in abuse in their family den—these are not the images our male legislators had in mind when the criminal codes were written.

8   We've learned a lot since then about the psychology of abusive relationships, about the cruelty, oppression and inescapability of child abuse and molestation, about the terror that marks virtually every moment for the victims of chronic domestic violence. Despite this knowledge, the media, the self-anointed pundits and the self-promoting denizens of the law schools' ivory towers sanctimoniously declare their outrage when an abused person recounts a life of torment to explain why he or she succumbed at last to terror and struck out at the abuser.

These critics label such explanations the "abuse excuse." They lament our loss of "personal responsibility."

9   This male model of justice pervades the public consciousness and explains why many people say they would sympathize with O.J. Simpson even if they believe he killed Nicole Brown Simpson and Ronald Goldman. It wouldn't matter, they say, even if they believed that these killings followed years in which this strong, physically fit professional athlete beat and emotionally abused his five-foot-eight 125-pound wife. O.J. Simpson may indeed be innocent, as he is now legally presumed to be. What makes much of his support in the community troubling, however, is that it derives not from this presumption, but from the undercurrent of entitlement that the killing of an ex-wife engenders.

A CASE OF PSYCHOLOGICAL ABUSE

10   The best and worst example of this double standard was graphically displayed to me in a case I handled a decade ago. My client, then a woman of fifty, had been raped on her way home from work years before and traumatized by the experience. Twenty years later she married a widower with a four-year-old daughter—and a shadowy past. Only after marrying this wealthy, domineering man did my client discover that he had produced his widowerhood by shooting his unarmed first wife to death as she spoke to a friend on the telephone while his infant daughter slept in the next room. He was convicted of manslaughter, served less than two years in prison and regained custody of the little girl upon his release.

11   During the course of their ten-year marriage the husband's highest form of amusement was to play the role of my client's former rapist by sneaking up on her from behind and grabbing her. He was the textbook battering husband, jealous, possessive, controlling his wife's every movement and human contact, belittling, explosively angry, sexually demanding. Finally, after a period of especially frequent outbursts, he threatened to do to my client what he had done to his first wife. She shot him, once, in the head while he was sleeping. She ran screaming down the hallway, called the police, confessed her crime. At her first trial she was convicted of second-degree murder and sentenced to five

years to life in state prison. Her conviction was reversed on appeal due to prosecutorial and judicial misconduct.

12   That's when I entered the case. In her second trial, we presented evidence of the extreme psychological impairment this woman suffered. The jury hung; subsequently, she pleaded guilty to manslaughter and the judge granted her probation. At the sentencing hearing, the male deputy D.A. took my client's hand and said: "I want to apologize to you for that first conviction. You are not a murderer. I just didn't understand."

13   Score one for equal justice.

Understanding Meaning

1. What is Abramson's thesis? How would you restate it in your own words?
2. What does Abramson mean by "male justice"?
3. Why does Abramson believe that the justice system was unbalanced, favoring men over women? Does the justice system give men special entitlements?
4. *Critical Thinking:* Does Abramson see any risk of an "abuse excuse" encouraging vigilante justice? How should society deal with those who act violently in response to abuse?

Evaluating Strategy

1. Abramson includes personal experiences in her essay. Does this give her writing greater credibility? Does firsthand experience provide powerful support?
2. What appeals does Abramson use to support her thesis?
3. Abramson provides several examples to support her thesis. Do you find them effective?

Appreciating Language

1. Abramson uses the term "abuse defense" rather than "abuse excuse." Consider the connotations these words have for readers. How does Abramson use language to justify use of the abuse defense?
2. *Critical Thinking:* How do word choice and connotation affect the way people view criminal cases? When does a "defendant" become an "accused killer," and how do those accused of crimes use the word "victim" to defend their actions?

Connections across the Disciplines

1. Refer to "Why More Women Are Going to Prison" by Jeff Gammage (page 522). Are many women imprisoned for retaliating against abusive partners?
2. Consider the opinions expressed by Rene Denfeld (page 284) and Gloria Steinem (page 514). How would they view Leslie Abramson's concept of "male justice"?

Writing Suggestions

1. Write an essay stating your opinion on the use of the abuse defense. Support your thesis with examples of situations in which people's past abuse should or should not be considered a justifiable defense for violent behavior.
2. *Collaborative Writing:* With a group of students, discuss a recent criminal case in which the abuse excuse was used as a defense. Have a member record comments. Write an essay advocating your group's opinion. If members have differing views, consider drafting pro and con versions.

PRO AND CON VIEWS: GLOBAL WARMING

JODI JACOBSON

Jodi Jacobson is a senior researcher at the World Watch Institute, an environmental organization that monitors the impact human activity has on the planet. She is also the author of Environmental Refugees: A Yardstick of Habitability.

Swept Away

In this World Watch *(1989) article, Jodi Jacobson describes the effects global warming will have in the future. Theorists claim that pollution is causing atmospheric changes that will trap heat and slowly cause the earth to become warmer. Climate changes will alter weather patterns and plant growth and raise ocean levels as the polar ice caps melt. Read Jacobson's account of the effects of global warming, and then read Jocelyn Tomkin's opposing piece.*

1   "Don't buy land in New Orleans," warns John Milliman of the Woods Hole Oceanographic Institution in Massachusetts. The scientist's comment stems from his knowledge of how sea level rise—an expected consequence of global warming—will affect the habitability of low-lying coastal regions around the world. In the 21st century, waves now breaking on the shores of Louisiana's coast could be lapping at the doors of homes in the Big Easy. Miami is another case in point. The first settlements in this city were built on what little high ground could be found, but today most of greater Miami lies at or just above sea level on swampland reclaimed from the Everglades. Water for its three million residents is drawn from the Biscayne aquifer that flows only feet below the city streets. That the city exists and prospers is due to what engineers call a "hydrologic masterwork" of natural and artificial systems that hold back swamp and sea.

2   Against a three-foot rise in ocean levels, which is expected by the year 2050, the city's only defense would be a costly system of sea walls and dikes. But that might not be enough to spare the city from insidious assault. Fresh water floats atop salt water, so as sea levels rise the water table would be pushed three feet closer to the surface. The elaborate pumping and drainage system that currently maintains the integrity of the highly porous aquifer could be overwhelmed. Roads would buckle, bridge abutments sink, and land revert back to swamp.

3   Miami's experience would not be unique. Large cities around the world—New Orleans, New York, Venice, Bangkok and Taipei, to name a few—would face the prospect of inundation by invading seas. For each, the choice would be fight or flight.

4   Protecting infrastructure and water supplies of coastal cities, not to mention saving shorelines and wetlands, will require many billions of dollars, perhaps even more than most well-off nations could afford. Sea levels have only gone up several inches over the past century, but their rise is sure to accelerate in the coming decades as global warming sets in motion an expansion of ocean volume and a melting of mountain glaciers and polar icecaps. While some universal increase in sea level is now inevitable, the rate and extent of change depends on preemptive action adopted by society today.

THE EXPANDING OCEAN

5   Most scientists now agree that a global warming has begun. Its causes are by now depressingly familiar: greenhouse gases generated by human activity are accumulating in the atmosphere and trapping the sun's radiant heat. These gases include carbon dioxide and nitrous oxides from the combustion of wood and fossil fuels, chlorofluorocarbons (used as a refrigerant and in industrial applications), and methane (from ruminant animals and rice paddies). Meanwhile, population pressures in the Third World are forcing wholesale forest clearing for fuel, farmland and living space. The result is fewer trees left to recapture the chief greenhouse gas, carbon dioxide.

6   It is now all but certain that the delicate balance between incoming sunlight and reflected heat that keeps the earth at a relatively constant average temperature has been upset. What is not certain is just how much higher the temperature will go, and how quickly the increase will take place. Estimates based on current trends project that an average global rise of between three and eight degrees Fahrenheit can be expected within the next 40 years.

7   As temperatures rise the waters of the earth will expand. Glaciers and icecaps will melt. Still higher sea levels may occur if the warming breaks loose such large frozen ice masses as the West Antarctic sheet. If correct, the predicted temperature changes would escalate sea level by five to seven feet over the next century. Some climatologists now estimate that the rate of increase will accelerate after 2050, reaching about an inch per year.

8   The heat and dryness of the summer of 1988 drew attention to the withering effects global warming could have on agricultural productivity, but its most lasting legacy could well be the displacement of peoples, the abandonment of entire delta regions, and the destruction of vital coastal ecosystems caused by inundation.

AN UNAFFORDABLE BILL

9   China's 1,500-mile-long Great Wall is considered the largest construction project ever carried out, but it may soon be superseded in several countries by modern-day analogues: the "Great Seawalls." If nothing is done to slow global warming, then building structures to hold back the sea will become essential, but their multi-billion dollar price tags may be higher than even some well-to-do countries can afford.

10   Nowhere is the battle against the sea more actively engaged than in the Netherlands. The Dutch are perhaps best known for their achievements in building a nation on the deltas of the Meuse, Rhine and Schedule rivers. And well they should be: Without the carefully maintained stretches of dikes (250 miles long) and sand dunes (120 miles) built by Holland's engineers to hold back the sea, more than half the country would be under water.

11   As the engineers know, the ocean doesn't relinquish land easily. In early 1953, a storm surge that hit the delta region caused an unprecedented disaster. More than 100 miles of dikes were breached, leading to the inundation of 600 square miles of land and the deaths of more than 1,800 people. In response, the Dutch government put together the Delta Plan, a massive public works project that took two decades and the equivalent of 6 percent of the country's gross national product each year to complete.

12   The Dutch continue to spend heavily to keep their extensive system of dikes and pumps in shape, and are now protected against storms up to those with a probability of occurring once in 10,000 years. But, due to sea level rise, maintaining this level of safety may require additional investments of up to $10 billion by 2040.

13   Large though these expenditures are, they are trivial compared with what the United States, with more than 19,000 miles of coastline, will have to spend to protect Cape Cod, Long Island, the Maryland, Massachusetts and New Jersey shores, North Carolina's Outer Banks,

most of Florida, the bayous of Louisiana, the Texas Gulf Coast and the San Francisco Bay Area.

14   Even so, industrial countries are in a far better financial position to protect their coastal regions than are developing nations. Bangladesh, for instance, can ill afford to match the Dutch mile for mile in seawalls. But its danger is no less real. The cyclones originating in the Bay of Bengal before and after the monsoon season already devastate the southern part of Bangladesh on a regular basis. Storm surges 18 feet higher than normal can reach as far as 125 miles inland and cover a third of the country.

15   In addition to lifting the ocean's level, global warming is likely to increase the frequency of these tropical storms. When added to the ongoing alteration of the Bengal Delta's natural processes by human activity, these conditions may wreak so much damage that Bangladesh as it is known today may virtually cease to exist.

SUBSIDING AWAY

16   Low-lying delta regions, vulnerable even to slight increases in sea level, will be among the first land areas lost to inundation. Residents of these regions are joined in activities that amount to a lowering of defenses. By overpumping groundwater and interfering with the natural ground-building that rivers achieve through sedimentation, they are causing the land to sink. In a vicious circle, the more populated these regions become, the more likely this subsidence—and the more devastating and immediate the hike in the level of the sea.

17   Under natural conditions, deltas are in a state of dynamic equilibrium, forming and breaking down in a continuous pattern of accretion and subsidence. Over time, these sediments accumulate to form marshes and swamps. But regional and local tectonic effects, along with compaction, cause the land to subside by as much as 4 inches a year if additional sediments are not laid down.

18   Channeling, diverting or damming rivers can greatly reduce the amount of sediment that reaches a delta. Where humans interfere with river systems, sediment either shoots past lowlands and is borne out to sea, as with the Mississippi River, or it is blocked upriver, as with the Nile. When this happens, sediment accumulation does not offset subsidence. The result is more severe shoreline erosion and a relative

increase in sea water levels. Subsidence also occurs where subterranean stores of water or oil are drained. In Bangkok, Thailand, net subsidence has reached 5 inches per year due to a drop in the water table caused by excessive withdrawals of groundwater over the past three decades.

19   In Louisiana, reduced sedimentation along with extensive tapping of groundwater and underground stores of oil and gas have accelerated the disintegration of the Mississippi Delta. That state now loses more land to subsidence and sea level rise on an annual basis—50 square miles per year—than any other state or country in the world.

20   According to Woods Hole's Milliman, the combined effects of sea level rise and subsidence in Bangladesh and Egypt, whose populations are concentrated on deltas, threaten the homes and livelihoods of some 46 million people.

21   To arrive at that figure Milliman's research team started with two estimates of sea level rise: a minimum of 5 inches by 2050 and 11 inches by 2100, and a maximum of 31 inches by 2050 and 85 inches by 2100. They then calculated the effects under three scenarios.

22   Under the "best case" scenario, the researchers assume the minimum rise in sea level and a delta region in equilibrium. The second scenario, called the "worst case," assumes the maximum rate of sea level rise and the complete damming or diversion of the river system draining into the delta. As mentioned, the resulting subsidence must then be added to the absolute rise in sea level. The third scenario is referred to as the "really worst case." It assumes that excessive groundwater pumping from irrigation and other uses accelerates subsidence.

23   To calculate the economic implications of these three cases on both Egypt and Bangladesh, Milliman and his colleagues assumed present-day conditions, such as the estimated share of total population now living in areas that would be inundated and the share of economic activity that is derived from them. Continued settlement and population growth in these areas will only make for more environmental refugees.

SEVEN FEET FROM DISASTER

24   Milliman's calculations bode poorly for Bangladesh, which is nothing more than the world's largest deltaic plain. The Bengal Delta, built at

the confluence of the Ganges, Brahmaputra and Meghna rivers, occupies about 80 percent of Bangladesh's total area. Much of the remainder is water. As a result, the nation's inhabitants are subject to annual floods from the rivers and from ocean storm surges.

25   Just how severely sea level rise will affect Bangladesh depends in part on the pace at which damming and channeling proceeds on the three giant rivers and their tributaries. Although annual flooding is severe and can damage crops grown on the flood plains, large areas of the delta region suffer drought for the rest of the year. The diversion of river water to parched fields leaves Bangladesh in its present predicament: sedimentation is decreasing and subsidence is increasing.

26   The Woods Hole researchers have also concluded that the increasing withdrawal of groundwater in Bangladesh is exacerbating subsidence. Between 1978 and 1985, there was at least a sixfold increase in the number of wells drilled in the country. Sediment samples suggest that the withdrawal of well water may have doubled the natural rate of subsidence.

27   Taking these factors into account, Milliman and his colleagues estimate Bangladesh is going to experience the "really worst case" scenario. The effect of sea level rise will be as much as 82 inches along the coast by 2050, in which event it's likely 18 percent of the habitable land will be under water. More than 17 million people would become environmental refugees. The 57-inch rise in the worst case wouldn't spare the nation: 16 percent of its land would be lost.

28   By the year 2100, the really worst case scenario would have progressed to the point that 38 million Bangladeshis will be forced to relocate. The social and economic effects will be jarring. Because nearly a third of the country's gross national product is generated within the land area that will be lost, an already poor country will have to accommodate its people on a far smaller economic base. Coastal mangrove forests, upon which 30 percent of the country's population depends to some extent for its livelihood, will be the first victims of advancing seas and extensive river diversion.

29   Where will those displaced by rising seas go? Moving further inland, millions of refugees will have to compete with the local populace for scarce food, water and land, perhaps spurring regional clashes. Moreover, existing tensions between Bangladesh and its large neighbor to the west, India, are likely to heighten as the trickle of environmental refugees from the former becomes a torrent.

UP THE NILE

30   Egypt's habitable area is even more densely populated than that of Bangladesh. By and large, Egypt is desert except for the thin ribbon of productive land along the Nile River and its delta. Egypt's millions crowd onto less than 4 percent of the country's land, leading to a population density there of 700 people per square mile.

31   Milliman's study points out that because the Nile has already been dammed—which means most of the sediment that would offset subsidence of the delta is trapped upstream—only the "worst" and "really worst" cases are relevant for Egypt. Consequently, local sea level rise would range between 16 and 22 inches by 2050, rendering up to 19 percent of Egypt's good land uninhabitable.

32   If the increase is 22 inches, more than 8.5 million people would be forced to relinquish their homes to the sea, and Egypt would lose 16 percent of its gross national product. By 2100, local sea level rise will range between 101 and 131 inches, submerging up to 26 percent of habitable land and affecting an equal portion—24 percent—of both population and domestic economic output.

33   While neither Bangladesh nor Egypt is likely to influence the global emission of greenhouse gases or sea level rise, they do wield considerable control over local sea levels. The development policies they choose in the near future will have a significant effect on the future of their deltas and the people who live on them.

ECOSYSTEMS AT RISK

34   Coastal swamps and marshes are areas of prodigious biological productivity. The ecological and economic benefits derived from areas such as Louisiana's wetlands are inestimable. Nearly two-thirds of the migratory birds using the Mississippi flyway make a pitstop in those wetlands, while existing marshlands and barrier islands buffer inland areas against devastating hurricane surges. Marshes not only hold back the intrusion of the Gulf of Mexico's salt water into local rivers but are a major source of fresh water for coastal communities, agriculture and industry. Louisiana's wetlands supply 25 percent of the U.S. seafood catch and support a $500-million-a-year recreational industry devoted to fishing, hunting and birding.

35   What was laid down over millions of years by the slow deposit of silt washed off of land from the Rockies to the Appalachians could be jeopardized in a little over a century. Louisiana's famous bayous and marshland may be overrun by the year 2040, when the Gulf of Mexico surges up to 33 miles inland. With the delicate coastal marsh ecology upset, fish and wildlife harvests would decline precipitously and a ripple effect would flatten the coastal economy. Communities, water supplies and infrastructure will all be threatened.

36   According to U.S. Environmental Protection Agency estimates, erosion, inundation and salt water intrusion could reduce the area of coastal wetlands in the United States by 30 to 80 percent if today's projections of sea level rise are realized. Vital wetlands such as the Mississippi Delta and Chesapeake Bay regions would be irreparably damaged. No one has yet calculated the immense economic and ecological costs of such a loss for the United States, much less extrapolated it to the global level.

37   Were it not for the enormous pressure human encroachment puts on them, coastal swamps and marshes might have a chance to handle rising seas by reestablishing upland. But heavy development of beach resorts and other coastal areas throughout the United States means that few wetlands have the leeway to "migrate."

38   Highly productive mangrove forests throughout the world will also be lost to the rising tide. Mangroves are the predominant type of vegetation on the deltas along the Atlantic coast of South America. On the north coast of Brazil active shoreline retreat is possible because there is little human settlement; the mangroves can possibly adapt. In the south, however, once-extensive mangroves have been depleted or hemmed in by urban growth, especially near Rio de Janeiro in Brazil. No more than 40 square miles of mangroves remain where once thousands of square miles stood. As sea level rises, these remaining areas will disappear.

MODERN-DAY ATLANTIS

39   In 2100, cartographers will likely be redrawing the coastlines of many countries. They may also make an important deletion: By that year, if current projections are borne out, the Maldives will have been washed from the earth. The small nation, made up of a series of 1,190 islands

in atolls, is nowhere higher in elevation than six feet. A mean sea level rise of equal height would submerge the entire country. With a three-foot rise, well within the expected increase of the next century, a storm surge would, in the words of President Maumoon Abdul Gayoom, be "catastrophic and possibly fatal." Other such endangered places include the Pacific islands of Kiribati, Tuvalu and the Marshalls.

40   By 2050, the Florida Keys "will no longer exist," according to Elton J. Gissendanner, past executive director of the Florida Department of Natural Resources. Loss of the Keys will displace thousands of permanent residents and wipe out a tourist industry that brings 100,000 people to the area each year. Approximately 70 percent of Florida's residents live right on the mainland coast, but no study has been done to determine how many will become environmental refugees.

41   Although increases in sea level will occur gradually over the next several decades—accelerating in 2030, when the greenhouse effect is expected to really kick in—the issue has already sparked a number of current debates.

42   For one, should society continue on its current path and accept sea level rise as inevitable, or should it change consumption patterns for fossil fuels and chemicals to mitigate a global warming? How long should local and national governments wait before investing heavily to defend their shores against a future threat, especially when other needs are pressing? When will it be too late? Conversely, should they seek to protect these areas at all? How can coastal residential and resort development be allowed to continue if the land is projected to disappear within a few decades? And who should provide insurance against catastrophe to those living in high-risk areas? Perhaps most important, who will help the Third World cope with the massive dislocations envisioned?

43   The industrial nations, heavily reliant on the burning of fossil fuels over the past century, are primarily responsible for initiating global warming. But, today virtually every citizen of every nation engages in activities that make the problem worse. Meanwhile, development strategies currently being adopted by many poorer countries—water projects that lead to subsidence, policies that encourage deforestation, and development programs based on fossil-fuel-intensive technologies—are likely to exacerbate, rather than abate, the warming and its effects.

44   If current trends persist, global warming and the subsequent rise in sea level will accelerate. If, on the other hand, concerted action is taken now—to raise energy efficiency and curtail overall fossil fuel use, to find substitutes for chlorofluorocarbons and other industrial chemicals that aggravate the greenhouse effect, to stem the tide of deforestation that destroys carbon-fixing trees—then sea level rise can be kept to a minimum.

45   President Gayoom of the Maldives frames the situation in blunt terms: "The predicted effects of the change are unnerving. . . . Reconstruction, rehabilitation and strengthening of coastal defense systems could turn out to be crippling for most affected countries." When the economic and environmental consequences are added in, no citizen of the planet is likely to remain unaffected.

Understanding Meaning

1. What is global warming?
2. What causes these changes, according to Jacobson?
3. How will global warming affect the planet? When will these changes occur?
4. How will governments be forced to respond to changes wrought by global warming?
5. *Critical Thinking:* What proof does Jacobson offer that these changes are likely to take place? How difficult is it to predict the future? What changes could alter the impact of global warming?

Evaluating Strategy

1. Jacobson begins the essay with a quote warning against buying land in New Orleans. Is this an effective attention getter, or does it risk being too sensational?
2. How does Jacobson explain complex scientific theories to a general audience?

Appreciating Language

1. How much technical language does Jacobson use? What does this reveal about her intended audience?

2. How does Jacobson use language to dramatize her view of the effects of global warming?

Connections across the Disciplines

1. How does this article support the argument made by Carl Sagan's "Why We Need to Understand Science" (page 589)?
2. *Critical Thinking:* Read Jocelyn Tomkin's refuting article (page 549). How does this article change your way of viewing Jacobson's assertions?

Writing Suggestions

1. Consider Jacobson's worst-case scenario. In your opinion, could the nations of the world cope with the slow rise of the oceans? Would the expenditure be much more than that spent on armaments? Write a short essay explaining how governments could respond to the crisis Jacobson describes.
2. *Collaborative Writing:* Discuss this essay with a group of students. Are they accustomed to reading articles full of gloom, predicting dire events in the future? Do writers overstate their cases to capture attention? Discuss instances where past predictions have been proven wrong. Work together to write a short paper outlining the issues raised in your group. You can develop the paper using comparison or cause and effect.

JOCELYN TOMKIN

Jocelyn Tomkin is an astronomer at the University of Texas at Austin. He wrote this article for Reason *(1993), a publication of the Reason Foundation based in Los Angeles. Tomkin argues that the effects of a rise in carbon dioxide are over-stated. Instead of seeing global warming as an environmental threat, Tomkin asserts it "has been an essential ingredient in the evolution of life on earth."*

Hot Air

Read Tomkin's article after studying the preceding essay by Jodi Jacobson. As you read Tomkin's piece, refer to Jacobson's. Which writer seems better at applying critical thinking skills?

1   In his best-selling book, *Earth in the Balance*, Vice President Al Gore speculates that global warming caused by the greenhouse effect will throw "the whole global climate system . . . out of whack," dramatically reducing rainfall in parts of the world already troubled by drought, melting the polar icecaps, raising ocean levels, and devastating low-lying countries such as Bangladesh, India, Pakistan, Egypt, Indonesia, Thailand, and China. "In the lifetimes of people now living, we may experience a 'year without winter,'" Gore writes. "We are carelessly initiating climate changes that could well last for hundreds or even thousands of years."

2   Do such predictions have a basis in reality? Central to this question is the greenhouse effect. Contrary to the impression given by the mainstream media, the greenhouse effect is not of recent origin; it has been around for billions of years. But the link between this indisputable phenomenon and Gore's doomsday scenarios is tenuous at best. To understand why, you have to know something about the mechanics of the greenhouse effect.

3   The sun bathes the earth in sunshine. Some of the sunshine is reflected straight back into space, either by clouds or by the earth's surface. The remainder is absorbed by the earth's surface and thus heats it. Predictions about global warming hinge on the question of where this heat goes. Answering this question requires a brief trip into

4   the world of electromagnetic radiation—light in all its forms, both visible and invisible.

5   All bodies radiate heat. A simple physical law says that the cooler a body is, the longer the wavelength at which it radiates its heat. The hot plate of a stove, for example, glows an orange-red when it's running at full blast. But turn it down, and as it cools it radiates its heat at longer and longer wavelengths, until it cools to the point where it's radiating exclusively in the infrared. To the eye it now appears to be off, although it is still too hot to touch.

6   Even everyday objects at everyday temperatures are busy radiators of heat in the infrared. A block of ice at melting point, for instance, has a temperature of 273 degrees Kelvin and is a raging furnace compared to a block of ice at absolute zero. (The Kelvin temperature scale is the same as the Celsius scale, except its zero is absolute zero, instead of the freezing point of water.) The earth itself continually radiates heat from both its dayside and its nightside. The balance between sunshine's heating effect and the cooling effect of the radiation the earth pours back into space allows the planet's surface to maintain a roughly constant temperature (apart from diurnal and seasonal variations).

7   But the earth's surface, with an average temperature of 288 degrees Kelvin, is much cooler than the sun's, with a temperature of 5,800 degrees Kelvin. So while the sun pumps most of its heat into space in the form of user-friendly visible light, the earth returns this heat to space in the form of much-longer-wavelength, invisible, infrared radiation. A greenhouse gas is a gas that is transparent at visible wavelengths but opaque at infrared wavelengths. It thus admits sunshine but blocks the escape of the earth's infrared radiation, thereby warming the planet's surface. As a rule, gases whose molecules have three or more atoms, such as carbon dioxide, are greenhouse gases, while gases whose molecules have only two atoms, such as oxygen, are not.

8   Among the greenhouse gases, carbon dioxide gets the lion's share of attention because its concentration is increasing, largely due to industrial activity. But it is actually a minor player. If the concentration of carbon dioxide in the atmosphere doubled, the blocking of the earth's infrared radiation would rise from 150 to 154 watts per square meter, an increase of roughly 3 percent. This means that the increasing level of carbon dioxide in the atmosphere is not matched by a corresponding increase in the greenhouse effect.

9   Over the last 100 years, for example, the level of carbon dioxide has increased by 25 percent, while the greenhouse effect has increased

by around 1 percent. (This 1-percent figure assumes that other things have stayed equal in the meantime, but in the real world "other things" are usually not so obliging, so the actual behavior of the greenhouse effect during this time is unknown. Nonetheless, its variation has been much closer to 1 percent than to 25 percent.)

10   Ordinary water vapor is actually the main contributor to the greenhouse effect. The balance between the natural processes of evaporation, which pumps water vapor into the atmosphere, and condensation into clouds, which squeezes it out, sets the level of water vapor in the atmosphere.

11   This means that the greenhouse effect and global warming are an integral part of the biosphere. They have been around at least since the formation of the first oceans and must therefore have preceded mankind's appearance by a few billion years. Indeed, if there were no global warming, if the earth's atmosphere were perfectly transparent at infrared wavelengths, the planet's average surface temperature would be a brisk zero degrees Fahrenheit, instead of the pleasant 59 degrees that we enjoy. Global warming has been an essential ingredient in the evolution of life on the earth.

12   Yet the illusion that carbon dioxide is the dominant greenhouse gas is extremely widespread. In an impromptu, totally nonscientific survey, I asked 10 of my fellow astronomers, "What is the major greenhouse gas?" Six said carbon dioxide. One added, "But isn't water vapor in there?" Two said water vapor. And one said, "Don't know."

13   Evidently a surprisingly large number of astronomers think that carbon dioxide is the major greenhouse gas, despite the fact that astronomers need to know how the earth's atmosphere stamps its spectral imprint on the radiation from heavenly bodies and what gases are responsible. In scientific disciplines that do not deal with the earth's atmosphere on a professional basis, the illusion that carbon dioxide is the major greenhouse gas is probably even more prevalent. Among the general public it must be well-nigh universal.

14   But even if carbon dioxide is a minor greenhouse gas, its level is increasing. Doesn't this mean global warming is increasing? Yes. But the real question is at what level, and is it significant compared to the changes in global warming that take place independent of mankind's activities? Will it cause an 8-degree increase during the next century, as predicted in the most alarming scenarios, or will there be a much more gradual, and mostly beneficial, increase of 1 degree or so?

15   We cannot answer this question by means of mere calculation, because our theoretical understanding of the biosphere is too incomplete. The *immediate* result of increased carbon dioxide is, indeed, an increase of global warming. The slightly higher average temperature leads to increased evaporation from the oceans, which leads to a further increase in global warming because water vapor is also a greenhouse gas. But this is far from the end of the story.

16   More water vapor in the atmosphere leads to increased cloudiness over the earth as a whole. This means more sunshine is reflected straight back into space and so never reaches the earth's surface. This, in turn, means less heating of the earth's surface and hence lower temperatures.

17   We don't know which one of these opposing mechanisms wins, so we don't know if the increase in the greenhouse effect is amplified or dampened by the time it feeds through to global warming. The availability of faster computers promises that during the next decade we will be able to get a better grip on these factors and many other, more complicated ones that are currently neglected.

18   In the meantime, the observational evidence that global warming is actually increasing is very shaky. Some researchers claim to see an increase in global warming of about 0.8 degree since 1860. Although average temperatures since then have increased by this much, it's doubtful that the rise reflects carbon-dioxide-induced global warming.

19   The large year-to-year fluctuations of average temperature—which are in the neighborhood of 1 degree—mean that the behavior of average global temperature is somewhat like that of a stock market index. Spotting a "real" temperature trend is like deciding if one is in a bull or a bear market. It's not impossible, but no bell rings when one trend ends and a new one begins.

20   Moreover, natural causes, rather than the increase in carbon dioxide, are a more likely explanation of the temperature increase. Most of the rise took place prior to 1940, *before* the main increase in the carbon-dioxide level.

21   Some climatologists interpret this pre-1940 temperature increase as an after-effect of the so-called Little Ice Age, a period of unusual worldwide cold that prevailed from 1600 to 1850. If we look at the 50 years or so from 1940 to the present, which have seen the major part of the increase in carbon-dioxide concentration, the increase in average global temperatures has been only 0.2 degree. This small increment is within the noise of natural variation. Although the level of carbon

dioxide in the atmosphere is increasing, it does not seem to be affecting global temperatures much.

22 In examining the historical record, we also have to consider the urban heat island effect. The buildings and pavement of a city give it a microclimate slightly warmer than that of the surrounding countryside. As cities have grown, their heat islands have grown with them, so their weather stations, which tend to be in downtown locations, have been more and more prejudiced in favor of higher temperatures.

23 Phoenix is a dramatic example. Between 1960 and 1990, as its population grew from 650,000 to 2.1 million, its mean annual temperature heated up by 5 degrees, almost in lockstep with the population increase.

24 Climatologists who have tried to quantify the urban heat island's influence on the global temperature record estimate that it accounts for somewhere in the neighborhood of 0.2 degree of the 0.8-degree increase seen since 1860. And when Kirby Hanson, Thomas Karl, and George Maul of the National Oceanic and Atmospheric Administration conducted a study of the U.S. temperature record that took into account the urban heat island effect, they found no long-term warming. They confirmed the temperature rise prior to 1940 but found that temperatures have fallen since then.

25 Another consideration is that most of the earth's surface is covered with water. Temperature data over the oceans is extremely sparse, so the record of the earth's historic average temperature over both land and water is much vaguer than the land record. The recent advent of satellites with the capability to measure global temperatures accurately over both land and sea may solve the problem, but so far their time base is limited to a few years. However, global measurements by satellite of atmospheric (as distinct from surface) temperatures over the last decade show no sign of increasing temperatures.

26 Far more than historical evidence, the hullabaloo about global warming is based on predictions by computer models. The global climate modeler gives his computer some basic facts, plus a program that recognizes the relevant physical processes and principles insofar as we know them and insofar as they can be calculated. With luck, the computer arrives at a climate not unlike that of the earth. Then the model gets a retroactive "tuning," so that its average global temperature is right.

27   A calculation of the greenhouse effect and associated global warming is one step in the procedure. Assuming a doubling of atmospheric carbon dioxide, these models predict an increase in global warming of somewhere between 3 degrees and 8 degrees during the next century.

28   When they are judged by their verifiable accomplishments, however, these computer models are not very impressive. They predict that the temperatures at the poles are lower than those at the equator, and they predict that it's hotter in summer than in winter. But they are weak on specifics. One model predicts an annual rainfall in the central Sahara that is the same as Ireland's.

29   Clearly, these global climate models are still in a primitive stage of development. They neglect many important factors—both known, such as the poleward transport of heat from the equatorial regions by ocean currents and the atmosphere, and unknown. When it comes to telling us things we don't know already, such as trends in global warming during the next century, they are not far removed from the crystal-ball school of climatology.

30   Alarmists such as the vice president are impatient with people who point this out. Gore writes: "If, when the remaining unknowns about the environmental challenge enter the public debate, they are presented as signs that the crisis may not be real after all, it undermines the effort to build a solid base of support for the difficult actions we must soon take. . . . The insistence on complete certainty about the full details of global warming—the most serious threat that we have ever faced—is actually an effort to avoid facing the awful, uncomfortable truth: that we must act boldly, decisively, comprehensively, and quickly, even before we know every last detail of the crisis."

31   But one of the "details" we still don't know is whether we are in fact facing a crisis requiring drastic action. The burden of proof is on the alarmists. They have failed to meet it.

Understanding Meaning

1.   How does Tomkin define global warming?
2.   When did the process of global warming begin, according to Tomkin?
3.   What is the principal element causing the greenhouse effect?
4.   What are the opposing effects of the greenhouse effect? Does Tomkin suggest outcomes?

5. *Critical Thinking:* What problems does Tomkin cite in making accurate predictions about global warming? In Tomkin's view, does enough evidence exist to make a prediction?

Evaluating Strategy

1. What impact does the article's opening have? Does Tomkin's questioning of Al Gore directly suggest that Jacobson's views lack credibility?
2. Tomkin is writing to a general audience about complex issues. Does his analogy of measuring climatic changes to making judgments about the stock market serve to enlighten or confuse readers?

Appreciating Language

1. What level of scientific language does Tomkin use? What does this reveal about his readers?
2. How does Tomkin refer to those he calls "alarmists"? Does he see them as fellow scientists making honest errors in judgment or as determined ideologues?

Connections across the Disciplines

1. Does Tomkin's article suggest that some environmentalists are motivated by political rather than scientific considerations? Does Joel Connelly's article (page 319) indicate that some environmentalists are more interested in making an impression than advocating sound science?
2. Compare Tomkin's and Jacobson's articles. Is one writer more interested in making a political point than a scientific one?

Writing Suggestions

1. Consider the pro and con arguments by Jacobson and Tomkin. Which author's article, in your opinion, is more persuasive? Write an essay that defends your point of view.
2. *Collaborative Writing:* Discuss the two articles with a group of students, and decide which author is correct. If you feel you do not know enough about the topic to decide, make a list of information you would need before making a judgment. Work together to draft a brief analysis of your group's views on the subject.

THOMAS JEFFERSON ET AL.

During the hot summer of 1776, the Second Continental Congress met in Philadelphia. Following a call for a resolution of independence from Britain, John Adams, Thomas Jefferson, Benjamin Franklin, Robert Livingston, and Roger Sherman were charged with drafting a declaration. Jefferson wrote the original draft, which was revised by Adams and Franklin before being presented to the entire Congress. After further changes, the Declaration of Independence was adopted and signed.

The Declaration of Independence

The Declaration of Independence presents a theory of government greatly influenced by the concept of natural rights espoused by Locke and Rousseau and then provides evidence that the British have failed to respect these rights. Notice that most of the declaration is a list of grievances or causes for the colonies to seek independence.

1   *In Congress, July 4, 1776. The unanimous Declaration of the thirteen united States of America,*

2   When in the Course of human events, it becomes necessary for one people to dissolve the political bands which have connected them with another, and to assume among the powers of the earth, the separate and equal station to which the Laws of Nature and of Nature's God entitle them, a decent respect to the opinions of mankind requires that they should declare the causes which impel them to the separation.

3   We hold these truths to be self-evident, that all men are created equal, that they are endowed by their Creator with certain unalienable Rights, that among these are Life, Liberty and the pursuit of Happiness.

4   That to secure these rights, Governments are instituted among Men, deriving their just powers from the consent of the governed,

5   That whenever any Form of Government becomes destructive of these ends, it is the Right of the People to alter or to abolish it, and to institute new Government, laying its foundation on such principles and organizing its powers in such form, as to them shall seem most likely to effect their Safety and Happiness. Prudence, indeed, will dictate

that Governments long established should not be changed for light and transient causes; and accordingly all experience hath shown, that mankind are more disposed to suffer, while evils are sufferable, than to right themselves by abolishing the forms to which they are accustomed. But when a long train of abuses and usurpations, pursuing invariably the same Object evinces a design to reduce them under absolute Despotism, it is their right, it is their duty, to throw off such Government, and to provide new Guards for their future security.

6 Such has been the patient sufferance of these Colonies; and such is now the necessity which constrains them to alter their former Systems of Government. The history of the present King of Great Britain is a history of repeated injuries and usurpations, all having in direct object the establishment of an absolute Tyranny over these States. To prove this, let Facts be submitted to a candid world.

7 He has refused his Assent to Laws, the most wholesome and necessary for the public good.

8 He has forbidden his Governors to pass Laws of immediate and pressing importance, unless suspended in their operation till his Assent should be obtained; and when so suspended, he has utterly neglected to attend to them.

9 He has refused to pass other Laws for the accommodation of large districts of people, unless those people would relinquish the right of Representation in the Legislature, a right inestimable to them and formidable to tyrants only.

10 He has called together legislative bodies at places unusual, uncomfortable, and distant from the depository of their public Records, for the sole purpose of fatiguing them into compliance with his measures.

11 He has dissolved Representative Houses repeatedly, for opposing with manly firmness his invasions on the rights of the people.

12 He has refused for a long time, after such dissolutions, to cause others to be elected; whereby the Legislative powers, incapable of Annihilation, have returned to the People at large for their exercise; the State remaining in the mean time exposed to all the dangers of invasion from without, and convulsions within.

13 He has endeavoured to prevent the population of these States; for that purpose obstructing the Laws for Naturalization of Foreigners; refusing to pass others to encourage their migrations hither, and raising the conditions of new Appropriations of Lands.

14 He has obstructed the Administration of Justice, by refusing his Assent to Laws for establishing Judiciary powers.

15   He has made Judges dependent on his Will alone, for the tenure of their offices, and the amount and payment of their salaries.

16   He has erected a multitude of New Offices, and sent hither swarms of Officers to harrass our people, and eat out their substance.

17   He has kept among us in times of peace, Standing Armies without the Consent of our legislatures.

18   He has affected to render the Military independent of and superior to the Civil power.

19   He has combined with others to subject us to a jurisdiction foreign to our constitution, and unacknowledged by our laws; giving his Assent to their Acts of pretended Legislation:

20   For quartering large bodies of armed troops among us:

21   For protecting them, by a mock Trial, from punishment for any Murders which they should commit on the Inhabitants of these States:

22   For cutting off our Trade with all parts of the world:

23   For imposing Taxes on us without our Consent:

24   For depriving us in many cases, of the benefits of Trial by Jury:

25   For transporting us beyond Seas to be tried for pretended offences:

26   For abolishing the free System of English Laws in a neighbouring Province, establishing therein an Arbitrary government, and enlarging its Boundaries so as to render it at once an example and fit instrument for introducing the same absolute rule in these Colonies:

27   For taking away our Charters, abolishing our most valuable Laws, and altering fundamentally the Forms of our Governments:

28   For suspending our own Legislatures, and declaring themselves invested with power to legislate for us in all cases whatsoever.

29   He has abdicated Government here, by declaring us out of his Protection and waging War against us.

30   He has plundered our seas, ravaged our Coasts, burnt our towns, and destroyed the lives of our people.

31   He is at this time transporting large Armies of foreign Mercenaries to compleat the works of death, desolation and tyranny, already begun with circumstances of Cruelty & perfidy scarcely paralleled in the most barbarous ages, and totally unworthy the Head of a civilized nation.

32   He has constrained our fellow Citizens taken Captive on high Seas to bear Arms against their Country, to become the executioners of their friends and Brethren, or to fall themselves by their Hands.

33   He has excited domestic insurrections amongst us, and has endeavoured to bring on the inhabitants of our frontiers, the merciless

Indian Savages, whose known rule of warfare, is an undistinguished destruction of all ages, sexes and conditions.

34   In every stage of these Oppressions We have Petitioned for Redress in the most humble terms: Our repeated Petitions have been answered only by repeated injury. A Prince, whose character is thus marked by every act which may define a Tyrant, is unfit to be the ruler of a free people.

35   Nor have We been wanting in attentions to our Brittish brethren. We have warned them from time to time of attempts by their legislature to extend an unwarrantable jurisdiction over us. We have reminded them of the circumstances of our emigration and settlement here. We have appealed to their native justice and magnanimity, and we have conjured them by the ties of our common kindred to disavow these usurpations, which, would inevitably interrupt our connections and correspondence. They too have been deaf to the voice of justice and consanguinity. We must, therefore, acquiesce in the necessity, which denounces our Separation, and hold them, as we hold the rest of mankind, Enemies in War, in Peace Friends.

36   We, therefore, the Representatives of the united States of America, in General Congress, Assembled, appealing to the Supreme Judge of the world for the rectitude of our intentions, do, in the Name, and by Authority of the good People of these Colonies, solemnly publish and declare, That these United Colonies are, and of Right ought to be, Free and Independent States; that they are Absolved from all Allegiance to the British Crown, and that all political connection between them and the State of Great Britain, is and ought to be totally dissolved; and that as Free and Independent States, they have full Power to levy War, conclude Peace, contract Alliances, establish Commerce, and to do all other Acts and Things which Independent States may of right do.

37   And for the support of this Declaration, with a firm reliance on the protection of divine Providence, we mutually pledge to each other our Lives, our Fortunes and our sacred Honor.

Understanding Meaning

1.   What are the principal causes for the Congress to declare independence?
2.   Why do Jefferson and the other authors argue that these grievances cannot be resolved in any other fashion?

3. *Critical Thinking:* When was the last time you read the Declaration of Independence? Do some items strike you as relevant to current conditions?
Should Americans be more familiar with a document that helped create
their own country and establish its values?

Evaluating Strategy

1. How does the Declaration of Independence use induction and deduction?
2. How much space is devoted to the list of causes? Is enough evidence provided to support severing ties with Britain?
3. The causes are placed in separate paragraphs rather than combined.
What impact does this have?

Appreciating Language

1. How does the document refer to the king?
2. This document was drafted in 1776. How readable is it today? How has
language changed in two hundred years?

Connections across the Disciplines

1. The opening of the Declaration of Independence asserts that the "pursuit of happiness" is a right. How does this concept relate to the search
for happiness described by John Ciardi (page 192)? Do Americans believe they have a right to be happy?
2. Compare the Declaration of Independence to Albert Einstein's letter to
President Roosevelt (page 622). What characteristics do many of the
world's most important writings seem to have?

Writing Suggestions

1. Write a personal analysis of the Declaration of Independence. What do
you think is the most significant feature of the document? What does the
phrase "Life, Liberty and the pursuit of Happiness" mean to you?
2. *Collaborative Writing:* Discuss the declaration with a group of students.
Does the current government reflect the ideals of Jefferson? How has
America changed since 1776? For further discussion, look up the original
draft, which contained a passage denouncing slavery, a passage Jefferson
had to delete to pacify southern delegates. Develop a statement with
other students reflecting your opinion of the Declaration of Independence's importance in the twenty-first century.

Cause-and-effect writing is often used in manuals, textbooks, training guides, and consumer information packets. Hewlett-Packard includes this troubleshooting guide in the owner's manual of a laser printer.

Solving Printer
Operation Problems

As you examine the cause-and-effect guide, consider the intended audience and the use of a chart. How easy would this information be to follow if written in standard paragraphs?

1   Use the following steps to help solve problems you experience with your printer. If you need more help, refer to the service and support information. . . . That chapter will guide you in getting help from your dealer or, if necessary, contacting Hewlett-Packard for help.

SYMPTOM	POSSIBLE CAUSE	SOLUTION
The printer does not respond when you send a print job from software.	The printer's parallel cable is loose.	Check the connections on the printer and on the computer. Make sure the cable on the printer is not attached upside-down (some cables have a flexible plastic sleeve that allows an improper connection).
		Secure the cable to the computer with screws and to the printer with the wire clips.

2

3

4	**The printer does not respond when you send a print job from software, continued.**	The parallel cable is defective.	Try your cable on another system with a print job that you know works.
5		The printer is malfunctioning.	If the printer is in Intelligent Off mode, press the front panel button to turn on the Ready light. Then press it again to print a self test page. If the self test page prints, the printer is working correctly.
6			If all the lights are on, there is a hardware error. Disconnect the printer from its power source and wait 15 minutes. Then reconnect it. If all four lights come back on, contact your HP authorized service representative. . . .
7		You did not select the correct printer through your software.	Check your software's printer selection menu to see if you selected the HP LaserJet 4L printer.
8		Your software or your printer is not yet configured for the correct printer port.	Check your software's configuration menu to make sure it is accessing the correct printer port.
9			If your computer has more than one parallel port, make sure you are connected to the correct one.

10	**The printer does not respond when you send a print job from software, continued.**	The printer is not connected to power, or the power source is not active.	Check your power cord, switches, and fuses.
11		You did not reset the printer after clearing a paper jam.	Press the front panel button, or open and close the top printer door to reset the printer after a jam.
12		The printer's top door or rear door is open.	Make sure both doors are closed securely.
13		The printer is connected to a switch box, and the switch box is not set up to receive data from your printer.	Check the switch box setting.
14	**The Error light is on steadily.**	The printer's top door is open, or the toner cartridge is not installed completely.	Open the door, reinstall the toner cartridge, then close the door firmly.
15	**The Error light is blinking.**	There was a memory error in your print job.	Press the front panel button to resume printing. (There may be some data loss.)
16			Change your page to make it less complex, or add optional printer memory.
17	**The Paper light is on steadily.**	The paper cassette is empty.	Load more paper into the paper cassette.
18	**The Paper light is blinking.**	There is a paper jam.	See . . . instructions on how to clear paper jams.
19	**Both the Data light and the Ready light are on steadily.**	There is unprinted data in the printer. (Your software did not send an "end of job" command.)	Briefly press the front panel button to print the rest of the data.

20	*The Data light is blinking.*	The printer is in Manual Feed mode and the manual feed slot is waiting for paper.	Insert a piece of paper into the manual feed slot.
21	*All the printer's lights are off.*	The printer is in Intelligent Off mode.	Briefly press the front panel button to activate the Ready light. If the Ready light does not come on, check the power cord and your power source. If the printer still does not respond, contact your local HP authorized service representative. . . .
22	*All the printer's lights are on.*	The printer has a hardware error.	Disconnect the printer from its power source and wait 15 minutes. Then reconnect it. If all four lights come back on, contact your HP authorized service representative. . . .
23	*The printer is feeding multiple sheets or jams frequently.*	The paper does not meet HP's specifications for print media (embossed, damaged, too slick or too rough, too much moisture, wrong weight).	Try another kind of paper. See the paper specifications. . . .
24		The paper is sticking together.	Take the paper out of the cassette and fan it to separate the sheets.
25		The paper cassette is too full.	Remove some of the paper.
26		The printer may need service.	Contact your HP authorized service representative. . . .

27	*The printer jams when you attempt a manual feed.*	You removed and reinserted your paper while trying to do a manual feed.	Once the printer senses that the paper is in the manual feed slot (you feel it grab the corner), do not remove it and reinsert it. This causes the printer to pull the paper through the paper path too late, and results in a paper jam. Let the printer automatically realign the paper to straighten it in the paper path.

Understanding Meaning

1. What causes the "Paper light" to blink?
2. When should you call a service representative?
3. What should you try when the printer jams or feeds multiple sheets?

Evaluating Strategy

1. How readable is this guide? Is it clearly stated?
2. What impact does the format have?
3. *Critical Thinking:* What would be the best way for technical writers to test their owner's manual before printing and shipping it to hundreds of thousands of consumers worldwide?

Appreciating Language

1. Does any of the wording seem confusing to you? Could this set of instructions be read by nontechnical consumers?
2. Why do all the solution statements open with verbs?

Connections across the Disciplines

1. Compare these instructions with "Cleaning Battery Terminals" (page 493). Do they share common features?

2.   Compare these instructions with "Communications Styles: United States and Taiwan" (page 290). When are chartlike presentations of text acceptable?

Writing Suggestions

1.   Write a similar cause-and-effect chart about a product you are familiar with.
2.   *Collaborative Writing:* Discuss manuals you have encountered as students or consumers with a small group. What problems and frustrations do people report having? Work together to write a list of causes of reader confusion. You may place these in a chart.

STRATEGIES FOR CAUSE-AND-EFFECT WRITING

1. **Determine your goal.** Are you attempting to explain a cause or to predict future outcomes?
2. **Evaluate your readers' needs.** What evidence does your reader require in order to accept your conclusions? Are government statistics more impressive than the testimony of experts? Does any background information or do any definitions need to be presented?
3. **Offer logical, acceptable evidence.** Present support that comes from reliable sources readers will accept. Present evidence in a clearly organized manner. Use brief narratives or analogies to dramatize data.
4. **Review your use of deduction or induction.** Does your major premise contain unproven assumptions? Is it clearly stated, or is it subject to different interpretations? Does your inductive leap move beyond reasonable doubt? Do you provide enough evidence to support your inductive conclusion?
5. **Qualify assertions and conclusions.** A writer who admits that alternative interpretations or conflicting evidence exists can appear more credible to readers than one who narrowly insists he or she has the only possible conclusion.
6. **Evaluate sources.** Do not allow yourself to automatically assume everything you read is valid. Experts have made errors of judgment. Read books, articles, and studies carefully. Look for signs of bias, unproven assumptions, or mistakes in logic. Look for what is missing.
7. **Use other modes to organize information.** It may be beneficial to use a narrative, comparison, extended definition, or division and classification to present your cause-and-effect thesis.

SUGGESTED TOPICS FOR CAUSE-AND-EFFECT WRITING

General Assignments

Write a cause-and-effect paper on any of the following topics. Your paper may use other modes to organize and present evidence. Cause-and-effect papers usually require research. It is possible to use cause and effect in less formal papers, in which you offer personal experience and observations as examples. However, the more objective facts you can cite, the stronger your writing will be.

Write a paper explaining the cause(s) of the following topics:

- Teenage pregnancy
- Sexual harassment
- Divorce
- The success or failure of a local business
- The victory or defeat of a political candidate

Write a paper predicting the effects of the following topics:

- The information superhighway
- Immigration
- Harsher drunk-driving laws
- An aging population
- The death of a spouse or loved one

Writing in Context

1. Analyze in a short essay a recent event on campus, in your community, or at your place of work. Examine what caused this event to take place. If several causes exist, you may use division to explain them or classification to rank them from the most important to the least important.
2. Write a letter to the editor of the campus newspaper predicting the effects of a current policy change, incident, or trend in student behavior.
3. Imagine a job application asks you to write a 250-word essay presenting your reasons for choosing your career. Write a one-page essay that lists your most important reasons. As you write, consider how an employer would evaluate your response.

STUDENT PAPER: CAUSE AND EFFECT

This paper was written by a student who is active in a campus environmental movement. She intended to use the essay both to fulfill a composition assignment and as an article for the college newspaper.

Can the Devon Be Saved?

1   For decades the back cover of the college catalog featured a photograph of a stone bridge crossing the Devon River. Fund raising brochures and alumni publications often include pictures of students

admiring Devon Falls on the north side of the campus. The river is as much associated with the college as Old Main and the hundred-year-old library clock tower. The Devon's grassy banks have been popular places for students to relax, picnic, read, or sunbathe. The Devon has been one of the college's main draws. Campus visitors are universally drawn by the sound of water rushing over massive boulders to the river bank.

2   Now massive development has come to the Devon River. The university has approved building a 300-room dorm along the river, clearing ten acres of woodland for the building and parking lot. Upriver, the county's largest subdivision, Devoncrest, nears completion. Some 200 condominiums and 450 apartments will be occupied by next spring. The surge in population will greatly increase the amount of sewage flowing into the fifty-seven-year-old treatment plant at English Beach. In addition, new storm sewers will feed more water into the river, as will runoff from the new parking lots being built on the banks.

3   The Riverwest project on the opposite shore will have even a greater impact on the Devon. Three high-rise office towers and a new shopping mall with parking for 800 cars will occupy a half-mile strip of newly cleared riverbank. Designed on an incline, the mall parking lots will send rainwater cascading into the river, eroding the denuded riverbank. Already mud slides have shorn ten feet off the edge. In winter tons of snow will likely be plowed from the new parking lots and dumped into the river.

4   This development will cause the narrow Devon River to flood in the spring. Five years ago the state erected a series of levees to protect the marshes from floods and possible oil spills. These levees protect the bird sanctuary very effectively, but they limit the marshland's ability to act like a mammoth sponge which previously absorbed much of the spring runoff.

5   As a result, we can expect flooding as more water enters the river near the new parking lots. Mud slides will add to the problem. The sewage treatment plant, located on the flood plain, may easily be overwhelmed and release raw sewage into the bay. Sewage spills could contaminate beaches and have a dramatic effect on fishing, boating, and tourism. The value of beach property could plummet.

6   In our rush to capitalize on the beauty of our river, we are threatening the bay which generates jobs and income. We must lobby the university and developers to take steps now to limit runoff from parking

lots and to plant fresh vegetation to prevent further erosion of the riverbanks. If steps are not taken now, the new condos and office towers will overlook nothing but a stream of mud and debris.

Questions for Review and Revision

1. How effective is the introduction? Does the student assume readers are familiar with the locale and the importance of the river?
2. This essay was directed to a local audience. How would it have to be revised for a wider readership unfamiliar with the campus?
3. What transitional devices does the student use? Could you suggest improvements?
4. *Other Modes:* How much of this essay contains *argument and persuasion?*
5. How does the student describe the river? Do words and connotations dramatize the importance of the river? Could added details create more striking images of the predicted environmental damage?
6. Read the paper aloud. Could revisions or reorganization clarify the writer's purpose?

Writing Suggestions

1. Using this student's essay as a model, write a cause-and-effect paper detailing results of an environmental, technological, or social change in your area. For example, how has a new computer system improved record keeping? Has a change in employee benefits affected morale?
2. *Collaborative Writing:* Discuss with a group of students the causes or effects of new construction, a new trend, or a new technological development. Brainstorm to list effects, both positive and negative. Create an essay listing the significant changes that may occur. You may divide the paper into two lists, detailing the beneficial and the detrimental results.

CAUSE-AND-EFFECT CHECKLIST

Before submitting your paper, review these points.

1. Is your thesis clearly stated?

2. Are causes clearly stated, logically organized, and supported by details?

3. Are conflicting interpretations disproven or acknowledged?

4. Are effects supported by observation and evidence? Do you avoid sweeping generalizations and unsupported conclusions?

5. Do you anticipate future changes that might alter predictions?

6. Do you avoid making errors in critical thinking, especially errors such as making hasty generalizations and confusing time relationships for cause and effect?

7. Have you tested your ideas through peer review?

 WebTutor

See www.harcourtcollege.com/english/sundance for information on writing cause and effect

10

ARGUMENT AND PERSUASION

INFLUENCING READERS

WHAT IS ARGUMENT AND PERSUASION?

We are bombarded by argument and persuasion every day. Newspaper editorials encourage us to change our opinions about abortion, gun control, or public financing of religious schools. Sales brochures convince us to invest in stocks or buy life insurance. Fundraising letters ask us to contribute to homeless shelters or the local symphony. Billboards, magazine ads, and television commercials urge us to buy automobiles and soft drinks. Political candidates solicit our votes. Public service announcements warn us against smoking and drunk driving.

As a student you have to develop persuasive arguments in essays and research papers to demonstrate your skills and knowledge. After graduation you will need a persuasive résumé and cover letter to secure job interviews. In your career you will have to impress clients, motivate employees, justify decisions, and propose new ideas to superiors with well-stated arguments and persuasive appeals.

Arguments are assertions designed to convince readers to accept an idea, adopt a solution, or change their way of thinking. Writers use reason and facts to support their arguments, often disproving or disputing conflicting theories or alternative proposals in the process. Attorneys prepare written arguments stating why a client has a valid claim or deserves a new trial. Scientists present the results of experiments to argue for new medical treatments or to disprove current assumptions. Economists assemble data to support arguments to raise or lower interest rates. In "Why We Need to Understand Science" (page 579), Carl Sagan urges his readers to appreciate the need for greater education in science. To impress his audience, he prepares a broad-based argument, demonstrating how science and technology are essential in solving current and future problems:

> We live in a society exquisitely dependent on science and technology, in which hardly anyone knows anything about science and technology. This is a clear prescription for disaster. It's dangerous and stupid for us to remain ignorant about global warming, say, or ozone depletion, toxic and radioactive wastes, acid rain. Jobs and wages depend on science and technology. If the United States can't manufacture, at high quality and low price, products people want to buy, then industries will drift out of the United States and transfer a little prosperity to another part of the world. Because of the low birthrate in the '60s and '70s, the National Science Foundation projects a shortage of nearly a million professional scientists and engineers by 2010. Where will they come from? What about fusion, supercomputers, abortion, massive reductions in strategic weapons, addiction, high-resolution TV, airline and airport safety, food additives, animal rights, superconductivity, Midgetman versus rail-garrison MX missiles, going to Mars, finding cures for AIDS and cancer? How can we decide national policy if we don't understand the underlying issues?

The way writers present evidence depends on their discipline or profession. Each field has specific methods and standards of presenting evidence and stating arguments.

The audience plays a critical role in the way writers shape an argument, especially when they suspect readers may hold alternative viewpoints or be prejudiced against them or the ideas they advocate. In his article "Why Prisons Don't Work" (page 579), Wilbert Rideau, a convicted murderer, understands that few readers have sympathy for convicts. He begins by agreeing with those who advocate punishing criminals but then presents his own views:

> Prison has a role in public safety, but it is not a cure-all. Its value is limited, and its use should also be limited to what it does best: isolating young criminals long enough to give them a chance to grow up and get a grip on their impulses. It is a traumatic experience, certainly, but it should be only a temporary one, not a way of life.

In directing an argument to readers, writers often use *persuasion*, making emotional or dramatic statements that stir people's passions and beliefs. Advertisers use sex appeal to sell everything from toothpaste to cars. Commercials for charities flash 800-numbers over images of starving children to motivate people to make donations. In creating persuasive arguments, you should consider the perceptual world of your readers (page 10).

Persuasive Appeals

Writers traditionally use three basic appeals to convince readers to accept their ideas or take action: logic, emotion, and ethics. Because each appeal has advantages and disadvantages, writers generally use more than one.

LOGIC supports a point of view or proposed action through reasoned arguments and a presentation of evidence:

Test results   Findings established by experiments or standard research methods.

Statistics   Data represented by numbers and percentages.

Expert testimony   Opinions or statements made by respected authorities.

Eyewitness testimony   Statements by those who experienced or witnessed events and situations.

Surveys   Measurements of public opinion or sample audiences.

Logic is widely used in academic, business, and government reports.

Advantages: Provides evidence needed for major decisions, especially group decisions.

Disadvantages: Can demand a high degree of reader attention and specialized knowledge.

EMOTION uses images, sensations, or shock appeals to lead people to react in a desired manner. Emotional appeals call on people's deeply felt needs and desires:

Creativity   The desire for recognition by self-expression.

Achievement   The need to attain money, fame, or fulfillment.

Independence   The drive to be unique, to stand out, and to be individual.

Conformity   The desire to be part of a group, to be included, and to be *in*.

Endurance   To achieve satisfaction by bearing burdens others could not or feeling successful by simply surviving.

Fear   To resist, avoid, or defeat threats to the self or society, such as cancer, crime, or terrorism.

Emotional appeals are found most frequently in public relations, marketing, and advertising.

Advantages: Produces immediate results.
Disadvantages: Has limited impact, can backfire, and provides limited factual support for readers to share with others.

ETHICS use shared values to influence people. Ethics may call on reasoning but do not rest wholly on logical analysis of data. Like emotional appeals, ethics reflect deeply held convictions rather than personal motivations.

Religion   The desire to follow the rules and behavior espoused by one's faith, such as to be a good Christian or practicing Jew.

Patriotism   The urge to place one's country before personal needs: "Ask not what your country can do for you; ask what you can do for your country."

Standards   The desire to be a good citizen, a good lawyer, or a good parent, to express the higher ideals of a community, profession, or family role.

Humanitarianism   A secular appeal to help others, save the environment, protect the weak, or to be a "citizen of the world."

Ethical appeals form the basis of many sermons, editorials, and political speeches.

Advantages: Can be very powerful, especially if the writer is addressing an audience with the same value system.

Disadvantages: Depends on readers who accept the principles espoused by the writer. A Muslim cleric's appeal, for example, may have little impact on Catholics or atheists.

To be effective, writers frequently mix factual detail with emotionally charged human interest. An article on homeless children might use the story of a single child to arouse sympathy, then provide statistics to illustrate the severity of the problem, and, finally, outline possible solutions.

Appealing to Hostile Readers

Perhaps most challenging is attempting to persuade a hostile audience, readers you anticipate having negative attitudes toward you, the organization you represent, or the ideas you advocate. Although no technique will magically convert opponents into supporters, you can overcome a measure of hostility and influence those who may still be undecided with a few approaches:

1. **Openly admit differences.** Instead of attempting to pretend no conflict exists, openly state that your view may differ from that of your readers. This honest admission can win a measure of respect.
2. **Responsibly summarize opposing viewpoints.** By fairly restating your opponents' views, you force readers to agree with you and demonstrate impartiality.
3. **Avoid making judgmental statements.** Do not label your opponents' ideas with negative language. Use neutral terms to make distinctions. If you call your ideas intelligent and your readers' naive, you will have difficulty getting people to accept your points because in the process they will have to accept your insults as being valid.
4. **Point to shared values, experiences, and problems.** Build common bridges with your readers by demonstrating past cooperation and common goals.
5. **Ask your readers to keep an open mind.** Don't demand or expect to convert readers. But almost everyone will agree to try to be open-minded and receptive to new ideas.
6. **Work to overcome negative stereotypes.** Play the devil's advocate, and determine what negative stereotypes your readers might have about you and your ideas. Then work to include examples, references, and evidence in your paper to counter negative assumptions.

CRITICAL THINKING FOR WRITING ARGUMENT AND PERSUASION

Perhaps no other form of writing demands more critical thinking than argument and persuasion. When using logical, emotional, and ethical appeals, avoid the common traps or fallacies writers often fall into:

- **Absolute statements**   Although it is important to convince readers by making a strong impression, avoid making absolute claims that can be dismissed with a single exception. If you state "all lawyers are honest," a reader has only to think of a single dishonest attorney to repudiate your argument. A qualified claim can make a strong impression and leave room for exceptions: "The legal profession is known for its high standards of ethical conduct."
- *Non sequitur* **(it does not follow)**   Avoid making assertions based on irrelevant evidence: "Bill Smith was a great football coach—he'll make a great mayor." Although a coach may possess leadership and skills in strategy, he may lack the political knowledge and diplomatic skills needed in government.
- **Begging the question**   Do not assume what has to be proved: "Nancy is lying because she never tells the truth." Asserting that Nancy never tells the truth offers no evidence that she is lying.
- **False dilemma**   Do not offer or accept only two alternatives to a problem: "Either employees must take a wage cut, or the company will go bankrupt." This statement ignores other possible solutions such as raising prices, lowering production costs, or increasing sales.
- **False analogy**   Comparisons make very weak arguments: "Crack cocaine should be legalized since Prohibition did not work." Alcohol and crack cocaine are not like substances. Alcohol has been consumed by humans for thousands of years. Crack cocaine has never been socially acceptable to most Americans.
- **Red herring**   Resist the temptation to dodge the real issue by drawing attention to something controversial: "How can you endorse the budget proposal of a congressman indicted for soliciting bribes?" Corruption charges alone do not invalidate a politician's policies.
- **Borrowed authority**   Avoid assuming that an expert in one field can be accepted as an authority in another: "Senator Johnson is convinced Dallas will win by ten points." A respected senator may have no more insight into the National Football League than a cab driver or a hairdresser. Celebrity endorsements are common examples of borrowed authority.
- *Ad hominem* **(attacking the person)**   Attack ideas, not the people who advocate them: "The only people who oppose gun control are paranoid

Nazis and Uzi-toting drug dealers." The merits of the issue and not the personalities have to be discussed to create a convincing argument.

STRATEGIES FOR READING ARGUMENT AND PERSUASION

When reading the argument and persuasion entries in this chapter, keep these questions in mind:

Meaning

1. What is the author's thesis? What does he or she want readers to accept?
2. How credible is the thesis? Does it make sense? Are alternatives discussed?
3. How does the writer characterize those who advocate differing views? Does the writer appear to have an unfair bias?

Strategy

1. Which appeals are used—logic, emotion, or ethics?
2. Do the appeals seem to work with the intended audience?
3. Are the factual details interesting, believable, and effective?
4. Are emotional appeals suitable, or do they risk backfiring or distorting the issue?
5. Are the logical fallacies avoided?
6. Does the writer appear to anticipate rejection or approval?

Language

1. What role does connotation play in shaping arguments using logical, emotional, or ethical appeals?
2. What does the author's choice of words suggest about the intended audience?
3. Does word choice indicate a bias?

WILBERT RIDEAU

Wilbert Rideau is a convicted murderer serving a life sentence at Algoma prison in Louisiana. He has been incarcerated since 1962. Rideau is the editor of the Louisiana State Penitentiary newsmagazine The Angolite *and coeditor of* Life Sentences.

Why Prisons Don't Work

This essay appeared in Time *magazine (1994). As you read the article, consider Rideau's situation as an inmate denouncing prison policies. Notice how the essay weaves emotional appeals based on personal experience and observation with factual support.*

1   I was among 31 murderers sent to the Louisiana State Penitentiary in 1962 to be executed or imprisoned for life. We weren't much different from those we found here, or those who had preceded us. We were unskilled, impulsive and uneducated misfits, mostly black, who had done dumb, impulsive things—failures, rejects from the larger society. Now a generation has come of age and gone since I've been here, and everything is much the same as I found it. The faces of the prisoners are different, but behind them are the same impulsive, uneducated, unskilled minds that made dumb, impulsive choices that got them into more trouble than they ever thought existed. The vast majority of us are consigned to suffer and die here so politicians can sell the illusion that permanently exiling people to prison will make society safe.

2   Getting tough has always been a "silver bullet," a quick fix for the crime and violence that society fears. Each year in Louisiana—where excess is a way of life—lawmakers have tried to outdo each other in legislating harsher mandatory penalties and in reducing avenues of release. The only thing to do with criminals, they say, is get tougher. They have. In the process, the purpose of prison began to change. The state boasts one of the highest lockup rates in the country, imposes the most severe penalties in the nation and vies to execute more criminals per capita than anywhere else. This state is so tough that last

year, when prison authorities here wanted to punish an inmate in solitary confinement for an infraction, the most they could inflict on him was to deprive him of his underwear. It was all he had left.

3   If getting tough resulted in public safety, Louisiana citizens would be the safest in the nation. They're not. Louisiana has the highest murder rate among states. Prison, like the police and the courts, has a minimal impact on crime because it is a response after the fact, a mop-up operation. It doesn't work. The idea of punishing the few to deter the many is counterfeit because potential criminals either think they're not going to get caught or they're so emotionally desperate or psychologically distressed that they don't care about the consequences of their actions. The threatened punishment, regardless of its severity, is never a factor in the equation. But society, like the incorrigible criminal it abhors, is unable to learn from its mistakes.

4   Prison has a role in public safety, but it is not a cure-all. Its value is limited, and its use should also be limited to what it does best: isolating young criminals long enough to give them a chance to grow up and get a grip on their impulses. It is a traumatic experience, certainly, but it should be only a temporary one, not a way of life. Prisoners kept too long tend to embrace the criminal culture, its distorted values and beliefs; they have little choice—prison is their life. There are some prisoners who cannot be returned to society—serial killers, serial rapists, professional hit men and the like—but the monsters who need to die in prison are rare exceptions in the criminal landscape.

5   Crime is a young man's game. Most of the nation's random violence is committed by young urban terrorists. But because of long, mandatory sentences, most prisoners here are much older, having spent 15, 20, 30 or more years behind bars, long past necessity. Rather than pay for new prisons, society would be well served by releasing some of its older prisoners who pose no threat and using the money to catch young street thugs. Warden John Whitley agrees that many older prisoners here could be freed tomorrow with little or no danger to society. Release, however, is governed by law or by politicians, not by penal professionals. Even murderers, those most feared by society, pose little risk. Historically, for example, the domestic staff at Louisiana's Governor's mansion has been made up of murderers, hand-picked to work among the chief-of-state and his family. Penologists have long known that murder is almost always a once-in-a-lifetime act. The most dangerous criminal is the one who has not yet killed but has a history of escalating offenses. He's the one to watch.

6   Rehabilitation can work. Everyone changes in time. The trick is to influence the direction that change takes. The problem with prisons is that they don't do more to rehabilitate those confined in them. The convict who enters prison illiterate will probably leave the same way. Most convicts want to be better than they are, but education is not a priority. This prison houses 4,600 men and offers academic training to 240, vocational training to a like number. Perhaps it doesn't matter. About 90 percent of the men here may never leave this prison alive.

7   The only effective way to curb crime is for society to work to prevent the criminal act in the first place, to come between the perpetrator and crime. Our youngsters must be taught to respect the humanity of others and to handle disputes without violence. It is essential to educate and equip them with the skills to pursue their life ambitions in a meaningful way. As a community, we must address the adverse life circumstances that spawn criminality. These things are not quick, and they're not easy, but they're effective. Politicians think that's too hard a sell. They want to be on record for doing something now, something they can point to at re-election time. So the drumbeat goes on for more police, more prisons, more of the same failed policies.

8   Ever see a dog chase its tail?

Understanding Meaning

1. Why does Rideau consider "getting tough" a "'silver bullet,' a quick fix"?
2. Why, in Rideau's opinion, do prisons fail to make society safer?
3. How does Rideau argue that murderers are less dangerous to society than other inmates?
4. What effect does prison have on inmates? Do prisons deter crime?
5. *Critical Thinking:* Rideau argues that older prisoners should be released. He also argues that murderers pose little danger to society. Rideau is a murderer who has been in prison for more than thirty years. How much of this article is really a personal appeal?

Evaluating Strategy

1. How effective is the opening?
2. How does Rideau use statistics to support his point of view? Are they convincing?
3. *Other Modes:* Where does Rideau use *cause and effect* and *narrative?*

Appreciating Language

1. What are the general style and tone of the essay? Is it suited for the readers of *Time?*
2. How does Rideau's language reveal his attitude toward politicians?

Connections across the Disciplines

1. Compare this article to "Why More Women Are Going to Prison" (page 522). Do you see similarities in the view of prisons?
2. Could John Holt's theories of self-discipline (page 417) be applied to prison rehabilitation?

Writing Suggestions

1. Write a letter to *Time* magazine supporting or criticizing Rideau's argument. What should prisons do—rehabilitate or warehouse?
2. *Collaborative Writing:* Discuss Rideau's essay with a group of students. Do you want to know more about the murder he was convicted of committing? Does focusing on the inmates obscure the plight of victims? How would family members feel if the man or woman who took the life of their loved one was released because he or she was deemed no longer a threat to the community? Should prisons punish? Work together on writing a letter to *Time* reflecting your opinions. Your group may divide and compose two letters in a point/counterpoint pair of arguments.

Leonce Gaiter is an African-American writer living in Los Angeles who has commented frequently on social issues. A graduate of Harvard, Gaiter has worked in media, including network television. He has been long concerned with the media depiction of African-Americans. Gaiter argues that well-intentioned whites maintain a sense of black inferiority, an attitude embraced by many African-American young people.

The Revolt of the Black Bourgeoisie

This article, written for the New York Times *in 1994, argues that young African-Americans are presented crippling stereotypes by both mainstream and black media. Gaiter blends personal observation and experience with factual support.*

1   At a television network where I once worked, one of my bosses told me I almost didn't get hired because his superior had "reservations" about me. The job had been offered under the network's Minority Advancement Program. I applied for the position because I knew I was exceptionally qualified. I would have applied for the position regardless of how it was advertised.

2   After my interview, the head of the department told my boss I wasn't really what he had in mind for a Minority Advancement Program job. To the department head, hiring a minority applicant meant hiring someone unqualified. He wanted to hire some semiliterate, hoop-shooting former prison inmate. That, in his view, was a "real" black person. That was someone worthy of the program.

3   I had previously been confronted by questions of black authenticity. At Harvard, where I graduated in 1980, a white classmate once said to me, "Oh, you're not really a black person." I asked her to explain. She could not. She had known few black people before college, but a lifetime of seeing black people depicted in the American media had taught her that real black people talked a certain way and were raised in certain places. In her world, black people did not attend elite colleges. They could not stand as her intellectual equals or superiors. Any African-American who shared her knowledge of Austen and Balzac—

while having to explain to her who Douglass and Du Bois were—had to be *willed* away for her to salvage her sense of superiority as a white person. Hence the accusation that I was "not really black."

4   But worse than the white majority harboring a one-dimensional vision of blackness are the many blacks who embrace this stereotype as our true nature. At the junior high school I attended in the mostly white Washington suburb of Silver Spring, Md., a black girl once stopped me in the hallway and asked belligerently, "How come you talk so proper?" Astonished, I could only reply, "It's proper*ly*," and walk on. This girl was asking why I spoke without the so-called black accent pervasive in the lower socioeconomic strata of black society, where exposure to mainstream society is limited. This girl was asking, Why wasn't I impoverished and alienated? In her world view, a black male like me couldn't exist.

5   Within the past year, however, there have been signs that blacks are openly beginning to acknowledge the complex nature of our culture. Cornel West, a professor of religion and the director of Afro-American Studies at Princeton University, discusses the growing gulf between the black underclass and the rest of black society in his book "Race Matters"; black voices have finally been raised against the violence, misogyny, and vulgarity marketed to black youth in the form of gangsta rap; Ellis Cose's book "The Rage of a Privileged Class," which concentrates on the problems of middle- and upper-income blacks, was excerpted as part of a *Newsweek* magazine cover story; Bill Cosby has become a vocal crusader against the insulting depiction of African-Americans in "hip-hop generation" TV shows.

6   Yes, there are the beginnings of a new candor about our culture, but the question remains, How did one segment of the African-American community come to represent the whole? First, black society itself placed emphasis on that lower caste. This made sense because historically that's where the vast majority of us were placed; it's where American society and its laws were designed to keep us. Yet although doors have opened to us over the past 20 years, it is still commonplace for black leaders to insist on our community's uniform need for social welfare programs, inner-city services, job skills training, etc. Through such calls, what has passed for a black political agenda has been furthered only superficially; while affirmative action measures have forced an otherwise unwilling majority to open some doors for the black middle class, social welfare and Great Society-style programs aimed at the black lower class have shown few positive results.

7   According to 1990 census figures, between 1970 and 1990 the number of black families with incomes under $15,000 rose from 34.6 percent of the black population to 37 percent, while the number of black families with incomes of $35,000 to $50,000 rose from 13.9 percent to 15 percent of the population and those with incomes of more than $50,000 rose from 9.9 percent to 14.5 percent of the black population.

8   Another reason the myth of an all-encompassing black underclass survives—despite the higher number of upper-income black families—is that it fits with a prevalent form of white liberalism, which is just as informed by racism as white conservatism. Since the early 70's, good guilt-liberal journalists and others warmed to the picture of black downtrodden masses in need of their help. Through the agency of good white people, blacks would rise. This image of African-Americans maintained the lifeline of white superiority that whites in this culture cling to, and therefore this image of blacks stuck. A strange tango was begun. Blacks seeking advancement opportunities allied themselves with whites eager to "help" them. However, those whites continued to see blacks as inferiors, victims, cases, and not as equals, individuals or, heaven forbid, competitors.

9   It was hammered into the African-American psyche by media-appointed black leaders and the white media that it was essential to our political progress to stay or seem to stay economically and socially deprived. To be recognized and recognize oneself as middle or upper class was to threaten the political progress of black people. That girl who asked why I spoke so "proper" was accusing me of political sins—of thwarting the progress of our race.

10   Despite progress toward a more balanced picture of black America, the image of black society as an underclass remains strong. Look at local news coverage of the trial of Damian Williams and Henry Watson, charged with beating the white truck driver Reginald Denny during the 1992 South-Central L.A. riots. The press showed us an African-print-wearing cadre of Williams and Watson supporters trailing Edi M. O. Faal, William's defense attorney, like a Greek chorus. This chorus made a point of standing in the camera's range. They presented themselves as the voice of South-Central L.A., the voice of the oppressed, the voice of the downtrodden, the voice of the city's black people.

11   To anyone watching TV coverage of the trial, all blacks agreed with Faal's contention that his clients were prosecuted so aggressively because they are black. Period. Reporters made no effort to show

opposing black viewpoints. (In fact, the media portrait of the Los Angeles riot as blacks vs. whites and Koreans was a misrepresentation. According to the Rand Corporation, a research institute in Santa Monica, blacks made up 36 percent of those arrested during the riot; Latinos made up 51 percent.) The black bourgeoisie and intelligentsia remained largely silent. We had too long believed that to express disagreement with the "official line" was to be a traitor.

12   TV networks and cable companies gain media raves for programs like "Laurel Avenue," an HBO melodrama about a working-class black family lauded for its realism, a real black family complete with drug dealers, drug users, gun toters and basketball players. It is akin to the media presenting "Valley of the Dolls" as a realistic portrayal of the ways of white women.

13   The Fox network offers a differing but equally misleading portrait of black Americans, with "Martin." While blue humor has long been a staple of black audiences, it was relegated to clubs and records for *mature* black audiences. It was not peddled to kids or to the masses.

14   Now the blue humor tradition is piped to principally white audiences. If TV was as black as it is white—if there was a fair share of black love stories, black dramas, black detective heroes—these blue humor images would not be a problem. Right now, however, they stand as images to which whites can condescend.

15   Imagine being told by your peers, the records you hear, the programs you watch, the "leaders" you see on TV, classmates, prospective employers—imagine being told by virtually everyone that in order to be your true self you must be ignorant and poor, or at least seem so.

16   Blacks must now see to it that our children face no such burden. We must see to it that the white majority, along with vocal minorities within the black community (generally those with a self-serving political agenda), do not perpetuate the notion that African-Americans are invariably doomed to the underclass.

17   African-Americans are moving toward seeing ourselves—and demanding that others see us—as individuals, not as shards of a degraded monolith. The American ideal places primacy on the rights of the individual, yet historically African-Americans have been denied those rights. We blacks can effectively demand those rights, effectively demand justice only when each of us sees him or herself as an individual with the right to any of the opinions, idiosyncrasies and talents accorded any other American.

Understanding Meaning

1. What is the "black bourgeoisie"?
2. Why does Gaiter argue that the definition of a "'real' black" is crippling to young African-Americans?
3. Why does Gaiter believe that negative stereotypes of blacks are more destructive when embraced by African-Americans rather than whites?
4. Why does Gaiter argue for individual rather than group rights?
5. *Critical Thinking:* Gaiter argues that many liberals have a vested interest in keeping a black underclass. Do people gain political power by using the disadvantaged as a power base, a voting bloc? At some point do reformers realize that if they are successful they will be out of a job?

Evaluating Strategy

1. What kinds of appeals does Gaiter use in his argument?
2. *Other Modes:* How does Gaiter use *narration* and *definition* in his essay?
3. How much factual support does Gaiter offer?

Appreciating Language

1. What is the tone of this essay? What words and phrases help shape it?
2. Is Gaiter angry or disillusioned with anyone or any institution? What do his connotations suggest?

Connections across the Disciplines

1. Would Gaiter likely see Charles Jamison's article "Why My Business Failed" (page 484) as a kind of positive example for young African-Americans?
2. How do Gaiter's observations compare to William Raspberry's (page 310)?

Writing Suggestions

1. Write an essay reflecting your views of how your ethnic group is depicted in the media. How are Jews, Koreans, the Irish, Italians, or Poles portrayed? Is your group ignored? Are the representations accurate or stereotyped? Argue for a more balanced approach, or approve of fair reporting.

2. *Collaborative Writing:* Discuss with a group of students the way African-Americans are portrayed in the media. Are middle-class African-Americans eclipsed by images of an underclass? Are black success stories missing in black history? Write an open letter to television networks advocating your group's position. If members have different opinions, draft additional letters. Read all members' versions to the group. Ask members to comment on the clarity of each thesis and the quality of supporting detail.

Carl Sagan (1934–1996) was born in New York City and educated at the University of Chicago, where he received his doctorate in 1960. A widely published astronomer, Sagan became widely known to American television audiences through a popular series called Cosmos. *An expert on the atmospheres of Venus, Mars, and Titan, he is also noted for his ability to explain scientific issues for a general audience.*

Why We Need to Understand Science

This article originally appeared in the popular magazine Parade *(1993). As you read the article, notice how Sagan moves from humorous narrative to a serious argument, supported by facts, that Americans are woefully lacking in their knowledge of science.*

1   As I got off the plane, he was waiting for me, holding up a sign with my name on it. I was on my way to a conference of scientists and TV broadcasters, and the organizers had kindly sent a driver.

2   "Do you mind if I ask you a question?" He said as we waited for my bag. "Isn't it confusing to have the same name as that science guy?"

3   It took me a moment to understand. Was he pulling my leg? "I *am* that science guy," I said. He smiled. "Sorry. That's my problem. I thought it was yours too." He put out his hand. "My name is William F. Buckley." (Well, his name wasn't *exactly* William F. Buckley, but he did have the name of a contentious TV interviewer, for which he doubtless took a lot of good-natured ribbing.)

4   As we settled into the car for the long drive, he told me he was glad I was "that science guy"—he had so many questions to ask about science. Would I mind? And so we got to talking. But not about science. He wanted to discuss UFOs, "channeling" (a way to hear what's on the minds of dead people—not much it turns out), crystals, astrology. . . . He introduced each subject with real enthusiasm, and each time I had to disappoint him: "The evidence is crummy," I kept saying. "There's a much simpler explanation." As we drove on through

the rain, I could see him getting glummer. I was attacking not just pseudoscience but also a facet of his inner life.

5   And yet there is so much in real science that's equally exciting, more mysterious, a greater intellectual challenge—as well as being a lot closer to the truth. Did he know about the molecular building blocks of life sitting out there in the cold tenuous gas between the stars? Had he heard of the footprints of our ancestors found in 4-million-year-old volcanic ash? What about the raising of the Himalayas when India went crashing into Asia? Or how viruses subvert cells, or the radio search for extraterrestrial intelligence or the ancient civilization of Ebla? Mr. "Buckley"—well-spoken, intelligent, curious—had heard virtually nothing of modern science. He *wanted* to know about science. It's just that all the science got filtered out before it reached him. What the society permitted to trickle through was mainly pretense and confusion. And it had never taught him how to distinguish real science from the cheap imitation.

6   All over America there are smart, even gifted, people who have a built-in passion for science. But that passion is unrequited. A recent survey suggests that 94 percent of Americans are "scientifically illiterate."

A PRESCRIPTION FOR DISASTER

7   We live in a society exquisitely dependent on science and technology, in which hardly anyone knows anything about science and technology. This is a clear prescription for disaster. It's dangerous and stupid for us to remain ignorant about global warming, say, or ozone depletion, toxic and radioactive wastes, acid rain. Jobs and wages depend on science and technology. If the United States can't manufacture, at high quality and low price, products people want to buy, then industries will drift out of the United States and transfer a little prosperity to another part of the world. Because of the low birthrate in the '60s and '70s, the National Science Foundation projects a shortage of nearly a million professional scientists and engineers by 2010. Where will they come from? What about fusion, supercomputers, abortion, massive reductions in strategic weapons, addiction, high-resolution TV, airline and airport safety, food additives, animal rights, superconductivity, Midgetman versus rail-garrison MX missiles, going to Mars, finding cures for

AIDS and cancer? How can we decide national policy if we don't understand the underlying issues?

8   I know that science and technology are not just cornucopias pouring good deeds out into the world. Scientists not only conceived nuclear weapons; they also took political leaders by the lapels, arguing that *their* nation—whichever it happened to be—had to have one first. Then they arranged to manufacture 60,000 of them. Our technology has produced thalidomide, CFCs, Agent Orange, nerve gas, and industries so powerful they can ruin the climate of the planet. There's a *reason* people are nervous about science and technology.

9   And so the image of the mad scientist haunts our world—from Dr. Faust to Dr. Frankenstein to Dr. Strangelove to the white-coated loonies of Saturday morning children's TV. (All of this doesn't inspire budding scientists.) But there's no way back. We can't just conclude that science puts too much power into the hands of morally feeble technologists or corrupt, power-crazed politicians and decide to get rid of it. Advances in medicine and agriculture have saved more lives than have been lost in all the wars in history. Advances in transportation, communication, and entertainment have transformed the world. The sword of science is double-edged. Rather, its awesome power forces on all of us, including politicians, a new responsibility—more attention to the long-term consequences of technology, a global and transgenerational perspective, an incentive to avoid easy appeals to nationalism and chauvinism. Mistakes are becoming too expensive.

10   Science is much more than a body of knowledge. It is a way of thinking. This is central to its success. Science invites us to let the facts in, even when they don't conform to our preconceptions. It counsels us to carry alternative hypotheses in our heads and see which best match the facts. It urges on us a fine balance between no-holds-barred openness to new ideas, however heretical, and the most rigorous skeptical scrutiny of everything—new ideas *and* established wisdom. We need wide appreciation of this kind of thinking. It works. It's an essential tool for a democracy in an age of change. Our task is not just to train more scientists but also to deepen public understanding of science.

HOW BAD IS IT?

11   Very bad. "It's Official," reads one newspaper headline: "We Stink in Science." Less than half of all Americans know that the Earth moves

around the Sun and takes a year to do it—a fact established a few centuries ago. In tests of average 17-year-olds in many world regions, the U.S. ranked dead last in algebra. On identical tests, the U.S. kids averaged 43 percent and their Japanese counterparts 78 percent. In my book, 78 percent is pretty good—it corresponds to a C+, or maybe even a B−; 43 percent is an F. In a chemistry test, students in only two of 13 nations did worse than the U.S. Compared to us, Britain, Singapore, and Hong Kong were so high they were almost off-scale, and 25 percent of Canadian 18-year-olds knew just as much chemistry as a select 1 percent of American high school seniors (in their second chemistry course, and most of them in "advanced" programs). The best of 20 fifth-grade classrooms in Minneapolis was outpaced by every one of the 20 classrooms in Sendai, Japan, and 19 out of 20 in Taipei, Taiwan. South Korean students were far ahead of American students in all aspects of mathematics and science, and 13-year-olds in British Columbia (in Western Canada) outpaced their U.S. counterparts across the boards (in some areas they did better than the Koreans). Of the U.S. kids, 22 percent say they dislike school; only 8 percent of the Koreans do. Yet two-thirds of Americans, but only a quarter of the Koreans, say they are "good at mathematics."

WHY WE'RE FLUNKING

12   How do British Columbia, Japan, Britain, and Korea manage so much better than we do? During the Great Depression, teachers enjoyed job security, good salaries, respectability. Teaching was an admired profession, partly because learning was widely recognized as the road out of poverty. Little of that is true today. And, so, science (and other) teaching is too often incompetently or uninspiringly done, its practitioners, astonishingly, having little or no training in their subjects—sometimes themselves unable to distinguish science from pseudoscience. Those who do have the training often get higher-paying jobs elsewhere.

13   We need more money for teachers' training and salaries, and for laboratories—so kids will get hands-on experience rather than just reading what's in the book. But all across America, school-bond issues on the ballot are regularly defeated. U.S. parents are much more satisfied with what their children are learning in science and math than are, say, Japanese and Taiwanese parents—whose children are

doing so much better. No one suggests that property taxes be used to provide for the military budget, or for agriculture, or for cleaning up toxic wastes. Why just education? Why not support it from general taxes on the local and state levels? What about a special education tax for those industries with special needs for technically trained workers?

14   American kids don't do enough schoolwork. The average high school student spends 3.5 hours a week on homework. The total time devoted to studies, in and out of the classroom, is about 20 hours a week. Japanese *fifth*-graders average 33 hours a week.

15   But most American kids aren't stupid. Part of the reason they don't study hard is that they've received few tangible benefits when they do. Competency (that is, actually knowing the stuff) in verbal skills, mathematics, and science these days doesn't increase earnings for average young men in their first eight years out of high school—many of whom take service rather than industrial jobs.

16   In the productive sectors of the economy, though, the story is different. There are furniture factories, for example, in danger of going out of business—not because there are no customers but because few entry-level workers can do simple arithmetic. A major electronics company reports that 80 percent of its job applicants can't pass a *fifth*-grade math test—and that's an American, not a Korean, fifth-grade test. The United States is already losing some $25 billion a year (mainly in lost productivity and the cost of remedial education) because workers, to too great a degree, can't read, write, count, or think. Parents should know that their children's livelihoods may depend on how much math and science they know. Now, while the kids are in school, is the time for them to learn. Parents might encourage their schools to offer—and their kids to take—comprehensible, well-taught advanced science courses. They might also limit the amount of mind-numbing TV their children watch.

WHAT WE CAN DO

17   Those in America with the most favorable view of science tend to be young, well-to-do, college-educated white males. But three-quarters of new American workers between now and 2001 will be women, non-whites, and immigrants. Discriminating against them isn't only unjust, it's also self-defeating. It deprives the American economy of desperately needed skilled workers.

18   Black and Hispanic students are doing better in standardized science tests now than in the late 1960s, but they're the only ones who are. The average math gap between white and black U.S. high school graduates is still huge—two to three grade levels; but the gap between white U.S. high school graduates and those in, say, Japan, Canada, Great Britain, or Finland is more than *twice* as big. If you're poorly motivated and poorly educated, you won't know much—no mystery here. Suburban blacks with college-educated parents do just as well in college as suburban whites with college-educated parents. Enrolling a poor child in a Head Start program doubles his or her chances to be employed later in life; one who completes an Upward Bound program is four times as likely to get a college education. If we're serious, we know what to do.

19   What about college and university? There are obvious steps similar to what should be done in high schools; salaries for teachers that approach what they could get in industry; more scholarships, fellowships, and laboratory equipment; laboratory science courses required of everyone to graduate; and special attention paid to those traditionally steered away from science. We should also provide the financial and moral encouragement for academic scientists to spend more time on public education—lectures, newspaper and magazine articles, TV appearances. This requires scientists to make themselves understandable and fun to listen to. To me, it seems strange that some scientists, who depend on public funding for their research, are reluctant to explain to the public what it is that they do. Fortunately, the number of scientists willing to speak to the public—and capably—has been increasing each year. But there are not yet nearly enough.

20   Virtually every newspaper in America has a daily astrology column. How many have a daily science column? When I was growing up, my father would bring home a daily paper and consume (often with great gusto) the baseball box scores. There they were, to me dry as dust, with obscure abbreviations (W, SS, SO, W-L, AB, RBI), but they spoke to him. Newspapers everywhere printed them. I figured maybe they weren't too hard for me. Eventually I too got caught up in the world of baseball statistics. (I know it helped me in learning decimals, and I still cringe a little when I hear that someone is "batting a thousand." But 1.000 is not 1,000. The lucky player is batting one.)

21   Or take a look at the financial page. Any introductory material? Explanatory footnotes? Definitions of abbreviations? None. It's sink or

swim. Look at those acres of statistics! Yet people voluntarily read the stuff. It's not beyond their ability. It's only a matter of motivation. Why can't we do the same with math, science, and technology?

22   By far the most effective means of raising interest in science is television. There's lots of pseudoscience on TV, a fair amount of medicine and technology, but hardly any science—especially on the three big commercial networks, whose executives think science programming means ratings declines and lost profits, and nothing else matters. Why in all America is there no TV drama that has as its hero someone devoted to figuring out how the universe works?

23   Stirring projects in science and technology attract and inspire youngsters. The number of science Ph.D.s peaked around the time of the Apollo program and declined thereafter. This is an important potential side-effect of such projects as sending humans to Mars, or the Superconducting Supercollider to explore the fine structure of matter, or the program to map all human genes.

24   Every now and then, I'm lucky enough to teach a class in kindergarten or the first grade. Many of these children are curious, intellectually vigorous, ask provocative and insightful questions, and exhibit great enthusiasm for science. When I talk to high school students, I find something different. They memorize "facts." But, by and large, the joy of discovery, the life behind those facts, has gone out of them. They're worried about asking "dumb" questions; they're willing to accept inadequate answers; they don't pose follow-up questions; the room is awash with sidelong glances to judge, second-by-second, the approval of their peers. Something has happened between first and 12th grade, and it's not just puberty. I'd guess that its partly peer pressure *not* to excel (except in sports); partly that the society teaches short-term gratification; partly the impression that science or math won't buy you a sports car; partly that so little is expected of students; and partly that there are so few role models for intelligent discussion of science and technology or for learning for its own sake.

25   But there's something else. Many adults are put off when youngsters pose scientific questions. Children ask why the Sun is yellow, or what a dream is, or how deep you can dig a hole, or when is the world's birthday or why we have toes. Too many teachers and parents answer with irritation or ridicule, or quickly move on to something else. Why adults should pretend to omniscience before a 5-year-old, I can't for the life of me understand. What's wrong with admitting that you don't

know? Children soon recognize that somehow this kind of question annoys many adults. A few more experiences like this, and another child has been lost to science.

26   There are many better responses. If we have an idea of the answer, we could try to explain. If we don't, we could go to the encyclopedia or library. Or we might say to the child: "I don't know the answer. Maybe no one knows. Maybe when you grow up, you'll be the first to find out."

27   But mere encouragement isn't enough. We must also give children the tools to winnow the wheat from the chaff. I'm haunted by the vision of a generation of Americans unable to distinguish reality from fantasy, hopefully clutching their crystals for comfort, unequipped even to frame the right questions or to recognize the answers. I want us to rescue Mr. "Buckley" and the millions like him. I also want us to stop turning out leaden, incurious, unimaginative high school seniors. I think America needs, and deserves, a citizenry with minds wide awake and a basic understanding of how the world works.

28   Public understanding of science is more central to our national security than half a dozen strategic weapons systems. The sub-mediocre performance of American youngsters in science and math, and the widespread adult ignorance and apathy about science and math, should sound an urgent alarm.

Understanding Meaning

1. What is the difference between pseudoscience and science?
2. Why is American "scientific illiteracy" dangerous?
3. Why are people, in Sagan's view, disinterested in science?
4. What does Sagan persuade readers to accept? What must be done to improve our nation's understanding of science?
5. What does Sagan mean when he says that science is more than "knowledge" but "a way of thinking"? What is the difference?
6. *Critical Thinking:* Sagan argues that the media has portrayed science in a way children find unappealing. What image of scientists did you develop as a child? Were scientists depicted as less glamorous than police officers or lawyers?

Evaluating Strategy

1. How important is the opening narrative? What does it suggest about Sagan's intended readers?

2. What factual appeals does Sagan make?
3. How does he attempt to make his concerns about science relevant to general readers?
4. How does he present statistics? Are they understandable?

Appreciating Language

1. What level of language does Sagan use? How does it differ from that expected in a scientific paper or textbook?
2. How does Sagan use language to arouse reader concern about scientific illiteracy?

Connections across the Disciplines

1. How does Richard Preston's "Ebola River" (page 67) dramatize the need for scientific education and research?
2. Sagan argues that science is driven by facts and truth. How does Sagan's argument relate to Samuel Scudder's nineteenth-century article (page 45)?

Writing Suggestions

1. Write a short essay arguing that Americans lack a general knowledge of an important topic—science, mathematics, the Constitution, the environment, or their own bodies.
2. *Collaborative Writing:* Discuss Sagan's article with a group of students. What impressions of science and scientists did the group have in childhood? Write a brief, persuasive, open letter to parents encouraging them to invest more in their children's knowledge of science. You may use facts from Sagan's article for support.

DAVID BLANKENHORN

> *David Blankenhorn is founder and president of the Institute for American Values, a nonpartisan organization dedicated to research and education on family issues. He has published numerous articles about the status of American families in* The New York Times, USA Today, Newsday, *and* The Los Angeles Times. *His book* Fatherless America: Confronting Our Most Urgent Social Problem *was published in 1995.*

Fatherless America

Before reading Blankenhorn's essay, consider your own attitudes toward fatherhood. How important are fathers in your experience? Do children without fathers face greater risks, in your view?

1   The United States is becoming an increasingly fatherless society. A generation ago, an American child could reasonably expect to grow up with his or her father. Today, an American child can reasonably expect not to. Fatherlessness is now approaching a rough parity with fatherhood as a defining feature of American childhood.

2   This astonishing fact is reflected in many statistics, but here are the two most important. Tonight, about 40 percent of American children will go to sleep in homes in which their fathers do not live. Before they reach the age of eighteen, more than half of our nation's children are likely to spend at least a significant portion of their childhoods living apart from their fathers. Never before in this country have so many children been voluntarily abandoned by their fathers. Never before have so many children grown up without knowing what it means to have a father.

3   Fatherlessness is the most harmful demographic trend of this generation. It is the leading cause of declining child well-being in our society. It is also the engine driving our most urgent social problems, from crime to adolescent pregnancy to child sexual abuse to domestic violence against women. Yet, despite its scale and social consequences, fatherlessness is a problem that is frequently ignored or denied. Especially within our elite discourse, it remains largely a problem with no name.

4   If this trend continues, fatherlessness is likely to change the shape of our society. Consider this prediction. After the year 2000, as people born after 1970 emerge as a large proportion of our working-age adult population, the United States will be a nation divided into two groups, separate and unequal. The two groups will work in the same economy, speak a common language, and remember the same national history. But they will live fundamentally divergent lives. One group will receive basic benefits—psychological, social, economic, educational, and moral—that are denied to the other group.

5   The primary fault line dividing the two groups will not be race, religion, class, education, or gender. It will be patrimony. One group will consist of those adults who grew up with the daily presence and provision of fathers. The other group will consist of those who did not. By the early years of the next century, these two groups will be roughly the same size.

6   Surely a crisis of this scale merits a response. At a minimum, it requires a serious debate. Why is fatherhood declining? What can be done about it? Can our society find ways to invigorate effective fatherhood as a norm of male behavior? Yet, to date, the public discussion on this topic has been remarkably weak and defeatist. There is a prevailing belief that not much can—or even should—be done to reverse the trend.

7   When the crime rate jumps, politicians promise to do something about it. When the unemployment rate rises, task forces assemble to address the problem. As random shootings increase, public health officials worry about the preponderance of guns. But when it comes to the mass defection of men from family life, not much happens.

8   There is debate, even alarm, about specific social problems. Divorce. Out-of-wedlock childbearing. Children growing up in poverty. Youth violence. Unsafe neighborhoods. Domestic violence. The weakening of parental authority. But in these discussions, we seldom acknowledge the underlying phenomenon that binds together these otherwise disparate issues: the flight of males from their children's lives. In fact, we seem to go out of our way to avoid the connection between our most pressing social problems and the trend of fatherlessness.

9   We avoid this connection because, as a society, we are changing our minds about the role of men in family life. As a cultural idea, our inherited understanding of fatherhood is under siege. Men in general, and fathers in particular, are increasingly viewed as superfluous to family life: either expendable or as part of the problem. Masculinity itself, understood as anything other than a rejection of what it has traditionally meant to be male, is typically treated with suspicion and even

hostility in our cultural discourse. Consequently, our society is now manifestly unable to sustain, or even find reason to believe in, fatherhood as a distinctive domain of male activity.

10   The core question is simple: Does every child need a father? Increasingly, our society's answer is "no," or at least "not necessarily." Few idea shifts in this century are as consequential as this one. At stake is nothing less than what it means to be a man, who our children will be, and what kind of society we will become.

11   In addition to losing fathers, we are losing something larger: our idea of fatherhood. Unlike earlier periods of father absence in our history, we now face more than a physical loss affecting some homes. We face a cultural loss affecting every home. For this reason, the most important absence our society must confront is not the absence of fathers but the absence of our belief in fathers.

12   In a larger sense, this is a *cultural* criticism because fatherhood, much more than motherhood, is a cultural invention. Its meaning for the individual man is shaped less by biology than by a cultural script or story—a societal code that guides, and at times pressures, him into certain ways of acting and of understanding himself as a man.

13   Like motherhood, fatherhood is made up of both a biological and a social dimension. Yet in societies across the world, mothers are far more successful than fathers at fusing these two dimensions into a coherent parental identity. Is the nursing mother playing a biological or a social role? Is she feeding or bonding? We can hardly separate the two, so seamlessly are they woven together.

14   But fatherhood is a different matter. A father makes his sole biological contribution at the moment of conception—nine months before the infant enters the world. Because social paternity is only indirectly linked to biological paternity, the connection between the two cannot be assumed. The phrase "to father a child" usually refers only to the act of insemination, not to the responsibility for raising a child. What fathers contribute to their offspring after conception is largely a matter of cultural devising.

15   Moreover, despite their other virtues, men are not ideally suited to responsible fatherhood. Although they certainly have the capacity for fathering, men are inclined to sexual promiscuity and paternal waywardness. Anthropologically, human fatherhood constitutes what might be termed a necessary problem. It is necessary because, in all societies, child well-being and societal success hinge largely upon a high level of paternal investment: the willingness of adult males to devote energy and resources to the care of their offspring. It is a problem

because adult males are frequently—indeed, increasingly—unwilling or unable to make that vital investment.

16   Because fatherhood is universally problematic in human societies, cultures must mobilize to devise and enforce the father role for men, coaxing and guiding them into fatherhood through a set of legal and extralegal pressures that require them to maintain a close alliance with their children's mother and to invest in their children. Because men do not volunteer for fatherhood as much as they are conscripted into it by the surrounding culture, only an authoritative cultural story of fatherhood can fuse biological and social paternity into a coherent male identity.

17   For exactly this reason, Margaret Mead and others have observed that the supreme test of any civilization is whether it can socialize men by teaching them to be fathers—creating a culture in which men acknowledge their paternity and willingly nurture their offspring. Indeed, if we can equate the essence of the antisocial male with violence, we can equate the essence of the socialized male with being a good father. Thus, at the center of our most important cultural imperative, we find the fatherhood script: the story that describes what it ought to mean for a man to have a child.

18   Just as the fatherhood script advances the social goal of harnessing male behavior to collective needs, it also reflects an individual purpose. That purpose, in a word, is happiness. Anthropologists have long understood that the genius of an effective culture is its capacity to reconcile individual happiness with collective well-being. By situating individual lives within a social narrative, culture endows private behavior with larger meaning. By linking the self to moral purposes larger than the self, an effective culture tells us a story in which individual fulfillment transcends selfishness, and personal satisfaction transcends narcissism.

19   In this respect, our cultural script is not simply a set of imported moralisms, exterior to the individual and designed only to compel self-sacrifice. It is also a pathway—indeed, our only pathway—to what the founders of the American experiment called the pursuit of happiness.

20   The stakes on this issue could hardly be higher. Our society's conspicuous failure to sustain or create compelling norms of fatherhood amounts to a social and personal disaster. Today's story of fatherhood features one-dimensional characters, an unbelievable plot, and an unhappy ending. It reveals in our society both a failure of collective memory and a collapse of moral imagination. It undermines families, neglects children, causes or aggravates our worst social problems, and

makes individual adult happiness—both male and female—harder to achieve.

21   Ultimately, this failure reflects nothing less than a culture gone awry: a culture increasingly unable to establish the boundaries, erect the signposts, and fashion the stories that can harmonize individual happiness with collective well-being. In short, it reflects a culture that increasingly fails to "enculture" individual men and women, mothers and fathers.

22   In personal terms, the end result of this process, the final residue from what David Gutmann calls the "deculturation" of paternity, is narcissism: a me-first egotism that is hostile not only to any societal goal or larger moral purpose but also to any save the most puerile understanding of personal happiness. In social terms, the primary results of decultured paternity are a decline in children's well-being and a rise in male violence, especially against women. In a larger sense, the most significant result is our society's steady fragmentation into atomized individuals, isolated from one another and estranged from the aspirations and realities of common membership in a family, a community, a nation, bound by mutual commitment and shared memory.

Understanding Meaning

1.   Briefly summarize Blankenhorn's thesis. What is he saying about fatherhood?
2.   Why is fatherhood declining in America?
3.   What are the social implications of millions of children growing up without fathers?
4.   How does fatherhood change men and their behavior? Do you agree with Blankenhorn's view that "men are inclined to sexual promiscuity and paternal waywardness"?
5.   *Critical Thinking:* Could the role of fatherhood be analyzed by studying children separated from their fathers for extensive periods of time, as in WWII? If the children of veterans who served overseas for several years grew up with more problems than those who had fathers in the home, would that support Blankenhorn's argument?

Evaluating Strategy

1.   Can a writer stress the importance of fatherhood without implying that single mothers are unable to properly rear and nurture children? How might women rearing children alone respond to his argument?

2. What support does Blankenhorn present to support his thesis?
3. *Other Modes:* Where does Blankenhorn use *comparison, cause and effect,* and *analysis* to construct his argument?

Appreciating Language

1. How would you define "fatherlessness"? At what point does a divorced father become an "absentee" father?
2. What does Blankenhorn mean by the term "decultured paternity"?
3. How would you characterize the tone and style of this passage, which formed the preface to Blankenhorn's book? Would it motivate you to continue reading?

Connections across the Disciplines

1. Do E. B. White's "Once More to the Lake" (page 151) and José Antonio Burciaga's "My Ecumenical Father" (page 127) demonstrate the importance of fatherhood?
2. Refer to the comments of Gloria Steinem (page 514) and Rene Denfeld (page 284). How might feminists and their critics respond to Blankenhorn's argument?

Writing Suggestions

1. Write a short autobiographical essay analyzing how the presence or absence of a father shaped your childhood. Do your experiences support or contradict Blankenhorn's observations?
2. In response to this article, write a short essay outlining your definition of a good father.
3. *Collaborative Writing:* Discuss Blankenhorn's article with a group of students, and measure their acceptance or rejection of his views. Work together to write a response in the form of a letter to the editor. If opinions within the group differ, consider writing opposing statements.

BLENDING THE MODES

NAT HENTOFF

Nat Hentoff (1925–) was born in Boston. The author of more than twenty-five books, Hentoff is also known for his numerous articles in the Village Voice, New Yorker, *and the* Washington Post. *A committed liberal, he has been outspoken on issues ranging from drug testing and the draft to racism and abortion. Although considered a leftist, Hentoff has criticized those on the Left who have advocated suppressing what they call "hate speech."*

Should This Student Have Been Expelled?

In this 1991 article from the Village Voice, *Hentoff persuades readers to accept "hate speech," no matter how offensive it is, as "speech" and therefore protected by the Constitution. As you read Hentoff's essay, notice how he uses* definition, narration, *and* comparison *to build his argument.*

> *The day that Brown denies any student freedom*
> *of speech is the day I give up my presidency of the university.*
> —Vartan Gregorian, president of Brown University,
> February 20, 1991

1   Doug Hann, a varsity football player at Brown, was also concentrating on organizational behavior and management and business economics. On the night of October 18, 1990, Hann, a junior, was celebrating his twenty-first birthday, and in the process had imbibed a considerable amount of spirits.

2   At one point, Hann shouted into the air, "Fuck you, niggers!" It was aimed at no one in particular but apparently at all black students at Brown. Or in the world. A freshman leaned out a dormitory window and asked him to stop being so loud and offensive.

3   Hann, according to reporters on the *Brown Daily Herald*, looked up and yelled, "What are you, a faggot?" Hann then noticed an Israeli flag in the dorm. "What are you, a Jew?" he shouted. "Fucking Jew!"

4   Hann had achieved the hat trick of bigotry. (In hockey, the hat trick is scoring three goals in a game.) In less than a minute, Hann had engaged in racist, anti-Semitic, and homophobic insults.

5   He wasn't through. As reported by Smita Nerula in the *Brown Daily Herald,* the freshman who had asked Hann to cool it recruited a few people from his dorm "and followed Hann and his friends.

6   "This resulted in a verbal confrontation outside of Wayland Arch. At this time, [Hann] was said to have turned to one of the freshman's friends, a black woman, and shouted, 'My parents own your people.'"

7   To the Jewish student, or the student he thought was Jewish, Hann said, "Happy Hanukkah."

8   There are reports that at this juncture Hann tried to fight some of the students who had been following him. But, the *Brown Daily Herald* reports, he "was held back by one of his friends, while [another] friend stretched his arm across the Wayland Gates to keep the students from following Hann."

9   John Howard Crouch—a student and Brown chapter secretary of the American Civil Liberties Union there—tells me that because Hann had friends restraining him, "nobody seriously expected fighting, regardless of anyone's words."

10   Anyway, there was no physical combat. Just words. Awful words, but nothing more than speech. (Nor were there any threats.)

11   This was not the first time Hann's graceful drunken language had surfaced at Brown. Two years before, in an argument with a black student at a fraternity bar, Hann had called the student a "nigger." Thereupon he had been ordered to attend a race relations workshop and to get counseling for possible alcohol abuse. Obviously, he has not been rehabilitated.

12   Months went by after Hann's notorious birthday celebration as Brown's internal disciplinary procedures cranked away. (To steal a phrase from Robert Sherrill, Brown's way of reaching decisions in these matters is to due process as military music is to music. But that's true of any college or university I know anything about.)

13   At last, the Undergraduate Disciplinary Council (five faculty or administration members and five students) ruled that Doug Hann was to leave the university forevermore. Until two years ago, it was possible for a Brown student to be dismissed, which meant that he or she could reapply after a decent period of penance. But now, Brown has enshrined the sentence of expulsion. You may go on to assist Mother

Teresa in caring for the dying or you may teach a course in feminism to 2 Live Crew, but no accomplishments, no matter how noble, will get you back into Brown once you have been expelled.

14 Doug Hann will wander the earth without a Brown degree for the rest of his days.

15 The president of Brown, Vartan Gregorian—formerly the genial head of the New York Public Library—had the power to commute or even reverse the sentence. But the speech code under which Hann was thrown out had been proposed by Gregorian himself shortly after he was inaugurated in 1989, so he was hardly a detached magistrate.

16 On January 25, 1991, Vartan Gregorian affirmed, with vigor, the expulsion decision by the Undergraduate Disciplinary Council.

17 Hann became a historic figure. Under all the "hate speech" codes enacted around the country in recent years, he is the first student to actually be expelled for violating one of the codes.

18 The *New York Times* (February 12) reported that "Howard Ehrlich, the research director of the National Institute Against Prejudice and Violence, said that he did not know of any other such expulsions, but that he was familiar with cases in which students who had harassed others were moved to other dormitories or ordered to undergo counseling."

19 But that takes place in *educational* institutions, whose presidents recognize that there are students who need help, not exile.

20 At first, there didn't seem to be much protest among the student body at Brown on free speech grounds—except for members of the Brown chapter of the ACLU and some free thinkers on the student paper, as well as some unaffiliated objectors to expelling students for what they say, not for what they do. The number of these dissenters is increasing, as we shall see.

21 At the student paper, however, the official tone has changed from the libertarian approach of Vernon Silver, who was editor-in-chief last semester. A February 13 *Brown Daily Herald* editorial was headed: *"Good Riddance."*

22 It began: "Doug Hann is gone, and the university is well to be rid of him."

23 But President Gregorian has been getting a certain amount of flack and so, smiting his critics hip and thigh, he wrote a letter to the *New York Times*. Well, that letter (printed on February 21) was actually a press release, distributed by the Brown University News Bureau to all sorts of people, including me, on February 12. There were a few

changes—and that *Brown Daily Herald* editorial was attached to it—but Gregorian's declaration was clearly not written exclusively for the *Times*.

24   Is this a new policy at the *Times*—taking public relations handouts for the letters page?

25   Next week I shall include a relentlessly accurate analysis of President Gregorian's letter by the executive director of the Rhode Island ACLU. But first, an account of what Gregorian said in that letter to the *Times*.

26   President Gregorian indignantly denies that Brown has ever expelled "anyone for the exercise of free speech, nor will it ever do so." Cross his heart.

27   He then goes into self-celebration: "My commitment to free speech and condemnation of racism and homophobia are well known. . . .

28   "The university's code of conduct does not prohibit speech; it prohibits *actions*."

29   Now watch this pitiable curve ball:

30   "Offence III [of the Brown code]—which deals with harassment—prohibits inappropriate, abusive, threatening, or demeaning actions based on race, religion, gender, handicap, ethnicity, national origin, or sexual orientation."

31   In the original press release, Gregorian underlined the word *actions*. There, and in the letter to the *Times*—lest a dozing reader miss the point—Gregorian emphasizes that "The rules do not proscribe words, epithets, or slanders, they proscribe behavior." Behavior that "shows flagrant disrespect for the well-being of others or is unreasonably disruptive of the University community."

32   Consider the overbreadth and vagueness of these penalty-bearing provisions. What are the definitions of "harassment," "inappropriate," "demeaning," "flagrant," "disrespect," "well-being," "unreasonably"?

33   Furthermore, with regard to Brown's termination of Doug Hann with extreme prejudice, Gregorian is engaging in the crudest form of Orwellian newspeak. Hann was kicked out for *speech*, and only speech—not for *actions*, as Gregorian huffily insists. As for behavior, the prickly folks whose burning of the American flag was upheld by the Supreme Court were indeed engaged in behavior, but that behavior was based entirely on symbolic speech. So was Hann's. He didn't punch anybody or vandalize any property. He brayed.

34   Art Spitzer, legal director of the ACLU's National Capital Area affiliate, wrote a personal letter to Gregorian:

35   "There is a very simple test for determining whether a person is being punished for his actions or his speech. You just ask whether he would have received the same punishment if he had spoken different words while engaging in the same conduct.

36   "Thus, would your student have been expelled if he had gotten drunk and stood in the same courtyard at the same hour of the night, shouting at the same decibel level, 'Black is Beautiful!' 'Gay is Good!' or 'Go Brown! Beat Yale!' or even 'Nuke Baghdad! Kill Saddam!'?

37   "I am confident," Spitzer said, that "he would not have been expelled for such 'actions.' If that is correct, it follows that *he was expelled for the unsavory content of his speech,* and not for his actions. I have no doubt that you can understand this distinction. (Emphasis added.)

38   "Now, you are certainly entitled to believe that it is appropriate to expel a student for the content of his speech when that content is sufficiently offensive to the 'university community.' . . .

39   "If that is your position, why can't you deliver it forthrightly? Then the university community can have an open debate about which opinions it finds offensive, and ban them. Perhaps this can be done once a year, so that the university's rules can keep pace with the tenor of the times—after all, it wouldn't do to have outmoded rules banning procommunist or blasphemous speech still on the books, now that it's 1991. Then students and teachers applying for admission or employment at Brown will know what they are getting into.

40   "Your recent statements, denying the obvious, are just hypocritical. . . ."

41   And what did the *New York Times*—in a stunningly fatuous February 21 editorial—say of Vartan Gregorian's sending Doug Hann into permanent exile? "A noble attempt both to govern and teach."

42   The *Times* editorials should really be signed, so that the rest of the editorial board isn't blamed for such embarrassments.

Understanding Meaning

1. What events led to Hann's expulsion? Why does Hentoff call him "a historic figure"?
2. Can one make both a "commitment to free speech" and a "condemnation of racism"?
3. What are "hate speech" codes? Does it strike you as odd that no one seemed offended by Hann's use of the infamous "f-word"? Is obscenity less disturbing than racial slurs?

4. Would comments about Irish drunks or Italian gangsters be considered "hate speech"?
5. *Critical Thinking:* How do you separate "speech" from "action"? Does the concept of free speech, for instance, allow us to insult a person without facing the legal consequences that would arise from a physical assault?

Evaluating Strategy

1. Hentoff opens his article with a quote from the president of Brown University. How does this set up the rest of his argument?
2. Label where Hentoff uses logical, emotional, and ethical appeals.
3. Do you find Hentoff's inclusion of the press release effective?
4. *Other Modes:* Where does Hentoff use *narration, comparison,* and *definition?*

Appreciating Language

1. Hentoff refers to Hann's activity as a "hat trick of bigotry"—scoring racist, anti-Semitic, and homophobic insults in one outburst. Does the use of this hockey term suggest mockery? Would "triple threat" have different connotations?
2. What tone does Hentoff create with comments about military music and statements such as "Doug Hann will wander the earth without a Brown degree for the rest of his days"? How serious does he take the issue of "hate speech" and those who condemn it?

Connections across the Disciplines

1. What free speech and hate speech issues are raised by the Internet? Review Michel Marriott's "CyberSoul Not Found" (page 509), which includes the story of an African-American woman who encountered racial hostility in a chat room.
2. *Critical Thinking:* Consider the impact the word "nigger" had on Nathan McCall (page 51). When speech has a devastating effect on people, does it become an "action" as opposed to speech or "expression"?

Writing Suggestions

1. Assume you were a student at Brown University during the Hann controversy. Write a letter to the editor of the college paper arguing whether or

  not Hann should be expelled. Support your argument with more than one persuasive appeal.

2. *Collaborative Writing:* Discuss the concept of "hate speech" with a group of students. Ask members to consider the fate of Doug Hann. Should he have been expelled? Is "hate speech" protected by the Bill of Rights? Record comments, and write a brief argument for or against disciplining students for expressing racist comments.

PRO AND CON VIEWS: CULTURAL IDENTITY

ARMANDO RENDÓN

Armando Rendón (1939–) was raised in San Antonio, Texas. He is currently vice president of ATM Systems, a Chicago-based counseling firm. He has published articles in The Washington Post *and* Civil Rights Digest. *Rendón also wrote a film script,* El Chicano. *In 1971 he published* Chicano Manifesto, *which outlined his views of the place of Mexicans in American society.*

Kiss of Death

In this section of Chicano Manifesto, *Rendón argues the importance of Hispanics to resist assimilation into mainstream American society and maintain their language and culture to avoid being "sucked into the vacuum of the dominant society."*

1   I nearly fell victim to the Anglo. My childhood was spent in the West Side barrio of San Antonio. I lived in my grandmother's house on Ruiz Street just below Zarzamora Creek. I did well in the elementary grades and learned English quickly.

2   Spanish was off-limits in school anyway, and teachers and relatives taught me early that my mother tongue would be of no help in making good grades and becoming a success. Yet Spanish was the language I used in playing and arguing with friends. Spanish was the language I spoke with my *abuelita*, my dear grandmother, as I ate *atole* on those cold mornings when I used to wake at dawn to her clattering dishes in the tiny kitchen; or when I would cringe in mock horror at old folk tales she would tell me late at night.

3   But the lesson took effect anyway. When, at the age of ten, I went with my mother to California, to the San Francisco Bay Area where she found work during the war years, I had my first real opportunity to strip myself completely of my heritage. In California the schools I attended were all Anglo except for this little mexicanito. At least, I never knew anyone who admitted he was Mexican and I certainly never thought to ask. When my name was accented incorrectly, Réndon instead of Rendón, that was all right; finally I must have gotten tired of correcting people or just didn't bother.

4   I remember a summertime visit home a few years after living on the West Coast. At an evening gathering of almost the whole family—uncles, aunts, nephews, nieces, my *abuelita*—we sat outdoors through the dusk until the dark had fully settled. Then the lights were turned on; someone brought out a Mexican card game, the *Lotería El Diablito*, similar to bingo. But instead of rows of numbers on a pasteboard, there were figures of persons, animals, and objects on cards corresponding to figures set in rows on a pasteboard. We used frijoles (pinto beans) to mark each figure on our card as the leader went through the deck one by one. The word for tree was called: *Arbol!* It completed a row; I had won. Then to check my card I had to name each figure again. When I said the word for tree, it didn't come at all as I wanted it to; AR-BOWL with the accent on the last syllable and sounding like an Anglo tourist. There was some all-around kidding of me and good-natured laughter over the incident, and it passed.

5   But if I had not been speaking much Spanish up until then, I spoke even less afterward. Even when my mother, who speaks both Spanish and English fluently, spoke to me in Spanish, I would respond in English. By the time I graduated from high school and prepared to enter college, the break was nearly complete. Seldom during college did I admit to being a Mexican-American. Only when Latin American students pressed me about my surname did I admit my Spanish descent, or when it proved an asset in meeting coeds from Latin American countries.

6   My ancestry had become a shadow, fainter and fainter about me. I felt no particular allegiance to it, drew no inspiration from it, and elected generally to let it fade away. I clicked with the Anglo mind-set in college, mastered it, you might say. I even became editor of the campus biweekly newspaper as a junior, and editor of the literary magazine as a senior—not bad, now that I look back, for a tortillas-and-beans Chicano upbringing to beat the Anglo at his own game.

7   The point of my "success," of course, was that I had been assimilated; I had bought the white man's world. After getting my diploma I was set to launch out into a career in newspaper reporting and writing. There was no thought in my mind of serving my people, telling their story, or making anything right for anybody but myself. Instead I had dreams of Pulitzer Prizes, syndicated columns, foreign correspondent assignments, front-page stories—that was for me. Then something happened.

8   A Catholic weekly newspaper in Sacramento offered me a position as a reporter and feature writer. I had a job on a Bay Area daily as a

copyboy at the time, with the opportunity to become a reporter. But I'd just been married, and there were a number of other reasons to consider: there'd be a variety of assignments, Sacramento was the state capital, it was a good town in which to raise a family, and the other job lacked promise for upward mobility. I decided to take the offer.

9   My wife and I moved to Sacramento in the fall of 1961, and in a few weeks the radicalization of this Chicano began. It wasn't a book I read or a great leader awakening me, for we had no Chávezes or Tijerinas or Gonzálezes at the time; and it was no revelation from above. It was my own people who rescued me. There is a large Chicano population in Sacramento, today one of the most activist in northern California, but at the time factionalized and still dependent on the social and church organizations for identity. But together we found each other.

10   My job soon brought me into contact with many Chicanos as well as with the recently immigrated Mexicans, located in the barrios that Sacramento had allocated to the "Mexicans." I found my people striving to survive in an alien environment among foreign people. One of the stories I covered concerned a phenomenon called Cursillos de Cristiandad (Little Courses in Christianity), intense, three-day group-sensitivity sessions whose chief objective is the re-Christianization of Catholics. To cover the story properly I talked my editor into letting me take a Cursillo.

11   Not only was much revealed to me about the phony gilt lining of religion which I had grown up believing was the Church, but there was an added and highly significant side effect—cultural shock! I rediscovered my own people, or perhaps they redeemed me. Within the social dimension of the Cursillo, for the first time in many years I became reimmersed in a tough, *macho ambiente* (an entirely Mexican male environment). Only Spanish was spoken. The effect was shattering. It was as if my tongue, after being struck dumb as a child, had been loosened.

12   Because we were located in cramped quarters, with limited facilities, and the cooks, lecturers, priests, and participants were men only, the old sense of *machismo* and *camarada* was revived and given new perspective. I was cast in a spiritual setting which was a perfect background for reviving my Chicano soul. Reborn but imperfectly, I still had a lot to learn about myself and my people. But my understanding deepened and renewed itself as the years went by. I visited bracero camps with teams of Chicanos; sometimes with priests taking the sacraments; sometimes only Chicanos, offering advice or assistance with badly needed food and clothing, distributed through a bingo-game

technique; and on occasion, music for group singing provided by a phonograph or a guitar. Then there were barrio organization work; migrant worker programs; a rural self-help community development project; and confrontation with antipoverty agencies, with the churches, with government officials, and with cautious Chicanos, too.

13   In a little San Francisco magazine called *Way,* I wrote in a March 1966 article discussing "The Other Mexican-American":

14   The Mexican-American must answer at the same time: Who am I? and Who are we? This is to pose then, not merely a dilemma of self-identity; but of self-in-group-identity. . . . Perhaps the answer to developing a total Mexican-American concept must be left in the hands of the artist, the painter, the writer, and the poet, who can abstract the essence of what it is to be Mexican in America. . . . When that understanding comes . . . the Mexican-American will not only have acculturized himself, but he will have acculturized America to him.

15   If anyone knew what he was talking about when he spoke of the dilemma of who he was and where he belonged, it was this Chicano. I very nearly dropped out, as so many other Mexican-Americans have, under the dragging pressure to be someone else, what most of society wants you to be before it hands out its chrome-plated trophies.

16   And that mystique—I didn't quite have it at the time, or the right word for it. But no one did until just the last few years when so many of us stopped trying to be someone else and decided that what we want to be and to be called is Chicano.

17   I owe my life to my Chicano people. They rescued me from the Anglo kiss of death, the monolingual, monocultural, and colorless Gringo society. I no longer face a dilemma of identity or direction. That identity and direction have been charted for me by the Chicano—but to think I came that close to being sucked into the vacuum of the dominant society.

Understanding Meaning

1. What kind of childhood did Rendón have?
2. What represented his early success? What does Rendón mean by the statement "I had bought the white man's world"? What were his goals?
3. What is the "Anglo kiss of death"?
4. How did Rendón respond to people who mispronounced his name?

5. What led to Rendón's "radicalization"?
6. The Chicanos Rendón encountered were the poor of the barrios and bracero camps. Would his sense of identity be different if the Mexicans he encountered in California were affluent professionals and entrepreneurs?
7. *Critical Thinking:* Rendón describes the Gringo society as "monolingual, monocultural, and colorless." Does he overlook the diversity of cultures in mainstream America, which includes Jews, the Irish, Italians, Germans, Greeks, Russians, and the French? Is this the perception that immigrants have of any culture, such as that all Mexicans or Nigerians seem alike?

Evaluating Strategy

1. What tone is established in the first sentence? Does the use of the word "victim" indicate hostility?
2. Rendón includes a quote from one of his articles. Is this an effective device? Would it be better to simply restate his ideas within "Kiss of Death"?
3. *Other Modes:* How does Rendón use *narration, description*, and *comparison* in developing "Kiss of Death"?

Appreciating Language

1. What does the term "kiss of death" mean to you? Do you associate it with the Bible or Hollywood images of the Mafia?
2. Rendón uses several Spanish words without providing definitions in English. What does this suggest about his idea of America becoming "acculturized" to the Mexican American?
3. Rendón uses both "Mexican-American" and "Chicano." What definitions of these terms are you familiar with? Do "Latino" and "Hispanic" have different meanings and connotations?
4. What does Rendón mean by "cautious Chicanos"?

Connections across the Disciplines

1. How might Rendón view the Chicano police officer described by Ramon "Tianguis" Pérez in "The Fender-Bender" (page 62)? Might he see this officer as a "cautious Chicano"?
2. How does Rendón's concept of cultural identity compare with the concerns of William Raspberry (page 310) and of Leonce Gaiter (583), who

questions the stereotypes offered of "genuine African-Americans"? Does Rendón assume that "real" Chicanos live in the barrio and not in suburbs?

Writing Suggestions

1. Write your own version of a "kiss of death" you have escaped in your own life. Perhaps you nearly lost yourself or compromised your future by taking a job or entering a relationship you found initially appealing but now view as an error. Your essay should emphasize how you altered your sense of identity.

2. Write a short essay analyzing your role in society. Do you see yourself as an individual in a collective society or as part of a group within society? Do others view you as a member of an ethnic group, one of the handicapped, or a product of your neighborhood or generation? Does an in-group identity provide support or heighten your sense of alienation from the greater society?

3. *Collaborative Writing:* Discuss Rendón's essay with a group of students, and ask each one to briefly respond to the notion of an "Anglo Kiss of Death." How do members of the group define this? Do they feel it is appropriate or unnecessarily harsh? Does it presume that mainstream American society is a malevolent force? Work together to write a few paragraphs expressing the views your group raises. You may organize your statement by using *comparison* or *division/classification*.

Barbara Ehrenreich (1941–) was born in Butte, Montana and attended Reed College in Oregon, where she received a bachelor's degree in chemical physics. In 1968 she completed a doctorate in cell biology at Rockefeller University in New York. While in graduate school, she became active in political and social issues such as education, low-income housing, and the war in Vietnam. She has published numerous articles in Time, Ms, Mother Jones, New Republic, *and* The Nation, *as well as several collections of essays.*

Cultural Baggage

Unlike Armando Rendón who embraces his ethnic heritage, Barbara Ehrenreich refuses to accept an ethnic identity, calling herself one of "the race of 'none.'"

1   An acquaintance was telling me about the joys of rediscovering her ethnic and religious heritage. "I know exactly what my ancestors were doing 2,000 years ago," she said, eyes gleaming with enthusiasm, "and *I can do the same things now.*" Then she leaned forward and inquired politely, "And what is your ethnic background, if I may ask?"

2   "None," I said, that being the first word in line to get out of my mouth. Well, not "none," I backtracked. Scottish, English, Irish—that was something, I supposed. Too much Irish to qualify as a WASP; too much of the hated English to warrant a "Kiss Me, I'm Irish" button; plus there are a number of dead ends in the family tree due to adoptions, missing records, failing memories and the like. I was blushing by this time. Did "none" mean I was rejecting my heritage out of Anglo-Celtic self-hate? Or was I revealing a hidden ethnic chauvinism in which the Britannically derived serve as a kind of neutral standard compared with the ethnic "others"?

3   Throughout the 60's and 70's, I watched one group after another— African-Americans, Latinos, Native Americans—stand up and proudly reclaim their roots while I just sank back ever deeper into my seat. All this excitement over ethnicity stemmed, I uneasily sensed, from a past in which their ancestors had been trampled upon by *my* ancestors, or at

least by people who looked very much like them. In addition, it had begun to seem almost un-American not to have some sort of hyphen at hand, linking one to more venerable times and locales.

4   But the truth is, I was raised with none. We'd eaten ethnic foods in my childhood home, but these were all borrowed, like the pasties, or Cornish meat pies, my father had picked up from his fellow miners in Butte, Mont. If my mother had one rule, it was militant ecumenism in all matters of food and experience. "Try new things," she would say, meaning anything from sweetbreads to clams, with an emphasis on the "new."

5   As a child, I briefly nourished a craving for tradition and roots. I immersed myself in the works of Sir Walter Scott. I pretended to believe that the bagpipe was a musical instrument. I was fascinated to learn from a grandmother that we were descended from certain Highland clans and longed for a pleated skirt in one of their distinctive tartans.

6   But in "Ivanhoe," it was the dark-eyed "Jewess" Rebecca I identified with, not the flaxen-haired bimbo Rowena. As for clans: Why not call them "tribes," those bands of half-clad peasants and warriors whose idea of cuisine was stuffed sheep gut washed down with whisky? And then there was the sting of Disraeli's remark—which I came across in my early teens—to the effect that his ancestors had been leading orderly, literate lives when my ancestors were still rampaging through the Highlands daubing themselves with blue paint.

7   Motherhood put the screws on me, ethnicitywise. I had hoped that by marrying a man of Eastern European-Jewish ancestry I would acquire for my descendants the ethnic genes that my own forebears so sadly lacked. At one point, I even subjected the children to a seder of my own design, including a little talk about the flight from Egypt and its relevance to modern social issues. But the kids insisted on buttering their matzohs and snickering through my talk. "Give me a break, Mom," the older one said. "You don't even believe in God."

8   After the tiny pagans had been put to bed, I sat down to brood over Elijah's wine. What had I been thinking? The kids knew that their Jewish grandparents were secular folks who didn't hold seders themselves. And if ethnicity eluded me, how could I expect it to take root in my children, who are not only Scottish-English-Irish, but Hungarian-Polish-Russian to boot?

9   But, then, on the fumes of Manischewitz, a great insight took form in my mind. It was true, as the kids said, that I didn't "believe in God." But this could be taken as something very different from an accusa-

tion—a reminder of a genuine heritage. My parents had not believed in God either, nor had my grandparents or any other progenitors going back to the great-great level. They had become disillusioned with Christianity generations ago—just as, on the in-law side, my children's other ancestors had shaken their Orthodox Judaism. This insight did not exactly furnish me with an "identity," but it was at least something to work with: we are the kind of people. I realized—whatever our distant ancestors' religions—who do *not* believe, who do not carry on traditions, who do not do things just because someone has done them before.

10   The epiphany went on: I recalled that my mother never introduced a procedure for cooking or cleaning by telling me, "Grandma did it this way." What did Grandma know, living in the days before vacuum cleaners and disposable toilet mops! In my parents' general view, new things were better than old, and the very fact that some ritual had been performed in the past was a good reason for abandoning it now. Because what was the past, as our forebears knew it? Nothing but poverty, superstition and grief. "Think for yourself," Dad used to say. "Always ask why."

11   In fact, this may have been the ideal cultural heritage for my particular ethnic strain—bounced as it was from the Highlands of Scotland across the sea, out to the Rockies, down into the mines and finally spewed out into high-tech, suburban America. What better philosophy, for a race of migrants, than "Think for yourself"? What better maxim, for a people whose whole world was rudely inverted every 30 years or so, than "Try new things"?

12   The more tradition-minded, the newly enthusiastic celebrants of Purim and Kwanzaa and Solstice, may see little point to survival if the survivors carry no cultural freight—religion, for example, or ethnic tradition. To which I would say that skepticism, curiosity and wide-eyed ecumenical tolerance are also worthy elements of the human tradition and are at least as old as such notions as "Serbian" or "Croatian," "Scottish" or "Jewish." I make no claims for my personal line of progenitors except that they remained loyal to the values that may have induced all of our ancestors, long, long ago, to climb down from the trees and make their way into the open plains.

13   A few weeks ago, I cleared my throat and asked the children, now mostly grown and fearsomely smart, whether they felt any stirrings of ethnic or religious identity, etc., which might have been, ahem, insufficiently nourished at home. "None," they said, adding firmly, "and the

world would be a better place if nobody else did, either." My chest swelled with pride, as would my mother's, to know that the race of "none" marches on.

Understanding Meaning

1. Why does Ehrenreich have difficulty defining her heritage?
2. Does Ehrenreich see something negative in embracing one's ethnic roots?
3. *Critical Thinking:* Armando Rendón (page 611) suggests that he avoided the "vacuum of the dominant society" that would have erased his identity. Does Ehrenreich suggest that embracing "nothingness" is liberating, freeing one from cultural mindsets, Old World limitations, bias, and inhibiting traditions?

Evaluating Strategy

1. What is Ehrenreich's thesis? How would you restate it in your own words?
2. How effective is the opening narrative?
3. *Other Modes:* Where does Ehrenreich use *comparison* and *narration* to develop her essay?

Appreciating Language

1. What do the tone and style of this essay suggest about the intended audience?
2. What words does Ehrenreich use to describe those who embrace their cultural heritage?

Connections across the Disciplines

1. Review "My Ecumenical Father" (page 127). Is there a difference between embracing the "race of none" and being ecumenical—identifying with one's own culture while respecting that of others?
2. Consider the observations made by David Blankenhorn in "Fatherless America" (page 598). If family structures are changing and children are growing up without the traditional support of two parents, can a strong ethnic or cultural identity provide them with role models, additional guidance, and moral standards they might otherwise miss?

Writing Suggestions

1. Write an essay explaining your attitude about your own ethnic identity. Persuade readers to accept your view of identity. Do you embrace a culture or celebrate being "none"?

2. *Collaborative Writing:* Discuss Ehrenreich's essay with a group of students. Do they share her views on race and identity, or do they see it as a form of denial? Does the "race of none" risk masking racial injustice and oppression? Record members' comments, and work to create a response. If members have differing opinions, draft opposing essays.

ALBERT EINSTEIN

Albert Einstein (1879–1955) was born in Ulm, Germany. He completed a doctorate at the University of Zurich in 1905. He developed his noted theory of relativity at this time and held several teaching positions in physics. His work soon received international attention. In 1921 Einstein was awarded the Nobel Prize in Physics. Nazi persecution forced him to leave Germany, and he took a teaching position at Princeton. As noted in the Introduction, Einstein's reputation led Leo Szilard to ask him to alert the United States government about the possibility of nuclear weapons.

Letter to President Roosevelt, August 2, 1939

As you read the letter, consider the problem Einstein and the other scientists, for whom English was a second language, faced in explaining an abstract scientific theory to a political official.

1
Albert Einstein
Old Grove Rd.
Nassau Point
Peconic, Long Island

August 2nd, 1939

2 F. D. Roosevelt,
President of the United States,
White House
Washington, D.C.

Sir:

3   Some recent work by E. Fermi and L. Szilard, which has been communicated to me in manuscript, leads me to expect that the element uranium may be turned into a new and important source of energy in the immediate future. Certain aspects of the situation which has arisen seem to call for watchfulness and, if necessary, quick action

on the part of the Administration. I believe therefore that it is my duty to bring to your attention the following facts and recommendations:

4   In the course of the last four months it has been made probable—through the work of Joliot in France as well as Fermi and Szilard in America—that it may become possible to set up a nuclear chain reaction in a large mass of uranium, by which vast amounts of power and large quantities of new radium-like elements would be generated. Now it appears almost certain that this could be achieved in the immediate future.

5   This new phenomenon would also lead to the construction of bombs, and it is conceivable—though much less certain—that extremely powerful bombs of a new type may thus be constructed. A single bomb of this type, carried by boat and exploded in a port, might very well destroy the whole port together with some of the surrounding territory. However, such bombs might very well prove to be too heavy for transportation by air.

6   The United States has only very poor ores of uranium in moderate quantities. There is some good ore in Canada and the former Czechoslovakia, while the most important source of uranium is Belgian Congo.

7   In view of this situation you may think it desirable to have some permanent contact maintained between the Administration and the group of physicists working on chain reactions in America. One possible way of achieving this might be for you to entrust with this task a person who has your confidence and who could perhaps serve in an inofficial capacity. His task might comprise the following:

8   a) to approach Government Departments, keep them informed of the further development, and put forward recommendations for Government action, giving particular attention to the problem of securing a supply of uranium ore for the United States;

9   b) to speed up the experimental work, which is at present being carried on within the limits of the budgets of University laboratories, by providing funds, if such funds be required, through his contacts with private persons who are willing to make contributions for this cause, and perhaps also by obtaining the co-operation of industrial laboratories which have the necessary equipment.

10   I understand that Germany has actually stopped the sale of uranium from the Czechoslovakian mines which she has taken over. That she should have taken such early action might perhaps be understood on the ground that the son of the German Under-Secretary of State,

von Weizäcker, is attached to the Kaiser-Wilhelm-Institut in Berlin where some of the American work on uranium is now being repeated.

11

Yours very truly,

Albert Einstein

Understanding Meaning

1. What does Einstein want the president to realize?
2. What specific recommendations does Einstein urge Roosevelt to carry out?
3. *Critical Thinking:* How does Einstein end the letter? Does the mere mention of Germany and nuclear research appear alarming? Remember that in August 1939 Hitler had already taken the Rhineland and Czechoslovakia. That month he was stepping up pressures on Poland. Within a month World War II would begin.

Evaluating Strategy

1. What appeals does Einstein use?
2. How does Einstein suggest that the president accept his recommendations?
3. Does Einstein assume his name alone will command attention? Is that why he uses first person in the letter?

Appreciating Language

1. What level of language does Einstein use? How does he explain physics in common terms?
2. Is the tone of this letter alarmist?

Connections across the Disciplines

1. How would this letter provide added support to Carl Sagan's "Why We Need to Understand Science" (page 589)?
2. Compare this letter to the fund-raising ad on page 626. How are they similar in attempting to make a persuasive argument in a brief statement?

Writing Suggestions

1. Write a persuasive letter to the president or other official to persuade him or her to follow your recommendations on a subject you feel is important.
2. *Collaborative Writing:* Discuss the letter with some students. Did Einstein manage to communicate effectively? Is this a lost art today? Work together to write a persuasive essay on the need for experts to communicate with the public and officials.

The Irish American Partnership is a nonprofit organization supported by Irish American politicians and business executives. Tip O'Neill, former Speaker of the House, and the retired commandant of the U.S. Marine Corps, General Paul X. Kelley, were among the founding members. The organization raises funds to support job training and business development programs in both the Republic of Ireland and Northern Ireland.

Irish Need Apply

This advertisement appeared in Irish American magazines and newspapers. The headline is a variation of the infamous "No Irish Need Apply" notices that greeted many Irish immigrants seeking work. Well into the twentieth century, want ads in American newspapers included this statement as a standard feature, often abbreviating it to "N.I.N.A."

Irish need apply.

1

2   Ireland needs us.

3   Unemployment above 20 percent. Young people forced to leave their homeland to find hope and work. Parents saying good-bye to their children everyday.

4   Ireland is a small island of abundant beauty but scarce financial resources. To survive and grow, this land of 5 million needs our help.

5   There are 44 million of us of Irish descent in America. We overcame our own struggles, and found comfort and prosperity in our new land.

6   Now it is time for us to apply that same determination to help those back home. Through the Irish American Partnership. The Partnership is a unique organization committed to peace and economic recovery in Ireland, North and South.

7   The Partnership needs you to support its work. Work like 600 jobs for people in Tralee, Ballymun, and West Belfast. Financial aid for graduate students in science and technology. Management training for Irish youth in U.S. companies.

(Continued)

(Continued from previous page)

8   Ireland has much to build on. Breathtaking beauty. A proud, educated, motivated work force. Some 375 American companies on its soil.

9   Above all, Ireland has us—deeply loyal Irish Americans able to help those in need.

10   Just fill out the coupon, and return it with a contribution to the Irish American Partnership. The needs are too great to ignore. Apply yourself.

❏ Yes, I want to apply. I want to support the Irish American Partnership. Enclosed is my contribution for
❏ $35   ❏ $50   ❏ $100 $_____ (amt.)
❏ I am not ready to contribute. Please send me more information.
Call toll-free 1-800-722-3893 or fill out and mail to:
Irish American Partnership, 4 Faneuil Hall Marketplace, Boston, MA 02109

Name (please print)

Address

City   State   Zip
The Irish American Partnership is a non-profit organization supported by American business executives and endorsed by political, religious and business leaders in Ireland, North and South. Its mission is a strong, healthy, peaceful Ireland through economic development, job creation and education

11   # The Irish American Partnership

Understanding Meaning

1.   How effective is the headline in getting attention? Would people of other ethnic groups recognize the historical allusion?
2.   What appeals are used?
3.   How much factual support is included in the ad? Why is factual support needed?
4.   Is an emotional appeal to an ethnic loyalty to the "Old Sod" evident?

Evaluating Strategy

1.   Ads must communicate in a glance. How effective is this ad?
2.   *Critical Thinking:* How does this ad fit a problem/solution pattern?

Appreciating Language

1.   What level of language is used? What words would strike the reader?
2.   How does word choice reinforce the use of appeals?

Connections across the Disciplines

1. How does this ad compare to the 3M ad on page 161?
2. How does an ad such as this, calling on Irish Americans to support Irish causes, relate to the issues of cultural identity raised by Rendón, Rowan, Pérez, and others you may have read in this book?

Writing Suggestions

1. Invent a similar organization raising money to help a group you identify with. Consider your readers carefully in devising your appeal.
2. *Collaborative Writing:* Working with a group of students, discuss the implied ethical appeal in this ad—that those who have achieved prosperity have an obligation to help others. Do middle-class African Americans or prominent Hispanics have a similar obligation? Work together to write a persuasive letter or ad urging people to "take care of their own."

STRATEGIES FOR WRITING ARGUMENT AND PERSUASION

1. **Determine your purpose.** Clearly establish your thesis, and define what ideas you want readers to accept and what actions you want them to take. Do not try to communicate too many separate actions in one document.
2. **Evaluate your readers carefully.** Examine the perceptual world of your audience. Do barriers to your message exist that must be overcome? What information do your readers need in order to accept your ideas?
3. **Determine which appeals will be effective.** Recognize the advantages and disadvantages of each appeal, and consider blending more than one.
4. **Craft your introductions and conclusions carefully.** Your opening paragraphs must arouse interest and prepare readers for your argument or appeal. Your conclusion should end with a statement that will reinforce acceptance of your ideas or the taking of recommended action.
5. **Present factual detail in ways readers can understand.** In presenting facts and statistics, use methods such as analogies and narratives to dramatize their significance.
6. **Do not mistake propaganda for persuasion.** Do not assume that hurling accusations, using questionable facts, or employing shock tactics will make your argument or appeal successful. People dislike feeling manipulated, and often potential supporters will find overstated appeals objectionable and offensive.

SUGGESTED TOPICS FOR WRITING ARGUMENT AND PERSUASION
General Assignments

Write a persuasive argument to a general audience on one of the following topics. You may use one or more appeals. You can frame your paper in the form of an essay, a letter, a flyer, or an advertisement.

- Community and police relations
- The drinking age
- The way colleges prepare or fail to prepare graduates for the job market
- Censorship
- Affirmative Action
- Labor unions
- Welfare programs

- Out-of-wedlock births
- Sexual harassment
- A national sales tax

Select one of the following issues, and craft a persuasive essay targeted to one of the audiences listed.

Issues: Medicare reform, distribution of condoms in public schools, school prayer, bilingual education, recycling, gun control, legalization of drugs
Audiences: Suburban residents, retired schoolteachers, small-business owners, an organization of minority police officers, inner-city health care providers

Writing in Context

1. Imagine you have become close to a highly respected member of your community. This person is well regarded by your family and may have a key role in your future. He or she invites you to join an organization that actively supports a view on abortion that is opposite to yours. Write a letter persuading this person to accept your reasons for declining the offer. Try to make your disagreement known without creating animosity.

2. Write a letter to the editor of the campus newspaper about an issue that you have heard discussed but that no one else seems willing to raise. Urge the community to pay attention.

STUDENT PAPER: ARGUMENT AND PERSUASION

This paper was written in response to the following assignment:

> *Write a 500–750-word persuasive essay about a current social or political is-sue. Avoid writing about subjects such as abortion or capital punishment un-less you can provide a new or unique angle. Document use of any outside sources.*

Why a Black Student Union?

1   Before any controversial issue can be discussed, there is usually a certain amount of misinformation to deal with. This is clearly the case with the Black Student Union. Many students have voiced concern and written letters to the editor since the college paper revealed that $540,000 was being allocated to the Union (Kane 1). The article stated that $52,000 was going to salaries, making the Black Student Union the only student organization with a paid staff.

2   First of all, the bulk of the money allocated to the Union is dedicated to renovating the building, which is university property. Constructed in 1962, the building has not had major repairs since 1974. Roof leaks, first reported to the administration three years ago, have led to sub-stantial and costly damage. In addition, it is the only building that was not retrofitted with new heating and air conditioning systems in 1996 (*CSU* 22). Also, the building still does not comply with the Americans with Disabilities Act. Wheelchair ramps must be installed by court order (*CSU* 23).

3   Second, no one at the Union receives a salary for student activities. Five graduate students are paid to tutor remedial classes. Given the lack of space in the cramped Academic Support Center, use of the Black Student Union makes sense and creates more openings in the Center. Many non-black students attend classes and remedial seminars at the Union. Less than half the graduates of the Internet course last semes-ter were African-American (Kane 2).

4   But there are other objections to the Union. Why should blacks have their own facility? Many on campus see the presence of a black student union as a kind of self-imposed apartheid. The Union has also been crit-icized for being the center of racially hostile militancy.

5   The Black Student Union hardly threatens to impose a new kind of segregation. We live in integrated dorms, attend integrated classes, participate in integrated sports, and serve on mostly white and Asian academic committees. The few hours a week a student might spend at the BSU hardly threatens racial isolation — any more than the women's center risks ending co-education or the Newman Center pits Catholics against Protestants. From my own observations, I see little evidence of the radical and extremist politics union opponents mention. The most popular event the Black Student Union holds is Career Week when black students line up to meet representatives from AT&T, IBM, Bank One, and 3M. Most students are concerned about academic performance and career options rather than radical politics. True, the Union has sponsored some controversial speakers, but so has the university itself. Much of the "extremist literature" cited in a campus editorial is not distributed by the Union. The Union receives a lot of free literature in the mail, which has been traditionally displayed in the lobby. When it was brought to the attention of the board that some of the pamphlets were anti-Semitic, members took quick steps to screen incoming publications and discard "hate literature."

6   The real purpose of the Union is to assist African-Americans to succeed on campus. Comprising less than 5% of the student body, blacks easily feel alienated, particularly those who graduated from predominately black high schools. According to Dean Smith, "Since only one of eight black males entering a university will graduate, it is imperative that we seek remedies to support their academic achievement and professional advancement" (12). Many black students have difficulty forming friendships and joining organizations. Often there were only a handful of college-bound students in their schools. To survive, they had to isolate themselves, studying alone to avoid associating with peers resentful of their dedication to academics. Outcasts in high school, these students find college bewildering. They are not accustomed to participating in class or working in groups. They often discover that they are woefully unprepared for college. Coming from schools with 50–75% dropout rates, many suffered from "social promotion." They discover that their A's and B's are only equal to C's and D's in better suburban schools. The Black Student Union offers African-American students a place to relax, interact with older students, and work to make the university a more hospitable place to minorities.

7   Given the history of discrimination and disadvantage faced by African-Americans, the Union can be a positive asset. Is it a crutch, an undeserved luxury? No one can deny that black students feel handicapped on campus. No one complains about the cost of wheelchair ramps and elevators which benefit a handful of physically disabled students. Why should we ignore the crippling legacy of racism?

WORKS CITED

CSU Facilities Report: 1999 Sacramento: State University Budget Office, 1999.
Kane, Kelly. "BSU Funding Furor." *Campus Times* May 24, 1999, 1–2.
Smith, Dean. *Black Males in Crisis.* New York: Random House, 1998.

Questions for Review and Revision

1.   What is the student's thesis?
2.   What negative assumptions does the student seek to address? How does he counter them?
3.   What audience does the writer appear to address? What appeals does the student use?
4.   How much of the paper is driven by responding to opponents' criticisms? Is this a useful device?
5.   How effective is the conclusion? Does comparing disabled students to African-Americans make a valid point? Would you suggest an alternative ending?
6.   Read the paper aloud. Are there passages that should be deleted or expanded? Do the tone and style suit the writer's purpose?

Writing Suggestions

1.   Using this paper as a model, write a similar essay taking a position on a current campus controversy. Assume you are addressing a hostile audience. Respond to their objections without criticizing or demeaning those who disagree with your thesis.
2.   *Collaborative Writing:* Discuss this paper with a group of students. Have a member record comments by the group. Work together to write a short statement approving or disapproving of the concept of establishing separate student unions. If members disagree, consider writing pro and con versions.

ARGUMENT AND PERSUASION CHECKLIST

Before submitting your paper, review these points.

1. Is your message clearly defined?

2. Does your paper meet readers' needs? Do you provide the support they need in order to accept your thesis?

3. Do you support your views with adequate evidence?

4. Do you anticipate reader objections and alternative points of view?

5. Do you balance the strengths and weaknesses of logical, ethical, and emotional appeals?

6. Do you avoid overstated, sentimental, or propagandistic appeals?

7. Do you avoid preaching to the converted? Will only those who already agree with you accept your arguments?

8. Do you make it easy for undecided readers to accept your position without feeling manipulated or patronized?

9. Have you tested your argument with peer review?

WebTutor

See www.harcourtcollege.com/english/sundance for further information on writing argument and persuasion

CREDITS

Abbey, Edward, "First Morning." From *Desert Solitaire* by Edward Abbey. Reprinted by permission of Don Congdon Associates, Inc. Copyright © 1968 by Edward Abbey, renewed 1996 by Clarke Abbey.

Abramson, Leslie, "Unequal Justice" by Leslie Abramson. From *Newsweek*, July 24, 1994. Copyright © 1994 Newsweek, Inc. All rights reserved. Reprinted by permission.

Austin, James, "Four Kinds of Chance." From *Chase, Chance and Creativity: The Lucky Art of Novelty* by James Austin. Copyright © 1978 by Columbia University Press. Reprinted with the permission of the publisher.

Baker, Russell, "The Plot Against People." From the *New York Times*, June 18, 1968. Copyright © 1968 by The New York Times. Reprinted by permission.

Blankenhorn, David, "Fatherless America." From *Fatherless in America* by David Blankenhorn. Copyright © 1995 by the Institute for American Values. Reprinted by permission of Basic Books, a member of Perseus Books, L.L.C.

Budish, Armond, "Fender Bender Do's and Don't's." As appeared in *Family Circle*, July 19, 1994. Reprinted by permission of the author.

Burciaga, José Antonio, "My Ecumenical Father." From *Drink Cultura* by José Antonio Burciaga. Copyright © 1993. Reprinted by permission of Cecilia P. Burciaga.

Carter, Bonnie, "Kinds of Sentences." Excerpt from *The Rinehart Guide to Grammar Usage*, Third Edition by Bonnie Carter and Craig Skates. Copyright © 1993 by Holt, Rinehart and Winston. Reprinted by permission of the publisher.

Castro, Janice, Dan Cook, and Cristina Garcia, "Spanglish." From *Time*, July 11, 1988, vol. 132, no. 2, p. 53. Copyright © 1988 Time Inc. Reprinted by permission.

Catton, Bruce, "Grant and Lee." Reprinted by permission of U.S. Capitol Historical Society. All rights reserved.

John Ciardi, "What is Happiness?" Reprinted by permission of the Ciardi Family Publishing Trust.

Connelly, Joel, "A Growing Awareness: Environmental Groups and the Media." Excerpted from *Beyond Wilderness Issue* #120, Aperture, New York, NY 1990. Copyright © Joel Connelly. Reprinted by permission.

Denfeld, Rene, "The New Victorians." From *The New Victorians* by Rene Denfeld. Copyright © 1995 by Rene Denfeld. By permission of Warner Books.

Dershowitz, Alan, "The 'Abuse Excuse' Is Detrimental to the Justice System." From *The Abuse Excuse* by Alan Dershowitz. Copyright © 1994 by Alan M. Dershowitz. By permission of Little, Brown and Company.

Didion, Joan, "Marrying Absurd." From "On Keeping a Notebook" from *Slouching Towards Bethlehem* by Joan Didion. Copyright © 1968 and copyright renewed © 1996 by Joan Didion. Reprinted by permission of Farrar, Straus & Giroux, Inc.

Dolnick, Edward, "Deafness as Culture." As appeared in *The Atlantic Monthly*, September 1993. Reprinted by permission of the author.

Einstein, Albert, "Letter to President Roosevelt, August 2, 1939." Reprinted by permission of Frank D. Roosevelt Library.

Elbow, Peter, "Desperation Writing." From *Writing Without Teachers* by Peter Elbow. Copyright © 1973, 1998 by Peter Elbow. Used by permission of Oxford University Press, Inc.

Ehrenreich, Barbara, "Cultural Baggage." From the *New York Times Magazine*, April 5, 1992, p. 16. Copyright © 1992 by The New York Times. Reprinted by permission.

Ehrlich, Gretel, "A Storm, the Cornfield, and Elk." From *The Solace of Open Spaces* by Gretel Ehrlich. Copyright © 1985 by Gretel Ehrlich. Used by permission of Viking Penguin, a division of Penguin Putnam Inc.

Frye, Northrup, "Our Three Languages." From *The Educated Imagination* by Northrup Frye. Copyright © 1963 by Northrup Frye. Published by House of Anansi Press Limited. Reprinted by permission of Indiana University Press and the Canadian Broadcasting Corporation.

CREDITS

INDEX

Abbey, Edward
  "The First Morning", 143
Abramson, Leslie
  "The Abuse Defense Balances the Justice System", 533
Absolute statements, 577
Abstracts, 159
"Abuse Defense Balances the Justice System, The" (Abramson), 533
"'Abuse Excuse' Is Detrimental to the Justice System, The" (Dershowitz), 528
Ad hominem, 577
Adams, John, 557
"Addicted to Plastic: The Overspent American" (Schor), 306
Agassiz, Louis, 45
Age, 11
allusion, illusion, 110
Analysis, 4, 299–382
  checklist, 382
  critical thinking, 303, 304
  detailed observation, 302
  readings, 306–377
  strategies for reading, 304, 305
  strategies for writing, 378
  student paper ("Nostalgia: Why We Need and Love the Past"), 379
  subjective vs. objective, 300–302
Argument and persuasion, 6, 572–634
  checklist, 634
  critical thinking, 577
  emotion, 574, 575
  ethics, 575, 576
  hostile readers, 576
  logic, 574
  readings, 579–628
  strategies for reading, 578
  strategies for writing, 629
  student paper ("Why a Black Student Union?"), 631
Arguments, 572
Asking questions, 18
Associations, 507
Audiences, 8–10

Austin, James
  "Four Kinds of Chance", 411

Baker, Russell
  "The Plot Against People", 388
Begging the question, 577
Berryman, John, 177
Bias, 303
"Birth of a TV Show: A Drama All Its Own" (Kolbert), 445
"Black is Beautiful: Tokyo Style" (Zielenziger), 314
"Black Political Leadership" (West), 35
"Black Wasn't Beautiful" (Mebane), 392
Black's Law Dictionary ("homicide"), 427
Blair, Eric, 72
Blankenhorn, David
  "Fatherless America", 598
Blending the modes
  "Deafness as Culture" (Dolnick), 212
  "Growing Up Old in L.A." (Rodriquez/Greenfield), 358
  "Man Who Mistook His Wife for a Hat, The" (Sacks), 81
  "New Victorians, The" (Denfeld), 284
  "Once More to the Lake" (White), 151
  "Our Three Languages" (Frye), 422
  "Should This Student Have Been Expelled" (Hentoff), 604
  "Why More Women Are Going to Prison" (Gammage), 522
  "Why My Business Failed" (Jamison), 484
Bookhout, James W., 93n
"Border Story" (Urrea), 118
Borrowed authority, 577
Brainstorming, 16, 17
Budish, Armond D.
  "Fender Benders: Legal Do's and Don't's", 451
Burciaga, José Antonio
  "My Ecumenical Father", 127

"Can the Devon Be Saved?" (student paper), 568
Capote, Truman
  "Out There", 114

Castro, Janice
  "Spanglish", 183
Catton, Bruce
  "Grant and Lee", 253
Cause and effect, 5, 501–571
  checklist, 571
  critical thinking, 507, 508
  deduction, 502, 503
  establishing causes, 504, 505
  induction, 503, 504
  predicting results, 505, 506
  readings, 509–566
  strategies for reading, 508
  strategies for writing, 567
  student paper ("Can the Devon Be Saved?"), 568
Checklists. *See also* Strategies
  analysis, 382
  argument and persuasion, 634
  cause and effect, 571
  comparison and contrast, 298
  definition, 237
  description, 170
  division and classification, 438
  narration, 105
  process, 500
"Chinese Space, American Space" (Yi-Fu Tuan),
  245
Ciardi, John
  "What is Happiness?", 192
"Cities of the Dead" (student paper), 168
Classification, 385–387. *See also* Division and
  classification
"Cleaning Battery Terminals" (Treganowan), 493
Clichés, 111, 112
Clustering, 18
Collaborative writing, 28–30
"Communication Styles: United States and Taiwan"
  (Kenna/Lacy), 290
Comparison and contrast, 4, 238–298
  checklist, 298
  organization, 239–243
  point-by-point organization, 241–243
  purpose, 239
  readings, 245–293
  strategies for reading, 243, 244
  strategies for writing, 294
  student paper ("Parallel States:Israel and Ire-
    land"), 295
  subject-by-subject organization, 240, 241
Computer, writing on, 27, 28
Concrete words, 110

Connelly, Joel
  "A Growing Awareness: Environmental Groups
    and the Media", 319
Connotation, 112
conscience, conscious, 110
Context, 2, 3
Contrast. See Comparison and contrast
Cook, Dan
  "Spanglish", 183
Crawford, Kimberly A.
  "Surreptitious Recording of Suspects' Conver-
    sations", 366
Critical reading, 32–34
Critical thinking
  analysis, 303, 304
  argument and persuasion, 577
  cause and effect, 507, 508
  classification, 386, 387
  directions, 442, 443
  division, 384, 385
  explanations, 440, 441
  logical fallacies, 303, 304, 507, 508, 577
"Cultural Baggage" (Ehrenreich), 617
Cultural definitions, 172, 173
"CyberSoul Not Found" (Marriott), 509

"Deafness as Culture" (Dolnick), 212
Declaration of Independence (Jefferson et al.),
  557
Deduction, 502, 503
Defensive writing, 10
Defining by comparison, 173
Defining by description, 173
Defining by example, 173
Defining through synonyms, 173
Definition, 4, 171–237
  checklist, 237
  context, 174, 175
  methods of, 173, 174
  purpose of, 174
  readings, 177–232
  strategies for reading, 175, 176
  strategies for writing, 233
  student paper ("Disneyland Dads"), 235
  types of definitions, 172, 173
Denfeld, Rene
  "The New Victorians", 284
Denotation, 112
"Depression" (*Encyclopedia of Psychology*), 230,
  231
"Depression" (Rosenberg), 230, 231

Dershowitz, Alan M.
"The "Abuse Excuse" Is Detrimental to the Justice System", 528
Description, 4, 106–170
    checklist, 170
    diction, 109–113
    objective vs. subjective, 107–109
    readings, 114–165
    strategies for reading, 113
    strategies for writing, 166
    student paper ("Cities of the Dead"), 168
"Desperation Writing" (Elbow), 461
Detailed observation, 302
Diction, 109–113
Didion, Joan
    "Marrying Absurd", 122
Diluted verbs, 111
Directions, 441–443. *See also* Process
Disciplines, 12–14
"Disneyland Dads" (student paper), 235
Division and classification, 5, 383–438
    classification, 385–387
    critical thinking (classification), 386, 387
    critical thinking (division), 384, 385
    division, 383–385
    readings, 388–433
    strategies for reading, 387
    strategies for writing, 434
    student paper ("Hispanics on Campus"), 435
"Documentation Tips" (Martin), 466
Dolnick, Edward
    "Deafness as Culture", 212
"Dyslexia" (Simpson), 177

"Ebola River" (Preston), 67
Education, 10, 11
Effect. See Cause and effect
Ehrenreich, Barbara
    "Cultural Baggage", 617
Ehrlich, Gretel
    "A Storm, the Cornfield, and Elk", 197
Einstein, Albert
    Letter to President Roosevelt, 622
Elbow, Peter
    "Desperation Writing", 461
Emotional appeals, 574, 575
Encyclopedia of Psychology, 230
Essay writing, 20–22
Ethical appeals, 575, 576
Ethical issues and connotation, 112
"Evaluating a Job Opportunity" (Grinslade), 479

Evolving definitions, 172
Explanations, 439–441. *See also* Process
Extended definitions, 174
Extended readerships, 10

Facts, 303
False analogies, 304
False analogy, 577
False dilemma, 577
"Fatherless America" (Blankenhorn), 598
FBI
    "Interrogation of Lee Harvey Oswald", 93
"Fender-Bender, The" (Pérez), 62
"Fender Benders: Legal Do's and Dont's" (Budish), 451
Filtering data, 304
"First Morning, The" (Abbey), 143
Five Ws, 18
"Four Kinds of Chance" (Austin), 411
Franklin, Benjamin, 557
Freewriting, 15, 16
Frequently misused words, 110
Frye, Northrop
    "Our Three Languages", 422

Gaiter, Leonce
    "The Revolt of the Black Bourgoisie", 583
Gammage, Jeff
    "Why More Women Are Going to Prison", 522
Garcia, Cristina
    "Spanglish", 183
Generalizations, 303, 304
Grammar handbook (kinds of sentences), 431
"Grant and Lee" (Catton), 253
Greenfield, Lauren
    "Growing Up Old in L.A.", 358
Greenfield, Meg
    "Why Nothing is 'Wrong' Anymore", 406
Grinslade, Liz
    "Evaluating a Job Opportunity", 479
Group (collaborative) writing, 28–30
"Growing Awareness: Environmental Groups and the Media" (Connelly), 319
"Growing Up Asian in America" (Noda), 397
"Growing Up Old in L.A." (Rodriquez/Greenfield), 358

"Handicap of Definition, The" (Raspberry), 311
Harris, Marvin
    "How Our Skins Got Their Color", 456
Hasty generalizations, 303, 304

Hentoff, Nat
  "Should This Student Have Been Expelled?",
    604
Hewlett-Packard (solving printer operation prob-
  lems), 563
"Hispanics on Campus" (student paper), 435
Holt, John
  "Three Kinds of Discipline", 417
"Homicide" (*Black's Law Dictionary*), 427
"Hot Air", (Tomkin), 549
"How Our Skins Got Their Color" (Harris), 456
"How to Lie with Statistics" (Huff), 326
Huff, Darrell
  "How to Lie with Statistics", 326

illusion, allusion, 110
imply, infer, 110
Individual readers, 9
Induction, 503, 504
Inductive leap, 504
infer, imply, 110
Inflated phrases, 111, 112
Instructions, 439–441. *See also* Process
"Interrogation of Lee Harvey Oswald" (FBI), 93
"Irish Need Apply" (Irish American Partnership),
  626
Ivins, Molly
  "A Short Story about the Vietnam War Memor-
    ial", 57

Jacobson, Jodi
  "Swept Away", 538
Jamison, Charles N., Jr.
  "Why My Business Failed", 484
"Japanese and American Workers: Two States of
  Mind" (Ouchi), 267
Jefferson, Thomas
  Declaration of Independence, 557

Kelley, Paul X., 626
Kenna, Peggy
  "Communication Styles: United States and Tai-
    wan", 290
Kennedy, John F., 93
Kinds of sentences (*Reinhart Guide to Grammar and
  Usage*), 431
King, Martin Luther, Jr.
  "The Ways of Meeting Oppression", 401
"Kiss of Death" (Rendón), 611
Kolbert, Elizabeth
  "Birth of a TV Show: A Drama All Its Own", 445
Kuper, Jessica, 175

Lacy, Sondra
  "Communication Styles: United States and Tai-
    wan", 290
"Language of Discretion, The" (Tan), 274
"Lesson, The" (McCall), 51
Livingston, Robert, 557
Logic, 574
Logical fallacies, 303, 304, 507, 508, 577
Lord, Walter
  "The Reconstructed Log Book of the *Titanic*", 98

MacGregor, Douglas, 267
"Man Who Mistook His Wife for a Hat, The"
  (Sacks), 81
Manhattan Project, 2
Marriott, Michel
  "CyberSoul Not Found", 509
"Marrying Absurd" (Didion), 122
Martin, Fran, 14
  "Documentation Tips", 466
McCall, Nathan
  "The Lesson", 51
Mebane, Mary
  "Black Wasn't Beautiful", 392
Menendez, Erik, 533
Metaphors, 111
Michaels, Leonard, 274
Miller, Russell, 109
Mizell, Louis R., Jr.
  "Who's Listening to Your Cell Phone Calls?", 337
Modes, 6
Momaday, N. Scott
  "The Way to Rainy Mountain", 137
Moving from topic to thesis, 19, 20
"My Ecumenical Father" (Burciaga), 127

Narration, 4, 39–105
  checklist, 105
  chronology, 42, 43
  focus, 42
  readings, 45–100
  strategies for reading, 43, 44
  strategies for writing, 101
  student paper ("Spare Change"), 103, 104
  writer's purpose, 39–42
Negative instructions, 442, 443
"New Victorians, The" (Denfeld), 284
Noda, Kesaya
  "Growing Up Asian in America", 397
Non sequitur, 577
"Nostalgia: Why We Need and Love the Past" (student paper), 379

O'Neill, Tip, 626
Objective analysis, 301
Objective description, 107, 108
Ogilvy, David, 13
"Once More to the Lake" (White), 151
Opinions, 303
Orwell, George
    "Shooting an Elephant", 72
Oswald, Lee Harvey, 93
Ouchi, William
    "Japanese and American Workers: Two States of
    Mind", 267
"Our Three Languages" (Frye), 422
"Out There" (Capote), 114
Overview of text, 37, 38

"Parallel States: Israel and Ireland" (student paper),
    295
Past experiences, 10
Perceptual world, 10, 11
Pérez, Ramon "Tianguis"
    "The Fender-Bender", 62
Personal definitions, 173
Perspective, 7
Persuasion. See Argument and persuasion
Pilipp, Frank
    "TV Movies of the First Decade of AIDS", 343
    "TV Movies of the First Decade of AIDS (Ab-
    stract)", 159
"Plot Against People, The" (Baker), 388
Point-by-point method, 241–243
Predicting results, 505, 506
Preston, Richard, "Ebola River", 67
Prewriting, 15–17
principle, principal, 110
Pro and con views
    abuse excuse
        "The 'Abuse Excuse' Is Detrimental to the
        Justice System" (Dershowitz), 528
        "The Abuse Defense Balances the Justice
        System" (Abramson), 533
    cultural identity
        "Cultural Baggage" (Ehrenreich), 617
        "Kiss of Death" (Rendón), 611
    global warming
        "Hot Air" (Tomkin), 549
        "Swept Away" (Jacobson), 538
Process, 5, 439–500
    checklist, 500
    critical thinking (directions), 442, 443
    critical thinking (explanations), 440, 441
    directions, 441–443

explanations, 439–441
readings, 445–495
strategies for reading, 443, 444
strategies for writing, 496
student paper ("Securing Your Home"), 498
Professional experience, 11

Qualifying definitions, 172

Ramos, Monica, 163
Raspberry, William
    "The Handicap of Definition", 311
Raudsepp, Eugene
    "Seeing Your Way Past Interview Jitters", 474
Reader, 8–12
Rechy, John, 108
"Reconstructed Log Book of the *Titanic*, The"
    (Lord), 98
Recursive, 21
Red herring, 577
Reference groups, 11
Regulatory definitions, 172
Reinhart Guide to Grammar and Usage
    "Kinds of sentences", 431
Rendón, Armando, "Kiss of Death", 611
Résumé of Monica Ramos, The (Ramos), 163
"Resumes That Rate a Second Look" (Weisbord),
    471
"Revolt of the Black Bourgeoisie, The" (Gaiter),
    583
Ricks, Christopher, 274
Rideau, Wilbert
    "Why Prisons Don't Work", 579
Ritter, Jonathan
    "The World View of a Computer Hacker", 187
Rodriquez, Richard
    "Growing Up Old in L.A.", 358
Roosevelt, Franklin D., 2, 622
Rosenberg, Don R., 231
Rowan, Carl T.
    "Unforgettable Miss Bessie", 131

Sacks, Oliver
    "The Man Who Mistook His Wife for a Hat", 81
Sagan, Carl
    "Why We Need to Understand Science), 589
Schor, Juliet B.
    "Addicted to Plastic: The Overspent American",
    306
Scudder, Samuel
    "Take This Fish and Look at It", 45
"Securing Your Home" (student paper), 498

"Seeing Your Way Past Interview Jitters" (Raud-
sepp), 474
Sherman, Roger, 557
"Shooting an Elephant" (Orwell), 72
"Short Story about the Vietnam War Memorial, A"
(Ivins), 57
"Should This Student Have Been Expelled?"
(Hentoff), 604
Shull, Charles
"TV Movies of the First Decade of AIDS", 343
"TV Movies of the First Decade of AIDS (Ab-
stract)", 159
Similes, 111
Simpson, Eileen, "Dyslexia", 177
Slippery slope interpretations, 507
Social roles, 11
"Solving printer operation problems" (Hewlett-
Packard), 563
"Spanglish" (Castro/Cook/Garcia), 183
"Spare Change" (student paper), 103
Standard definitions, 172
Stark, Steven D.
"A Tale of Two Sitcoms", 259
Status, 11
Steinem, Gloria
"Words and Change", 514
"Storm, the Cornfield, and Elk, The" (Ehrlich),
197
Strategies. See also Checklists
collaborative writing, 29
creating a composing style, 22
critical reading, 33, 34
reading analysis, 304, 305
reading argument and persuasion, 578
reading cause and effect, 508
reading classification and contrast, 387
reading comparison and contrast, 243, 244
reading definitions, 175, 176
reading descriptions, 113
reading narration, 43, 44
reading process, 443, 444
writer's block, 30, 31
writing analysis, 378
writing argument and persuasion, 629
writing cause and effect, 567
writing classification and contrast, 434
writing comparison and contrast, 294
writing definitions, 233
writing descriptions, 166
writing narration, 101
writing on a computer, 27, 28
writing process, 496

Student papers
analysis ("Nostalgia: Why We Need and Love the
Past"), 379
argument and persuasion ("Why a Black Student
Union?"), 631
cause and effect ("Can the Devon Be Saved?"),
568
comparison and contrast ("Parallel States: Israel
and Ireland"), 295
definition ("Disneyland Dads"), 235
description ("Cities of the Dead"), 168
division and classification ("Hispanics on Campus"), 435
narration ("Spare Change"), 103
process ("Securing Your Home"), 498
Subject-by-subject method, 240, 241
Subjective analysis, 300
"Surreptitious Recording of Suspects' Conversations" (Crawford), 366
"Swept Away" (Jacobson), 538
Synonyms, 173
Szilard, Leo, 1

"Take This Fish and Look at It" (Scudder), 45
"Tale of Two Sitcoms, A" (Stark), 259
Tan, Amy
"The Language of Discretion", 274
Teller, Edward, 1
Text, overview, 37, 38
Thesis, 20
Three Cs of group dynamics, 29
"Three Kinds of Discipline" (Holt), 417
3M Pharmaceutical Sales Representative Want Ad,
161
Tomkin, Jocelyn, "Hot Air", 549
Topics for writing. See Writing topics
"Transaction, The" (Zinsser), 248
Transitional phrases, 441
Treganowan, Lucille
"Cleaning Battery Terminals", 493
"TV Movies of the First Decade of AIDS (Abstract)"
(Pilipp/Shull), 159
"TV Movies of the First Decade of AIDS"
(Pilipp/Shull), 343

"Unforgettable Miss Bessie" (Rowan), 131
Unnecessary words, 111
Urrea, Luis Alberto
"Border Story", 118

Values, 11
Visual aids, 442

Want ads, 161
"Way to Rainy Mountain, The" (Momaday), 137
"Ways of Meeting Oppression, The" (King, Jr.), 401
WebTutor, 38
Weisbord, Anne
    "Resumes That Rate a Second Look", 471
West, Cornel
    "Black Political Leadership", 35
"What is Happiness?"t (Ciardi), 192
White, E. B.
    "Once More to the Lake", 151
"Who's Listening to Your Cell Phone Calls?"
    (Mizell), 337
"Why a Black Student Union?" (student paper), 631
"Why More Women Are Going to Prison" (Gam-
    mage), 522
"Why My Business Failed" (Jamison), 484
"Why Nothing is "Wrong" Anymore" (Greenfield),
    406
"Why Prisons Don't Work" (Rideau), 579
"Why We Need to Understand Science" (Sagan), 589
Williams, Terry Tempest, "Yucca", 203
Wordiness, 111
"Words and Change" (Steinem), 514
"World View of a Computer Hacker, The" (Ritter),
    187
Writer, 3–8
Writer's block, 30–32
Writer's purpose, 4–6
Writer's role, 7, 8
Writing beyond the classroom
    Cleaning Battery Terminals (Treganowan), 493
    Communication Styles: United States and Tai-
        wan (Keena/Lacy), 290
    Declaration of Independence (Jefferson et al.),
        557
    "Depression" (*Encyclopedia of Psychology*), 230
    "Depression" (Rosenberg), 231

Homicide (*Black's Law Dictionary*), 427
Interrogation of Lee Harvey Oswald (FBI), 93
Irish Need Apply (Irish American Partnership),
    626
Kinds of Sentences (Rinehart Guide to Grammar
    and Usage), 431
Letter to President Roosevelt (Einstein), 622
Reconstructed Logbook of the *Titanic* (Lord), 98
Résumé of Monica Ramos (Ramos), 163
Solving Printer Operation Problems (Hewlett-
    Packard), 563
Surreptitious Recording of Suspects' Conversa-
    tions (Crawford), 366
3M Pharmaceutical Sales Representative Want
    Ad, 161
TV Movie of the First Decade of AIDS (Ab-
    stract), 159
Writing contexts, 14, 15
Writing process, 15–27
Writing topics
    analysis, 378, 379
    argument and persuasion, 629, 630
    cause and effect, 567, 568
    comparison and contrast, 294, 295
    definition, 233, 234
    description, 167
    division and classification, 434, 435
    narration, 101, 102
    process, 496–498

Yi-Fu Tuan
    "Chinese Space, American Space", 245
"Yucca" (Williams), 203

Zielenziger, Michael
    "Black is Beautiful: Tokyo Style", 314
Zinsser, William
    "The Transaction", 248